I0890694

Anthropological Approaches to Understanding Consumption Patterns and Consumer Behavior

Valentina Chkoniya
University of Aveiro, Portugal

Ana Oliveira Madsen
CEGE, Católica Porto Business School, Portugal & Universidade Católica Portuguesa, Porto, Portugal

Paata Bukhrashvili
Ilia State University, Georgia

A volume in the Advances in Marketing, Customer Relationship Management, and E-Services (AMCRMES) Book Series

IGI Global
DISSEMINATOR OF KNOWLEDGE

Published in the United States of America by
IGI Global
Business Science Reference (an imprint of IGI Global)
701 E. Chocolate Avenue
Hershey PA, USA 17033
Tel: 717-533-8845
Fax: 717-533-8661
E-mail: cust@igi-global.com
Web site: http://www.igi-global.com

Copyright © 2020 by IGI Global. All rights reserved. No part of this publication may be reproduced, stored or distributed in any form or by any means, electronic or mechanical, including photocopying, without written permission from the publisher.
Product or company names used in this set are for identification purposes only. Inclusion of the names of the products or companies does not indicate a claim of ownership by IGI Global of the trademark or registered trademark.

Library of Congress Cataloging-in-Publication Data

Names: Chkoniya, Valentina, 1977- editor. | Madsen, Ana, 1977- editor. | Buxrašvili, Paata, 1960- editor.
Title: Anthropological approaches to understanding consumption patterns and consumer behavior / Valentina Chkoniya, Ana Madsen, and Paata Bukhrashvili, editors.
Description: Hershey : Business Science Reference, 2020. | Includes bibliographical references and index. | Summary: “”This book provides an anthropological approach to the study of consumption patterns and consumer behavior”--Provided by publisher”-- Provided by publisher.
Identifiers: LCCN 2019048540 (print) | LCCN 2019048541 (ebook) | ISBN 9781799831150 (hardcover) | ISBN 9781799831167 (paperback) | ISBN 9781799831174 (ebook)
Subjects: LCSH: Consumption (Economics) | Consumer behavior.
Classification: LCC HB801 .A648 2020 (print) | LCC HB801 (ebook) | DDC 306.3--dc23
LC record available at https://lccn.loc.gov/2019048540
LC ebook record available at https://lccn.loc.gov/2019048541

This book is published in the IGI Global book series Advances in Marketing, Customer Relationship Management, and E-Services (AMCRMES) (ISSN: 2327-5502; eISSN: 2327-5529)

British Cataloguing in Publication Data
A Cataloguing in Publication record for this book is available from the British Library.

All work contributed to this book is new, previously-unpublished material. The views expressed in this book are those of the authors, but not necessarily of the publisher.

For electronic access to this publication, please contact: eresources@igi-global.com.

Advances in Marketing, Customer Relationship Management, and E-Services (AMCRMES) Book Series

Eldon Y. Li
National Chengchi University, Taiwan & California Polytechnic State University, USA

ISSN:2327-5502
EISSN:2327-5529

Mission

Business processes, services, and communications are important factors in the management of good customer relationship, which is the foundation of any well organized business. Technology continues to play a vital role in the organization and automation of business processes for marketing, sales, and customer service. These features aid in the attraction of new clients and maintaining existing relationships.

The Advances in Marketing, Customer Relationship Management, and E-Services (AMCRMES) Book Series addresses success factors for customer relationship management, marketing, and electronic services and its performance outcomes. This collection of reference source covers aspects of consumer behavior and marketing business strategies aiming towards researchers, scholars, and practitioners in the fields of marketing management.

Coverage

- Cases on Electronic Services
- Data mining and marketing
- Telemarketing
- Social Networking and Marketing
- Text Mining and Marketing
- Electronic Services
- Ethical Considerations in E-Marketing
- CRM and customer trust
- Customer Retention
- Legal Considerations in E-Marketing

IGI Global is currently accepting manuscripts for publication within this series. To submit a proposal for a volume in this series, please contact our Acquisition Editors at Acquisitions@igi-global.com or visit: http://www.igi-global.com/publish/.

The Advances in Marketing, Customer Relationship Management, and E-Services (AMCRMES) Book Series (ISSN 2327-5502) is published by IGI Global, 701 E. Chocolate Avenue, Hershey, PA 17033-1240, USA, www.igi-global.com. This series is composed of titles available for purchase individually; each title is edited to be contextually exclusive from any other title within the series. For pricing and ordering information please visit http://www.igi-global.com/book-series/advances-marketing-customer-relationship-management/37150. Postmaster: Send all address changes to above address. Copyright © 2020 IGI Global. All rights, including translation in other languages reserved by the publisher. No part of this series may be reproduced or used in any form or by any means – graphics, electronic, or mechanical, including photocopying, recording, taping, or information and retrieval systems – without written permission from the publisher, except for non commercial, educational use, including classroom teaching purposes. The views expressed in this series are those of the authors, but not necessarily of IGI Global.

Titles in this Series

For a list of additional titles in this series, please visit:
http://www.igi-global.com/book-series/advances-marketing-customer-relationship-management/37150

International Approaches to Marketing, Communication Media, and Management of Government Policies
Oscar Odiboh (Covenant University, Nigeria) Eno Akpabio (University of Namibia, Namibia) and Piet Kommers (University of Twente, The Netherlands)
Business Science Reference • © 2020 • 280pp • H/C (ISBN: 9781799830726) • US $225.00

Emotional, Sensory, and Social Dimensions of Consumer Buying Behavior
Ana Maria Soares (School of Economics and Management, University of Minho, Portugal) and Maher Georges Elmashhara (School of Economics and Management, University of Minho, Portugal)
Business Science Reference • © 2020 • 424pp • H/C (ISBN: 9781799822202) • US $215.00

Examining Cultural Perspectives in a Globalized World
Richard Brunet-Thornton (University of Economics, Prague, Czech Republic)
Business Science Reference • © 2020 • 350pp • H/C (ISBN: 9781799802143) • US $215.00

Managing Social Media Practices in the Digital Economy
Shirin Alavi (Jaypee Institute of Information Technology, India) and Vandana Ahuja (Amity Business School, Amity University, Noida, India)
Business Science Reference • © 2020 • 312pp • H/C (ISBN: 9781799821854) • US $215.00

Handbook of Research on Decision-Making Techniques in Financial Marketing
Hasan Dinçer (Istanbul Medipol University, Turkey) and Serhat Yüksel (İstanbul Medipol University, Turkey)
Business Science Reference • © 2020 • 646pp • H/C (ISBN: 9781799825593) • US $395.00

Impacts of Online Advertising on Business Performance
Tereza Semerádová (Technical University of Liberec, Czech Republic) and Petr Weinlich (Technical University of Liberec, Czech Republic)
Business Science Reference • © 2020 • 262pp • H/C (ISBN: 9781799816188) • US $225.00

Handbook of Research on Innovations in Technology and Marketing for the Connected Consumer
Sumesh Singh Dadwal (Northumbia University, London, UK)
Business Science Reference • © 2020 • 532pp • H/C (ISBN: 9781799801313) • US $295.00

IGI Global
DISSEMINATOR OF KNOWLEDGE

701 East Chocolate Avenue, Hershey, PA 17033, USA
Tel: 717-533-8845 x100 • Fax: 717-533-8661
E-Mail: cust@igi-global.com • www.igi-global.com

Editorial Advisory Board

Pedro Anunciação, *Polytechnic Institute of Setúbal, Portugal*
Elodie Attié, *Université Toulouse, France*
Belem Barbosa, *University of Aveiro, Portugal*
Bodil Stilling Blichfeldt, *University of Southern Denmark, Denmark*
José Luís Cacho, *Port of Sines, Portugal*
Alice Duarte, *University of Porto, Portugal*
Francesco Facchini, *Polytechnic University of Bari, Italy*
Sandra Filipe, *University of Aveiro, Portugal*
Mariantonietta Fiore, *University of Foggia, Italy*
Luis Gouveia, *Universidade Fernando Pessoa, Portugal*
Manuel Luiz, *Boston Consulting Group, Brazil*
Mara Madaleno, *University of Aveiro, Portugal*
Liraz Margalit, *IDC Interdisciplinary Center Herzliya, Israel*
Joao Lourenço Marques, *University of Aveiro, Portugal*
Luís Marques, *Catolica Porto Business School, Portugal*
Armando Mateus, *TouchPoint Consulting, Portugal*
Raquel Meneses, *University of Porto, Portugal*
Sérgio Monteiro-Rodrigues, *University of Porto, Portugal*
Álvaro Nascimento, *Catolica Porto Business School, Portugal*
Mogens R. Nissen, *Dansk Centralbibliotek for Sydslesvig, Denmark*
Helena Nobre, *University of Aveiro, Portugal*
Nino Okrostsvaridze, *Ilia State University, Georgia*
Almiro de Oliveira, *Information Systems Governance European Club, Portugal*
René Taudal Poulsen, *Copenhagen Business School, Denmark*
Alexandre Silva Quevedo, *Universidade Federal do Rio Grande do Sul, Brazil*
Roberto Rana, *University of Foggia, Italy*
Mario Romao, *ISEG – Lisbon School of Economics and Management, Portugal*
Floortje Schilling, *University of Vienna, Austria*
Nandini Sen, *Heriot Watt University, UK*
Dora Simões, *University of Aveiro, Portugal*
Kevin J. Tuite, *Université de Montréal, Canada*
Seda Yildirim, *Tekirdag Namık Kemal University, Turkey*

Table of Contents

Section 2
Globalization

Section 3
Identity

Section 4
Tendencies

Detailed Table of Contents

Consumption patterns have always been an important indicator of a generation's identity, but in a world where globalization tends to standardize everything and digital technology tends to accelerate the globalization process, some might predict that identities are dissolving faster than ever. This chapter aims to help understand how new Portuguese generations perceive fish products. Throughout this research, it became very evident that young consumers are very aware of the ultimate emergency of sustainability. This chapter uses the example of Docapesca's pioneer initiative to prove that it is worth investing in consumer education and that, when we adopt a generation focused approach to implement a national marketing campaign, it is possible to obtain valuable advances in consumption for a sustainable future.

Approaches that attempt to predict consumer behavior have come a long way since the inception of socio-demographic profiling. This development is, on the one hand, driven by the desire of businesses to perform better and connect better with consumers. On the other hand, this is also driven by consumers

Logistic services are central to the design and management of any supply chain. Due to recent technological advances, modern supply chains are challenging traditional market boundaries in ways that both influence and are influenced by consumer behavior (e.g., Amazon, Alibaba, or JD.com). Economically speaking, corporations are changing along the way resources are being used in production. At the firm level, management decisions follow cost efficiency and risk management principles, pursuing a cost-risk tradeoff equilibrium. Theoretically, operations organized within the boundaries of the firm are just those for which the markets are unable to offer a more efficient alternative, whereas the link between buyers and sellers (i.e., demand and supply in the market) is intermediated by logistics services, such as transport, to mention but one. As technological innovation, social transformation, and consumer behavior threaten firms' traditional boundaries, logistics need to adjust and adapt to new and emerging challenges, its costs, and risks to end consumers.

This chapter evaluates the role on container shipping and development of ports and terminals around the world on globalization and consumer behavior. Container shipping is the unsung hero of globalization. It is remarkable that despite containerization and container shipping having such an all-encompassing impact and consequences on consumption, consumption patterns, consumer behavior, and societies in every corner of the world, container shipping is simply invisible to the world at large. The chapter also looks at impact of ever-growing large ports on the society and economy of the cities the ports are located in.

The internet of things (IoT) allows companies to better understand consumers' needs while improving sales conditions (e.g., easier access to products and information, gain of time for employees and consumers, smart entertaining environments, etc.). However, digitalizing a store is an investment. Therefore, it is necessary for managers to know consumers' expectations and the perceived benefits and risks for both managers and consumers. This chapter studies the academic literature and managers opinions about consumers' attitudes toward the acceptance of smart retail stores. More specifically, the roles of consumer well-being, social image, utility value, human value, privacy concerns, technology trust, health concerns, and different personality traits toward smart retail stores are discussed.

The purpose of the chapter is to recognize how customers perceive the value proposition content of network companies providing restaurant services. This is theoretical and empirical research in equal measure. The chapter presents the results of the restaurants value proposition study in Saint Petersburg (Russia) according to industry data and identifies the target audience key needs and industry characteristics in the market, semantic core formation, and clustering in order to identify the main criteria affecting the value proposition formation. The study was conducted among 16 chain restaurant holdings located in St. Petersburg, using statistical data based on the marketing statistical tool Google KeyWord Planner analytic database. The results made it possible to highlight key criteria of the value proposition by which consumers make their choice. This approach will allow standardizing decision-making systems on the possibility of identifying the innovative potential of the company's transition to a qualitatively new level of service and use of production resources.

Chapter 9
Cross-Cultural Differences and Similarities in Retailers' Branding and Digital Maturity: A Cross-Border Case Study 159
Andreas Hesse, Koblenz University of Applied Sciences, Germany
Pieter Steenkamp, Cape Peninsula University of Technology, South Africa
Holger J. Schmidt, Koblenz University of Applied Sciences, Germany
Virimai V. Mugobo, Cape Peninsula University of Technology, South Africa

Digital disruption is not something that may happen in the future; it is currently happening and impacting all types of businesses, including retail. This chapter reflects cross-cultural similarities and differences. German and South African consumers increasingly use the internet to look for product information and to purchase online products and services. Nevertheless, about 25% of German and South African companies in the study sample are more or less offline, not offering even basic digital services, while a significant number of companies ignore opportunities for branding. The digital maturity and branding practices of 933 businesses located within the central business districts of two international cities of similar regional importance, namely Koblenz in Germany and Stellenbosch in South Africa, were investigated. Retailers were analysed in order to compare and contrast their progression along a digital maturity scale as well as their branding practices. The case study presented in this chapter aimed to provide a starting point for the development of such a picture.

Chapter 10
If You Want to Trigger an Emotional Purchase, Don't Make Your Customers Think: Understanding Customer Decision Making 176
Liraz Margalit, IDC Interdisciplinary Center Herzliya, Israel

The classic economic theory describes consumers as rational economic actors that select an alternative only after considering all the relevant information. However, while the logical process is certainly a key factor in considered purchases such as insurance or financial products, it is actually detrimental to the retail-consumer industry, where emotional decision making or the impulse purchase plays a central role. Although we like to think of ourselves as rational creatures, absorbing information, weighing it carefully, and making thoughtful decisions, many of our most crucial choices are made by what we call hunches, gut feelings and a somewhat automatic reaction that is beyond or beneath consciousness. We like to refer to this feeling as intuition ("I have a very good feeling about this house"), but the reality is that this "intuition" is an established part of emotion-based learning. This chapter deals with the significant role of emotions in everyday purchase decisions.

Section 3
Identity

The chapter discusses the influence and impact of product placement of Bollywood cinema. It examines the different strategies adopted in Bollywood movies for promotional purposes in India and internationally. It does an evaluation of the effectiveness of this type of communications, including deciding about travel destinations and concentrates on the viewer's recall on the consumption of the product and its impact on improving brand image. The chapter is also to understand the consumer buying behaviour in terms of Bollywood. It assesses the product placement of Bollywood in India based on its popularity and the diversity in the types of placements and was analysed using ethnography as a method tool. From the study it was observed that the importance of Bollywood movies on masses is evident in India and internationally. Consumers feel that the advertisements should be entertaining and the same should be conjoined with the storyline in order to convey the brand message in the best possible way. The chapter tries to locate the solutions and recommendations of the Bollywood film crisis.

This chapter, from a historical anthropological perspective, discusses the role of heritage museums in Danish coastal tourism. It is argued that the museum experience is highly contextual making it necessary to understand how place specific heritage interacts with tourist holiday motivations and museums understanding of their role as heritage suppliers. The interplay of these factors must be understood to create better bonds between museums and visitors especially in a tourism context. In order to do this, new questions must be asked, and research should move away from binary understandings of demand and supply.

This research examines the strength of the Turkish Georgians ethnic identity in Turkey and Germany, issues of socialization with German society, and perception of "home" and "consumption" of the past to define ethnic identity. Consumption is not only a way of behaving, but it is also part of a way of life, which is defined by ethnic and religious identity, which itself defines consumer behaviour. A perception of self-identification, linkage with forefathers, and a search for a long-lost past are particularly necessary in foreign countries, and different reminders regarding the past and origin are considered to be the best means. Consumption of "past" and (re)construction of memories form a tight-knit ethnic unit in a foreign country, and institutionalization of own culture is so strong that many of the ethnic participants feel as if they were living in their own country. Ethnic "retailers" (communities, membership groups) provide the "emotional glue" that sticks ethnic participants together giving them a sense of identity.

As a consequence of long-term organic integration with their homeland, a characteristic lifestyle developed among the Georgians. This is particularly evident in the richly variegated customs, traditions, and norms of everyday behavior. To a significant degree they are conditioned by thousands of years of adaptation to the environment, and its associated biocultural and socio-economic forms. From the earliest times these complexes of economic-cultural relations implied the possession of the land by social units – families – on the basis of juridical norms founded upon blood relationship. Such relations were firmly grounded upon common tribal shrines, through which was acknowledged the tribal territory's chief patron and regulator. It follows that each land-owning family of the tribe, on the basis of vassalage to the shrine, was directly responsible before the shrine, and, accordingly, the moral comportment of each tribal member was marked by deep and honest respect for the deity.

Housing is more than a living space; it represents a social status capable of promoting several forms and levels of socialization and segregation. Housing is characterized by a set of attributes and functions that are valued differently, in which the consumption of "good housing" is made considering the preferences of their attributes, perceived tangibly/intangibly by the consumers. The reciprocal relation between housing and space, and the lack of structured information capable of apprising the key drivers of such dimensions increase the complexity of understanding the rational mechanisms of evaluating the real housing value. Despite the challenges associated with the modelling of housing markets, urban studies and spatial econometric literature provide a broad (but unfinished) theoretical framework and practical tools that are able to describe, understand, and predict households' housing consumption. Thus, the aim of this chapter is to present concepts and techniques to rationally capture individual and collective housing preferences, and the way in which they interact.

The chapter analyses alpaca (Vicugna pacos) meat production and consumption in Peru. The analysis highlights what affects alpaca meat consumption, drawing from exploratory studies in the Andean high zone of Arequipa, Puno, and Cusco. The reasons that are behind alpaca meat consumption decisions are anthropological aspects related to historical and cultural processes, as well as the commercial channels and the presentation of the product. In this sense, the authors link the theoretical approach on consumption, emphasizing the influence of the consumer in the market and vice versa. Nevertheless, it is interesting to note that even in the current conditions of the market there is a growth in the demand for alpaca meat resulting from the increase in tourism flows, not only of foreigners but also Peruvians.

Wine has been a part of human history for thousands of years, serving both social and religious roles. Just a few centuries ago, it became possible to store wine in good conditions, allowing it to be bottled and aged, which created a luxury product, consumed as a token of prestige. This study aimed to analyse wine brand managers' perceptions on the motivations behind luxury wine consumption. Given the exploratory nature of the study, eight interviews with Portuguese luxury wine producers and distributors' managers have been undertaken. The content analysis of the interviews seems to indicate that, overall, there is a strong understanding of the consumers' motivations. Yet, there are certain more specific aspects with the potential to be explored in order to raise the efficiency of the strategies being employed.

The term sustainable consumption is not only a behavior type in marketing and a just consumption behavior, it is more than this. Sustainable or responsible consumption behavior can change the world. Sustainable consumption concept has been investigated widely in the literature and factors that effecting sustainable consumption or being a green consumer has been investigated recently, too. But the relationship between sustainable development and consumer behavior isn't investigated sufficiently. After 2030 Sustainable Development Goals set up, responsibilities and roles have been an important issue to achieve sustainable development in the long term. In this point, this study aims to investigate the consumer role for sustainable development goals through sustainable consumption patterns and trends.

The global automotive industry is both vast in its complexity and vital to the lifestyles of many residents in the industrialized world. Cars not only make transportation easier, but are associated with a sense of freedom and economic accomplishment. A better understanding of people's lifestyles, values, and mobility needs has led the automakers to redefine their long-term strategies as a base to a new development of products/services to support the new mobility. This chapter highlights the challenges and the main disrupting factors for the automotive sector to move towards mobility companies. This chapter gives a

Foreword

While the best predictor of your next purchase often happens to be your last purchase, mainly in high frequency sectors, there are three fundamental shifts that turn the future of consumption much harder to predict than ever. The demographic aging, the pivot to health or environment conscience and the ubiquitous progress of technology in our lives, all point into greater frugality or deflation. If the past tells us apparently little, if anything, about this future, these new behaviours to be discovered or leveraged are nevertheless already here, somewhere, just not widely distributed, yet.

Is Japan grey hair society a glimpse of our future societies? Will Chinese people grow old before they become rich? Will we become farmers again? Is China a blueprint for booming Africa consumption? Will we print our own meat or shirts at home? Will machines replenish automatically our fridges? And more importantly, is the future of shopping no shopping at all?

Our ability to believe together in collective myths such as nations, religions or even money is what made us human in the first place (Harari, Y. N., in Sapiens*: A Brief History of Humankind*). In this context, shopping appears to be serving a broader purpose than just fulfilling needs, as our choices tell something about who we are, about who we want to be. Or about how we want to be perceived. Shopping choices are often the visible manifestation of the empires previously imprinted in our minds and this book is a formidable attempt at uncovering the infinite aspects – shall we say empires- of consumption. A must read for any marketing and sales practioner and researcher. A must consult for whoever seeks inspiration around the role consumption is likely to play in our future societies.

Luis Simoes
Kantar, France

Luis Simoes *is Global Chief Strategy Officer at Kantar, Worldpanel Division. More than 20 years of deep professional services in FMCG (Fast-moving consumer goods) across all continents. Wide range of interests from actual behaviour analytics, innovative data application, business and corporate strategy. Worked at Nielsen, now Kantar and led WPP investment in Infoscout/ Numerator (SF) where he served as board member.*

Foreword

Marketing, consumer research and anthropology used to be strange bed fellows, and for many they remain a fairly incompatible set of disciplines. There was, and is in many ways, fairly thick theoretical and practical walls between these domains, in terms of academic discipline as well as practice. It is, however, a wall with not only an increasing number of cracks in it but also a number of big, blatant (and welcome!) holes.

In terms of business practice, the Ethnographic Practice in Industry Conference is one public stage witnessing the both increasing and successful application of principles of anthropological method and theory in business-oriented problem solving. Many corporate entities worldwide now embrace ethnographic studies as part of their knowledge generation and managements systems. Last but not least, the increase in the use of data analytics and Artificial Intelligence tools in the business world also calls for an increasing use of anthropological analytical skills which are able to discern the social patterns revealed through 'big data'. On the academic front, there is a similar steeply rising tendency to couple anthropological insights with market-oriented studies. The present volume is just one element in a stream of academic literature mobilizing many, some or a few elements of anthropological concepts and methods for business research. Indeed, while far from all contributions here can be said to be clear-cut examples of anthropological insight, the chapters are witnessing the scope of interactions between anthropology and business. We find here examples of the application of ethnographically inspired methods for very classical business problems such as consumer motivations – actually a more psychologically oriented notion - and brand management issues. But we also find studies pertaining to historical anthropology, market systems in developing economies, analyses of the culture of specific markets, and anthropological insights into market devices, including a focus on the "unsung hero of globalization", the shipping container. The latter draws attention to a growing interest in networks of materiality and relations underpinning consumption.

The entire research domain of what is today known Consumer Culture Theory, complete with an international association, conferences and workshops, doctoral education programs, can be said to be an outcome of the idea, that business programs in general would benefit tremendously from a more culturally informed, socio-anthropologically theorized and methodologically inspired approach to consumption practices beyond the predominant focus on consumer decision making, rooted in economics or psychology. The nexus is also visible in academic educational programs. From one side, the interest in market conditions is increasingly visible in the topics in masters' theses from the anthropological educational programs in Denmark. While these are predominantly of critical approach, they do demonstrate the increasing willingness to engage with business related issues, not exclusively from a critical point but also in order to improve and rethink business practices in order to generate larger respect for cultural and natural environments. The power and instrumentality of ethnographic skills is, on the other hand, not lost on a good number of business education contexts. Anthropologically inspired classes in ethnographic methods and cultural knowledge are becoming standard elements in many business programs across the world. In other words, there are quite a few attempts to include, what anthropology has to offer into business academia. Maybe none or only a few of these are as thorough in their insistence on the crossroad between anthropology and market intelligence as University of Southern Denmark's BSc program in Market and Management Anthropology. Incorporating courses from as well anthropology as critical business studies, regular business courses and a bit of political science and law to top it off, this is a truly interdisciplinary program. "The business of business is business", Milton Friedman famously quipped, thereby laying the ground for the landslide of the shareholder perspective overtaking much of the world's enterprise ethos in the decades around the recent turn of the Millennium. Obviously, this dictum leaves only a very limited space for ethics in business, basically making it enough to obey the law and to the extent possible even stretch it to the maximum whenever there is an opportunity for extra profit. The number of business scandals making the headlines in the local and global press witness the sometimes quite meagre impact of ethical principles on business. But maybe we should not put the blame exclusively on the individual corporations. The fierce competition in the neo-liberalized global market is making profitability at all (ethical) cost a tempting and possibly even necessary goal to pursue. Hence, a good part of the problem is of systemic character. Anthropology has its own share of historical issues concerning ethics. For a start it is obviously historically connected to the explorations and exploitations of colonialism, a legacy lasting well into the twentieth century. Furthermore, the discipline is not free from its own scandals and abuse in more recent times, including usage of anthropological insight in various military interventions around the world. Finally, contemporary development projects also at times mobilizes anthropological knowledge in order to facilitate the inclusion of tribal and other indigenous people in a global world economy with the resources that these indigenous groups possess – far from always to the benefits of the tribal and indigenous groups. The tools of ethnographic method and anthropological theory are powerful tools, maybe the most powerful tools in cultural understanding. This raises important ethical questions, not least when put to instrumental use in such a significant sector for the global and local wellbeing – a significance that is most of the time ambiguous, ambivalent and complex – as the contemporary business world. It is therefore worthwhile to remind the reader in this context, of the general ethical motto prevailing in anthropology (at least as an ideal if not always practiced): Do no harm! Or, expressed slightly differently and with a Scandinavian touch, as a final remark I will remind the reader of the Pippi Longstocking principle: If you are very strong, you also should be very sweet.

Søren Askegaard
University of Southern Denmark, Denmark

Søren Askegaard *is Professor at Department of Marketing and Management, University of Southern Denmark, and Chair, Danish Institute for Advanced Study. MA in social sciences, DESS political and social communication, PhD business studies. Associate Editor of the Journal of Consumer Research. Founder of the Market and Management Anthropology study program. President-elect of the Consumer Culture Theory Consortium. Current research interests: consumer culture theory and logics, the anthropos of marketing, ideologies of health.*

Preface

Learn from the past if you want to predict the future – Confucius (551 BC - 479 BC)

Anthropological Approaches to Understanding Consumption Patterns and Consumer Behavior bridges the gap between what marketers say about the specialized topic called consumer behavior, and what social anthropologists really know about why people want things. And what a spectacular conversation these two fields of research will have throughout the book. It is like putting the two sides of a coin, which have always been with their backs turned on to each other, facing each other – finally!

The disciplines of Anthropology and Consumer Research have long been separated in silos and this book is an innovative way to join them in a unique perspective that leads to a more profound knowledge and unique understanding of the behaviors, as a way to predict the future.

This book is a truly international, interdisciplinary and integrated vision on the topic of consumption, bringing the academy and industry together. It offers a unique perspective of 70 highly professional and experienced researchers and practitioners from all continents of the world, leading to interesting and worthwhile work.

Readers can inspire on lessons from ancient civilizations and on perspectives of modern societies for the future of consumption. This book has contributions from authors from 20 countries, including Australia, Austria, Belgium, Brazil, Canada, Denmark, France, Georgia, Germany, Israel, Italy, Netherlands, Peru, Poland, Portugal, Russia, South Africa, Turkey, United Kingdom and United States of America – which just by itself is an example of globalization. It is notorious that each and every one of them is proud of their heritage but at the same time, they all defend that it is crucial to create a common value, which can be reached by working together and learning from each other's identities.

"Anthropological Approaches to Understanding Consumption Patterns and Consumer Behavior" offers a compilation of 24 chapters presenting a holistic approach and is organized in four sections: "Essential", "Globalization", "Identity" and "Tendencies". The spread of this orientation has meant foregoing other ways of seeing the place of consumption in social life and predict tendencies.

ESSENTIAL

Consumption is part of a way of life (Douglas, 2002) and Section 1 (Essential) intends to bring a holistic approach to the specialized topic called Consumption Patterns and Consumer Behavior. To be able to understand the evolution of consumption, nothing better than checking what anthropology has to say about the topic.

Anthropology is the study of humans, the study of human behavior and of societies, both in the past and in the present (Hannerz, 2001) and anthropologists have unique perspectives on the deep history of human experience. Consequentially, consumer behavior arose as an inter-disciplinary social science that examines how emotions, attitudes and preferences affect buying behavior and decision making.

Consumer behavior has established itself as a discipline in its own right (Solomon, 2020), blending elements from psychology, sociology, social anthropology, anthropology, ethnography, marketing and economics, especially behavioral economics.

The four chapters that compose the first section of the book introduce the conceptualization of the Anthropology and Consumption.

In the first chapter, "Leading the Way to a Sustainable Future: The Positive Impact of a Generation Marketing Campaign", Teresa Coelho, Valentina Chkoniya, Ana Oliveira Madsen, and Carlos Figueiredo show the importance of the consumption patterns as an indicator of a generation's identity in a world where globalization tends to standardize everything and digital technology tends to accelerate the globalization process. This chapter brings the academy and industry together and gives the example of Docapesca's pioneer initiative to prove that it is worth to invest in consumer's education, and that, when we adopt a generation focused approach to implement a national marketing campaign, it is possible to obtain valuable advances in consumption for a sustainable future

The second chapter, "Personalization 3.0: How Personality Can Predict Consumer Behavior", by Katharina Sophie Kuehn, discusses the approaches that attempt to predict consumer behavior. The author proposes a biopsychological framework to understand personality based on evolutionary studies of primal emotion systems and explains how this framework can predict preferences and behavioral tendencies in consumers. To ascertain the validity of the theory, four experiments were conducted to test and confirm personality-specific predictions regarding the effectiveness of personalized advertising campaigns, product choices, and brand preference.

In the third chapter, "Gifts as Language: Gift Code Between Relatives", anthropologist Alice Duarte addresses the issue of gifts as a language of sociability. This chapter proposes to analyze consumption as a cultural practice, pointing out the instrumental role of commodities as a language available to social actors to express and communicate. It also highlights some aspects of the gift code between relatives, the key purpose of which is to explain how interpersonal relations are produced through the exchange of gifts between subjects, in this case linked by family ties.

The fourth chapter, "How to Deal with Corporations' Complicatedness: A Brazilian Example", by Manuel Luiz from Boston Consulting Group, discusses how companies in the 21st century need to simplify their internal processes in order to become competitive in the external market and foster productivity. The authors focus the discussion in Brazil, an emerging economy that suffers the effect of Globalization (as much as other developed economies). The chapter suggests a possible framework to address the need for simplifying the company's internal context and driving performance in order to fight the growing external complexity.

GLOBALIZATION

Section 2 of this book (Globalization) addresses the common denominator in all the contributions that were being submitted while this book was being put together from all around the world: globalization. Globalization is omnipresent in this book since, nowadays, there is a complete interdependence between the world's economies, between cultures, populations, technology and information. It is almost unthinkable to imagine how planet hearth would keep moving without cross-border trade of goods and services, and how people would react if suddenly travelling was no longer possible.

The next four chapters show that there are frontiers of consumption all around us and that companies and individuals are now encouraged to think of themselves as in a relationship with in a global market. Globalization is the word used to describe the growing interdependence of the world's economies, cultures, and populations, brought about by cross-border trade in goods and services, technology, and flows of investment, people, and information (Kolb & Trade and Investment Policy Watch, 2018).

The fifth chapter, "Customer-Oriented Global Supply Chains: Port Logistics in the Era of Globalization and Digitization", brings the academy, Port of Sines and Rangel Logistics Solutions together. José Luís Cacho, Luís Marques and Álvaro Nascimento suggest that logistic services are central to the design and management of any supply chain. Due to recent technological advances, modern supply chains are challenging traditional market boundaries in ways that both influence and are influenced by consumer behavior. The authors underline the need to adjust logistic services and adapt to new and emerging challenges, its costs and risks to end consumers.

Following supply chain evolution, the sixth chapter is devoted to "Impact of Container Shipping and Ports on Globalization and Consumer Behavior" and was written by Santosh Kumar Singh from APM Terminals – Maersk Group. The author defends that container shipping is the unsung hero of globalization and underlines that despite containerization and container shipping having such an all-encompassing impact and consequences on consumption, consumption patterns, consumer behavior and societies in every corner of the world, container shipping is simply invisible to the world at large. The chapter also looks at impact of ever-growing large ports on the society and economy of the cities the ports are located in.

In the seventh chapter, "Consumers' Acceptance and Resistance Factors Toward Smart Retail Stores", Elodie Attié, Lars Meyer-Waarden and Eric Bachié suggest that the Internet of Things (IOT) allows companies to better understand consumers' needs while improving sales conditions (e.g., easier access to products and information, gain of time for employees and consumers, smart entertaining environments, etc.). This chapter brings the academy and Percall (company expert in the integration of PLM and IOT systems in the major high-tech industries) together in order to discuss the roles of consumer well-being, social image, utility value, human value, privacy concerns, technology trust, health concerns, and different personality traits toward smart retail stores.

The eighth chapter, "Value Proposition of Network Companies Providing Restaurant Services in Russia: Analysis and Evaluation", by Elizaveta Fainshtein and Elena Serova, tries to explain how customers perceive the value proposition content of network companies providing restaurant services. The chapter presents the results of the restaurants value proposition study in Saint Petersburg (Russia) according to industry data, as well as identifies the target audience key needs and industry characteristics in the market, semantic core formation and clustering in order to identify the main criteria affecting the value proposition formation.

In the ninth chapter, "Cross-Cultural Differences and Similarities in Retailers' Branding and Digital Maturity: A Cross-Border Case Study", Andreas Hesse, Pieter Steenkamp, Holger J. Schmidt and Virimai V. Mugobo focus on digital disruption and the way it is impacting all types of businesses, including retail. This chapter reflects cross-cultural similarities and differences. German and South African consumers increasingly use the Internet to look for product information and to purchase online products and services. Retailers were analyzed in order to compare and contrast their progression along a digital maturity scale as well as their branding practices.

In the tenth chapter, "If You Want to Trigger an Emotional Purchase: Don't Make Your Customers Think – Understanding Customers' Decision Making", Liraz Margalit explains that the classic economic theory describes consumers as rational economic actors that select an alternative only after considering all the relevant information. However, while the logical process is certainly a key factor in considered purchases such as insurance or financial products, it is actually detrimental to the retail-consumer industry, where emotional decision-making or the impulse purchase plays a central role. This chapter deals with the significant role of emotions in everyday purchase decisions.

IDENTITY

One of the greatest challenges that humanity faces today is to balance forces of globalization with national identities (Beriss, 2019). Values are fundamental to our life in a community, to avoid becoming a nihilist society that knows nothing but money and commerce … and the reason why there is hope (Lipovetsky, 2019).

"Identity" is addressed in Section 3, and as we now know, it derives mainly from the work of psychologist Erik Erikson in the 1950s, failing to capture the word's current meanings in everyday and social science contexts (Erikson, 1968). Deep concern with identity issues, joined eight chapters in this section.

In the eleventh chapter, "How Bollywood Filmdom Operate in India and in International Arena: Consumption of Bollywood", social anthropologist Nandini Sen discusses the influence and impact of product placement of Bollywood cinema. The chapter examines the different strategies adopted in Bollywood movies for promotional purposes in India and internationally. Consumers feel that the advertisements should be entertaining and the same should be conjoined with the storyline in order to convey the brand message in the best possible way. The chapter tries to locate the solutions and recommendations of the Bollywood film crisis.

The twelfth chapter, "Not a 'Coke and Chips' Holiday: Museums in Danish Coastal Tourism", by Barbora Gulisova and Lulu Anne Hansen, from a historical anthropological perspective, discusses the role of heritage museums in Danish coastal tourism. It is argued that the museum experience is highly contextual, making it necessary to understand how place specific heritage interacts with tourist holiday motivations and museums understanding of their role as heritage suppliers.

In the thirteenth chapter, "'Consumption'" of Past to Define Ethnic Identity in Real Time and Space: The Case of Turkish Georgians in Turkey and Germany", Nino Okrostsvaridze and Elisabed Bzhalava examine the strength of Turkish Georgians ethnic identity in Turkey and Germany, issues of socialization with German society, perception of "home" and "consumption" of the past to define ethnic identity. The authors defend that, ethnic "retailers" (communities, membership groups) provide the 'emotional glue' that sticks ethnic participants together giving them a sense of identity.

Following the topic, in the fourteenth chapter, "Dwelling and Cult in the Life and Culture of the Ancient Georgians", Paata Bukhrashvili shows that the housing construction phenomenon is particularly interesting since the anthropological tolls/ materials which have been discovered and collected on different sites, reflect many aspects of the economic, social and spiritual life of the people who lived in a specific place.

The fifteenth chapter, "Housing Consumption: A Territorial Analysis of Housing Market Drivers", by Joao Lourenço Marques, Paulo Batista, Eduardo Anselmo Castro and Arnab Bhattacharjee, gives a modern perspective on housing topic. The chapter defends that, housing is more than a living space; it represents a social status able of promoting several forms and levels of socialization and segregation. Thus, this chapter presents concepts and techniques to rationally capture individual and collective housing preferences, and the way in which they interact.

In the sixteenth chapter, "Alpaca Meat: Constraints and Reinforcements on Consumption", Yezelia Danira Caceres, Sara Calado Gonzalez and Juan Rivera Medina analyze alpaca (vicugna pacos) meat production and consumption in Peru. The reasons that are behind alpaca meat consumption decisions are anthropological aspects related to historical and cultural processes, as well as the commercial channels and the presentation of the product.

In the seventeenth chapter, "The Portuguese Luxury Wine Market: A Study on the Perceptions of Wine Brand Managers", Nuno Metello de Nápoles, Helena Nobre and Raquel Meneses explain that wine has been a part of human history for thousands of years, serving both social and religious roles. This chapter pays special attention to wine brand managers' perceptions on the motivations behind luxury wine consumption.

The eighteenth chapter is devoted to "The Consumer Role for Sustainable Development: How Consumers Contribute Sustainable Development Goals" and was written by Seda Yildirim. It explains the term of sustainable consumption and 2030 Sustainable Development Goals, aiming to investigate consumer's role for sustainable development goals through sustainable consumption patterns and trends.

TENDENCIES

Section 4 (Tendencies), addresses the study of consumer behavior and how it is concerned with all aspects of purchasing behavior – from pre-purchase activities through to post-purchase consumption, evaluation and disposal activities. It is also concerned with all persons involved, either directly or indirectly, in purchasing decisions and consumption activities including brand-influencers and opinion leaders. Research has shown that consumer behavior is difficult to predict, even for experts in the field. However, new research methods such as ethnography and consumer neuroscience are shedding new light on how consumers make decisions.

The last six chapters address some business and research trends, strategies and opportunities in Artificial Intelligence (AI) era.

In the nineteenth chapter, "Automotive Sector Moving Towards Mobility Companies: The New Mobility Landscape", Marlene Almeida, as working for a major automotive company expert, explains how the industry has been influenced by different trends in an evolving society.

The twentieth chapter, "The Roles of Time Orientation and Innate Innovativeness on Intentioned Adoption of an AI Innovation: The Study of Millennial Consumers in London, UK", by Giorgi Antadze, examines the extent of innovation adoption to personality traits, namely time orientation and innate innovativeness, and how they influence the intention to adopt a specific innovation - the virtual nurse assistant.

In the twenty-first chapter, "Decision-Making as a Socio-Cognitive Process", Monique Borges, Joao Lourenço Marques and Eduardo Anselmo Castro underline that researchers from multidisciplinary scientific fields have been puzzled by human behavior in dynamic and complex decision-making contexts. This chapter focuses on how socio-cognitive theories have been introduced as analytic tools to explain individual and collective behaviors, decision rules and cognitive mechanisms.

The twenty-second chapter, "Neuromarketing as an Environmental Awareness Tool: The Sustainable Consumption", by Alexandre Silva Quevedo, Daniela Müller Quevedo, Paola Schmitt Figueiró, and

Elissa Kerli Fernandes, shares one of the greatest concerns of the last century: that human activities can extinguish the living conditions on the planet. This chapter presents a critical review of the main studies conducted by researchers in the last decade related to the theme of sustainable consumption associated with neuromarketing.

In the twenty-third chapter, "Merging Explicit Declarations With Implicit Response Time to Better Predict Behavior", Rafal Ohme, Michał Matukin and Paula Wicher explain that declarations and actions do not always overlap and thus predicting future behavior solely on the basis of self-reported measures seems to be ineffective. The authors propose a Confidence Index (CI) - a measure based on Fazio's attitude accessibility model. The chapter provides actionable insights on how to improve sales team performance.

Finally, in the twenty-fourth chapter, "The Neuromarketing Revolution: Bringing Science and Technology to Marketing Insight", Elissa Moses and Kimberly Rose Clarkhis examine the advent of the Neuromarketing Revolution which over the past 10 years changed the way market research is conducted worldwide to include nonconscious measures in everyday studies. Authors show that neurometrics are considered of high value for understanding consumer response and of great potential value for improving prediction leveraging AI and machine learning.

As the book demonstrates, the deep belief of the authors is that to be able to supplant the global challenges put in front of us by the future of consumption and by the occurrence of unpredictable events - in times where trade is indispensable for the survival of our habits and for the maintenance of our status quo - researchers need to start working in a connected way across various disciplines and across different sectors, and the resulting knowledge needs to be shared with the rest of the world, so that through the exchange of new ideas, multi-disciplinary solutions can be created.

By bridging the gap between Anthropology and Consumer Research, this book belongs to the niche of pioneering researcher, in where authors are encouraged collaborating with their peers from other disciplines and industries, so to reach multi-disciplinary solutions.

Featuring practice and research on topics such as consumer behavior, social anthropology, market research, customer experience, consumer insights, trends studies, consumption tendencies, housing phenomenon and ethnographic research, this book is ideally designed for academicians, researchers and business professionals in marketing, management, marketing strategy, shopper marketing, market intelligence, supply chain and social anthropology seeking coverage on the use of anthropology in understanding how people interact with goods, redesigning the customer experience and predicting trends in consumer behavior.

"Anthropological Approaches to Understanding Consumption Patterns and Consumer Behavior" is meant to be used as a basis for further research, but also as an essential reference source for practice and for those that are concerned with their contribution to a better world.

Editors of this book wish, that by looking at the past the future becomes brighter, contributing to a better understanding of people and their behavior!

Valentina Chkoniya
University of Aveiro, Portugal

Ana Oliveira Madsen
CEGE, Católica Porto Business School, Portugal & Universidade Católica Portuguesa, Porto, Portugal

Paata Bukhrashvili
Ilia State University, Georgia

REFERENCES

Beriss, D. (2019). Food: Location, Location, Location. *Annual Review of Anthropology, 48*. doi:10.1146/annurev-anthro-102317-050249

Confucius. (2006). *The Analects of Confucius*. ReadHowYouWant.com, Limited.

Douglas, M. (2002). *The World of Goods: Towards an Anthropology of Consumption*. Routledge. doi:10.4324/9780203434857

Erikson, E. H. (1968). *Identity: Youth and Crisis*. W. W. Norton.

Hannerz, U. (2001). Anthropology. Oxford: Pergamon;

Lipovetsky, G. (2019). *Agradar e Tocar: ensaio sobre a sociedade da sedução*. Edições 70.

Solomon, M. R. (2020). *Consumer Behavior: Buying, Having, And Being (6th ed.)*. Pearson Education.

Acknowledgment

The editors would like to acknowledge the contribution of all the people involved in this project and, more specifically, the authors, the editorial advisory board and the reviewers that accepted embarking in the challenge of bridging the gap between Anthropology and Consumer Research, between Marketeers and Anthropologists, between Academia and Industry.

The path has been long and those who prevailed, will have their names written on the future of a unique perspective about people and consumption, about a way to unveil the future by looking at the past.

We hope you are as proud as we are of the final result, and wish you the best for your future projects. Thank YOU for your contribution!

Valentina Chkoniya
University of Aveiro, Portugal

Ana Oliveira Madsen
CEGE, Católica Porto Business School, Portugal & Universidade Católica Portuguesa, Porto, Portugal

Paata Bukhrashvili
Ilia state University, Georgia

Section 1
Essential

Chapter 1
Leading the Way to a Sustainable Future:
The Positive Impact of a Generation Marketing Campaign

Teresa Coelho
Docapesca – Portos e Lotas, S.A., Portugal

Valentina Chkoniya
https://orcid.org/0000-0003-1174-3216
University of Aveiro, Portugal

Ana Oliveira Madsen
CEGE, Católica Porto Business School, Portugal & Universidade Católica Portuguesa, Porto, Portugal

Carlos Figueiredo
Docapesca – Portos e Lotas, S.A., Portugal

ABSTRACT

Consumption patterns have always been an important indicator of a generation's identity, but in a world where globalization tends to standardize everything and digital technology tends to accelerate the globalization process, some might predict that identities are dissolving faster than ever. This chapter aims to help understand how new Portuguese generations perceive fish products. Throughout this research, it became very evident that young consumers are very aware of the ultimate emergency of sustainability. This chapter uses the example of Docapesca's pioneer initiative to prove that it is worth investing in consumer education and that, when we adopt a generation focused approach to implement a national marketing campaign, it is possible to obtain valuable advances in consumption for a sustainable future.

DOI: 10.4018/978-1-7998-3115-0.ch001

Copyright © 2020, IGI Global. Copying or distributing in print or electronic forms without written permission of IGI Global is prohibited.

INTRODUCTION

One of the greatest challenges humanity faces today is to balance the forces of globalization with national identities (Beriss, 2019). This chapter highlights the growing importance of the testimony that passes to the new generations of consumers and that preserves a country's uniqueness. It presents the results of a very recent campaign that was created to increase consumers' awareness regarding sustainability; the campaign was implemented by Docapesca Portos e Lotas, SA Portugal (a state-owned company, under the Ministry of Finance and the Ministry of Sea).

In the last few years a lot has been said – and published – regarding the possibility and the advantages of making campaigns to increase the awareness of consumers to various prominent and urgent issues. Food sustainability, namely fish sustainability, has been one of the most crucial of those issues. Marketing communications are one of the most difficult but crucially important components of modern marketing (Reynolds & Phillips, 2019). One of the most challenging and critical aspects when implementing marketing campaigns is the ability to better understand consumers' sensibility to extremely important issues and to inform consumers of some aspects of the product or service. Every year thousands of campaigns are planned and implemented all over the world, trying to reach consumers so to make them buy a specific product, service or solution (Ettenson et al., 2013) or change their attitude towards something. But somehow the analyses and the discussion of a campaign's results is a quite rare topic in the scientific literature. When national campaigns are over - after all the initiatives and communication approaches have been used and after all the money has been spent - who shows the results and where are they published? Was it worth it? It is this missing type of analyses that this chapter brings. Plus, it gives special attention to the importance of educating consumers towards a more sustainable consumption.

In 2019, consumption of fish in EU increased for nearly all of the main commercial species. Portugal is the absolute champion, with an average consumption of 57 kg of fish and seafood per person, per year. This is more than double the EU's average per capita (European Commission, 2020). The Portuguese follow the Mediterranean diet which actively encourages the consumption of fish and represents the crystallization of the centuries-old cooking legacies of different civilizations (Hidalgo-Mora et al., 2020). Culture theorists like Claude Fischler, Leon Rappoport, Mary Douglas, Poul Rozin, Massimo Montanari, Pierre Bourdieu and Cornelius Castoriadis agree that the basic determinant of population's diet is its culture, and food has always been much more than a source of physical nourishment (Madsen & Chkoniya, 2019b). In Portugal fish is such an important dietary element of the countries *cuisine* that it is difficult to imagine how people could survive without it (Simoons, 1994). Consumers target their food orientations towards fish because they have symbolic and emotional weight attached. Of course consumers also eat fish because of the rational side of it: consumers perceive fish as being particularly healthy, valuable for children because it has valuable supplements of protein, calcium, and vitamin B12, and higher fish consumption in pregnancy may confer protection against the harmful effect of prenatal exposure to toxins (Jedrychowski et al., 2010). However, in Portugal fish is much more than *just that*: in Portugal fish is impregnated with identity. But in a world where globalization tends to standardize everything and digital technology tends to accelerate the globalization process, some could predict that this heavy presence of fish in the construct of Portuguese identity is going to dissolve quickly in a near future. There is an eternal *love story* between Portugal and fish (Madsen, 2014), that is transmitted through out generations and so this heavy testimony is inherited.

This chapter uses the example of Docapesca's pioneer initiative to prove that it is worth it to invest in consumer's education, it is possible to maintain the testimony updated when we adopt a generation focused approach to implement a national marketing campaign, and it is possible to obtain valuable advances in consumption for a sustainable future.

BACKGROUND

Food Consumption, Identity and Globalization

Everybody needs to eat but the truth is that people all over the world eat different things. Food is more than just a collection of nutrients; it has always been much more than a source of physical nourishment, being an important part of everyday culture (Sanjur, 1982). Food has many different meanings attached, like identity, personal relationships and power; food is a mean to distinguish us from the rest of the world (Madsen, 2014). Food, people and society are intertwined in such a complex way that it is very difficult to disassociate one from the others (Grunert, Brunsø, Bredahl, & Bech, 2001). Food behavior is closely tied to humans' sense of personal identity and social-adjustment habits (Rappoport, 2010), where identity and identification (with a group or society) are both of vital and symbolic importance (Fischler, 1988). Politics, religion, traditions and languages, create and reinforce the idea of identity by connecting it with favorable views of society (Brewer & Trentmann, 2006). The foods eaten, like the language spoken and the groups to which we belong to, are part of our identity. The food we eat is such an important issue that it even has the strength to define us (Fischler et al., 2011).

Culture - a particularly aspect when dealing with fish consumption in Portugal - is a complex whole that includes knowledge, beliefs, art, morals, law, customs, and any other capabilities and habits acquired by man as a member of society (Fieldhouse, 1986; Scupin, 2016). Different cultures give consumers different habits and traditions, and in the end, different identities. We perceive food through our senses, which can create strong associations and memories (Holtzman, 2006). According to Farb and Armelagos 1980, food preparation and consumption is often associated with particular ritual events, which can be easily understood by the example of fish consumption in Portugal: fish is the main component of the Christmas dinner and no disadvantage is perceived by consumers when including it in their celebrations (Grunert et al., 2001).

But how does all of this survive in a global world, where food is mostly produced and distributed by global corporations? Nowadays most of us know little about who grows our food or where it comes from - which is often seen as a sign of deep alienation from the sources of food. For example, consumers from the U.S.A. or from Italy buy bananas from Ecuador; consumers from Sweden buy vegetables from Spain; English bacon – essential food in the so traditional English breakfast - actually comes from Denmark. Cod (salted and dried), does not exist in Portuguese waters but it is the second most consumed fish species in the country, representing around 38% of the national seafood demand, and it is imported from Norway, Iceland and Russia (Almeida et al., 2015).

Consumers do not care that most of the food that they commonly eat are the product of globalization (Sproesser et al., 2019). A product like coffee has its maximum levels of production in Brazil but it is Finland that shows the highest consumption per capita (International Coffee Organization, 2020). Ivory Coast has the highest production levels of chocolate in the world but its highest consumption levels per capita are in Switzerland (International Cocoa organization, ICCO – 2020). There is no other country producing as much potatoes as China but it is in Belarus that consumers eat it the most per capita (FAO, Food and Agriculture Association, 2020). The world has never been as global as now!

Globalization is a very popular word these days. It is the word used to describe the growing interdependence of the world's economies, cultures, and populations, brought about by cross-border trade in goods, services, technology, flows of investment, people, and information (Kolb, 2018). Improvements in conditions of production and transport facilities, along with the international communication possibilities, immigration and tourism, have caused great upheavals in the majority of European traditional food cultures (Kiss et al., 2019). Regarding food, the world is controlled by 10 brands: Mondelez, Coca-Cola, Nestle, PepsiCo, Associated British Products, Mars, Danone, General Mills, Kellogg's and Unilever (Business Insider, 2016). These giant corporations are in charge of almost all the food products we consume. And we are talking about all-over-the-world-consumption.

Already in 1983 Harvard Business School professor Theodore Levitt provocatively said in his work, *The Globalization of Markets,* that a global market for uniform products and services had emerged. Back then, he argued that corporations should exploit the *economics of simplicity* and grow by selling standardized products all over the world. Managers interpreted his ideas to mean that transnational companies should standardize products, packaging, and communication to achieve a least-common-denominator positioning that would be effective across cultures (Holt et. al., 2004). Since 1983 the world has implemented an incredible food system dominated by mega brands/corporations that tend to control a complex web of activities involving the production, processing, transportation, and consumption of food (Ericksen, 2008; Ingram, 2011; Zhang & Mao, 2016). It is impossible to hide from globalization and its resulting homogenization. Consumers all over the world are encouraged to try out *that new* product (Kotler, 2019), and to eat that *new* food that is spread worldwide through heavy marketing communication. In the end, consumers tend to fall for those global brands/products and the world is becoming more and more standardize. The challenge today is to balance these forces of globalization with national identities (Beriss, 2019) and to be able to survive without damaging our surroundings.

Why Sustainability Is The Future For All Businesses

On the surface, there has seemingly never been a better time to launch a sustainable offering. Consumers - particularly Millennials, generation Y - increasingly say they want brands that embrace purpose and sustainability (White et al., 2019).

Sustainable consumption is the use of goods and services that responds to basic needs and promotes a better quality of life, while minimizing the use of natural resources, toxic materials and emissions of waste and pollutants over the life cycle, in order to avoid jeopardizing the needs of future generations (Bathmanathan et al., 2018). It includes the governance and economics of food production, the degree to which we waste food, and how food production affects the natural environment (Reed & Ryan, 2019). Sustainability has become an important topic in the modern twenty-first century society; the world population continues to grow, technologies evolve, relationships between economies change while other important topics also influence economic issues - such as population, poverty, health, oil, preservation of ecosystems, food, water, climate change, and so on (Martin & Schouten, 2012). The conviction that individuals can contribute significantly to achieve long-term sustainability goals by adopting sustainable behavior patterns is one of the main premises of sustainable consumption (Zralek & Burgiel, 2020). Thus, as environmental, social, and governance (ESG) issues have become more important influencers of customer and employee expectations, organizations have tightened their embrace of sustainability programs

(Coucke et al., 2019). Indulgence, health and universalism are key features that motivate consumers to decide in favor of more sustainable alternatives. The combination of self-interest and environmental values is considered to be the most effective strategy. Faced with this combination, consumers do not have to decide between fulfilling only one of these values (Eberhart & Naderer, 2017). A global study published by Harvard Business Review in June 2019 concluded that world investors have been voicing concerns about sustainability for several decades but not until recently have they translated their words into action, in order to make the world a better place (Eccles & Klimenko, 2019).

From Generation to Generation

Generations are interconnected by common experience, life experiences and common values (Li et al., 2019). The values and the way of thinking of young people (Generation Y and Z) are distinct from the previous generations (Garia-Fodor & Csiszárik-Kocsír, 2018). The environment which surrounds the generations is changing significantly; thus the socialization of new generations takes place under these altered circumstances, which means that they are not the same as the former young generations. International studies show that the behavior and ways of life of today's young generation are different from previous generations, e.g. from their parents and grandparents (Troncoso-Pantoja, 2019). Their references are different and the most discussed ones in the scientific literature are resumed in Table 1. For example, the preferred means of communication of young generations are the smartphone, SMS's and social networks, while in their parents the reference is email, and for their grandparents it is the telephone or formal letter.

MAIN FOCUS OF THE CHAPTER

Generation Marketing Campaign

About 85% of expert marketers agree that generation marketing is the most important element in their marketing arsenal, but yet only 42% of business owners have an active plan in place (Pardot, 2020).

On the other hand, marketing communications are one of the most difficult but essential components of modern marketing (Reynolds & Phillips, 2019). Many years ago, in 1976, Jürgen Habermas considered the market as the greatest generator of national wealth known to mankind (Habermas & Fultner, 2002). In recent years the challenge of understanding markets and consumers has been made even more complicated by the explosion of new digital media options (Berger et al., 2020; Ettenson et al.,2013; Keller, 2016). The rapid development of digital technology has greatly changed the way that consumers receive business product and service information (Duralia, 2018; Xue & Lin, 2017). It is undeniable that consumers are daily assaulted by a multitude of stimuli, the vast majority of which are the result of marketing communication activities initiated by organizations operating on the domestic, international or global market (Bault & Rusconi, 2020). Since its introduction into the marketing literature - in the early 1990s - integrated marketing communications have become well accepted as an important marketing communication perspective. The idea is that integrated marketing communications may lead to higher levels of marketing performance (Tafesse & Korneliussen, 2013) and many issues related to designing and implementing marketing strategies are better understood by taking into account a perspective based on generational cohorts (Parment, 2013). This has gained widespread recognition in the marketing com-

Table 1. Differences between generations (adapted from Atkins et al., 2016; Barska, 2018; Bathmanathan et al., 2018; Ceballos & Bejarano, 2018; Chung & Lee, 2017; Chkoniya et al., 2019; Crappell, 2015; Gursoy et al., 2019; Huang et al., 2019; Lin, 2011; Kamenidou et al., 2019; Lindner Radons et al., 2016; Loroz & Helgeson, 2013; Minnema et al., 2016; Rea, 2019; Nadeem et al., 2017; Rodrigues, 2018; Roy et al., 2015; Sandy et al., 2013; Ulver, 2019)

Generation	Born	Signature Product (Defining Technology)	Communication Media	Communication Preference
Generation R (The Silent Generation)	Pre-1945	Automobile	Formal letter	Face-to-Face
Generation B (Baby Boomers)	1945-1960	Television	Telephone	Face-to-Face ideally, but telephone or e-mail if required
Generation X (Xennials)	1961-1980	Personal Computer	e-mail and text message	Text-messaging or e-mail
Generation Y (Millennial Generation)	1981-1995	Smart Phone / Tablet	Text message and Social Media	On-line and mobile (text messaging)
Generation Z (IGen)	1996-2010	Mobile devices, 3-D printings, Google and Facebook	Handheld device	Face time
Generation α (Generation Alpha)	Born after 2010	Artificial Intelligence	Too early to define	Too early to define

munication literature but concrete empirical evidences that demonstrate the contribution of implementing integrated marketing communications to campaign-level marketing performance are still limited (Tafesse & Korneliussen, 2013). In an effort to make a contribution to this area, this chapter describes a high stock fish species promotion campaign, oriented for the young generation, developed in Portugal by Docapesca - Portos e Lotas, S. A. (Docapesca).

The Example of Docapesca (in brief)

Docapesca - Portos e Lotas, S. A. is a state-owned company responsible for the management of all fishing ports in mainland Portugal and for the public service of the first sale of fish in auction. The company is present throughout the entire coastal area of mainland Portugal from Vila Praia de Âncora (on the country's top north) to Vila Real of Santo António (the country's southeast border). Since 2014 it has been a port authority in fishing and has recreational ports under his jurisdiction. Docapesca involves a cycle from "sea to the table" (whole fresh fish distribution channel) and ensures its consistency with all the actors, whether they are the master of the vessel or the fishmonger at the market or supermarket (as well as the amateur and professional cook). As an anchor in the fishing sector, Docapesca strives to transfer value to the fisheries and aquaculture sector, being decisive in the innovation of its processes and its growth. Besides giving tremendous importance to sustainability, Docapesca guarantees the high standards of food quality and safety and, more than just encouraging consumers to include more fish in its daily meals, Docapesca teaches them how to choose the best fish.

In an attempt to increase consumers' awareness of less consumed species, the company has developed a long-term campaign, divided into several parts: the *CCL – Proof of Purchase in Auction, the Chub Mackerel* Promotion Campaign and most recently the *Horse Mackerel Promotion Campaign.*

The campaign promoted by Docapesca is a reflex of the company strategic goals (Docapesca, 2020) and the sustainability of the fishing sector has been, in the recent years, one of the most important of those strategic goals. This long-term campaign relies on three pillars: *economic*, through the increase in consumption of fish and the increase of the average price of some species (thus increasing the income of fishermen); *environmenta*l, through the promotion of less captured species sold in auction by the national fishing fleet in Portuguese waters (respecting minimum fish sizes); and *social*, through the promotion of a healthy diet.

Before starting the campaign, targeted to young Portuguese generation, Docapesca carefully studied some very important elements of the integrated marketing communication: it has made a thorough market characterization, it has inquired tendencies regarding fish consumption and it has made a profile of Generation Y and Generation Z. Results were very positive.

Young Portuguese Consumers Profile

Generation Y and generation Z are relevant actors for this business, since they show a great purchasing power (Arli et al., 2019), and this group will make up 75% of the workforce by 2025 (Delloitte, 2014; Pendergast, 2007). Being generation Y and Z so pertinent in consumption, it is important to design an integrated marketing communication that targets them based on creating sustained value for society underpinned by a relation of cooperation and proximity.

The relationship between current young generations and the ones preceding them has always been ambivalent. The environment has changed significantly thus the socialization of new generations takes place under altered circumstances, which means that they are not the same as the former (once upon a time) young generations. Parents, teachers and decision makers have to accept that new values have emerged and understand the new behavioral patterns (Törőcsik et al., 2015) from young generations. Generation Y includes people born between 1980 and 1995. They are called generation Y because they came after Generation X (or maybe because of the English word youth) but most of them prefer to be known as the Millennium generation (Riedy, 2018). Being born between 1995 and 2010, generation Z was raised having internet, cannot conceive the world without ICTs (Chkoniya et al., 2019), and has no idea how the previous generations managed to survive without the digital world (Zemke & Raines, 2012). Also known as the "Facebook-generation" or the "iGeneration", they think and communicate using intrinsic digital natives (Tari, 2011). It is crucial to closely follow generation Z as they come of age and move into their prime earning and spending years, replacing their parents as the most coveted market segment (Loroz & Helgeson, 2013).

An aspect that turned out to be extremely relevant in the elaboration of the national campaign was a pre-study which was (as the name says) made before it all started. Results indicated that there is a set of characteristics common to all these people (Chkoniya et al., 2019): they are high-tech and hyper-connected (90% have a Facebook profile and 80% sleep with their mobile device), they are individualistic and ambitious (77% attach great importance to being well treated and 54% want to achieve something more in life), and they trust the experience of others (74% like to learn new things on YouTube and 57% trust the opinion of their colleague / family member more than the opinion of an expert).

However, there is also a lot that separates them and, in fact, there is not a homogeneous group of young people but rather seven segments with different philosophies of life (Coelho et al., 2018). While birth age has been a useful way to create groups, it describes segments but it does not help to understand segment motivations (Parment, 2013). The results shown in the table below reveal that seven factor groups were retained and assigned the following labels: (1) Trendy Seekers, (2) Conservatives, (3) Extreme Lifers, (4) Traditional Families, (5) Social Techies, (6) World Protectors and (7) Simple Lifers.

Table 2. The seven segments of young people with different philosophies of life (adapted from Coelho et al., 2018)

Segments	Who They Are	How They Are Characterized
Trendy Seekers (23%)	mostly 25-34 years old, balanced men and women	They are happy people and are concerned with having many friends, a successful professional career and being admired by people. Financial security is of great importance. For this reason, they seek to invest in material goods and build a solid heritage.
Conservatives (18%)	mostly 16-29 years old, both men and women	They prefer a life always with the same rhythm and live the traditional way. They are stable, discreet and calm people. They are concerned about being organized, disciplined, economical and homely.
Extreme Lifers (18%)	mostly men aged between 16 and 24 years	They consider that life is to be lived to the limit. They like to stand out from other people/crowds. They are people concerned about their food. They are very optimistic and also believe that next year their economic situation will be better.
Traditional Families (15%)	mostly women aged between 25 and 34 years	They spend most of their free time with their family. They identify themselves with the Portuguese lifestyle. They are serious, responsible and hardworking people. They prefer to save money than to enjoy it.
Social Techies (9%)	mostly men aged between 20 and 24 years	They are modern, sophisticated and sexy people. They give a lot of importance to be treated well. For them, the best part of the week is to be with their friends away from home. They invest in leisure activities (cinema, music) and are among the first to try new technologies.
World Protectors (9%)	mostly women aged between 20 and 24 years	They are people concerned with helping to build a better world. They do not make an important decision until they speak to people they trust. The opinion of friends is extremely important. They like to buy products / brands that support a social / environmental cause.
Simple Lifers (8%)	mostly women aged between 25 and 34 years	They like simple things in life, try new things / explore. They are very concerned about their food.

When talking about generations Y and Z, we are talking about people highly influenced by their peers, in constant search for information and affirmation. Over 50% of them does not make an important decision until they speak to the people they trust and look for the information they feel they need to have; they like to ask and give advice; they look for new recipes on social networks and they feel more motivated on what to do when their friends agree. The Y / Z generations like to watch online advertising because it has creative pieces (52% / 45%), and also because it introduces content on the web (48% / 46%). Movies and TV shows are equally important means of communication for 55% of them (Madsen & Chkoniya, 2019b).

It was also found that, contrary to what one could think, young Portuguese consumers know and like to cook, something that distinguishes them, for example, from what is happening with young Anglo-Saxons. Over 50% of young Portuguese like to search for new recipes on social networks, with 28% being active promoters of brands (they will continue to buy and speak well of products or services). About 57% of young Portuguese consumers like/or even love to cook and enjoy being creative in the kitchen. To 31% of them, cooking is just one of the things they do - they do not mind cooking. On the bottom end of this chart, answering "I do not like to cook, it is an annoyance", we have less than 12%. Regarding their health, 54% of young Portuguese consumers pay attention/demand good food and 46% practice a sport. When asked which changes they should implement into their diet so to eat healthier, the results were the following: cut in sweets (46%), control the amount of fat consumed (40%), eat less processed foods (39%) and follow a diet low in carbohydrates and rich in omega 3 (30%). There is also a general belief that fresh fish is the most suitable food for meals, but unfortunately it is more expensive than meat *(Coelho, et al., 2018).* What young Portuguese people like the most about fresh fish is its taste (67%) and its quality and freshness (26%). As for the main limitations when eating fish, results showed that the biggest limitation is fish-smell (42%), followed by price (25%) and difficulty to prepare (11%) (Madsen & Chkoniya, 2019a).

This study also asked young consumers who did they considered as a good national ambassador for the campaign and results indicated that young consumers perceived nautical athletes as being the most credible.

Docapesca Campaign Strategy

Following the indications of the pre-campaign study, Docapesca implemented a substantial fish campaign with nautical athletes as the front figure. The campaign included an awareness program in schools, with nautical athletes Fernando Pimenta, Francisco Lufinha, Hugo Vau, Joana Pratas and Teresa Almeida. The message emphasized on the importance of sustainability, on the benefits of consuming fish, and on the importance of children and young adults adopting healthy eating habits (Figure 1).

The "*horse mackerel* promotion campaign" (Figure 1) was developed in 2018 and 2019. It had a very clear objective of promoting the consumption of this particular species, *horse mackerel*, among 3 target audiences: final consumers, distributors and caterings (giving particular attention to young people - generations Y and Z). *Horse mackerel* was the second species to be included in this long-term oriented campaign. Already in 2012, in the beginning of this long-term national campaign, Docapesca launched the *chub mackerel*, another "top 3" species regarding fish catches/landing quantity, and that specific species was the star of the campaign until 2017 (developing this integrated marketing communication for *chub mackerel* was a different challenge than the *horse mackerel* one, since the consumption of *chub mackerel* was minimal and with no tradition in Portuguese *cuisine).* With a strategy oriented towards culinary schools and gourmet chefs, Docapesca promoted *chub mackerel* at several points of sale (such as municipal markets or the main supermarkets chains), with showcookings and workshop classes. For example, to create a gourmet style fish burger, Docapesca launched in 2014 the "Fish Gourmet Challenge". This initiative consolidated the promotion of *chub mackerel* consumption and it was aimed at students of catering courses, with the objective of developing a recipe that could be produced and packaged industrially as ready-to-eat and accessible, both from the point of view of the quality / price ratio and from the point of view of preparation and confection at home, contributing to the promotion of new uses of this fish species.

Figure 1. One of the photos with nautical athletes used in the 2018 – 2019 Campaign. Translation: "Eh Mackerel! The mackerel of our coast is good in all ways. It is healthy and sustainable."

In order to achieve this goal, a diversified approach was implemented in various media, through a television spot that ran on the three generalist Portuguese channels (RTP, SIC and TVI), advertising on ATM machines, outdoor advertising, advertisements in regional press, online presence on social networks (Facebook and Instagram), cooking classes and showcookings in municipal markets and gastronomic events (Figure 2), which obtained wide national news coverage. Just as an example of the coverage, in 2019, during week 2 of the campaign, ATM advertisement reached 2,775,086 contact (Portuguese population is around 10,000,000 people). As for the outdoor advertising, it was implemented in 22 municipalities in 2018 and 36 municipalities in 2019.

Figure 2. Photos from cooking classes, showcookings and fish gourmet challenge

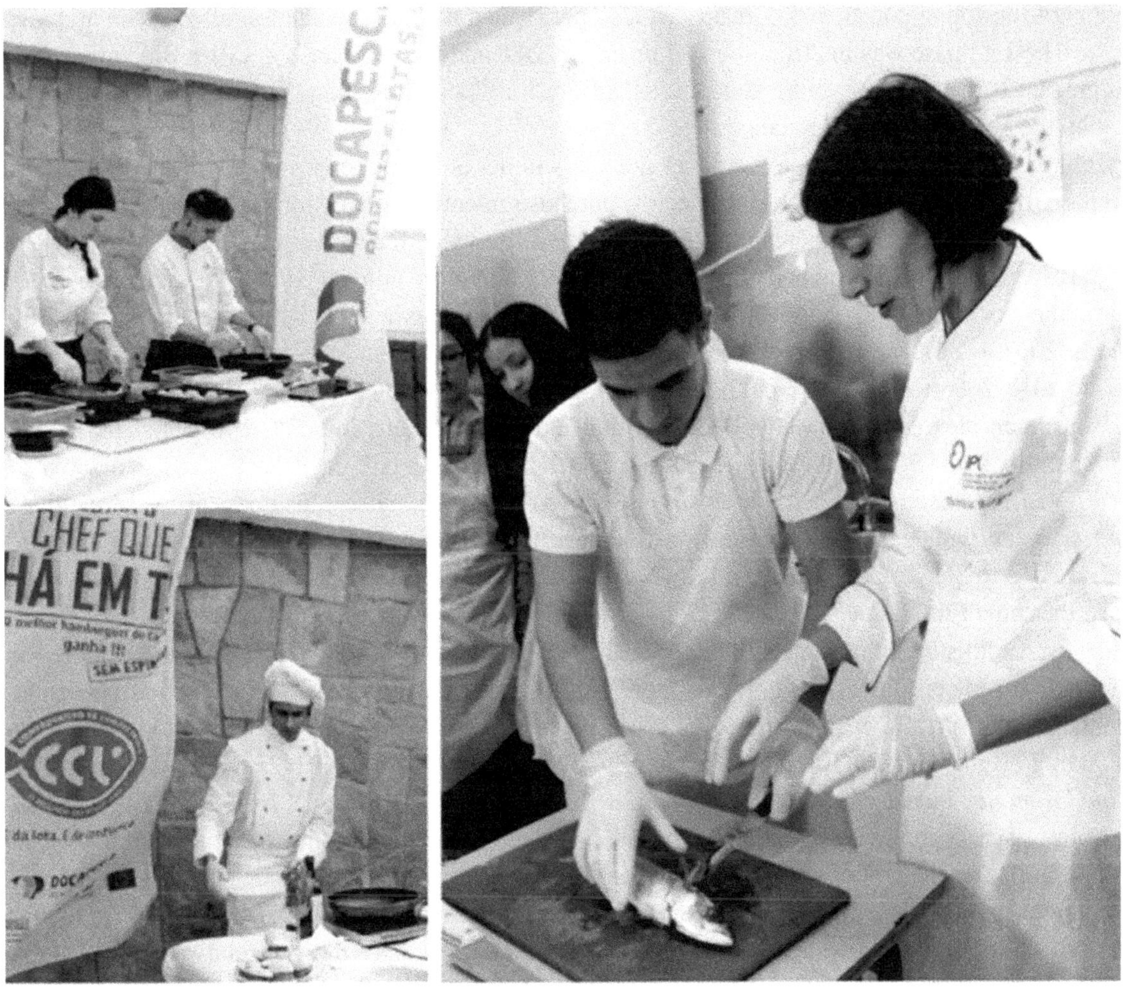

The Positive Impact of Docapesca Generation Marketing Campaign

Docapesca long-term campaign turned the page on the valuation of national fish and made undervalued species like *chub mackerel* and *horse mackerel* to be included in the Mediterranean diet. Nowadays the awareness that the food we eat is a key factor in health on a global scale has stemmed and that means that diet is receiving increasing attention as a key factor in healthy lifestyle strategies (Hidalgo-Mora et al., 2020). Since the beginning of the campaign, consumption of *chub mackerel* has risen as well as its average price at auction - 28% between 2011 and 2017 (INE 2012; INE 2018). Following a similar trend, in 2018, consumption and average price of *horse mackerel* has increased, with the latter increasing by 30%, which contributed to the increase in fishermen's income (INE, 2019).

Besides considering INE's (National Statistics Institute) data, to better understand the impact of the campaign for young consumers, Docapesca also performed a yearly evaluation after each campaign's phase. The 1st phase was in 2017, the 2nd phase in 2018 and the 3rd phase in 2019. Since the goal of this chapter is the study of young generations, a filter for Generation Z and Generation Y data was applied to the general population data.

Table 3 shows clear evidence that, over the years under analysis, there was an increase in terms of purchase intention for high stock fish species, purchase intention for fresh fish, perception of sustainability of fish species, value perception - including origin, value for money perception and knowledge about fish availability. Young consumers are now more and more convinced that Portuguese fish is the best in the world and there is a strong association of fish as being healthy. The first one increased from 68% in 2017 to 82% in 2019 ($p<0.01$, Khi2=209.10, dof=7(VS)) and the second one increased from 70% in 2018 to 86% in 2019 ($p=0.00$, Khi2=257.49, dof=6(VS).

Consumers have good knowledge about fish and understand that it is imperative to eat fish that respects sustainability quotas. The indicator increased from 61% in 2018 to 65% in 2019 ($p<0.01$, Khi2=209.10, dof=7(VS)), indicating that it is a relevant issue for young Portuguese consumers. Together with *Perception of healthiness* it shows the most positive results with an increase of 16% only in one year, from 70% in 2018 to 86% in 2019, ($p<0.01$, Khi2=632.44, dof=3(VS))).

At the same time *Knowledge about high stock fish species* availability also starts to show a growing tendency. Another big achievement of this campaign (reinforcing the idea that consumers give more value to fresh fish and consumers are more and more willing to eat fresh fish), is the fact that purchase intention increased from 50% in 2017 to 56% in 2019 ($p<0.01$, Khi2=67.57, dof=15 (VS)). *Value perception* (including origin) increased from 49% in 2017 to 60% in 2019 ($p<0.01$, Khi2=81.39, dof=4(VS)) and *Value for money* increased 24% ($p<0.01$, Khi2=949.67, dof=13(VS)).

Data was collected with quota sampling, by using a socio-demographic variable such as sex, age, and region representative of population as non-probability sampling technique. The questionnaire was anonymous in order to guarantee a higher level of participation and honesty. Each question was debated by a multidisciplinary team composed of nutritionists, marketing and survey specialists, representatives of commercial companies, statisticians, and people experienced in the seafood sector. Furthermore, the attained preliminary questionnaire was sent to a group of twenty individuals outside the expert group with the purpose of assaying the clarity, simplicity, and appropriateness of the various questions. During this process, several changes were implemented in the questionnaire keeping its original structure. It is also important to note that perception of sustainability of Portuguese high stock fish species and perception of fish as healthy food (benefits for health) were only added/evaluated after 2017 due to its growing relevance and changes in the consumption tendencies. In order to reach a large universe and

Table 3. The Positive Impact of Docapesca Campaign on the Generation Z and Generation Y

	Year of Campaign	2017	2018	2019
	After	1st phase	2nd phase	3rd phase
Purchase intention for high stock fish species	Top Two Box	50%	52%	56%
	Mean	3.17	3.26	3.4
Perception of Portuguese fish as a "best in the world"	Top Two Box	68%	75%	82%
	Mean	4.0	4.2	4.4
Perception of sustainability of Portuguese high stock fish species	Top Two Box	-	61%	65%
	Mean	-	3.83	3.84
Perception of ðsh as healthy food (benefits for health)	Top Two Box	-	70%	86%
	Mean	-	3.97	4.4
Value perception, including origin	Top Two Box	49%	58%	60%
	Mean	3.3	3.5	3.6
Value for money perception	Top Two Box	32%	53%	56%
	Mean	3	3.5	3.6
Knowledge about high stock fish species availability	Top Two Box	-	54%	58%
	Mean	-	3.72	3.75

different geographical regions of the country, a telephonic medium was the natural option. For the purpose of this chapter, the authors decided to present a filtered version of the total results (which include the general population), so to specify on Generation Z and Generation Y (392 respondents in each year).

The distribution of the importance variables of choice criteria used values in 5-point Likert type scale. Statistical analysis was carried out using the SphinxIQ software (Sphinx Company, Montréal, Canada). The difference of means between pairs was resolved by using confidence intervals in a Tukey HSD test. Level of significance was set for $p < 0.01$.

SOLUTIONS AND RECOMMENDATIONS

The challenge today is to balance the forces of globalization with national identities (Beriss, 2019), guaranteeing that cultural testimonies continue to pass from generation to generation. On the other hand, the results presented in this chapter indicate that many issues related to designing and implementing marketing strategies are also better understood and implemented by taking into account a perspective based on generational cohorts, offering an especially rich vehicle for marketing campaigns.

Docapesca is an example of success in a very challenging sector; nevertheless, and against all odds, it has managed to capture consumers' attention and is showing very positive results. Many can learn from this initiative and for sure some should follow this company's example and implement similar approaches. The most important recommendation for other companies, operating in other categories and other environments, is to follow the example described in this chapter.

Retail and mass consumption professionals can grab the challenge and take this study as a best practice example and apply it to each of the categories in which they operate. It should be done by understanding the needs of generation Y and Z, perceiving their preferred channels of communication, and hopefully, understanding how to get their message across.

Docapesca's effort was rewarded with positive results, an achievement that can be adopted by others.

FUTURE RESEARCH DIRECTIONS

After focusing the study of young generations and fish (Generations Y and Z), it would be very interesting to study other generations (generations R, B, X and alpha) and to compare the results – evaluate the changes in the last years and explore the differences in fish consumption. Another interesting direction in research would be to find out how big is the role of senior consumers in young consumers' preferences, how do they influence the youngsters. As it was mentioned before, today's young generations have a behavior and ways of life different from previous generations, their parents and grandparents (Troncoso-Pantoja, 2019). It would be extremely valuable to study the impact of senior consumers as influencers.

CONCLUSION

Globalization tends to standardize everything. From the music we hear, to the food we eat. One might say that this homogenization is inevitable and that in a near future we will all be consuming in a similar way and that the evolution of digital technology will end personalization and the tailor-made. But the fact is that identity is a strong construct that is inherited and that can be stimulated through the education of new generations. Being generation Y and Z so pertinent in consumption, it is important to design communication strategies that target them based on creating sustained value for society underpinned by a relation of cooperation and proximity. But an efficient communication requires the implementation of an integrated marketing communication. Understand the target (generations Y and Z in our chapter), how they gather information, how they decide, which sources of information they search for, who they trust, and understand the specific market are mandatory factors in a winning equation. In the case described in this chapter, consumers are high-tech, hyper-connected, individualistic, ambitious and they trust the experience of others. Portuguese fish market - with its cultural norms and traditions - is where habits for consuming are created, as it is the base where perception, socialization and cognitions are formed (Madsen, 2014). However, one must be cautious in assuming that the identification of similar attitude patterns or groups in different countries will necessarily imply the existence of similar behavior and response patterns (Douglas, 2002).

This chapter defends that it is important to identify and analyze as many terms of the equation as possible and take safe steps to fulfill the needs of each consumer, always taking into consideration that identity is a vital element in the unique solution of satisfy consumers' needs. The case of Portugal and fish is very pertinent: fish is (still) a considerable part of Portuguese identity and has a very high symbolic currency on the countries commercial marketplace – considering Eric Arnould and Craig Thompson's work we would go even further and say that *fish has identity value* (Arnould & Thompson, 2005). It is undeniable that globalization is the heavy player in the consumption set but it is also true that in this global society it is possible to maintain (and even increase) the consumption of some products like *horse mackerel.*

Some might say that fish with identity value in Portugal in the 21st century is an obvious consequence of past preferences. Though, the constant reinforcement made by Docapesca in preserving this situation has had a significant impact on its maintenance. The implementation of an integrated marketing communication has allowed Docapeca to understand consumers' needs, understand the importance of fish in Portuguese Mediterranean diet and, by taking all of that in consideration, Docapesca has managed to increase the consumption of more sustainable fish species – of less known fish species which are abundant in Portuguese waters.

Identity value does not come out of the blue, it is indispensable that companies invest in well-designed campaigns to reach the desirable outputs. This chapter has showed that the time and the money invested in a national campaign for the increase in consumption of two less known fish species which are abundant in Portuguese waters (chub mackerel and horse mackerel) will be refunded in the future by more sustainable habits that are now going to be adopted. This pioneer successful initiative has proven that it is worthy to invest in consumer's education and it is possible to have a positive return when companies adopt a generational approach to implement a campaign.

There is concrete empirical evidence demonstrating that Docapesca gave a huge help towards the valuation of national fish and towards fish sustainability and it has managed to successfully increase value of *chub mackerel* and of *horse mackerel* in Portugal. To conclude, there is evidence that when adopting a well-programed generation focused approach to implement a marketing campaign, it is possible to obtain valuable advances in consumption for a sustainable future.

REFERENCES

Almeida, C., Karadzic, V., & Vaz, S. (2015). The seafood market in Portugal: Driving forces and consequences. *Marine Policy*, *61*, 87–94. doi:10.1016/j.marpol.2015.07.012

Arli, D., Tkaczynski, A., & Anandya, D. (2019). Are religious consumers more ethical and less Machiavellian? A segmentation study of Millennials. *International Journal of Consumer Studies*, *43*(3), 263–276. doi:10.1111/ijcs.12507

Arnould, E., & Thompson, C. (2005). Consumer Culture Theory (CCT): Twenty Years of Research. *The Journal of Consumer Research*, *31*(4), 868–882. doi:10.1086/426626

Atkins, K. G., Kumar, A., & Kim, Y.-K. (2016). Smart grocery shopper segments. *Journal of International Consumer Marketing*, *28*(1), 42–53. doi:10.1080/08961530.2015.1082080

Barska, A. (2018). Millennial consumers in the convenience food market. *Management*, *22*(1), 251–264. doi:10.2478/manment-2018-0018

Bathmanathan, V., Rajadurai, J., & Sohail, M. S. (2018). Generational Consumer Patterns: A Document Analysis Method. *Global Business and Management Research*, *10*(3), 958–970. Retrieved from http://search.ebscohost.com/login.aspx?direct=true&db=bth&AN=133618190&site=eds-live

Bault, N., & Rusconi, E. (2020). The Art of Influencing Consumer Choices: A Reflection on Recent Advances in Decision Neuroscience. *Frontiers in Psychology, 10*, 3009. doi:10.3389/fpsyg.2019.03009 PMID:32038387

Berger, J., Humphreys, A., Ludwig, S., Moe, W. W., Netzer, O., & Schweidel, D. A. (2020). Uniting the Tribes: Using Text for Marketing Insight. *Journal of Marketing*, *84*(1), 1–25. doi:10.1177/0022242919873106

Brewer, J., & Trentmann, F. (2006). *Consuming cultures, global perspectives: historical trajectories, transnational exchanges*. Retrieved from https://books.google.pt/books?id=XACSAAAAIAAJ

Beriss, D. (2019). Food: Location, Location, Location. *Annual Review of Anthropology*, *48*. doi:10.1146/annurev-anthro-102317-050249

Ceballos, L. M., & Bejarano, M. (2018). Value segmentation of adolescents: A performance of appearance. *International Journal of Fashion Design. Technology & Education*, *11*(2), 148–159. doi:10.1080/17543266.2017.1352039

Chkoniya, V., Madsen, A. O., & Coelho, T. (2019). The impact of information and communication technologies in fish consumption in Portugal: Building a support for the coming generations. *Economia Agro-Alimentare*, *21*(3), 855–872. doi:10.3280/ECAG2019-003016

Chung, H., & Lee, E. (2017). Store Brand Quality and Retailer's Product Line Design. *Journal of Retailing*, *82*(4), 349–355. doi:10.1016/j.jretai.2006.08.008

Coelho, T., Chkoniya, V., & Queiroga, A. P. (2018, January). Quem são os Jovens Portugueses? Como consomem e como compram? *Distribuição Hoje*, 21–24. Retrieved from https://www.distribuicaohoje.com/insights/quem-sao-os-jovens-portugueses-como-consomem-e-como-compram/

Coucke, N., Vermeir, I., Slabbinck, H., & Van Kerckhove, A. (2019). Show Me More! The Influence of Visibility on Sustainable Food Choices. *Foods*, *8*(6), 186. doi:10.3390/foods8060186 PMID:31151326

Crappell, C. (2015). The ABCs of Gen X, Y(P), Z. *American Music Teacher, 65*(3), 40–43. Retrieved from http://search.ebscohost.com/login.aspx?direct=true&db=a9h&AN=111188950&site=eds-live

Delloitte. (2014). *The Millennial Survey 2014*. Retrieved from http://www2.deloitte.com/al/en/pages/about-deloitte/articles/2014-mil-lennial-survey-positive-impact.html

Docapesca, (2020). *Mission and Strategy*. Retrieved from www.docapesca.pt/pt/docapesca/missao-e-estrategia.html

Douglas, M. (2002). *The World of Goods: Towards an Anthropology of Consumption*. Routledge. Retrieved from https://books.google.pt/books?id=goBCb-RGfU4C

Duralia, O. (2018). Integrated Marketing Communication and Its Impact on Consumer Behavior. *Studies in Business & Economics*, *13*(2), 92–102. doi:10.2478be-2018-0022

Eberhart, A. K., & Naderer, G. (2017). Quantitative and qualitative insights into consumers' sustainable purchasing behaviour: A segmentation approach based on motives and heuristic cues. *Journal of Marketing Management*, *33*(13/14), 1149–1169. doi:10.1080/0267257X.2017.1371204

Eccles, R. G., & Klimenko, S. (2019). The Investor Revolution. *Harvard Business Review*. Retrieved from http://search.ebscohost.com/login.aspx?direct=true&db=edb&AN=135981990&site=eds-live

Ericksen, P. J. (2008). Conceptualizing food systems for global environmental change research. *Global Environmental Change*, *18*(1), 234–245. doi:10.1016/j.gloenvcha.2007.09.002

Ettenson, R., Conrado, E., & Knowles, J. (2013). Rethinking the 4 P's. *Harvard Business Review*.

European Commission. (2020). *The EU Fish Market 2019 edition is out: everything you wanted to know about the EU market for fish and seafood.* Retrieved from https://ec.europa.eu/fisheries

Fieldhouse, P. (1986). *Food & Nutrition: Customs & Culture*. Croom Helm. Retrieved from https://books.google.pt/books?id=TicOAAAAQAAJ

Fischler, C. (1988). Food, self and identity. *Information*, *27*(2), 275–292. doi:10.1177/053901888027002005

Fischler, C., Nemer, M., & France, N. (2011). *Manger mode d'emploi: entretiens avec Monique Nemer*. Fondation Nestlé France. Retrieved from https://books.google.pt/books?id=ePGyngEACAAJ

Garia-Fodor, M., & Csiszárik-Kocsír, Á. (2018). The validity of value-based consumer behavioral models in the financial consciousness of the z generation. Online Journal Modelling the New Europe, (27), 107–131. doi:10.24193/OJMNE.2018.27.05

Grunert, K. G., Brunsø, K., Bredahl, L., & Bech, A. C. (2001). Food-Related Lifestyle: A Segmentation Approach to European Food Consumers BT - Food, People and Society: A European Perspective of Consumers' Food Choices. Berlin: Springer Berlin Heidelberg. doi:10.1007/978-3-662-04601-2_14

Gursoy, D., Chi, O. H., Lu, L., & Nunkoo, R. (2019). Consumers acceptance of artificially intelligent (AI) device use in service delivery. *International Journal of Information Management*, *49*, 157–169. doi:10.1016/j.ijinfomgt.2019.03.008

Habermas, J., & Fultner, B. (2002). *On the Pragmatics of Social Interaction: Preliminary Studies in the Theory of Communicative Action*. MIT Press. Retrieved from https://books.google.pt/books?id=CQtDResLBQ8C

Hidalgo-Mora, J. J., García-Vigara, A., Sánchez-Sánchez, M. L., García-Pérez, M.-Á., Tarín, J., & Cano, A. (2020). The Mediterranean diet: A historical perspective on food for health. *Maturitas*, *132*, 65–69. doi:10.1016/j.maturitas.2019.12.002 PMID:31883665

Holt, D., Quelch, J., & Taylor, E. (2004). How Global Brands Compete. *Harvard Business Review*, *82*, 68–75,136. PMID:15449856

Holtzman, J. (2006). Food and Memory. *Annual Review of Anthropology*, *35*(1), 361–378. doi:10.1146/annurev.anthro.35.081705.123220

Huang, M.-H., Rust, R., & Maksimovic, V. (2019). The Feeling Economy: Managing in the Next Generation of Artificial Intelligence (AI). *California Management Review*, *61*(4), 43–65. doi:10.1177/0008125619863436

INE - Instituto Nacional de Estatística. (2012). *Estatísticas da Pesca: 2011*. Lisboa: INE.

INE - Instituto Nacional de Estatística. (2018). *Estatísticas da Pesca: 2017*. Lisboa: INE.

INE - Instituto Nacional de Estatística. (2019). *Estatísticas da Pesca: 2018*. Lisboa: INE.

Ingram, J. (2011). A food systems approach to researching food security and its interactions with global environmental change. *Food Security*, *3*(4), 417–431. doi:10.100712571-011-0149-9

International Cocoa organization. (2020). *Quarterly Bulletin of Cocoa Statistics*. Retrieved from https://www.icco.org/

International Coffee Organization. (2020). *Trade Statistics - January 2020*. Retrieved from http://www.ico.org/

Jedrychowski, W., Perera, F., Mrozek-Budzyn, D., Flak, E., Mroz, E., Sochacka-Tatara, E., & Spengler, J. D. (2010). Higher Fish Consumption in Pregnancy May Confer Protection against the Harmful Effect of Prenatal Exposure to Fine Particulate Matter. *Annals of Nutrition & Metabolism*, *56*(2), 119–126. doi:10.1159/000275918 PMID:20134157

Kamenidou, I. C., Mamalis, S. A., Pavlidis, S., & Bara, E.-Z. G. (2019). Segmenting the Generation Z Cohort University Students Based on Sustainable Food Consumption Behavior: A Preliminary Study. *Sustainability*, *11*(3), 837. doi:10.3390u11030837

Keller, K. L. (2016). Unlocking the Power of Integrated Marketing Communications: How Integrated Is Your IMC Program? *Journal of Advertising*, *45*(3), 286–301. doi:10.1080/00913367.2016.1204967

Kiss, K., Ruszkai, C., & Takács-György, K. (2019). Examination of Short Supply Chains Based on Circular Economy and Sustainability Aspects. *Resources*, *8*(4), 161. doi:10.3390/resources8040161

Kolb, M. (2018). *What Is Globalization?* Retrieved from https://www.piie.com/microsites/globalization/what-is-globalization

Kotler, P. (2019). The market for transformation. *Journal of Marketing Management*, *35*(5/6), 407–409. doi:10.1080/0267257X.2019.1585713

Li, Y. J., Haws, K. L., & Griskevicius, V. (2019). Parenting Motivation and Consumer Decision-Making. *The Journal of Consumer Research*, *45*(5), 1117–1137. doi:10.1093/jcr/ucy038

Lin, C.-H. (2011). Personality, Value, Life Style and Postmodernism Consumer Behavior: A Comparison Among Three Generations. *International Journal of Organizational Innovation*, *3*(3), 203–230. Retrieved from http://search.ebscohost.com/login.aspx?direct=true&db=bth&AN=59220375&site=eds-live

Lindner Radons, D., Flores Battistella, L., & Zampieri Grohmann, M. (2016). Geração e gênero como moderadores no comportamento de compra pró-ambiental. *Pensamiento & Gestión*, (41), 148–171. Retrieved from http://search.ebscohost.com/login.aspx?direct=true&db=bth&AN=122029597&site=eds-live~

Loroz, P. S., & Helgeson, J. G. (2013). Boomers and their Babies: An Exploratory Study Comparing Psychological Profiles and Advertising Appeal Effectiveness Across Two Generations. *Journal of Marketing Theory and Practice*, *21*(3), 289–306. doi:10.2753/MTP1069-6679210304

Madsen, A. O. (2014). *La influencia del sistema del mercado en comportamiento: el caso del pescado en Portugal y Dinamarca*. Universidad Rey Juan Carlos.

Madsen, A. O., & Chkoniya, V. (2019). Tendencies Regarding Fish Consumption – The Case of Portugal (Europe's Leader & 3rd in the World). *European Journal of Interdisciplinary Studies, 6*(1), 33–50.

Madsen, A. O., & Chkoniya, V. (2019a). Fish Consumption in the Age of the Information Society - The Evolution of the Fish Sector in Portugal. *European Journal of Social Sciences, 2*(2). Retrieved from http://journals.euser.org/index.php/ejss/article/view/4251

Martin, D., & Schouten, J. (2012). *Sustainable marketing*. Upper Saddle River, NJ: Pearson Prentice Hall.

Minnema, A., Bijmolt, T. H. A., Gensler, S., & Wiesel, T. (2016). To Keep or Not to Keep: Effects of Online Customer Reviews on Product Returns. *Journal of Retailing, 92*(3), 253–267. doi:10.1016/j.jretai.2016.03.001

Nadeem, W., Juntunen, M., & Juntunen, J. (2017). Consumer segments in social commerce: A latent class approach. *Journal of Consumer Behaviour, 16*(3), 279–292. doi:10.1002/cb.1632

Pardot. (2020). *B2B Marketing Trends | Insights from the Frontlines of B2B Marketing*. Retrieved from https://www.pardot.com/

Parment, A. (2013). Generation Y vs. Baby Boomers: Shopping behavior, buyer involvement and implications for retailing. *Journal of Retailing and Consumer Services, 20*(2), 189–199. doi:10.1016/j.jretconser.2012.12.001

Rappoport, L. (2010). *How We Eat: Appetite, Culture, and the Psychology of Food*. ECW Press. Retrieved from https://books.google.pt/books?id=srj_y0b8Mh8C

Rea, A. (2019). Reading Through the Ages: Compare all five generations of adult readers to ensure you're giving all your patrons what they want. *Library Journal*. Retrieved from http://search.ebscohost.com/login.aspx?direct=true&db=edsglr&AN=edsgcl.609310951&site=eds-live

Reed, K., & Ryan, P. (2019). Lessons from the past and the future of food. *World Archaeology, 51*(1), 1–16. doi:10.1080/00438243.2019.1610492

Reynolds, T. J., & Phillips, J. M. (2019). The Strata Model Predicting Advertising Effectiveness: A Neural-Network Approach Enhances Predictability of Consumer Decision Making. *Journal of Advertising Research, 59*(3), 268–280. doi:10.2501/JAR-2018-037

Riedy, C. (2018). Cross-Generational Counseling Strategies: Understanding Unique Needs of Each Generation. *Journal of Counselor Practice, 9*(1), 6–23.

Rodrigues, J. (2018). Smartphones: fundamentally reshaping today's teenagers: iGen: Why today's super-connected kids are growing up less rebellious, more tolerant, less happy: and completely unprepared for adulthood (Jean M. Twenge). *Church. Communication and Culture VO, 3*(1), 75–79. doi:10.1080/23753234.2018.1429223

Roy, S., Guha, A., & Biswas, A. (2015). Celebrity endorsements and women consumers in India: How generation-cohort affiliation and celebrity-product congruency moderate the benefits of chronological age congruency. *Marketing Letters, 26*(3), 363–376. doi:10.100711002-015-9354-1

Sandy, C. J., Gosling, S. D., & Durant, J. (2013). Predicting Consumer Behavior and Media Preferences: The Comparative Validity of Personality Traits and Demographic Variables. *Psychology and Marketing, 30*(11), 937–949. doi:10.1002/mar.20657

Sanjur, D. (1982). *Social and cultural perspectives in nutrition*. Englewood Cliffs, N.J.: Prentice-Hall. Retrieved from https://catalog.hathitrust.org/api/volumes/oclc/7572902.html

Simoons, F. (1994). *Eat Not this Flesh: Food Avoidances from Prehistory to the Present*. University of Wisconsin Press. Retrieved from https://books.google.pt/books?id=JwGZTQunH00C

Sproesser, G., Ruby, M. B., Arbit, N., Akotia, C. S., Alvarenga, M. dos S., Bhangaokar, R., & Renner, B. (2019). Understanding traditional and modern eating: The TEP10 framework. *BMC Public Health, 19*(1). doi:10.118612889-019-7844-4

Tafesse, W., & Korneliussen, T. (2013). Examining the effect of using multiple media tools on the marketing performance of organizations in a trade campaign environment. *Journal of Marketing Communications, 19*(3), 215–227. doi:10.1080/13527266.2011.619556

Tari, A. (2011). Z generáció. Budapest: Tercium Könyvkiadó.

Törőcsik, M., Szűcs, K., & Kehl, D. (2015). Lifestyle Segments in Generation Z – A New Approach to Identify Groups among Youth. *International Journal of Business Insights & Transformation, 9*(1), 64–68. Retrieved from http://search.ebscohost.com/login.aspx?direct=true&db=bth&AN=131717881&site=eds-live

Troncoso-Pantoja, C. (2019). Comidas tradicionales: Un espacio para la alimentación saludable. *Perspectivas en Nutricion Humana, 21*(1), 105–114. doi:10.17533/udea.penh.v21n1a08

Ulver, S. (2019). From Mundane to Socially Significant Consumption: An Analysis of How Foodie Identity Work Spurs Market Formation. *Journal of Macromarketing, 39*(1), 53–70. doi:10.1177/0276146718817354

White, K., Hardisty, D. J., & Habib, R. (2019). The Elusive Green Consumer. *Harvard Business Review*. Retrieved from http://search.ebscohost.com/login.aspx?direct=true&db=edb&AN=137120584&site=eds-live

Xue, H., & Lin, Y. (2017). The omni-channel consumer segmentation method based on consumption data stream mining. 2017 IEEE 2nd International Conference on Big Data Analysis (ICBDA)(, Big Data Analysis (ICBDA), 2017 IEEE 2nd International Conference On. 10.1109/ICBDA.2017.8078814

Zemke, R. R., & Raines, C. (2012). Generations at Work: Managing the Clash of Veterans. Baby Boomers, Xers, and Nexters in You Workplace. Academic Press.

Zhang, J., & Mao, E. (2016). From Online Motivations to Ad Clicks and to Behavioral Intentions: An Empirical Study of Consumer Response to Social Media Advertising. *Psychology and Marketing, 33*(3), 155–164. doi:10.1002/mar.20862

Zralek, J., & Burgiel, A. (2020). Prospects for a Sustainable Future: Mapping Sustainable Behaviors According to Consumer Perceptions. *Review of Business, 40*(1), 35–50. Retrieved from http://search.ebscohost.com/login.aspx?direct=true&db=bth&AN=141137614&site=eds-live

KEY TERMS AND DEFINITIONS

Cohort: Is the age of an individual at which life events and transitions take place; period is what happens within an individual's lifetime; a cohort is a group of individuals who have shared experiences and events in their formative years that could lead to similar attitudes and behaviors for the rest of their lives.

Consumer's Education: Is the preparation of a consumer to be capable of making informed decisions when it comes to purchasing products. Consumer education is the answer to the common phrase found in the business world, "buyer beware."

Consumption Patterns: The process by which people search, purchase and consume products in a way to meet all their needs or desires.

Cuisine: Is the style of cooking, including its practices, traditions and recipes, associated with a specific culture.

Generation Marketing Campaign: Is a series of activities carried out by a company for informing, reminding or persuading its target generation audience about its product or service, by using two or more generational marketing tactics at once.

Globalization: The word used to describe the growing interdependence of the world's economies, cultures, and populations, brought about by cross-border trade in goods and services, technology, and flows of investment, people, and information.

Identity: The fact of being who or what a person or thing is. Unique features about something or someone. Two important factors determining identity are cultural tradition and religion.

Mediterranean Diet: Is a diet inspired by the eating habits of Italy and Greece with a heart-healthy eating approach that emphasizes eating fresh, whole foods.

One Generation: Means all of the people born and living at about the same time, regarded collectively. Generations are defined by age, period, and cohort.

Sustainable Consumption: Is the use of goods and services that respond to basic needs and bring about a better quality of life, while minimizing the use of natural resources, toxic materials and emissions of waste and pollutants over the life cycle, so as not to jeopardize the needs of future generations.

Chapter 2
Personalization 3.0:
How Personality Can Predict Consumer Behavior

Katharina Sophie Kuehn
Deep Sphere, Australia

ABSTRACT

Approaches that attempt to predict consumer behavior have come a long way since the inception of socio-demographic profiling. This development is, on the one hand, driven by the desire of businesses to perform better and connect better with consumers. On the other hand, this is also driven by consumers who are explicitly seeking personalized guidance in a crowded marketplace and implicitly, nonconsciously, seeking to fulfill underlying emotional needs and goals by consuming brands and products. The author proposes a biopsychological framework to understand personality based on evolutionary studies of primal emotion systems and explains how this framework can predict preferences and behavioral tendencies in consumers. To ascertain the validity of the theory, four experiments were conducted to test and confirm personality-specific predictions regarding the effectiveness of personalized advertising campaigns, product choices, and brand preference.

INTRODUCTION

The goal of this chapter is to introduce a new framework for predicting consumer behavior and personalizing consumer experiences, grounded in the latest findings of neuroscience and biopsychological personality research. The author argues that, contrary to currently prevalent socio-demographic and behavioral personalization approaches, underlying consumer personalities, including their innate primal emotions and resulting temperaments, psychological needs, and goals must be understood for personalization efforts to finally become more personal and meaningful on an individual level, as well as more predictive.

DOI: 10.4018/978-1-7998-3115-0.ch002

Copyright © 2020, IGI Global. Copying or distributing in print or electronic forms without written permission of IGI Global is prohibited.

Further, this chapter aims to pinpoint the operating principles of the nonconscious, emotional *system 1* in the minds of consumers and its emotional relevance detectors that constantly work to evaluate the saliency of available options as consumers navigate their environments. It aims to make transparent the hidden, underlying forces that drive consumer decision making, by understanding how the instructions of the ancient primal emotion systems guide and influence the choices of different personality types.

BACKGROUND

The topic of personalization has attracted wide interest in business in recent times, driven by the insight that, in saturated, multi-optional markets, consumers not only want to be catered to in more personal ways and be assisted with navigating today's sea of similar products but are also more effectively influenced by stimuli that target and work on a personal, emotional level. Coinciding with this is the rise of unprecedented capabilities to utilize data and technology to personalize communications and propositions in real-time. As a result, personalization is on the agendas of many organizations. However, meaningful approaches that link a holistic understanding of consumer personality and emotion to proven strategies for personalization are still the exception in practice.

Businesses today, when attempting to understand consumption patterns and consumer behavior to personalize their experience, often neglect the underlying patterns and real reasons for those behaviors. Here, it is argued that behaviors are mere cues that expose deeply held, underlying personality patterns about consumers and by failing to recognize these underlying patterns, many personalization attempts fail. Many consumers today have received recommendations to book a hotel they were already staying in while using the hotel's WiFi network, been emailed endless offers of more engagement rings after already buying one, have received recommended "movies for you" that didn't match their interests, or yet another dating partner whose only commonalities were that they also like ocean sports and sleeping with the windows open.

A BRIEF HISTORY OF PERSONALIZATION

Between the beginning of anonymous mass consumerism and now, many businesses have moved from treating every customer the same to clustering customers into demographic segments. The author refers to this as *Personalization 1.0* because demographic segmentations were the first rudimentary attempt to categorize customers into different segments. The first socio-demographic market segmentation tool of this kind was developed in 1916 by Paul Cherington, director of research for J. Walter Thompson, a marketing communications brand, and member of the census advisory committee for the American Statistical Association (Lockley, 1950). His research department, using the socio-demographic ABCD typology of households, quickly became an epicenter for market and consumer research in the United States. Demographic segments are still widely used in business today. According to a Marketing Week survey (2019) with a sample of more than 800 professionals working across 23 sectors, the currently most commonly used methods of segmentation are age (38%), location (42%) and, increasingly, behavior (44%).

More recently, data and technology-driven businesses such as Netflix and Amazon have dedicated large investments into personalizing their customer experience based on user behavior and engagement with different products and titles.

To date, the main focus of Netflix's product recommendations engine has been to analyze how subscribers search, click, watch, and pause, creating "doppelganger" profiles for users with similar behavioral histories. Nevertheless, getting it right is a complex and elusive endeavor, as anyone who has ever desperately searched for inspiration and relevant recommendations on new content to watch can attest.

Similarly, Amazon's recommendation system is based on several behavioral elements, including what a user bought in the past, items in the cart, items rated and liked, and what other customers viewed and purchased. Amazon calls its recommender system "item-to-item collaborative filtering", generating approximately 35% of consumer purchases on the website according to a MacKenzie, Meyer and Noble (2013) report. This behavior-based personalization paradigm appears to be the current focus of advanced businesses' personalization efforts and is referred to as *Personalization 2.0* by the author.

The problem with Personalization 2.0 approaches, however, is that they are missing an explanatory framework for understanding the human behind the behavior. In other words, they are missing the *reason why* for observed behaviors—something that is required to attempt personally relevant recommendations, especially when it comes to the recommendation of options outside of the observable history of existing behaviors as well as personalized ways in which to present them. Consequently, Personalization 2.0 not only frequently leads to suboptimal recommendations, but to comical ones too. Several bloggers, including Jac Rayner, have started entire social media accounts sharing Personalization 2.0 malfunctions as shown in the example in Figure 1.

Figure 1. Blogger Jac Rayner's message to Amazon on Twitter (GirlFromBlupo, 2018, April 6)

In summary, Personalization 2.0 approaches are certainly superior to demographic personalization approaches (or no personalization at all) in terms of increasing customer conversion rates, revenue, lead generation, and basket size (Barilliance, 2015; Evergage, 2018; Gartner, 2018; Salesforce, 2017). However, in the process, they often lead to alienation at an individual level, when it becomes apparent that consumers are being targeted not as humans, but based on past behaviors and mere behavioral correlations, resulting in personalized content that is either too repetitive, too inaccurate and irrelevant or too creepy (as in too literally personalized, resulting in consumers feeling stalked).

PERSONALIZATION 3.0: UNDERSTANDING CONSUMER PERSONALITY AND DECISION MAKING

Only if underlying consumer personalities are understood, including their innate primal emotions and resulting temperaments, psychological needs, and goals that all influence decision making, will personalization really become more personal and meaningful. This approach doesn't only focus on which products should be recommended (although it can include the selection of more relevant products and brands), but also on how products should be recommended in a way that is personally relevant and appealing. Most importantly, it can explain the underlying reasons for observed consumer preferences and behaviors, therefore allowing more accurate, human, and individually relevant predictions. This is the goal of *Personalization 3.0*.

Principle 1: Consumer Decision Making is Highly Emotional

Every day, consumers make countless decisions, with an average of 226.7 decisions made each day on food alone according to researchers at Cornell University (Wansink & Sobal, 2007). As people shop a website, visit a physical store, or watch an advertisement, their senses take in between 11 and 20 million bits of information every second (Lipton, 2015). Only approximately 40 out of these 11–20 million bits get processed by the cognitive system in the neocortex of the brain, which is, from an evolutionary perspective, the newest part of the human brain. It corresponds with cognition, deliberation, abstraction, reason, analysis, strategic planning, and voluntary control and has been conceptually coined as *system 2* by the economic Nobel Prize laureate Daniel Kahneman (noting that Kahneman uses the terminology of systems 1 and 2 as organizing metaphors for processing modes, not actual systems or regions in the brain).

Most of the information gets filtered through predominantly emotional, automatic, involuntary, nonconscious processing structures in the subcortical regions of the brain, below the neocortex. This emotional *system 1* acts as a filter or emotional "relevance detector" (Montagrin & Sander, 2016) to evaluate within split seconds, and below the radar of conscious awareness, the saliency of available options. As discussed by Kahneman (2011), system 1 influences a large part of human behavior, has no capacity for language, and typically precedes the reasoning and analysis of system 2. It has been generally recognized that by the time we intentionally initiate an action, the brain has already done its work. In 1996, Libet found an electrophysiological neural potential causing action 100 ms before the conscious decision. In 2018, a full-scale replication of Libet's study was conducted and the authors were able to replicate Libet's original outcomes in principle (Dominik et al., 2018). System 1 is also the seat of human intuition, motivation, and emotion and is where all sensory inputs get integrated and evaluated as to whether they are salient and should, therefore, pass through into conscious awareness. System 2 only engages when the circumstances require because this mode of thinking is costly and energy consuming for the brain. Therefore, all choices in life, including important and consequential ones, are strongly moderated by system 1.

Damasio's (2000) patients with damage to the ventromedial part of the prefrontal lobe (where cognition and secondary emotions are thought to be integrated) showed that their lives dramatically fell apart as they lost the capacity to empathize with others or themselves and became incapable of making even the smallest decisions. Why? To them, all conceivable options appeared equal and were given equal attention, with no emotional predisposition. Thus, "selective reduction of emotion is at least as prejudicial for rationality as excessive emotion" (Damasio, 2000, p.13).

It is widely accepted today that emotions are tightly interwoven with structures of cognition and memory (Sapolsky, 2017), with emotions influencing—and enabling—decision making in a bottom-up fashion. As LeDoux (2000, p. 225) wrote: "Emotional arousal has powerful influences over cognitive processing. Attention, perception, memory, decision-making and the conscious concomitants of each are all swayed in emotional states. The reason for this is simple: emotional arousal organizes and coordinates brain activity." This operating principle is shown in Figure 2.

Figure 2. Human decision making as an interplay of system 1 (bottom up emotional bursts) and system 2 (top down executive control) (© 2020, Deep Sphere™. Used with permission)

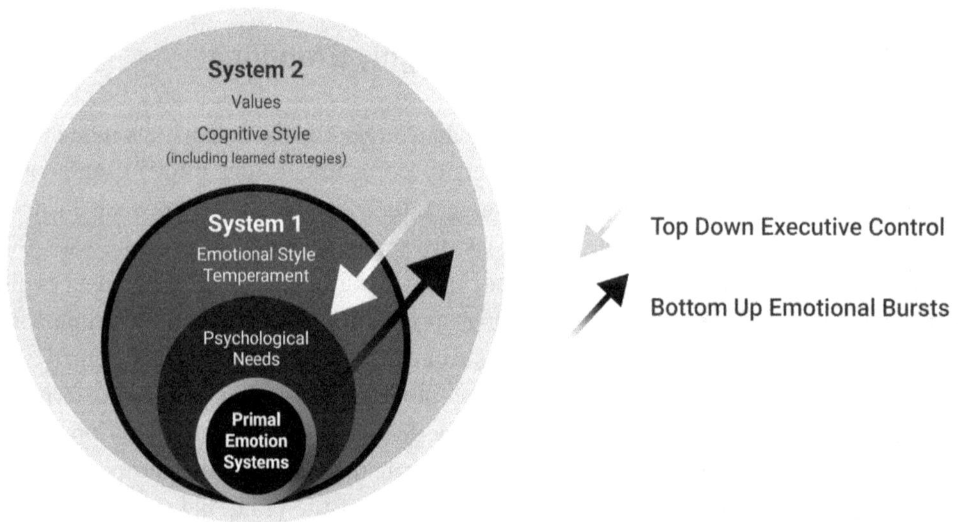

Principle 2: Personality Congruence Can Predict Decision Making

When it comes to predicting which consumers are going to be attracted to which brands and messages, the theory of personality congruence suggests that personality congruence has a strong impact, often the greatest, on brand preference, consumer attitude, brand awareness and purchase decisions (Grimm, 2005; Maymand & Razmi, 2017). These findings are in line with Aaker's (1997, p. 347) early observations stating that "the greater the congruity between the human characteristics that consistently and distinctively describe an individual's actual or ideal self and those that describe a brand, the greater the preference for the brand." Further studies also suggest that tailoring messages to the personality traits of a target audience can be an effective way of increasing purchases and engagement with a message (Hirsh, Kang, & Bodenhausen, 2012; Matz, Kosinski, Nave & Stillwell, 2017; Wall, Campbell, Kaye, Levy, & Bhullar, 2019).

Principle 3: Personality Must Account For System 1 Not Just System 2

The limitation of the majority of existing studies that attempt to quantify the predictive strength of personality on behavior lies in their usage of exclusively language based (system 2) frameworks of personality. The studies of Grimm (2005), Hirsh et al,. (2012), Matz, Kosinski, Nave, & Stillwell (2017) and Wall et al,. (2019) all rely on the well-established and most widely used model of the NEO Five Personality Inventory. However, the NEO Five (or BIG Five) framework is based on the lexical hypothesis that assumes that existing personality traits of a group eventually become part of the group's language. Accordingly, the model was built using an extraction of around 4,500 adjectives from the dictionary. The original extraction was done by Allport & Odbert (1936), further developed by Eysenck (1967), and finally evolved into its latest form of the NEO Personality Inventory Revised (NEO PI-R) (Costa & McCrae, 1992), with the final five dimensions of neuroticism, extraversion, openness, agreeableness and conscientiousness, which emerged using factor analysis (Holgado-Tello, Carrasco-Ortiz, del Barrio-Gándara, & Chacón-Moscoso, 2007).

Given the largely unconscious nature of human emotion and motivation that gives rise to traits and behaviors, system 1 contents form a critical part of an explanatory model of personality. Any lexical model of personality is inherently limited as it can only scratch the surface layers of personality. It merely provides system 2 descriptions of people's conscious perceptions of others' personality traits.

A more contemporary, explanatory, bottom-up approach that accounts for the largely nonconscious nature of human personality and decision making must, therefore, be based on an understanding of how biology, specifically genetics, evolution and environmental factors influencing brain development cause individual variation from the general human design. However, integrating such a perspective into studies assessing the predictive nature of personality on behavior still remains a sparsely developed topic, besides a few exceptions (Fisher, Island, Rich, Marchalik, & Brown, 2015; Haeusel, 2008; Haeusel, 2011; Klotz & Akinalp, 2013).

From a biopsychological perspective, personality can be described as the emergence of relatively stable dispositional traits and behaviors, which are due to a person's genes, environment, upbringing, and their resulting epigenetics, leading to individual variations from the general human design. These differences manifest in individual emphasis of primal emotion systems, basic psychological needs, and temperament, which act as bottom-up emotional bursts—summarized as system 1 in Figure 2—resulting in individual decisions, preferences, and behavioral patterns.

Second, these bottom-up bursts are supervised and partially shaped by people's system 2 top-down cortical control mechanisms, which develop over the course of a lifetime, especially until the age of 25 during the maturation of the prefrontal cortex (Sapolsky, 2017), into environment-specific values, cognitive styles, and learned strategies for goal attainment. This is often referred to as character or characteristic adaptations (DeYoung, 2014; McAdams & Pals, 2006), which describes the consequences generated by processes of learning and adaptation of the individual, responding to and developing in a specific culture, context, and upbringing. Together, these two layers (system 1 and system 2) result in different

Figure 3. A layered view of personality, including systems 1 and 2 (© 2020, Deep Sphere™. Used with permission)

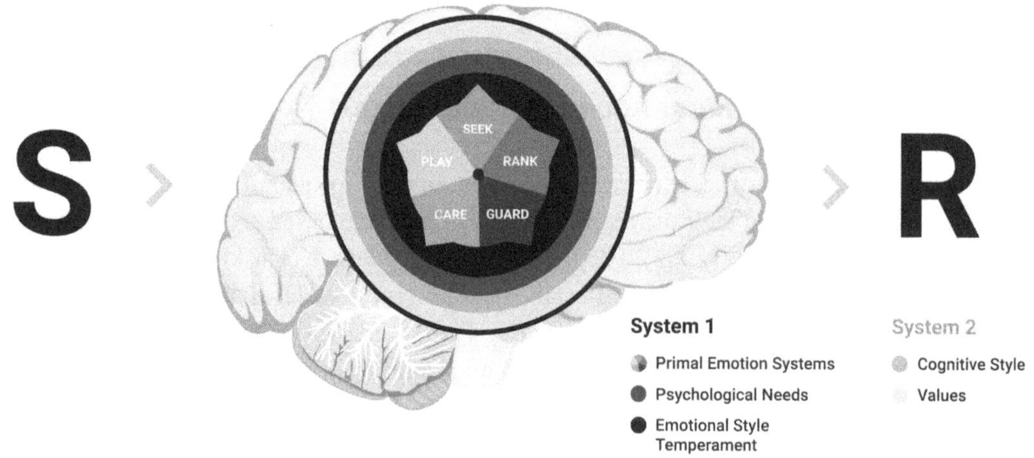

personality patterns and characteristic behavioral tendencies or responses (R) in response to different classes of environmental stimuli (S), as shown in Figure 3.

Because of the powerful role of the emotional, nonconscious component of decision making and its particular relevance when it comes to consumer behavior, the following sections will focus on the influence of the inner three layers of primal emotion systems, basic psychological needs, and emotional style (also referred to as temperament in the literature, e.g., Fisher, Island, Rich, Marchalik, & Brown, 2015) and here conceptually attributed to the emotional, nonconscious system 1.

The Biopsychological Foundation of Personality: Primal Emotion Systems

The most prominent proponent of the primal emotion systems theory and the scientist who coined the term *affective neuroscience*, Jaak Panksepp, posited that primary process emotions provide the biopsychological foundation of personality. To link these primary process emotions (referred to as primal emotion systems throughout) to personality traits and behavioral patterns, Panksepp developed the Affective Neuroscience Personality Scales, which show that at the deepest level, constellations of traits emerge from the activational and organizational activities of primal emotion systems that have evolved to ensure the basic survival and functioning of all mammals, including humans (Panksepp, 2006, 2010). As shown in Figure 4, there are nine primal emotion systems with dedicated functions to ensure basic survival and functioning.

These primal emotion systems are organized within the subcortical regions of the brain and the positive and negative affects they create are designed to inform mammals how they are doing in their quest to survive. Positive affect signalizes survival and functioning, negative affect signalizes survival threat. These affects or emotions have evolved to move animals into action in ways that promote survival and are "evolutionary memories of such importance that they were coded into the genome in rough form"

(Panksepp, 2010, p. 1). Each emotion system has a distinct brain anatomy, neuropharmacology, and physiology (Panksepp and Biven, 2012).

Emotion systems come into effect through specific neural circuitry that is affected by a combination of neurotransmitters, neuromodulators, hormones, and cytokines, leading to the development of associated personality traits (summarized in Figure 4). These traits give rise to characteristic goals and behavior patterns, which originally enhanced survival, to different degrees in different individuals.

Seeking

The first primal emotion system responsible for basic individual functioning is the seeking system, which has evolved to make mammals explore for resources, mating partners, and new territories and to provide them with the psychological energy and enthusiasm to explore the environment and seek rewards. Newer evidence (Berridge & Robinson, 2016) additionally suggested that the seeking system consisted of two subcomponents—a motivational, appetitive, "wanting" side and a hedonic appraisal, consummatory, "liking" or pleasure side. These systems also play an essential role in learning, by attaching a positive value and arousal to specific activities and thereby inducing repetition of these activities (Tyng, Amin, Saad, & Malik, 2017). Food, drugs, sex, social media usage, monetary reward, and electrical stimulation are just some of these activities activating the mesolimbic dopamine system implicated in the neural basis of reward (Toronchuk & Ellis, 2013).

Key neuromodulators of the seeking system include dopamine, opioids, endorphins, neurotensin, and orexin. Dopamine, in particular, plays an important role in the anticipation of reward- and goal-directed behavior. Dopamine neurons also play a key role in the motivation to explore, be curious, learn, and tell the brain which stimuli lead to reward and which ones don't (Kidd & Hayden, 2015). Norbury and Husain's (2015) systematic review of data relating sensation seeking to neurotransmitter systems in humans showed that individuals higher in sensation seeking had higher endogenous dopamine levels and greater dopamine response to cues of upcoming reward. The dopamine system is further associated with the traits of intense stimulation and novelty-seeking, risk-taking, impulsivity, attentional problems, and extroversion. On the contrary, chronic levels of stress can deplete the mesolimbic system of dopamine, bringing on anhedonia and depression (Sapolsky, 2017).

Disgust

The second primal emotion system responsible for basic individual survival is the disgust system, which has evolved to help animals avoid harmful foods, substances, and environments, but also to trigger moral and esthetic disgust that is designed to detect morally flawed conspecifics and avoid cooperation with them and is critical to the human capability of social evaluation (Toronchuk & Ellis, 2007a, 2007b) and serves as an out-group marker. For example, pictures of drug addicts and homeless people typically activate the insula (disgust) rather than the amygdala (fear) in the brain (Sapolsky, 2017). This system was omitted by Panksepp (1998, 2010); however, it is thought to have originally evolved in ancient vertebrates to protect against infection and toxins, and meets all the criteria of primal emotion systems as outlined by Toronchuk and Ellis (2013).

Figure 4. Personality traits and their evolutionary function

Evolutionary Function	Primal Emotion System	Specific Evolutionary Functions	Temperament/ Personality Traits
Individual Needs			
Basic Functioning	Seeking (Hedonic and Motivational)	Facilitates learning, motivational, appetitive, hedonic appraisal, incentive salience	Open to experience, curious, pleasure-seeking, risk-taking, novelty-seeking, extravert, impulsive
Basic Survival	Disgust	Avoiding harmful foods, substances, environments. Also, moral disgust, avoiding cooperation with harmful conspecifics	Neurotic, fearful, low-sensation-seeking (seeking reduction of sensory stimuli)
	Fear	Monitoring danger and moving away from it, limiting tissue damage	Neurotic, fearful, control-seeking
	Anger	Mobilizing resources to defend, protect, and compete for territory	Competitive, aggressive, motivated, determined
Social Needs			
Reproduction	Lust	Procreation and bonding	-
Group Cohesion	Care	Caring for offspring and conspecifics	Agreeable, nurturing, empathetic, trusting, sensitive to social approval, and reinforcement
	Panic/ Attachment	Protection of vulnerable individuals, bonding	-
	Play	Forming social bonds, learning motor skills, and testing social limits	Extravert, experimental, curious, humorous
Group Functioning	Rank	Regulating conflict, limiting aggression in social groups, and allocating sexual and material resources	Confident, optimistic, impulsive, risk-taking, territorial, assertive, rank-seeking

Serotonin plays a key role in the disgust system (Kavaliers, Ossenkopp, & Choleris, 2018), as its release is essential for the activation of disgust mechanisms and their use by the gut, vagus nerve, and brainstem (Rubio-Godoy, Aunger, & Curtis, 2007). Oxytocin is involved in the recognition and avoidance of infected individuals as well as the social avoidance of potentially threatening situations (Kavaliers, Ossenkopp, & Choleris, 2018). Personality-wise, high disgust sensitivity is inversely correlated with sensation-seeking, suggesting that disgust and sensation-seeking represent opposing emotional operating systems with contrasting behavioral traits.

Fear

The primal emotion system of fear is equally responsible for basic individual survival and has evolved to monitor danger and activate the impulse to move away from it to limit tissue damage.

Key neuromodulators of the fear system are glutamate, diazepam binding inhibitor, corticotropin releasing factor, cholecystokinin, alpha-MSH, and neuropeptide Y (Alcaro, Carta, & Panksepp, 2017). With higher levels of fear, people have higher survival chances compared to personalities who prioritize the seeking of rewards, partners, and resources over the careful monitoring of the environment and the avoidance of injury. Low-fear individuals end up having higher chances of being hospitalized due to accidents but on the upside have, on average, more children and mating partners over the course of their lifetime (Montag & Panksepp, 2017). On the contrary, high-fear personalities are likely to forgo many such rewards and, rather, spend their attentional resources on monitoring danger. Their motto in life could be summarized as: "No fun, no risk."

Anger

The primal emotion system of anger (also referred to as rage) is the third system responsible for basic individual survival and has evolved to mobilize resources to compete as well as to facilitate the defense and protection of territory. Anger can also arise when an expected reward is absent.

Substance P, acetylcholine, glutamate, and vasopressin play a role in the anger system (Alcaro et al., 2017; Panksepp and Harro, 2004). Anger has been shown to motivate prolonged effort during slow goal attainment and is associated with increased levels of determination as well as aggression and competitiveness (Lebel, 2017; Pettersson & Turkheimer, 2013).

Lust

The primal emotion system of lust has evolved to ensure the survival and reproduction of the group, driving individuals to identify potential mates, bond, and procreate.

Vasopressin, oxytocin, and steroids modulate the lust system (Alcaro et al., 2017) and are associated with parental behavior as well as adult social bonds. In males, vasopressin is also associated with sexual competition (Carter, 2017).

Care including Panic/Attachment

Survival chances for mammals are higher in social groups. Therefore, the primal emotion system of care is critical for the cohesion of the group and has evolved to ensure the care and nurturing of offspring and conspecifics, and elicits the need to bond, form connections, and fit into the group to survive. This program is coded into our brains as the care system, which craves human connection and works to avoid being ostracized. An infant screaming in panic as their mother moves away or a lover killing themselves after being rejected can equally be attributed to the care system at play, the flipside of which is panic and separation distress. Several authors including Panksepp (1998, 2010) list panic and attachment as separate from the care system; however, because it is a negative affect in response to being separated from the caregiver or another important person and the drive to reunite and reconnect with this person (care drive), the two systems of care and panic/attachment are treated as linked here. As Montag and Panksepp (2017) also pointed out, care activities downregulate the arousal of panic/sadness.

The care system is fueled by oxytocin, vasopressin, prolactin and dopamine (Alcaro et al., 2017; Panksepp and Harro, 2004). In particular, the neuropeptides, oxytocin and vasopressin play an important role in caring behaviors. Oxytocin prepares the female body for birth and lactation and facilitates maternal behaviors such as synchronized eye gazing, touch, and finding babies more appealing, while vasopressin plays a role in paternal behavior. Oxytocin's reputation has been impeccable for a long time, being renowned to decrease aggression (except when it comes to the defense of own children), and making people more socially attuned, trusting, and empathetic. It is also known to strengthen monogamous pair bonding, creating more faithful partners and nurturing parents. Oxytocin fosters social interest, competence, and theory of mind and makes people more sensitive to social approval and social reinforcement. All in all, as Sapolsky (2017) stated, oxytocin has been "coasting in a teflon presidency" (p. 107). However, he also pointed out some nuances to the above generic statement. Oxytocin enhances the competence to detect an Us versus Them and makes people more prosocial but only to an Us, and worse to everyone else. Implicit reaction time tests, for example, have shown that people with high levels of these two neuropeptides have a stronger in-group bias and higher aggression toward members of the out-group. They are also not more cooperative in general; but only under the circumstance that the other party is not anonymous. If the other party is anonymous, these individuals show more gloating, backstabbing, envy, and decreased cooperation (Sapolsky, 2017).

Play

The primal emotion system of play also contributes to the cohesion of the group. This system can be seen in hyenas, lions, elephants and other animals in the wild. Rough and tumble play exists in all of them, just as it does in humans, because it is play that enables mammals to form social bonds, learn new skills, including motoric skills, and test social limits. In humans, play extends to representational and intellectually imaginative play. The play system is necessary for healthy human cognitive development and was evolutionarily facilitated by cortical enlargement and the long lactation period in humans prolonging social interaction and mother–infant play (Kerney, Smaers, Schoenemann, & Dunn, 2017; MacLean, 1990).

Key neuromodulators include opioids, glutamate, and acetylcholine (Alcaro et al., 2017) and traits such as extraversion, intellectual and creative curiosity, humor and celebratory behavior depend on the play system and its neuromodulators (Montag & Panksepp, 2017).

Rank

To ensure the functioning of the group, there needs to be not only mechanisms for group cohesion but also for resolving conflict and tensions around the allocation of resources. Accordingly, the primal emotion system of rank was proposed by Toronchuk and Ellis (2013) in addition to Panksepp's (1998, 2010a) identified affective systems. The rank system deals with power, rank, dominance and subordination and has evolved to ensure the functioning of the group by regulating conflict, limiting aggression in social groups and allocating sexual and material resources. The higher the social rank, the better the access to partners and material resources within a given community (Fedigan, 2015). This dynamic is firmly installed in the brain, making animals seek rank and humans seek status, power and significance, and is associated with feelings of pride, elevated mood and high self-esteem during success as well as low self-esteem and depression during defeat (Wetherall, Robb, & O'Connor, 2019), thus allowing lower-ranking individuals to communicate acceptance of their rank and cope with forgoing reward (Price et al., 2007).

Key hormones in humans' drive for rank are testosterone and related hormones collectively called androgens (Sapolsky, 2017). Unlike what was assumed in the past, heightened testosterone levels do not predict or increase aggression and violence; rather, testosterone prompts whatever behaviors are required to obtain and maintain status, and drive the psychology of dominance, identification, and self-esteem (Eisenegger, Naef, Snozzi, Heinrichs, & Fehr, 2010). This is where context (modeled in the system 2 layer of Figure 3) comes in. As Sapolsky (2017, p. 107) states: "(...) the problem in society is not that testosterone can increase aggression - it's the frequency with which we reward aggression." In other words, most societies and developmental contexts teach individuals that an effective strategy for status attainment and defense is to display aggressive behaviors. Instead, in more collectivist human societies, as well as groups of bonobos, aggression is punished and cooperation rewarded. For example, in bonobos, females with the strongest alliances and most cooperative behaviors are the highest ranking ones (DeWaal, 2010). Therefore, if circumstances were socially engineered to reward cooperation with an improvement in rank, testosterone will drive exactly those behaviors (Sapolsky, 2017).

However, some personality traits and characteristic behavioral patterns that high testosterone levels do causally bring about are a decrease in empathy (measured by a decrease in empathic mimicry and a lower capability of reading conspecifics emotions by looking at their eyes), heightened confidence and optimism, decreased anxiety and fear, heightened impulsivity and risk-taking and, as mentioned, more than anything, an intense focus on reading rank and applying themselves to any learned behaviors associated with improving or defending their rank (Sapolsky, 2017).

Consumption as an Unconscious Biopsychological Goal Pursuit

As shown in the preceding section, humans experience and navigate their environments in response to the subjective emotions induced by the primal emotion systems whose mechanisms underpin psychological needs and temperaments and, thereby, produce goals and behaviors without any conscious awareness of their evolutionary origins and functions.

In the same way, many consumer choices happen as nonconscious responses to external stimuli as well as internal processes that consumers remain largely unaware of. Primal emotion systems not only cause different personality traits, as outlined, but they also produce different associated consumer goals. These goals can be understood as actualizations of people's primal emotion instructions and include mental representations of a desired future state in the quest by humans to survive and thrive. Importantly, these goals divide the world into salient and non-salient cues where only those products, brands, or messages cut through the emotional relevance detectors and filters in the minds of consumers, which indicate that they will be rewarding in the pursuit of goals.

It is especially those strong and consistent biopsychological motivators of behavior arising from an individual's dominant primal emotion instructions and their resulting personality traits that are potent predictors of certain classes of behavior and decision-making patterns.

Accordingly, Personalization 3.0 is the attempt to understand consumers' unconscious biopsychological goal pursuits and to address those goals by signalizing that a choice will be rewarding for the consumer's pursuit of rank, safety, care, play or hedonic pleasure.

Personalization 3.0 Experimental Design

To test the premise of Personalization 3.0, several emotionally tailored experiments were devised to demonstrate how certain stimuli appeal to specific audiences, while they are ineffective or even alienating to other audiences. These responses to certain stimuli can, in turn, expose underlying biopsychological personality patterns and characteristics of the audience. In this sense, consumer responses and behaviors are cues that hint at deeply held, underlying personality patterns and their primal emotion instructions at play.

For the practicality of the personalization application and testing, as well as for maintaining a manageable amount of distinct consumer segments, primal emotion systems were clustered into the following five primary instructions as visualized in Figure 3 (lust was removed owing to the difficulty in reliably testing this system with consumers):

- Guard: Disgust, Fear, and Anger
- Play: Play
- Seek: Seek
- Rank: Rank
- Care: Care, Attachment, and Sadness

Experiment Overview

To test and extend the validity of the proposed theory, personality-related predictions were made to see whether the evidence confirms the theory. For that purpose, large samples of consumers were invited on a number of occasions, on an opt-in basis, to take a standardized self-report questionnaire assessing primal emotion instructions located in system 1 of the Deep Sphere personality framework shown in Figure 3. Then, four different experiments were devised to test hypotheses 1–7 as shown in Figure 5, on personality-based predictions of consumer responses.

The first and the second experiment consisted of personalized Facebook ads, using emotionally tailored messaging and imagery with the first appealing to the guard system and the second to the seek system, to assess a predicted increase in engagement rates over the generic control ads. The first experiment was conducted with a total sample of 279,780 consumers (59,239 consumers on mobile devices and 220,541 consumers on desktop devices) and the second experiment consisted of 181,615 consumers.

Figure 5. Hypotheses regarding data values in relation to primal instructions

Experiment	Hypothesis	Variable	Personalized Value	Primal Instruction
1	1	Ad preference	Traditional	Guard
2	2	Ad preference	Unconventional	Seek
3	3	Kitchen preference	Warm, natural	Care
3	4	Kitchen preference	Sleek, premium design	Rank
3	5	Kitchen preference	Vibrant design	Seek
4	6	Brand preference	Premium	Rank
4	7	Brand preference	Mass market	Care

The third experiment assessed consumer preference of three different kitchens with different consumer personality segments in a sample of 27,773 consumers.

The fourth experiment was designed to directly test Aaker's (1997) and Grimm's (2005) personality congruence theory, stating that a fit between human personality and brand personality has the greatest direct impact on brand preferences. This experiment tested consumer preference of two different brand personalities, based on consumer personality types in a sample of 115,744 consumers.

Hypotheses and Predictions

Hypothesis 1: Individuals with a high guard instruction respond favorably to traditional, nostalgic looking ads (black and white hero image showing blue-collar workers), a message of trust, quality, durability, and reliability (in copy), combined with a 2-year warranty promise to cater to their primal goal for safety and their basic psychological need for predictability and managing risk.

Because guard, especially with its primal system of disgust, is inversely correlated with sensation-seeking, sensationalist and exaggerated (often typical) marketing language, such as speaking about exceptional value, as well as vibrant colors were avoided. The resulting ad was tested for superiority compared to the brand's generic, non-personalized control ad, which included the brand's usual, generic components of lifestyle imagery, focusing on value for money, environmental efficiency, and how appliances fit lifestyle.

Hypothesis 2: Individuals with a high seek instruction respond favorably to a message of individuality and challenging conventions (high appeal of the unconventional).

However, the purpose of this second Facebook experiment was not only to test the seek instruction prediction but also to determine whether the ad with personalized copy only, but not imagery, is still effective at increasing engagement with targeted personality types over a generic control ad. Accordingly, the control ad uses the brand's usual copy and creative ("Smeg fridges feature a timeless style and trusted, robust Italian design. Browse the range at Appliances Online"), while the seek-personalized ad only varies in terms of its copy, personalizing it to say, "Who wants a boring old white fridge? Smeg's colourful, retro range brings some fun and personality to your kitchen."

Hypothesis 3: Individuals with a high care instruction prefer warm, natural kitchen designs, signalizing a sense of family friendliness, nurturance, and care.
Hypothesis 4: Individuals with a high rank instruction prefer sleek, premium kitchen designs, signalizing social status, achievement, and success.
Hypothesis 5: Individuals with a high seek instruction prefer vibrant kitchen designs, signalizing a sense of novelty and pleasure.

The purpose of the third experiment was to test whether hypotheses 3–5 can be confirmed by observing an above-average preference with each of the three personalized kitchen designs for each of the predicted types.

Hypothesis 6: In line with the theory of personality congruence, individuals with a high rank instruction and, therefore, a desire to stand out prefer premium brands, signalizing status.

Hypothesis 7: In line with the theory of personality congruence, individuals with a high care instruction and, therefore, a desire to fit in, along with a heightened sensitivity toward social approval prefer mass-market brands, signalizing popularity and reassuring the individual that this is everybody's choice.

Results

Personalization 3.0 Drives Increased Engagement with Facebook Advertisements

Experiment 1

In the first experiment, which tested hypothesis 1, the control ad (left side of Figure 6) was displayed to all types, excluding guard type customers who were identified via direct profiling on the Appliances Online website and a Facebook lookalike audience. The variant ad (right side of Figure 6) was displayed to guard type customers only. Then, engagement rates, i.e., the number of people who took action (e.g., like, link click, comment, share, view picture) out of the total people reached (e.g., number of people who saw the ad at least once), were monitored for both advertising executions.

As Figure 7 shows, the guard type personalized ad on mobile devices achieved a significantly higher engagement rate of 2.50% versus 1.99% for the generic control ad, signifying a 25.81% increase in the engagement rate.

On desktops, the effects were dramatically stronger, as shown in Figure 8. The personalized ad achieved a 618.60% increase in engagement rate compared to the control ad, with a 2.23% engagement rate versus a control engagement rate of 0.31%. This mobile–desktop difference in magnitude was likely because high guard type individuals tend to be risk-averse late adopters of new ways of doing things, including mobile shopping, and, therefore, still prefer using desktop devices over mobile devices.

In summary, experiment 1 confirmed hypothesis 1 and showed that the deployment of personalized ads can significantly increase engagement rates on mobile and desktop devices in the context of digital Facebook advertising.

Figure 6. Facebook advertising experiment 1: Generic control ad versus personalized guard ad (Appliances Online Facebook Campaign, March 16th, 2018 – March 30th, 2018, n = 279,780)

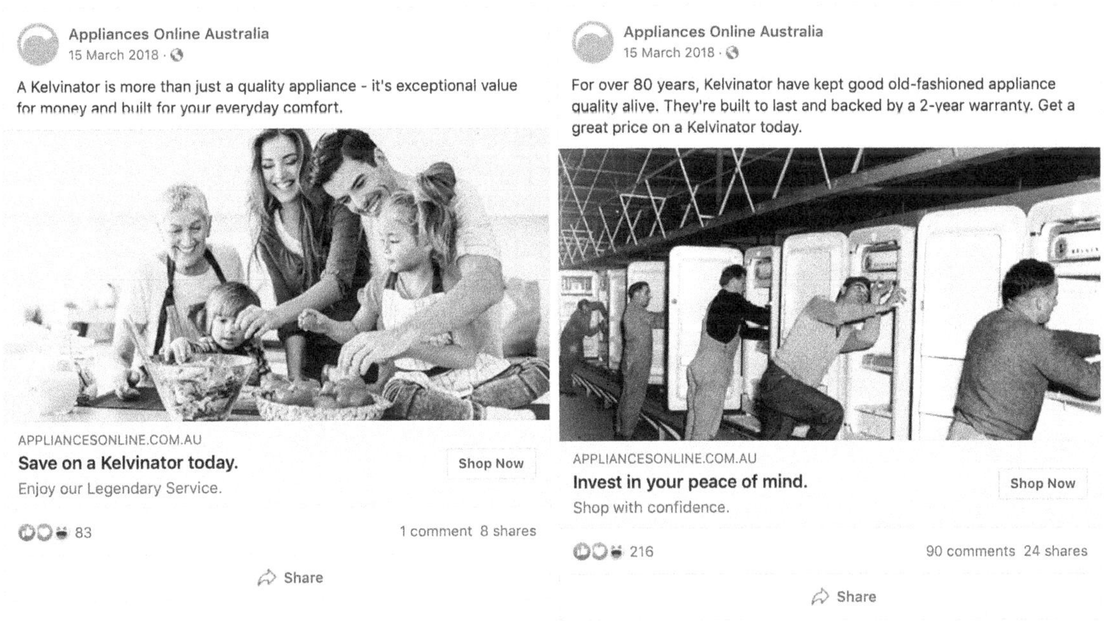

Figure 7. Guard-personalized ad, mobile (Appliances Online Facebook, March 16, 2018 – March 30, 2018 (14 days), n =59,239)

	Reach	Engagement	Engagement Rate	Engagement Rate Change	P Value	Z Score
Control	27,743	551	1.99%			
Guard Variation	31.496	787	2.50%	25.81%	0.0000	4.2208
Note: Engagement rate calculated by comparing the number of people who took action (like, link click, comment, share, viewed picture) to total reach (number of people who saw the ad at least once). *Confidence interval = 95%. At 95% confidence, a P value <0.05 indicates statistical significance.*						

Experiment 2

In the second experiment, displayed in Figure 9, which tested hypothesis 2, the control ad (left side) was displayed to all types, excluding customers with a high seek instruction who were identified via direct profiling on the Appliances Online website and a Facebook lookalike audience. The seek type personalized ad (right side) was displayed to high seek customers only. Again, engagement rates for both executions were monitored.

Figure 8. Guard type personalized ad, desktop (Appliances Online Facebook, March 16, 2018 – March 30, 2018 (14 days), n = 220,541)

	Reach	Engagement	Engagement Rate	Engagement Rate Change	P Value	Z Score
Control	197,657	613	0.31%			
Guard Variation	22,974	512	2.23%	618.60%	0.0000	19.5389
Note: Engagement rate calculated by comparing the number of people who took action (like, link click, comment, share, viewed picture) to total reach (number of people who saw the ad at least once). *Confidence interval = 95%. At 95% confidence, a P value <0.05 indicates statistical significance.*						

Figure 9. Facebook advertising experiment 2: Generic control ad versus personalized seek ad (Appliances Online Facebook, May 18, 2019 – June 8, 2019 (21 days), n = 181,615)

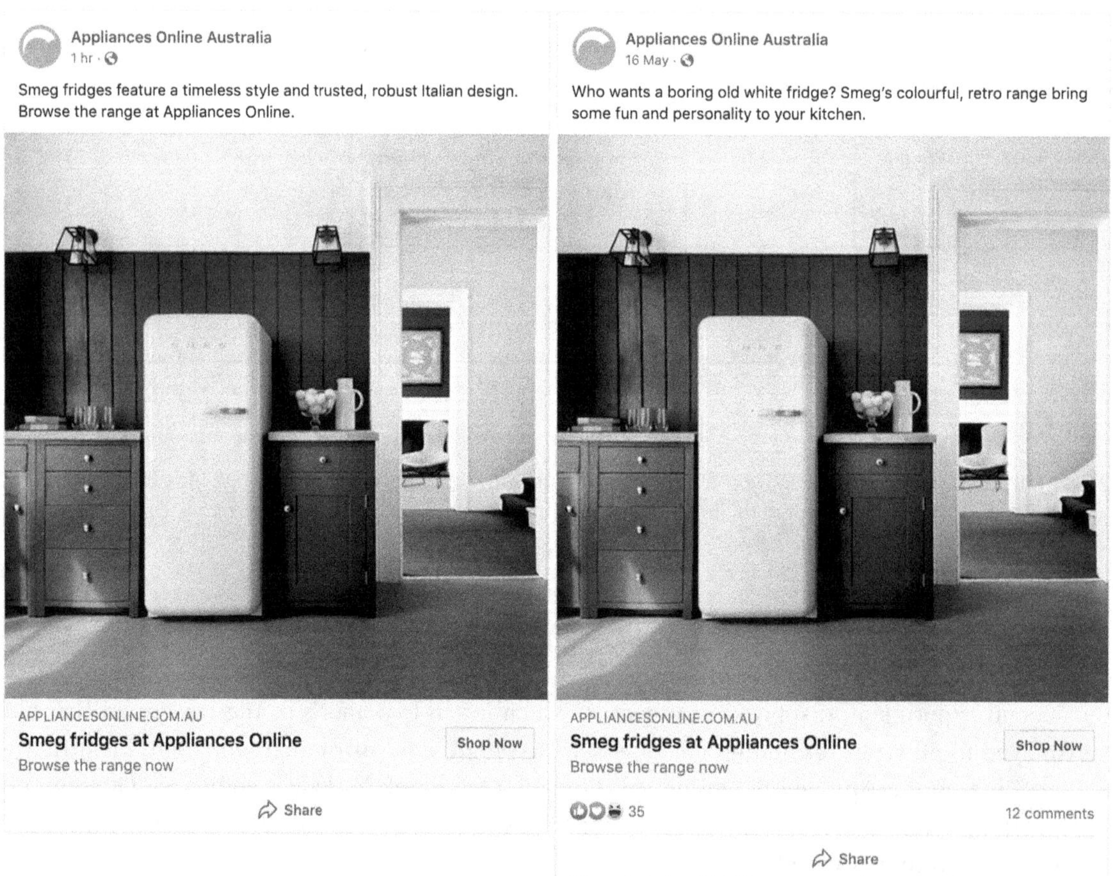

As Figure 10 shows, the seek type personalized ad achieves a significantly higher engagement rate of 0.66% (versus an engagement rate of 0.47% in the control ad), representing a 40.29% increase in engagement rate of the seek type personalized ad compared to the generic control ad. In summary, experiment 2 confirmed hypothesis 2, showing that the deployment of personalized seek ads significantly increased the engagement rate with consumers with a high seek instruction, in the context of digital Facebook advertising. The effect of a 40% lift is very strong, even though the copy was the only personalized element that spoke to primal goals.

Figure 10. Seek type personalized ad (Appliances Online Facebook, May 18, 2019 – June 8, 2019 (21 days), n = 181,615)

	Reach	Engagement	Engagement Rate	Engagement Rate Change	P Value	Z Score
Control	77,488	366	0.47%			
Seek Variation	104,127	690	0.66%	40.29%	0.0000	5.4073

Note: Engagement rate calculated by comparing the number of people who took action (like, link click, comment, share, viewed picture) to total reach (number of people who saw the ad at least once). *Confidence interval = 95%. At 95% confidence, a P value <0.05 indicates statistical significance.*

Personality Predicts the Preference of Different Personalized Kitchens

Experiment 3

During the third experiment, which tested hypotheses 3, 4, and 5, three different personalized kitchens were presented in an online customer survey with a total sample of 27,773 participants, as shown in Figure 11. The survey question asked respondents, "Which style of kitchen would you select for yourself/ your family?" to test whether care respondents preferred the care-personalized kitchen above average (kitchen number 1), rank respondents preferred the rank-personalized kitchen above average (kitchen number 2), and seek respondents preferred the seek-personalized kitchen above average (kitchen number 3 in Figure 11).

As Figure 12 shows, of all respondents who chose kitchen 1, the care group was overrepresented by 11%, confirming hypothesis 3. High guard and play consumers also responded favorably to the care personalized kitchen, i.e., they were overrepresented by 6% and 7% above average, respectively. Correlations as these are typical and expected as guard and play are the neighbors to care from a primal emotion perspective, as shown previously in Figure 3. The emotionally opposite end of the personality spectrum, high seek types, strongly disliked this kitchen, i.e., they were 30% underrepresented compared to the average consumer in the survey to select this kitchen for their home, as were rank-driven consumers with -35%.

Figure 11. Kitchen preference by personality type (Appliances Online Customer Insights Survey, 2016, n = 27,773. July 12, 2016 – July 28, 2016. Q15 Which style of kitchen would you select for yourself / your family? Select by clicking on the image that spontaneously appeals most to you)

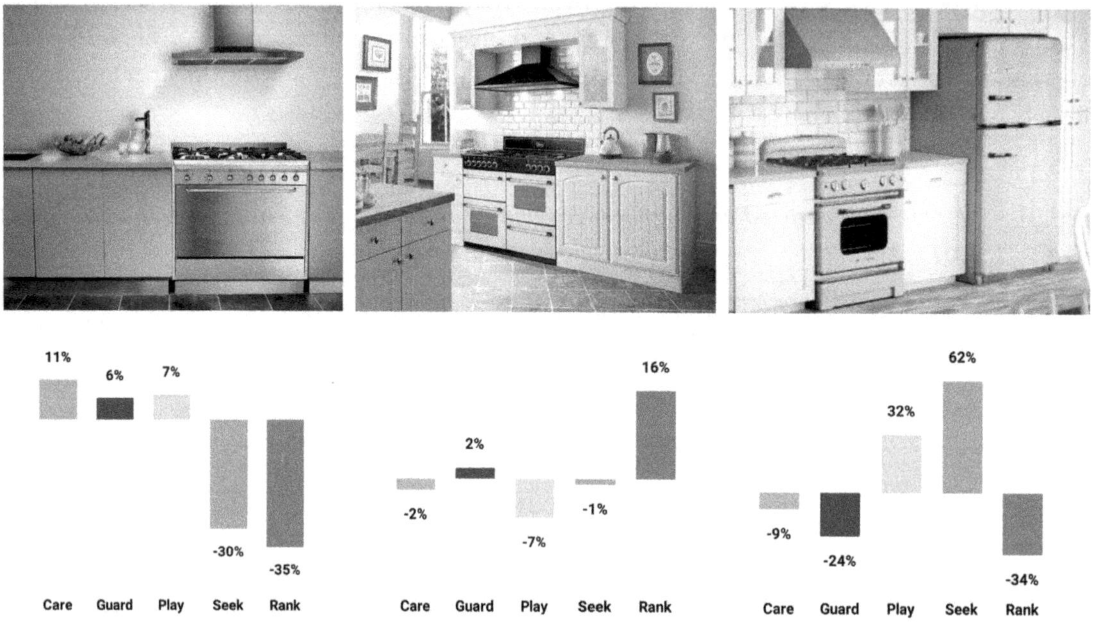

Figure 12. Kitchen preference by type - Kitchen 1 (care) (Appliances Online Customer Insights Survey, 2016. July 12, 2016 – July 28, 2016)

	Number of people who selected this kitchen as their preference	% of people who selected this kitchen as their preference	Representation versus survey population	Z score	P value
Care	1,344	50%	11%	17.0523	0.0000
Guard	460	17%	6%	4.4193	0.0000
Play	515	19%	7%	1.3138	0.1889
Seek	190	7%	-30%	-8.0202	0.0000
Rank	206	8%	-35%	6.1861	0.0000
Confidence interval = 95%. At 95% confidence, a P value <0.05 indicates statistical significance.					

High rank respondents preferred kitchen 2 as predicted and shown in Figure 13, with a 16% higher representation than the average consumer to select this rank-personalized kitchen, confirming hypothesis 4. This personalized kitchen is a good example for a very one-dimensional (one dimension meaning rank specifically) and well-tailored stimulus, only influencing high rank consumers to select it above chance.

Figure 13. Kitchen preference by type - Kitchen 2 (rank) (Appliances Online Customer Insights Survey, 2016. July 12, 2016 – July 28, 2016)

	Number of people who selected this kitchen as their preference	% of people who selected this kitchen as their preference	Representation versus survey population	Z score	P value
Care	4,186	44%	-2%	20.4186	0.0000
Guard	1,551	16%	2%	6.3824	0.0000
Play	1,570	16%	-7%	-3.8952	0.0001
Seek	936	10%	-1%	-6.5578	0.0000
Rank	1,291	14%	16%	38.2649	0.0000
Confidence interval = 95%. At 95% confidence, a P value <0.05 indicates statistical significance.					

Figure 14 shows that high seek respondents most strongly resonated with their personalized kitchen, as they were overrepresented by 62% to select it, thus confirming hypothesis 5. Notably, seek's neighbor type play also liked this kitchen a lot, with play types overrepresented by 32% in selecting this kitchen.

When looking at the absolute numbers and percentages of people selecting kitchens as their preference, Figure 12, 13 and 14 indicate the different sizes of each of the five segments across the sample population, which is also broadly representative for the personality distribution in the Australian population when factoring out the magnitudes of over- and under-representations. For example, the care segment is the largest segment in the population, while rank and seek are much smaller segments overall.

Personality Predicts Brand Preference

Experiment 4

During experiment 4, consumer preference of brand was measured by brand pageview split versus site average and two distinctly different brand personalities were selected to test hypotheses 6 and 7. Fisher & Paykel was selected representing a mass market, care personality brand (brand preferences shown on the left side of Figure 15), while Bosch was selected to represent a more premium, rank personality brand (brand preferences shown on the right side of Figure 15).

Figure 14. Kitchen preference by type - Kitchen 3 (seek) (Appliances Online Customer Insights Survey, 2016. July 12, 2016 – July 28, 2016)

	Number of people who selected this kitchen as their preference	% of people who selected this kitchen as their preference	Representation versus survey population	Z score	P value
Care	621	41%	-9%	5.4803	0.0000
Guard	184	12%	-24%	-2.2059	0.2745
Play	359	23%	32%	5.5907	0.0000
Seek	246	16%	62%	4.9313	0.0000
Rank	118	8%	-34%	4.8830	0.0000
Confidence interval = 95%. At 95% confidence, a P value <0.05 indicates statistical significance.					

Figure 15. Brand preference by personality type (Appliances Online Website Analytics, all time brand pageview split vs. site average for the top eight viewed brands., April 2, 2017 – September 30, 2018, n = 115,744)

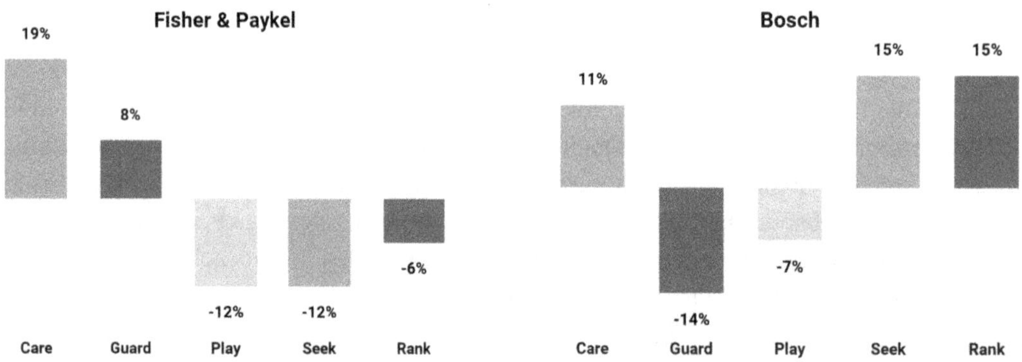

As Figure 16 shows, in line with the theory of personality congruence, individuals with a care instruction and, therefore, a desire to fit in prefer the mass market brand Fisher & Paykel, with a brand pageview representation of 19% above average, confirming hypothesis 7.

Individuals with a high rank instruction and, therefore, a desire to stand out gravitate more strongly toward Bosch, a sleek, premium brand, confirming hypothesis 6, with a 15% above average representation. However, Bosch brand preferences do not show an as clear and polarizing result as that of the Fisher & Paykel brand, with care consumers also being overrepresented by 11% in Bosch brand pageviews (Figure 17).

Figure 16. Brand preference by type - Fisher & Paykel (Appliances Online Website Analytics, April 2, 2017 – September 30, 2018)

	Number of people who viewed this brand	% of people who viewed this brand	Representation versus website user population	Z score	P value
Care	1,406	33%	19%	7.6409	0.0000
Guard	515	12%	8%	2.4708	0.0135
Play	947	22%	-12%	-5.3137	0.0000
Seek	609	14%	-12%	-2.8117	0.0049
Rank	748	18%	-6%	-2.1471	0.0318
Confidence interval = 95%. At 95% confidence, a P value <0.05 indicates statistical significance.					

Figure 17. Brand preference by type - Bosch (Appliances Online Website Analytics, April 2, 2017 – September 30, 2018)

	Number of people who viewed this brand	% of people who viewed this brand	Representation versus website user population	Z score	P value
Care	1,894	31%	11%	5.3630	0.0000
Guard	589	10%	-14%	-3.3259	0.0009
Play	1,444	24%	-7%	-4.0942	0.0000
Seek	849	14%	15%	-4.3989	0.0000
Rank	1,317	22%	15%	5.2031	0.0000
Confidence interval = 95%. At 95% confidence, a P value <0.05 indicates statistical significance.					

DISCUSSION AND RECOMMENDATIONS

These results show that the proposed biopsychological personality framework provides a clear link between consumers' nonconscious primal emotion instructions and their behavior. This correlation enables the predictive selection of adequate, emotionally tailored stimuli for different consumer personalities in order to improve existing personalization practices.

The relationship was demonstrated to extend across a range of different applications, including advertising, product and brand personalization. As the Facebook advertising results in experiments 1 and 2 confirmed, significant increases in user engagement rates, ranging between 25%, 40% and up to 618%, can be observed when applying personalized ads compared to generic, non-personalized ads. Equally, when it comes to the choice of product, including its visual style, personality can predict consumer behavior, as experiment 3 suggested. All consumer segments responded favorably to the kitchens that were tailored to match their personality styles, with preferences ranging between 11%, 16% and 62% above average, whilst at the same time repelling consumer personality types located at the opposite end of the personality spectrum by up to -35%. Finally, Aaker's (1997) and Grimm's (2005) theory of personality congruence could also be supported, showing that when there is a direct match of brand personality and consumer personality, consumers take a higher interest in the brand that matches their own personality with 15% and 19% above average brand pageviews in those instances in experiment 4.

Predictions such as these work because the link between consumers' primal emotion instructions and their in-market behaviors reveals the underlying reasons for these behaviors. This allows practitioners to plan for different attentional and perceptual processes in consumers' minds. In the current war for attention, only those who understand these processes and cater to their dynamics will be able to cut through consumers' individual emotional relevance detectors.

While the evolution of primal emotion systems originally enhanced the survival and fitness of humanity's earliest ancestors living in ancient tribes, they simultaneously gave rise to different personality traits, characteristic goals and behavior patterns that can help explain how modern individuals navigate the wilderness of an oversaturated consumer landscape today. Practitioners creating brand and marketing strategies—including products, social media campaigns, advertisements, user experiences and recommender systems—are well-advised to pay attention to the emotional, nonconscious and often unintended signals their communications are sending. Every single element of a proposition, from how it looks to how it's framed, sounds, feels and behaves is an emotional cue communicating to consumers, whether or not the proposition will be able to satisfy their personality-related, intrinsic, individual needs and goals. For example, research into how colors activate specific emotions shows that the yellow spectrum is associated with joy, creativity and play while blue hues are associated with fear and a desire for trustworthiness, predictability and control (e.g., Dael, Perseguers, Marchand, Antonietti & Mohr, 2016). A message of trust, durability and reliability speaks to fearful, control seeking individuals (emotional systems of disgust and fear as part of guard) while a message of individuality and challenging conventions speaks to curious, novelty-seeking, impulsive individuals (motivated by the emotional system of seek), as shown in experiments 1 and 2. As the neuroscientific literature reviewed in this chapter suggests, this matters precisely because consumer decision making is highly emotional. Consumer choices are largely nonconscious responses to external stimuli and internal processes of evolutionary origin and function.

The more a stimulus is targeted and congruent in its primal instruction (e.g., a specific ad, copy or product), the less noise there is in the prediction of behavior. Accordingly, brands should aim to portray one clear, congruent personality to their matching target audience or select emotionally tailored messages for different audiences when undertaking personalized communications.

Nevertheless, demographic Personalization 1.0, as well as malfunctions in behavioral Personalization 2.0, are still dominating business practices. This current state of personalization was entertainingly illustrated by Jac Rayner's (2018) toilet seat example, and empirically supported by research across 23 industry sectors by Marketing Week (2019). As described above, both approaches fail to address the underlying needs and motivations of different consumer personalities. Therefore, such attempts may at best succeed in presenting the right product at the right time (for example, a fridge when someone exhibits a digital cue of being in the market for replacing a broken-down fridge). However, there remains a lack of relevant information on how to present that product in a personally relevant way. Furthermore,

Personalization 1.0 and 2.0 provide no opportunity to predict future demand for previously unobserved needs. The Amazon toilet seat buyer may also be in the market for a bungee jump, which could only be accurately predicted by knowing the buyer's underlying primal emotion instruction of high seek (producing a stable disposition for exciting risk-taking). However, a different Amazon customer who also bought the toilet seat but who has a high guard instruction (producing a disposition for safety, control and predictability) would recoil from the proposition of a bungee jump. Instead, they are more likely to respond favorably to the offer of taking up life insurance for their pet. Both consumers displayed the same initial purchase behavior but have vastly different personalities and motivations. Future opportunities for engagement with these two customers must vary accordingly. Applying a biopsychological understanding of consumer personality provides a more predictive and meaningful approach to personalization.

FUTURE RESEARCH DIRECTIONS

Because of the crucial role of the emotional, nonconscious component of consumer decision making and its particular relevance when it comes to brand, product, or marketing appeal, this research zoomed in on the influence of primal emotion systems as well as resulting basic psychological needs and traits, which have been conceptually attributed to system 1.

Future research lies in the deeper exploration of the interplay of system 1 and system 2 or emotional and cognitive processes when studying and modeling personality for consumer behavior prediction purposes. Because environmental influences shape the characteristic adaptations of consumers, including learned strategies for goal pursuit, understanding key environmental influencing factors on personality development is important to predict consumer behaviors across different environmental contexts. For example, it is well documented that collectivist and individualist cultures operate in different paradigms and cultural norms (Taras, Kirkman, & Steel, 2010), thereby influencing an individual's strategies and behavioral expressions when pursuing goals such as rank. While someone in the US (individualist score of 91 out of 100; Hofstede, Hofstede, & Minkov, 2010) seeks uniqueness and personal accomplishment, someone in Hong Kong (individualist score of 25 out of 100; Hofstede, Hofstede, & Minkov, 2010) places higher importance on their obligations to the group and the achievement of the group as a whole. Even though two individuals across the two cultures may show an equally dominant rank drive in the standardized test, their strategies to achieve and maintain rank, together with the associated consumer behaviors, may vary strongly. Understanding these culture-specific influences on characteristic adaptations could prove a useful step forward in reducing prediction noise.

CONCLUSION

Consumers welcome personalized experiences and respond positively toward options that resonate with their innate goals and dispositions, as shown in the preceding four experiments. In this sense, personalization can simplify decision making by reducing today's overload of irrelevant choices and improving consumer experiences for the better. For businesses, Personalization 3.0 provides an avenue to better plan and predict the success of their advertising, marketing, and brand initiatives, reduces wastage, treats consumers more respectfully as whole human beings, and increases the chance of success of personalization investments. However, the marketing application of this frontier is not without its ethical challenges.

As the presented empirical evidence shows, understanding humans' evolutionary and psychological impulses and personal tendencies is a powerful tool for influencing behavior at scale. Consequently, causes for its application should always be selected with environmental, societal, and individual health considerations in mind.

ACKNOWLEDGMENT

This research received no specific grant from any funding agency in the public, commercial, or not-for-profit sectors. However, the research was supported by consumer research samples of the Winning Online Group Pty Ltd. The author thanks John Winning for the use of data collected on Appliances Online and Jon-Claude Raad and Christopher Knight for their research and experimentation support.

REFERENCES

Aaker, J. (1997). Dimensions of brand personality. *JMR, Journal of Marketing Research*, *34*(3), 347–356. doi:10.1177/002224379703400304

Alcaro, A., Carta, S., & Panksepp, J. (2017). The affective core of the self: A neuro-archetypical perspective on the foundations of human (and animal) subjectivity. *Frontiers in Psychology*, *8*, 1424. doi:10.3389/fpsyg.2017.01424 PMID:28919868

Barilliance. (2015). The most effective types of personalized product recommendations. *Barilliance*. Retrieved from https://www.barilliance.com/the-most-effective-types-of-personalized-product-recommendation

Berridge, K., & Robinson, T. (2016). Liking, wanting, and the incentive-sensitization theory of addiction. *The American Psychologist*, *71*(8), 670–679. doi:10.1037/amp0000059 PMID:27977239

Carter, C. (2017). The Oxytocin–Vasopressin Pathway in the Context of Love and Fear. *Frontiers in Endocrinology*, *8*, 8. doi:10.3389/fendo.2017.00356 PMID:29312146

Dael, N., Perseguers, M., Marchand, C., Antonietti, J., & Mohr, C. (2016). Put on that colour, it fits your emotion: Colour appropriateness as a function of expressed emotion. *Quarterly Journal of Experimental Psychology*, *69*(8), 1619–1630. doi:10.1080/17470218.2015.1090462 PMID:26339950

Damasio, A. (2000). *The feeling of what happens: Body and emotion in the making of consciousness*. Fort Worth, TX: Harcourt College Publishers.

DeWaal, F. (2010). *The age of empathy*. New York: Harmony Books.

DeYoung, C. (2014). A cybernetic big five theory for personality psychology. *Personality and Individual Differences*, *60*, S18. doi:10.1016/j.paid.2013.07.381

Dominik, T., Dostál, D., Zielina, M., Šmahaj, J., Sedláčková, Z., & Procházka, R. (2018). Libet's experiment: A complex replication. *Consciousness and Cognition*, *65*, 1–26. doi:10.1016/j.concog.2018.07.004 PMID:30007132

Eisenegger, C., Naef, M., Snozzi, R., Heinrichs, M., & Fehr, E. (2010). Prejudice and truth about the effect of testosterone on human bargaining behaviour. *Nature*, *463*(7279), 356–359. doi:10.1038/nature08711 PMID:19997098

Evergage. (2018). 2018 Trends in personalization. *Evergage*. Retrieved from https://www.evergage.com/wp-content/uploads/2018/04/Evergage-2018-Trends-in-Personalization-Survey.pdf

Fedigan, L. (2015). Dominance rank in primates. In P. Whelehan & A. Bolin (Eds.), *The International Encyclopedia of Human Sexuality* (pp. 305–306). Oxford: John Wiley & Sons, Ltd. doi:10.1002/9781118896877.wbiehs116

Fisher, H., Island, H., Rich, J., Marchalik, D., & Brown, L. (2015). Four broad temperament dimensions: Description, convergent validation correlations, and comparison with the Big Five. *Frontiers in Psychology*, *6*, 6. doi:10.3389/fpsyg.2015.01098 PMID:26284018

Gartner. (2018). 2018 State of personalization report. *Gartner*. Retrieved from https://www.gartner.com/en/documents/3892113/2018-state-of-personalization-report

GirlFromBlupo. (2018, April 6). *Dear Amazon, I bought a toilet seat because I needed one. Necessity, not desire. I do not collect them. I am not a toilet seat addict. No matter how temptingly you email me, I'm not going to think, oh go on then, just one more toilet seat, I'll treat myself* [Twitter Post]. Retrieved from https://twitter.com/GirlFromBlupo/status/982156453396996096?s=20

Grimm, P. (2005). Ab components' impact on brand preference. *Journal of Business Research*, *58*(4), 508–517. doi:10.1016/S0148-2963(03)00141-3

Haeusel, H. G. (2008). *Think Limbic*. Freiburg: Haufe Gruppe.

Haeusel, H. G. (2011, March). *The scientific foundation of the Limbic approach.* Retrieved from https://www.nymphenburg.de/tl_files/pdf/LimbicScience110220.pdf

Hirsh, J., Kang, S., & Bodenhausen, G. (2012). Personalized Persuasion. *Psychological Science*, *23*(6), 578–581. doi:10.1177/0956797611436349 PMID:22547658

Hofstede, G., Hofstede, G., & Minkov, M. (2010). Cultures and organizations: Software of the mind (3rd ed,). Johanneshov: MTM.

Kahneman, D. (2011). *Thinking, fast and slow*. New York: Farrar, Straus and Giroux.

Kavaliers, M., Ossenkopp, K., & Choleris, E. (2018). Social neuroscience of disgust. *Genes Brain & Behavior*, *18*(1), e12508. doi:10.1111/gbb.12508 PMID:30062689

Kerney, M., Smaers, J., Schoenemann, P., & Dunn, J. (2017). The coevolution of play and the cortico-cerebellar system in primates. *Primates*, *58*(4), 485–491. doi:10.100710329-017-0615-x PMID:28620843

Kidd, C., & Hayden, B. (2015). The Psychology and Neuroscience of Curiosity. *Neuron*, *88*(3), 449–460. doi:10.1016/j.neuron.2015.09.010 PMID:26539887

Klotz, C., & Akinalp, C. (2013). Identifying Limbic Characteristics on Twitter. In *The 9th International Conference on Computing and Information Technology. Advances in Intelligent Systems and Computing*, (vol. 209, pp. 19-27). Springer. 10.1007/978-3-642-37371-8_6

Lebel, R. (2017). Moving Beyond Fight and Flight: A Contingent Model of How the Emotional Regulation of Anger and Fear Sparks Proactivity. *Academy of Management Review*, *42*(2), 190–206. doi:10.5465/amr.2014.0368

LeDoux, J. E. (2000). Emotion circuits in the brain. *Annual Review of Neuroscience*, *23*(1), 155–184. doi:10.1146/annurev.neuro.23.1.155 PMID:10845062

Libet, B. (1996). Cerebral time factors in conscious and unconscious mental functions. *Journal of Clinical Neurophysiology*, *13*(4), 350. doi:10.1097/00004691-199607000-00027

Lipton, B. (2015). *The biology of belief.* Hay House Publishing.

Lockley, L. (1950). Notes on the history of marketing research. *Journal of Marketing*, *14*(5), 733–736. doi:10.1177/002224295001400511

MacKenzie, I., Meyer, C., & Noble, S. (2013). *How retailers can keep up with consumers.* Retrieved from https://www.mckinsey.com/industries/retail/our-insights/how-retailers-can-keep-up-with-consumers

MacLean, P. D. (1990). *The triune brain in evolution: Role in paleocerebral functions.* New York: Plenum Press.

Marketing Week. (2019). *Marketing effectiveness survey.* Retrieved from https://www.marketingweek.com/carlsberg-demographics-waterwipes-5-things-that-mattered-this-week-and-why/

Maymand, M., & Razmi, R. (2017). On the Effect of the Congruence between the Brand Image and Brand Personality on the Consumers' Brand Preference and Purchase Intent: A Case Study of Aquafina Bottled Water. *International Journal of Economic Perspectives*, *11*(1), 1369–1383.

McAdams, D., & Pals, J. (2006). A new Big Five: Fundamental principles for an integrative science of personality. *The American Psychologist*, *61*(3), 204–217. doi:10.1037/0003-066X.61.3.204 PMID:16594837

Montag, C., & Panksepp, J. (2017). Primary emotional systems and personality: An evolutionary perspective. *Frontiers in Psychology*, *8*, 464. doi:10.3389/fpsyg.2017.00464 PMID:28443039

Montagrin, A., & Sander, D. (2016). Emotional memory: From affective relevance to arousal. *Behavioral and Brain Sciences*, *39*, 39. doi:10.1017/S0140525X15001879 PMID:28347365

Norbury, A., & Husain, M. (2015). Sensation-seeking: Dopaminergic modulation and risk for psychopathology. *Behavioural Brain Research*, *288*, 79–93. doi:10.1016/j.bbr.2015.04.015 PMID:25907745

Panksepp, J. (1998). *Affective neuroscience: The foundations of human and animal emotion.* New York, NY: Oxford University Press.

Panksepp, J. (2006). Emotional endophenotypes in evolutionary psychiatry. *Progress in Neuro-Psychopharmacology & Biological Psychiatry*, *30*(5), 774–784. doi:10.1016/j.pnpbp.2006.01.004 PMID:16554114

Panksepp, J. (2010). Affective neuroscience of the emotional BrainMind: Evolutionary perspectives and implications for understanding depression. *Dialogues in Clinical Neuroscience*, *12*(3), 533–545. PMID:21319497

Panksepp, J., & Biven, L. (2012). *The Norton series on interpersonal neurobiology. The archaeology of mind: Neuroevolutionary origins of human emotion*. New York, NY: W. W. Norton & Company.

Panksepp, J., & Harro, J. (2004). The future of neuropeptides in biological psychiatry and emotional psychopharmacology: Goals and strategies. In J. Panksepp (Ed.), *Textbook of Biological Psychiatry* (pp. 627–660). Hoboken, NJ: Wiley.

Pettersson, E., & Turkheimer, E. (2013). Approach temperament, anger, and evaluation: Resolving a paradox. *Journal of Personality and Social Psychology*, *105*(2), 285–300. doi:10.1037/a0033046 PMID:23773039

Price, J., Gardner, R. Jr, Wilson, D., Sloman, L., Rohde, P., & Erickson, M. (2007). Territory, rank and mental health: The history of an idea. *Evolutionary Psychology*, *5*(3), 531–554. doi:10.1177/147470490700500305

Rubio-Godoy, M., Aunger, R., & Curtis, V. (2007). Serotonin – A link between disgust and immunity? *Medical Hypotheses*, *68*(1), 61–66. doi:10.1016/j.mehy.2006.06.036 PMID:16928421

Salesforce Inc. (2017). The Power of Personalized Shopping. *Salesforce.com Inc*. Retrieved from https://www.salesforce.com/products/commerce-cloud/resources/resources-assets-for-filter/the-power-of-personalized-shopping/

Sapolsky, R. (2017). *Behave*. London: Vintage.

Taras, V., Kirkman, B., & Steel, P. (2010). Examining the impact of culture's consequences: A three-decade, multilevel, meta-analytic review of Hofstede's cultural value dimensions. *The Journal of Applied Psychology*, *95*(3), 405–439. doi:10.1037/a0018938 PMID:20476824

Toronchuk, J., & Ellis, G. (2007a). Disgust: Sensory affect or primary emotional system? *Cognition and Emotion*, *21*(8), 1799–1818. doi:10.1080/02699930701298515

Toronchuk, J., & Ellis, G. (2007b). Criteria for basic emotions: Seeking DISGUST? *Cognition and Emotion*, *21*(8), 1829–1832. doi:10.1080/02699930701334419

Toronchuk, J., & Ellis, G. (2013). Affective neuronal selection: The nature of the primordial emotion systems. *Frontiers in Psychology*, *3*, 589. doi:10.3389/fpsyg.2012.00589 PMID:23316177

Tyng, C., Amin, H., Saad, M., & Malik, A. (2017). The Influences of Emotion on Learning and Memory. *Frontiers in Psychology*, *8*, 8. doi:10.3389/fpsyg.2017.01454 PMID:28883804

Wall, H., Campbell, C., Kaye, L., Levy, A., & Bhullar, N. (2019). Personality profiles and persuasion: An exploratory study investigating the role of the Big-5, Type D personality and the Dark Triad on susceptibility to persuasion. *Personality and Individual Differences*, *139*, 69–76. doi:10.1016/j.paid.2018.11.003

Wansink, B., & Sobal, J. (2007). Mindless eating. *Environment and Behavior*, *39*(1), 106–123. doi:10.1177/0013916506295573

Wetherall, K., Robb, K., & O'Connor, R. (2019). Social rank theory of depression: A systematic review of self-perceptions of social rank and their relationship with depressive symptoms and suicide risk. *Journal of Affective Disorders*, *246*, 300–319. doi:10.1016/j.jad.2018.12.045 PMID:30594043

KEY TERMS AND DEFINITIONS

Characteristic Adaptations: Consequences generated by cybernetic processes of learning and adaptation of the individual. Characteristic adaptations evolve through changes in the brain function within one human lifetime, in relation to particular life circumstances of the individual. Characteristic adaptations can be conceptually attributed to the system 2 layer of personality and consist of goals, interpretations, and strategies, and can be conscious or nonconscious.

Epigenetics: The study of gene-environment interactions, explaining how the same genotype leads to different phenotypes.

Motivation and Goals: At the core of personality stands motivation, in an evolutionary sense, the motivation to ensure basic survival and functioning, in a psychological sense the motivation to fulfill basic human needs. These needs, in turn, give rise to goals.

Personality: An individual's variation to the general evolutionary design, which encompasses a set of relatively stable dispositional traits and behaviors that can be identified across all human societies as well as other mammals.

Primal Emotion Systems: Mammal's core operating systems that have evolved to ensure individual survival and functioning as well as the survival, cohesion, and functioning of the group. These remain universally influential in humans.

Saliency: An important attentional mechanism in cognitive neurosciences, focusing on an organism's limited amount of cognitive and perceptual resources toward stimuli that are key to their survival, functioning, and goal pursuit, while not allocating limited attention toward less pertinent stimuli.

Traits: Characteristic patterns of emotions, motivations, strategies, behaviors, or styles for pursuing need fulfilling goals. Traits are probabilistic, so even an error-free measure of a trait cannot predict behavior at any given moment with 100% accuracy. Nevertheless, they provide significant predictive power in aggregate and can in many cases also predict single instances of behavior better than chance.

Chapter 3
Gifts as Language:
Gift Code Between Relatives

Alice Duarte
University of Porto, Portugal

ABSTRACT

This chapter addresses the issue of gifts as a language of sociability. The culture of our industrial and post-industrial societies over the last centuries has largely become a culture based on mass-produced and mass-distributed objects. There is no doubt that people use these commodities as part of processes within which social and moral considerations come into play, but this is hardly explained in phenomenological terms. This chapter proposes to analyse consumption as a cultural practice, pointing out the instrumental role of commodities as a language available to social actors to express and to communicate. It highlights some aspects of the gift code between relatives, the key purpose of which is to explain how interpersonal relations are produced through the exchange of gifts between subjects, in this case linked by family ties. There is a significant degree of diversity in the exchange of gifts between relatives, encompassing emotionally charged contexts. The author conducted a qualitative research consisting of in-depth interviews and ethnography in Northern Portugal.

INTRODUCTION

This chapter feeds on the communication presented at the Conference *Interaction Order: Contribution to a Multidisciplinary Approach to Social Interactions*, wherein E. Goffman's expression "interaction order" (1983) appeared as a condensed message used to guide a line of thought that links various speakers, who should give their contribution to an "analysis of social practice as interaction order". In other words, building on E. Goffman's expression (or taking it as a pretext), the Conference hoped to do its part towards a "practice theory" able to give some phenomenological and analytical details about some private social interactions.

Having re-read E. Goffman (1983), the author was determined to address the issue of *gifts* as language of sociability and, through him, respond to the proposed challenge and, at the same time, contribute to overcoming the simplistic view – yet persistently dominant in place since the Frankfurt School – of

DOI: 10.4018/978-1-7998-3115-0.ch003

Copyright © 2020, IGI Global. Copying or distributing in print or electronic forms without written permission of IGI Global is prohibited.

consumption as "mass consumption" and, therefore, as an anti-social activity. Still building on these thoughts, long after this chapter was written.

BACKGROUND

In the current chapter, the author does take due note of E. Goffman's idea of "interaction order" as the conceptual map underlying the relationships between individuals in particular social situations, and his emphasis that interactions need not be understood as being limited to strictly conversational situations. At the same time, the author also acknowledges E. Goffman's central idea concerning the organised and recurring nature of the interaction order, and of its precariousness and instability which gives it a substantial dynamic potential. Bearing this in mind, the author proposes to highlight some aspects of the gift code between relatives, to explain how interpersonal relations are produced within the exchange of gifts between specific individuals. The choice of relatives as the focus of observation of the code rules on the exchange of gifts results from the fact that their interactions embody a significant degree of diversity, encompassing emotionally charged contexts, as in the case of gifts exchanged between spouses. In other words, the gift code between more or less close relatives, clearly illustrates the emotional load that E. Goffman (1983) insisted on always crossing and constantly threatening the inter-relational process.

Now that the author has clarified that she intends to address social interactions from the viewpoint of consumption for others, she needs to refer to the conceptual and methodological framework of the research that has enabled her to collect the material under analysis (Duarte, 2015, 2011, 2009). The research falls within the area of anthropology of consumption, and is guided by the concern for showing the consumption process as a cultural practice, that is, one in which goods and services consumed are addressed in terms of their re-socialization by the social actors (Miller, 1987; McCracken, 1988). The culture of industrial society has, over the last century, largely become a culture based on mass-produced and mass-distributed objects. However, there is no doubt that people use these commodities as part of the process within which social and moral considerations come into play. The research was based on the fundamental idea that commodities (even if mass produced) are inevitably something socialized and, at the same time, its main objective was to demonstrate the plurality of possible appropriations performed on the same commodities. The analysis of the consumption process as cultural practice – in other words, as a process of attributing meanings – needs to be trivialised so that one is able to better understand how it works in peoples' lives[1]. With this in mind, the investigator self-imposed access to specific consumers, considering them in their regular consumption practices and locating them in their households' contexts. With the intention of understanding the socio-cultural basis of demand, the researcher supports a conception of consumption as a set of practices socially and personally meaningful, through which commodities are re-appropriated – or re-socialised – by social actors and used with the purpose of expressing themselves and communicating. In short, rather than being limited to any act of buying, consumption includes all acts and decisions made before and after the purchase itself; all goods and services available in the market are commodities, but this does not render them immune to social and moral readings; through the consumption process, social actors withdraw the commodities from the impersonal situations in which they were produced and (re)contextualise them through specific appropriations. Seen as a cultural practice, consumption is, therefore, a potential means for social actors to express themselves and communicate, through which one can examine how they build values and attribute meanings.

When the researcher decides to approach consumption as a practical and circumstantial activity and defends a clear poststructuralist position in respect of the actors' agency, the next requirement will be to operationalize the research taking into account the real practices of actual consumers. This will be the way to provide, as far as possible, a phenomenological character to the research. It was with this in mind that the author formed an empirical sample of 24 households from the new middle classes, to which a qualitative methodology was applied, based on in-depth long-term interviews and on ethnography. The intention was to show the co-existence of plural processes of appropriation of commodities carried out by social actors who enjoy the greatest possible structural proximity with one another.[2] The successful achievement of these goals, however, made two supplementary analytical developments possible. On the one hand, it provided quite a comprehensive understanding of the values, representations and ambitions operating in the lives of those households from the new Portuguese middle classes (Duarte, 2009, 2015). On the other hand, it also allowed access to the subjective experiences of consumption of the informants, abundantly illustrating the possibilities of re-socialization of the commodities. One of the most interesting axes of analysis within of the many ways in which social actors can appropriate commodities is the consumption for others in the form of gifts, through which one can take account of how social actors create and maintain sociability networks (Duarte,2011)[3].

At this point, it should be briefly explained that the potential informants were first approached randomly while visiting a shopping centre in the Greater Porto area, and it was established a quite informal verbal contact with them. About half of those people initially contacted, which together with their households would became the research analysis units, were selected *a posteriori,* after they gave their consent and having fulfilled some pre-set conditions. These conditions consisted basically of choosing only households whose characteristics placed them in the pre-defined "middle-class" category[4]. It was, therefore, possible to organise what might be called a thematic research, i.e., a research unfolded into various units of analysis without them forming a "community", in the sense that they don't form a socio-spacial continuity. This strategy allowed to avoid the methodology practice, often used in anthropology, of selecting an empirical study object as a unit of analysis, intensively researching it, but also atomising it many times. Instead, the 24 households selected form the same number of case studies that constitute the "territory" of analysis due to their link to the "middle class" category. Visitors to the shopping centre initially contacted were about 50 persons, with whom the author of the chapter established quite informal verbal contact, asking them to talk "a bit of their usual shopping behaviours" and explaining the research objectives. These initial talks could be shorter or longer depending on the availability of people. In all cases they served to obtain consent to subsequent encounters with the investigator, as well as to collect some conventional class indicators and other information relating to the life of individuals and their households (e.g. professional occupations, composition of the households, educational qualifications). In basis of information from and the agreement of the people to continue in the investigation, it is formed the sample of research that brings together 24 households, to which we access from one of their members contacted before.

Geographically speaking, these households are spread across the metropolitan area of Porto and beyond that within a 50 km radius. Having formed the universe of study, in which the informants-consumers appear as members of their respective households, the research was continued with to hold a first interview, more formally defined and recorded, carried out in the family home or other location as indicated by persons, as their workplace or the same shopping center. On average, the duration of these first interviews overtook two and a half hours. Two or three months later, the author started a second round of interviews (and in some cases yet later, a third interview), made in the same way, but now almost all carried in the respective family home. The main topic of conversation during the first interviews was the gifts and the circuits of family gifts exchanging. In the second round of interviews (and third, when existing), the central topic was the patterns of consumption and the services used by the household. The articulated method of in-depth interviews and ethnography allowed the research to achieve the desired contextual understanding of their consumer practices. This methodological framework lasted about 19 months during which two (or three) successive rounds of interviews were carried out, resulting in more than 150 hours of recordings, as well as in an effective approach to the spaces and daily routines of the informants[5]. The format of the interviews in increasingly personalized and private spaces, often with the presence of two family members (the couple or members of the two generations present in the household), allowed incorporating an ethnographic approach that helped overcome the merely speech level of the data. The ethnographic strand of the research – translated into an effective approach to the everyday life of the subjects, in the repetition of successive interactions with the same individuals and in the progressive character of the relationships – allowed achieving an improved understanding of the consumption practices of households and their valuations. The important heuristic complement provided by the ethnographic component must be emphasised, as it enabled the researcher to access materials that far exceed the strictly discursive level, and to increase the understanding of the subjectivities acting in the consumption process.

INTERPERSONAL RELATIONS AND COMMODITIES

In a Goffmanian perspective, interaction is a field of microanalysis par excellence. It is only through a sufficiently thorough empirical analysis, capable of revealing the various versions of the entrenched interrelations, that the researcher can attain the recurring dimensions of those situations. The data tabled below, with which the author seeks to illustrate some facets of the performance of consumer goods as relational complements of the individuals, comes from an analysis of the consumption process that deserves the label "micro", not only due to its markedly qualitative nature, but also because it effectively refers to concrete individuals. It should be clarified that the author examined the networks of family sociability, whose dynamics places the individuals in more or less defined positions of mutual obligations, but also the networks of friendship, of neighbourhood and professionals, the composition of which depends more on various types of elective processes. On the other hand, as for the goods offered and/or exchanged, all types of gifts are considered, provided they are in its material version, including cash gifts. The author carried out an exhaustive analysis of all the cases of gift offers or exchanges involving the study units, or its members individually. The wealth of information collected is both extensive and consistent, covering all gift exchange situations – from the most recurring to the more sporadic – and also clarifies which gifts were actually offered and received on each of the gift offering or exchange occasions.

It is useful to recall the theoretical notion of "consumption work" (Miller, 1987: 190) to explain the process through which goods can connect the people who buy them and those who receive them as gifts, thus becoming vehicles for the creation and strengthening of interpersonal relationships. Consumption work need not entail the physical transformation of objects, and refers to the long and complex process in which the consumer works on a commodity to re-contextualise it. Through this process, people can transform any commodity from its generically sellable condition – i.e., that can be bought in the market for a price – into a unique commodity linked to a specific person – and, as such, basically unsellable. In respect of the interactions under analysis, consumption work concerns the practices through which objects bought on the market are appropriated and made into relational complements of the subjects involved in this exchange of gifts.

When viewed in terms of their use towards the building of sociabilities, the consumption practices of informants are surprising for their intricate mix of actual work, imagination and sentimentality. It becomes clear that feelings such as love, affection or gratitude can be expressed through material goods. But what also stands out is that this requires, in an objective way, the accomplishment of many practical actions, supported by considerable amount of real work. A whole range of tasks have to be done in the process of obtaining a gift with which to perform an exchange ritual able to materialise the linkage between two subjects and bring together the three elements – the donor, the relationship, and the recipient. Briefly, these tasks include the process of giving some thought as to which gift would be appropriate for a given situation and the subject in question; collect, more or less surreptitiously, and cross information about the future recipient's preferences, wishes or needs at any given time; visit shopping centres and specific shops; making sure that the wrapping is suitable and that the gift arrives at its destination on time.

They say that gifts are worth the time people spend buying them. (Elsa)[6]

I get so stressed when it comes to buying gifts, it's agony! Because I don't know what to buy! I get so stressed because I have to think well about it. (Cidália)

It's torture for me! I never buy anything on my first attempt. (Inês)

The comprehensive analysis of these appropriation processes through which anonymous commodities are transformed into personal gifts that can establish ties between people brings us to what the author has termed *gift code,* i.e., a set of recurrent tendencies. One of its main manifestations is the principle of individualising the gift according to its recipient. The persistent emphasis on this topic and the informants' unanimous opinion that it is important – as opposed to their disappointment or even disgust for standard gifts, or gifts chosen without having a specific person in mind – allows us to understand that one is looking at a dominant cultural representation, whose outlines include some idealization[7]. But, as a matter of fact, this is the most feasible conduct in the daily life of individuals, since the reasons for offering a gift cannot be justified abstractly, but only by reference to a specific subject. For the donor, any individual to whom she/he gives a gift does not exist as an isolated being, but rather as a member of networks of relations, wherein all his or her contacts – private and public – are arranged according to a hierarchy of importance. Each step in this hierarchy makes sense, especially when measured comparatively on a scale. The position of each recipient in that hierarchy will determine not only the type of gift thought of as appropriate, but also the justified efforts required to buy this gift. Moreover, alongside the more personal and emotional considerations, normative schemes exist at a social level to support supra-individual assessments generally associated with the gender and age of recipients, as well as with the type of social relationship between the two people involved. Finally, regardless of the particular intentions behind a gift offer, the ultimate goal of the donor is to always ensure that the selected gift is appreciated and to the liking of the recipient. Therefore, for all these considerations to be done and the exchange of gifts to be a means for maintaining and strengthening the existing emotional and social relationships, we need to proceed with specific recipients in mind.

I forgot to mention a gift I gave, a very important one! My middle child has a girlfriend, a girl with a very special attitude; I sent her the little spoon he used to eat with when he was a baby! I got a little box, put a little bow on it and send it to her. It's a present that shows love; special love. It was a way of showing that I care about her. (Isabel)

However, to argue that gifts are thought-out and bought for specific recipients is not the same as arguing that consumption work never suffers inattention, or that it is always done with the same degree of commitment. Underlying the cultural representation which crops up in the informants' discourses in quite straightforward terms, when it comes to the issue of gifts actually offered, it becomes evident that there are varying degrees of individualisation. It's only logical that it be so. The efforts put into the purchase of gifts vary according to the emotional and social relations established between the donor and each specific recipient of their gifts. These efforts can be, for example, the money to be spent, and the time, energy and diligence considered adequate according to the ranking of relationships. Taken together, the actions and efforts put into each gift reflect the differentiated commitment that each relationship needs to be maintained or renewed. If the effort level is high, it is because the recipients of those gifts are identified as deserving of special emotional, loving or social attention. This is why relationships between people are, in fact, measured by the gifts bought and offered, and how gifts become objectifications of relationships, connecting the individuals involved in each interaction.

THE FAMILY SYSTEM OF GIFT GIVING EXCHANGE

The focal point of the family as the origin and destination of gifts comes across very clearly in the networks of sociability that catalyse the circulation of gifts the most.

Among the informants, in all contexts of gift exchanging, a large share of the gifts exchanged and/or offered are among relatives, which in itself should be seen as a mechanism that reinforces the network of ties already existing among them. The analysis of all the empirical material shows that there are few situations in which other relationships stand on equal terms with relatives. In this respect, an overview of the universe of study produces an image that, in general, is in line with what R. Pahl (1995) advocates when he states that family relationships are more robust than ever, presenting as an essential network of affinities and social obligations. Underlying this dynamic there is a second tendency that materializes one more component of the aforementioned *gift code*: in the family circulation of gifts, it is perceptible that its distribution appears differentiated by three concentric circles of relatives.

Depending on the degree of kinship, gifts are distributed across three increasingly blurred exchange circles. The first and most intense of the three circles consists of the nuclear family, wherein the privileged recipients are the children and spouses. In the second circle, the boundary of the nuclear family is crossed, largely due to the normal course of the households' life cycle and to the fact that the children have now formed their own households. As a result, even though they live in distinct spaces, some of the relatives included in this circle are still the same: parents, children and siblings. However, new relatives are also added to the previous ones: grandchildren and in-laws. This second circle, therefore, contains various categories of relatives, each of which comprise a set of people formally defined as identical, but in fact not all of them occupy similar positions in emotional terms. This is also evident in the gift exchanging process. Apart from this second level, a third circle can still be found, consisting of countless uncles and cousins among which the exchange of gifts occurs, or not, according to the emotional ties most valued in each family.

Within this broad ambit of the family, it is so quite clear that the circulation of gifts embodies a language and a means of structuring the intimacy of people. The author notes that the informants' hierarchy of affections determines: the level of effective consumption work done, the degree of individualization of the gift, and the money made available for its purchase[8].Specifically for this last variable, one can speak again of a universally applicable principle: the money spent on gifts for relatives spread across the three concentric circles of exchange increases from the periphery to the centre. Apart from any variation between the households under consideration, in all of them the most distant relatives always receive less expensive gifts and the pre-set spending threshold for these relatives tends to be strictly followed. On the opposite end, the members of the nuclear family – especially children and spouses – always receive the most expensive gifts and, in most cases, there is no strict price limit defined; and if there is one, it is systematically exceeded. Such a family gift exchange system is, at the same time, a clear example of how gifts can be used to express love and affection, and of how their appropriation process is shaped by monetary considerations that are also used to express affection and feelings. The fact that the hierarchy of importance of the recipients of gifts finds correspondence in the different spending also shows how the individualisation of gifts is multifaceted. The more one is appreciated, the higher the price paid for the gift he or she will receive. In this sense, it can be said that the purchase and circulation of gifts serve to show affection, but the way these affections are ranked in importance is also reflected on the differentiated price/value of the gifts purchased[9].

In analytical terms, we need to understand that gifts are a language used to promote affection and feelings also through their differentiated market value. Claiming otherwise, i.e., claiming that all financial issues are not part of the process of using gifts as mediators of interpersonal relationships, is to forget that we have, for some centuries now, lived in societies where money is a fundamental standard value. And it is also forgetting that the social actors in these societies, regardless of their financial situation, always have to deal with money constraints. But this is, however, an idealization that reaches not only common people, but also some academics. The difficulty in regarding financial issues as being wholly part of the appropriation of gifts is related to a rather widespread cultural representation (Duarte, 2009: 14-17), based on the idea that *materiality* and *spirituality* are radically different (Carrier, 1995). It is important to understand and recognise that the relative cost of a gift itself can be a means to express either affections, or gradations in these affections. By understanding that in this way, too, do gifts become objectifications of flows of sociability, it will be possible to no longer identify the desire to receive a gift and/or the ambition to receive "good gifts" as "selfish" behaviours, as inappropriate to the spirit of gratuity that should exist in this type of interaction. On the contrary, we will see that receiving – as well as, giving – is a way of confirming that we are part of a relational network, and that receiving the "best gifts" (whatever that may mean, even in money terms) can clearly come through as a confirmation that one is loved. At the same time, the same principle also works in the opposite way. In respect of people understood as being on the same level of affection or loving care, an exact financial equivalence is pursued to the gifts given to them. The rule seems to be clear: if spending varies according to the types of relations in place, equivalent affective relations require exactly the same financial equivalence.

I usually define a specific amount and try not to spend much more than that. I make a list and attach a number to each recipient; daughters: 75 euros; husband: 25 or 30; father: 15; and then the other people too. Except for my daughters– obviously their gifts are the most expensive –I always try to stick to what I intended to spend. (Raquel)

I'm always careful about what I spend with my brother and sister: whatever one gets, the other gets it too. She's 24 and he's 19. I try to be careful! I gave my brother exactly what I gave to my sister! The gifts were different, but I spent with each one the same 100 euros, more or less. (Marta)

As for the aforementioned first circle of relatives, i.e., the nuclear family, we shall now focus on the directions of giving and receiving gifts among the relatives included therein and, in particular, on their underlying reciprocity or otherwise. On one hand, children offer gifts to their parents from very early on, even before they have any financial autonomy, or even before they are able to do the actual buying by themselves. With very small children, the other parent often chooses and buys the gift, and the child only delivers it personally. As they grow, and especially from early adolescence on, they do get involved themselves in buying the gift, either by continuing to receive financial help, entirely or partially, from the other parent, or by digging into their piggy banks and allowances. In general, children are expected to offer gifts on their parents' birthday, Mother's or Father's Day, and at Christmas, and they usually do so. These procedures fairly explain the fact that the very act of offering gifts to the parents is part of the socialisation process taught by parents on a daily basis. The same applies to gift exchange between siblings. Although this does not happen in their early childhood, it does tend to occur even before they have any financial autonomy, using savings in their piggy banks or asking their parents to pay for the birthday and Christmas gifts exchanged between them.

In parallel with these observations, it should be noted also that children and spouses are the main recipients of gifts within the nuclear family, although for both the question of reciprocity puts on quite differently. Between parents and children, the exchange is usually uneven "in quantity and in value" as already stated by T. Caplow (1984: 1316). The ruling standard is that fathers/mothers are the greatest gift donors, and children appear as their asymmetrical recipients. This parents' behaviour is clearly manifested at birthdays and Christmas, in the number of gifts and/or their value. But other indicators also stand out, for instance, the frequent use of one-off and/or occasional gifts[10]. In this case, little or no concerns with reciprocity arise, related with the emotional closeness between donor and receiver, among whom a strictly symmetrical idea of reciprocity makes no sense[11]. The issue of reciprocity neither is nor should be construed as being strictly balanced, and the actual asymmetry is the element that confirms how far-flung the relationship is from being a merely accounting logic.

As for the spouses and the gifts giving between them, on the one hand, the already marked tendency of the increased attention devoted to the gifts to the most loved ones is notorious. But on the other hand, although the emotional closeness between spouses is identical, gift exchanges among them present clear contrasts with the pattern found between parents and children. This, therefore, deserves special attention.

GIFT CODE BETWEEN SPOUSES

The Importance of Reciprocity and the Danger of the Bad Gift

Although with some variations, the majority of couples in the universe of study exchanged gifts among themselves (sometimes more than one): on birthdays, at Christmas and on their wedding anniversaries. Interestingly, even couples who have been together for long exchange gifts on Valentine's Day, a relatively recent commemoration in Portugal. Besides these occasions, some couples also exchange gifts on other significant occasions, for example, the day they met, the day when they started dating, the day they made up, etc. However, the practice of the one-off or occasional gift (frequent from parents to children) is hardly found between spouses.

As can be seen from the contexts of exchanges listed, the gift exchange between spouses is dominated by moments of mutual giving. In other words, when a gift is offered this almost always implies that another gifts counter-offered at the same time. While among the other relatives, only the Christmas gifts involve this expectation; between the couple only the birthdays of each spouse do not imply the simultaneous exchange of gifts. This pattern indicates – but also potentiates – a kind of eagerness into to reciprocate or the need to affirm balanced reciprocity, which should be understood as a symbolic reinforcement of the bond between the two spouses. In this case, one can say that reciprocity takes on great importance precisely because the simultaneous return of each present is like a repeated statement of the mutual existing relationship and, for this reason too, the exchange of gifts between spouses tends to entail an anxiety, or underlying tension, not found on the gifts circulation among, namely, the other members of the immediate family. This is especially so with regard to wedding anniversary gifts, or other dates equally meaningful for the couple, but only for the couple, and, therefore, that cannot be remembered by any more general shopping bustle, as is the case of Christmas gifts or Valentine's Day. The first signs of anxiety regarding "wedding anniversary" gifts appear the minute one wonders if the other has forgotten the date. In this case, possible forgetfulness triggers a very tangible fear, which is however manifested in a diffuse form, since if it were to happen, it would force the other spouse to consider the possibility that it should be understood as a sign of lack of interest in the common relationship. Bearing in mind A. Giddens's proposition (1992: 80 ff.) on the transformation of personal and sexual intimacy in modernity being based on the idea of personal trust as a project that needs to be "worked on" by the parties involved, it is easy to understand the deep-rooted threat of any action likely to be understood differently. Forgetting a special day for the couple (or the likelihood that this will happen) undermines the *ethos* of romantic love and parallel constellation of values that brings out the demand for proof of the continuous and increasing intimacy of lovers. Between spouses, the expectations raised as to the gifts to be received and the corresponding added commitment in the gifts to be given are based on this romantic idealisation of love, and this ideal is also shown in the desire to feel that the relationship is strengthened through gifts assessed as especially satisfying. More than in any other context of circulation of gifts – and in complete opposition to what occurs between parents and children – in this case the issue of reciprocity becomes particularly relevant. Mutual expectations and the desire to not be outmatched by the other spouse in terms of the impact and the surprise effect of their gifts are quite recurring patterns. On the other hand, given the tensions, struggles and latent competition detected, the author also questions the fact that gift exchange between spouses should also be analysed in the light of the existing power relations within the nuclear family. Some of the evidence found confirms that this social unit should not be analysed exclusively as a unit of converging interests.

Ok, I always give her a gift! ...- the best gift is for her: I give her a piece of jewellery, a watch, or some clothes that I know she'd love to have! (...) The gift I give that gives me more expectations as to the reaction of whoever receives it is usually her gift; this year, maybe [the most important one]it was her watch; because it's for her and because I care more... about her gift than anyone else's! I mean, I worry more when it comes to my wife (...). (Jorge)

I know that my husband is always carefully about finding the perfect gift for me; I must also be careful about choosing something for him! It has to please him! It doesn't have to be something too expensive ...but it has to be something already made and chosen according to what I know, I hope, he'll be very delighted with. (Isabel)

The tensions and implication in gift exchanging between spouses become clearer when analysed under the light of what the author has termed *unhappy gift,* meaning a gift that is unable to achieve the desired result despite the fact that the donor may have fulfilled the extensive consumption work that should be undertaken before the offering of a gift. Sometimes, on the part of the recipient, the gift is assessed as not fulfilling the expectations, thus becoming an example of an *unhappy gift*. Covering any gift received that is perceived as unsatisfactory or undesirable, the *unhappy gift* translates a frustrated expectation of the recipient as to her/his importance in the relationship with the donor, or of the outlines of such a relationship. Through a gift received as inappropriate, the recipient is faced with the lack of coincidence of her/his feelings regarding the relationship between the two people in interaction. Not surprisingly, the impact upon receiving these gifts varies according to the personal and emotional degree of the relationship of the people involved. If the individuals in question are linked through a professional relationship– for example, among mere co-workers – receiving an *unhappy gift* will tend to trigger no more than an appeased comment about it. The same is true for other equally less close personal and emotional relationships, for example, involving neighbours and even distant relatives. At this level, expectations are in fact lower, both in terms of the potential identification with the gifts received, or of the potential communion with the donor. The situation, however, changes radically when the *unhappy gifts* are exchanged within relational networks based on close emotional ties. In this case, there is no getting away from the interpretation that the relationship will have been underestimated or disregarded by the donor.

Some of the couples in the universe of study seemed to be particularly aware of the devastating impact that *unhappy gifts* exchanged between them would entail. In the context of this relationship, marked by ambition and desire for emotional closeness and communion with the other, the negative appreciation of a gift received cannot be mitigated by justifications valid in other contexts. In these other cases, the inappropriateness of the gift – conveyed in sentences like "it doesn't suit me", "it's not my type" or "it's not to my taste" – is understood as comprehensible, owing to a particular taste or self-image of the recipient. In contrast, in the interaction between spouses, damages would not be mitigated using any "justification" related to the identitary peculiarities or taste of the people involved. The premise is that these peculiarities be recognised and catered for. It is, therefore, understandable that the possibility of an *unhappy* gift could become a dark shadow hanging over the couple. Specifically, two couples in the universe of study, fearing that this could happen – in particular, by some potencial inattention of the husband – found ways to prevent this by adopting different tactics. These included "giving hints", that is, the intentional communication, more or less disguised, of the wife's preferences by herself. Through this expedient, the predictable frustration of the expectation of the wife was avoided, but, above all, it was ensured that gift exchanging between spouses was not a corrosion factor of the relationship and of their feelings. Gifts would, therefore, continue to play the role of mediators in the relationship, and the spouses continued using them as their relational complements.

Following what was said earlier, one last topic in connection with the gift code between spouses that merits some comments has to do with gender issues. Broadly speaking, research has confirmed the tendency for consumption activities to be marked by gender issues, and one should not hide the fact that in many ethnographic situations the work in consumption was delegated to women. At the same time, however, this finding cannot be taken as an absolute assumption, since equally relevant nuances was found.

More specifically in relation to consumption for others in the form of gifts, yet again one sees that much of the work is delegated to women, in particular to the *family's mothers*, but again one cannot talk about an absolute assumption. In this particular context, four *family fathers* were found who, in general and indiscriminately, performed all the tasks needed to obtain either their personal gifts or some gifts offered by their households[12]. At the same time, however, based on the overall view of the universe of research, one can only say that almost all male informants carry out, by themselves and autonomously, the gift for their wives (or girlfriends)[13]. When it comes to doing more than just purchase the gift for the partner – and, in fewer cases, the specific gifts for children – the generalisation no longer applies. The author suggested elsewhere (Duarte, 2011) the idea that underlying this generalised tendency of delegation there is a perception of the practices of consumption work as substitutes similar to other acts of caring, which is what justifies its frequent assignment to the female member of the couple. It should be noted that one of the few contexts in which this general tendency of male delegation undergoes an inflection, that can be named as universal among informants, is that of the circulation of gifts between spouses and its gift code.

SOLUTIONS AND RECOMMENDATIONS

The analysis of the consumption process as cultural practice – that is, as a process of attributing meanings – needs to be trivialised in order to better understand how it works in peoples' lives. At the same time, the objective of understanding the socio-cultural basis of demand requires providing, as far as possible, a phenomenological character to the research.

FINAL COMMENTS

Albeit limited by the inevitable space restrictions of a chapter, the author hopes she has succeeded in demonstrating how consumption is without a doubt a socialised process, and how the meanings of commodities are eminently performative. Moreover, she also sought to explain how consumer goods can effectively mediate relations between people. It was important to demonstrate that the analysis of some social interactions is remarkably amplified by the consideration of ties established between people with the help of gifts. These deserve to be considered as key elements of the sociability construction process of social actors and corresponding "interaction orders".

Gifts, and all work related to their purchase, objectify the feeling that connect people in each relationship. Material goods and feelings thus appear as interchangeable, it being possible to use ones as the expression of others. It would be good if one could trivialise this perception of the gift's expressive potential. The author tried to contribute to this providing a "practice theory" capable of shedding light, in detail, on the process through which one can obtain a gift able to fulfil the ritual of its exchange and correlative transfer of meaning from the consumer good to the recipient through the donor, connecting the three in a particular and specific manner.

Through a theoretically sustained interpretation, the author sought to systematise in a uniform voice the polyphony of the informants' voices. The major aim was to substantiate the statement that fatigue, full effort, and actual work are integral and inescapable parts of the consumption activities directed at other people. Given some of the informants' discourses, and their emphasis on the difficulty of obtaining suitable gifts to offer, one could almost doubt that the background context is that of a "consumer society" and its corresponding overabundance of products. Though this is a mere curiosity, it is nevertheless symptomatic that to qualify the gifts they offer, informants mainly use, in addition to terms such as "pretty" and "useful", adjectives such as "different," "special," and "original".

My husband is hard to please! Because he is very fussy and if I want to buy him clothes I have to go with him, but I can't buy them without him seeing them first! It's so difficult ... to give him anything. Last year, my daughters gave him a sweater, but to do that we had to put together a scheme. There was someone who got some sweaters and my oldest daughter brought several home; as if they weren't meant to be for us, but at the same time she showed him the sweaters; and father even said: "I actually like this one!". – "Oh Dad, but these sweaters are for Maria's father; I just bought them to see the model...". That's how we knew which one he liked! So, this is how we have to do it. (Raquel)

ACKNOWLEDGMENT

This research was supported by FCT – Foundation for Science and Technology - within the scope of UID/SOC/00727/2019

REFERENCES

Almeida, J. F., Costa, A. F., & Machado, F. L. (1994). Recomposição socioprofissional e novos protagonismos. In A. Reis (Ed.), *Portugal: 20 Anos de Democracia* (pp. 307–330). Lisbon: Círculo de Leitores.

Bourdieu, P. (1979). *La Distinction. Critique Sociale du Jugement.* Paris: Éditions du Minuit.

Carrier, J. (1995). *Gifts and Commodities: Exchange and Western Capitalism since 1770.* London: Routledge.

Duarte, A. (2009). *Experiências de Consumo. Estudos de caso no interior da Classe Média.* Porto: Universidade do Porto Editorial.

Duarte, A. (2011). *O Consumo para os Outros: Os Presentes como Linguagem de Sociabilidade.* Porto: Universidade do Porto Editorial.

Duarte, A. (2012). Emergência e Queda das Novas Classes Médias: a Improvável Consolidação das suas Práticas de Consumo. In C. M. Silva & J. V. Aguiar (Eds.), Classes, Políticas e Culturas de Classe (pp. 165-181). V. N. Famalicão: Edições Húmus/Universidade do Minho.

Duarte, A. (2015). The Short Life of the New Middle Classes in Portugal. *Anthropologica*, *57*(2), 557–570.

Giddens, A. (1992). *As Consequências da Modernidade*. Oeiras: Celta Editora.

Goffman, E. (1983). The Interaction Order. *American Sociological Review*, *48*(1), 1–17. doi:10.2307/2095141

McCracken, G. (1988). *Culture and Consumption*. Bloomington: Indiana University Press.

Miller, D. (1987). *Material Culture and Mass Consumption*. Oxford: Basil Blackwell.

Pahl, R. (1995). *After Success. Fin de Siècle Anxiety and Identity*. Cambridge: Polity Press.

Savage, M., Leroux, B., Rouanet, H., & Warde, A. (2008). Class and Cultural Division in the UK. *Sociology*, *42*(6), 1049–1072. doi:10.1177/0038038508096933

KEY TERMS AND DEFINITIONS

Consumption as Culture: Conception of the consumption process as a set of practices socially and personally meaningful, through which commodities are re-appropriated – or re-socialised – by social actors and used with the purpose of expressing themselves and communicating. Seen as a cultural practice, consumption is, therefore, a potential means for social actors to express themselves and communicate, through which one can examine how they build values and attribute meanings.

Family Sociability: Networks of household relations, whose dynamics places the individuals – the relatives – in more or less defined positions of mutual obligations. One can also speak of friendship networks, of neighbourhoods, or of workmates, but in these cases, their composition depends more on elective processes.

Gift Code: A set of recurring trends that express the normative schemes on the exchange of gifts. There is a social level of analysis that supports supra-individual assessments usually associated with the gender and age of the recipients, as well as the type of social relationship between the two people involved. And there are also more personal and emotional considerations. The gift code defines the type of gift considered appropriate for a specific person and also justifies the efforts required to purchase it.

Gift Giving Exchange: The goods offered and/or exchanged by individuals covering all gift exchange situations, and the circuits of this circulation, considering all types of gifts, either in their material version or in services, including gifts in cash. One can talk about consumption for others in the form of gift giving exchange.

Gifts as Relational Complements: The exchange of gifts between specific individuals used to produce and strengthen interpersonal relationships. The performances of the gifts exchanged between the individuals involved transform the gifts into vehicles for creating and strengthening interpersonal relationships

Greater Porto Area: Metropolitan region of the city of Porto, the second largest city in Portugal, located in the north of the country.

ENDNOTES

1 In a language closer to that of sociology, one could say in a very similar sense that such trivialisation could occur through the affirmation of a sociology of interaction, regarded as a sociology of the situation.

2 The intention was not, therefore, to grant the existence of a "middle-class culture" (along the lines of M. Savage et al., 2008), nor equate the role of "cultural consumption" as a mechanism of social differentiation or reproduction of dominance (along the lines of P. Bourdieu, 1979).

3 Another relevant line of analysis concerns the study of the role of consumption in crafting private, personal and household identities (Duarte, 2009).

4 The "middle class" as the universe of study largely derives from the typology proposed by the Almeida, Costa and Machado team of researchers (Almeida, Costa and Machado, 1994), although it is more restrictive that that typology would allow due to the addition of two criteria: it excluded professional occupations in the primary sector and required informants to live in an urban setting and lifestyle. The underlying intention was to build a universe of study as "unitary" as possible, by maximising access to "new middle class" households. This universe would clearly show the mixture of different ways of appropriating commodities, by individuals of relatively similar social standing. In terms of analysis results, this research design further allowed a comprehensive understanding of the instrumental role of consumption in peoples' lives, while at the same time it allowed to characterise that segment of the Portuguese social structure in detail (Duarte, 2015, 2012).

5 In some households, contacts and interviews were made in the presence of the couple or of two persons of consecutive generations. However, in these cases and where testimonials were collected from one family member only, the context of reference was always the whole household.

6 Each informant was given a fictional name that refers not only to the individual alone, but also to his/her household. Thus, the author termed each household by the name given to its member, male or female, with whom she established initial contact in the shopping centre. This was the strategy found to protect the anonymity of informants and, at the same time, to facilitate the reference to households.

7 The principle of personalizing the gift and its real implementation, or not, will be addressed later in this chapter.

8 Both the dominant trend of the family as recipient and donor of gifts, and the different distribution of gifts across the three concentric circles are readily observable during the Christmas gift giving ritual. As this is an occasion in which many people receive - and give - gifts at the same time, it is easier to detect where the dominant exchanges point to. These trends, however, can also be observed outside the Christmas gift circuit.

9 Although this chapter has only addressed the family network of sociabilities, the same interpretation thereof also applied to all other sociability networks.

10 This is the name the author choses for those unexpected gifts, or gifts that mark private epiphenomena viewed as significant, for e.g., "I saw it and it reminded me of her" or "he has made a tremendous effort, he deserves to be pampered".

11 In contrast to the exchange of gifts in both the third circle of relatives and in the friendship networks.

12 These *family fathers* were of different ages: Alberto, 70; Diogo, 44; Jorge, 34; André, 24.

13 In the universe of study, only one male informant– seventy-year old Anselmo – said he was not involved in any task related to buying gifts for his wife. At the same time, these spouses hardly ever exchanged gifts.

Chapter 4
How to Deal With Corporations' Complicatedness:
A Brazilian Example

Manuel Luiz
Boston Consulting Group, Brazil

ABSTRACT

This chapter discussed how companies in the 21st century need to simplify their internal processes in order to become competitive in the external market and foster productivity. The authors focus the discussion in Brazil, an emerging economy that suffers the effect of globalization (as much as other developed economies) but, at the same time, is plagued by structural factors that hinder the country's competitiveness, a concept that is referred to as "Brazil cost." The chapter suggests a possible framework to address the need for simplifying the company's internal context and driving performance in order to fight the growing external complexity.

INTRODUCTION

Twenty-one century corporations currently face a business environment that can be best characterized as more complex and sophisticated. This environment demands adaptation and is facing external challenges such as dealing with increased customer demands and dealing with a more intense competitive environment. To respond to this external challenge, many corporations increase their structures (adding more departments, hiring layers and creating more functions), design new performance indicators, create new decision committees and thicken performance reports, among others responses. Because of these practices, which The Boston Consulting Group (BCG) has labeled as increased "Complicatedness", corporate managers spend 70-90% of their time in meetings and in the production of corporate reports, lacking time for what should be their focus: managing people (BCG, 2019). In a developing country such as Brazil, fighting complicatedness emerges as an opportunity to reduce bureaucracy and increase competitiveness. This chapter discusses how companies in the 21st century need to simplify their internal processes in order to become competitive in the external market and foster productivity. The authors

DOI: 10.4018/978-1-7998-3115-0.ch004

Copyright © 2020, IGI Global. Copying or distributing in print or electronic forms without written permission of IGI Global is prohibited.

focus the discussion in Brazil, an emerging economy that suffers the effect of Globalization (as much as other developed economies) but, at the same time, is plagued by structural factors that hinder the country's competitiveness, a concept that is referred to as "Brazil cost". The chapter suggests a possible framework to address the need for simplifying the company's internal context and driving performance in order to fight the growing external complexity. Fostering the desired corporate behaviors, namely promoting cooperation among employees, could be a solution to simplify organizations and increase their competitive advantage (Luiz, 2017).

BACKGROUND

Brief Summary of the Most Relevant Studies (for This Chapter) on Management

The world's first glimpse regarding management practices was brought to us by Frederick Winslow Taylor, an American mechanic engineer, through his 1911's work, entitled *The Principles of Scientific Management* (Taylor, 2010), which, in 2001, Fellows of the Academy of Management voted the most influential management book of the twentieth century (Bedeian & Wren, 2001). Taylor was a man of his times and sought solutions to the problems of his times. However, many of his ideas remain relevant to the modern day and have inspired further innovations. Only five years later, Jules Henri Fayol, founder of the Classical Administration Theory, published his master piece, *Administration Industrielle et Générale* – General Industrial Administration (Fayol, 1999). In those days, the important topics were basically the study of standard production time, the supervision of the functionality of the production line, the use of standardized tools and equipment, the planning of work processes, the definition of positions and duties and employee awards. Many of these topics are still very relevant (one would say that they are now – more than 100 years latter – the foundation of the basics in a company). But let's face it, 100 years have passed and the business world changed dramatically. Like Alvin Toffler predicted in the 70´s (Toffler, 1983).

Toffler was a visionary. He told the world that, like Darwin did before him, if one wanted to survive (to have success in the business world one can say), one had to adapt. Alvin Toffler's "rule" of permanent adaptation is more updated than ever. We live in a fast and extremely unstable world (we might even use the term turbulent if we follow Alvin Toffler' thoughts). It is amazing to see how in 1970 Alvin Toffler wrote an easy and called it: "Future Shock". He predicted that in a not so far away future, there would be a generation (that we now call generation Z) that had to live in permanent adaptation, if they wanted to survive, of course. In his capacity to predict the future, Toffler taught us (50 years ago) the rule for surviving: constantly adapt to the immense changes that occur in the world; change is the process by which the future invades our lives. And it is amazing to see that Toffler recommends that that would live in a not so far away future to be extremely vigilant, always aware, always in contact with everything and everyone – because - changes are inevitable (Chkoniya et al., 2019).

Another relevant understanding on management was given to us by Henry Mintzberg. Manager is responsible to integrates all the activities which are performed in an organisation. In other words, he has to co-ordinate the talents of people working under him for the purpose of achieving the organisational goals. The role of a manager gets much importance than other executives in an organisation. Hence, a manager's job is very much complex and requires some special qualities to be a head. According to Mintzberg, managers have a big range of roles that might need to be performed during a normal day at work (Mintzberg, 1973). Yes, there is a big range of roles but the manager never knows what a "normal" day at the company really implies. It is important to know "what managers actually do". Managers play a variety of roles in organisation to manage the work. Henry Mintzberg criticized the traditional functional approach. He concluded that functions "tell us little about what managers actually do. At best they indicate some vague objectives managers have when they work. Managers do not act out the classical classification of managerial functions. Instead, they engage in a variety of other activities." Roles are organized set of behaviours. These are behavioural patterns (Azevedo & Gates, 2019). After studying several managers at work, in 1990 Mintzberg identified some basic roles that a manager would have to be prepared to perform on a daily bases (table 1) depending on the external challenges: he defined an interpersonal category (in where the manager had to perform roles as figurehead, leader and liaison), also identified another category - the informational category (in where managers had to show their skills as monitor, disseminator and spokesperson) and a third category related with decision making - the decisional category – that would include the roles of resource allocator, disturbance handler, entrepreneur and negotiator (Mintzberg, 1990).

Table 1. The 10 roles key roles of a manager are then divided up into three categories, as follows (adopted from Mintzberg, 1990)

Category	Roles	Resource Allocator
Interpersonal	Figurehead	Doing ceremonial duties like receiving visitors, attending the wedding of subordinates. Signing documents. Delivering speeches at social gatherings
	Leader	Motivating subordinates and directing them towards goal accomplishment
	Liaison	Integrating organization internally and externally. Integrating individuals with the organization vertically and horizontally. Integrating the organization with its environment to assess the level of competition, magnitude of social change, impact of Government policies, and legislative enactment, etc.
Informational	Monitor	Receiving from several sources to obtain thorough knowledge about environments influencing organization
	Disseminator	Transmitting information collected from different sources to other members of the organization
	Spokesperson	Representing organization to the outside world and explaining goals, policies decision, programs and results of certain actions
Decisional	Entrepreneur	Whenever opportunities manifest, he initiates action for capitalizing it. Absorbing changes or bringing in changes into the organization to capitalize opportunities identified through environmental scanning. Conducting viability study, organizing strategy meeting with the project manager and R&D personnel.
	Disturbance Handler	Intervening whenever unexpected events unfold like strike, grievances, cash flow shortage, accident, etc.
	Resource Allocator	Deciding the priorities of organizational activities and allocating resources to those activities
	Negotiator	Representing an organization in negotiating deals within the organization and also with external agencies like suppliers' contractors, banks and the like.

So even though one might think that a day of a manager is basically spent dealing with big contracts, thinking about the company's strategy, planning the right approach to enter new markets or maybe working closer with its employees so to better take advantage or their knowledge and skills,..., reality shows that there are many other *not-so-glamorous* activities that occupy the managers time – like writing reports or participating in never-ending meetings (Morieux, 2011). In short, unpredictable variables from the crazy 21st century's intense competitive environment are always *popping up* and change turns out to be the only constant variable. And so we have it: managers having shortage of time to understand their employee's knowledge and skills since they spend most of their time dealing with different unplanned issues that completely change their daily agendas; managers need to adapt constantly to the unpredictable, due to the constant change. And so managers have little faith in their employees' ability to survive the twists and turns of a rapidly evolving economy (Fuller et al., 2019).

A Quick Snapshot of the Brazilian Economy

Brazil has a population of a bit more than 210 million people, is the 5th largest nation in the world by size and is currently the World's eighth largest economy (2017) in terms of GDP, based on the International Monetary Funds' (IMF) data (IMF, 2020). It is also the second largest economy in the Americas, only lagging behind the United States. The IMF also positions Brazil on the World's 65th position in terms of GDP per capita, with a US$10.019 (ten thousand and nineteen US dollar per person - 2017) (IMF, 2020). Brazil is the 22nd largest export economy in the world and the 37th most complex economy according to the Economic Complexity Index (ECI), (OCE, 2019).

According journal The Economist, in 2001 Brazil was a country with a meagre growth rate as skimpy as its swimsuits, prey to any financial crisis that was around, a place of chronic political instability, whose infinite capacity to squander its obvious potential was as legendary as its talent for football and carnivals, did not seem to belong with those emerging titans (The Economist, 2009). But a lot has been done and today Brazil is actually one of the largest "emerging" economies in the World. The "B" in the famous BRIC economies, represents Brazil - alongside with Russia, India and China. Today Brazil is a member of several economic organizations, such as Mercosul (the Southern Common Market) and G20 (an international forum for the governments and central bank governors from 19 countries and the European Union), (OCE, 2019).

Brazil experienced a remarkable transformation in the 2000's decade, which *The Economist* portrayed, in 2009, as "Brazil takes off". In the 5 years leading into 2011, according to the statistics of EIU (Economist Intelligence Unit) and IBGE (Brazilian Statistics & Geography Institute), GDP Compound Annual Growth Rate (CAGR) was 4.2%, credit as a percentage of GDP climbed to 61.4% (from 30.4% in 2001) and unemployment was cut in half to 6.0% (from 11.3% in 2001). During this same period, a significant rise of Brazilian middle class (an increase of 13 percentage points of "C" class in the Brazilian socio-economical pyramid) led to significant increase in consuming market (Lang & Mauerer, 2010).

But in the years that followed, according statistics presents by The Economist Intelligence Unit (The EIU), World Bank and Instituto Brasileiro de Geografia e Estatistica (IBGE) Brazil faced its worst ever recession. Productivity stagnation driven by wages growth (31%) highly surpassing productivity growth (15%) between 2006 and 2013, public finance in delicate situation, peak inflation (10.7%) and deficit (10.6%), both registered in 2015 and the lowest investment rate since 2006 (16.6%), bundled together with a large corruption scandal (Carwash Operation) and President Impeachment (2016) led to significant economics' deterioration. Brazil GDP contracted 3.8% and 3.6% in 2015 and 2016, respectively, currency depreciated 30% against the US dollar from 2010 and 2013 and credit rating was downgraded by Standard & Poors (EIU, 2020; IBGE, 2020; World Bank, 2020).

Leading into 2017 and 2018, the Brazilian economy started to show signs of recovery, with several fiscal and economic reforms being discussed or, even better, already implemented (pension reform, approved in the second half of 2019) and Brazil seems to be on the growth track again, as informed by Oxford Economics projections for the coming years (Oxford Economics, 2019).

Brazil is an amazing country with lots of touristic place that overwhelmed the almost 7 million international tourists every year (IBGE, 2020). Brazil has innumerous economic resources like gold, bauxite, diamonds, platinum, iron, tin and coal, but the country has also a huge potential in oil & gas and hydropower. Actually, in 2018 Brazil rose as one of the largest hydro energy producers in the World, with an installed capacity closer to 105 gigawatts - with this type source of energy representing roughly 65% of the country production matrix (ANEEL, 2019; EWEA, 2019). When added up the contributions of other renewable sources (like Solar and Wind), the total weight of renewables in the Brazilian energy matrix sums up 75% of total installed capacity (GWEC, 2019). Brazil is the second-largest producer of hydroelectric power in the world, after only China, and hydropower accounted for more than 70% of the country's electricity generation in 2018 (EIA, 2019). It is easy to see that hydro energy is the most important source of energy in Brazil and will continue being. Brazil's latest 10-year energy plan seeks to maintain this level of hydro generation while increasing the share of nonhydro renewables, particularly solar. Most of Brazil's hydroelectric plants are located in the country's Amazon River basin in the north, but Brazil's demand for electricity is mainly along the eastern coast, particularly in the southern portion (ANEEL, 2019). Reliance on hydropower for most of the country's electricity generation, combined with the distant and disparate locations of its demand centers, has presented electricity reliability challenges (EPE, 2019).

In addition, in 2006, after the discoveries of the Brazilian pre-salt layer, Brazil joined the top 15 countries in the World with the greatest proven oil reserves (in 11th place), with a recoverable volume of 42 billion barrels (from the previous 16 billion barrels) (Azevedo Filho et al, 2019). Venezuela is on the top of the ranking with an amazing 297 million barrels (Figure 2), followed closely by Saudi Arabia, and then Canada, Iran, Iraq, Kuwait, United Arab Emirates, Russia, Libya and the USA. Petrobras, Petróleo Brasileiro, S.A., which is the National Oil & Gas Corporation, is the owner of roughly 75% of these reserves (according to Rystad Energy and Reuteurs), and also by more than 90% of total Brazilian Oil & Gas production (Rystad,2019; OPEP, 2019).

Some economists from the American Bank Goldman Sachs point out to a strong consolidation of the Brazilian economy in the coming years, anticipates that the Brazilian economy will become the fourth largest in the World by 2050 (Goldman Sachs, 2020). Nonetheless, and despite all the progress and economy consolidation achieved in the past 20-30 years, Brazil still suffers from a large competitiveness deficit, when compared against the vast majority of the Northern Hemisphere economies. Some of the factors are the (low) infrastructure quality and development, the (low) institutional maturity (from local governments, to the Federal Government up to the States' Government) and the very high state dependency. These factors create the large competitiveness gap and determine a significant "Brazil cost", which is an expression used to characterize the increased operational costs associated with doing business in Brazil.

The Brazilian Association for the Machinery and Equipment Industry - Abimaq – publish in 2010 a unique study focused on agro products (Neto et al., 2010). That study concluded that there was a 35% cost aggravation for producing a specific basket of agriculture products in Brazil, when comparing with producing the same basket in the United Stated or in Germany. After this study was published, several other studies, in different other industries, have confirmed a similar type of situation: Brazil's cost disadvantage is notorious and very harmful for the economy. These other studies also highlighted other weaknesses of the Brazilian economy, such as a much longer lead times from production to consumption (given poorer infrastructures) and a longer timeline for customs clearance. In fact, the World Bank positioned Brazil in the very-far-from-the-top 123rd position in a total of 195 countries studied, regarding "easiness to doing business" (World Bank, 2020). There is no other way of interpretation this, the study was quite clear in its conclusions: it is not easy to do business in Brazil.

To prosper in this new environment, companies must look for new ways to create shareholder value that are less dependent on growth. The right strategy will be different for each company. However, adjusting business portfolios and improving productivity will be important value drivers in most cases.

The next decade in Brazil will impose new challenges but also offer high rewards. What worked in the past may not be a recipe for the future. Companies able to meet these challenges—particularly by boosting productivity—will be well positioned to serve Brazil's sizable domestic market, take advantage of the country's advantaged position in natural resources, and continue to create value (Ukon et al., 2013).

MAIN FOCUS OF THE CHAPTER

"The Brazil Cost"

The authors focus the discussion in Brazil, an emerging economy that suffers the effect of Globalization (as much as other developed economies) but, at the same time, is plagued by structural factors that hinder the country's competitiveness, a concept that is referred to as "Brazil cost" (the increased cost associated with doing business in Brazil in comparison with doing business in other countries). In a very practical and direct way, several factors are prevalent in Brazil:

- High public administration corruption (and the consequent increase in Justice Cost burden),
- Excessive bureaucracy for creating and maintaining companies,
- High banking spread (Brazil has one of the largest in the World),
- High tax burden,
- A very high pension cost (although a reform is currently being discussed – Q4 2019),
- Low education levels,
- Expensive labor cost,
- Legal uncertainty,
- Among others.

Brazil not only spends a lower percentage of its GDP in Research & Development (1.5%), but also spends as much in Justice as it invests in R&D. In fact, there is a 1.0 ratio of R&D to Justice cost in Brazil while, for example, the United States and Germany present "healthier" ratios, in the order of magnitude of 5.0-6.0. Countries with higher R&D spend can build and enhance their competitive advantage.

Economy "Complexity" and Organization's "Complicatedness"

As it was mentioned before, the current business environment is increasingly complex. This greater complexity is a result of the appearance of new competitors, a result of the increased level of available information (with data availability and bid data analysis), a result of the development of new technologies and, of course, a result of globalization. Globalization is the word used to describe the growing interdependence of the world's economies, cultures, and populations, brought about by cross-border trade in goods and services, technology, and flows of investment, people, and information. Countries have built economic partnerships to facilitate these movements over many centuries. But the term gained popularity after the Cold War in the early 1990s, as these cooperative arrangements shaped modern everyday life (Kolb & Trade and Investment Policy Watch, 2018). The Boston Consulting Group (BCG) estimated that the *Complexity index*, which describes the compounded effect of the above-mentioned effects, has grown six times (6x) in the last 50 to 60 years. It is worth highlighting that this *Complexity Index* solely reflects the company's External factors (BCG, 2018).

In such a complex context, companies have a desperate need to adapt in order to be able to compete in the market. For that purpose, in an attempt to successfully adapt, companies create (or expand) their organizational structure and tend to redesign their processes and their information systems - which became slow and unproductive. Nowadays we see how new integration committees proliferate – companies attempt to better handle multi-disciplinary and complex issues. New performance indicators are added to the corporation's scorecards. Performance review meetings became more frequent. Each event became longer. New reports are produced. All of these are the common reactions, typical of companies that try to adapt to a more complex environment; and these are what the Boston Consulting Group reports labeled as "*Complicatedness*". One curious aspect is that the Boston Consulting Group reports also mentioned is that *Complicatedness* has suffered a 35x (disproportional to the 6x) growth in the same 50 to 60 years analyses (Oxford Economics, 2019; The Economist, 2009; Ukon et al., 2013).

Just by itself this would be alarming, but it is severely more serious since this *Complicatedness* translates into the reduction of the company competitiveness (which is the capacity to produce, with high patterns of productivity, at the lowest cost, what the client needs, and satisfying consumers' demanding conditions (Oliveira, 2004). It is completely understandable and obvious that, with all of these extra and heavy time consuming and non-productive activities, employees tend to lose focus from the key activities and corporate environment tends to generate frustrated and demotivated employees. In fact, in companies that suffer from *Complicatedness*, managers use 40% of their time producing reports and use 30% to 50% of their time in alignment meetings – which means that they are cutting their time availability for what should be the core of their functions: managing the company and managing people.

To conclude, corporations' exaggerated response towards the market external factors (in an attempt to adapt) in a country such as Brazil (that already presents several structural weaknesses, as a consequence of the mentioned "Brazil cost"), can further hinder competitiveness.

Rapid Change in Corporate World

The rapid development of new technologies in this extremely global world has completely changed the way business is done. The fundamental question is not whether to deploy with new technology – companies have no choice if they want to remain competitive; the fundamental question is how to deploy. New technology offers opportunities for companies to establish a distinct strategic positioning – much better than in previous generations (Porter, 2001). The fast moving environments I where companies operate on a daily bases has created many changes and has had many consequences (Madsen & Chkoniya, 2019). Nowadays managers need to follow up with all of that unpredictability – if they want to survive of course. It is because of technological innovations that today there is free access to markets everywhere – and amazingly, when companies are born, they are already global companies. New technologies allow diversification of supplied goods and services – companies can diversify their portfolio of products and services to infinity and there is no market that they cannot reach (Rangan & Adner, 2001). New technologies and globalization have increased consumers' sophistication and, at the same time, have shortened innovation cycles, determining that the products that are demanded today might no longer be the ones demanded in the near future. In this context of rapid change corporate success demands the ability to operate in an agile and flexible way (Toffler, 1973) – making rapid decision making a fundamental key to a company's ability to deploy competitive advantage. As so the impact of such a context is huge and is global, and does not distinguish between developed and emerging economies - Brazil is exposed to this same situation.

The Big Opportunity Comes With the Simplification - Fighting Complicatedness

Businesses compete in a world that is growing ever more complex. Disruptive technologies emerge with increasing frequency. Customers' needs and demands change at breakneck speed. New competitors are always entering the fray. n their attempts to reduce uncertainty and reestablish control amid this new complexity, companies tend to introduce new reports, new rules, and new processes. Such reactions, however, simply translate external complexity into internal "complicatedness"— the counterproductive proliferation of cumbersome structures, processes, and systems (Jaap Backx, 2017). Complicatedness hinders productivity by creating a work environment that leaves employees disengaged and unmotivated. To be successful in today's complex and fast-changing world, companies must be highly agile and flexible — able to identify opportunities and make informed decisions quickly in order to exploit those opportunities. To be able to successfully fight *Complicatedness* company's and its managers need to understand the following three main principles:

1. Company's performance depends on what people are capable of delivering;
2. What people deliver is a result of all the employees' individual behaviors. Therefore, it is of great importance to analyze how employees interact, which information they use, how employees relate with their managers/leaders, how employees relate with consumers, what they look after and which attributes they value;
3. Employees' behavior is a result of the context they live in. Since behavior is visible (and measurable), it is possible to understand what motivates each person, and what does not. Consequently, if a company wants to improve its performance, it needs to "facilitate" the adoption of the required behavior, by changing its context.

Context is a construct that aggregates the company's organizational design, the company's governance model, the company's incentives scheme and the employee's career path - these are some of the variables that create a context. So to improve performance, companies need to change all or a segment of these.

The end goal of a simplification process should be to deeply understand which behaviors need to be addressed and which interventions are necessary to stimulate the desired behaviors. At the end of the day, each company should work towards implementing a context that incentivizes all employees to behave in line with the desired performance goals.

Companies that fight *Complicatedness* in an effective way realize that the achieved outcomes are highly relevant. For example, The Boston Consulting Group recently supported the simplification process of one of its Brazilian clients, with direct support on two very specific context elements. On one side, in terms of organizational structure, in where The Boston Consulting Group supported the elimination of more than 30% of managerial positions, which translated into a flattening out of the organization structure, into the empowering of managerial decisions and the increasing of the speed of the company's decision-making process. On the other side, in also had a huge impact in terms of process redesign, in where The Boston Consulting Group has revised all procurement processes and has eliminated low value added activities, which translated into a reduction of total procurement time from specification to purchasing by 45% (BCG, 2019).

SOLUTIONS AND RECOMMENDATIONS

As leaders in organizations of all kinds grapple with the forces reshaping their world, and with challenging questions about business's role in society, they are finding that the keys to business success have changed. In many industries, growth is harder to sustain, survival is not a given, and a narrow focus on financial performance is not enough (BCG, 2020).

In today's increasingly complex world, disruptive technologies emerge with accelerating frequency, customer demands change at breakneck speed, and new competitors relentlessly enter the fray. Some companies respond by adding new reports, new rules, and new processes to master complexity. Such responses increase complicatedness, are counterproductive, and hinder performance.

Many companies have the knowledge and skills they need to address the challenges that lead to low performance. But ultimately, they fail because they use the wrong approach. Historical approaches and classical rules of management often fall short in today's world because they don't address the fact that performance is driven by what people do—their behaviors—and that people behave in their self-interest and, thus, rationally, given the situation or context. To improve performance, companies have to make the desired behaviors rational (Jaap Backx, 2017).

To successfully address complicatedness, companies need to start by recognizing the principles that form the foundation of BCG's approach to simplification, or *Smart Simplicity*. There are two key principles:

- Performance is a result of what people do (behaviors). A company's performance is ultimately driven by employee and customer behaviors. These include the behaviors of leaders (for example, how they lead, whom they promote or make company heroes, what they measure, and what they talk about in meetings) and employees (for example, how they interact, what they do and do not do, and how readily they share information).
- Behaviors of people are driven by rational reactions to their context. People do what they do because it is the logical solution given the context in which they work. Therefore, if a company wants to improve performance, it has to make the desired behaviors rational. Behaviors are observable: they are what people actually do, day in and day out. Behaviors — not a discussion of what people are not (but maybe should be) doing — should be the focus. If it is possible to articulate what motivates people, what they aim for, the means they have to achieve their goals, and what is in

their way, it is also possible to understand what causes their behaviors. Behaviors can, therefore, be influenced by smart adjustments to the company environment — the "context" — to make the desired choices the logical ones.

Simplifying organizational context, determined by the elements of organization, processes, decision rights, performance indicators, among others, in order to drive superior performance and compete in global, increasingly complex markets, should be the focus of corporate managers in the 21st century in order to become competitive in the external market and foster productivity.

Using this approach, management can deliver lasting improvement in performance.

FUTURE RESEARCH DIRECTIONS

Globalization is in the midst of a profound change, its basic tenets pressured by rising protectionism and the diverging growth paths of emerging markets. At the same time, digital integration is accelerating. For every barrier to globalization, it seems, there's a catalyst for a new kind of connectivity. Companies must understand the new realities. The formula for business success that worked a decade ago doesn't necessarily work today. And leaders can't know for sure what will work ten years from now (BCG, 2020a). Business leaders need a new agenda, get ahead of the social, technological, and political trends that will define the future of business, and seize the opportunity to play new roles and carve out new competitive spaces (BCG, 2020b). The successful companies in the future won't ignore the massive shifts all around them. They'll meet those shifts head-on.

This chapter discussed how companies in the 21st century need to simplify their internal processes in order to become competitive in the external market and foster productivity by suggesting a possible framework to address the need for simplifying the company's internal context and driving performance in order to fight the growing external complexity. The present chapter does not present a clear link between reducing a Company's complicatedness and competitive advantage. Creating a clear link between these two variables can create a compelling narrative to motive companies to act. That would be the author's recommendation for future research.

CONCLUSION

Creating a corporate context that fosters appropriate behavior (in an economic and social perspective), that incentives autonomy and empowerment in the decision making process and that focuses on cooperation, is fundamental to guarantee corporate success in this global world of constant market evolution. In a country such as Brazil, in which the business environment presents structural (very deep) challenges, simplifying corporations could be an important tool to foster productivity (productivity is seen as the maximum production/ per unit of production factors). Leveraging process simplification in the corporate world is, in fact, a state of art approach when solving business problems, when the company wants to add value and when gaining competitive advantage. Companies need to foster a strong collaboration environment in which employees are capable of solving problems individually or in teams. In such environment, managers are released from all the noise and all the *Complicatedness* and can dedicate their time and expertise into fostering cooperation and teamwork. Successful leaders mobilize people without having to impose a strong set of rules (Drucker, 1964) and let context determine behavior and hence performance. Thinking a bit further about Brazil, the country suffers currently an important growth challenge but it a very well-known fact that Brazilian economy still lags behind significantly in terms of productivity, in a society and business environment that is characterized and intensely bureaucratic (with a strong reflex on "Brazil cost"). The above mentioned simplification points – based on acting upon context and aiming at changing employees' behaviors to drive the desired performance – could be considered as important tools to drive agility in organizations, which would then become leaner and flatter. This way, companies could rise as leaders of their own industries and be the drivers of the (so needed) economic growth. The author of this chapter is convinced that company's investment in more empowered employees and investment in agility - associated with less *Complicatedness* contexts - could be an extremely successful weapon in the path for growth and for reducing "Brazil cost" in the coming years.

ACKNOWLEDGEMENT

I would like to give a special thanks to Professor Ana Oliveira Madsen for her valuable and constructive suggestions during the planning and development of this chapter. This chapter would not have been possible without the exceptional support of my friend of more than 20 years. Throughout the process of writing this chapter Professor Ana Oliveira Madsen was always extremely helpful and encouraging, and she enriched this chapter with adequate literature review and has helped me get the chapter into a point where it's actually publishable. It is not easy for a corporate person like myself to write an article that complies with all the academic preforms. Her assistance was essential in the writing process and her willingness to give her time so generously has been very much appreciated.

REFERENCES

ANEEL- Agência Nacional de Energia Elétrica. (2019). *Retrospectiva ANEEL*. Retrieved from https://www.aneel.gov.br/

Azevedo, G., & Gates, A. (2019). Wake Up! The World Is Out of Balance and If You Do Nothing You Are Part of the Problem: An Interview With Henry Mintzberg. *Journal of Management Inquiry*, *28*(2), 180–186. doi:10.1177/1056492618761811

Azevedo Filho, E. T., Palma, M. A. M., Perestrelo, M., da Hora, H. R. M., & Lira, R. A. (2019). The pre-salt layer and challenges to competitiveness in Brazil: Critical reflections on the local content policy in the oil and gas Sector. *The Extractive Industries and Society*, *6*(4), 1168–1173. doi:10.1016/j.exis.2019.09.009

Backx, J., Hilberath, C., Messenböck, R., & Morieux, Y. H. S. (2017). Mastering Complexity Through Simplification: Four Steps to Creating Competitive Advantage. *Boston Consulting Group*. Retrieved from https://www.bcg.com/publications/2017/people-organization-operations-mastering-complexity-through-simplification.aspx

BCG - Boston Consulting Group. (2018). *Complicatedness Survey: BCG's Complicatedness Survey pinpoints problem areas.* Retrieved from https://www.bcg.com/capabilities/smart-simplicity/complicatedness-survey.aspx

BCG - Boston Consulting Group. (2019). *Risk Management &Compliance in the Financial Industry.* Retrieved from https://www.bcg.com/industries/financial-institutions/risk-management.aspx

BCG - Boston Consulting Group. (2020a). *The New Globalization: A Collection.* Retrieved from https://www.bcg.com/featured-insights/thought-leadership-ideas.aspx

BCG - Boston Consulting Group. (2020b). *What will it take to win in the 2020s?* Retrieved from https://www.bcg.com/featured-insights/winning-the-20s/overview.aspx

Bedeian, A. G., & Wren, D. A. (2001). Most influential management books of the 20th Century. *Organizational Dynamics, 29*(3), 221–225. doi:10.1016/S0090-2616(01)00022-5

Boglioti, E., Lyon, V., & Morieux, I. (2016). The Smart Solution to the Productivity Paradox. *The Boston Consulting Group.* Retrieved from https://www.bcg.com/publications/2016/technology-digital-people-organization-smart-solution-productivity-paradox.aspx

Chkoniya, V., Madsen, A. O., & Coelho, T. (2019). The impact of information and communication technologies in fish consumption in Portugal: Building a support for the coming generations. *Economia Agro-Alimentare, 21*(3), 855–872. doi:10.3280/ECAG2019-003016

de Oliveira, A. (2004). *Análise do investimento em sistemas e tecnologias da informação e da comunicação.* Lisboa: Sílabo.

Drucker, P. F. (1964). *Managing for results. Economics task and risk-taking decision.* Retrieved from https://books.google.pt/books?id=ZMj2uQEACAAJ

Economics, O. (2019). *Country Economic Forecasts.* Retrieved from https://www.oxfordeconomics.com/my-oxford/publications/399091

EIA- U.S. Energy Information Administration. 2020. *Analysis - Energy Sector Highlights.* Retrieved from https://www.eia.gov/international/overview/country/BRA

EIU - The Economist Intelligence Unit. (2020). *Brazil Economy, Politics and GDP Growth Summary.* Retrieved from http://country.eiu.com/Brazil?utm_content=buffer3fe2c&utm_medium=social&utm_source=plus.google.com&utm_campaign=buffer#

EPE - Empresa de Pesquisa Energética. (2019). *Anuário Estatístico de Energia Elétrica.* Retrieved from http://www.epe.gov.br/

EWEA - The European Wind Energy Association. (2019). *Reports.* Retrieved from https://www.ewea.org/

Fayol, H. (1999). *Administration industrielle et générale. Dunod.* Retrieved from https://books.google.pt/books?id=HqsCHAAACAAJ

Fuller, J. B., Raman, M., Wallenstein, J. K., & de Chalendar, A. (2019). Your Workforce Is More Adaptable Than You Think. *Harvard Business Review.* Retrieved from http://search.ebscohost.com/login.aspx?direct=true&db=edb&AN=135981992&site=eds-live

GWEC - Global Wind Energy Council. (2019). *Global Wind Report 2018*. Retrieved from www.gwec.net

IBGE - Instituto Brasileiro de Geografia e Estatistica. (2020). *Estatísticas*. Retrieved from https://www.ibge.gov.br/

IMF - International Monetary Fund. (2019). *World Economic Outlook Reports*. Retrieved from https://www.imf.org/

Kolb, M., & Trade and Investment Policy Watch (2018). *What Is Globalization?* Retrieved from https://www.piie.com/microsites/globalization/what-is-globalization

Lang, N. S., & Mauerer, S. (2010). *Winning the BRIC Auto Markets: Achieving Deep Localization in Brazil, Russia, India, and China*. Retrieved from www.bcg.com

Luiz, M. (2017). *"A Simplificação como Protagonista do Sucesso Empresarial", as part of the "Presente para o Futuro" compilation, a Project that presents expectations and perceptions of The Boston Consulting Group Brazil partners for the coming 20 years*. The Boston Consulting Group.

Madsen, A. O., & Chkoniya, V. (2019). Fish Consumption in the Age of the Information Society - The Evolution of the Fish Sector in Portugal. *European Journal of Social Sciences, 2*. Retrieved from http://journals.euser.org/index.php/ejss/article/view/4251

Mintzberg, H. (1973). *The Nature of Managerial Work. Harper & Row*. Retrieved from https://books.google.pt/books?id=9HmdkQEACAAJ

Mintzberg, H. (1990). The Manager's Job: Folklore and Fact. *Harvard Business Review Reprint Service*. Retrieved from https://books.google.pt/books?id=NAUXnQEACAAJ

Morieux, Y. (2011). Smart rules: Six ways to get people to solve problems without you. *Harvard Business Review*, *89*, 78–84, 86,136. PMID:21939130

Neto, L. A., De, D., Diretor, C., Bueno, F., Schaefer, A.-R. M., Bernardini-Assessor Da, M., … Zanella, C. (2010). A*BIMAQ - Associação Brasileira da Indústria de Máquinas e Equipamentos*. Retrieved from www.abimaq.com

OCE - The Observatory of Economic Complexity. (2019). *Brazil*. Retrieved from https://oec.world/en/profile/country/bra

OPEP - Organization of the Petroleum Exporting Countries. (2019). *Oil Market Report*. Retrieved from https://www.opec.org/opec_web/en/publications/338.htm

Porter, M. E. (2001). Strategy and the Internet. *Harvard Business Review*. Retrieved from http://search.ebscohost.com/login.aspx?direct=true&db=bth&AN=4147416&site=eds-live

Rangan, S., & Adner, R. (2001). Profits and the Internet: Seven Misconceptions. *MIT Sloan Management Review*. Retrieved from http://search.ebscohost.com/login.aspx?direct=true&db=bth&AN=4834377&site=eds-live

RYSTAD. (2019). *Energy Annual Review of World Oil Recoverable Resources*. Retrieved from https://www.rystadenergy.com/

Sachs, G. (2020). *Insights: Through the Trough.* Retrieved from https://www.goldmansachs.com/insights/pages/eurozone-outlook-2020.html

Taylor, F. W. (2010). The Principles of Scientific Management. *Cosimo, Incorporated.* Retrieved from https://books.google.pt/books?id=G_vTmZvRkhEC

The Economist. (2009). Brazil takes off. *Economist,* (8657). Retrieved from https://www.economist.com/leaders/2009/11/12/brazil-takes-off

Toffler, A. (1973). Future Shock. *Saturday Evening Post.* Retrieved from http://search.ebscohost.com/login.aspx?direct=true&db=a9h&AN=17947865&site=eds-live

Ukon, M., Bezerra, J., Cheng, S., Aguiar, M., Xavier, A., & Le Corre, J. (2013). Brazil: Confronting the Productivity Challenge. *Boston Consulting Group.* Retrieved from https://www.bcg.com/publications/2013/globalization-leadership-talent-brazil-confronting-productivity-challenge.aspx

World Bank. (2020). *Brazil.* Retrieved from https://www.worldbank.org/en/country/brazil

ADDITIONAL READING

Messenböck, R., Morieux, I., Backx, J., & Wunderlich, D. (2018) "How Complicated is your Company?" *The Boston Consulting Group.* Retrieved from https://www.bcg.com/publications/2018/complicated-company.aspx

Morieux, I., & Tollman, P. (2014) "Why Managers Need the Six Simple Rules". *The Boston Consulting Group.* Retrieved from https://www.bcg.com/publications/2014/behavior-culture-change-management-why-managers-need-six-simple-rules.aspx

KEY TERMS AND DEFINITIONS

Boston Consulting Group (BCG): Is a global management consulting firm. BCG partners with leaders in business and society to tackle their most important challenges and capture their greatest opportunities. BCG was the pioneer in business strategy when it was founded in 1963. To succeed, organizations must blend digital and human capabilities. BCG's diverse, global teams bring deep industry and functional expertise and a range of perspectives to spark change through leading-edge management consulting as well as data science, technology and design, digital ventures, and business purpose. We work in a uniquely collaborative model across the firm and throughout all levels of the client organization to deliver results that help our clients thrive.

Brazil Cost: The increased cost associated with doing business in Brazil in comparison with doing business in other countries.

Complexity: Reflects the increased number of market variables that affect the decision making process of Corporations. These variables exist in the Corporation's environment (improved client sophistication, fiercer competition, increased information availability, etc.) and therefore they are externally given.

Complicatedness: Reflects the (over-proportional) effects of Corporation's response to dealing with the Complexity (more layers, thicker governance, committees, etc.). Complicatedness arises from businesses' reaction to complexity (and therefore is internally driven).

Context: Refers to the different corporate elements that are shapeable with the purpose of driving employee's desired behaviors.

G20: The Group of 20 is an organization of finance ministers and central bank governors from 19 individual countries and the European Union. It includes Argentina, Australia, Brazil, Britain, Canada, China, France, Germany, India, Indonesia, Italy, Japan, Mexico, Russia, Saudi Arabia, South Africa, South Korea, the United States and Turkey. It bills itself as the "premier forum for international economic cooperation - The group meets every year and collectively, its members represent more than 80 percent of the world's gross domestic product. Established in 1999 after a series of major international debt crises, the G20 aims to unite world leaders around shared economic, political and health challenges. It is a creation of the more select Group of 7, an informal bloc of industrialized democracies. (Based on information from The New York Time, 2019).

Gross Domestic Product (GDP): Is the standard measure of the value added created through the production of goods and services in a country during a certain period. As such, it also measures the income earned from that production, or the total amount spent on final goods and services (less imports). While GDP is the single most important indicator to capture economic activity, it falls short of providing a suitable measure of people's material well-being for which alternative indicators may be more appropriate.

MERCOSUL: The Southern Common Market (MERCOSUR for its Spanish initials from *Mercado Comum do Sul*) was created by the Treaty of Asunçión in 1991 which is a free trade purposed association for goods, people and currency, and that includes Brazil, Argentina, Paraguay and Uruguay. Venezuela became a member in 1995 but has been suspended since 2016.

People Management: Includes all activities that managers promote in order to attract and retain employees and ensure that they have high performance and contribute to the organizational goals.

Sma rt Simplicity Concept: While complexity is a fact of business life, complicatedness doesn't have to be. Smart Simplicity, BCG's innovative approach to solving this issue, can simplify organizations by helping them identify and resolve unnecessary complicatedness and deliver lasting, measurable change. More information in "The Smart Solution to the Productivity Paradox," BCG article, January 2016, and Yves Morieux and Peter Tollman, *Six Simple Rules: How to Manage Complexity without Getting Complicated*, Harvard Business School Publishing, 2014. This publication references the work of Herbert A. Simon, who, in 1978, was awarded the Nobel Prize in economics for his "pioneering research into decision-making processes within economic organizations."

Section 2
Globalization

Chapter 5
Customer-Oriented Global Supply Chains:
Port Logistics in the Era of Globalization and Digitization

José Luís Cacho
https://orcid.org/0000-0001-7854-871X
Port of Sines, Portugal

Luís Marques
https://orcid.org/0000-0001-9028-5799
Rangel Logistics Solutions, Portugal & Catolica Porto Business School, Portugal

Álvaro Nascimento
https://orcid.org/0000-0001-5570-8039
Catolica Porto Business School, Universidade Católica Portuguesa, Portugal

ABSTRACT

Logistic services are central to the design and management of any supply chain. Due to recent technological advances, modern supply chains are challenging traditional market boundaries in ways that both influence and are influenced by consumer behavior (e.g., Amazon, Alibaba, or JD.com). Economically speaking, corporations are changing along the way resources are being used in production. At the firm level, management decisions follow cost efficiency and risk management principles, pursuing a cost-risk tradeoff equilibrium. Theoretically, operations organized within the boundaries of the firm are just those for which the markets are unable to offer a more efficient alternative, whereas the link between buyers and sellers (i.e., demand and supply in the market) is intermediated by logistics services, such as transport, to mention but one. As technological innovation, social transformation, and consumer behavior threaten firms' traditional boundaries, logistics need to adjust and adapt to new and emerging challenges, its costs, and risks to end consumers.

DOI: 10.4018/978-1-7998-3115-0.ch005

Copyright © 2020, IGI Global. Copying or distributing in print or electronic forms without written permission of IGI Global is prohibited.

INTRODUCTION

The forces of globalization and changes in consumption behaviour coupled with technological advances in information systems are changing the way firms organize production. In short, supply chains are increasingly fragmented. To satisfy rapidly changing demand patterns, Global Supply Chains (GSC) must be consumer oriented and flexible enough. Components and parts originated in countries and regions apart are assembled in a way that final goods can be fast delivered to customers and at the most competitive price. Theoretically, the technology – i.e., where and how to produce and assemble – must be chosen in order to remain competitive. Some firms go further and develop its customer value proposition based on a characteristic of the supply chain.

Falling barriers to trade saw firms unbundling production into smaller tasks performed at different locations, benefiting from the lower costs of some countries. The result was the fragmentation of production, where intermediate goods – to be accurate, also services, when embedded in manufactured goods – had to physically travel and cross borders along the value supply chain. This new architecture is having strong implications not only to international trade, but also to the transportation industry, in ways that will be highlighted next.

Over the last 100 plus years, supply chain management has evolved from an initial focus on improving relatively simple, but very labour-intensive, processes to the present day engineering and managing of extraordinarily complex global networks (Panday and Panday, 2018). The increased complexity can be seen in the percentage of foreign value added to the exports of each country, which has been increasing steadily almost without exception. In the EU alone, foreign value added of gross exports increased from 14% to 16% between 2005 and 2016, after reaching a 19% peak in the aftermath of the crisis, in 2012.[1]

The authors attempt to show the challenges sea ports are currently facing, as global supply chain management switches and becomes increasingly consumer driven. There are many topics left out of the scope of this paper. Questions addressed are the challenges this new trend is posing to port authorities, market participants and regulators along. In concrete, how is logistics expected to react to a wave of technological breakthroughs that twist supply chains to become consumer driven?

A discussion is warranted on how ports add attrition to global value chains, and what can be done to increase efficiency – i.e., cost reduction and risk management. Specifically, how can consumer-oriented supply chains – defined as being triggered by consumption patterns – be implemented, in strong collaboration between port authorities, shippers and key stakeholders (such as manufacturing companies), in order to contribute positively to welfare, and achieve a more efficient answer to consumer needs.

The rest of the chapter is organised as follows. The next section lays out the forces of globalisation and innovation, setting the scene to better understand the competitive environment firms are currently facing. Following, a critical review of supply chain management, with a focus on global supply chains, places sea ports as nodes of a connectivity network and explores its interdependency with shipping, logistics, and manufacturing companies. Before the concluding remarks, a list of logistic challenges to port authorities is presented, and the options thoroughly discussed.

BACKGROUND

Illustrating the rising trend in global value chain participation, Ignatenko et al. (2019) show that, in 2013, about 70% of total exports from the European countries involved global value chains – either backward and forward linkages – comparing with only 60% in 2010. Although the distribution is not homogeneous across the globe, growth in participation rates is a common feature for most of the countries and regions. Over the same period, the ratio increased by 5 percentage points for the Western World and Asia, rising participation levels to close to 50%. Similarly, in a special report – "The World is Flat" – published just recently, The Economist sustains that a majority of world trade involves global value supply chains:[2]

The combination of the information-technology revolution, which made communications affordable and reliable, and the entry of China into the World economy, which provided bountiful cheap labour, had transformed manufacturing into a global enterprise. [...] Multinational corporations (MNCs), that once kept manufacturing close to home stretched supply chains thin as they chased cheap labour and economies of scale on the other side of the world.

Technology is the biggest force underlying change. Emerging trends – such as big data, data analytics, robotics, and artificial intelligence – show new means of supply chain coordination, other than the traditional hierarchical structure – in many instances, a chain of command – within the firm. Internet platforms are already being used to support new and more flexible business models, where buyers and sellers interact with each other, assembling products in multiple and varied ways, depending on individual tastes and initiative.

The exponential growth of e-commerce in recent years is just a reflection of this trend. Exhibiting two digit growth rates, Intracen[3] estimates that by 2020 it will account for approximately 15% of total retail sales. E-commerce is not just a dumb substitute for brick and mortar street stores. It rethinks the whole value chain strategically, around a new retailing ecosystem with strong implications for both production and distribution. As Zeng (2018) explains:

Alibaba today is not just an online commerce company. It is what you get if you take all functions associated with retail and coordinate them online into a sprawling, data-driven network of sellers, marketers, service providers, logistics companies, and manufacturers. In other words, Alibaba does what Amazon, eBay, PayPal, Google, FedEx, wholesalers, and a good portion of manufacturers do in the United States, with a healthy helping of financial services for garnish. [...] new capabilities in network coordination and data intelligence [are] put to use [by these companies]. The ecosystems they steward are vastly more economically efficient and customer-centric than traditional industries.

In short, technology is changing not only the way products and services are made and delivered, but also how firms incorporate consumer preferences when defining their strategies. The Economist (2019: 4) points out there are people dreaming of autonomous supply chains, requiring little or no human intervention, a world where predictive analytics, 3-D printing, and real-time interaction with final consumers are put to use, targeting the specific needs of each individual. No matter how distant in the future this "utopia" lies, it is feeding an unprecedented pace of innovation.

Because of this, logistics services are elevated to the core of modern global supply chains. In contrast with the past, when transportation of raw materials and final goods accounted for a great proportion of international trade, logistic companies are required to have its operations better intertwined with manufacturing firms and even consumers, blurring the division between internal and external logistics. Components and parts of unfinished goods travel back and forth, before being finally assembled at a particular location – when not in different countries – and delivered to either close or faraway customers.

Insofar, search for efficiency has been the driving force of change of GSC. While risk is certainly to be taken into consideration when firms analyse the performance of its supply chain, the truth is that this aspect has been neglected, given the savings achieved on the cost side. Time is now arriving for aggregating risks into the analysis, not only operational and financial, but strategic risks also:[4]

Firms embraced such practices as lean inventory production and just-in-time delivery, that pursued efficiency and cost control, while making little provisions for risk.

For countries, seamless and lower handling costs are not the only competitive factors to increase participation in GSC. The ability to perform positively in a global economy depends critically on creating the necessary conditions for firms to enter and participate in decentralized and coordinated production arrangements. As such, governments should aim at policies that increase country connectivity. Product and service markets can then be expanded beyond domestic boundaries and foster economic growth, while consumers reap the benefits of competitive pricing, due to specialization.[5]

Further, the choice of sea port location is affected by the reengineering of GSC. The increasing flows of trade of intermediate products, requires physical space to assemble plants in close proximity to ports that are central to the transport network. One possibility is that sea ports, as mere entry and exit gates to local or regional markets in close connection with the "hinterland", are substituted for nodes of a complex logistics network, going beyond the handling of goods alone – i.e., "transhipment" – and where transformation activities take place.

The transportation industry must meet the requirements created by this emerging trend on GSC, and the trade opportunities opened by commerce and other purposes platforms. In customer oriented GSC, the decisive factor is the ability to satisfy various demands at the lowest cost. Considering that container shipping is the most economical means of transportation in international trade, port authorities must rethink their participation in the physical movement of goods, given the new industrial and consumption context.

Summing up, a new role for sea ports is envisaged. Current business models of "transhipment" –feeding the development of many ports – have to be revised and extended, as to encompass local transformation of goods that are distributed to neighbour markets, according to customers' requirements. Ports regain a close relationship with a redesigned hinterland, i.e., its manufactures and consumers. How are ports likely to perform transformation operations, while letting local and more distant consumers participate in the new game of global value chains? Which are the key success factors that sea ports must have? These are questions that are addressed in following sections.

SUPPLY CHAIN MANAGEMENT (SCM)

Starting from the definition, a supply chain consists of two or more separated organizations linked by operational – material and information – and financial flows. In general, organisations are identified as firms producing parts, components and end products, and logistic service providers. Ascencio et al. (2014: 446). The same way, Dai (2010: 604) defines supply chain as:

[...] a system of organizations, people, technology, activities, information and resources involved in moving a product or service from supplier to customer.

Supply chain management requires coordination of flows between organisations. For competitive reasons, flows must be coordinated as to maximise efficiency and reduce risks. The efficiency of any supply chain can be measured by the degree of integration between its distinct partners. On top of this, Govindan (2018) adds three levels of sustainability – economic, environmental and social – as a defining characteristic of modern supply chain management, emphasising the new challenges producers are facing.

Transaction Costs and Supply Chain Complexity

A seamless integrated supply chain means its transaction costs are small. When stakeholders agree to and execute a common plan, they can improve the competitiveness of the value chain as a whole. Therefore, we can establish a relationship between the competitiveness of the value chain and the ability to adapt its structure according to market and consumer needs.[6]

Dai (2010: 604) argues that modern firms are consumer oriented, and the core of their strategies lies on the choice of the best performing supply chain. Therefore, competition is between supply chains, rather than between companies. The performance of a supply chain is assessed on its ability to efficiently coordinate complicated, and continuously changing, collaboration arrangements among stakeholders.

Within this context, logistics service providers are not restricted to the transportation of goods alone. They are required to interact efficiently with buyers and sellers, upstream and downstream, in a collaborative fashion, where "timely delivery" becomes as important as cost of transport. The existing trade-off between time and cost must be continuously weighted and monitored, as the ability of firms to compete depends on combining these two value drivers effectively.

Govindan (2018: 424) stresses what others said about dynamic capabilities, that in a rapidly changing environment and markets, firms need to be able to reconfigure internal and external competencies using its own resources, in order to offer higher economic value and survive its competitors.[7] Dynamic capabilities are core for firms operating in industries facing disruption from technological and sociological moves. This changing of boundaries calls for renewed supply chain management, particularly where transportation – i.e., moving of physical goods, to reach markets, suppliers and customers, the aspect that concerns us on this paper – is relevant.

Information, Coordination and Integration

Traceability is at the core of modern supply chain management. For this to happen, information must be easily shared and freely exchanged amongst participants with a single objective in mind: address customer needs in accordance to firms' value proposal. In a dynamic environment, intense use of IT technologies, adoption of standards, and harmonization of processes are key.

In turn, better supply chain coordination requires further integration. Theoretically, the ability of a network to carry signals from consumers to producers needs to be improved, reducing inventory costs along the supply chain, while achieving a prompt response to rapidly changing customer preferences. This reorganisation has strong implications for management, from the perspective of both risk exposure and cost efficiency.

One can find already adaptative supply chains networks, in replacement of traditional linear organisation models. The ideal supply chain delivers the right product, to the right customer, at the right place, at the right cost, at the right time.[8] Dai (2010) proposes a grid based model, where the supply chain possesses three characteristics: "anyone", "anywhere" and at "anytime" – 3A – can place an order, which has to be routed to the corresponding suppliers, to activate production – of goods or services – and subsequent delivery.

His model is just an illustration on how communication and information technologies are reshaping the boundaries of the firm and the logistics, i.e., changing supply chain management. An iterative optimization solution that matches buyers and sellers based on the characteristics that customers require. The example of Dai (2010) on flower trading, suggests that in a dynamic business environment, supply chains must have agile and flexibility capabilities.

Sustainable Supply Chain Management, Cost Reductions and Welfare Gains

Several authors argue that enhanced supply chain coordination induces welfare gains. Traditional cost reduction goals can be passed on to consumers, increasing consumer surplus. Further, on a long-term perspective, i.e., from a sustainability perspective, integrated performing supply chains offer better coordination of economic, social and environmental goals, which benefit producers and consumers individually, as well as the whole society. And, though sustainable supply chain management is still dominated by environmental issues, the social implications begin to be taken into consideration. Govindan (2018) offers a good literature review on this respect.

Companies gain competitive advantage when they have control over their supply chain in regard to economic, social and environmental performance. Such is needed to acquire and retain consumer's trust and choice. In the case of food supply chains, customers need to be assured of the quality of the product. In other cases, reliable information must be shared to keep the buyer informed about availability and delivery dates, one of demand attributes. In every industry firms should take a sustainable approach to supply chain management if they want to succeed in the modern world.

Nonetheless, attention should be given to institutional constraints restricting options and corporate strategies available.[9] Social norms and institutions governing life in society – either formal, as the law and its enforcement mechanism, or informal, as culture and tradition – have a non-negligible impact on the way sustainable supply chains are designed. Modern day concerns about the environment, and social and economic cohesion are to be taken into account.

Govindan (2018: 424) says, on this respect:

Consumers may pay special attention and prefer products that have been produced with low levels of harmful emissions, such as low inputs of land, water, and energy, as well as respect for animal welfare, low transportation distances, and low carbon footprints. [...] In addition, exports and sales to foreign customers are two more drivers that claim manufacturers to adopt sustainable practices.

As we write, it is not clear whether globalisation and the search for cost reduction is expanding or shrinking supply chains, due to international threats looming in the horizon. No matter what direction it takes, there is no decrease in complexity. Yet, arguments can be put forward that getting closer to consumers is needed to help companies expand customisation and speed up delivery. From a risk management perspective, shorter supply chains, facilitate quality control and the adoption of risk mitigation strategies.[10]

Risk Factors, Contagion and Supply Chain Realignment

In comparison to traditional vertically integrated value chains, GSC raise systemic risks, as factories and countries become increasingly interconnected partners in a dense and complex logistics network. Similarly, to what happens in financial markets, failure at one node – e.g., delay in production of a given component – cascades to the rest of the network in various directions. Efficiency gains, aiming at being more competitive and achieve price cuts, are likely to come at a cost of a new plethora of risk factors. The extent of potential damage depends on the idiosyncrasy and centrality of the asset, or stakeholder, that is being deployed at the faulting node.

Usually, the quest for cost reduction[11] translates into squeezing inventories along the production value chain, also in order to obtain the needed flexibility to rapidly respond to changing consumer needs. The fragility of the network increases to the extent that inventory buffers – which are useful to withhold and absorb shocks – are progressively eliminated. Further, the required coordination in the value chain needs a new approach, where hierarchical control is substituted for cooperation, which has implications for determining whom is ultimately accountable. Finally, not the least, the entire value supply chain becomes more vulnerable to external attacks – such as cyber-attacks – requiring more posts of protection to increase security.[12]

In case of disruption, the realignment of a global supply chain may be very expensive. The costs being higher, the less alternatives there are to replace broken links and faulty nodes. If breaks are structural, global supply chains need to be redesigned, a process in which the flexibility to find alternative paths or connections, to replace the old ones, works as an advantage to reduce vulnerability. Sea ports connectivity might play an important role in this aspect, facilitating the geographic switching of suppliers, without incurring significant losses and operating changes within a short time frame.

PORT LOGISTICS CHALLENGES

Complexity of logistic operations increased greatly along with the growth in International trade. In 2018, world container port throughput grew 4,7%, after 6,7% from 2016 to 2017[13]. There are problems of congestion in port facilities, leading to high logistic costs and requiring better coordination of resources and collaboration among ports' stakeholders. The port community encompasses a wide range of public and private players involved in logistics, which are managed under a given governance structure, attributing roles and responsibilities and facilitating communication.

There is a new and growing interest in port studies, as suggested by the number of papers written on the subject. Port performance is the dominant theme in maritime transport research, addressing issues such as economic efficiency, logistic flows and the changing role of ports to supply chains. The hot topic is how can ports improve on the "tax burden" that transport costs add to the price of final goods.

Ascencio et. Al (2014: 445) argue that transportation is becoming a strategic business function. First, transport accounts for a larger proportion of the costs of goods sold. Secondly, delivery delays may undermine firm competitiveness in a world where markets are being reshaped by globalization and increasingly dominated by e-commerce trends. As such:

[Sea] ports are now seriously exploring the potential of the supply chain management concept. Effective SCM is an essential strategy for enterprise success in global and e-markets to get products to market faster and at a minimal total cost.

It has been mentioned already that GSC perform better and become more competitive when the activities are well coordinated and integrated. A higher level of integration – i.e., increased efficiency might be achieved through collaboration – i.e., when the supply chain is managed collaboratively – or in isolation – when the firms act independently.[14] Ports can play a role on improving the management of GSC, increasing its competitiveness.

There are constraints to port management. The changing environment and the volatility in freight markets are stressing port operations, introducing structural changes in logistics and new patterns of distribution. The large number of public and private stakeholders that interact in transport operations and the logistics of international trade generate coordination problems, requiring a considerable amount of information to be exchanged (mostly paperwork and bureaucracy).

Regarding terminal efficiency, several strategies to improve port performance and reduce terminal congestions have been suggested, adopting new technologies, work organization models and information systems. Examples go from adoption of dry port's use in optical port configurations, water transport in inland waterway, to robotic cargo handling systems[15].

Connectivity Gates to the Hinterland

In the era of free trade and globalisation, the role of container ports to the regional economy is undisputable. Changes in transportation, produce changes to firm's behaviour and trade patterns, with economic implications at the regional and national level, measured by the impact on employment and income. In hyper-globalised supply chains firms produce anywhere and use maritime transportation to move goods around the world. Container ports cannot be avoided and need to be able to respond efficiently to requested functions.

Ascencio et. Al (2014: 446) say that, traditionally, ports are interfaces between ships and shore, providing shelter and berthing space, temporary storage for cargo and loading and unloading operations. Emerging trends in supply chains and consumer preferences is changing the pattern of trade, requiring logistic service providers to rethink their business – i.e., their role, their processes. Sea ports, functional nodes in logistics networks, must go beyond traditional transhipment and reinvent its connection to the hinterland. A similar description can be found in Vieira et al. (2015: 76), among others.

Port efficiency in this context means granting access and connection to the supply chain at the lowest price and the fastest time delivery. In modern times, as supply chains are increasingly demand driven, time is the edge competitive factor, to which one should add traceability, allowing buyers and sellers to know the very delivery stage of any order at each moment in time precisely. When ports gain efficiency, they can increase competitiveness of firms and industries within its catchment area, i.e., the hinterland.[16]

Vieira et al. (2015: 83), synthetize the need to achieve efficiency gains through better management of the information flows, which could translate in better connectivity, reducing boats dwell times, and lead to better use of the port infrastructure, thus decreasing unit costs:

Ports, which are key links in logistics chain, need to be efficient and effective in order to respond adequately to their customers' demands. To do so, it is necessary to rationalise port logistics processes and the associated physical, financial and information flows. [...] From the proposed improvements it will be possible to [...] maximise the use of port infrastructure, decrease costs and improve service level to customers, mainly by reducing the dwell time of import and export.

Ports, however, need to respond to the hinterland specialization to a certain extent. Which means, the way the hinterland participates – or is willing and able to participate – in GSC. Industries show different patterns of fragmentation: clothing and footwear operate GSC, while the car industry is organised around regional hubs, for example. Inputs, mainly labour, and public policies directed to Foreign Direct Investment dictate the positioning of Ports and its alignment with the supply chains they are expected to serve. Some supply chains give privilege speed, while others are more focused on costs. On hindsight some ports need regional connectivity, while others must place globalisation first.

Transportation Technology and Container Ports

Container ports are centres for cargo, hubs for international trade. Its performance is core to the design and management of modern GSC. The expansion of transport network infrastructures and the technological advances in transportation are structural changes. Taken together with new IT capabilities, that support a new pattern of demand driven production, are impacting trade and product supply chains to a never seen extent.

Gelareh et al (2013: 3308) say that according to the United Nations:

[...] up to 90% of the total trade volume (excluding crude oil) is transported on vessels and up to 90% of that is transported in form of containerized cargo on fully cellular container vessels. These container vessels operate in fleets of Liner Service Providers (LSPs) and follow published itineraries. In fact, these published itineraries are what distinguishes liner shipping from tramp or industrial shipping. These itineraries specify routes (the rotations of vessels), the order in which ports are called at, the approximate arrival time at each port and the vessel type.

On a recent Mckinsey research article, Dekhne et al. (2019) say that the transportation and warehousing industry is a candidate for automation of high potential, ranking ahead of many other sectors. At most companies are having a cautious approach, perhaps taking timid steps to tap what might turn to be a structural shift, for fear of unknown risks and uncertainty about the future of global trade. Also, to see how other constituencies and competitors respond to the unfolding future.[17]

Automation is on the table for other transport related companies and organisations. Along with production, sea ports are compelled to change its structure, in a way not to compromise the fast and on time delivery that suppliers promise to its customers, while keeping competitive prices. That is, adjusting to the needs of shippers and port operators, to mention but two. On more general terms, permitting a sustainable consumption and production pattern on all layers: economic, social and environmental.

In the past, companies used to have a one-size-fits-all approach to supply chain management. Today, companies like Amazon or Alibaba are entering the business of delivering fast moving consumer goods. They want to fast track products to end consumers, particularly the perishables ones, which require better articulation of transportation modes and activities at the nodes of the logistics value chain. Goods must flow directly to end-users, instead of being dispatched to sit in warehouses waiting to be forwarded. Aggregation is giving place to fragmentation, impacting transportation strategies, to which carriers and stakeholders, who meet physically and informationally at the port level need to adjust.

Digitisation, which is changing how producers manage GSC, is also being used by logistics operators, aiming at preserving its functions. Upstream firms are investing in order to track its production through the supply chain, facilitating automation of transport and deliveries. In most recent examples, products can be tracked from the producer premises to the consumer home.[18] Using predictive demand models and artificial intelligence it is possible to render containerized transportation and existing routes efficient to the new supply chain ecosystem. The interesting point here is that manufacturers and logistics service operators are becoming more integrated, to an extent that manufacturers are gaining extended control of upstream and downstream transport flows.

Maritime Transport Industry Reorganisation

Promises of fast delivery are championed by modern retailers, mostly web-based (Amazon is just representative of a large number of other e-market places and e-commerce platforms), and are particularly intense in food retailing. To fulfil its value proposal, such companies are building up transport capacity, not only to serve at final stage of the physical transport flow, but also at earlier stages in the value chain, where aggregation is key to achieve economies of scale. Nowadays, not only intermediate but also final goods – much of them embedding a large share of services – can travel the world before reaching the end consumer.

Companies that are not big enough to achieve economies of scale, or lack the expertise and capabilities needed for efficient delivery, have the option of contracting out logistic services to offset any disadvantages vis-à-vis its competitors. Logistic contractors can exhibit superior performance if they are able to build up capacity to an extent that it reduces unit costs of production, while coping with the complexity arising from a diverse number of vendors and products.

When disentangling logistics from production, manufacturing firms are, in many cases, reducing indivisibilities of its production process, and distributing economies of scale more efficiently along the value chain. The expected outcome is reduction in production costs and improved service to customers.

The contrary is also possible where forward vertical integration of logistics operations allows companies to reap the benefits from network and agglomeration economies. There are numerous examples of shippers controlling port operations, and expanding its reach to encompass land transportation in both bulk cargo and parcel delivery, Amazon being the most well-known example of integration of e-commerce and logistics services at the consumer level, attempting to climb up the physical transport value chain, compounding the advantage it has from controlling information flows.

Other illustrative cases involve the maritime transport industry, as liners buying land logistics operators, moving forward in an attempt to be closer to final consumers. Multiple arrangements are possible, which is going to be the most successful is yet to be revealed. One thing for true, technology is reshaping the logistic transport chain, and new relationships at sea ports.

There is a trend of increasing integration of port and maritime industry. The answer to container ports is to adapt, engage and evolve to the changing environment, and be active in developing a new ecosystem, where its direct stakeholders might change rapidly. Not only a diverse range of logistics service companies want to go global – such as UPS and Uber, that we are used to see operating a restricted section of the transport flow – but also the emerging giant retailers see themselves fit and prepared to embrace logistics services at a higher level, beyond the last mile.

The Economist (2019: 10) reports that Singapore is building a massive new port with automated cranes and driverless vehicles. Also, they are leading a project to develop digital standards, like the SWIFT codes used in banking. Carriers, such Maersk[19], are using blockchain to make shipping paperless and more transparent, such that every participant in the transportation process uses and has real time access to the same information, to make decentralized decisions accordingly.

Governance and Management of Port Logistics

Theoretically, a port can be conceived as a logistics platform, where a group of enterprises interact and work together in order to increase the operational efficiency of each one and of the system as a whole, allowing competitive advantages that translate into gains to the community, such as consumers. As organisations, ports are local communities grouping several actors belonging to competing and complementary networks, who come together for both individual (e.g., own profitability) and collective (e.g., making the supply chain feasible) purposes.

Port authorities are expected to design governance structures that promote port network competitiveness, and global value chains feasibility. Ascencio et al. (2014: 447) report that empirical studies found it very difficult to achieve supply chain integration at the port level, because of data sharing problems, lack of coordination and trust among private and public stakeholders. Additional valued added services to foster efficiency should be provided, as well as improving the attractiveness of ports, reinforcing connection and access to the hinterland.

Port actors belong to several overlapping networks, the reach depending on the perspective and type of relationship they establish between themselves. For the purpose of this section, we take a narrow view, and address ports as confined networks of "port services provision". That is, as elements of GSC, or nodes where logistics operations – physical and informational – take place. A range of direct and indirect services to ships and cargos is provided at each port by both the port authority and a range of firms allowed to use the port facilities. For the sake of clarity, a brief identification of the players interacting directly at the port level is presented in Figure 1.

At the core, port authorities are responsible for writing concession contracts, a standard practice to grant exclusive permission to port operators to use the terminal adopted worldwide. It is a fundamental instrument for internal regulation because, not only it establishes the conditions to access port operations, but also sets service levels, investment obligations and pricing policy oversight. The attractivity of a port depends on how efficiently the overall community operates. As a logistics hub, services add to production costs – not only money, but also time – and impact the competitiveness of firms competing in GSC. The interface role – linking buyers and sellers in geographically distant markets – raises the importance and the interconnectedness of the hinterland with the port community and vice-versa.[20]

Customers are users of port services and can be organized into hinterlands – geographical spaces that are de origin and destination of cargo around ports. Ports usually search to be connected with the hinterland in order to access customer needs, creating port communities to share information and align objectives. Hinterland customers are, traditionally, manufacturing or retail companies. However, if the cargo comprises mostly final products, hinterlands can be a sum of consumers geographically concentrated and, in this perspective, should directly influence port supply-chain design, particularly its ability to respond to consumer behaviour change.

Traditionally, as no relationship is built between port actors and final consumers, existing manufacturing and retail companies tend to act as consumer behaviour watchers, sharing their views with port authorities, which nonetheless carry their own strategic decisions. This might change as multinational companies operating globally and giving voice to customers, might want to get customers increasingly involved in the value chain management, seeking to reduce port attrition and facilitating the flows of international trade, saving cost and time.

Figure 1. Port actors and logistics operations

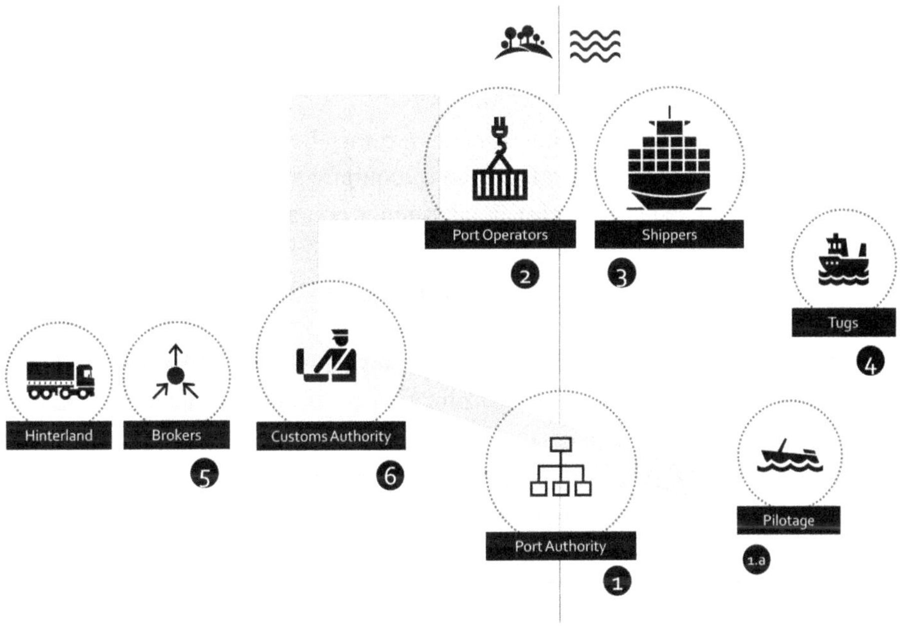

Source: adapted from Nascimento and Gonçalves (2017).

*Notes: [1] The **Port Authority** is responsible for infrastructure investments – e.g. terminal and sea entrances – and a range of ancillary services, such as security management, pilotage and internal navigation. They hold the power to franchise operations to third parties – port operators – through concession contracts, regulating service terms and investment commitments. [2] **Port Operators** are entities in-charge of equipment – e.g. cranes – which they are allowed to operate, offering services to shippers as required. Normally, they have their own labour force – "stevedores" – but temporary work systems are also implemented as to respond efficiently to cargo variability – mainly in dry bulk and general cargo, and not so often in containers' operations. [3] **Shippers** – and ship owners – are agents that take care of all document's procedures in ports, comprising both global companies – like Maersk or MSC – and more local and regional focused ones. Shippers use ports as logistic nodes where to load and unload cargo and arrange transportation according to destination. [4] **Brokers** provide services to customers in context of cargo consolidation, grouping cargo from several customers into a container, buying ship and port services on their behalf. Sea freight forwarders act as cargo brokers. Examples of other port actors includes [5] **Tugs**, offering assistance to ships in their port maritime manoeuvres, and [6] **Customs Authority**, seeking fiscal approval for exported and imported cargo.*

Although the majority of port actors aim at recovering their invested capital at a desired rate of return, they also have public service obligations. A public service obligation, for instance, is the way ships are allowed to enter the port – usually by ETA (Estimated Time of Arrival), and not the importance of the shipper to the port, or to some port actors. The definition and oversight of these obligations are encompassed within the regulatory duties the port authority is empowered with. They are imposed on all players based on welfare and competition grounds, having into consideration the externalities ports bring to regional and national economies.[21]

Potential for conflict exists when each player seeks to maximize individual return on invested capital, in a way that it decreases others' return on capital. Illustrations of these are, contractual obligations to invest in the terminal, imposed on port concessions, while not being allowed to price services freely – because of maximum prices clauses. The competitive advantage of the investment can benefit other players, such as shippers, who pay a price below market expectations, and do not transfer the port network advantage to final consumers. One of the consequences of such externalities is that the competitiveness of the port operator – due to its artificial low price – does not translate into a benefit to the community. The gains are privately internalized by the port network.

Conflicting interests arise also when investments are misaligned. For instance, if a port authority decides to invest in developing the port terminal and its equipment – e.g., capacity – in order to improve service – e.g. decrease time needed to perform a container operation – and the customs authority is a laggard, the efficiency of the port network remains stagnant. Simply, port operations will be faster, but shipping agents or custom brokers will have to wait for custom authority to conclude fiscal approval. In the present context of trade variability – both import and export flows – the uncertainty – regarding arrival time of ships or trucks at the port terminal – is requiring new investments to expand capacity and meet peak demand. However, because capacity utilization is different for each port actor, coordination is necessary to achieve a balanced value chain flow.

One expects port authorities to be entrusted with legal and regulatory powers to supervise and solve conflicts within the network, overcoming cases of lack of cooperation. As public agencies, they act on behalf of the Government based on a port management charter which, ideally, should set goals and targets using key performing indicators (KPI). However, the practice seems distant from ideal. Even if some authority is granted to port authorities in a formal governance model, some players have market power to balance, and even surpass, the influence of port authorities, reducing its effectiveness – e.g., shippers calling at different ports to increase bargaining power.

Port authorities face the challenge of integrating its operations with GSC. Seaports are interfaces where different stakeholders are brought together and need to be articulated. Therefore, when port authorities face powerful players, the balance has to be achieved through a complex network of internal governance instruments, some formal – e.g. concession contracts – and other informal – e.g. auto-regulation and trust. We will discuss this issue next.

Redesigning Corporate Relationships in Port Logistics

A new logistics mantra could be spelt as "get the information flowing". As Zeng (2018) cleverly explains in Alibaba new ventures, sharing common goals and having the right incentives is of tantamount importance. Besides the right technological IT infrastructures, contracting and incentives are pivotal for success:

Getting the technical infrastructure right is just the beginning. It took tremendous effort for us to build a common standard so that data could be used and interpreted in the same way across all of Alibaba's business units. Additionally, figuring out the right incentive structures to persuade companies to share the data they have is an important and ongoing challenge. Much more work is needed. Of course, the degree to which companies can innovate in this area will depend in part on the rules governing data sharing in the countries they're operating in. But the direction is very clear: The more data flows across the network, the smarter the business becomes, and the more value the ecosystem creates.

Vieira et. Al (2015), using the Port of Santos as a case study, analyse the logistics flows. Of the physical, financial and information flows present in any supply chain, ports are responsible for a number of activities, which should integrate with other stakeholders:

All [...] activities take place in ports of loading and discharge, are associated to physical, financial and informational flows and are performed by the different actors of port logistics chain such as exporters, importers, ocean carriers, ship agents, international freight forwarders, non-vessel owner common carriers, customs brokers, container terminals and port authorities. It is also important to highlight the public bodies which act as consenters in export and import operations and have impact over information and documents flows at the ports.

The authors highlight disfunctions in the information flow at the port level, which can be broadly classified as arising from discoordination, because of the multiplicity of systems being used to manage operations, the complexity of documental procedures, and the disconnection in the actions of different stakeholders. Gains could be achieved regarding dwell times using a new information flow, better aggregating, coordinating and simplifying the roles and activities performed by port stakeholders only.

Dekhne et al. (2019: 3) see great opportunities for ports, from wisely investing in automation. Some of this is already being seen in Singaporean maritime ports, as mentioned somewhere in this chapter:

Port operators can take several steps to get the most out of automation. Among other moves, they can build automation-ready capabilities rather than simply automating old processes. And they can apply better project discipline to ensure that automation investments account for all attributes of port operations.

Many port operations could be automated by 2030, the authors say, if artificial intelligence takes over. The complex relationship dynamics between manufacturing firms and customers, and logistic operators, is hindering the pace of adoption of new solutions, due to risks involved. The management paradigm must evolve from procurement and competition into cooperation, which is quite the opposite of has been happening in traditional value chains, where logistic operators are squeezed to reduce transportation and handling costs – i.e., transferrable benefits to buyers: cost reduction and speed delivery.

Port authorities have a range of formal and informal instruments to align port stakeholders' efforts around a common efficiency goal. Formal instruments include IT open sharing information systems, such as the Port Single Window[22] that is being further developed to become a Logistic Single Window. Initially aimed at becoming a means to supress paper from port administrative procedures, systems have evolved to become public sharing spaces, aligning service expectations and reinforcing auto-regulation. Being a peer-monitoring system, breaches are quickly identified and non performing players are made liable for damages caused to the whole network on real time.

The Logistic Single Window aim reveals the objective of enlarging the scope from port to logistic chains, having in mind the way retailers are – and are expected to, in the future – addressing consumer needs and accounting for their individual preferences. Thus, we speculate, Logistic Single Window solutions can be used as instruments to effectively integrate ports' responsive capability to the already anticipated change in consumer behaviour. Experiments include shippers and shipping agents input ETA and the customs authority inputs fiscal approval.

Other private strategies to increase port competitiveness have also been adopted. Shippers are for long acquiring and investing in port operations, a vertical integration move that aims at better coordination between the logistics operator at the port and the shipper, and improve the performance of the port. An illustrative example is the maritime transportation leader, Maersk, who owns a port operator company: APM Terminals. Further, Maersk is currently buying other logistic companies, and announcing its aim of becoming a logistic global provider, from start to end, i.e., from production to final consumer.

Mergers and acquisitions are not the only vertical integration strategy. Alliances have also been used a solution to share resources – all the same, Maersk has an alliance with MSC to share spare ship space.[23] Usually a shipper alliance goes beyond the narrow definition of transport only, and includes operations at port terminals. Gelareh et al (2013) refer that Liner Service Providers sometimes merge service routes (in a certain region) in order to optimize transit time and reduce fixed deployment costs. Reduced transportation costs in crucial for firms' competitiveness, as it allows goods to be sold at lower prices and reach more distant markets.

Following this concentration wave, shippers market power increases relative to other port actors, mainly the port authorities, whom became forced to compete globally in order to get the "alliances" resident to their ports. For instance, Algeciras – in Spain – Sines – in Portugal – and Tangier – in Morocco – all compete to have the same shippers calling and docking to their ports.

But port strategies are not restricted to classic port actors, i.e., incumbents like shippers, port operators or port authorities. New entrants, even if not yet identified as such, are making strategic moves that can disrupt port networks. Services such as those offered by Uber Freight or Amazon Freight – providing truck services to final customers – can be scaled up to maritime transportation. Amazon is also starting to provide air transport. For now, restricted to in line-hauls between main logistic platforms. Yet, a system that is easily scalable to Amazon partners, i.e., the companies that use Amazon web and logistic platforms to sell their products.[24]

Further, we see inland terminals starting to provide services to inland customers – in their hinterlands – aiming at integrating supply-chains locally through services such as transportation, packaging of good into containers, warehouse, depots and temperature-controlled handling and storage environments (Maersk, 2019). This decision encompasses a strategic option that approaches maritime transport companies to final customers. All these network characteristics are a challenge to ports. Network behaviour needs to address changes in consumer behaviour.

Effects of Global Supply Chains on Port Competition Capabilities

If a network behaviour is needed to respond quickly to changes in demand and supply, how can ports adapt to this environment switch? In concrete, how will ports organize themselves to operate a customized supply-chain that implies different products in a container, instead of mono-products containers? Will warehouse space be organized in the same way as today, by container? Or will it be organized by the type of products inside the containers? Or, even, will it be organized by fulfilment solutions, ready to be delivered to customers? Will ports expand their traditional relationships in hinterland to include final customers?

Ports seem to be 'elephants' trying to run a 100 meters competition. In face of more powerful players, that do not include only shippers but are ever expanding to include e-commerce global giants – like the ones Amazon and Alibaba – how will ports adapt to customized and responsive supply-chains?

Several strategic scenarios can be presented: network cooperation is a common characteristic. Ports are already facing internal network challenges – e.g. searching ways to have the actors cooperating in order to achieve common goals. Now, as traditional business models are under a threat of disruption, we must add broader global supply-chain network concerns, which require a powerful responsive solution to consumer behaviour. Will this new challenge lead a higher level of cooperation among port actors? Will port networks be disrupted by new comers, with powerful coordination capabilities? Will we have consumers interacting directly with ports? This are just a range of strategic questions port authorities should ask themselves, in order to design the ports of the future, as seamless interface nodes in global supply chains, economizing in cost and time.

When discussing these topics, one should bear in mind that port competition is not only about the competitive advantages of a single port, but how ports interact, combined in a network that is able to deliver superior performance, achieving efficiency gains. Vieira et al (2015) say that small to medium sized ports, usually presented in literature as exhibiting inefficiencies leading to higher transaction costs, can gain competitiveness identifying nearby influential central ports to which to connect, a strategy that Noteboom (2008, 2010) identifies as multi-port gateways. Ports do not operate alone anymore and modern supply chains need ports to act together to offer firms the needed flexibility (cost and time) and redundancy (risk management) to reach the market.

In a disruptive context, similar to what we have been addressing with this paper, port competitiveness can be enhanced if we add the ability to foster cooperation, improving the flow of information between stakeholders in the supply chain. Serving new partners in international trade – such as e-commerce companies – is very demanding for logistics service operators and, not least, port infrastructures. Imagine global value supply chains where inventories are reduced to a minimum[25], and one needs capacity and flexibility to deal with big swings in demand, such as seasonal Christmas orders. Spare capacity will be sitting there for a great part of the year, and pricing schemes should be capable to address fluctuations as presented in this example.

Dekhne et al. (2019) say that ports and transport logistic operators have been slow in embracing new challenges with further automation. Strong e-commerce players with large bargaining power threaten to reduce prices, making cost recovery from new investments, say if ports are going to be automatized, more difficult.[26] The point is then, how to facilitate the shift from a procurement and competition framework to a new one where cooperation is a shared interest. To be conducive to a fair distribution of value a new structure is required, pushing the discussion into the corporate governance arena, searching for a newly incentive-compatible management setting.

The WTO (2019: 10) report on global supply chains argues that connectivity is not confined to the physical supply chain of goods, it also includes effective communication between the different participants in global value chains, which using the internet can improve. Such connectivity is important for growth and country development as:

[...] the possibility of fragmenting production across borders gives rise to a finer international division of labor and greater gains from specialization. Global value chains allow resources to flow to their most

productive use, not only across countries and sectors, but also within sectors across stages of production. As a result, GVCs magnify the growth, employment, and distributional impacts of standard trade.

SOLUTIONS AND RECOMMENDATIONS

It is reasonable to conclude that the old model of loading containers with a single product to a handful of distribution centres, cannot meet today's demand for endless variety and speedy delivery. To match supply and demand of smaller and varied orders, loads must be organised differently, and IT comes to rescue, just to have decisions right.

Ports will quite likely have to invest in expanding capacity, but also to change logistics processes, to assist stakeholders in production and reduce its risks.[27] Logistics companies will attempt to share some of the technology upside and its risks with consumers, and smart pricing of logistic services is likely to ensue.[28] In short, ports should envisage to reduce attrition to trade, reducing transport and transaction costs.

FUTURE RESEARCH DIRECTIONS

Efficiency in a world of global supply chains requires cooperation which, however, is at odds with competition, raising an issue of how regulators will deal with the need to achieve economies of scale, when there are strong indivisibilities in the production function – such as it is shipping – and production capacity exceeds the size of demand.[29] In short, how are regulators going to balance the efficiency and competition trade-off?

Due to its nature, collective coordination problems arise in ports. Cooperative behaviour does not emerge spontaneously and individual port actors often free-ride (de Langen, 2003). Because of existing different and conflicting interests, port authorities may be required to intervene to solve collective action problems. But how are they expected to improve collaboration and integration among stakeholders at the port level, and beyond?

CONCLUSION

This paper attempts to show the challenges ports are currently facing, as global supply chain management switches and becomes increasingly consumer driven. Though, there are many other topics left out of the scope of this paper, some questions are crucial and must be addressed by port authorities, market participants and regulators along. How is logistics expected to react to a wave of technological breakthroughs that twist supply chains to become consumer driven? Economy globalisation, in the past, led to the fragmentation of production, and opened up an opportunity for increased participation of countries and economies in international trade, originating global value supply chains, as it is reflected in the data. Logistics operators around the world had to adapt to the increased demand for transportation, building up capacity and optimizing the logistics network. Innovation in IT of today suggests a new revolution is under way, as the shift to customer-centric strategies is forcing companies to restructure its operations. The boundaries of firms are moving in response to automation and artificial intelligence in ways that have not been possible before. In response, logistics services operators must adapt to newly redesigned value chains to remain competitive. Ports, as functional nodes of far reaching and complex logistics networks are not exempt from this challenge. Key stakeholders, that meet at each port location, require a level and scope of interaction different from the past. Competition should give place to cooperation, and a new port ecosystem must be built, so economic welfare gains can be achieved under the new paradigm of consumer driven supply chains. Though the future is uncertain, a goal that seems strongly entrenched is the need to get information flowing between value chain stakeholders with minimal attrition. E-commerce players – such as Amazon, Alibaba, or JD.com – have already understood the importance of logistics for its success, and are pioneering projects inbounding logistics into their business models. Incumbent logistics operators saw the opportunities also and try to anticipate mavericks moves. Liners such as MSC are integrating the logistics value chain downwards, from maritime transport to factory and home delivery. The final design is yet to be seen. This paper is aimed, primarily, to logistics service operators, offering a framework to analyse threats and opportunities, and support strategy. Secondly, policy makers, in particular Port Authorities, should be made aware of the regulatory challenge lying ahead and the actions needed to capture the economic benefit to the port community, and to the society as a whole.

REFERENCES

Ahmad, N. (2017). *Indicators on global value chains: A guide for empirical work.* OECD Statistics Working Papers, 2017/08.

Ascencio, L. M., González-Ramírez, R. G., Bearzotti, L. A., Smith, N. R., & Camacho-Vallejo, J. F. (2014). A Collaborative supply chain management system for a maritime port logistics chain. *Journal of Applied Research and Technology*, *12*(3), 444–458. doi:10.1016/S1665-6423(14)71625-6

Coase, R. H. (1937). The Nature of the Firm. *Economica*, *4*(16), 386–405. doi:10.1111/j.1468-0335.1937.tb00002.x

Dai, W. (2010, May). *Consumer Oriented Supply Chain Management Based on Mobile Agent System.* Paper presented at the 4th International Conference on New Trends in Information Service and Service Science, Gyeongju, South Korea.

De Langen, P. (2003). *The Performance of Seaport Clusters: a framework to analyse clusters performance and an application to the seaport clusters in Durban, Rotterdam and the lower Mississippi* (Unpublished doctoral dissertation). Erasmus Research Institute Management, Rotterdam School of Management, Erasmus University Rotterdam.

Dekhne, A., Hastings, G., Murnane, J., & Neuhaus, F. (2019, April). Automation in Logistics: Big opportunity, bigger uncertainty. *The McKinsey Quarterly.*

Dollar. (2019). Invisible Links: Value chains transform manufacturing and distort the globalization debate. *Finance & Development, 56*(2), 50-53.

Facchini, F., Digiesi, S., & Mossa, G. (2020). Optical dry port configuration for container terminals: A non-linear model for sustainable decision making. *International Journal of Production Economics*, *219*, 164–178. doi:10.1016/j.ijpe.2019.06.004

Foulquier, E., & Maugeri, S. (2012). The Port as a Territory: An Excepctional Space or a Common Good? Discussing Deficiency in Port Governance. *Investigación y Desarrollo*, *20*(1), 32–53.

Gelareth, S., Maculan, N., Mahey, P., & Monemi, R. (2013). Hub-and-spoke Network Design and Fleet Deployment for String Planning of Liner Shipping. *Applied Mathematical Modelling*, *37*(5), 3307–3321. doi:10.1016/j.apm.2012.07.017

Govindan, K. (2018). Sustainable consumption and production in the food supply chain: A conceptual framework. *International Journal of Production Economics*, *195*, 419–431. doi:10.1016/j.ijpe.2017.03.003

Hidalgo, C., & Hausmann, R. (2009). The building blocks of economic complexity. *Proceedings of the National Academy of Sciences of the United States of America*, *106*(26), 10570–10575. doi:10.1073/pnas.0900943106 PMID:19549871

Ignatenko, A., Raei, F., & Mircheva, B. (2019). *Global Value Chains: What are the Benefits and Why Do Countries Participate?* IMF Working Papers, WP/19/18.

Maersk. (2019). *Maersk to Accelerate Growth in Logistics and Services*. Retrieved from https://www.maersk.com/news/articles/2019/05/16/maersk-to-accelerate-growth-in-logistics-and-services

Ming, Z. (2018, Sept.). Alibaba and the Future of Business: Lessons from China's innovative digital giant. *Harvard Business Review*.

Nair, R. (2016). Study on Economic Regulation of Collaborative Strategies among Container Shipping Companies Following Repeal of European Union Regulation 4056/86. *The Asian Journal of Shipping and Logistics*, *32*(2), 89–97. doi:10.1016/j.ajsl.2016.05.002

Nascimento, A., Costa, A., Santos, F., & Cruz, C. (2016). *Terminais portuários e infra-estruturas logísticas em Portugal: análise da oportunidade para construção de um novo terminal de águas profundas*. Retrieved from: https://cciporto.com/downloads/acp_terminaisportuarios.pdf

Nascimento, A., & Gonçalves, R. (2017). *Porto de Sines: 3ª fase de ampliação do molhe leste: análise custo-benefício do investimento* (Unpublished technical report). CEGEA, Centro de Estudos em Gestão e Economia Aplicada – Universidade Católica Portuguesa.

Noteboom, T. (2008). *The Relationship Between Seaports and the Intermodal Hinterland in Light of Global Supply Chains: European Challenges*. OECD/International Transport Forum, Discussion Paper, 2008-10.

Noteboom, T. (2010). Concentration and the Formation of Multi-port Gateway Regions in the European Container Port System: An update. *Journal of Transport Geography*, *18*(4), 567–583. doi:10.1016/j.jtrangeo.2010.03.003

Oliver, E. W. (1973). Markets and Hierarchies: Some Elementary Considerations. *The American Economic Review*, *63*(2), 316–325.

Oliver, E. W. (2002). The Theory of the Firm as Governance Structure: From Choice to Contract. *The Journal of Economic Perspectives*, *16*(3), 171–195. doi:10.1257/089533002760278776

Panday, P. N., & Panday, S. (2018, March). *Leadership Strategies for supply chain Management*. Paper presented at the 3rd Global Leadership Research Conference 2018, Amity Business School, Noida, India.

Teece, D., Pisano, G., & Shuen, A. (1997). Dynamic Capabilities and Strategic Management. *Strategic Management Journal*, *18*(7), 509–533. doi:10.1002/(SICI)1097-0266(199708)18:7<509::AID-SMJ882>3.0.CO;2-Z

The Economist. (2019, June 13). The World is not flat, Special Report: Global Supply Chains. *The Economist*.

UNCTAD. (2019). *Handbook of Statistics*. United Nations.

Vieira, G., Kliemann Neto, F., & Ribeiro, D. (2015). The Rationalization of Port Logistics Activities: A Study at Port of Santos (Brazil). *International Journal of e-Navigation and Maritime Economy, 2*, 73-86.

WTO. (2019). *Global Value Chain Development Report: technological innovation, supply chain trade, and workers in a globalized world*. Geneva, Switzerland: The World Trade Organization.

ADDITIONAL READING

OECD. (2019). *Global Value Supply Chains*. Retrieved from http://www.oecd.org/sti/ind/global-value-chains.htm

Port Economics. (2019). Retrieved from http://www.porteconomics.eu/

UNCTAD. (2019). *Statistics*. Retrieved from https://unctadstat.unctad.org/EN/Index.html

World Bank. (2019). *Global Value Chains*. Retrieved from https://www.worldbank.org/en/topic/global-value-chains

KEY TERMS AND DEFINITIONS

Digitization: It is used to mean the increased use of information technologies (IT) to manage production and link stakeholders – various producers and consumers – in the value chain.

Efficiency: Efficiency within the context of this paper means using a production technology that minimizes incurred costs, and leading to the lowest effort – energy saving – needed to produce a unit of output.

Firm Organisation: Firms are hierarchical institutions managing resources (inputs) according to an internal set of rules. Such rules specify not only efficiency, but also risk sharing goals. A trade-off exists between efficiency and risk, and decisions regarding production are shaped by the way firms are organized – i.e., internal formal and informal rules.

Global Supply Chains: In a global supply chain, production takes place in different countries before being sold to final consumers. Once produced, the components – originated in places distant apart – are assembled in total or partly at a given location, before the good is placed in the market. IT facilitates coordination of global supply chain.

Globalization: In a globalized world, production can take place anywhere in the world, as firms chose to minimize costs of production. Globalization means increased interdependency between countries, and usually implies international specialization.

Innovation: Innovation is used interchangeably as meaning either new production processes, or new products and services. In a global supply chain context, it also means re-arranging production to take place at geographically distant plants in the world of the same or distinct corporations.

Logistics: Moving goods along the value chain implies two flows: goods and information. A logistic approach to the value chain involves an optimisation process, deciding on how to make production – i.e., a protocol of information exchange and physical transport.

Seaports: Seaports are nodes of a transport network, where cargo – either final or ongoing products – is aggregated and shipped overseas using vessels of varying purposes and capacities. Usually, a port performs a wide range of activities, including administrative paperwork, manoeuvres, safety operations, and inter-modality.

Sustainability: It means having the least impact upon the environment (e.g., decarbonisation), minimizing social unrest (e.g., income equality), and maximising economic efficiency (e.g., cost of production). We use it to mean environmental, social, and economic sustainability.

Transaction Costs: The explicit and implicit costs that firms incur when transacting with other firms in the market. The higher the costs, the more likely is the firm to internalize production.

Transportation Costs: When goods – either materials, final or ongoing products – are transported from the production site to the market, there is a cost to be paid, increasing the price to final consumers.

ENDNOTES

1 Cf. OECD Statistical database: https://www.oecd-ilibrary.org/trade/data/oecd-statistics-on-trade-in-value-added_36ad4f20-en. Accessed on: 15/09/2019.

2 The Economist (2019:3).

3 Retrieved from: http://www.intracen.org/uploadedFiles/intracenorg/Content/Publications/BRICS%20E-commerce%20_Status%20Opportunities%20and%20Challenges_22AUG2017_final.pdf

4 Cf. The Economist (2019: 3).

5 Studies point out several benefits for firms participating in global value chains, such as rapid learning, innovation, and industrial upgrading, in addition to better access to information, opening of new markets, and opportunities for fast technological learning and skill acquisition. See Ignatenko et al. (2019: 11), amongst others. Visit also the OECD and World Bank web sites for Global Supply Chains (links available in the web resources section).

6 Cf. Ascencio e al. (2014: 446).

7 Cf. the theory of dynamic capabilities, introduced by Teece et al. (1997), using the resource based view (RBV) of the firm framework. According to RBV all firms have resources to use in production and capabilities (i.e., organization and processes developed through experience and life-learning) upon which they can build a competitive advantage, if used creatively.

8 Cf. Dai (2010: 604).

9 Govindan (2018).

10 The Economist (2019: 5).

11 The supply chain traps companies in incremental thinking says The Economist (2019), as managers try to squeeze costs through sourcing, and customer-centric e-commerce platforms – such as Amazon, and Alibaba – push suppliers for 30% improvement in efficiency. Logistics is being used as a weapon to engineer a competitive advantage.

12 Illustratively, The Economist (2019) writes that "stretching supply chains thin to make goods ever cheaper carries risks. [...] Most MNCS do not know who supplies the supplier of its supplier, but they might be held hostage if that distant vendor cannot fulfil its obligations. The dangers are occasionally brought to light by external shocks. [...] More recently, shocks have been political. Brexit [...] could disrupt supply lines linking Britain and the continent."

13 UNCTAD (2019)

14 Ascencio et al. (2014: 446).

15 Facchini et al (2020).

16 Vieira et al (2015).

17 Dekhne (2019:2) argue that the delay is due to "the unusual competitive dynamics of e-commerce, a lack of clarity about which technologies will triumph, problems obtaining the new gizmos, uncertainties arising from shippers' new omnichannel-distribution schemes and an asymmetry between the length of contracts with shippers and the much-longer lifetimes of automation equipment and distribution centres."

18 As we write, Walmart is offering customers who order online deliveries straight into their fridge (The Economist, 2019).

19 Maersk's TradeLens initiative.

20 Long gone are the days when port authorities operated all services at the port level directly, from cargo handling to the necessary paperwork at customs and navigation and docking support to ships approaching the pier. For economic and political reasons the structure of port organization is more complex and has several players with different duties, contracted out by the port authority. To a large extent, port authorities have withdrawn from most logistics operations, just to assume the roles of managers and regulators of the port community.

21 A discussion of externalities can be found elsewhere. See, for example, Nascimento et al. (2016).

22 A Port Single Window is a IT based system were the majority of port actors must input data about their services to be performed, and port global operation can be planned.

23 Though there are competition concerns regarding sharing capacity between competitors. EU and US hold opposing views on this respect. Nevertheless, this should be an issue to keep an eye on.

24 Maybe that is why, recently, Maersk – a shipping company - announced that it will accelerate growth in logistic services through further integration of APM Terminals Inland – a part of APM Terminals, a Maersk group port operator company – into Maersk Logistics from 1 august 2019.

25 For reasons explained in the previous section.

26 The threat comes as much from excess capacity in transport industry, as from e-commerce players building logistics capabilities. So far, entrants are deploying their own logistics in very lucrative niche markets, slowly climbing the ladder of investment.

27 Cf. Ascencio et al. (2014).

28 Dekhne et. Al (2019).

29 Nair (2016).

Chapter 6
Impact of Container Shipping and Ports on Globalisation and Consumer Behaviour

Santosh Kumar Singh
APM Terminals, The Netherlands

ABSTRACT

This chapter evaluates the role on container shipping and development of ports and terminals around the world on globalization and consumer behavior. Container shipping is the unsung hero of globalization. It is remarkable that despite containerization and container shipping having such an all-encompassing impact and consequences on consumption, consumption patterns, consumer behavior, and societies in every corner of the world, container shipping is simply invisible to the world at large. The chapter also looks at impact of ever-growing large ports on the society and economy of the cities the ports are located in.

INTRODUCTION

Container shipping is the unsung hero of globalization. It is remarkable that in spite of containerization and container shipping having such an all-encompassing impact and consequences on consumption, consumption patterns, consumer behavior and societies in every corner of the world, container shipping is simply invisible to the world at large. Remarkably, there is not an inch of our life and our lifestyle which is not touched, influenced, affected, impacted and transformed by the end-of-line act of container shipping. Without container shipping, amazon would not be the largest retailer in the world and Apple the largest tech company. Samsung would not be the largest phone company while Huawei snaps at its heels to dethrone it from its temporary perch. Toyota would not be the largest automotive company. Nike will not be the largest shoe company and Zara would not be the largest apparel company worldwide. One could go on.

Fact is, container shipping is made up of dull looking metal containers, large ships, heavy industrial machinery and transport equipment which does not receive even a second glance from consumers. Why? The containers could be carrying the latest iPhone, the newest Tesla, the high-in demand Nike trainer,

DOI: 10.4018/978-1-7998-3115-0.ch006

Copyright © 2020, IGI Global. Copying or distributing in print or electronic forms without written permission of IGI Global is prohibited.

the latest video gaming console, the critical life-saving drug against the deadly Zika virus, the expensive 18-year old scotch or the rare fish caught in freezing waters off the coast of Alaska. Consumers will gaze lovingly at the iPhone in the nearest mall, rave about the latest Ferrari in the popular auto shop and devour the Alaskan fish in the Michelin star restaurants without an inkling of what has gone in ensuring that the consumer gets their sought-after phone, car or meal or whiskey.

Container Shipping is like the closing credits that roll in once the movie finishes and the audience is rushing to leave without finding out the work put into the film they just watched. So why exactly is this whole other dimension that is so crucial and paramount to the market today hidden behind the scenes? One may gather that this is simply because of the fact that consumers do not come in contact with container ships like they do with the phones, cars, food and clothes. And this leads to an entire industry basically staying invisible. The industry is given no credit for driving world trade, increasing globalization, fueling consumption, and changing consumption patterns. One reason is the poor research done on the impact of the industry per se. Another reason is that the industry itself is very *unsexy*. Why bother about dull boxes and ships and rails and trucks when the mind of the consumer is filled with thoughts of the next best product; the latest movies, the most popular video games, new cars, shoes and clothing?

BACKGROUND

Let's begin with the start of transportation. In its very basic sense, transportation is the movement of goods, animals and humans from one point to another. There can be different modes of transportation – rail, road, air, water, cable, pipes and so forth. The very first means of transportation for humans was through walking running and swimming. The domestication of animals was a significant milestone on history of transportation for humans. It allowed heavier weights to be carried for longer distances. It also allowed humans to be carried to large distances on animals as well. This increased the speed and duration of humans to transport goods. The invention of the wheel was another significant milestone in the development of means of transportation. Along with the wheel, the development of sleds helped better the transporting of goods, other animals and humans by animal-power.

Now, as for water transportation; its history travels back several thousand years. While humans could travel shallow waters to transport goods at short distances, long water transportation was not possible by humans alone. Animals, especially large animals like elephants, camels and horses could assist in carrying goods, other animals and humans over shallow waters and for short distances. However, to cover larger distances on water – on rivers, lakes and along the coast- as early civilizations were settled along rivers and lakes and along the coast, a new mode of transportation was needed. It was this need which led to the development of the earliest mode of transportation on water. The earliest records indicate that a raft made by tying several logs together with creepers was the first kind of object which could float on water, could cover longer distances and could be steered. Then came the development of the basket boat, a frame boat build like basket and covered with animal skin. Various things were tried to keep the basket frame boat watertight. It is also estimated that the first boats were dugout canoes which were independently developed by various stone age populations and used for trade, fishing and transportation.

Soon there was the development of boats which could cover even longer distances and were equipped with sailing technologies. In 4000BC, builders in ancient Egypt used reeds to build what can be called the first sailing boats. By 2500BC, the Egyptians were building wooden boats which could sail a greater amount of distance and possibly travel across the oceans. Northern European Vikings also developed oceangoing vessels and used them for transporting goods, animals and humans prior to 1000AD. In early India and Arabia, dhows were developed for sailing across oceans. Dhows are what are known as Lateen-sail ships. Lateen or Latin-rig is a triangular sail set on a long yard mounted at an angle on the mast on the dhow. It was used on the waters of the red sea, Indian Ocean and the Persian Gulf. China had developed as early as 200AD what were called 'junk ships' (Barbosa, 1866). These were ships with multiple masts and could as much as 200 people in one go. The south-East Asians and Polynesians societies also developed seagoing vessels and relied heavily on these for trade and transportation (Hourani & Carswell, 1995).

Ships with sailing technologies were plying around the world from 1400 AD. Exploration was flourishing as populations expanded around the world. The period from early 15th century to the early 17th century is known as the Age of discovery (Mancall & Weiss, 1999; Parry, 2010). During this time, European ships travelled around the world, across oceans to find trading routes and trading partners to fee the burgeoning population and industrial growth in Europe. Historians refer to the Age of Discovery as the pioneer Portuguese and later Spanish long-distance maritime travels in search of alternative trade routes to the East Indies, in search of spices, gold and silver. These pioneer explorations and expeditions led to various encounters with people of different civilizations and mapping on lands unknown before this.

The most famous of all expeditions is that of Christopher Columbus who backed by Spanish monarchs led the first expedition in 1492 to sail westwards across the Atlantic and then onto Asia and to the lands where spice, gold and silver was. Between 1492 and 1503 Columbus completed three round trip voyages between Spain and Americas. These voyages were milestones. These voyages could be termed as the start of European exploration and more importantly; the beginning of colonization of the American continents and thereafter to the colonization of other parts of the world. The Spanish quickly conquered most of South America and Central America and large parts of North America. The Portuguese conquered Brazil. The British, French and the Dutch conquered islands in the Caribbean. By early 15th century, Europeans were exploring the African coast in search of alternate water route to India. The Portuguese were the most active at this time.

This was also the time when the slave trade mushroomed along the African coast with the Europeans using their ocean-going sail boats to the maximum. In the 17th, 18th and 19th century a network of maritime trade formed in the Atlantic, connecting Europe, Africa and the Americas through a triangular trade. Europeans would buy slaves from Africa, ship them to plantations in the Caribbean, the sugar and molasses they produced was shipped to the British American colonies and distilled into Rum. The rum was then consumed by the colonizers in colonies and largely also shipped to Europe. Slowly, the Europeans started carrying finished goods to Africa to trade for slaves. This triangular trade brought immense riches to Europe and Americas and at the same time pulled them deeply into the slave trade, reverberations of which can be felt even today (Ryden, 2001; Andrew White, 2007; Ostrander, 1956).

The early 15th century exploration by the Europeans to find an alternate route to India in search of, to start with spice, Gold and silver, and thereafter for other commodities was no small development. This development could be described as the key milestone in the rise of today's modern world of globalization and capitalistic commerce. The competition among European nations for political power, influence, commerce and culture, led to many European companies establishing colonies in India by beginning of the 16th century.

Very soon the age of the steam dawned. Steam was first applied to boats in 1770s. Initially boats combined steamships and sailing technologies together. However, as the steam propulsion technologies developed, steamships came to the fore. Steamships gradually replaced sailing boats for commercial shipping in the course of the 19th century. At this time ships were still mainly built with wood. However soon iron-clad steam engine ships were introduced in warships. The iron clad was developed as the wooden ships were vulnerable to fire of explosives. The first source of fuel for steamships was wood, then coal and later; fuel oil (Hill & Keegan, 2002).

In the 20th century, heavy fuel oil began to replace coal as the fuel of choice for steamships. Advantages of fuel oil were convenience, reduced manpower and reduced space needed for fuel bunkers. In the second half of 20th century, around 1960 onwards, newest ships were built with diesel engines. Now a days LNG-Liquified Natural gas is being introduced as fuel in commercial ships as these are less polluting.

How did trade between nations start? At the very start, trading was a local discourse. Traders in a village, town, cluster of villages or a small group of close towns would trade within and with each other. Lack of transportation modes would restrict travel beyond the known confines of the geography. Slowly trade started to expand on land across farther distances. This was possible with domestication of animals for carrying oneself and goods and families. Traders started to travel to villages and cities afar in search of markets to sell their wares. Or they would travel to buy merchandise and bring back to their local markets. Most of these travels will be on land routes. At the start, it was a rarity for trading routes to be transnational. There was an immense amount of danger in undertaking such a dangerous proposition. However, with time, these land trading routes become safer and better and thereby more used. Many trading routes become more popular than others as different merchandise could be traded across the route at various 'market-centers'. The silk -route was one of them where many types of goods were transported across thousands of kilometers and across multiple countries. Goods transacted in in value also increased phenomenally over time.

Water routes also started to develop as time progressed. The Egyptians had trade routes through the Red Sea, importing spices from East Africa and Arabia. The eastern Mediterranean region also developed extensive trade routes in the black sea and around the North African coast.

In Asia, South-East Asian countries had trade routes with China and also with India and Middle-East. This was a key trade route which facilitated the spread of south-East and Indian spices to the west, through middle-east and led to the spread of Hinduism and Buddhism to the East. Now that was a phenomenal side-effect, the credit for which is not duly given to international trade.

The Indian sub-continent has multiple sub-trade routes with South-East Asian nation states. The trading routes along the water developed along rivers and river civilizations. These were the first trading routes on water, driven mainly by the fact that by far the easiest method of transporting goods is by water, in an era where towns and villages are connected by trails and footpaths and not by well-developed roads. The first ones were developed along the great rivers which became the backbone of early civilizations – the Nile, the Euphrates, The Tigris, The Indus, The Yellow river. Merchants would carry goods from their villages and towns, either upstream or downstream the river and sell their goods at other markets. There they would purchase merchandise not available in their markets and sail down to their villages and towns with those goods. In most parts these trades were within the same country. However, this wasn't always the case in some places. Rivers cut across multiple communities and habitations and at times across countries. Hence the first shorts of international trade, if you will, were on these early river trading routes. Along with these river trading routes, there were also parts of the world where trading took place along the coastline of a country and sometime along the coastlines of many countries.

As noted earlier, there was trading along the coastline of India, Pakistan, middle-east and East Africa. Traders would sail along the coast in boats carrying merchandise across many countries. The way this works is that the boats stay close to the coastline and stop at multiple places to transact business.

Sailing along the coast and staying close to the shore helped the merchants stay safer avoiding attack from pirates and also not have to develop advanced boats to sail across open seas. Remarkably this multi-country coastal trade is in operation even today. The boats, known as dhows are in operation even today and continue to carry international trade along the rim of India Ocean touching many countries from India to East Africa.

Short-haul international trading slowly started to take shape as merchants started to sail across smaller sea distances around the world.

As noted earlier, by 1500-1600, long-haul international started to show the first shoots. Governments started to fund sea expeditions in search of spices, gold and at times fineries. As the world economy started to grow at a faster pace, trading across countries gained pace. The industrial revolution gave a significant push to global trade and thereby long-haul ocean shipping and trading, an area which could be researched with more seriousness.

With the industrial revolution, factories in Europe needed immense quantities of raw materials to manufacture shoes, fabrics, machinery and so forth. They then also needed to sell the production in markets locally and in various parts of the world.

MAIN FOCUS OF THE CHAPTER

Now, this is where shipping companies entered the picture. Shipping companies established sailings of suitable ships between main centers of raw material production and the main centers of manufacturing and processing. They then also established regular sailings between the centers of production and places where the merchandise was consumed.

This aspect of regular ships between places of raw materials to, places of manufacture to places of consumption gained speed as ships started to be propelled by steam instead of sail boats. In early 20th century motorized ships came to be employed in long-haul trading routes. The motorized ships slowly edged out steam ships. By mid-20th century steam was used for propulsion only in specialized ships. However, while the propulsion mechanism took a giant leap from steam to motorized, the process of carrying cargo did not undergo much change. Ships continued to carry goods into break-bulk or what is known as cargo in conventional manner.

In conventional shipping, merchandise is loaded unit by unit, either manually or with low-tech machines into the belly of the ship. As this was mainly a manual process, conventional shipping was a very slow process. One would recall old movies or movies made on historical events like the first world war, and if they have sections showing the docks, where a long queue of men and women are engaged in carrying a sack of rice, sugar or like on their backs, marching in and out of the belly of the ship. Ships would stay for days at each port. There would be a small portion of cargo lost due to pilferage or a small portion is damaged due to inclement weather, or faulty packing or due to rough journey of the ship. In the 1940 and 50s conventional shipping did eventually improve its game to use low-tech machines to move merchandise faster in and out of ships. However, it still was quite a long stay for all ships around the world.

The world of international maritime trade was at the cusp of being revolutionized. The credit of this revolution should be rightly given to Malcolm Purcell Maclean. He was an entrepreneur who started as a truck driver and reinvented worldwide shipping in the 1950s. A farmer's son born in Maxton, North Carolina, the man dubbed father of Containerization began to haul empty tobacco barrels in an old trailer when he was a teenager. Together with his two other siblings he opened the Mclean trucking company in

1934. While this was the time of the great depression, Malcolm and his siblings managed to build their company into one of the largest trucking concerns over the next two decades. Malcolm McLean said the idea of shipping large boxes came to him one day in 1937 in Hoboken, N.J. He was carrying a load of cotton bales from Lafayettlville, North Carolina Hoboken, New Jersey (Saxon, 2001).

When he arrived at the docks in Hoboken, McLean was bored out of his mind, sitting around waiting for the hundreds of men and women to painfully unload the bales from many trucks, one bale at a time and then watched the workers make their way to get the bales loaded onto the ship. Malcolm was not only bored. He was fuming at the fact that his income and growth in his income depended on him getting back to North Carolina with his truck to carry more cargo. The more he waited around in docks watching cargo getting unloaded and loaded in slow motion, the more earning opportunity he was losing. Out of this frustration, inspiration struck. He thought: *"wouldn't it be great if his truck could be lifted and out directly on the ship, without his cotton bales being touched?"*.

Malcolm nursed the idea for 16 years and he finally put his idea to work in 1955 when he sold his share of McLean trucking and bought the Pan Atlantic Steamship Company of Mobile, Alabama. In April 1956, Malcolm McLean bought a rusty World War II tanker to execute his plan. He converted the tanker, named it Ideal X, which sailed from Port Newark with 58 containers on specially rigged decks and unleashed the era of containerization and changed the face of world trade, globalization and thereby consumption, consumption patterns and behavior-forever.

At the crux of the entire idea of containerization was the hypothesis to transport goods in standard sized containers. In this way cargo could be packed in these standard-sized containers from the place it was manufactured and then that standard-sized unit could be loaded onto ships which then sail across the seas and arrive at ports where they are unloaded at the port and then loaded onto waiting trucks to be delivered at a customer's warehouse. In this way, the entire journey time for the cargo would be dramatically reduced. There would be very little chance of cargo being tampered with and pilfered. The cargo could also be packed safely in a container and arrive relatively damage free at the importers' warehouse. This was a revolutionary idea, way ahead of its time. At the time Mr Mclean was devising this idea, there was very little infrastructure around the world which was ready for handling containers (Cudahy 2006).

For having the idea to save time and increase the speed of moving cargo was revolutionary. However, executing this idea meant massive changes in the entire supply chain and more so in the way ships were built, the type of machinery and equipment needed at ports to load and unload containers in a safe manner, the capabilities for trucks to transport these containers methodically over roads and multiple other requirements. However, moving ocean trade and transportation in containers was an idea whose time had come. World economy was rising on the back of growing population and consumption. There were visible changes in the manufacturing landscape. Companies were looking at cheaper places to manufacture and in most cases these places were in faraway countries. The companies were also looking for a way to reduce costs and improve speeds at which they could provide goods manufactured in far off places in their local markets. This led to rapid growth of containerization of the global trade in the 1960 and 1970s. Starting with various sizes. Over time container sizes normalized to mainly into 8 x 8 and ½ x 20-foot, 8 x 8 and ½ x 40 foot or 8 x 9 and ½ x 40 foot. With passage of time more types of standard container types were devised to carry different shapes and sizes of cargo. However, it was important to define the base sizes as then the other parts of the supply chain- like the machinery in ports and terminals, the rail companies, the trucking companies and the associated machinery for handling containers across the supply chain could be standardized to allow for faster movement of the standard sized container.

Maersk entered the container trade in 1972, a relatively late entrant. However, once it entered, over the 1970and 80s, it worked on improving services and increasing number of services around the world. It introduced a number of services connecting markets across the world and by 1999, Maersk became the worlds' largest shipping line in the world.

The rapid growth of containerization is visible in numbers. In 1996 the entire container trade was 45 million TEUS. In 2005 this has almost doubled to about 90 million Twenty-foot equivalent units (TEUs). In 2015 container trade had jumped to 135 mn TEUS. In 2019 containerized trade is expected to be at 170 mn TEUS.

At the same time, the size of container ships also gained pace. Ideal X, Malcolm McLean's first container ship carried 58 boxes. The largest ship in the 1960s had the ability to carry up to 500 20-foot containers in a sailing. In 1977 the largest ship could carry 3,000 20-foot containers. In 1990 the largest ship was able to carry 4,800 20-foot containers in a sailing. In 2006 the ship capacities jumped exponentially. The largest ship could carry 15,000 20-foot containers. In 2017, the largest ship was carrying Currently the largest ships can carry twenty-three thousand 20-foot containers in each sailing.

Without the container the global village would still be a concept, not a reality, because manufacturing would still be a local process

- C.C. Tung, Ex-CEO of Orient Overseas Container Lines (Gilmore, 1999)

Mr Tung's sagacious words echo what Mr McLean perhaps had visions of when he was waiting around docks for cargo to be loaded or unloaded onto his truck. This is a very fundamental aspect of world trade for all to spend a few minutes reflecting on. Without the container, many companies simply would not have survived. Local manufacturing would have required much more expensive manpower and more expensive raw materials, which would have then involved more power, land and capital expenses and more expensive maintenance of assets. This in turn would have led to higher cost of merchandise, which may or may not have been successful at finding many buyers. The world has simply been brought closer because of advent of containerization and container shipping. And thereby altering the face of consumption in the world.

Another development which has transformed global trade and with it, the consumer behavior and consumer patterns is the development of the 'refrigerated container'.

A refrigerated container is a standard size container which can transport temperature sensitive goods over long distances. Like the normal 'dry' container, the refrigerated container is available in different sizes with majority being 8 x 8 and ½ x 20-foot, 8 x 8 and ½ x 40 foot or 8 x 9 and ½ x 40 foot. A refrigerated container can carry various types of cargoes requiring transportation under temperature-controlled atmosphere. Today refrigerated containers carry bananas, pineapples, apples, lemons, onions, various cuts of beef, almost all types of fish, different types and cuts of lamb, dairy, diverse dairy products, different types of processes foods like juices, eggs, almost all types of medicines, multiple vaccines, variety of enzymes, flowers of all kinds, live flowers, buds, various kinds of chemicals, explosives, multiple liquified gases and so forth.

One has to only look at this list to pause and reflect that many of these types of commodities and merchandise cannot make their journeys across seas and across thousands of kilometers on sea and on land if container shipping had not come about and totally transformed world trade and also the way the world consumes. The various types of bananas and apples one sees in supermarkets, the wide variety of lemons, the different sizes of tomatoes, the different types of watermelons, the pineapples, the onions, the paprika, the coriander, the ginger and the cabbage. The different types of potatoes, kiwifruits, grapes, strawberries, pears, and oranges. And the different types of chilies, jackfruits, tamarinds and berries. From avocados to peaches, from forest mushrooms to organic ones, to the various cuts of lamb and differently aged beef one can choose from in a super market, the list is endless. One can choose from so many kinds of fish in the local shop, from salmons to Tuna to sharks to squids to Octopuses to scallops to shellfishes to oysters, to crabs to lobsters, from sole to the sea bass, which was simply not possible only 50 years back. What kind of chicken or turkey do you want? You only have to wish and it is available. From chicken wings to minced chicken, from boneless chicken pieces to whole chicken, from India curried chicken to barbecue marinated chicken, from chicken nuggets to chicken popcorn, from bone turkey to boneless turkey, from marinated turkey to whole turkey.

Dairy in all its forms is processes thousands of miles away and transported to your door-step for consumption. The large selection of dairy products like cheese, yoghurt and milk one sees lined up in in the nearby superstore, from ice-creams to cakes, from 4-cheese pizzas to chicken pizzas, from beef pizzas to all-vegetarian pizzas, all are just a click away. Another key item transported in refrigerated containers is medicines. Today one can find all kinds of medicines in the local drug store. From enzymes to vaccines, from proteins to vitamin supplements, from insulin packs to life-saving emergency drugs, from drugs for your pets to vaccines for your horse.

Another group of key items transported in refrigerated containers are products for industrial use. From industrial grade explosives, to water purification self-heating chemicals, from liquified gases in refrigerated tanks to frozen chemicals for heavy industries. Now a days even fresh flowers and live plants are being transported in refrigerated containers. These could be from roses to lilies to marigolds, from daisies to chrysanthemums, from medical plants to decorative plants. Popular wines from around the world are packed in refrigerated containers and made available at the nearest store.

Let me take a walk down the memory lane. In 1950 before container shipping arrived on the world scene, one would go to the nearest vegetable shop and buy the local vegetables. And the local vegetable available is the cute shop will the ones for the season. One could go to the local butcher and get a portion of local beef, local pork or the locally reared chicken. One could go to the local fishmonger and select from the fish available according to the season and catch of the day. One could then go to the local grocery store and pick up the potatoes if in Europe, Rice if in Asia, Wheat or Rice if in India, Sweet potato in West Africa and potatoes if in USA. One would bring the purchases, all locally grown and reared as the case may be, and whip up a lip-smacking meal for oneself. If for any reason one fell ill, a visit to the local doctor will be needed. Depending on the ailment afflicting the person, the doctor will prescribe medicines which are only made locally. As you can imagine, in many parts of Asia, Latin America and Africa and even in parts of Europe, life expectancy was low and many ailments could not be cured in time. While advancement in medicine research and innovation has dramatically improved life expectancy across the world, back then one was still reliant on advancement in medicine research and innovation locally.

Cut to 2019, among many other developments, containerization has changed the way goods are moved and consumed and one can only marvel at the phenomenal way in which life has changed. One walks gingerly to the local super market in a small city in Germany to buy things for a meal later this evening. One looks at tomatoes from turkey, or the ones from California, or the ones from Spain or the ones from India. One could also pick cherry tomatoes all the way from New Zealand. And importantly it does not matter which season it is. Tomatoes and many types of tomatoes are available all years round. One then looks at potatoes for frying from Spain, potatoes for making a puree from Netherlands, peeled potatoes from Malta, large-size cut potatoes from Greece, small-size cut potatoes from Morocco. One picks up organic coriander from France, sage from Italy, chilies from Argentina and carrots from India. One picks up green apples from China, pineapples from Costa Rica and bananas from Ecuador. Again, the fruits and vegetables are available all year around, no matter what the season is. One then looks at brown rice from Vietnam, Basmati rice from India, sticky rice from Indonesia and rice and quinoa mix from Argentina. One looks at naan from India or wraps from Mexico. One can pick up Cuadril from Argentina, Angus beef from USA, Rump steak from Australia, sirloin from New Zealand or Kobe beef from Japan. Or one can pick up chicken drumsticks from USA, or boneless chicken from Brazil or a whole chicken from Vietnam. Or one can fancy picking up the sea bass or the sole, the oysters, or the octopus, the salmon or the tuna, the crabs or the lobster. One can choose from the never-ending rows of wines from around the world. Malbecs from Argentina or the Merlot from South Africa, the choicest shirazs from New Zealand or the Shiraz from Spain. If one is taken ill for any reason, the doctors today have the ability to prescribe the best medicines and drugs one can get. The medicines may have been produced in country thousands of miles away and carried in refrigerated containers to all countries where they are needed. In fact, the containerization of pharmaceuticals has completely changed the face of healthcare in most countries around the world. While research and innovation in pharmaceuticals thrive in few centers around the world, the entire world is benefiting from the result of the pharmaceuticals research and innovation. This is because majority of medicines, vaccines, vitamins, enzymes are now manufactured in cheaper locations around the world. Places like India, China, and some South-East Asian countries manufacture the newest drugs at fraction of cost at which they can be manufactured in western countries. This also benefits poorer countries as the cost of these medicines is kept low and is thus available to people in poorer countries. Had this not been the case, many countries in Asia, Africa and Latin America would not be able to afford regular medicines, vaccines, vitamins and so forth. In short, the entire world is at one's doorstep today. The global village is alive and thriving and more to go. The containerization revolution has truly transformed the way people around the world live, what we eat, how we eat, what we cook, how we cook, in how many ways we can cook, discover new flavors and simply be.

As with the development of ships and eventually the dominance of container ships, it is fascinating to look at how ports developed.

At the very start, ports as we know them today simply do not exist. As river trading developed and coastal trading showed green shoots, basic docking structures got build to transfer merchandise off the ships or on to the ships. This was handled in a completely manual manner. Use of muscle and lots of sweat. Animal trading used to be a reasonable portion of river and coastal trading and animals of various kinds – from sheep, to goats to camels to horses were merchandised. This required some docks to be made in a way suitable for animals to be led off the boat on solid land or from the river bank or sea coast onto the boat.

As ships became bigger and started carrying larger sized merchandise, the original 'docks' started to become more formal structure. They usually had well defined, solid pier structures – initially made of wood and then made with stones and then will concrete and metal pilings. As ports were area of merchandise it attracted all kinds of people, including thieves. This was a good hunting ground for thieves to pilfer cargo and sell it off at cheap prices in the market. Unsavory characters would also make earlier docks their den as contraband goods would exchange hands here. Over time, docks started to plan for securing their entire premises. The docks, and ports and harbors now are ultra-secure zones with high-tech gates, wired premises, round the clock security and entry banned for un-authorized persons.

Today's ports are multiple acre complexes with heavy-duty machinery to handle ships of gigantic proportions. Shanghai port is 100 acres and can handle 45 million 20 - foot containers every year. Singapore port is 700 hectares and can handle 35 million 20 -foot containers in a year. Shenzhen port is spread over a multiple set of ports and can handle 26 million 20 - foot containers in a year. Dubai port is a large- mega port and can handle 16 million 20 - foot containers per annum. Port of Rotterdam is spread of 26 thousand acres and can handle 15 million 20 - foot containers in a year.

Maersk entered the terminal industry to provide reliable services to its customers and to have control over the overall supply chain. As market grew its market share and the container market boomed, Maersk came across delays in multiple places around the world. To mitigate this, Maersk started evaluating ports and terminals which could help it to deliver reliable service to its customers. One of its first investments was a share in the Modern container terminal in Hong Kong where Maersk had large business passing through its gates. In in 1975, Maersk McKinney Moller inaugurated a 51-hectare dock in Area 51 in New Jersey, not far from Newark airport for exclusive use of Maersk's container ships. APM Terminals was established as an independent terminal operating company with the AP Moller Maersk group in 2001. Over the next 16 years APM Terminals expanded at a massive pace around the world. It invested billions on dollars in terminals around the world. Today APM Terminals operates a global network of 74 operating port facilities in 58 countries around the world. The company provides port management and operations to over 60 companies which serve the world's leading importers and exporters of containerized, bulk, liquid bulk, general cargo and other commodities (Jephson & Morgen, 2014).

The port facilities of APM Terminals are an important part of the overall global trade. As such they play an important role in the economies of the countries they are located in. The ports are the places where ships laden with cargo of all kinds – from grains to oil, to pulses to paints, from eggs to phones, from computers to clothes – dock. The ports then are the gateways for global trade for the countries they operate in. As a terminal operator, APM terminals play a key role in the communities around their ports. The ports provide employment to the communities they operate in. As ports and terminals moves out of many cities with development of world trade and increase in ship sizes, many ports and terminals are located in areas which do not always have the necessary social infrastructure. In many places, ports and terminals are the only employer in the vicinity. This aspect of ports and terminals is not thoroughly researched. Reality is that ports and terminals have played and continue to play an important role in transformation of a society. With jobs, the communities are able to raise the standard of living. They are then able to provide better opportunities to the next generation – their kids. Another important aspect where ports play an important role is in the development of overall human wellbeing. APM Terminals have played their part of the cooperate citizen, part of the conscientious citizen, of taking care of their wellbeing of the community. In almost all places where APM Terminals have operations, APM Terminals have worked with local communities for the betterment of the community's health and wellbeing. APM Terminals operates schools in many communities. At some places, APMT supports, either with funds or materials in establishment of school, dispensaries, hospitals and toilets. In a few places APM Terminals runs and supports community health services for communities around the port and also for users of the port. For example, the container terminal in Nhava Sheva near Mumbai in India runs health clinics for truck drivers who use the container terminal. Port of Pipavav runs courses for skills development of youth from the nearby communities and works on provision of clean drinking water for surrounding communities. In Lazaro Cardenas, APM Terminals a shelter house for children from the community. It is for education, support and also give love and care. In med-port Tangier the container terminal runs a crèche and school for children of the community. While these are a few examples, the impact these community initiatives have on social development of the surrounding communities is immense. Social development metrics become better and the next generation the has the right platform to join the progressive society and take part in its development and also contribute to its development. This by no means is a small impact.

Container shipping also changed the fate of many cities and changed lives of citizens of many cities and transformed economies of many cities. This was because the container ships started growing in size and required deeper waters to dock at ports. In olden times, traditional ports were usually built on a river and were the center of the city. In fact, the cities grew because of the port. As the ports transacted more business, more people started living near the traditional ports and the city expanded outward with the port as the center of the city. As the ships grew in size and especially as the container ships started growing in size, the traditional city-center ports could not expand freely as the city had grown around them, with residential layouts, schools, restaurants, spice markets, godowns and slaughterhouses. As the traditional ports were built on rivers, there was a limit to how much the rivers could be deepened. This led ports to move out of the city center to deeper banks of the river. More often the ports edged out towards the open sea. Many times, the ports would completely out of the city, and away from the rivers and towards the deeper waters on the nearest coast.

Let's take a pause here to reflect on this change. While the change here is laid down in simple words and in matter of fact manner, the full import of this change was anything but simple. This was a monumental change for the society at large. This transition of ports moving away from city centers and from river banks out to the sea changed the very way of life for people in the city, the way people consumed, the way trade was done, the way people lived, and the way civilizations interacted. This was a dramatic change with profound impact on the economy of the city. It also changed the lifestyle of majority of the city inhabitants. With the port no longer in the city center, the micro-economy which thrives around the port was destroyed. Workers had to move out of cites to stay closer to ports or commute longer distances to ports out of the city. Many cities also declined in importance not only economically but also culturally. Brugge in Belgium was a major port of Europe in 19th century. It was also a major city where art and music thrived and it attracted artistes, writers, musicians, dancers and artistes from many parts of Europe and even the world. With the advent of containerization, Brugge could no longer accommodate bigger ships which needed deeper waters. The port shifted 20 kilometers further towards the sea and a new port city developed known as Zeebrugge, 'Brugge on Sea'. The city of Brugge lost its economic glory right then. It also lost is pre-eminent position as the cultural magnet of Europe. The port of Mumbai in India lost its place as key maritime port with the advent of container shipping as the bigger ships moves to the new port 40 kilometers away in Nhava Sheva. The port of Mumbai is smack in the middle of the bustling city of Mumbai. In the 1970 and 80s it was the busiest port in India. As ships began to grow in size, and international trade ramped up to and from Mumbai, the city port of Mumbai took longer and longer to serve increasing amounts of cargoes at its piers. A new port was built 40 Kilometers away from the Mumbai port in late 1980s to cater for the increasing international trade and increasing size of ships. Over the 1990s and early 2000s, the port of Mumbai lost its pre-eminent place as the busiest port in India to the new port 40 kilometers away.

With this the economic epicenter of trade shifted away from the city of Mumbai forever. In similar vein, New York lost its glory as newer ports were built in New Jersey which could handle large containerships and have railroads which could transport goods away from the ports efficiently. New York at one time was one of world's largest ports. In America it was the largest port from the time of the Civil war till the 1970s. However, it soon started to lose that distinction to Houston and Los Angeles as America's busiest port and also to New Jersey in its own backyard. The port of New York started to become less attractive as ships started to grow in size. There was a need to get cargo in and out of the port and its vicinity quickly. Port of New York was not suited for this change. Port of New York also started to become more attractive for real estate development as demand for residential housing and offices started to grow on the island of Manhattan. The port of Rotterdam also paints a similar picture. The port of Rotterdam came into being in 1283 when a tract of land was reclaimed at the mouth of the Rotte River. It soon became an important center for transfer of cargoes between England and Germany.

Many infrastructural developments followed as a result of Netherlands becoming a strong Naval power in the 18th and 19th centuries. As business boomed across Europe, Rotterdam started to attract more and more cargo. And as the number of ships grew and the size of the ships, the port started to shift outwards towards the North Sea. In the early 20th century the port shifted 40 kilometers westward from its original place at the mouth of Rotte river. Now the port of Rotterdam is the largest port in Europe and sits right on the North Sea. However, the moving out of traditional ports was a step in the right direction for economic growth of the impacted cities, the country in which the port was located and eventually also for global economic growth and prosperity. Many traditional ports have been converted into cultural centers and have led to revival of their artistic, musical and cultural history and in some instances the traditional port cities have now the best of both worlds – as a place to rejoice in arts and culture and also as key maritime hub, like we see in Rotterdam. From a growth perspective, the traditional port cities had to undergo this pain to make a quantum leap in their own development.

SOLUTIONS AND RECOMMENDATIONS

Given the far-reaching impact of container shipping on global trade, globalization, consumer behaviour and changing patterns of consumption, it is important that there is deeper study to examine the role container shipping has played in shaping the world as we see it today. Similarly, the changing face of ports and terminals around the world has significantly impacted growth and decline of port cities and with that the micro-economies and sub-cultures of many a cities have changed dramatically. A thorough examination is needed in order to fully appreciate the cause and effect of container shipping and developments of ports and terminals on our society and economy.

FUTURE RESEARCH DIRECTIONS

As container shipping continues on connecting geographies and markets, cultures and economies, the concept of global village is now firmly entrenched. This also brings forth the fact that there is growing amount of interdependence between the countries of the world. An event in one part of the world will immediately impact other parts of the world. Supply chains continue to become more complex and longer and disruptions could potentially cause havoc in ways in which we live, travel, consume and even exist. There is an immediate need for nations to acknowledge the criticality of container shipping and ports on our lives and work at making the industry as fail-proof and robust as possible. A proposal is to study the under-researched impact of container shipping, ports and terminals on our economy, consumption patterns, and changing consumption patterns.

CONCLUSION

One area which is at the center of growth and development in container shipping and its impact on consumption is the impact of shipping as a whole on the environment. The shipping industry has an impact on the environment. However international shipping by far is the most efficient mode of commercial transport. At the same time, it is genuinely acknowledged by the industry that the Green House Gas (GHG) emissions of the industry need to reduce. Transporting goods over large distances does mean that the carbon footprint is increased for the goods transported. Consumers in some countries are making individual choices to reduce their impact on the environment. They are opting for consuming local products, which also has a social angle as it helps the local industry. In a few countries' consumers are choosing products with zero carbon footprint, low carbon foot print and are selecting products which are non-polluting and environmentally sustainable. These developing consumer trends retain the potential to radically impact shipping and consumption across the world. At the same time, it must be noted that all cargo which is transported may not necessarily have the bigger carbon footprint. For example, tomatoes produced in green-houses in Netherlands may have a bigger carbon footprint than tomatoes imported from Italy. This is because more energy is needed to produce the tomatoes in Netherlands than in Italy. This is an area of interest research and debate and deeper studies are needed to bring out the facts. Having said, it does not take away the fact that the shipping industry per se has an impact on the environment and that impact needs to be neutralized for sake of our children.

Global estimates put the impact of shipping industry on Green-House-Gas (GHG) emissions at 2.2%. Experts also estimate that the shipping industry will need to deploy multipole interventions to ensure that this share is reduced over time. Assisted by multiple authorities, including the UNO, The European Union, various national and multilateral bodies, and also required by many companies like Ikea and Walmart, the shipping industry is working hard to address their impact on environment and reduce their emissions. The shipping industry has implemented many technical and operational interventions to reduce their impact on the environment. Some of these interventions include reducing speed of vessels, adjusting routes according to weather patterns, changes in hull design, design of propellers and gaining efficiency in propulsion devices.

We have finally ditched the old paradigm of just having to be faster and faster. This is better both for the bottom line and the environment, says Climate and Environment Manager at Maersk Line, Jacob Sterling to Politiken, a Danish newspaper (Sterling, 2012).

Importantly, one of the key interventions to be implemented by shipping companies in 2020 is the use of low-sulphur fuel which drastically reduced the environmental impact from ships' fuel. Many shipping companies are putting tremendous effort in developing environmentally friendly engines which can propel ships with alternate fuels like LNG, hydrogen, methanol, vegetable oil, bio-diesel, bio-LNG, ammonia and alcohol. Renewable energy sources like wind and solar are not ideal for container ships which have large engines. However, these sources are being tested for meeting smaller requirements such as lighting on board ships. Every small step helps. The shipping industry's aim is to go to carbon neutral by 2050. Where industry leaders like Maersk take visible first steps, others will likely follow. For the shipping industry, regulators and consumers, this is an area of intense focus in the months and years to come and without a doubt one which will transform both shipping and consumption patterns around the world.

That this massive economic, societal, cultural and lifestyle change was due to the lowly container and container shipping is hardly noticed by anyone. Today, approximately 90% of global trade by volume is carried out through shipping, this includes tankers, tramps, break-bulk, car carriers and container carriers. As regards to container shipping, a rough estimate is that today container shipping carries 60% of the seaborne trade by value. Maersk transports every 5th container in global trade on it ships. With its network of 74 ports, APM Terminals, a sister concern of Maersk plays a significant role in the transportation chain. Maersk has played a not so-small role in the past 50 years in accelerating globalization, growing economies, fueling consumption and in changing consumption patterns and consumer behavior. In fact, Maersk has been at the forefront of this change.

ACKNOWLEDGMENT

I would like to thank Maersk and APM Terminals' organizations who helped me immensely in researching the impact of container shipping and development of ports and terminals have had and continue to have on globalization, consumption and changing consumption patterns. I would also like to thank Keith Svendsen, COO APM Terminals and Jon Goldner, Global Head of Commercial, APM Terminals in encouraging me on this endeavour. A big thanks to Ana Oliveira Madsen (PhD), Professor at Católica Porto Business School & CEGE who persevered with me on the development of this chapter.

REFERENCES

Barbosa, D., & Stanley, H. E. J. S. B. (1866). *A Description of the Coasts of East Africa and Malabar in the Beginning of the Sixteenth Century*. Hakluyt Society.

Cudahy, B. J. (2006). *The Containership Revolution: Malcom McLean's 1956 Innovation Goes Global.* Retrieved from http://onlinepubs.trb.org/onlinepubs/trnews/trnews246containerrevolution.pdf

Gilmore, F. (1999). *Brand Warriors: Corporate Leaders Share Their Winning Strategies*. Profile Books.

Hill, R., & Keegan, J. (2002). *War at Sea in the Ironclad Age*. Cassell Military.

Hourani, G. F., & Carswell, J. (1995). *Arab Seafaring in the Indian Ocean in Ancient and Early Medieval Times*. Princeton University Press.

Jephson, C., & Morgen, H. (2014). *Creating Global Opportunities: Maersk Line in Containerisation 1973-2013*. Cambridge University Press. doi:10.1017/CBO9781139795340

Mancall, P. C., & Weiss, T. (1999). Was Economic Growth Likely in Colonial British North America? *The Journal of Economic History*, *59*(1), 17–40. doi:10.1017/S0022050700022270

Ostrander, G. M. (1956). The Colonial Molasses Trade. *Agricultural History*, *30*(2), 77–84.

Parry, J. H. (2010). *The Age of Reconnaissance: Discovery, Exporation and Settlement, 1450-1650*. Orion.

Ryden, D. (2001). Producing a Peculiar Commodity: Jamaican Sugar Production, Slave Life, and Planter Profits on the Eve of Abolition, 1750-1807. *The Journal of Economic History*, *61*(2), 504–507. doi:10.1017/S0022050701268107

Saxon, W. (2001). M. P. McLean, 87, Container Shipping Pioneer. *The New York Times*.

Sterling, J. (2012). The Carbon Footprint of the Shipping Industry - More Than Shipping. *Politiken*. Retrieved from https://www.morethanshipping.com/green-shipping/

White, A. (2007). A "Consuming" Oppression: Sugar, Cannibalism and John Woolman's 1770 Slave Dream. *Quaker History*, *96*(2), 1–27. doi:10.1353/qkh.2007.0003

ADDITIONAL READING

Frame, C., & Cross, R. (2013). *The Evolution of the Transatlantic Liner*. History Press Limited. Retrieved from http://www.chriscunard.com

ICS - International Chamber of Shipping. (2014). *Shipping, World Trade and the Reduction of CO 2 Emissions United Nations Framework Convention on Climate Change (UNFCCC)*. Retrieved from https://www.ics-shipping.org/docs/default-source/resources/environmental-protection/shipping-world-trade-and-the-reduction-of-co2-emissions.pdf?sfvrsn=6

Levinson, M. (2016). The Box: How the Shipping Container Made the World Smaller and the World Economy Bigger - Second Edition with a new chapter by the author. Princeton University Press.

KEY TERMS AND DEFINITIONS

Container Shipping: Carriage of cargo in standardised steel containers.

Container Terminals: Place where cargo is unloaded from ships onto land or vice versa.

Conventional Shipping: Conventional shipping, merchandise is loaded unit by unit, either manually or with low-tech machines into the belly of the ship.

Green House Gases: These are emissions which adversely impact the environment.

Refrigerated Containers: Cargo containers which carry perishable goods like meat, fish, vegetables at controlled temperatures.

Trade Routes: Shipping routes, which connected one geography to another.

Triangular Trade: Network of maritime trade formed in the Atlantic, connecting Europe, Africa and the Americas in the 17-19 century.

Chapter 7
Consumer Acceptance and Resistance Factors Toward Smart Retail Stores

Elodie Attié
https://orcid.org/0000-0003-3400-8927
Toulouse School of Management Research, Université Toulouse I Capitole, France

Lars Meyer-Waarden
Toulouse School of Management Research, Université Toulouse I Capitole, France

Eric Bachié
Percall, France

ABSTRACT

The internet of things (IoT) allows companies to better understand consumers' needs while improving sales conditions (e.g., easier access to products and information, gain of time for employees and consumers, smart entertaining environments, etc.). However, digitalizing a store is an investment. Therefore, it is necessary for managers to know consumers' expectations and the perceived benefits and risks for both managers and consumers. This chapter studies the academic literature and managers opinions about consumers' attitudes toward the acceptance of smart retail stores. More specifically, the roles of consumer well-being, social image, utility value, human value, privacy concerns, technology trust, health concerns, and different personality traits toward smart retail stores are discussed.

INTRODUCTION

The Internet of Things (IoT) and smart technologies considerably influence the retail industry and consumer shopping experiences (Inman & Nikolova, 2016; Manyika et al., 2013; Renko & Druzijanic, 2014). Strategies now extend product displays to fully immersive retail stores, like with the connected mirror that allows consumers to virtually try on clothes, create outfits from the inventory, request matching

DOI: 10.4018/978-1-7998-3115-0.ch007

Copyright © 2020, IGI Global. Copying or distributing in print or electronic forms without written permission of IGI Global is prohibited.

products, and connect to social networks. In France, managers and consumers are witnessing a timely metamorphosis of the point of sale with different technologies (i.e., smart mirror in the fitting room, application for smartphone, website dedicated). For example, Decathlon, a French store specialized in sports, digitized a store in Paris to improve consumer experience (e.g., real-time product information and inventory consultation, store transformed into a fitness room with coaches who are the salespeople at the same time). Moreover, the brand Bonobo insures its consumers to find their clothing size thanks to real-time stock information. Another example is with the brand Nike which launched digital stores with touch pads to pay for products, wall screens to consult the catalogue, emails or QR codes to memorize a product, and smartphones to test the Nike mobile app. Indeed, smart retail technologies give managers tools to enhance consumer experience and service personalization (Toch et al., 2012). Smart retail stores seem to be a valuable way to create greater benefits, customer loyalty and personalized interactions with consumers on the long term (Pantano & Timmermans, 2014; Wünderlich et al., 2013). Consequently, retailers are aware of the IoT potential and are interested to use smart technologies in retailing strategies (Foroudi et al., 2018).

As empirical studies on the topic are missing, there are many calls for research about these kinds of smart environments (Dennis et al., 2014; Foroudi et al., 2018; Garaus et al., 2016; Gao & Bai, 2014; Inman & Nikolova, 2017; Oh et al., 2007; Verhoef et al., 2009). Therefore, it becomes of high academic and managerial relevance to understand how the IoT is shaping the future of retailing (Kotler et al., 2017). Consequently, this research contributes to theory and practice by discussing theoretical and managerial highlights regarding consumers' acceptance of smart retail stores and consumer buying intentions. To do this, few investigated factors of consumer acceptance and resistance are simultaneously taken into account, namely social influence, consumer well-being, and privacy concerns, as little research has investigated consumer acceptance and resistance of innovations (Talke & Heidenreich, 2014; Laukkanen, 2016). Moreover, this study extends existing theory on individual consumer differences with consumer traits like innovativeness, empowered and well-being personalities (e.g., Venkatesh & Bala, 2008; Gelderman et al., 2011).

This chapter is organized as follows: the next section describes the background of smart retailing; this is followed by a literature review about the acceptance and resistance factors of smart retail stores; then, solutions and recommendations are stated, followed by future research directions and a conclusion.

BACKGROUND

Smart retail stores are interactive retailing systems which deliver services for consumers and employees through a network of smart devices. These smart connected devices sense their surroundings and can engage in real-time data collection, interaction, and feedback (Wünderlich et al., 2015). Engineering researchers also talk about physical Internet stores which use networking technology, wireless and cloud manufacturing to upgrade traditional retail industries into smart stores (Montreuil et al., 2012). Therefore, the IoT is leading the retail industry to more digitalized in-store interactions with consumers and personalized shopping experiences (Roy et al., 2016; Barthel et al., 2015; Immonen & Sintonen, 2015; Xu et al., 2011). This involves a consumer's cognitive, affective, emotional, social, and physical response to retailers through technology (Verhoef et al., 2009). Investments in smart retail stores are predicted to reach $36 billion by 2020 (Research and Markets, 2015). In a high and growing competitive market, smart retail stores seem to be a promising tool to reduce consumer churns with a personalized in-store experience (Kim et al., 2017).

The IoT should influence consumer behaviours and perceptions toward smart retail stores (Foroudi et al., 2018; Sivarajah et al., 2015). Consumers should be more willing to buy when they have positive attitudes toward new technologies (Foroudi et al., 2018; Ngo & O'Cass, 2013). Behavioural intentions to buy are also linked to brand images (Laroche & Sadokierski, 1994; Teng & Laroche, 2007). Furthermore, smart retail stores acceptance should depend on the trust consumers have into data management (Hoffman et al., 1999). The way smart retail stores collect real-time data can be seen as intrusive, arousing privacy concerns (Awad & Krishnan, 2006; Hong & Thong, 2013; Phelps, et al., 2001). Privacy refers to consumers' perceived abilities to control disclosure and subsequent uses of their data (Westin, 1967; Milne & Culnan, 2004; Phelps et al., 2000). Therefore, privacy concerns refer to which extent consumers are concerned about the flow (i.e., collection and usage) of their personal information (Phelps et al., 2000). Besides, privacy concerns engender negative perceptions about smart technologies (Wüenderlich et al., 2015). Moreover, users can experience stress from technology that decreases feelings of well-being (Shin, 2010; Van der Heijden, 2004; Wüenderlich et al., 2015). Research focuses more and more on this concept of well-being (Su et al., 2014). It defines how and why consumers perceive experiences in positive ways, through cognitive judgments and affective reactions, without objective facts (Diener, 1984). Consequently, quality of life and hedonism are close-related concepts included in the broader concept of well-being (Ayadi et al., 2017; Costa & McCrae, 1980; Dolan et al., 2008; Hsee et al., 2009). In the context of smart retail stores, well-being is defined as consumers' global judgment of how these stores influence their satisfaction in their consumer, social, leisure, and community journey, which should all significantly improve quality of life (El Hedhli et al., 2013). Thus, well-being focuses on the emotional and hedonic benefits of performing a specific behaviour (Dabholkar, 1996). Furthermore, perceived well-being is linked to consumer choices (Gilovich et al., 2015) and is an antecedent of technology acceptance (Bruner & Kumar, 2005; Çelik & Yılmaz, 2011; Chiu et al., 2014; Dabholkar & Bagozzi, 2002; Hirschman & Holbrook, 1982; Johar & Awalluddin, 2011; Kim & Forsythe, 2008; Kulviwat et al., 2007; Sherman et al., 2001; Van der Heijden, 2004). Indeed, consumer well-being can come from perceived enjoyable experiences (Ryan & Deci, 2001). Consequently, hedonic experiences bring greater well-being than acquiring material possessions (Ayadi et al., 2017; Van Boven & Gilovich, 2003). Perceived well-being thus comes from the anticipated positive emotions from experiences (Perugini & Bagozzi, 2001). In turn, these perceived emotions positively influence behavioural intentions (Andreasen et al., 2012; Dabholkar & Bagozzi 2002; Koufaris 2002; Curran & Meuter 2007; Davis & Pechmann, 2013; Perugini & Bagozzi, 2001; Weijters et al. 2007). Also, well-being can be experienced with activities improving social satisfaction (Naci & Ioannidis, 2015). Social image is defined as the visible and perceived inputs used to enhance a social status and image within a specific social group (Moore & Benbasat, 1991). A positive social image has positive effects on well being (Hoffman, 2012; Kuisma et al., 2007). Therefore, the more consumers believe that visiting and buying in smart retail stores can enhance their social image, the more their well-being should consequently increase. Moreover, research has shown that social image positively influences consumer acceptance (Bandura, 1986; Compeau & Higgins, 1995; Foroudi et al., 2018; Venkatesh & Davis, 2000). Consumers who perceive smart retail stores as conforming socially are thus more likely to visit them (Kaul, 2005). Indeed, a behaviour that is consistent with group norms allows people to enhance their perceived social image (Kiesler & Kiesler, 1969; Pfeffer, 1981), increasing acceptance.

Furthermore, people may react differently to innovations due to personality traits such as innovativeness, which is the degree of attraction toward innovations (Rogers, 1983). Innovativeness is said to be a relevant moderator of new technology acceptance models (Argawal & Prasad, 1998; Mittal & Kamakura, 2001) as innovative consumers are more likely to accept smart environments than others (Argawal & Karahanna, 2000). Besides, other personality traits, such as well-being and empowered personalities, influence smart connected stores acceptance. High-wellbeing consumers are defined as autotelic people with an emotional intelligence, with feelings readily expressed (Csíkszentmihályi, 1975), who are predisposed to feel, accept and share feelings of hedonism (Attié & Meyer-Waarden, 2018). They favour group activities, social interactions and social environments (e.g., Hock, 1962). Positive emotions, entertainment and well-being benefits lead their choices. Therefore, these consumers use technology as a way to experience well-being (Seligman, 2011) and smart retail stores could be a way to feel positive emotions. On the opposite, low-wellbeing consumers are people less predisposed to accept, feel and share senses of well-being than the average people (Attié & Meyer-Waarden, 2018). They privilege utilitarian benefits rather than hedonism when making choices (Harris & Westin, 1991). These consumers own a natural prudence and inform themselves before accepting new things (e.g., Mill, 2012) so the acceptance process might be longer. Consequently, the opinions of their entourage influence strongly their decisions. As smart retail stores are not well developed yet, these people might not feel confident about visiting this kind of new unknown stores. Then, high-empowered consumers are people predisposed to get, feel, then use senses of power over themselves, other people, companies or situations (Attié & Meyer-Waarden, 2018). High-empowered people tend to be self-confident (Hock, 1962) and should look for improving their social status. Smart retail stores should improve their perceived social status by giving them an innovative image. On the other hand, low-empowered consumers are people not predisposed to feel, get, and therefore use power (Attié & Meyer-Waarden, 2018), and consequently should be less attracted to the benefits of smart retail stores. They are rather rational and wise (Hock, 1962). Therefore, they inform themselves about any eventual issues (e.g., health impacts, technical problems, privacy issues) before accepting new technologies (e.g., Mill, 2012). Privacy is the most important value to them so they tend to reject personalization benefits to protect their personal information (Attié & Meyer-Waarden, 2018). Therefore, the acceptance process of low-empowered people should be longer, as for low well-being consumers.

ACCEPTANCE AND RESISTANCE FACTORS

The IoT enables personalized offers and responds to consumer needs of innovation, self-awareness and consumer well-being. However, the IoT is also a source of concerns that can lead to rejection toward the technology. This next part aims to define the acceptance and resistance factors of smart retail stores.

The Connected Consumer and Consumer Needs

The new consumer is becoming more and more connected. If Internet technologies are initially mainly used by younger generations, they appear now widely accepted by all generations (Foroudi et al., 2018). Personality traits, such as innovativeness, have more impact on consumer behaviors toward technologies (Rogers, 1983). Therefore, it is highly recommended to define types of consumers attracted to smart retail stores.

Personality Traits

Consumers react differently to innovations due to their degree of innovativeness (Rogers, 1983). The more consumers are characterized by a high level of innovativeness, the more smart environments are accepted (Argawal & Karahanna, 2000). Regarding the high versus low empowered and well-being personality, the authors believe that each personality can find appealing aspects in accepting IoT environments. High-empowered consumers are naturally more attracted to smart environments (Attié & Meyer-Warden, 2018), favouring the acceptance process of smart retail stores. As for innovators, high-empowered consumers have an ability to convince peers through word-of-mouth actions if performing a specific action (e.g., visiting a smart retail store) improves their social image and ascertain a specific social status within their social group (Hellström, 2004). Low-empowered consumers could also easily accept smart retail stores as technology decreases social interactions, which are not favoured by these personalities. For high-wellbeing personalities, hedonism is the main goal in life (e.g., Mill, 1998). Therefore, since they are very socially orientated, they might dislike the idea to replace employees by automatized smart objects, which decreases social interactions. So to convince this type of personality, smart retail stores should emphasize the hedonic and entertaining aspects with hedonic innovations, and not just regular innovations. Furthermore, low-wellbeing personalities could be seduced by smart retail stores. Indeed, visiting a smart retail store could be a way to gain time and share with other people a smart personalized experience, decreasing privacy concerns (e.g., Xu et al., 2011). Furthermore, they might enjoy receiving notifications and personalized feedback, which lowers their sense of loneliness and sadness, and increasing well-being. To measure these personalities, Attié and Meyer-Waarden (2018) defined a scale inspired by the literature. Table 1 shows the items kept to measure each personality based on statistical tests.

Table 1. Scales to measure well-being and empowered personalities

High-wellbeing personalities rate higher on:	Low-wellbeing personalities rate higher on:
I would describe myself as: 1. Talkative 2. Full of energy 3. Able to generate a lot of enthusiasm 4. Open to others 5. Curious 6. Often enthusiastic 7. Inspired	I would describe myself as: 1. Reserved 2. Somewhat calm 3. Often sad 4. Often tensed 5. Often in a bad mood 6. Easily upset 7. Rather irritable
High-empowered personalities rate higher on:	**Low-empowered personalities rate higher on:**
I would describe myself as: 1. Affirmed 2. Sociable 3. Managing well stressful situations 4. Self-controlled 5. Rather proud 6. Mentally strong 7. Active	I would describe myself as: 1. Shy 2. Erased 3. Often worried 4. Distressed 5. Rather anxious 6. Easily ashamed 7. Rather nervous

Consumer Needs

New technologies are an integral part of the connected consumer's daily life with connectivity available anywhere and anytime, favoring a place with free Wi-Fi for example. Stores have become a way to attract consumer. They are perceived as places of relaxation, pleasure, and well-being. The connected consumer expects a retail experience full of entertainment and emotions, with personalized and real-time interactions with the brand. The connected consumer thus looks for a store which simplifies the purchase experience and brings emotions through smart features. If consumer needs change with time and technology evolution, consumer purchasing power increases as well according to the numbers of the INSEE (2018). Therefore, consumers are willing to pay more for a more reliable, fast, personalized and connected service: stores are no more selling only products but a connected experience as well. Therefore, value is not only perceived from utilitarian benefits but also from the relational, well-being and experience associated benefits (Novak et al., 2000; Bruner & Kumar, 2005; Çelik & Yılmaz, 2011; Chiu et al., 2014; Curran & Meuter, 2007; Dabholkar & Bagozzi, 2002; Hirschman & Holbrook, 1982; Johar & Awalluddin, 2011; Kim & Forsythe, 2008; Koufaris 2002; Kulviwat et al., 2007; Sherman et al., 2001; Van der Heijden, 2004). Research has shown that shopping is fun to do (Arnold & Reynolds, 2003; Wakefield & Baker, 1998). However, this result might depend on the context (Wang, 2017). For example, a supermarket self-checkout is more a utilitarian service where consumers prefer to not spend too much time, and therefore do not need or expect fun from this consuming experience (Wang, 2017); on the opposite, well-being has a stronger impact in hedonic service contexts (Van der Heijden, 2004). Consumers prefer a store with no queue at the checkout, products available and real-time personalized information. They are also more willing to buy when they initially have positive beliefs and attitudes toward the brand (Foroudi et al., 2018; Ngo & O'Cass, 2013). Shopping can fulfil fundamental human needs like autonomy, competence, and relating to others (Tauber, 1972). Satisfaction of these needs play an important role in improving perceived well-being (e.g., Deci & Ryan, 2002). To sum up this part, table 2 shows the main characteristics of consumers and their needs.

Table 2. The main traits of personality of consumers and their main needs

Types of users	Main traits	Main needs
Innovative	Attracted to new technologies, curious, open-minded, intuitive, technophile.	Discover new technologies and services, easy and fast access to connectivity through Wi-Fi networks
High-empowered	Self-controlled, energetic, strong-minded, with a strong leadership, proud.	Improve social status through a social action (i.e., visiting a smart retail store)
Low-empowered	Diplomatic, vigilant, hesitant, suspicious.	Be reassured regarding safety of technologies and less social interactions with people
High-wellbeing	Positive, dynamic, talkative, inconstant, irrational, thoughtless.	Be entertained through smart devices like virtual headsets, virtual games, smart screens and robots, and more social interactions with people or personalized features
Low-wellbeing	Thinker, listener, careful, rational, easily tensed, anxious, distressed.	Increase productivity with a gain of time (i.e., less queue at the check-out, information about each products and location in the store) and personalized features

Improving Consumer Experience with the IoT

IoT Services for Stores

The shopping experience in a physical store can combine the ease of an online transaction with the simple pleasure and social interaction of shopping. For example, a virtual assistant might help consumers and retailers to select and locate items in the store on a smartphone or from a store tablet; the digital virtual assistant interacts via a voice interface (i.e. Siri), suggests items or ensembles to upsell, suggests alternative sizes or colors to try, and allows consumers to request different sizes or colors within the virtual fitting room. The retailers get the notification in real-time and can easily find the products thanks to the geolocation of each product to respond in real time to consumers' needs. These solutions based on the principles of the nudge economy (i.e., detecting hesitant buyers to incentivize them to complete a purchase) offer the opportunity to create a more efficient point of sale leading to greater productivity and profits. The nudge economy allows tracking and analyzing footfall of customers, sending on-the-spot offers to phones of logged-in customers and collecting feedback from no-buy shoppers. Retail technologies then monitor and analyze customer traffic and behavior in order to send immediate and interactive offers to customers.

The IoT aims at answering to different needs according to consumers, retailers and managers. The advantages for the customer is the ability to identify where the clothes are located in the store on his/her smartphone, to choose another size or color inside the fitting room via the smart mirror, and receive some special offers by notification on his/her smartphone. For the retailer, the advantages are to receive notifications from the fitting room when the customer asks for another size or color, identify where the clothes are located thanks to a RFID tag and support each customer visiting the store. Finally, for managers, they can get alerts about the stock to manage it in real time (analytics), define and send personalized notifications, analyze the customer journey in store to better define the merchandising strategy, and analyze customers profiles (i.e., man, woman, age, etc.). Eric Bachié, Percall's Director of IoT business comments that companies "have invested significantly in putting together a realistic taster of what shoppers can look forward to in tomorrow's Connected World and it is all achievable today."

Business-to-business companies offer a global solution from the hardware to the soft up with the right solution. This stage is developed in three phases, through strategic recommendation (i.e., feasibility study, interest for the brand, analysis of the problem to solve, recommendation about the solution to develop), audit and consulting (i.e., definition of the context of the brand, technical study, technologies choice, integration in the information system of the brand), and scoping (i.e., collection of needs, adjustment of use cases, quotation of the solution, planning of deployment).

Big Data Collection for a Personalized Experience

The connected consumer is identifiable through a large amount of collected data (i.e., purchases, geolocation, reviews on social media, smart connected objects data). Each shopping experience can be analyzed in real time as smart devices connect themselves to the Internet automatically to collect consumer data. This aims at improving the store efficiency, accuracy and economic benefits, in addition to reducing retailers' interventions. According to customers' characteristics, the IoT is able to define the best personalized offer for them at the right time (i.e., send a personalized offer for shoes when the clients are in the shoes' department). Companies collecting the data ensure that the data collection is anonymous (except data linked to the loyalty program). The system takes into account only the sex, age, purchase path, etc.

Resistance Factors Toward Smart Connected Stores

Intrusion and Privacy

A smart retail store implies that consumers allow their personal information to be collected and analyzed and that companies can target them according to this data (i.e., gender, age, desired products, purchase frequency, time spent looking at a product, etc.). Privacy concerns generally negatively affect the acceptance process (Wüenderlich et al., 2015). Consumers want to know how their data is managed: is it stored securely, used for personalized features, or sold to third parties? Since May 2018, the European Data Protection Regulation regulates the data market. Data centers ensure that there is no historic follow up of the customers. But, little research has investigated privacy concerns in the context of smart connected environments yet (Verhoef et al., 2017; Fox & Royne, 2018). An increasing number of people give up privacy concerns simply by aiming to live a personalized experience and belong to a desired social group (Turow et al., 2008). Thus, there should be no increase of stress if the benefits of personalization are higher than the loss of privacy (Xu et al., 2011). On the other hand, privacy concerns differ according to individual's perceptions and values and might be contingent to contexts (Donaldson & Dunfee, 1994; Malhotra et al., 2004). Indeed, there could be a difference between sensitive and more general data: data sharing should be clear with the volume of data collected and analyzed to define the acceptable perimeter of privacy sharing. Therefore, trust and transparency are necessary for a better consumer acceptance (Hoffman et al., 1999).

Human Value

Another concern of companies and consumers is about the reduction of people in stores. Machines can replace employees and thus decrease human interactions between buyers and retailers. This also implies that the IoT creates new kinds of jobs in engineering, network, computer science, or that sellers will have to become image consultants for example to provide an added value in a near future. Moreover, current events have highlighted some very worrying technical problems. Connected alarms can be hacked and deactivated remotely, facilitating burglary for example. More dangerous, professional hackers were able to hack a connected car and apply its brake remotely as it was driving. These risks about technology are real and people are being aware of them through the media. Thus, if safety standards are continuously reviewed by professional technical teams, the consumer's apprehension towards the IoT is still justified. Therefore, if there are still retailers to reassure the consumer, and if the technology never fails, both consumers and managers should be more willing to accept smart retail stores.

Health Controversies

In the literature, fear is often studied as a persuasive strategy used to influence consumer attitudes and behaviors (Fishbein & Ajzen, 1975). For example, fear has been used to address public health issues such as smoking prevention, driving under the influence of alcohol, or poor eating habits (e.g., Freimuth & Mettger, 1990). Another problem with the IoT is that a connected environment necessarily implies the presence of electromagnetic pollution. In 2011, the International Agency for Research on Cancer judged the radiation from connected objects to be potentially carcinogenic. According to other specialists, these objects emit very low-frequency radiation that is then harmless to humans. In reality, it is still too early to analyze the real effects of prolonged and cumulative exposure to these small radiations. It will take more time to obtain significant results regarding these health controversies.

SOLUTIONS AND RECOMMENDATIONS

Understanding the needs of the connected consumer implies to change the way companies used to define their strategies (Verhoef et al., 2009). Strategies should focus more on consumers, their characteristics, needs, beliefs, interests and values, rather than on the average purchase. The connected consumer wants services with a 360°C vision: consultation of the availability of each product and its location in the store, real-time information, a fast checkout, etc. A controlled e-logistics system allows consumers to find a fast, reliable and flexible service, leading to greater consumer satisfaction. Figure 1 summarizes the global view of smart retail stores market according to consumers, companies and IoT solutions.

Figure 1. Global view of smart retail stores market

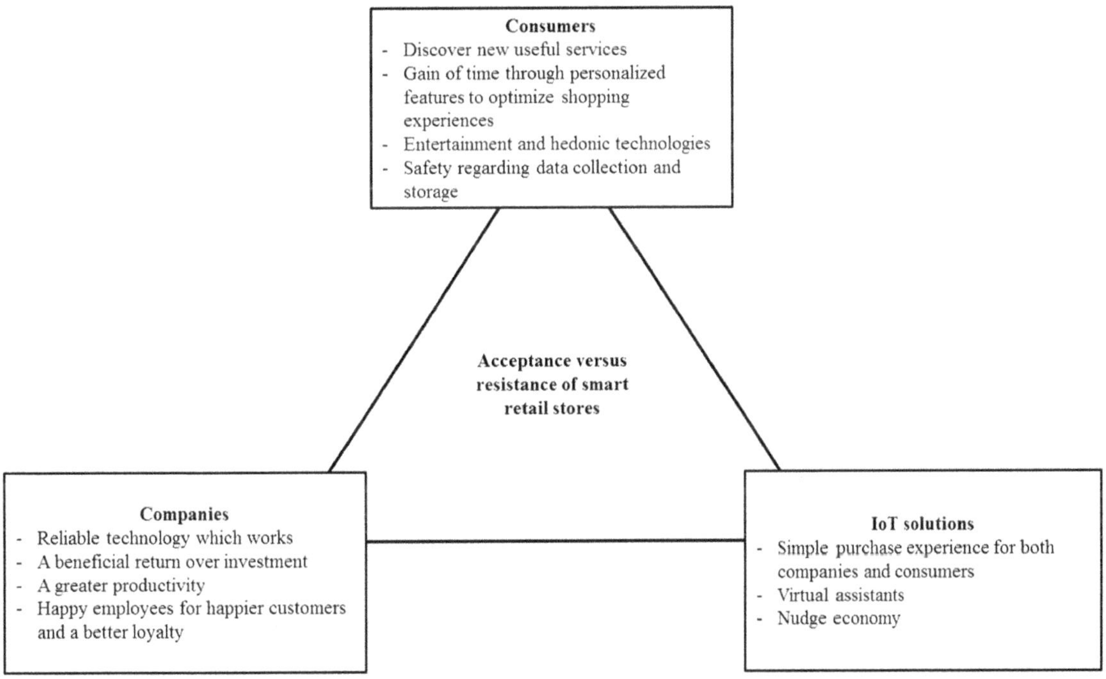

The evolution of the IoT brings some implications for retail managers. If consumers' expectations are satisfied, they are more likely to adopt these new technologies and become buyers (Applebaum, 1998; Levinas, 1997). Even if prices and utility are important, consumer experience, well-being and social benefits appear to become more and more significant for consumers, adding meaningful value to differentiate stores from competitors (Kim et al., 2017; Novak et al., 2000). Therefore, it is important to connect stores according to consumer targets, and then to enhance consumer experience through self-congruence. Consumers can be loyal to brands but connectivity pushes them to be loyal to several brands through notification push for example. It is important for companies to differentiate them through quality because dissatisfaction will push consumers to other brands while satisfaction should keep them loyal. Furthermore, trust is a key to improve social relationships, including between consumers and brands, because behind each smart device is the recording of consumers' private data. It is thus necessary to continually rethink privacy policies and have the IoT technology tested regularly by high-performance technology and software companies. If and when consumers have doubts, they naturally turn to their relatives who will then exert a certain social influence. Companies must therefore try to reconcile with unhappy consumers and convince them to give them a second chance through exemplary behavior, while maintaining a privileged relationship with loyal consumers. More specifically, the best way to convince high innovative and empowered consumers is to create an innovative brand image and personalized service experiences. Then, price does not appear to be a drawback as long as visiting smart retail stores improves social image. Marketing strategies should thus focus on reinforcing innovative brand status, image and recognition, in order to fit with these consumers' values. Moreover, regarding low well-being consumers, personalized feedback and encouragements should please them as they are rather anxious and lonesome. For low-empowered users, the policies of data privacy and use should be clear and transparent. However, people with a high well-being personality might be more attracted to real social interactions, so keeping employees in stores is a way to increase smart retail stores acceptance, or with hedonic innovations (e.g., environments adapting to consumers moods, interactive robots). Therefore, increasing distractions and entertainment through relationships and immersion with personalized features should improve smart environments acceptance (Seligman, 2011). Kaul (2005) also shows that stores with modern equipment, good and clean facilities, and ease in transactions improve satisfaction and behavioral patronage intentions. Furthermore, a huge amount of big data can be obtained and analyzed through analytical tools (Lee & Lee, 2015). This can be very useful for management and marketing decisions to create an individual value-added service experience for consumers through real-time event feedback (Lee & Lee, 2015; Remondes & Afonso, 2018). However, there is still a need to overcome the security hurdle that slows down the extension of IoT opportunities (Lee & Lee, 2015; Suo et al., 2012). Indeed, ethical issues can arise, due to the ubiquity, omnipresence, and unpredictable characteristics of the IoT (Van der Hoven, 2013). Confidentiality, privacy, and trust between users, companies and smart devices, still need to be better regulated and transparent with consumers (Lee & Lee, 2015). However, it appears that privacy concerns do not increase stress when consumers believe that the personalization and social benefits are higher than the loss of privacy (Xu et al., 2011). Thus, data security must be a central topic in product/service development, data policies and communication to increase trust towards the brand (Bhattacherjee, 2000; Hengstler et al., 2016; Shieh et al., 2013).

FUTURE RESEARCH DIRECTIONS

Some questions regarding smart retail stores remain unanswered. It would be interesting to use "real" smart retail store data and field experiments to study consumers' perceptions and behaviors before, during and after their outlet visit, and do longitudinal investigations about loyalty and other benefits (i.e., consumer well-being, purchase behavior). Future research should also compare results between smart versus non-smart stores, and hedonic (e.g., perfume and beauty stores) versus utilitarian (e.g., grocery stores like Amazon Go) retail contexts to see if there are differences between the type of stores and consumer targets, as well as with other types of smart environments like smart homes, smart hospitals or smart cities.

CONCLUSION

This research advances earlier research on technology acceptance (Atkins & Kim, 2012) in the context of smart retail stores. The roles of privacy concerns, perceived social image, perceived well-being, innovativeness, and types of personalities are highlighted. The IoT can generate well-being or bad-being, so it is important for companies to find the best strategy according to their target. Finally, researchers have seen a change in consumer behavior and this IoT changing environment should modify the coming consumer behavior as well.

ACKNOWLEDGMENT

This research was supported by Percall.

REFERENCES

Andreasen, A. R., Goldberg, M. E., & Sirgy, M. J. (2012). Foundational research on consumer welfare: Opportunities for a transformative consumer research agenda. In Transformative consumer research for personal and collective well-being, (pp. 25-65). Academic Press.

Applebaum, K. (1998). The sweetness of salvation: Consumer marketing and the liberal-bourgeois Theory of Needs. *Current Anthropology*, *39*(3), 323–349. doi:10.1086/204737

Arnold, M. J., & Reynolds, K. E. (2003). Hedonic shopping motivations. *Journal of Retailing*, *79*(2), 77–95. doi:10.1016/S0022-4359(03)00007-1

Atkins, K. G., & Kim, Y.-K. (2012). Smart shopping: Conceptualization and measurement. *International Journal of Retail & Distribution Management*, *40*(5), 360–375. doi:10.1108/09590551211222349

Attié, E., & Meyer-Waarden, L. (2018). The acceptance process of the Internet of Things: How to improve the acceptance of the IoT technology? In Smart Marketing With the Internet of Things. doi:10.4018/978-1-5225-5763-0

Awad, N. F., & Krishnan, M. S. (2006). The personalization privacy paradox: An empirical evaluation of information transparency and the willingeness to be profiled online for personalization. *Management Information Systems Quarterly*, *30*(1), 13–28. doi:10.2307/25148715

Ayadi, N., Paraschiv, C., & Vernette, E. (2017). Increasing consumer well-being: Risk as potential driver of happiness. *Applied Economics*, *49*(43), 4321–4335. doi:10.1080/00036846.2017.1282142

Bandura, A. (1986). *Social foundations of thought and action: A social cognitive theory*. Prentice-Hall, Inc.

Barthel, R., Hudson-Smith, A., & de Jode, M. (2015). Future retail environments and the internet of things (IoT). London Global University, UCL.

Bhattacherjee, A. (2000). Acceptance of e-commerce services: The case of electronic brokerages. *IEEE Transactions on Systems, Man, and Cybernetics*, *30*(4), 411–420. doi:10.1109/3468.852435

Bruner, G. C. II, & Kumar, A. (2005). Explaining consumer acceptance of handheld internet devices. *Journal of Business Research*, *58*(5), 553–558. doi:10.1016/j.jbusres.2003.08.002

Çelik, H. E., & Yilmaz, V. (2011). Extending the Technology Acceptance Model for Adoption of E-shopping by Consumers in Turkey. *Journal of Electronic Commerce Research*, *12*(2), 152–164.

Chiu, C. M., Wang, E. T., Fang, Y. H., & Huang, H. Y. (2014). Understanding Customers' Repeat Purchase Intentions in B2C e-Commerce: The Roles of Utilitarian Value, Hedonic Value and Perceived Risk. *Information Systems Journal*, *24*(1), 85–114. doi:10.1111/j.1365-2575.2012.00407.x

Compeau, D. R., & Higgins, C. A. (1995). Computer self-efficacy: Development of a measure and initial test. *Management Information Systems Quarterly*, *19*(2), 189–211. doi:10.2307/249688

Costa, P. T., & McCrae, R. R. (1980). Influence of Extraversion and Neuroticism on Subjective Well-Being: Happy and Unhappy People. *Journal of Personality and Social Psychology*, *38*(4), 668–678. doi:10.1037/0022-3514.38.4.668 PMID:7381680

Csíkszentmihályi, M. (1975). *Beyond Boredom and Anxiety: Experiencing Flow in Work and Play*. San Francisco: Jossey-Bass.

Curran, J. M., & Meuter, M. L. (2007). Encouraging existing customers to switch to self-service technologies: Put a little fun in their lives. *Journal of Marketing Theory and Practice*, *15*(4), 283–298. doi:10.2753/MTP1069-6679150401

Dabholkar, P. A. (1996). Consumer evaluations of new technology-based self-service options: An investigation of alternative models of service quality. *International Journal of Research in Marketing*, *13*(1), 29–51. doi:10.1016/0167-8116(95)00027-5

Dabholkar, P. A., & Bagozzi, R. P. (2002). An attitudinal model of technology-based self-service: Moderating effects of consumer traits and situational factors. *Journal of the Academy of Marketing Science*, *30*(3), 184–201. doi:10.1177/0092070302303001

Davis, B., & Pechmann, C. (2013). Introduction to the special issue on transformative consumer research: Developing theory to mobilize efforts that improve consumer and societal well-being. *Journal of Business Research*, *66*(8), 1168–1170. doi:10.1016/j.jbusres.2012.08.008

Deci, E. L., & Ryan, R. M. (2002). *Handbook of self-determination research*. Rochester, NY: University of Rochester Press.

Dennis, C., Brakus, J. J., Gupta, S., & Alamanos, E. (2014). The effect of digital signage on shoppers' behavior: The role of the evoked experience. *Journal of Business Research*, *67*(11), 2250–2257. doi:10.1016/j.jbusres.2014.06.013

Diener, E. (1984). Subjective Well-Being. *Psychological Bulletin*, *95*(3), 542–575. doi:10.1037/0033-2909.95.3.542 PMID:6399758

Dolan, P., Peasgood, T., & White, M. (2008). Do We Really Know What Makes Us Happy? A Review of the Economic Literature on the Factors Associated with Subjective Well-Being. *Journal of Economic Psychology*, *29*(1), 94–122. doi:10.1016/j.joep.2007.09.001

Donaldson, T., & Dunfee, T. W. (1994). Toward a Unified Conception of Business Ethics: Integrative Social Contracts Theory. *Academy of Management Review*, *19*(2), 252–284. doi:10.5465/amr.1994.9410210749

El Hedhli, K., Chebat, J.-C., & Sirgy, J. (2013). Shopping well-being at the mall: Construct, antecedents, and consequences. *Journal of Business Research*, *66*(7), 856–863. doi:10.1016/j.jbusres.2011.06.011

Fishbein, M., & Ajzen, I. (1975). *Belief, Attitude, Intention and Behavior: An Introduction to Theory and Rresearch*. Reading, MA: Addison-Wesley.

Foroudi, P., Gupta, S., Sivarajah, U., & Broderick, A. (2018). Investigating the effects of smart technology on customer dynamics and customer experience. *Computers in Human Behavior*, *80*, 271–282. doi:10.1016/j.chb.2017.11.014

Fox, A. K., & Royne, M. B. (2018). Private information in a social world: Assessing consumers' fear and understanding of social media privacy. *Journal of Marketing Theory and Practice*, *26*(1-2), 72–89. doi:10.1080/10696679.2017.1389242

Freimuth, V. S., & Mettger, W. M. (1990). Is there a Hard to Reach audience? *Public Health Reports*, *105*(3). PMID:2113680

Gao, L., & Bai, X. (2014). A unified perspective on the factors influencing consumer acceptance of internet of things technology. *Asia Pacific Journal of Marketing and Logistics*, *26*(2), 211–231. doi:10.1108/APJML-06-2013-0061

Garaus, M., Wolfsteiner, E., & Wagner, U. (2016). Shoppers' acceptance and perceptions of electronic shelf labels. *Journal of Business Research*, *69*(9), 3687–3692. doi:10.1016/j.jbusres.2016.03.030

Gelderman, C. J., Paul, W. T., & Van Diemen, R. (2011). Choosing self-service technologies or interpersonal services—The impact of situational factors and technology related attitudes. *Journal of Retailing and Consumer Services*, *18*(5), 414–421. doi:10.1016/j.jretconser.2011.06.003

Gilovich, T., Kumar, A., & Jampol, L. (2015). A Wonderful Life: Experiential Consumption and the Pursuit of Happiness. *Journal of Consumer Psychology*, *25*(1), 152–165. doi:10.1016/j.jcps.2014.08.004

Harris, L., & Westin, A. F. (1991). *Harris-Equifax Consumer Privacy Survey 1991*. Atlanta: Equifax Inc.

Hellström, T. (2004). Innovation as social action. *Organization, 11*(5), 631–649. doi:10.1177/1350508404046454

Hengstler, M., Enkel, E., & Duelli, S. (2016). Applied artificial intelligence and trust, the case of autonomous vehicles and medical assistance devices. *Technological Forecasting and Social Change, 105*, 105–120. doi:10.1016/j.techfore.2015.12.014

Hirschman, E., & Holbrook, M. (1982). Hedonic consumption: Emerging concepts, methods and propositions. *Journal of Marketing, 46*(3), 92–101. doi:10.1177/002224298204600314

Hock, C. R. (1962). *The Four Temperaments.* Milwaukee: The Pallotine Fathers, Inc.

Hoffman, D. L. (2012). Internet indispensability, online social capital, and consumer well-being. In Transformative consumer research for personal and collective well-being. New York, NY: Routledge.

Hoffman, D. L., Novak, T. P., & Peralta, M. (1999). Building consumer trust online. *Communications of the Advanced Conferences & Meetings, 42*(4), 80-85.

Hong, W., & Thong, J. (2013). Internet privacy concerns: An integrated conceptualisation and four empirical studies. *MIS Quaterly, 37*(1), 275–298. doi:10.25300/MISQ/2013/37.1.12

Hsee, C. K., Yang, Y., Li, N., & Shen, L. (2009). Wealth, Warmth, and Well-Being: Whether Happiness Is Relative or Absolute Depends on whether It Is about Money, Acquisition, or Consumption. *JMR, Journal of Marketing Research, 46*(3), 396–409. doi:10.1509/jmkr.46.3.396

Immonen, M., & Sintonen, S. (2015). Evolution of technology perceptions over time. *Information Technology & People, 28*(3), 589–606. doi:10.1108/ITP-12-2013-0219

Inman, J., & Nikolova, H. (2016). *Shopper-Facing Retail Technology: An Adoption Decision Calculus.* Academic Press.

Johar, M. G. M., & Awalluddin, J. A. A. (2011). The Role of Technology Acceptance Model in Explaining Effect on e-Commerce Application System. *International Journal of Managing Information Technology, 3*(3), 1–14. doi:10.5121/ijmit.2011.3301

Kaul, S. (2005). Impact of performance and expressiveness value of store service quality on the mediating role of satisfaction. *IIMA*, 3.

Kiesler, C. A., & Kiesler, S. B. (1969). *Conformity*. Menlo Park: Addison-Wesley.

Kim, J., & Forsythe, S. (2008). Adoption of virtual try-on technology for online apparel shopping. *Journal of Interactive Marketing, 22*(2), 45–59. doi:10.1002/dir.20113

Kim, W., Smolders, A., Brengman, M., Luyten, K., & Schöning, J. (2017). The path-to-purchase is paved with digital opportunities: An inventory of shopper-oriented retail technologies. *Technological Forecasting and Social Change, Elsevier, 124*(C), 228–242. doi:10.1016/j.techfore.2016.11.023

Kotler, P., Kartajata, H., & Setiawan, I. (2017). Marketing 4.0 – Moving from traditional to digital. Academic Press.

Koufaris, M. (2002). Applying the technology acceptance model and flow theory to online consumer behavior. *Information Systems Research, 13*(2), 205–223. doi:10.1287/isre.13.2.205.83

Kuisma, T., Laukkanen, T., & Hiltunen, M. (2007). Mapping the reasons for resistance to Internet banking: A means-end approach. *International Journal of Information Management, 27*(2), 75–85. doi:10.1016/j.ijinfomgt.2006.08.006

Kulviwat, S., Bruner, G. C. II, Kumar, A., Nasco, S. A., & Clark, T. (2007). Toward a unified theory of consumer acceptance of technology. *Psychology and Marketing, 24*(12), 1059–1084. doi:10.1002/mar.20196

Laroche, M., & Sadokierski, R. W. (1994). Role of confidence in a multi-brand model of intentions for a high involvement service. *Journal of Business Research, 29*(1), 1–12. doi:10.1016/0148-2963(94)90022-1

Laukkanen, T. (2016). Consumer adoption versus rejection decisions in seemingly similar service innovations: The case of the Internet and mobile banking. *Journal of Business Research, 69*(7), 2432–2439. doi:10.1016/j.jbusres.2016.01.013

Lee, I., & Lee, K. (2015). The Internet of Things (IoT): Applications, investments, and challenges for enterprises. *Business Horizons, 58*(4), 431–440. doi:10.1016/j.bushor.2015.03.008

Levinas, E. (1997). *Time and the other* (R. Cohen, Trans.). Pittsburgh: Duquesne University Press.

Malhotra, N. K., Kim, S. S., & Agarwal, J. (2004). Internet Users' Information Privacy Concerns (Iuipc): The Construct, the Scale, and a Causal Model. *Information Systems Research, 15*(4), 336–355. doi:10.1287/isre.1040.0032

Manyika, J., Chui, M., Bughin, J., Dobbs, R., Bisson, P., & Marrs, A. (2013). *Disruptive technologies: Advances that will transform life, business, and the global economy*. McKinsey Global Institute.

Mill, J. S. (1998). Utilitarianism (R. Crisp, Ed.). Oxford: Oxford University Press.

Mill, J. S. (2012). Utilitarianism. Spark Notes Editors.

Milne, G., & Culnan, M. (2004). Strategies for Reducing Online Privacy Risks: Why Consumers Read (Or Don't Read) Online Privacy Notices. *Journal of Interactive Marketing, 18*(3), 15–29. doi:10.1002/dir.20009

Mittal, V., & Kamakura, W. (2001). Satisfaction, repurchase intent, and repurchase behavior: Investigating the moderating effect of customer characteristics. *JMR, Journal of Marketing Research, 38*(1), 131–142. doi:10.1509/jmkr.38.1.131.18832

Montreuil, B., Ballot, E., & Fontane, F. (2012). An Open Logistics Interconnection Model for the Physical Internet. *Information Control Problems in Manufacturing, 14*(1), 327–332. doi:10.3182/20120523-3-RO-2023.00385

Moore, G. C., & Benbasat, I. (1991). Development of an instrument to measure the perceptions of adopting an information technology innovation. *Information Systems Research, 2*(3), 173–191. doi:10.1287/isre.2.3.192

Naci, H., & Ioannidis, J. P. A. (2015). Evaluation of Wellness Determinants and Interventions by Citizen Scientists. *Journal of the American Medical Association*, *314*(2), 121. doi:10.1001/jama.2015.6160 PMID:26068643

Ngo, L. V., & O'Cass, A. (2013). Innovation and business success: The mediating role of customer participation. *Journal of Business Research*, *66*(8), 1134–1142. doi:10.1016/j.jbusres.2012.03.009

Novak, T. P., Hoffman, D. L., & Young, F. (2000). Measuring the Customer Experience in Online Environments: A Structural Modeling Approach. *Marketing Science*, *19*(1), 22–44. doi:10.1287/mksc.19.1.22.15184

Oh, H., Fiore, A. M., & Jeoung, M. (2007). Measuring experience economy concepts: Tourism applications. *Journal of Travel Research*, *46*(2), 119–132. doi:10.1177/0047287507304039

Pantano, E., & Timmermans, H. (2014). What is smart for retailing? *Procedia Environmental Sciences*, *22*, 101–107. doi:10.1016/j.proenv.2014.11.010

Perugini, M., & Bagozzi, R. (2001). The role of desires and anticipated emotions in goal directed behaviours: Broadening and deepening the theory of planned behaviour. *British Journal of Social Psychology*, *40*(1), 79–98. doi:10.1348/014466601164704 PMID:11329835

Pfeffer, J. (1981). *Power in organizations*. Marshfield: Pitman.

Phelps, J. E., D'Souza, G., & Nowak, G. J. (2001). Antecedents and consequences of consumer privacy concerns: An empirical investigation. *Journal of Interactive Marketing*, *15*(4), 2–17. doi:10.1002/dir.1019

Phelps, J. E., Nowak, G. J., & Ferrell, E. (2000). Privacy concerns and consumer willingness to provide personal information. *Journal of Public Policy & Marketing*, *19*(1), 27–41. doi:10.1509/jppm.19.1.27.16941

Remondes, J., & Afonso, C. (2018). *An overview of main IoT trends applied to business and marketing. In Smart Marketing With the Internet of Things*. doi:10.4018/978-1-5225-5763-0

Renko, S., & Druzijanic, M. (2014). Perceived usefulness of innovative technology in retailing: Consumers' and retailers' point of view. *Journal of Retailing and Consumer Services*, *21*(5), 836–843. doi:10.1016/j.jretconser.2014.02.015

Research and Markets. (2015). *Retail IoT Market Growth and Forecast 2015 to 2020*. Accessed from http://www.marketsandmarketsblog.com/retail-iot-market.html

Rogers, E. M. (1983). *Diffusion of Innovations*. New York: The Free Press.

Roy, S. K., Balaji, M. S., Sadeque, S., Nguyen, B., & Melewar, T. C. (2016). Constituents and consequences of smart customer experience in retailing. *Technological Forecasting and Social Change*.

Ryan, R. M., & Deci, E. L. (2001). On Happiness and Human Potentials: A Review of Research on Hedonic and Eudaimonic Well-Being. *Annual Review of Psychology*, *52*(1), 141–166. doi:10.1146/annurev.psych.52.1.141 PMID:11148302

Seligman, M. E. P. (2011). *Flourish: A Visionary New Understanding of Happiness and Well-being*. New York: The Free Press.

Sherman, E., Schiffman, L.G., & Mathur, A. (2001The Influence of Gender on the New Age Elderly's Consumption Orientations. *Psychology and Marketing*, *18*(10), 1073–1089. doi:10.1002/mar.1044

Shieh, L.-F., Chang, T.-H., Fu, H.-P., Lin, S.-W., & Chen, Y.-Y. (2013). Analyzing the factors that affect the adoption of mobile services in Taiwan. *Technological Forecasting and Social Change*, *87*, 80–88. doi:10.1016/j.techfore.2013.11.004

Shin, D. (2010). The effects of trust, security & privacy in social networking: A security-based approach to understand the pattern of adoption. *Interacting with Computers*, *22*(5), 428–438. doi:10.1016/j.intcom.2010.05.001

Sivarajah, U., Irani, Z., & Weerakkody, V. (2015). Evaluating the use and impact of Web 2.0 technologies in local government. *Government Information Quarterly*, *32*(4), 473–487. doi:10.1016/j.giq.2015.06.004

Su, R., Tay, L., & Diener, E. (2014). The Development and Validation of the Comprehensive Inventory of Thriving (CIT) and the Brief Inventory of Thriving (BIT). *Applied Psychology. Health and Well-Being*, *6*(3), 25171. doi:10.1111/aphw.12027 PMID:24919454

Suo, H., Wan, J., Zou, C., & Liu, J. (2012). Security in the Internet of Things: A Review. *Proceedings of the International Conference on Computer Science and Electronics Engineering*, 648-652. 10.1109/ICCSEE.2012.373

Talke, K., & Heidenreich, S. (2014). How to overcome pro-change bias: Incorporating passive and active innovation resistance in innovation decision models. *Journal of Product Innovation Management*, *31*(5), 894–907. doi:10.1111/jpim.12130

Tauber, E. M. (1972). Why do people shop? *Journal of Marketing*, *36*, 46–49.

Teng, L., & Laroche, M. (2007). Building and testing models of consumer purchase intention in competitive and multicultural environments. *Journal of Business Research*, *60*(3), 260–268. doi:10.1016/j.jbusres.2006.09.028

Toch, E., Wang, Y., & Cranor, L.F. (2012). Personalization and privacy: a survey of privacy risks and remedies in personalization-based systems. *Science & Business Media*, 203-220.

Turow, J., Hennessy, M., & Bleakley, A. (2008). Consumers' Understanding of Privacy Rules in the Marketplace. *The Journal of Consumer Affairs*, *42*(3), 411–424. doi:10.1111/j.1745-6606.2008.00116.x

Van Boven, L., & Gilovich, T. (2003). To Do or to Have? that Is the Question. *Journal of Personality and Social Psychology*, *85*(6), 1193–1202. doi:10.1037/0022-3514.85.6.1193 PMID:14674824

Van der Heijden, H. (2004). User acceptance of hedonic information systems. *Management Information Systems Quarterly*, *28*(4), 695–704. doi:10.2307/25148660

Van der Hoven, E. (2013). *Fact sheet- Ethics Subgroup IoT-Version 4.01*. Delft University of Technology Chair Ethics Subgroup IoT Expert Group.

Venkatesh, V., & Bala, H. (2008). Technology acceptance model 3 and a research agenda on interventions. *Decision Sciences*, *39*(2), 273–315. doi:10.1111/j.1540-5915.2008.00192.x

Venkatesh, V., & Davis, F. D. (2000). A theoretical extension of the technology acceptance model: Four longitudinal field studies. *Management Science*, *46*(2), 186–204. doi:10.1287/mnsc.46.2.186.11926

Verhoef, P. C., Lemon, K. N., Parasuraman, A., Roggeveen, A., Tsiros, M., & Schlesinger, L. A. (2009). Customer Experience Creation: Determinants, Dynamics and Management Strategies. *Journal of Retailing*, *85*(1), 31–41. doi:10.1016/j.jretai.2008.11.001

Verhoef, P. C., Stephen, A. T., Kannan, P. K., Luo, X., Abhishek, V., Andrews, M., ... Zhang, Y. (2017). Consumer connectivity in a complex, technology-enabled, and mobile-oriented world with smart products. *Journal of Interactive Marketing*, *40*, 1–8. doi:10.1016/j.intmar.2017.06.001

Wakefield, K. L., & Baker, J. (1998). Excitement at the mall: Determinants and effects on shopping response. *Journal of Retailing*, *74*(4), 515–540. doi:10.1016/S0022-4359(99)80106-7

Wang, C. (2017). Consumer acceptance of self-service technologies. *International Journal of Market Research*, *59*(6), 787–802. doi:10.2501/IJMR-2017-048

Weijters, B., Rangarajan, D., Falk, T., & Schillewaert, N. (2007). Determinants and outcomes of customers' use of self-service technology in a retail setting. *Journal of Service Research*, *10*(1), 3–21. doi:10.1177/1094670507302990

Westin, A. (1967). *Privacy and Freedom*. New York: Atheneum.

Wüenderlich, N. V., Heinonen, K., Ostrom, A. L., Patricio, L., Sousa, R., Voss, C., & Lemmink, J. G. A. M. (2015). Futurizing smart service: Implications for service researchers and managers. *Journal of Services Marketing*, *29*(6/7), 442–447. doi:10.1108/JSM-01-2015-0040

Xu, H., Luo, X., Carroll, J. M., & Rosson, M. B. (2011). The Personalization Privacy Paradox: An Exploratory Study of Decision Making Process for Location-Aware Marketing. *Decision Support Systems*, *51*(1), 42–52. doi:10.1016/j.dss.2010.11.017

KEY TERMS AND DEFINITIONS

Connected Consumer: Consumer connected to Internet networks through smartphones or connected devices, informed in real time about products and services, with an influence on social networks, representing an opportunity as well as a threat for companies.

Consumer Well-Being: Consumers' perceptions of how smart retail stores influence their satisfaction and quality of purchase experience.

Empowered Personality: People more or less predisposed to get, feel, and use senses of power over themselves, other people, companies, or situations.

Privacy Concerns: To which extent consumers are concerned about the collection, storage and use of their personal information.

Smart Retail Store: Interactive retailing systems which deliver services for consumers and employees through networks of smart devices.

Smart Retailing: The way of using new technologies in retailing strategies.

Well-Being Personality: People more or less predisposed to feel, accept and share feelings of hedonism.

Chapter 8
Value Proposition of Network Companies Providing Restaurant Services in Russia:
Analysis and Evaluation

Elizaveta Fainshtein
https://orcid.org/0000-0002-6503-7248
National Research University Higher School of Economics, Russia

Elena Serova
https://orcid.org/0000-0002-9510-3496
National Research University Higher School of Economics, Russia

ABSTRACT

The purpose of the chapter is to recognize how customers perceive the value proposition content of network companies providing restaurant services. This is theoretical and empirical research in equal measure. The chapter presents the results of the restaurants value proposition study in Saint Petersburg (Russia) according to industry data and identifies the target audience key needs and industry characteristics in the market, semantic core formation, and clustering in order to identify the main criteria affecting the value proposition formation. The study was conducted among 16 chain restaurant holdings located in St. Petersburg, using statistical data based on the marketing statistical tool Google KeyWord Planner analytic database. The results made it possible to highlight key criteria of the value proposition by which consumers make their choice. This approach will allow standardizing decision-making systems on the possibility of identifying the innovative potential of the company's transition to a qualitatively new level of service and use of production resources.

DOI: 10.4018/978-1-7998-3115-0.ch008

Copyright © 2020, IGI Global. Copying or distributing in print or electronic forms without written permission of IGI Global is prohibited.

INTRODUCTION

Innovation management, value proposition development and competitive strategy were classified as three main elements of the company's marketing system. Although a huge number of different research papers provided empirical support for the marketing strategy, most of them were based on market analysis and focused on innovative ways of presenting a company's product, enhancing the competitive advantage in the industry (Foss & Saebi, 2018). In the context of business modeling theory, researchers (e.g. Karmarkar & Pitbladdo, 1995; Morris et al., 2005; Chesbrough, 2010; Teece, 2018; Geissdoerfer et al., 2018) suggest that the simultaneous construction of the interrelated development of all three elements (innovation management, value proposition development and competitive strategy) would provide a list of competitive advantages. One of the recent streams of marketing research is related to the value proposition, especially in conditions of fierce competition and an unstable economic situation. For these firms the formation of a company's value proposition and innovative management have become hot topics. Currently, the development of innovative tools has developed significantly because of their relevance and because they can be implemented among companies immediately at the strategic level within the company, not only in the external marketing policy.

For service providers, innovation in business models is thought to be more profitable than selective innovation in products or processes (Arora & Singer, 2006; Sorescu et al., 2011). Sustainable business models based on a strategically sound value proposition can have the additional advantage of reducing risks and increasing sustainability in the long run (Clinton & Whisnant, 2019), creating opportunities for creating a competitive value proposition and increasing consumer demand (e.g. Chkoniya & Mateus, 2019; Fjeldstad & Snow, 2018, Snihur & Wiklund, 2019). The Fjedstad and Snow (2018) approach is based on five key elements (customers, value proposition, offer of services, value creation mechanisms and value assignment mechanisms), one of which is value proposition. This position is fully consistent with this study, which shows that a clear definition of the business model makes it possible to understand what to focus on when building a strategy and shaping a service with a customer-oriented approach and provides consistent guidance for managers. To realize these benefits, organizations are increasingly interested in implementing sustainable solutions.

However, many strategic innovations in management systems fail, making mistakes in forming a value proposition in the business model (Bocken et al., 2014; Chesbrough, 2007). This has serious managerial and economic implications for companies, as well as consumer perceptions of a company's brand (McGrath, 2010). In other words, most organizations do not have clearly focused strategies. They compile long lists of desired results, completely ignoring the need to focus on and clearly coordinate resources (Rumelt, 2012). All this leads to significant delays in making sustainable decisions internally regarding further business planning (Mitchell and Bruckner, 2004; Bocken et al., 2014). Despite the importance of these administrative problems, the causes of failure have a knowledge gap that needs to be eliminated.

The main research question is what the criteria are for choosing a company providing services, from the point of view of consumers, for the formation of an optimal value proposition. The answer to this question fills the gap in research related to the formation of value propositions and the basis of the enterprise strategy, considered from the perspective of consumer choice. In this chapter, the strategic choice is analyzed from the point of view of the value proposition and key criteria by which the consumers make their choice using the example of a chain of restaurants in St. Petersburg (Russia).

The central problem of the study is the lack of optimal developments for evaluating the value proposition of a chain of companies in the market for the provision of services. The knowledge gap lies in the quantitative assessment of the results of using a company's marketing capabilities to create a competitive value proposition demanded by the consumer. The hypothesis of the study is based on the assumption that in a competitive environment, a company should analyze the key requests of potential consumers and create an optimal value proposition based on this. Since the demand for competitive advantages in the face of growing competition is only beginning to grow, the main task of the study is to formulate a way to assess the creation of an optimal value proposition in the market for the provision of services, based on key consumer requests by the marketing innovation mechanism, for its practical application in business and a confirmation of the hypothesis.

In investigating this problem, the authors conducted an empirical study on the value proposition of a sustainable business model and determined which factors are significant for the business and for the consumers, and the key needs of the target audience were identified. The industry features and product offerings of companies in the market, the formation and clustering of the semantic core to identify the main criteria affecting the formation of the value proposition of a restaurant chain in St. Petersburg by industry data were also considered. This chapter suggests that these and similar issues be addressed by developing the suggested research programs and the proposed working calculations presented in the study.

The objective is to define the value proposition of a chain restaurant business based on high frequency data that is made available by Google KeyWord Planner marketing tool for the restaurant market with the subsequent possibility of using this methodology for similar and competing businesses. In other words, this chapter recognizes how customers perceive the content of the value proposition of companies providing restaurant services. In this vein, signals coming from consumers demand determined which factors are significant for the business value proposition. The research provides an understanding of how to transform customer expectations into a competitive advantage for companies in the service market. The case study of the restaurant chain market in St. Petersburg, becomes this study's focus in order to investigate the interrelationship between customer demand and the factors which effect the formation of the value proposition.

This is theoretical and empirical research in equal measure. The study sample contained 1,000 keywords of the semantic core of keywords among popular customers online query results and the optimization options, which allowed us to analyze the relationship between the elements of the service format and the value proposition of restaurant chains. The study was conducted using statistical data based on the marketing statistical tool Google KeyWord Planner analytic database. The methodology of this research is based on comparative analysis and cluster analysis, the case study, statistical data collection, analyzing the semantic core and CHAID (Chi-square Automatic Interaction Detector) analysis. Both content and statistical analysis are used in this research.

A wide range of factors influenced chain companies' value proposition was found. That is to say, reviews and ratings of visitors; value for money; delicious food, a variety of types of cuisine and the specifics of dishes; special offers; service; promotions and discounts; geographic location; and the brand that generated the targeted search were the most distinguishing characteristics identifying customers who are focused on the target purchase. In this sense, the companies that serve such customers and take into account the maximum number of identified demand factors, analyzed by CHAID analysis and adjust their strategies and value propositions to have a direct impact and have a competitive advantage over other companies. As a confirmation of the above thesis, this trend can be seen in chain restaurant companies, where there is a representative sample due to the larger volume of business and, as a result, greater provision of services and it is easier to see pronounced trends in customer preferences among restaurant chains.

The results of the study made it possible to highlight the key criteria of the value propositions by which consumers make their choice. This approach allow the standardization of the decision-making system to identify the innovative potential of the company's transition to a qualitatively new level of the service delivery and the use of production resources.

Due to the relatively unexplored nature of the phenomenon, this study opted for a unique approach to the analysis of the interrelationship between customer demand and the factors, which effect the formation of the value proposition in the restaurant chain industry.

This research contributes to the scientific literature on strategic management and restaurant chains, and recognizes how consumers perceive the services offered, in particular (1) what importance they attach to the elements of a value proposition to create a competitive advantage, (2) which parameters of service customers make choices based on, and (3) what elements should the company bear in mind in the context of strategic choice in the broad sense.

The structure of the chapter is as follows. In section 2, significant research gaps are identified and research questions are formulated based on the literature review. Section 3 presents the method used to organize the case studies. Section 4 presents the results and discussion. There are conclusions and implications for future research in section 5.

BACKGROUND

The value chain is an effective tool for strategic analysis giving a detailed review of the company's activities for the formation of strategic planning trends. Initially, the concept of creating a chain of consumer value was used to determine competitive advantages when using an analysis of the company's activities differentiated into segments. (Porter & Siggelkow, 2008).

This research examines the innovation of value propositions based on a mind-based approach. The literature review considers the approach of Okasio (1997) in the context of the formation of an innovative value proposition of a company that operates a restaurant chain. The main premise of the mind-based approach is that the strategic sustainability of the company in the long run is the result of decisions made regarding the structure of the company's business model. Since the basis of business modeling is the formation of a value proposition, the main focus of the work is to analyze the value proposition of a restaurant chain. In addition, management decisions at its core consist of attention to the specific issues of the value proposition and responses to consumer requests. Attention is paid to various issues depending on the context of the firm, its brand, structure, resources and internal interactions, which are influenced by consumer preferences (Ocasio, 1997). The main focus of this study is on this model, since it focuses on the analysis of the elements of a value proposition, namely, how to get out of direct competition and what criteria should be emphasized in order to create a unique competitive promotion in the market (Kim & Mauborgne, 1997).

Create a value proposition and strategic innovation brings a competitive advantage and creates new ways to form a competitive advantage (Serova & Bagiev, 2012; Matthyssens et al., 2008; Frow & Payne 2011). Kim & Mauborgne (1999) believe that the company's strategic thinking is strongly focused on overtaking competitors and comparing strategic actions with actions in the market. Consequently, direct competition is exhausting and leads to a reactive approach characterized by imitation rather than innovation. Major competitive advantages can be achieved by breaking away from traditional strategic logic and by adopting innovative thinking (Kim & Mauborgne, 1999; Kim & Mauborgne, 2005). This view is reproduced in the literature on both strategic and innovative value propositions, which are almost identical concepts.

From a broader perspective, a conception that developing further value propositions for customers can be found in different areas, such as market positioning, outsourcing, sales channels as distribution, and business-modeling (Serova & Krichevsky, 2015). Norman & Ramirez (1993) took the value chain as a level of analysis, noting the importance of creating value together with different players: suppliers, business partners and customers. This view is reflected in the later literature on innovation in the field of values by Gummesson (2010), emphasizing the possibility of joint value creation as part of creating a value proposition for companies.

From an analysis of the literature on marketing innovations and business modeling, it is possible to conclude that there are no solutions to issues such as the selection of key processes and resources for implementing marketing innovations when they are used specifically for chain businesses or the development and monitoring of marketing innovation in forming value propositions. According to the value chain analysis presented by many authors (e.g. Porter, 2019; Prahalad, 2004; Lindič & Marques da Silva, 2011; Geissdoerfer et al., 2016; Johnson, 2008; Trimi et al., 2012; Hernandez & Pedersen, 2017; Li, 2018) the importance of forming the company's value proposition is due to the growing globalization and convergence of industry and the complex environment that forces companies to enter new markets. New markets typically involve new customers, competitors, stakeholders, business knowledge and skills (Kafentzis et al., 2004). Since a market participant may not need to develop them internally, collaborating with other firms, the company must have a stable management structure.

The competitiveness of a value proposition can be defined as its ability to offer a service that meets the competitive requirements of the consumer in the required quantity, at the right time, and under the most favorable conditions (Pynnönen et al., 2012; Tukker & van den Berg, 2017). Consequently, the competitiveness of a value proposition is a property that characterizes its unique ability to provide an appropriate level of quality unique products in comparison with the best similar products on the market in which the consumer is interested. The degree of compliance with the technical, technological, organizational and other characteristics that the business offers in the services market, meeting the requirements of the consumer, which determine the attractiveness of the goods and services in the market, identifies the segments of this market that are accessible to the company and prevents the redistribution of this market in favor of other players.

Miles and Snow (1978) argue that various corporate strategies come from which companies make decisions on 3 main problems: entrepreneurial (how a company should manage its market share), development and management problem (how a company should implement its solution to an entrepreneurial problem) and an administrative problem (how should a company structure itself to manage the implementation of solutions to the first 2 problems). This statement hurts that the success of a company is ultimately determined not by a specific strategic orientation, but by formulating and maintaining a systematic strategy that takes into account the environment, technology and structure of the company.

As competition in the service markets increased and due to the lack of the internal organization flexibility and strategy of the company, the value proposition role gradually increased (Miles & Snow, 1986). Thus, the main directions of strategy formation are developed on the basis of determining the preferences of potential customers, which are taken into account when creating a value proposition. In the last decade, there has been a trend of increasing competition on a global scale. This has led organizations around the world to start changing their strategies. They began to move away from a centralized multi-level hierarchy and move on to more flexible structures, reminiscent of networks rather than traditional management pyramids. A network business is a collection of companies or specialized units whose activities are coordinated by market mechanisms instead of team methods. Networks or domestic markets involve creating a market economy within the company and a special approach to strategy development. The transfer of market relations, shifting the emphasis of development to the internal environment of companies, brought to life the considered type of structure - network organizations in the field of restaurant services, in which the customer-oriented approach is of fundamental importance, taking into account key criteria of current demand at a particular moment and timely adapting the company's value proposition for maintaining its competitiveness.

At present, during a period of active restructuring of economic systems and reforming business processes, many authors raise the question of assessing the innovative potential of marketing as a tool for the competitive advantage of a company in a competitive environment (Burnett, 1998). Interaction with a higher technical level of knowledge in the field of innovation has already led to a detailed analysis and development of new implementation processes in companies. As part of the study, they can be unified, generalized and used as an effective tool for transforming business processes.

Modern market encourages companies to achieve success by focusing on the analytical study of strategic management, because this can strengthen their position in the industry and have a constant stable income. In addition, enterprises that use analytical tools to form a value proposition have the opportunity to significantly increase brand sustainability and achieve the desired growth of the company under favorable business conditions in the restaurant market in Russia. The development of the direction opens up opportunities for better use of the theoretical knowledge gained, find a practical application for them and form common management standards when introducing and applying a value proposition.

The research discusses one of the key methods for creating a sustainable competitive advantage optimizing the company's business processes, and substantiates the need to introduce analytics regarding the criteria of a value proposition taking into account the consumer impact on the Russian restaurant market, as modern methods for assessing, planning and creating competitive strategies are attracting more attention. In the modern world, enterprises seeking a competitive advantage actively apply strategic business management tools in the current period and for forecasting and planning future actions. Strategies for analyzing the value proposition of business models are especially in demand among large chain companies, since business modeling provides arguments for decision-making in companies that are strategic and operational.

MAIN FOCUS OF THE CHAPTER

The methodology of this research is based on comparative analysis and cluster analysis, a case study, statistical data collection, analyzing the semantic core and CHAID analysis.

Cluster Analysis (CA) is a convenient way to identify homogeneous groups of objects. Groups of similar objects are called clusters. Objects in a particular cluster have similar characteristics but differ from objects that do not belong to this group. The purpose of CA is to identify a number of objects that are similar among themselves in a certain set of parameters (cluster variables). After selecting such variables, it is necessary to select a clustering procedure to form groups of objects.

There are many different clustering procedures (Everitt, 2011), but the practical difference is the differentiation between hierarchical methods and centroid-based clustering (primarily, the k-means clustering): hierarchical clustering and k-means clustering.

Each of these procedures has its own approach to grouping the most similar objects into clusters. Agglomerative procedures are probably the most widely used of the hierarchical methods. They produce a series of partitions of the data: the first consists of *n* single member 'clusters'; the last consists of a single group containing all *n* individuals. The basic operation of all such methods is similar, and will be illustrated for two specific examples, single linkage and centroid linkage. At each stage the methods fuse individuals or groups of individuals which are closest (or most similar). Differences between the methods arise because of the different ways of defining distance (or similarity) between an individual and a group containing several individuals, or between two groups of individuals (Everitt, 2011).

The k-means clustering method forms exactly *k* different clusters located at the greatest possible distances from each other. Its essence lies in the fact that the classification process begins with the assignment of some initial conditions (for example, the number of clusters being formed or the threshold for the classification process). As in hierarchical cluster analysis, in iterative methods there is the problem of determining the number of clusters. In general, their number may not be known. Not all iterative methods require the initial specification the number of clusters. But for the final decision about structure of set under study, several algorithms can be tried by changing either the number of clusters formed or the established proximity threshold for combining objects into clusters. Then the best partition can be chosen.

The data include 1,000 results of keywords among popular queries using statistics from the Google KeyWord Planner analytic database 02.16.2016 - 02.16.2019 (Table 1), which allows to analyze the relationship between the elements of the service format and the value proposition of restaurants and to conduct the cluster analysis. The study formed keywords semantic core and the optimization options, based on synonyms, "restaurant", "restaurants" and "restaurant chain". The Google search engine finds related words by keyword, as well as optimization options - similar keywords in related topic to popular requests from the selected industry.

During the study, statistical data collection methods were used, by keywords, Google KeyWord Planner. St. Petersburg was chosen as the target location, where, according to official Google data from Google KeyWord Planner marketing tool, the coverage is 5,850,000 registered users. The analysis was based on the search for keywords in Russian.

Table 1. Descriptive statistics by keywords, related topic to popular requests of St. Petersburg restaurant industry based on the Google KeyWord Planner analytical database, 2016-2019

Average monthly requests	Level of competition			Total
	High	Medium	Low	
10 - 100	48	123	345	516
100 - 1 000	8	42	326	376
1 000 - 10 000	1	11	82	94
10 000 - 100 000	1	1	12	14
Total	58	177	765	1000

Duplicate queries were excluded from the final analysis of keywords. Based on the data obtained, groups of the average number of requests per month were formed, as well as the level of competition, showing the ratio of the number of advertisers among restaurant companies using a specific keyword from the selection to the total number of keywords in Google, which allowed the sorting of the data by their frequency and the preparation of statistical information for cluster analysis.

Empirical quantitative research was chosen because it allows to verify the applicability of the methodology by analyzing the semantic core and CHAID analysis using the example of the format of the service industry of the chain restaurant industry in St. Petersburg (Table 2, 3, 4, 5). Both methods were based on statistical information from the Google KeyWord Planner analytic database. This keyword planner tool was created specifically to optimize search engine marketing and to obtain the most accurate quantitative data on the goods and services requested by consumers. As a result, a 4-factor model of the decision tree was formed, based on the chi-square method with 7 variables. During the analysis and the formation of the semantic core, the keywords of the queries of users of the Google search system were compared to the criteria for the service format of the restaurant industry in St. Petersburg.

Figure 1.

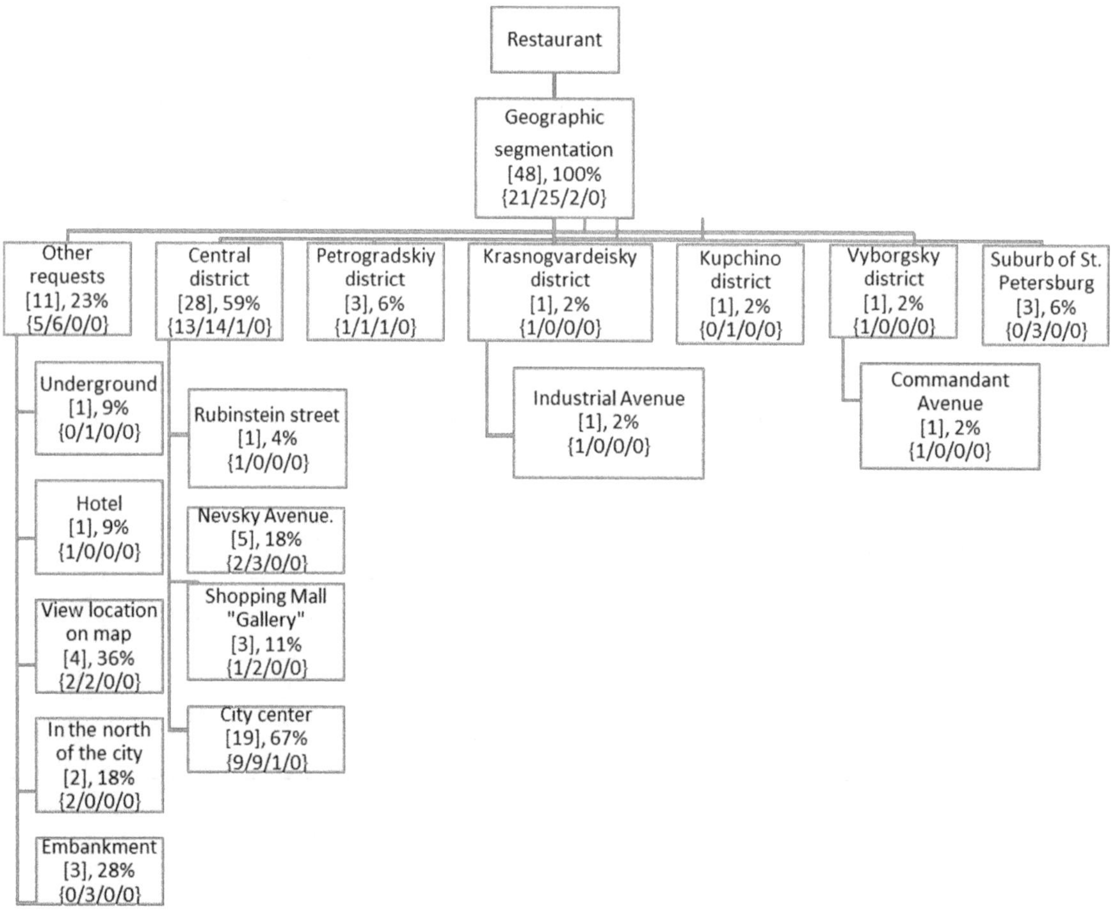

Google's keyword planner tools provide enhanced public access to statistics, including the ability to track not only the average number of queries per month, but also the level of competition, unlike other search engines. The open system of the keyword planner tool, based on the statistics of user requests from the Google search engine, allows you to objectively analyze relevant data on the most popular services related to the restaurant business in St. Petersburg and, as a result, form a semantic core.

Table 2. CHAID analysis. Semantic core clustering: geographic segmentation

Categories of average monthly searches	Number of requests
10-100	21
100-1000	25
1000-10000	2
10000-100000	0
Total	48
100% - the share of the target group of keywords in the entire sample of this segment; (48) – the size of the target group of keywords in the segmentation; {21/25/2/0} – the number of requests in accordance with the categories of the average number of requests per month.	

Table 3. CHAID analysis. Semantic core clustering: psychographic segmentation

Categories of average monthly searches	Number of requests
10-100	285
100-1000	206
1000-10000	53
10000-100000	7
Total	551
100% - the share of the target group of keywords in the entire sample of this segment; (551) - the size of the target group of keywords in the segmentation; {285/210/49/7} - the number of requests in accordance with the categories of the average number of requests per month.	

Table 4. CHAID analysis. Semantic core clustering: behavioral segmentation

Categories of average monthly searches	Number of requests
10-100	152
100-1000	95
1000-10000	23
10000-100000	4
Total	274
100% - the share of the target group of keywords in the entire sample of this segment; (274) - the size of the target group of keywords in the segmentation; {152/95/23/4} - the number of requests in accordance with the categories of the average number of requests per month.	

Table 5. CHAID analysis. Semantic core clustering: social demographic segmentation

Categories of average monthly searches	Number of requests
10-100	58
100-1000	46
1000-10000	20
10000-100000	3
Total	127
100% - the share of the target group of keywords in the entire sample of this segment; (127) - the size of the target group of keywords in the segmentation; {58/46/20/3} - the number of requests in accordance with the categories of the average number of requests per month.	

Figure 2.

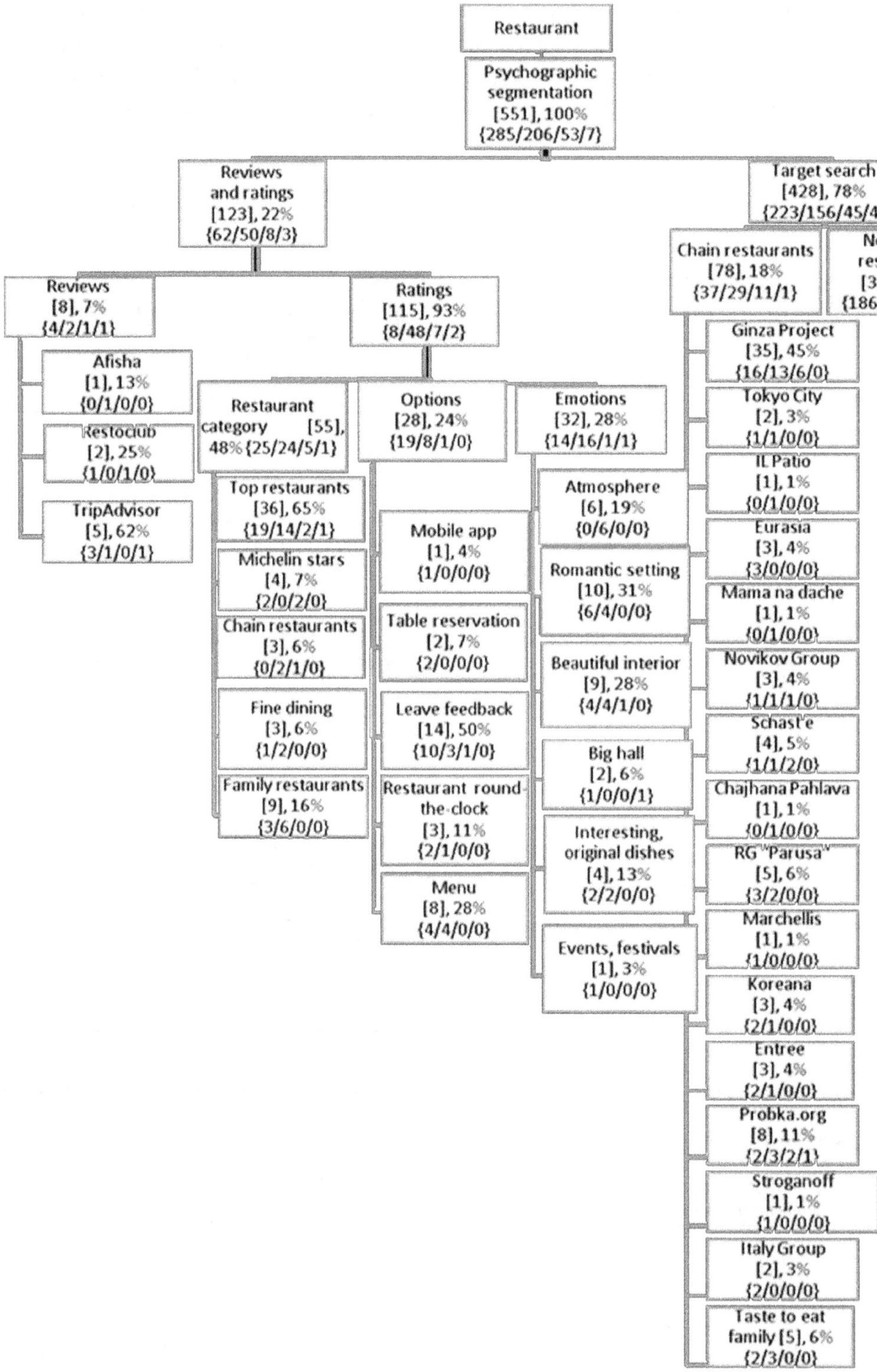
Restaurant
Psychographic segmentation [551], 100% {285/206/53/7}
Reviews and ratings [123], 22% {62/50/8/3}
Target search [428], 78% {223/156/45/4}
Reviews [8], 7% {4/2/1/1}
Ratings [115], 93% {8/48/7/2}
Chain restaurants [78], 18% {37/29/11/1}
Non-chain restaurants [350], 82% {186/127/34/3}
Afisha [1], 13% {0/1/0/0}
Restoclub [2], 25% {1/0/1/0}
TripAdvisor [5], 62% {3/1/0/1}
Restaurant category [55], 48% {25/24/5/1}
Options [28], 24% {19/8/1/0}
Emotions [32], 28% {14/16/1/1}
Top restaurants [36], 65% {19/14/2/1}
Michelin stars [4], 7% {2/0/2/0}
Chain restaurants [3], 6% {0/2/1/0}
Fine dining [3], 6% {1/2/0/0}
Family restaurants [9], 16% {3/6/0/0}
Mobile app [1], 4% {1/0/0/0}
Table reservation [2], 7% {2/0/0/0}
Leave feedback [14], 50% {10/3/1/0}
Restaurant round-the-clock [3], 11% {2/1/0/0}
Menu [8], 28% {4/4/0/0}
Atmosphere [6], 19% {0/6/0/0}
Romantic setting [10], 31% {6/4/0/0}
Beautiful interior [9], 28% {4/4/1/0}
Big hall [2], 6% {1/0/0/1}
Interesting, original dishes [4], 13% {2/2/0/0}
Events, festivals [1], 3% {1/0/0/0}
Ginza Project [35], 45% {16/13/6/0}
Tokyo City [2], 3% {1/1/0/0}
IL Patio [1], 1% {0/1/0/0}
Eurasia [3], 4% {3/0/0/0}
Mama na dache [1], 1% {0/1/0/0}
Novikov Group [3], 4% {1/1/1/0}
Schast'e [4], 5% {1/1/2/0}
Chajhana Pahlava [1], 1% {0/1/0/0}
RG "Parusa" [5], 6% {3/2/0/0}
Marchellis [1], 1% {1/0/0/0}
Koreana [3], 4% {2/1/0/0}
Entree [3], 4% {2/1/0/0}
Probka.org [8], 11% {2/3/2/1}
Stroganoff [1], 1% {1/0/0/0}
Italy Group [2], 3% {2/0/0/0}
Taste to eat family [5], 6% {2/3/0/0}

Figure 3.

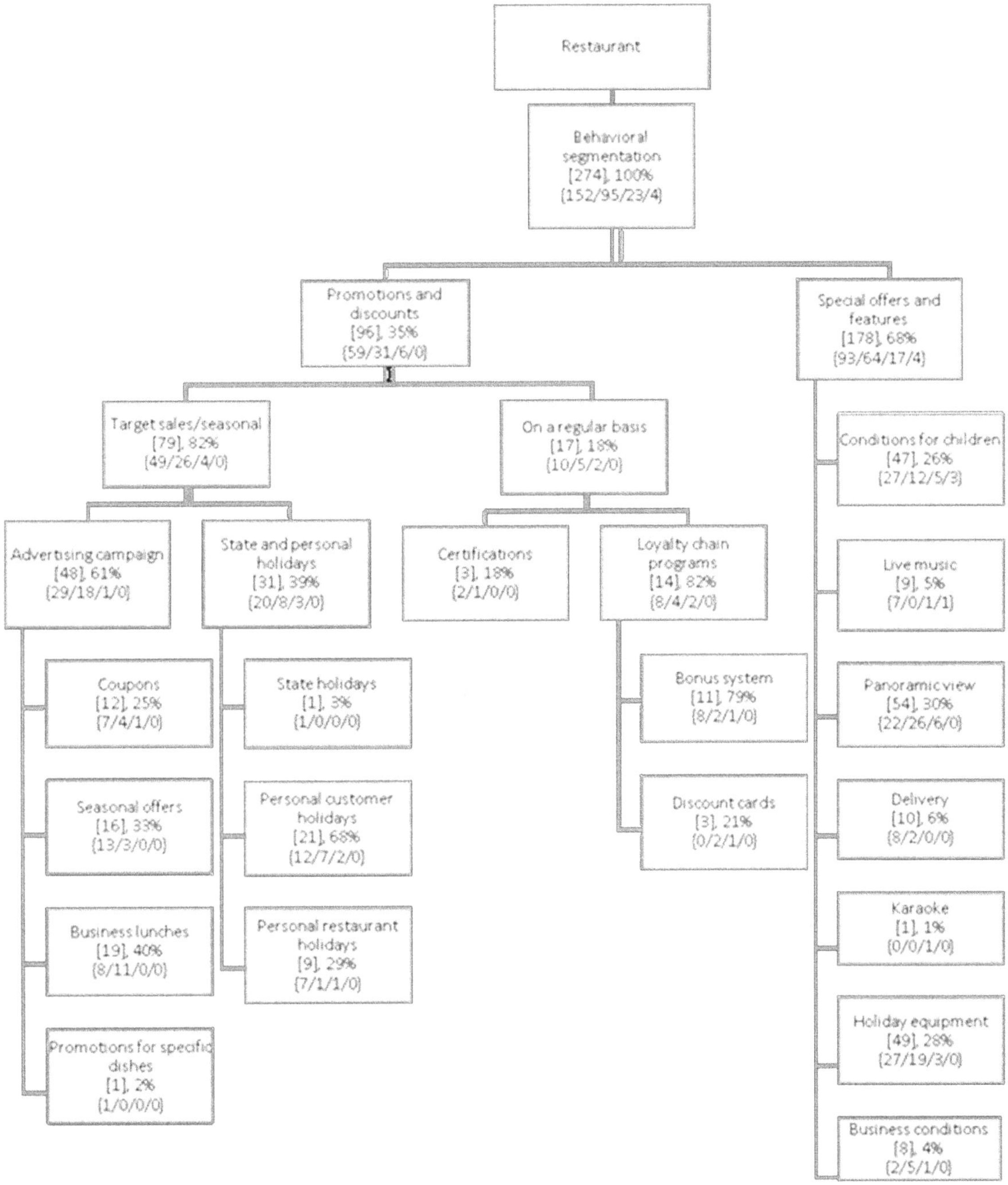
Restaurant
Behavioral segmentation [274], 100% {152/95/23/4}
Promotions and discounts [96], 35% {59/31/6/0}
Special offers and features [178], 68% {93/64/17/4}
Target sales/seasonal [79], 82% {49/26/4/0}
On a regular basis [17], 18% {10/5/2/0}
Conditions for children [47], 26% {27/12/5/3}
Advertising campaign [48], 61% {29/18/1/0}
State and personal holidays [31], 39% {20/8/3/0}
Certifications [3], 18% {2/1/0/0}
Loyalty chain programs [14], 82% {8/4/2/0}
Live music [9], 5% {7/0/1/1}
Coupons [12], 25% {7/4/1/0}
State holidays [1], 3% {1/0/0/0}
Bonus system [11], 79% {8/2/1/0}
Panoramic view [54], 30% {22/26/6/0}
Seasonal offers [16], 33% {13/3/0/0}
Personal customer holidays [21], 68% {12/7/2/0}
Discount cards [3], 21% {0/2/1/0}
Delivery [10], 6% {8/2/0/0}
Business lunches [19], 40% {8/11/0/0}
Personal restaurant holidays [9], 29% {7/1/1/0}
Karaoke [1], 1% {0/0/1/0}
Promotions for specific dishes [1], 2% {1/0/0/0}
Holiday equipment [49], 28% {27/19/3/0}
Business conditions [8], 4% {2/5/1/0}

Figure 4.

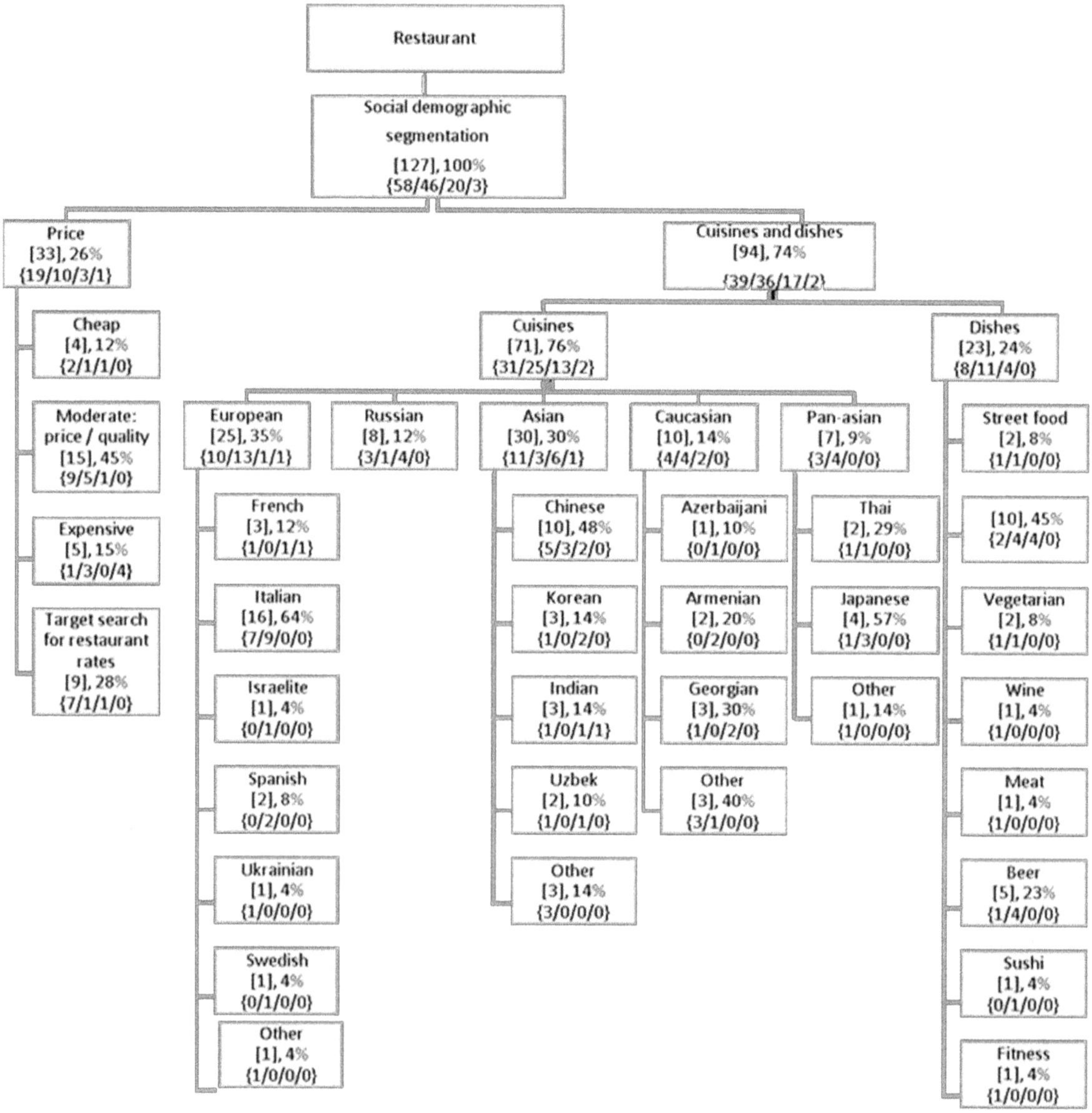

Another feature of choosing the Google KeyWord Planner tool, in contrast to alternative systems, is the expanded package of indicators provided. In addition to the standard statistics of the average number of search queries for a particular keyword and variants close to it, for evaluating the effectiveness of keywords in different periods, data is also provided on how competitive a query is for a keyword with certain geo-targeting and targeting settings in the search network. The level of competition (high, medium or low) allows you to evaluate the ratio of the number of advertisers using this keyword to the total number of keywords on Google for a given topic. In other words, one can trace the value orientation not only from the consumer side (the frequency of requests in a certain period), but also the demand for using the service described in the value proposition.

In this study, the semantic core represents key phrases that consumers use with the most pronounced frequency. The creation of a semantic core accurately characterizes the basic elements of value and market supply. The procedure for compiling it involves analyzing and selecting keywords from the maximum possible number of available sources in the search engine.

The semantic core is compiled by analyzing key concepts that reflect the needs of the target audience, popular search queries most often requested in search engines, industry specifics, the product offerings of companies in the market, the offers of related services.

Semantic analysis is used to identify and describe the features of the object of study in order to determine its qualities, with which the consumer chooses the company's service. Based on a quantitative assessment, this method provides the opportunity to form a cluster of the semantic core in order to identify key marketing innovations that can be used in the restaurant industry in St. Petersburg.

The approach of the research can be characterized as inductive, since there is no prior knowledge in the field of the formation of the company's value proposition in the restaurant industry in St. Petersburg. Consequently, the research approach is associated with new topics and interpretations about them (Dubois & Gadde, 2002). The focus is on interpreting perception (Welch et al., 2011), which is characterized by a subjective search for meaning.

SOLUTIONS AND RECOMMENDATIONS

The data on the selected analyzed groups of keywords were processed, which included the removal of duplicates. Based on these data, a cluster analysis was carried out. The study allows us to highlight the value segments of consumer demand for services and consider how a value proposition is appropriate for consumers.

The classification was carried out in accordance with the segmentation criteria: geographical, psychographic, behavioral, and socio-demographic and was further divided into clusters corresponding to segmentation. Based on the data obtained (Table 6), clusters are formed that have a certain level of influence on the restaurant service based on the level of demand frequency and search for services.

Table 6. Clustering the semantic core of the service industry format of the restaurant industry in St. Petersburg, 2016-2019

N°	Segmentation, criterion	Cluster	Number of keywords, %
1	Geographical	Geolocation	4,8
2	Psychographic	Reviews and ratings	12,3
3		Target search	42,8
4	Behavioral	Promotions and discounts	9,6
5		Special offers and features	17,8
6	Socio-demographic	Cuisine and dishes	9,4
7		Price	3,3
Total			100

Customer satisfaction is directly related to restaurant sales. Thus, it is important to determine which quality factors are perceived by potential customers to have a greater effect on satisfaction. The managerial task of the study was to identify the features of the value proposition based on the service format as an instrument for developing the innovative potential of companies using methods of semantic clustering.

The results of the study revealed seven factors (Table 6) that potential customers pay attention to, based on their searches: reviews and ratings of other visitors; value for money; quality food, variety of food and specifics of dishes; special offers and conditions of service; promotions and discounts; geographic location; and the brand. The results of the study and the clusters provide significant information for restaurateurs in creating a management strategy and introducing marketing innovations.

The segmentation of chain restaurants according to industry data based on cluster analysis made it possible to obtain a list of 16 of the most popular restaurant groups in Russia, which are popular in St. Petersburg and are the most popular Google searches among users: Ginza Project, Tokyo City, Il Patio, Eurasia, Mama na dache, Novikov Group, Schast'e, Chajhana Pahlava, RG Parusa, Marchellis, Koreana, Entree, Probka.org, Stroganoff, Italy Group, Taste to eat family.

Previously, no similar research was conducted in the industry due to the problem of collecting and standardizing aggregated market data. Commercial companies consider such information confidential and are not ready to provide information to researchers because of concerns about the use of data by competitors and the heterogeneous content of the data.

The collection of information was facilitated by a CHAID analysis of the restaurant industry in St. Petersburg based on statistical information from the Google KeyWord Planner analytical database for the period 2016-2019 (Table 2, 3, 4, 5). Data were also provided by the restaurant administration, including important business performance variables for each restaurant chain. All 16 restaurant chains in this study are at the top list of customer requests among more than 6,000 restaurants in St. Petersburg represented in Afisha restaurants online statistical database among all restaurant companies in Russia, especially in Saint-Petersburg.

The standardization of restaurant chain data is one of the most important tasks of this study, which can be seen in table 1. It was obtained as a result of analysis of Rambler & Co's open data provided in the Afisha restaurants analytical portal, specializing in restaurants of St. Petersburg and field interviews with administrators in all restaurant chains in the study.

The authors generated and analyzed the indicators of the 16 most popular restaurant chains in St. Petersburg, according to indicators of user requests (Table 7). To standardize the data for better analysis they were divided into four class categories by levels, as some of the 16 holdings use different methods of doing business and category of segments.

The data were compiled according to the categories of service provided, which is present in the city's restaurants and based on the segments of the restaurant market, which were tested earlier in studies of restaurant typologies based on the level of service (Muller & Woods, 1994) and practical studies of the National Restaurant Association (NRA) and CREST (Consumer Reports for Eating Share Trends), a national marketing research company that identified a four-segment restaurant typology. In accordance with the theoretical analysis for the study, all segments of the restaurant market were divided into classes by levels: high level (upscale); average level (midscale); moderate upscale and business dining; quick service.

1. Q_r – the number of restaurants in the chain, (pcs.).
2. The number of seats in the restaurant, (pcs.)

3. Average restaurant bill - the average restaurant bill, (according to the "Poster"), (₽).
4. Average place occupancy in a restaurant– the average turnover places in the restaurant, (%).
5. Average numbers of seats - the average number of seats, (pcs).
6. Average revenue per seat: Average bill x Average places occupancy rate – the average revenue per seat: average bill x average turnover of a place in a restaurant, (₽).
7. Average restaurant revenue - the average restaurant revenue per month, (₽).
8. Restaurant class - the class of a restaurant chain in the market.
9. Cumulative % of total amount of chain restaurants – the cumulative % of the total number of 16 chain restaurants, (%).

Table 7. Rating of chain restaurants in St. Petersburg, 2016-2019

Nº	Chain restaurants	Q_r^1	NS^2	ARB^3	AOR^4	ANS^5	AR_s^6	AR_r^7	$RClass^8$	%
1	Ginza Project (4)	3	270	700	3,5	90	2450	6 725 250	4	1,24
2	Ginza Project (3)	13	2691	1500	2,5	207	3750	23 675 625	3	5,39
3	Ginza Project (2)	25	4700	2500	2	188	5000	28 670 000	2	10,37
4	Ginza Project (1)	10	2130	3000	1,5	213	4500	29 234 250	1	4,15
5	Tokyo City	45	10575	1500	2,5	235	3750	26878125	3	18,67
6	IL Patio	6	996	1500	2,5	166	3750	18986250	3	2,49
7	Eurasia	71	7668	1500	2,5	108	3750	12352500	3	29,46
8	Mama na dache	2	184	1500	2,5	92	3750	10522500	3	0,83
9	Novikov Group (2)	1	184	2500	2	184	5000	28060000	2	0,41
10	Novikov Group (3)	3	180	1500	2,5	60	3750	6862500	3	1,24
11	Schast'e	3	318	1500	2,5	106	3750	12123750	3	1,24
12	Chajhana Pahlava	2	598	1500	2,5	299	3750	34198125	3	0,83
13	RG "Parusa" (2)	3	450	2500	2	150	5000	22875000	2	1,24
14	RG "Parusa" (1)	4	780	3000	1,5	195	4500	26763750	1	1,66
15	Marchellis	10	1480	1500	2,5	148	3750	16927500	3	4,15
16	Koreana	4	352	1500	2,5	88	3750	10065000	3	1,66
17	Entree	2	120	2500	2	60	5000	9150000	2	0,83
18	Probka.org	5	655	2500	2	131	5000	19977500	2	2,07
19	Stroganoff	3	1026	2500	2	342	5000	52155000	2	1,24
20	Italy Group (4)	3	150	700	3,5	50	2450	3736250	4	1,24
21	Italy Group (3)	10	1020	1500	2,5	102	3750	11666250	3	4,15
22	Italy Group (2)	8	1088	2500	2	136	5000	20740000	2	3,32
23	Taste to eat family	5	420	1500	2,5	84	3750	9607500	3	2,07
-	Total	241	-	-	-	-	-	-	-	100,00

The data in table 7 include important market performance variables, such as the average restaurant turnover, the average revenue per seat and the average restaurant revenue per month for each type, which are the main indicators used to assess the quality of the results of demand and the popularity of the restaurant chains. Table 7 confirms these points. Marketers can obtain information about the segments of restaurant chains and their characteristic market performance variables, for example, what the average check and the average turnover are in a restaurant typical for each category. All of this can be used to formulate value propositions for the business model and form long-term strategic policy.

The main contribution of the research described in this book chapter is the novelty of the approach to determining the value proposition in the market for the provision of chain restaurant services. The modern restaurant services market is characterized by a very rapid degree of growth and a high level of competition. Particular attention in the development of the company's strategy is given to a significant increase in quantitative indicators and improvement of the quality characteristics of the services provided. In connection with existing problems, attention should be paid to the progress of appropriate strategies, taking into account the causal relationship between the driving forces of the value proposition and the perception of customers about quality, which have a direct relationship. In other words, consumer preferences form demand and only those products that in their value proposition fully reflect consumer wishes will be competitive.

Catering refers to the rapidly developing sector of the economy. Network restaurant business strategies should also include such possible solutions to emerging problems as providing enhanced control over the quality of services and improving technical characteristics to create more favorable client-oriented conditions. Although enterprises of various formats are represented on the market of restaurant services, nevertheless, the level of satisfaction and compliance with consumer needs can be traced in table 7, based on indicators evaluating the level of their work in the market.

The results of the evaluation of consumer offers have a significant impact on innovation in the company. For the introduction of innovations taking into account consumer preferences, the value lies in the purposeful development of strategic management and the company's ability to personalize products, combining resources and activities at more efficient rates than other companies in the service delivery industry.

By analyzing the value proposition from the point of view of the market power of buyers, a company gains an advantage that leads to the development of a long-term strategy and a simplification of business processes. This facilitates the building of a business model, since this technology allows you to create a flexible data analysis system. The use of an analytical tool leads to a decrease in the cost of production processes and, as a result, the company's costs are reduced by removing the services that are not required by customers. It increases the flow of customer involvement in new services of the company, as it simplifies the processes of attracting customers and their interest in services. Thus, the service is best suited to the needs of the target segment and differs from the offers of other market players. Companies that use a long-term strategy focus on developing a value proposition in their segment, taking into account the dynamics of the market, and the features and needs of customers within it. Companies develop specialized products building strong brand loyalty.

FUTURE RESEARCH DIRECTIONS

Analysis is done only in on-line customers requests. The methodology capture only 'google' population. Other channels perspectives could be presented as the development of represented research and may be an opportunity for further research to expand the sample and extrapolate the data or compare it with data of related areas in the service market too see how it may impact. Further research may use other standardized tools for representative sampling, which would allow a more objective description.

CONCLUSION

Companies are trying to commercialize new ideas and technologies through their business models, forming innovative value propositions to detune from their competitors. While companies may have significant managerial knowledge, resources and investments to explore new ideas and technologies, they often have little opportunity for an objective analysis of the preferences of potential customers through which a value proposition is formed. The same idea or technology brought to market through two different business models will produce two different results. Thus, it is beneficial for companies to develop the ability to formulate a value proposition and implement their business models taking into account the analysis of customer preferences. Such an analysis is presented in this research.

The competitive advantage for modern companies is increasingly arising from the ability to optimally formulate a company's value proposition to provide unique properties to its product or service and will stimulate greater attraction of potential customers compared to other companies offering similar products. An analysis of the consumer's market power and customer audience preferences has a significant impact on the competitiveness of a company's product in the market. This creates the need to study the preferences of customers in order to formulate a value proposition and the strategy of the company. The research results presented here highlight the key consumer needs that affect the restaurant chain market. They include a choice regarding the process of creating and assigning value, a loyalty program, a strong brand, a high rating, location, quality food and a large selection of dishes, which are typical for all restaurant typologies based on the level of service.

The empirical study has a clearly structured analytical algorithm and high adaptability. Restaurant chains can track and analyze the key indicators of their target audience, select priority indicators for their company from them, and make calculations and use them to adjust the strategy.

For those, who make decisions, the particular value of the study is to disclose the industry strategy for the strategic management of restaurant chains, taking into account the main factors of the value proposition, which determine the ultimate competitiveness of targeted marketing.

The findings help to understand how analytical information about key concepts that reflect the needs of the target audience should be implemented in order to identify the main criteria for the value propositions of restaurant chains. This study outlined new opportunities by providing one of the first tests of resources for knowledge management in terms of organizational efficiency of using information about consumer inquiries on a specific topic in the market. The identification of various resources for strategic management and business modeling shows areas where the company can develop this ability, which is also confirmed by the results of other studies on building the competitiveness of the company (Table 7).

The main contribution of this article includes relevant theoretical and practical aspects that can be used scientifically and in strategic business planning. From a theoretical point of view, the article contributes to the literature on strategic management of enterprise chains by analyzing and forming a firm's value proposition and its elements based on consumer preferences. The semantic analysis shows that when analyzing keywords, clusters are formed that influence the format of restaurant service based on the level of demand frequency and service search, which are important for achieving the goals of the company and increasing its competitive advantages. From a practical point of view, the research presents principles on how to highlight the value segments of consumer demand for services in the restaurant business.

The transformation of a value proposition is possible by identifying factors in a value proposition. It depends on how well thought out and relevant the market is the success of the business in the moment. The company's ability to systematically create value determines success in the long run.

The chapter of the book presents a step-by-step design of empirical research that helps to determine the currently relevant value proposition factors that correspond to consumer demand; they involve four stages:

Stage 1. Selection of analyzed groups of keywords.

Stage 2. Unloading a list of keywords. Fixing and sorting the information provided by the system according to the result of requests within the framework of the service format of the restaurant industry of St. Petersburg.

Stage 3. Data processing. Removing duplicate keywords (repeated queries, identical phrases obtained from the results of the starting words in the sample).

Stage 4. Evaluation and sorting of data by their frequency remaining in the third stage. Preparation of statistical information for cluster analysis.

The results show the use of keywords from queries of restaurant users in St. Petersburg for clustering the semantic core and forming a descriptor of a value proposition. The study standardizes the description of restaurants, thereby improving the integration of scientific research and makes the results accessible to entrepreneurs for practical use. Recommendations on optimizing the use of restaurant classification help simplify the analysis of the empirical data and their comparison, thereby improving the information of practitioners and other researchers about achievements in the field of restaurant business knowledge management. The practical significance of the research results is widely used in management activities and can be used by specialists in the field of management and marketing, actively interacting with the processes of developing and promoting innovative products and services, drawing up a development plan and choosing a company's action strategy, creating a competitive advantage, market and industry research in restaurant business.

Limitations arise from the research methods used. Moreover, arketers can get information about the contribution of each customer segment in the overall analysis of the company strategy through correlation analysis or multiple regression analysis. As long as the core of marketing is experienced market knowledge, obtaining and understanding such market information is the best marketing practice. The only obstacle will be the difficulty of collecting market data. Although this empirical study applies to the restaurant chains in St. Petersburg, Russia, the same research methodology and design can be applied to all restaurant markets in any part of the world.

REFERENCES

Arora, R., & Singer, J. (2006). Customer satisfaction and value as drivers of business success for fine dining restaurants. *Services Marketing Quarterly*, *28*(1), 89–102. doi:10.1300/J396v28n01_05

Bocken, N. M., Short, S. W., Rana, P., & Evans, S. (2014). A literature and practice review to develop sustainable business model archetypes. *Journal of Cleaner Production*, *65*, 42–56. doi:10.1016/j.jclepro.2013.11.039

Burnett, J., & Moriarty, S. E. (1998). *Introduction to marketing communication: an integrated approach.* Prentice Hall.

Chan Kim, W., & Mauborgne, R. (2005). *Blue Ocean Strategy: How to create uncontested market space and make the competition irrelevant.* Boston: Harvard Business Review Press.

Chesbrough, H. (2007). Business model innovation: It's not just about technology anymore. *Strategy and Leadership*, *35*(6), 12–17. doi:10.1108/10878570710833714

Chesbrough, H. (2010). Business model innovation: Opportunities and barriers. *Long Range Planning*, *43*(2-3), 354–363. doi:10.1016/j.lrp.2009.07.010

Chkoniya, V., & Mateus, A. (2019). Digital Category Management: How Technology Can Enable the Supplier-Retailer Relationship. In D. Simões, B. Barbosa, & S. Filipe (Eds.), *Smart Marketing With the Internet of Things* (pp. 139–163). Hershey, PA: IGI Global. doi:10.4018/978-1-5225-5763-0.ch008

Clinton, L., & Whisnant, R. (2019). Business Model Innovations for Sustainability. In *Managing Sustainable Business* (pp. 463–503). Dordrecht: Springer. doi:10.1007/978-94-024-1144-7_22

Dubois, A., & Gadde, L. E. (2002). Systematic combining: An abductive approach to case research. *Journal of Business Research*, *55*(7), 553–560. doi:10.1016/S0148-2963(00)00195-8

Everitt, B. S., Landau, S., Leese, M., & Stahl, D. (2011). *Cluster Analysis.* New York: John Wiley & Sons. Ltd. doi:10.1002/9780470977811

Fjeldstad, Ø. D., & Snow, C. C. (2018). Business models and organization design. *Long Range Planning*, *51*(1), 32–39. doi:10.1016/j.lrp.2017.07.008

Foss, N. J., & Saebi, T. (2018). Business models and business model innovation: Between wicked and paradigmatic problems. *Long Range Planning*, *51*(1), 9–21. doi:10.1016/j.lrp.2017.07.006

Frow, P., & Payne, A. (2011). A stakeholder perspective of the value proposition concept. *European Journal of Marketing*, *45*(1/2), 223–240. doi:10.1108/03090561111095676

Geissdoerfer, M., Bocken, N. M., & Hultink, E. J. (2016). Design thinking to enhance the sustainable business modelling process–A workshop based on a value mapping process. *Journal of Cleaner Production*, *135*, 1218–1232. doi:10.1016/j.jclepro.2016.07.020

Geissdoerfer, M., Vladimirova, D., & Evans, S. (2018). Sustainable business model innovation: A review. *Journal of Cleaner Production*, *198*, 401–416. doi:10.1016/j.jclepro.2018.06.240

Gummesson, E., Mele, C., Polese, F., Nenonen, S., & Storbacka, K. (2010). Business model design: Conceptualizing networked value co-creation. *International Journal of Quality and Service Sciences*.

Hernandez, V., & Pedersen, T. (2017). Global value chain configuration: A review and research agenda. *BRQ Business Research Quarterly*, *20*(2), 137–150. doi:10.1016/j.brq.2016.11.001

Johnson, M. W., Christensen, C. M., & Kagermann, H. (2008). Reinventing your business model. *Harvard Business Review*, *86*(12), 57–68.

Kafentzis, K., Mentzas, G., Apostolou, D., & Georgolios, P. (2004). Knowledge marketplaces: Strategic issues and business models. *Journal of Knowledge Management*, *8*(1), 130–146. doi:10.1108/13673270410523961

Karmarkar, U. S., & Pitbladdo, R. (1995). Service markets and competition. *Journal of Operations Management*, *12*(3-4), 397–411. doi:10.1016/0272-6963(94)00014-6

Kim, W. C., & Mauborgne, R. (1999). Strategy, value innovation, and the knowledge economy. *MIT Sloan Management Review*, *40*(3), 41.

Kim, W. C., & Maubourge, R. (1997). Value innovation. *Harvard Business Review*, (1).

Li, W. S. (2018). Strategic Value Analysis: Value Search. In *Strategic Management Accounting* (pp. 159–170). Singapore: Springer. doi:10.1007/978-981-10-5729-8_9

Lindič, J., & Marques da Silva, C. (2011). Value proposition as a catalyst for a customer focused innovation. *Management Decision*, *49*(10), 1694–1708. doi:10.1108/00251741111183834

Matthyssens, P., & Vandenbempt, K. (2008). Moving from basic offerings to value-added solutions: Strategies, barriers and alignment. *Industrial Marketing Management*, *37*(3), 316–328. doi:10.1016/j.indmarman.2007.07.008

McGrath, R. G. (2010). Business models: A discovery driven approach. *Long Range Planning*, *43*(2-3), 247–261. doi:10.1016/j.lrp.2009.07.005

Miles, R. E., & Snow, C. C. (1986). Organizations: New concepts for new forms. *California Management Review*, *28*(3), 62–73. doi:10.2307/41165202

Miles, R. E., Snow, C. C., Meyer, A. D., & Coleman, H. J. Jr. (1978). Organizational strategy, structure, and process. *Academy of Management Review*, *3*(3), 546–562. doi:10.5465/amr.1978.4305755 PMID:10238389

Mitchell, D. W., & Bruckner Coles, C. (2004). Establishing a continuing business model innovation process. *The Journal of Business Strategy*, *25*(3), 39–49. doi:10.1108/02756660410536991

Morris, M., Schindehutte, M., & Allen, J. (2005). The entrepreneur's business model: Toward a unified perspective. *Journal of Business Research*, *58*(6), 726–735. doi:10.1016/j.jbusres.2003.11.001

Muller, C. C., & Woods, R. H. (1994). An expanded restaurant typology. *The Cornell Hotel and Restaurant Administration Quarterly*, *35*(3), 27–37. doi:10.1177/001088049403500312

Normann, R., & Ramirez, R. (1993). From Value Chain to Value Constellation: Designing Interactive Strategy. *Harvard Business Review*, *71*(4), 65–77. PMID:10127040

Ocasio, W. (1997). Towards an attention-based view of the firm. *Strategic Management Journal, 18*(S1), 187–206. doi:10.1002/(SICI)1097-0266(199707)18:1+<187::AID-SMJ936>3.3.CO;2-B

Porter, M., & Siggelkow, N. (2008). Contextuality within activity systems and sustainability of competitive advantage. *The Academy of Management Perspectives, 22*(2), 34–56. doi:10.5465/amp.2008.32739758

Porter, M. E., & Kramer, M. R. (2019). Creating shared value. In *Managing sustainable business* (pp. 323–346). Dordrecht: Springer. doi:10.1007/978-94-024-1144-7_16

Prahalad, C. K., & Ramaswamy, V. (2004). Co-creation experiences: The next practice in value creation. *Journal of Interactive Marketing, 18*(3), 5–14. doi:10.1002/dir.20015

Prusak, L. (1996). The knowledge advantage. *Planning Review, 24*(2), 6–8. doi:10.1108/eb054546

Pynnönen, M., Hallikas, J., & Ritala, P. (2012). Managing customer-driven business model innovation. *International Journal of Innovation Management, 16*(04), 1250022. doi:10.1142/S1363919612003836

Rumelt, R. P. (2012). Good strategy/bad strategy: The difference and why it matters. *Strategic Direction, 28*(8).

Serova, E., & Bagiev, G. (2012). Intelligent information technologies and systems in the systemic research of marketing space. In *ICMLG2016-4th International Conference on Management, Leadership and Governance: ICMLG2016* (p. 296-303). Academic Conferences and Publishing Limited.

Serova, E., & Krichevsky, M. (2015). Intelligent Models and Systems in Spatial Marketing Research. *Electronic Journal of Information Systems Evaluation, 18*(2), 159–171.

Snihur, Y., & Wiklund, J. (2019). Searching for innovation: Product, process, and business model innovations and search behavior in established firms. *Long Range Planning, 52*(3), 305–325. doi:10.1016/j.lrp.2018.05.003

Sorescu, A., Frambach, R. T., Singh, J., Rangaswamy, A., & Bridges, C. (2011). Innovations in retail business models. *Journal of Retailing, 87*, S3–S16. doi:10.1016/j.jretai.2011.04.005

Teece, D. J. (2018). Business models and dynamic capabilities. *Long Range Planning, 51*(1), 40–49. doi:10.1016/j.lrp.2017.06.007

Trimi, S., & Berbegal-Mirabent, J. (2012). Business model innovation in entrepreneurship. *The International Entrepreneurship and Management Journal, 8*(4), 449–465. doi:10.100711365-012-0234-3

Tukker, A., & van den Berg, C. (2017). Product-services and competitiveness. In *New Business for Old Europe* (pp. 35–71). Routledge. doi:10.4324/9781351280600-3

Welch, C., Piekkari, R., Plakoyiannaki, E., & Paavilainen-Mäntymäki, E. (2011). Theorising from case studies: Towards a pluralist future for international business research. *Journal of International Business Studies, 42*(5), 740–762. doi:10.1057/jibs.2010.55

KEY TERMS AND DEFINITIONS

CHAID Analysis: Relationship identification method of quantitative and / or qualitative ordinal signs of the studied values in order to build a predictive model based on a hierarchical data segmentation system by the type of decision tree structure.

Chain Restaurant Business Management: Entrepreneurial activity area aimed at making a profit and satisfying the needs of consumers through the provision of services to provide customers with food and drinks in a specially designated place, which corresponds basic hygiene and legal requirements.

Cluster Analysis: Multidimensional statistical procedure that collects data containing information about a sample of objects, and then organizes the objects into relatively homogeneous groups.

Competitive Strategy: Comprehensive plan of strategic management actions that helps company increase or maintain its position relative to other players in the market.

Customer-Oriented Approach: Individualized approach of meeting the needs of each individual client by creating high value, focused on long-term relationships.

Innovation Management: Preparation and adoption system of strategic decisions aimed at the formation, support and development of the technological company's potential by introducing new products, production processes and economic relations.

Knowledge Management: Strategy that transforms all types of intellectual assets into higher productivity, efficiency and new value.

Value Proposition: Strategic tool for positioning a product or service related to the exceptional properties of products, which, due to its unique characteristics, helps the company to rebuild from competitors in the market.

Chapter 9
Cross-Cultural Differences and Similarities in Retailers' Branding and Digital Maturity: A Cross-Border Case Study

Andreas Hesse
Koblenz University of Applied Sciences, Germany

Pieter Steenkamp
Cape Peninsula University of Technology, South Africa

Holger J. Schmidt
https://orcid.org/0000-0002-4252-7527
Koblenz University of Applied Sciences, Germany

Virimai V. Mugobo
Cape Peninsula University of Technology, South Africa

ABSTRACT

Digital disruption is not something that may happen in the future; it is currently happening and impacting all types of businesses, including retail. This chapter reflects cross-cultural similarities and differences. German and South African consumers increasingly use the internet to look for product information and to purchase online products and services. Nevertheless, about 25% of German and South African companies in the study sample are more or less offline, not offering even basic digital services, while a significant number of companies ignore opportunities for branding. The digital maturity and branding practices of 933 businesses located within the central business districts of two international cities of similar regional importance, namely Koblenz in Germany and Stellenbosch in South Africa, were investigated. Retailers were analysed in order to compare and contrast their progression along a digital maturity scale as well as their branding practices. The case study presented in this chapter aimed to provide a starting point for the development of such a picture.

DOI: 10.4018/978-1-7998-3115-0.ch009

Copyright © 2020, IGI Global. Copying or distributing in print or electronic forms without written permission of IGI Global is prohibited.

INTRODUCTION

Digital disruption is not something that may happen in the future; it is currently happening and impacting all types of businesses, including retail. This chapter reflects cross-cultural similarities and differences; how companies deal with digital disruption and branding. The digital maturity and branding practices of 933 businesses located within the central business districts of two international cities of similar regional importance, namely Koblenz in Germany and Stellenbosch in South Africa, were investigated. In particular, retailers were analyzed in order to compare and contrast their progression along a digital maturity scale as well as their branding practices. The United Nations Development Programme (UNDP) lists Germany as a developed country and South Africa as a developing country (UNDP, 2018). It is easy for one to assume that businesses situated within the advanced German economy would be more professional in branding practices and digitally more mature than their counterparts in the developing South African economy, but the findings from this study show otherwise and do not register advantage in respect of the advanced economy. Rather, they reveal slight differences built on the variations in tenure of retailers in connection with their local circumstances. Local retailers, in particular in the German city are lagging behind, for instance in the implementation of e-commerce and additional omnichannel services.

It can be expected that the professionalism and digital readiness of retailers varies across geographical areas and urban landscapes of different size. For example, the digital readiness of globally operating retail chains can be expected to be higher than that of local retailers. But thus far, there is no clear picture based on empirically valid information of the differences in branding professionalism and digital readiness, taking size and location into account. The study presented in this chapter aimed to provide a starting point for the development of such a picture. By revealing that local retailers are lagging behind to a great extend in offering digital services and utilizing the potential of branding practices, the findings have direct practical implications.

BACKGROUND

Digital maturity and branding professionalism are two constructs that need to be explained in order for readers to interpret and understand the present research. We therefore provide a brief overview of the key terms that will be used when we present the results of our study. For reasons of space, we will refrain from a detailed examination.

Digital Maturity

It is inevitable that businesses will be affected by the digital revolution, but it is projected that the retail industry will experience one of the highest degrees of digital disruption among all industries by 2020 (Rigby and Tager, 2014). Considering this, it is of relevance to assess the status of digital maturity of businesses. Accordingly, needs for action and potentials can be identified and addressed. Digital maturity is an important concept increasingly used to rate the technology-driven progress of industries, businesses and organizations (Berghaus and Back, 2016). Technology in this regard has a focus on digitalization, a process of transferring information into an electronic data format and evaluating its impacts on society and business (Brennen and Kreis, 2014). Shahiduzzaman et al. (2017) characterize digital maturation as a process whereby a company becomes increasingly digital over time by leveraging digital technologies.

Prior measurements for estimating digital maturity concentrate on the impact of digital maturity, or on a company's readiness to deal with digital disruption (Heinemann, 2017). Early regional studies promoted by the consultancy industry posited a positive impact of high digital maturity on firm performance, for instance on revenues and marketing costs (Chadha, 2018). Nevertheless, it remains unclear to what extent and how the maturity of retailers can be classified. And, in particular the predictors of different shapes of such digital maturity are unclear.

Digital disruption involves the transformation caused by emerging digital technologies and business models. Innovative technologies are making an impact on the value of existing products and services, and this is why the term 'disruption' is used: the emergence of new products and services can revolutionize the current market and provoke the need for re-evaluation (Oxford College of Marketing, 2016). Digital disruptions in the retail environment are pervasive. The emergence of e-commerce can be seen as digital disruption, in three main ways, namely: the proliferation of pure online players like Amazon; the opportunity to extend sales channels online for all retailers; and manufacturers' direct sales online and offline shops. The latter phenomenon appears to a strong extent in the fashion industry. Nearly all manufacturer brands built up direct sales via the internet and at least flagship stores in the offline world. Retailers with a traditional focus on stationary business on premises react by reducing their physical footprint and by focusing on customer experience across channels, in particular combining and intertwining customer touchpoints seamlessly – so-called omnichannelling (Heinemann, 2017). Operating through omnichannels reflects the variety of consumer behaviour and experience throughout the customer journey (Lazaris and Vrechopolous, 2014). Nevertheless, sustaining a physical presence still fulfils certain requirements of consumers; in particular the desire for immediate product availability, shopping atmosphere, curated shopping and after-sales service (Heinemann, 2017). Although consumers increasingly embrace online channels during the various stages in their purchase decision making, services that connect the online and offline worlds meet their needs even better (Hesse, 2019). Click-and-collect services combine online purchases with an immediate pick-up opportunity in a brick-and-mortar store or at various locations (Constantine, 2015). Similarly, retailers – in particular those with various on-site locations – offer same-day or next-hour delivery by setting up a local delivery service from the store to the customer (Hesse, 2019). For targeted purchases, numerous physical store retailers allow consumers to check real-time product availability online before travelling to the city. For the provision of services, more and more companies offer appointment tools on their websites or in an app, to allow consumers to request or set a time and date to meet up and interact, for instance with a hairdresser, physiotherapist or in a nail spa (Wang and Fung, 2015). Accordingly, omnichanneling reflects the need for retailers to keep all their channels up to date, with their digital appearances linking all their stores to their online platforms, and to be accessible on all the touchpoints that customers prefer (Heinemann, 2017). Similarly, this study unfolds whether, how and to what extent these developments are different or similar for both cities. Doing so, it is possible to reveal indicators of such developments.

Branding

Brands are a direct consequence of the strategy of market segmentation and product differentiation (Keller, 2013). A trusted brand increases expectations, reduces consumer perceptions of risk and simplifies decision making (Devasagayam et al., 2010). This is particularly true in product areas where functional differences have become less important. Brands have been defined in various ways (Kapferer, 2004). McGhie (2012) defines a brand as "emotional shorthand for accumulated or assumed information," to the extent that "a brand is present when the value of what a product, service or personality means to its audience is greater than the value of what it does for that audience" (p. 14).

Brand management comprises all the activities involved in the creation, management and termination of brands (Burmann et al., 2017). It involves building a promise, satisfying that promise and preserving it (Iglesias et al., 2013), in this way contributing to the long-term sustainable competitive advantage of a company (Todor, 2014). Branding is an aspect of brand management focussing on the more operational tasks (Schmidt, 2015). It usually refers to the management of brand elements, which Keller (2013) defines as "distinct devices that are trademarkable, which serve to differentiate and identify the brand" (p. 114). Examples of brand elements are colours, design, signs, labels, slogans and much more.

In the context of the retail industry, the brand of the retail store (a retailer's brand, also called a store brand) is of highest importance (Redler, 2018). Many retailers sell similar products: a Coca-Cola from Checkers does not taste different from a Coca-Cola from Woolworths. The brand of the retail store is one chance for the retailer to differentiate itself from its competitors. Studies have shown that retailers who incorporate the idea of the retailer brand in their strategies and behaviours are more successful than others (e.g., Schmidt et al., 2017). Since they are perceivable within the store, the brand elements described above (brand name, colour, logo, signs and digital signage, packaging) are the most obvious part of a brand management strategy from the customer's point of view. Examples like the grocery chain Walmart and the global fashion chain Hennes & Mauritz demonstrate best practice of how to establish a retailer brand. The brands' promises apply to the entire range of products and services offered.

MAIN FOCUS OF THE CHAPTER

The chapter offers a study that builds on a descriptive approach informed by observations to deductively examine retailers' digital habits and branding practices (Malhotra and Birks, 2007). A cross-border comparison was the driver of the data collection process, which started with the selection of two cities in two markets differing in their economic development. The study focused on retailers and other companies with physical premises located in the city business districts (CBDs) of the two cities. The analysis concentrated on the observable activities (e.g., offering a Facebook account) and visible artefacts (e.g., a brand logo as an outdoor sign) of retailers. In addition, companies in the CBDs were analyzed to cross-validate findings and identify differences from and similarities to other types of business.

The study was conducted in the cities of Koblenz (Germany) and Stellenbosch (South Africa). The Koblenz population is about 120,000. The city is home of Koblenz-Landau University and Koblenz University of Applied Sciences. The densest age range of the population is from 40 to 49 years. From a retail perspective, Koblenz offers a well-off clientele with considerable purchasing power and ubiquitous access to the Internet (Koblenz Stadtmarketing, 2017). Stellenbosch is an economic hub in its area with a population of about 175,000. It is home to Stellenbosch University and is surrounded by wine farms. The most prevalent age range is between 20 and 24 years, which can be accredited largely to the student population (Western Cape Government, 2015).

In the German market, according to the German Retail Federation, retail is still dominated by in-store sales (HDE, 2018). The retail turnover share of e-commerce in 2018 was still below 15 per cent but growing by around 10 per cent per year (HDE, 2018). The 'brandscape' in German cities is increasingly dominated by global and nationwide retailer brands and manufacturer brands. Local retailers that still exist to a large extent, are losing market share and are little by little disappearing (IHK Darmstadt, 2017).

The South African retail market, on the other hand, was chosen because it is a growing and emerging market (Hirsch, 2012). In recent years, international retailer brands like Walmart, Zara and H&M have started to open stores in South African cities, and e-commerce has experienced double-digit growth (Euromonitor International, 2018). E-commerce may close the gap between international trends and local needs (Schmidt et al., 2017). The growth of e-commerce in South Africa is a result of international and local businesses targeting the growing middle class in the country, offering convenience shopping to South Africa's fairly young population, with 20 per cent of Internet users availing themselves of e-commerce (Global Economic Governance Africa, 2017). Global online giants Amazon and Alibaba, as well as medium-size pure-online players like Gumtree.com, Spree.com and Onedayonly.com have already entered the South African market (Euromonitor International, 2018).

Describing the research setting, differences in the local circumstances for retailing must be mentioned (see Table 1). The criteria chosen to compare the commercial circumstances are the most salient differences between the two cities. The cityscape in the center of Koblenz is characterized by pedestrian areas, with 53 per cent of the companies analyzed located in these areas, while only 5 per cent of those in Stellenbosch were comparably sited; but more stores in Stellenbosch were located in shopping malls than in Koblenz (40% as opposed to 15%). Both cities represent attractive tourist destinations. Koblenz with the confluence of the rivers Moselle and Rhine and various fortresses, Stellenbosch as an important wine region of South Africa. The multi-branch ratio and the share of chain stores also differed between the two cities. The majority of stores still had local roots, notably in Koblenz, at 64 per cent, compared to Stellenbosch at 54 per cent. There was also a comparable landscape of types of business within the cities. The majority of businesses were retailers (including food-retailing) in both cities (Koblenz 55%, Stellenbosch 53%), besides a significant proportion of service providers (Koblenz 21%, Stellenbosch 33%). Twenty-four per cent of businesses in Koblenz and 14 per cent in Stellenbosch were classified as gastronomic and food services.

Commensurately, bases of comparison for digital commerce must be highlighted. While retailers in Koblenz enjoy a well-off clientele spread across the generations, Stellenbosch's shopping community has a younger average age. Although customers in Koblenz have easy access to the Internet right across the city, large customer groups are still reluctant to use digital services (Hootsuite, 2019). Conversely, in Stellenbosch the accessibility and bandwidth of the Internet are inferior, while the usage by consumers is much more intensive, in particular in regard to social media (Hootsuite, 2019).

Data Collection

Ethical clearance for the research project was obtained from the University of Technology in Cape Town South Africa, which included providing assurances of respect for privacy. Quantitative and qualitative data was collected from the Internet and from observation in the field. The data collection took place in February 2019 (in Stellenbosch, South Africa) and March 2019 (in Koblenz, Germany). For assessing the constructs of digital maturity and branding practices, dimensions were distilled from a literature review and a previous study (Hesse, 2019). In preparation for data collection, the list of dimensions (see Table 2-4) was verified in two pre-tests, one conducted by a researcher in Koblenz, and a second conducted by research assistants in Cape Town. In addition to the verification of the dimensions, scores of 0, 1 or 2 were defined and described to indicate digital and branding progress: a score of 0 meant limited progress and a score of 2 advanced progress.

Table 1. Business Demographics

	Koblenz	Stellenbosch
All companies included in the study	500	433
Circumstances		
- Streets	32% (160)	55% (238)
- Pedestrian areas	53% (265)	5% (22)
- Malls	15% (75)	40% (173)
Types of Business		
- Retailer (incl. food retailing)	55% (275)	53% (229)
- Service Provider	21% (90)	33% (144)
- Gastronomy (incl. food services)	24% (104)	14% (61)
Geographical Footprint		
- Local/regional	64% (320)	54% (234)
- National	18% (90)	25% (108)
- International	18% (90)	20% (87)

The first part of the data collection considered branding activities. The stores were all physically visited to collect the data, and all the data was recorded in an app and transferred onto Excel spreadsheets. Details of the physical presence of the companies – including name, type, industry, footprint and location – were also recorded. In order to ensure uniform recording, the field researchers were comprehensively briefed and a recording app was used. Inconsistencies were aligned and corrected immediately in the field. The second part of data collection was conducted by desk research and focused on how retailers dealt with digitalization, digital services and the Internet. Another Excel spreadsheet was used to assess the dimensions of digital maturity, including website marketing, e-commerce and omnichannel services, applications, search engine marketing, and social media marketing (see Table 2).

Data Analysis

The data, gathered in two locations, was united and standardized using Excel. After the data was prepared and validated for analysis, a first ad-hoc analysis was conducted, followed by a discussion within the research team, including authors and field workers in both countries. The identification of significant characteristics, whether similarities or differences, as well as peculiarities, further drove the process of data analysis.

The data was used first to describe and then compare and contrast the businesses' digital maturity and branding practices in the two cities (Walk, 1998). In addition to interpreting the analysis qualitatively, Langley's (1999) quantification strategy was applied (see Tables 2 and 3, below). First, a total branding score (a possible maximum of 20) and a total digital maturity score (a possible maximum of 44) were compiled. Four stages of digital maturity have been identified and are qualitatively described. Once again, by immediate exchange and alignment the researchers ensured that subjectivity only allows for a limited degree of different interpretation. Secondly, a cross-country analysis was conducted to identify similarities and differences between the two cities (Walk, 1998). Thirdly, using Pivot-tables specific propositions were examined in detail to extract findings appropriate to further research or practical implementation.

SOLUTIONS AND RECOMMENDATIONS

The results of the study offer broad insights into various characteristics of the digitalization and branding practices of retailers in the two cities involved. First, the branding practices of retailers in the two cities are evaluated. Secondly, digital engagement is discussed and four stages of digital maturity are characterized and described. Thirdly, the study homes in on locally-rooted smaller retailers. Finally, the interplay of digital maturity and branding practices is briefly examined.

Table 2. Branding practices of Koblenz and Stellenbosch retailers

	Koblenz			Stellenbosch		
	All companies (500) All retailers (273) All local retailers (155)			All companies (500) All retailers (273) All local retailers (155)		
brand name	1,22	1,28	0,99	1,53	1,54	1,28
brand logo	1,17	1,08	0,97	1,45	1,46	1,32
brand colour	1,18	1,16	0,86	1,56	1,55	1,41
building signs	1,49	1,48	1,23	1,57	1,63	1,64
entrance door	1,07	1,08	1,22	0,98	0,84	1,05
shop window	1,19	1,22	1,22	1,01	0,97	0,99
corporate fashion	0,54	0,42	0,23	0,95	0,94	0,49
store devign	0,72	0,77	0,4	1,1	1,13	0,82
packaging	0,81	1,11	0,7	0,89	1	0,63
branded price tags	0,55	0,69	0,45	0,85	1	0,79
sum (branding practices)	**10**	**10**	**8**	**12**	**12**	**10**

Branding Practices

The study reveals that in both cities companies utilize core branding elements, specifically names, logos, colours, and especially by branding buildings and shop windows (see Table 2). Contrary to the general expectation, retailers of any size located in Stellenbosch display these practices to a greater extent than retailers in Koblenz, where smaller locally-rooted retailers in particular are less likely to do so. The use of in-store branding practices, like corporate fashion, store design, brand price tags and branded packaging, could be identified to a lesser extent. Instead of using brand elements, the local dealers in Koblenz/ Germany practice a very reduced identification by their company names or owner names. Brands are exclusively used here at product level and manufacturer level. Again, in this regard, Stellenbosch companies are empirically proven to be more active in this regard than Koblenz companies. All in all, in

Koblenz 57 per cent of businesses have below-average branding practices, while for Stellenbosch the figure is 36 per cent.

Digital Engagement

The existence of a company's website is an important prerequisite for further digital activities, whether e-commerce or search engine marketing. The same is true for social media accounts, which serve as a base for social media marketing. It should be noted in advance that up to 25% of the businesses do not have a website nor a social media account and can therefore only be found on the Internet via indirect portals and providers. Both a website and a social media account are present for approximately 75 per cent of the companies in both cities. As might be expected, such companies are well represented in organic search engine results. In particular, nearly all the companies in Koblenz are displayed as a search result on the first page of Google's search engine. With regard to Google Maps, companies in both cities are easily accessible and most of the companies offer consumer-relevant information like opening hours, special offers or photos, and this information is widely accessed, particularly by students and tourists. Focusing on retailers, again, basic services such as e-commerce and delivery are widely distributed among Koblenz's international and national retailers. Most, however, do not utilize the more advanced applications that build on these, like appointment tools or product availability services (see Table 3). Conversely, and perhaps contrary to expectations, national and international retailers in Stellenbosch broadly offer omnichannel services. Overall, in general, locally-rooted smaller retailers are lagging behind with regard to developments in digital commerce in both cities.

Stages of Companies' Digital Maturity

The study found that digital maturity varies on a continuum. To arrive at a rigorous qualitative description, the dimensions of digital maturity can be characterized in four stages. According to Langley's (1999) quantification strategy, the average score of the companies was calculated to be 16 out of a possible maximum of 44 points. This average can be used as an indicator for a city's retailer digital maturity index. We would like to emphasize that the four stages should be understood as a rough indication and not as a quantified classification. The average is exactly the same for both cities involved in this study. Companies with a calculated total of between 0 and 11 were grouped in the cluster "Offliners", between 12 and 22 in the cluster "Basic Onliners", between 23 and 33 in the cluster "Advanced Onliners", and between 34 and 44 in the cluster "Digital Forerunners". Subsequently, the characteristics of digital maturity within the clusters are briefly described (see Table 3).

Table 3. Characteristics of Digital Maturity

Offliners (0-11)	**Basic Onliners (12-22)**	**Advanced Onliners (23-33)**	**Digital Forerunners (34-44)**
Stellenbosch: 30% (132) **Koblenz: 31% (155)**	**Stellenbosch: 46% (199)** **Koblenz: 46% (229)**	**Stellenbosch: 22% (94)** **Koblenz: 22% (108)**	**Stellenbosch: 2% (9)** **Koblenz: 2% (8)**
Frequently observed: ✓ Organic search (SEO) ✓ Google Maps ✓ Payment services ***Rarely or not observed:*** ☒ Website marketing (all) ☒ E-commerce and omnichannel services (all) ☒ Social media marketing (all) ☒ Paid search (SEA) ☒ Brand/company app ☒ Further smartphone services ☒ In-store WiFi	*Frequently observed:* ✓ Website marketing (some) ✓ Organic search (SEO) ✓ Google Maps ✓ Facebook account ✓ Payment services *Rarely or not observed:* ☒ Appointment tool ☒ Brand/company app ☒ Further smartphone services ☒ We Chat Account ☒ In-store WiFi	*Frequently observed:* ✓ Website marketing (all) ✓ E-Commerce and omnichannel services (some) ✓ Organic search (SEO) ✓ Google Maps ✓ Facebook account ✓ Instagram account ✓ Other social network accounts ✓ Payment services *Rarely or not observed:* ☒ We Chat Account	*Frequently observed:* ✓ Website marketing (all) ✓ E-Commerce and omnichannel services (all) ✓ Organic search (SEO) ✓ Paid Search (SEA) ✓ Google Maps ✓ Facebook account ✓ Instagram account ✓ Other social network accounts ✓ Payment services ✓ In-store WiFi ✓ *Rarely or not observed:* ☒ We Chat Account

Differences between retailers and other types of business as well as differences based on the geographical footprint of companies tend to be levelled out by clustering the companies as indicated above. The local peculiarities of Koblenz and Stellenbosch are briefly presented and described in the delineation of digital maturity stages that follows.

Offliners. "Offliners", elsewhere called "digital latecomers" or "digital laggards" (Tiago and Verissimo, 2014), typically appear in search engine results based on their Google Maps business account. Such companies do offer payment opportunities such as credit cards, debit cards and mobile payment services to their customers. Of particular note is the non-existence of a website or a social media account and, accordingly, any digital service within that stage. The cluster represents 31% of the companies in Koblenz and 30% in Stellenbosch. Typically, smaller companies, in particular locally-rooted companies, are to be found in this stage.

Basic Onliners. In contrast to the "Offliners", the group of "Basic Onliners" in addition employ website marketing, at least by having a website, and social media marketing, with an account, in most cases, on Facebook. This biggest group of companies is of the same proportion (46%) in both cities. Basic digital services and applications are prevalent, for instance the companies can easily be found on search engines' and Google Maps' top results, whereas specific services are only identified in scattered instances. The businesses classified here are thus findable, accessible and at least minimally present in the digital world of the Internet. This fundamental presence can also be seen as a starting point for further developments in the digital transformation.

Advanced Onliners. Companies advanced in digital habits can be characterized by their extensive application of website and social media marketing. First, companies (notably in Koblenz) start with search engine advertising activities. First omnichannel services are observed, albeit of a limited character. More and more service provider offer an appointment tool to their customers who may prearrange an appointment digitally to avoid any waiting time. In that regard and with the same intention of avoiding waiting time for customers, retailers increasingly offer product availability check. Consumers pre-check whether a specific good is available within a specific store. With services called "click-and-reserve" and "click-

and-collect" consumers minimize their efforts on-site on picking-up the selected goods. However, brand or corporate apps and other smartphone services are still not prevalent, although some do use these. In both cities around 22 per cent of the companies can be assigned to this stage of digital maturity. Local retailers, especially in Koblenz sample, are only marginally represented in this group.

Table 4. Digital engagement of Koblenz and Stellenbosch retailers

	Koblenz			Stellenbosch		
	All companies (500) All retailers (273) All local retailers (155)			All companies (500) All retailers (273) All local retailers (155)		
Website existence	1,14	1,14	1,17	1,14	1,08	0,85
Website responsiveness	1,79	1,78	1,59	1,38	1,38	1,01
Website usability	1,39	1,44	1,24	0,8	0,78	0,56
Contact opportunities	1,04	1,07	1,02	0,94	0,89	0,66
Opening hours	0,94	0,96	0,93	0,89	0,86	0,69
e-mail newsletter	0,73	1,06	0,47	0,62	0,7	0,36
e-commerce/delivery	0,76	1,6	0,66	0,54	0,54	0,38
Click&reserve/click&collect	0,31	0,49	0,23	0,44	0,49	0,25
Appointment tool	0,23	0,16	0,12	0,25	0,08	0,03
Product availability check	0,34	0,47	0,36	0,67	0,59	0,34
brand/cpompany app	0,17	0,19	0,01	0,36	0,36	0,05
Furrther smartphone	0,19	0,21	0,13	0,21	0,2	0,05
Organic search	1,93	1,9	1,89	1,4	1,38	1,22
Paid search	0,28	0,38	0,06	0,37	0,38	0,11
Google maps	1,83	1,83	1,74	1,45	1,46	1,3
Facebook	1,15	1,14	0,75	1,14	1,28	0,87
Instagram	0,77	0,89	0,45	0,74	0,85	0,37
We chat	0	0	0	0	0	0
Any other social media	0,38	0,52	0,1	0,48	0,55	0,27
Payment service	1,1	1,27	1,13	1,01	1,12	1,03
in-store wi-fi	1	1	0	0,29	0,22	0,1
Digital price labeling	0,9	0,95	0,92	0,76	0,97	0,7
Sum (digital mm)	**16**	**18**	**13**	**16**	**16**	**11**

Digital Forerunners. Finally, "Digital Forerunners" additionally employ search engine advertising on a regular basis and in some cases offer free WiFi in their locations. Nearly all digital services and applications are scored at an advanced level. Exceptionally, the social network We Chat is employed in a very few cases and targeted primarily at Chinese tourists. All in all, only 2% of the companies surveyed in both cities qualify as digital forerunners. Almost exclusively international corporations are to be found here.

Locally-Rooted Retailers Lagging Behind

Retailers' digital maturity is stronger and varies less than that of other types of business in both cities. Nevertheless, when it comes to small, locally-rooted retailers, there is a higher share of laggards and a lower share of forerunners in both towns. Accordingly, the computed digital maturity index is much lower for small, locally-rooted retailers (see Table 4).

A lot of the locally-rooted retailers make use of basic digital services and applications like a website with company information, a Google Maps account and a social network account on Facebook. However, such companies are lagging behind in the implementation of e-commerce and additional omnichannel services. Most smaller retailers still hesitate to invest in omnichannel services like a product availability check, even if such services will improve customers' experience and add to their existing on-site strength. One explanation for that can be seen in the lack of digital warehouse logistics encompassing all goods and items of a store. Without having established such a prerequisite the implementation of advanced digital services for customers is a huge challenge. However, local retailers are well advised to create these conditions when opportunities arise.

Table 5. Digital Maturity Index

	Stellenbosch	Koblenz
All companies	16	16
Locally-rooted retailers	11	13
National & international retailers	20	24

In regard to their branding practices, local retailers on the Koblenz database achieved an average of 8 points (which is much lower than the scores of international and national companies), whereas their counterparts in Stellenbosch scored more (an average of 10,4 points). The basic branding practices observed were signposting of the building, the entrance doorway and the shop window. Core brand elements like name, logo and colour are utilized rarely in Koblenz and much more often in Stellenbosch. Advanced practices like corporate fashion or in-store elements are not employed by most of the small retailers in either city. The branding rating model offered a range from 0 to 20. Again, applying Langley's (1999) quantification strategy, the average of the companies was calculated as 10 for Koblenz and 16 for Stellenbosch. In Koblenz, 57 per cent of the businesses have below-average branding practices, while in Stellenbosch this figure is 36 per cent. Companies in Koblenz, especially non-internationals of which there is a higher share than in Stellenbosch, are lagging behind in utilizing core branding practices and in-store branding opportunities.

Similar Tendencies of Digital Engagement and Branding Practices.

The study illustrates that the digital engagement of companies with an international footprint goes hand in hand with the level of intensity of branding practices. The reverse applies for locally-rooted smaller companies at the other end of the scale, in particular local retailers: according to the observational data, such companies are lagging behind in both constructs. Following this line of argumentation, it seems to be clear that the size of a company and the regional, supra-regional, national or international structure of the organisation in question is a decisive indicator and predictor of the characteristics of digital services and the use of brand practices.

FUTURE RESEARCH DIRECTIONS

A lot of research on digital commerce and branding practices has an empirical focus on one market (e.g., Berghaus and Back, 2016; Schmidt et al., 2017). By assessing the digital maturity and branding practices of retailers in two cities in two different countries, and comparing the results, this study offers a fresh perspective on the two constructs, construed as a continuum on which the businesses in the cities are located. The geographical footprint of companies (whether the businesses were considered to be local, national or international) is reported as a clear indicator and predictor for both constructs. Before this comparative assessment of digital maturity, it might have been assumed that companies in the more advanced economy (Koblenz, Germany) would have progressed further along the scales of digital maturity and branding practices. Yet it emerges that the opposite is the case or at least such an assumption would have been wrong. As mentioned above, in Koblenz 57 per cent of the businesses have below-average branding practices, while for Stellenbosch this figure is 36 per cent. Emerging markets are characterized by a high representation of international market entrants (UNDP, 2018). In this instance, the emerging market hosts more companies that are non-local (national and international) and thus feature a higher level of maturity in both constructs. Conversely, a large number of long-standing, established family-owned retailers can be identified in Koblenz, whereas in Stellenbosch there is a greater proportion of newcomers. Recently-founded companies as well as international market entrants are characterized by a more advanced level of digital maturity. On the other hand, the extensive presence of long-standing and established family-owned retailers is a strong indicator of resistance to digital engagement. A look at the development of this structural difference between the two cities shows that in Stellenbosch new settlements of international chains can be seen to a greater extent, while in Koblenz only slowly and sporadically small local retailers are being replaced by larger organizations with appropriate conditions.

Theoretical Implications

The study offers insight into two different markets and shows how digitalization is shaped within those markets. By illuminating which dimensions are represented or not, the research substantiates the understanding of digital maturity in the case of retailing as well as in the case of service providers. It also makes a contribution towards improving the definition and characterization of the term of digital maturity. By illustrating which kind of digital services contribute to the manifestation of the four stages of digital maturity the understanding of that term is improved. In this way, individual digital services can be distinguished from one another and characterised as essential basic elements or elements of advanced digitality. For example, findability in search engines on the Internet is one of the basic elements, whereas advertising in search engines is more of an advanced service. The study also demonstrates the characteristics of emerging markets that lead to an increasing level of digital maturity and branding professionalism in comparison to developed markets. The study innovatively indicates how digital maturity and branding practices correlate. Finally, methodologically speaking, the study offers an assessment of digital maturity and branding practices that can easily be applied in any city. Further application and implementation of the assessment of digital services and brand practices would help to further deepen the understanding of both constructs. By extending such field research to cities with different structures of organizations, for instance megacities like Cape Town and Berlin, or two geographical areas of different circumstances, like in China or the US, the digital disruption and development of retailing, in particular local retailing, could be analyzed and better understood.

Practical Implications

In both countries, practitioners – in particular owners of locally-rooted companies – may recognize areas for activities to extend (in particular) omnichannel services and in-store branding opportunities. For instance, offering free WiFi to visitors should be a priority for most businesses. Most notably, long-standing retailers in Koblenz are urged to invest in digitalization beyond a website, Google Maps and a social media account, and to extend their commitment to branding, using brand elements in-store and more generally. On the other hand, Stellenbosch retailers are advised to make more effective use of basic services, for example, through search engine optimization and Google Maps discoverability. Contrasting different developments in different markets, may help practitioners to initiate changes to progress to the next stage of development.

Recommendations for Practitioners:

- Complete basic digital services (e.g., search engine optimization to improve discoverableness in the Internet and within navigation apps, free WiFi services for customers)
- Utilize basic branding opportunities (e.g., labeling of the store, packaging, shopping window)
- Extend omnichannel services that may add value for customers (e.g., appointment tools, availability checks, click-and-collect services)
- Extend in store brand management (e.g., with corporate fashion, interieur, brand colours,)

Limitations

Limiting the assessment and comparison to two cities within two markets renders the study comparable to a case study, with its inherent limitations. Case studies offer rich insights and enable researchers to reach a deeper understanding of the case as representing a phenomenon. On the other hand, case study research is limited in generalizability (Yin, 2011). The selection of two cities in the study at hand shows a strong bias and limits the interpretation of the findings to the specific circumstances for retailing in the two cities. This limitation provides a springboard for extending the research to (a) other similar medium-sized cities in the same markets, and (b) bigger cities (e.g., comparing Berlin and Cape Town) or rural areas and (c) including other regions like Southern Asia or the US. A second limitation of the study is the lack of a weighting mechanism for the dimensions of the constructs within the assessment. The scales of the dimensions were used unweighted, because digitalization as a phenomenon is young, dynamic and unexplored. The importance of the specific dimensions of the constructs may vary over time. Nevertheless, there are dimensions with an antecedent character (e.g., the existence of a website) which should be considered in future research. Moreover, the observations conducted in the study do not extend to any impacts or effects related to the constructs. No observation was made of the behaviour of consumers, or of indicators of the financial performance of the retailers or other types of business, such as an increase in sales volume. The assessment is limited to observation of the appearance of the dimensions of the two constructs and scoring the character of a dimension. For instance, a retailer may offer a product-availability-check for all products available in a brick-and-mortar store. This advanced digital service would be awarded two points, whether or not customers are aware of the service, and whether or not the investment in such a service has led to an increase in sales.

CONCLUSION

German and South African consumers increasingly use the Internet to look for product information and to purchase online products and services such as flights, books, consumer electronics and fashion. Nevertheless, about 25 per cent of German and South African companies in the study sample are more or less offline, not offering even basic digital services, while a significant number of companies ignore opportunities for branding. The constructs are shown to be interconnected, digital engagement is displayed on a continuum and differences between the developed and the emerging economy are reported as unexpected. The geographical footprint and retailers' tenure seem to have a significant impact on both constructs. Thus, the company and retailer portfolio of the city in a developing market displays more mature digitalization and branding practices. Future research may allow for a further development of a digital maturity scale.

REFERENCES

Berghaus, S., & Back, A. (2016). Stages in digital business transformation: results of an empirical maturity study. *MCIS 2016 Proceedings*, 22. https://aisel.aisnet.org/mcis2016/22

Brennen, S., & Kreis, D. (2014). *Digitalization and digitalization.* http://culturedigitally.org/2014/09/digitalization-and-digitalization

Burmann, C., Halaszovich, T., Schade, M., & Hemmann, F. (2017). *Identity-based brand management.* Wiesbaden: Springer Gabler. doi:10.1007/978-3-658-13561-4

Chadha, S. (2018). *The CMO of 2020: navigating the journey towards digital marketing maturity in APAC.* https://bit.ly/2UGzakO

Constantine, C. (2015). *Landlords must adapt to demands of savvy customers.* Estate Gazette.

Darmstadt, I. H. K. (2017). *Vor Ort erfolgreich bestehen. Ein Leitfaden für den stationären Einzelhandel* [Successful on site. A guideline for the stationary retail trade]. https://www.darmstadt.ihk.de/produktmarken/standortpolitik/branchen/Handel_Absatzwirtschaft/Brancheninformationen/Check-Liste-fuer-den-stationaeren-Einzelhandel/3639562

Devasagayam, P. R., Buff, C. L., Aurand, T. W., & Judson, K. M. (2010). Building brand community membership within organizations: A viable internal branding alternative? *Journal of Product and Brand Management, 19*(3), 210–217. doi:10.1108/10610421011046184

Euromonitor International. (2018). *Digital disruption in retail*. https://blog.euromonitor.com/digital-disruption-in-retail/

Global Economic Governance Africa. (2017). *E-commerce country case study South Africa*. http://www.gegafrica.org/publications/e-commerce-country-case-study-south-africa

HDE. (2018). *Online-Monitor*. https://www.einzelhandel.de/online-monitor

Heinemann, G. (2017). *Die Neuerfindung des stationären Einzelhandels - Kundenzentralität und ultimative Usability für Stadt und Handel der Zukunft* [The reinvention of the stationary retail trade - customer centrality and ultimate usability for the city and trade of the future]. Wiesbaden: Springer-Verlag. doi:10.1007/978-3-658-15862-0

Hesse, A. (2019). Digitalisierung, Omnichanneling und Local-Commerce-Modelle aus Sicht des lokal-stationären Einzelhandels [Digitization, omnichanneling and local commerce models from the point of view of local-stationary retailing]. In Wissenschaftliche Schriften des Fachbereichs Wirtschaftswissenschaften, Hochschule Koblenz - University of Applied Sciences, Nr. 29.

Hirsch, M. (2012). The development of the retail environment in South Africa. *Retail Mark*, *8*(1), 82–85.

Hootsuite. (2019). *The global state of digital in 2019*. https://hootsuite.com/resources/digital-in-2019

Iglesias, O., Ind, N., & Alfaro, M. (2013). The organic view of the brand: A brand value co-creation model. *Journal of Brand Management*, *20*(8), 670–688. doi:10.1057/bm.2013.8

Kapferer, J. N. (2004). *The new strategic brand management: creating and sustaining brand equity long term*. London: Kogan Page.

Keller, L. K. (2013). *Strategic brand management: building, measuring, and managing brand equity* (4th ed.). London: Pearson.

Koblenz Stadtmarketing. (2017). *Shopping & Genuss* [Shopping and enjoyment]. https://www.koblenz-stadtmarketing.de/shopping-genuss/

Langley, A. (1999). Strategies for theorizing from process data. *Academy of Management Review*, *24*(4), 691–710. doi:10.5465/amr.1999.2553248

Lazaris, C., & Vrechopolous, A. (2014). 'From Multichannel to Omnichannel' retailing: review of the literature and calls for research. *2nd International Conference on Contemporary Marketing Issues (ICCMI)*, 18-20.

Malhotra, K., & Birks, D. F. (2007). *Marketing research: an applied approach*. Harlow, UK: Pearson Education Limited. doi:10.1108/S1548-6435(2007)3

McGhie, A. (2012). *Brand is a four letter word: positioning and the real art of marketing*. Charleston: Advantage Media Group.

Oxford College of Marketing. (2016). *Digital disruption: what is it and how does it impact businesses?* https://blog.oxfordcollegeofmarketing.com/2016/02/22/what-is-digital-disruption/

Redler, J. (2018). *Die Store Brand: Einkaufsstätten als Marken verstehen, aufbauen und steuern* [The store brand: understanding, building and managing shopping stores as brands]. Wiesbaden: Springer. doi:10.1007/978-3-658-09709-7

Rigby, D. K., & Tager, S. (2014). *Leading a digital transformation.* http://www.bain.com/publications/articles/leading-a-digital-transformation.aspx

Schmidt, H. J. (2015). *Markenführung* [Brand management]. Wiesbaden: Springer.

Schmidt, H. J., Mason, R., Steenkamp, P., & Mugobo, V. (2017). Does brand orientation contribute to retailers' success? An empirical study in the South African market. *Journal of Retailing and Consumer Services*, *38*, 210–222. doi:10.1016/j.jretconser.2017.06.012

Shahiduzzaman, M., Kowalkiewicz, M., Barrett, R., & McNaughton, M. (2017). *Digital business: towards a value-centric maturity model.* Academic Press.

Tiago, M. T. P. M. B., & Veríssimo, J. M. C. (2014). Digital marketing and social media: Why bother? *Business Horizons*, *57*(6), 703–708. doi:10.1016/j.bushor.2014.07.002

Todor, R. D. (2014). The importance of branding and rebranding for strategic marketing. *Bulletin of the Transilvania University of Braşov*, *7*(56), 60–64.

UNDP. (2018). *2018 Statistical update: United Nations Development Programme Human Development Reports.* http://hdr.undp.org/en/2018-update

Walk, K. (1998). *How to write a comparative analysis.* https://writingcenter.fas.harvard.edu/pages/how-write-comparative-analysis

Wang, J., & Fung, R. Y. (2015). Dynamic appointment scheduling with patient preferences and choices. *Industrial Management & Data Systems*, *115*(4), 700–717. doi:10.1108/IMDS-12-2014-0372

Western Cape Government. (2015). *Socio-economic profile Stellenbosch municipality.* www.western-cape.gov.za

Yin, R. K. (2011). *Applications of case study research.* Thousand Oaks, CA: Sage Publications.

KEY TERMS AND DEFINITIONS

Advanced Onliners: The term advanced onliners refers to a group of businesses that are advanced in digital habits characterized by their extensive application of website and social media marketing. In addition, omnichannel services are observed, albeit of a limited character.

Basic Onliners: The group of "Basic Onliners" refers to businesses that employ website marketing, at least by having a website, and social media marketing, with an account, in most cases, on Facebook. Basic digital services and applications are prevalent, for instance the companies can easily be found on search engines' and Google Maps' top results, whereas specific services are only identified in scattered instances.

Branding Practices: Branding practices refers to all kind of using brand elements like labelling, colours, slogans or else.

Digital Commerce: The term digital commerce is increasingly used encompassing all commercial services that build on electronic or digital platforms, processes, devices or applications. The term extends the term e-commerce which concentrates on electronic sales activities.

Digital Forerunners: The group of digital forerunners employ search engine advertising on a regular basis and in some cases offer free WiFi in their locations. Such companies offer various digital services and applications to their customers aiming for a better service.

Digital Maturity: Digital maturity is an important concept increasingly used to rate the technology-driven progress of industries, businesses and organizations. The term characterizes digital maturation as a process whereby a company becomes increasingly digital over time by leveraging digital technologies.

Local Retailers: The term local retailers refers in particular to businesses that focus on a brick-and-mortar store, in many cases family owned with a longer history of providing services or selling goods in a limited geographic are.

Offliners: Offliners are businesses that do not use digital services and the Internet, or only use them to a limited extent. In other sources these are also referred to as digital latecomers or digital laggards.

Omnichannel Behaviour of Customers: The term describes customers who switch touchpoints throughout their decision-making process.

Omnichanneling: Omnichanneling is an approach to sales that seeks to provide customers with a seamless shopping experience. Accordingly, omnichanneling reflects the need for retailers to keep all their channels up to date, with their digital appearances linking all their stores to their online platforms, and to be accessible on all the touchpoints that customers prefer.

Chapter 10
If You Want to Trigger an Emotional Purchase, Don't Make Your Customers Think:
Understanding Customer Decision Making

Liraz Margalit
IDC Interdisciplinary Center Herzliya, Israel

ABSTRACT

The classic economic theory describes consumers as rational economic actors that select an alternative only after considering all the relevant information. However, while the logical process is certainly a key factor in considered purchases such as insurance or financial products, it is actually detrimental to the retail-consumer industry, where emotional decision making or the impulse purchase plays a central role. Although we like to think of ourselves as rational creatures, absorbing information, weighing it carefully, and making thoughtful decisions, many of our most crucial choices are made by what we call hunches, gut feelings and a somewhat automatic reaction that is beyond or beneath consciousness. We like to refer to this feeling as intuition ("I have a very good feeling about this house"), but the reality is that this "intuition" is an established part of emotion-based learning. This chapter deals with the significant role of emotions in everyday purchase decisions.

INTRODUCTION

...People will forget what you said, people will forget what you did, but people will never forget how you made them feel. - Maya Angelou (2019)

Years ago, when retailers actually knew their individual customers in the physical world, the butcher knew to offer Mrs. Jones the nicer cuts, whereas Mr. Smith preferred whatever was on sale. The florist could subtly direct Mrs. Jones to the flowers nearing the end of their shelf-life, while making sure they matched the color scheme of her living room. Retailers knew that how each customer felt vis-à-vis their establishment could make or break their business.

DOI: 10.4018/978-1-7998-3115-0.ch010

Copyright © 2020, IGI Global. Copying or distributing in print or electronic forms without written permission of IGI Global is prohibited.

And there is much more to it. it's not only about customer's preferences. Interactions in the physical space enable salespeople to address a variety of needs, some functional and some emotional. "It's like a sixth sense. When a guy walks into the store, I can tell in, like, five seconds." The veteran clothing salesperson I'm interviewing warms quickly to my questions about his art. "I watch the way he walks, his eyes. I can tell if he's happy, sad or stressed. I can tell if he needs to talk, or just wants to get on with finding whatever he's looking for. I know how to respond to make my commission."

Today, the e-commerce ecosystem has reached a level of sophistication we could only have dreamed of a decade ago (Monroe & Barrett, 2019). With competition only a click away (Tesseras, 2013), online retailers truly appreciate what small-town retailers understood so well: successful product marketing is all about looking at your products and services from the customer's point of view.

In the digital arena, there are more customers and prospects than the local butcher or florist ever imagined. And there are endless sources of detailed data about these individuals. The challenge facing online retail today is no longer what we know about each of our millions of customers and prospects. Rather, retailers today need to focus on effectively harnessing this knowledge to treat each individual as an individual.

This chapter would like to take a look at the rational and emotional processes that impact shopper intent, behavior, decision making and content consumption and provide some concrete tips that can help online retailers leverage this practical and theoretical knowledge, to identify and respond to what the author likes to refer to as the customers' Digital Body Language - the digital signals made by customers and seek our interpretation (Niles-Hofmann & Celentano, 2015; Woods, 2009).

BACKGROUND

The Traditional Assumption Regarding Online Customers' Behavior

Classic economic theory describes consumers as rational creature, a rational economic actor who select an alternative only after considering all the relevant information, reading ratings and reviews and making all the necessary comparisons (Smith, 2019). Most theories of choice assume that decisions derive from an assessment of the future outcomes of various options and alternatives through some type of cost-benefit analyses (Berry et al., 2013).

The field of economics, which is concerned with formalizing the rules that govern human decision making, has begun to focus increasingly on forms of decision making that go beyond simple cost–benefit analysis. Traditional economic theory assumed that most decision making involves rational Bayesian maximization of expected utility (Cyert & DeGroot, 1987), as if humans were equipped with unlimited knowledge, time, and information-processing power. The prevalent assumption of this view was that a direct link exists between knowledge and the implementation of behavioral decisions - that is, that one does what one actually knows. In the 1970s and 1980s, decision-making researchers identified phenomena that systematically violated such normative principles of economic behavior. Kahneman & Tversky led this new approach to describe how people think and make decisions. They have developed an alternative model, called prospect theory in which choices among risky prospects exhibit several pervasive effects that are inconsistent with the basic tenets of utility theory (Kahneman & Tversky, 1979). In the 1990s, they began to show that many forms of decision making, especially those that involve a high level of risk and uncertainty, involve biases and emotions that act at an implicit level (Hastie & Dawes, 2010). Marketing professionals began to think about how individual identities shaped buying behaviors.

The influence of emotions on decision-making is largely ignored. Although there are many studies that aim to explore the mechanism of Impulse or emotional purchase, the literature of consumer behavior relates solely to its functional value - what needs does the purchase fulfill for the customer, social reinforcement, self-worth, status etc. or refers to the procedural aspects of impulse purchase, namely describes the stage in the decision-making process where consumers apply impulse purchase (mostly before checkout). However, the literature ignores the mechanism of purchase decision making and today, as the buying process moves online, it's critical to understand what are the components which drive customers to buy online.

The traditional theory speculates that our purchasing decisions follow the principle of "utility maximization." In other words, when we try to decide which item to buy, we measure each potential selection against the criteria most important to us (cost, warranty, features, safety, etc), and choose the option that most accurately meets our needs. This model also assumes that our preferences are well-defined and constant over time. But is this actually reflected in the 'real life' decisions we make every day? Behavior psychology suggests just the opposite. While the logical process is certainly a key factor in considered purchases such as insurance or financial products, it can actually be detrimental in the consumer retail context, wherein emotional decision-making or impulse purchasing plays a central role.

One of the most significant factors in the purchasing experience is the information we review about a certain product prior to the decision to purchase the product. The prevalent assumptions regarding e-commerce product pages dictate that exposure to reviews, product details and technical specifications increase the likelihood of purchasing the product.

Product information is considered to be a crucial factor in purchasing experience. According to the American Express Retail Monitor (2018), 85 percent of retailers view the provision of product information as a key factor in attracting consumers. The prevalent assumptions regarding ecommerce product pages dictate that exposure to reviews, product details and technical specifications increase the likelihood of purchasing the product.

However, analyses of e-commerce websites that the author conducted for a retail clients revealed surprising behavior: visitors who were exposed to additional details and information about the product were less likely to purchase the product, compared to visitors who were exposed only to the product image and general details. Not only is this strange, it contradicts everything we know about customer behavior and decision making in the digital arena.

To confirm these findings, author conducted an A/B test. The author created 2 versions of the same product page (please see Figure 1 and Figure 2) one version which contains detailed information about the product, reviews, technical specifications, closed description and the second version was identical version of the page wherein information was hidden behind tabs. In the second version customers could only see the product image, switch colors and size. After 1.5 months we decided to reveal the results. Surprisingly we obtained the same results: Customers who were exposed to additional details and information about the product were less likely to purchase compared to customers who were exposed only to the product image and general details (Figure 1). when the information was hidden behind tabs, the percentage of visitors who added the product to their cart was significantly higher.

Exposure to too much information and data forces customers to invest cognitive resources that they weren't planning on investing, and automatically triggers the rational process.

Figure 1. Product page without information (only to the product image and general details)

Once the rational system is involved, the purchase process becomes far more complicated. Visitors now feel the need to conduct research on the product, weighing its pros and cons against others on the market. Moreover, they may begin to second-guess their initial interest in the product, as thoughts such as "Do I really need this?" creep into their minds.

Ironically, customers are not aware of the effect that "too much information" has on their behavior. When asked, they repeatedly state that being provided with information about the product before purchasing plays a central role in their purchasing decisions.

What's Going on Here?

How can we explain those behavioral differences between customers who were exposed to product information and those we were not?

Over the last few decades, there has been a growing interest in the emotional basis of complex decision-making. This interest was, in large part, inspired by the well-established finding that neurological patients with lesions to ventromesial (VM) frontal lobes often showed normal intelligence, with near or near-to-normal performance on a range of "executive" tasks (Turnbull, et al, 2014). However, in spite of these domains of preservation, such individuals often displayed difficulties in learning from past mistakes, with real life manifestations such as entering repeatedly into inappropriate relationships, and unsuitable business agreements. Such decisions may immediately seem rewarding, but typically prove to be counter-productive in the long run, often leading to career termination and financial losses (Damasio et al., 1991; Bechara et al., 2000). Notably, such individuals display failures in using emotional feedback from previous situations (i.e., the punishing consequences of impulsive actions) in the guidance of their future choices.

Measuring these decision-making failures in the real-world is challenging, both ethically and methodologically. The Iowa Gambling Task (IGT) was developed as a simple neuropsychological tool to tap into such deficits in emotional-processing, which might be associated with complex decision-making difficulties, as observed in individuals with frontal lobe lesions (Rolls et al., 1994; Damasio et al., 1996; Lezak et al., 2012).

Figure 2. Product page with additional details and information about the product

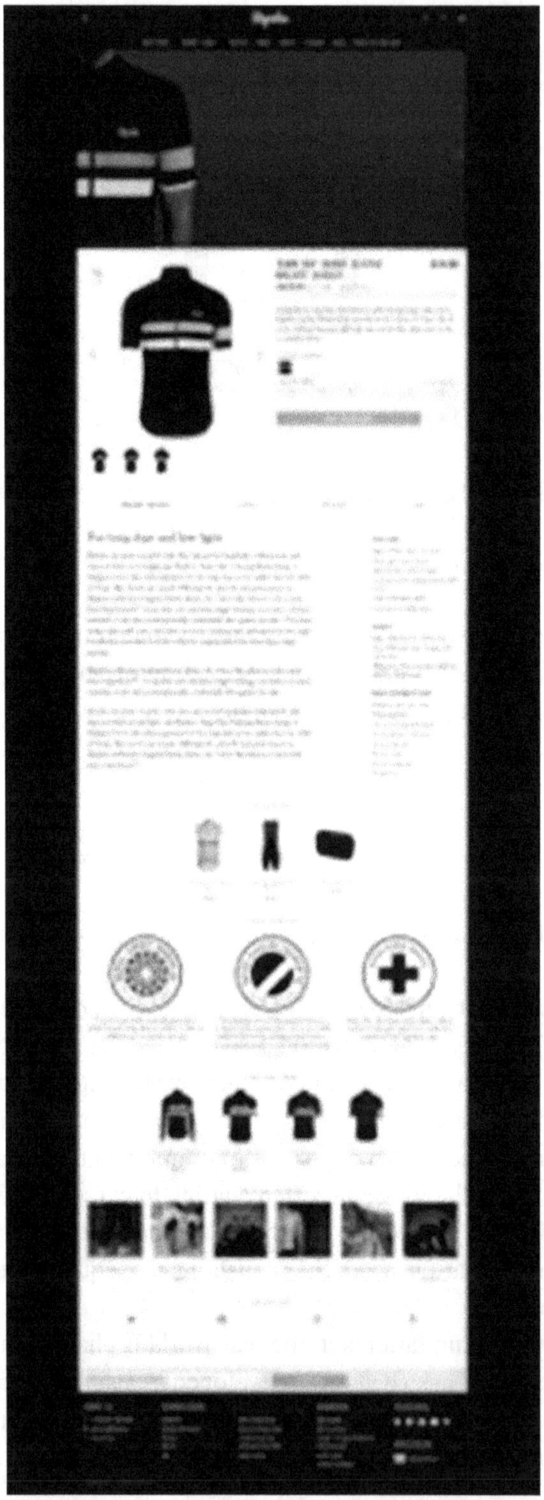

The Iowa Gambling Task (IGT)

The Iowa Gambling gambling task has penetrated somewhat into public consciousness via its discussion in Antonio Damasio's book Descartes' Error. The task involves four virtual card decks represented on a computer screen (Please see Figure 3). The object of the game is to win money, and when a card is drawn the result may be to add or subtract. The four decks are not created equal. Two of the decks that can be selected will reliably provide a profit in the long-term. They don't give big wins, but the losses (or "punishments") are smaller, and you'll come out on top if you stick to them. The other two decks however provide huge profits, but also huge losses, and over enough trials will leave you bankrupt. Of course, this information isn't revealed to the participant – just that they should win as much money as possible.

The Researchers at the University of Iowa asked participants to pick one card at a time from four different decks while their physiological responses were measured. The card decks were set up such that the first two led to an overall loss in score over the long run, while the other two led to an overall gain. After a time most people figure that out and begin exclusively sticking to "good decks", but even before they are consciously aware of this, the "bad decks" begin generating higher stress responses, for example in terms of galvanic skin conductance when the computer cursor hovers over a "bad deck".

Figure 3. The Iowa Gambling task involves four virtual card decks represented on a computer screen

The participants "figured out" the game after choosing about 50 cards and could then explain in a logical manner why choosing cards from the first two decks was a bad idea. But the logical process described above was not the only process that was observed. The Participants exhibited stress responses including increased skin conductivity and increased sweat gland activity in their palms when hovering over the losing decks after only 10 cards. In other words, the participants unconsciously anticipated punishment 40 cards before they could articulate it, and actually figured out the game subconsciously long before they had realized it consciously.

Decision-Making Outside Awareness

An important element in our understanding the nature of emotion-based-learning, and the factors that drive learning on the Iowa Gambling Task in particular, is the question of conscious awareness. Conscious awareness and good performance on the task are unrelated. The subjects can demonstrate good performance, or in other words, they can make decisions that are considered beneficial for them, without realizing what are the cognitive and somatic processes that guide and direst those decisions. As demonstrated in the Iowa gambling task and in following experiments, most time, we don't have accesses to the emotional processes behind our decisions and choices but interestingly, when asked, we are very good at providing rational reasons for why we choose the way we did.

The emotional stage of decision making is done outside of conscious awareness and reveal itself through hunches and got feelings. When it comes to purchase decision process, most crucial choices are actually based on hunches, gut feelings, or automatic reactions that are beyond our consciousness. If we want to truly understand what types of factors influence customers' decision-making, we first need to understand the cognitive and emotional processes that underlie our decisions.

MAIN FOCUS OF THE CHAPTER

Purchase Decision Id the Result of Two Competing Processes

The most important thing you should consider when trying to analyze and predict human behavior is that human behavior is not the product of a single process, but rather reflects the interaction of different specialized emotional and rational processes. There are two different types of decisions that people make. *Value-based* decisions are made in the orbitofrontal cortex (OFC). So, during those times when you really are comparing the Honda to the Subaru when you are shopping for a car, then you are making a value-based goal decision and the second type *is emotional based* decisions that are controlled by the limbic areas of our brain. The part of out brain that controls emotions.

The emotional process is generally automatic, affective and heuristic-based. It quickly proposes intuitive answers to problems as they arise. Emotion operates below the surface of consciousness, transfers messages through biological channels such as skin conductivity and sweat glands, and automatically makes many of our decisions. The rational process, on the other hand, is slow, effortful, conscious and rule-based. It generates logical and rational responses.

Although we like to think of ourselves as rational creatures, absorbing information, weighing it carefully, and making thoughtful decisions, many of our most crucial choices are made by what we call hunches, gut feelings and a somewhat automatic reaction that is beyond or beneath consciousness. We like to refer to this feeling as intuition ("I have a very good feeling about this house"), but the reality is that this "intuition" is an established part of emotion-based learning.

Purchase decisions are not the result of careful evaluation of various alternatives through cost-benefit analysis. Rather, they are guided by affective reactions arising directly from the decision itself at the time of deliberation. For the vast majority of products, it is preferable that visitors remain in emotional mode during the purchase process.

By understanding and adapting to the nuances of human intent, online retailers can optimize the shopping experience, maximize its ultimate outcome, and capitalize on consumer brand awareness. To understand the psychology driving human behavior, it's important to note that incidental variables affect the way visitors evaluate a product more than one might imagine. Often, browsers are not aware of the environmental cues affecting their online decision-making. If asked, customers will generally explain their decisions as completely rational and based on a logic thinking process. However, when web users choose between several options, most of the time their decisions are based on automatic evaluations that occur without conscious awareness. They are often unaware of the variables that influence automatic decisions so instead or hoping that your customers will do what is expected from them when using the site or app, if you understand what motivate them, you have the ability to influence their behavior in the right direction. If you give someone a lot of information, then they will switch from emotional to goal-directed. So if you want someone to make an emotional decision, don't give them too much information to review. If you want them to make a goal-directed decision then *do* give them information to review.

Site owners should strive to bring or keep visitors in an emotional mode, to encourage emotional purchases and avoid over-examination of product or service details. The secret of the impulse buy is to trigger your visitors' intuitive and emotional response, encouraging them to buy because of how it makes them feel, not for what it does or how well it stacks up.

The literature refers to the emotional vs rational systems as system 1 and system 2, or the Dual-process and dual-system theories, meaning that there are two distinct processing modes available for a cognitive task, which employ different procedures and may yield conflicting results. One process (system 1) is characterized as fast, automatic and non-conscious, the other (system 2) as slow, controlled and conscious. System 1 processes are also described variously as associative, heuristic or intuitive, and system 2 processes as rule-based, analytical or reflective. In addition, it is often claimed that System 2 is an evolutionarily recent, uniquely human system, which is the source of our capacity for decontextualized, abstract thinking in accordance with logical norms. The core of dual-process theory is present in the everyday distinction between intuition and reason – the former immediate, quasi-perceptual, sensitive to subconscious cues and sometimes biased; and the latter slow, effortful, explicit and more cautious.

The most important pre-modern account of the unconscious (historically, at least) was, of course, Freud's. Freud held that the human mind is composed of two systems: one conscious, and the other unconscious (Freud, 2018). He held that these systems operate in different modes ('primary process' and 'secondary process'): the former associative, and the latter logical. He also held that the contents of the unconscious were inaccessible to the conscious mind, and that the unconscious system was a source of motivation and mental conflict. With all of this, most modern dual-process theorists agree. Nevertheless, there are huge differences between Freud's unconscious and contemporary psychologists' System 1 (i.e. the system supporting fast, automatic, non-conscious processes). The Freudian unconscious consists largely of repressed impulses or memories; it is not a reasoning system and seeks only to maximize pleasure and minimize pain; and it can influence action and conscious thought only indirectly, through dreams, neurotic symptoms and symbolic activities (Frankish, 2010). By contrast, System 1 (the 'cognitive unconscious', as it is sometimes called) has its own knowledge base and goal structure, which are not the product of repression; it is a set of inferential mechanisms adapted for the control of everyday behavior; and it can directly influence action and conscious thought.

The Dual Process Theory and the Digital World

The dual process theory of the human mind defines, among other things, two distinct routes by which people process information: central and peripheral. These routes are reflected in or influence an individual's state of mind, and are themselves influenced by motivation (a desire to process the message) and ability (available cognitive resources).

Cacioppo and Petty () state that there are two "routes" to persuasion: central and peripheral. The central route to persuasion consists of thoughtful consideration of the arguments (ideas, content) of the message. When a receiver is doing central processing, he or she is being an active participant in the process of persuasion. Central processing has two prerequisites: It can only occur when the receiver has both the motivation and the ability to think about the message and its topic. If the listener doesn't care about the topic of the persuasive message, he or she will almost certainly lack the motivation to do central processing. On the other hand, if the listener is distracted or has trouble understanding the message, he or she will lack the ability to do central processing.

The peripheral route to persuasion occurs when the listener decides whether to agree with the message based on other cues besides the strength of the arguments or ideas in the message. For example, a listener may decide to agree with a message because the source appears to be an expert, or is attractive. The peripheral route also occurs when a listener is persuaded because he or she notices that a message has many arguments -- but lacks the ability or motivation to think about them individually. In other words, peripheral cues, like source expertise (credibility) or many arguments in one message, are a short-cut. The author does not want to or can't think carefully about the ideas in this persuasive message, but it is a fair gamble to go ahead agree with the message if the source appears to be knowledgeable or if there are many arguments in support of the message. This route occurs when the auditor is unable or unwilling to engage in much thought on the message. Receivers engaged in peripheral processing are more passive than those doing central processing.

- A central route is taken when a person is motivated to generate thoughts in response to substantive content – for example, a shopper who compares prices of similar products. The central route is controlled by higher-level brain areas, and reflects rational thinking.
- A peripheral route is taken when someone is unable or unwilling to execute a cognitive assignment. This route is controlled by emotional brain areas, and uses heuristics and cognitive biases when cognitive resources or the motivation required to process information are lacking.

The Takeaways

- It is important to bear in mind that a single user can apply each of the cognitive routes alternately and even shift routes during the same visit.
- In the absence of sufficient levels of stimulation, unintentional visitors will get bored and move on. Similarly, a sense of disorientation can lead your goal-oriented users to abandon your site permanently.

- Thus, it is mission-critical that your site be optimized for both types.
- On any given page, ensure that you provide sufficient levels of stimulation to engage unintentional visitors, as well as elements - such as navigation tools and search options – to help goal-oriented users take the minimum steps necessary to reach their goal.

As we saw in the two experiments described above, the customer's mindset affects his digital decision making, as in the case of impulse vs rational purchase, and it also affects the costomers' digital behavior i.e. how the customer is going to approach information on the website or app, but the dual process theory also influences the customers content consumption on websites.

Whether it's YouTube, Vine or integrated content -- video has quickly become one of the most impactful ways to speak to an audience. According to a recent study (Karppinen et al, 2005) shows that if you want visitors to your site to share and interact with your content, delivering it via video is the best way to go. Consumers are 39 percent more likely to share content if it's delivered via video, and 36 percent more likely to comment and 56 percent more likely to give that video a coveted "like."

But it's not time to bury print just yet. Watching a video and reading a print article require completely separate cognitive processes, and for businesses, it's important to understand the differences before you make a decision to use a video clip instead of print content.

Internet users do love video. The average consumer with an Internet connection watches roughly 206 videos per month, and Nielsen claims 64 percent of marketers expect video to dominate their strategies in the near future. Taking a look at the numbers, it seems like a no-brainer to say that video content is more engaging than text. But tapping into a little basic psychology, we can further break down these findings, and also describe the conditions that will drive visitors to prefer text.

Different Types of Cognitive Tasks

Videos are processed by the brain 60,000 times faster than text. Think about the heavy lifting your cognitive system has to do when reading an article vs. watching a video clip! Humans are hardwired to avoid demanding cognitive strain, so this tendency toward "laziness" will, more often than not, invite us to choose information that is easy to process over the form that makes us put out a lot of effort.

Reading articles and watching videos also require two different brain processes (please see Figure 4 - a comparison between these 2 cognitive task). When we read, the process requires us to be actively involved. The brain gets a much better workout when reading vs. watching, and the process requires a longer attention span and deeper cognitive efforts.

Reading is active. When we read an article, we don't just look at the words in front of us -- we create thoughts about that content, activating our mental structures. Reading requires the production of "inner voice," which dials up our attention span. That means that careful reading is not an automatic process, but rather occurs when we actively process what we are reading.

Watching a video, though, is passive. It's much less demanding and more of an automatic process, asking a lot less energy and effort on behalf of the person watching.

Figure 4. Video vs Text: two different brain processes

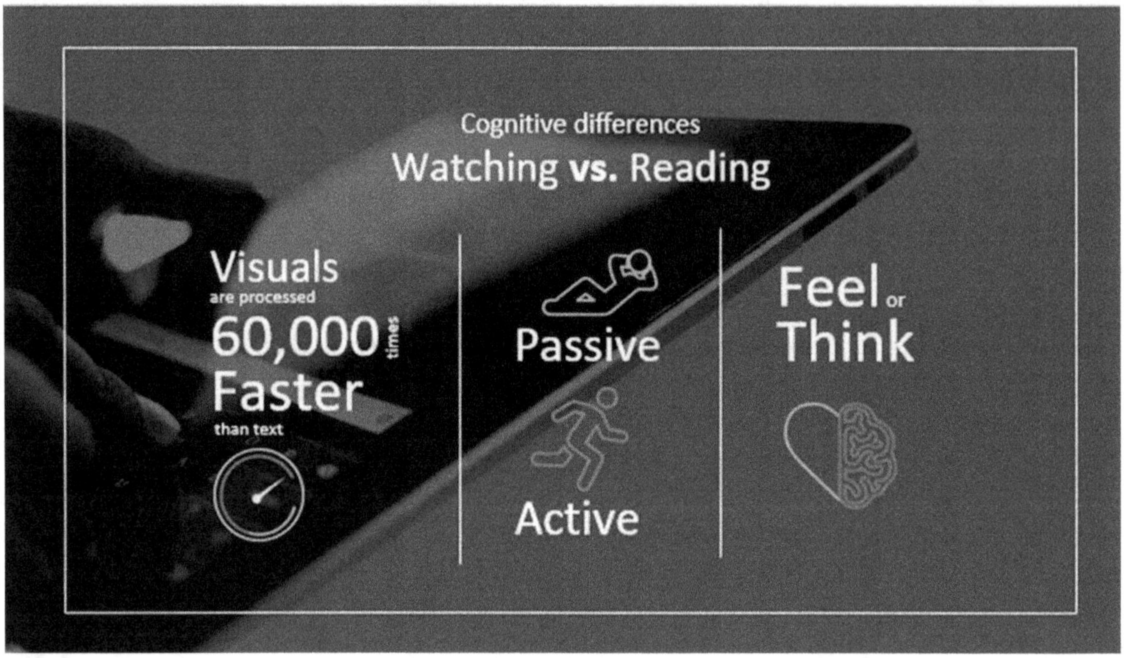

SOLUTIONS AND RECOMMENDATIONS

The dual process theory is key to understanding shopper intent. It is supported by the observable differences between goal-oriented visitors - who visit a website for a specific reason - and unintentional visitors - who are just passing time, checking out what a website has to offer, or seeking entertainment. A recent analysis the author has conducted, illustrates the distinctive patterns of behavior between these two groups in the digital world. The first group comprised visitors who arrived intentionally at a sub-section of a site using the site's primary navigation. The second group was made up of visitors who arrived at that same sub-section after being automatically redirected there from a video on the homepage. The differences in behavioral patterns were very clear. Goal-oriented visitors (those who navigated to the page on purpose) ignored the page's featured elements and went directly to navigational elements like search and the "Browse Alphabetically" menu that showcased the site's assets. For these visitors, the central route was clearly active. Visitors who were automatically redirected to the page, however, leisurely examined the featured articles and images, showing interest in colorful and captivating images. These visitors ignored informative text and demonstrated no interest in the Search box. For them, the peripheral route had taken control. I then analyzed the behavioral patterns of each group above, and uncovered a number of significant differences:

- Unintentional visitors were engaged with the page three times longer than intentional visitors
- Unintentional visitors scrolled all the way down the page; goal-oriented visitors did not
- Unintentional visitors were intrigued by evocative keywords like "temptation," "adultery" and "shocking," while goal-oriented visitors were less susceptible to sensational language

- Unintentional visitors viewed an average of eight pages on the site while goal-oriented visitors viewed far fewer pages and spent much less time on the site
- The next pages visited by goal-oriented visitors were from search results, while unintentional visitors mostly clicked through to featured content

FUTURE REASERCH AND RECOMMENDATIONS

In the digital sphere, there is an obvious limit to the sensory experiences that can be deployed. The challenge is to apply these insights and create as much cognitive involvement as possible with the senses available to us: sight and sound. Experience is more than just what meets the eyes. The decision to buy a product is mediated by a number of unconscious factors that shape the customers' final decision. The author encourages future research to explore what other factors influence the decision process and how brands can trigger the consumer's emotions by involving the maximum possible subconscious pathways in the online interaction.

CONCLUSIONS

The classic economic theory describes consumers as rational economic actors that select an alternative only after considering all the relevant information. However, while the logical process is certainly a key factor in considered purchases such as insurance or financial products, it is actually detrimental to the retail-consumer industry, where emotional decision-making or the impulse purchase plays a central role. Although we like to think of ourselves as rational creatures, absorbing information, weighing it carefully, and making thoughtful decisions, many of our most crucial choices are made by what we call hunches, gut feelings and a somewhat automatic reaction that is beyond or beneath consciousness. We like to refer to this feeling as intuition ("I have a very good feeling about this house"), but the reality is that this "intuition" is an established part of emotion-based learning. This chapter deals with the significant role of emotions in everyday purchase decisions.

Optimizing for Goal-Oriented Visitors

When visitors are highly motivated, willing to dive deeply into the information process, and equipped with the necessary cognitive resources, they will focus all their attention on the process. These visitors will ignore distractions such as ads and featured elements, take the minimum steps necessary to reach their goal, and rely on as much information as they can retrieve.

You can convert these visitors by providing navigational tools and search abilities that allow them to complete their tasks as quickly and easily as possible. It is also crucial that you equip goal-oriented visitors with all the information they need to make a calculated decision – including customer reviews, easy access to website assets, and even information from other websites.

Optimizing for Unintentional Visitors

When visitors are unwilling or unable to process featured content, they subconsciously use simple rules called heuristics to infer the validity of the content they are exposed to.

Examples of such heuristic rules would be: "Messages with many arguments are more likely to be valid than messages with fewer arguments"; or "A message coming from a man dressed like a doctor may seem more valid than the exact same message coming from a guy in shorts."

In addition, under the sway of emotion-based processing, these visitors will pay attention to colorful images, embedded video, attractive headlines and catchy slogans. In order to appeal to these visitors, the website should be colorful and attractive, have a limited amount of detail and use a lot of imagery and video.

Associative linkage is another winning tactic for keeping unintentional visitors engaged. In the absence of a defined goal, visitor behavior can be directed by associations that link one idea to another – which can greatly increase engagement time.

For example, visitors to sites like Buzzfeed and Facebook generally don't have a specific goal in mind, but are looking for amusement during a work break or at the end of the day. Smart websites know how to grab these visitors for long periods of time by posting links to very similar content at the bottom of each article, leading the visitors from one article of interest to the next. Major e-commerce sites like Amazon are also frequented by visitors just looking to kill time, and the most successful ones use mechanisms such as "Similar items" sections and "Recommended for you" pages that take into account not only the customer's purchase history but also recent browsing activity.

Decision-making is not limited to rational data processing, weighing the costs and benefits. Our senses and subconscious emotions play key roles in the process without us even knowing.

When we make a decision about buying a particular pair of shoes, we of course take into account the price, how we look in them and how often we will wear them. Yet we are also influenced by the aromas around us, whether we are standing or sitting, and whether we are hungry or sated, even though these factors have nothing to do with the shoes.

In this world of information that we live in, the growing flood of information, goods and services mingle and merge in our memories, and we cannot separate one brand from another. When the brain is asked to choose a product from the multitudes that more or less share the same characteristics, the deciding factor will be the emotions and memories associated with that product. The higher the intensity of that emotion, the greater the chance of selecting that product.

Compared to the rational system, which is slower and requires many cognitive resources, psychologically, our emotional path can process vast amounts of information more rapidly. So when a product is linked to a positive scent, our brains quickly create an association between this positive feeling and the product. Thus that product will be chosen much faster this way than through the computation of rational information. In other words, we feel faster than we think.

REFERENCES

American Express Retail Monitor. (2018). *Annual Report 2018*. Retrieved from https://ir.americanexpress.com/

Angelou, M. (2019). Staff spotlight. *Policy & Practice*, (19426828). Retrieved from http://search.ebscohost.com/login.aspx?direct=true&db=a9h&AN=135974225&site=eds-live

Bechara, A., Tranel, D., & Damasio, H. (2000). Characterization of the decision-making deficit of patients with ventromedial prefrontal cortex lesions. *Brain, 123*(11), 2189-2202. doi:10.1093/brain/123.11.2189

Berry, C. J., Paganelli, M. P., & Smith, C. (2013). *The Oxford Handbook of Adam Smit*h. OUP Oxford. Retrieved from https://books.google.pt/books?id=D7Bcf_1f_w0C

Cacioppo, J. T., Petty, R. E., Kao, C. F., & Rodriguez, R. (1986). Central and peripheral routes to persuasion: An individual difference perspective. *Journal of Personality and Social Psychology, 51*(5), 1032. Doi:10.1037/0022-3514.51.5.1032

Cyert, R. M., & DeGroot, M. H. (1987). *Bayesian Analysis and Uncertainty in Economic Theory*. Rowman & Littlefield. doi:10.1007/978-94-009-3163-3

Damasio, A. R., Everitt, B. J., Bishop, D., Roberts, A. C., Robbins, T. W., & Weiskrantz, L. (1996). The somatic marker hypothesis and the possible functions of the prefrontal cortex. *Philosophical Transactions of the Royal Society of London. Series B, Biological Sciences, 351*(1346), 1413–1420. doi:10.1098/rstb.1996.0125 PMID:8941953

Damasio, A. R., Tranel, D., & Damasio, H. C. (1991). Somatic markers and the guidance of behavior: Theory and preliminary testing. In H. S. Levin, H. M. Eisenberg, & A. L. Benton (Eds.), *Frontal lobe function and dysfunction* (pp. 217–229). Oxford University Press.

Frankish, K. (2010). Dual-Process and Dual-System Theories of Reasoning. *Philosophy Compass, 5*(10), 914–926. doi:10.1111/j.1747-9991.2010.00330.x

Freud, S. (2018). The Uncanny. *Dialogues in Philosophy, Mental and Neuro Sciences, 11*(2), 84–100. Retrieved from http://search.ebscohost.com/login.aspx?direct=true&db=a9h&AN=135254124&site=eds-live

Hastie, R., & Dawes, R. M. (2010). *Rational Choice in an Uncertain World: The Psychology of Judgment and Decision Making*. SAGE Publications.

Kahneman, D., Tversky, A., Foundation, R. S., & Press, C. U. (2000). *Choices, Values, and Frames*. New York: Russell sage Foundation. Cambridge University Press. doi:10.1017/CBO9780511803475

Lezak, M. D., Howieson, D. B., Bigler, E. D., & Tranel, D. (2012). *Neuropsychological assessment* (5th ed.). USA: Oxford University Press.

Monroe, R. W., & Barrett, P. T. (2019). The Evolving B2B E-Commerce and Supply Chain Management: A Chronological Mémoire. *Journal of Business and Management, 25*(1), 49–67. doi:10.6347/JBM.201903_25(1).0003

Niles-Hofmann, L., & Celentano, A. (2015). Learning Insights From Digital Body Language. *Chief Learning Officer.* Retrieved from http://search.ebscohost.com/login.aspx?direct=true&db=edb&AN=108887204&site=eds-live

Rolls, E. T., Hornak, J., Wade, D., & McGrath, J. (1994). Emotion-related learning in patients with social and emotional changes associated with frontal lobe damage. *Journal of Neurology, Neurosurgery & Psychiatry, 57*(12), 1518-1524. Doi:10.1136/jnnp.57.12.1518

Smith, A. (2019). *The Wealth of Nations.* BookRix.

Tesseras, L. (2013). A Business Opportunity That's Only a Click Away. *Marketing Week.* Retrieved from http://search.ebscohost.com/login.aspx?direct=true&db=bth&AN=89984421&site=eds-live

Turnbull, O. H., Bowman, C., Shanker, S., & Davies, J. (2014). Emotion-based learning: Insights from the Iowa Gambling Task. *Frontiers in Psychology, 162*(5). doi:10.3389/fpsyg.2014.00162 PMID:24711796

ADDITIONAL READING

Bechara, A., & Damasio, A. R. (2005). The somatic marker hypothesis: A neural theory of economic decision. *Games and Economic Behavior, 52*(2), 336–372. doi:10.1016/j.geb.2004.06.010

Cacioppo, J. T., & Petty, R. E. (1982). The need for cognition. *Journal of Personality and Social Psychology, 42*(1), 116–131. doi:10.1037/0022-3514.42.1.116

Capon, A., Handley, S. J., & Dennis, I. (2003). Working memory and reasoning: An individual differences perspective. *Thinking & Reasoning, 9*(3), 203–244. doi:10.1080/13546781343000222

Carruthers, P. (2006). *The architecture of the mind.* Oxford: Oxford University Press. doi:10.1093/acprof:oso/9780199207077.001.0001

Colom, R., Rebollo, I., Palacios, A., Juan-Espinosa, M., & Kyllonen, P. C. (2004). Working memory is (almost) perfectly predicted by g. *Intelligence, 32*(3), 277–296. doi:10.1016/j.intell.2003.12.002

Dube, C., Rotello, C. M., & Heit, E. (2010). Assessing the belief bias effect with ROCs: It's a response bias effect. *Psychological Review, 117*(3), 831–863. doi:10.1037/a0019634 PMID:20658855

Evans, J., & St, B. T. (2003). In two minds: Dual-process accounts of reasoning. *Trends in Cognitive Sciences, 7*(10), 454–459. doi:10.1016/j.tics.2003.08.012 PMID:14550493

Evans, J. S. B. T., Barston, J. L., & Pollard, P. (1983). On the conflict between logic and belief in syllogistic reasoning. *Memory & Cognition, 11*(3), 295–306. doi:10.3758/BF03196976 PMID:6621345

Gao, H., Mittal, V., & Zhang, Y. (2020). The Differential Effect of Local–Global Identity Among Males and Females: The Case of Price Sensitivity. *JMR, Journal of Marketing Research, 57*(1), 173–191. doi:10.1177/0022243719889028

Gao, J., Zhang, C., Wang, K., & Ba, S. (2012). Understanding online purchase decision making: The effects of unconscious thought, information quality, and information quantity. *Decision Support Systems*, *53*(4), 772–781. doi:10.1016/j.dss.2012.05.011

Huang, Y. F., & Kuo, F. Y. (2012). How impulsivity affects consumer decision-making in e-commerce. *Electronic Commerce Research and Applications*, *11*(6), 582–590. doi:10.1016/j.elerap.2012.09.004

Jonathan, St. B. T. (2001). Necessity, possibility and belief: A study of syllogistic reasoning. *The Quarterly Journal of Experimental Psychology Section A*, *54*(3), 935–958. doi:10.1080/713755983 PMID:11548042

Kahneman, D., & Frederick, S. (2002). Representativeness revisited: Attribute substitution in intuitive judgement. In T. Gilovich, D. Griffin, & D. Kahneman (Eds.), *Heuristics and biases: The psychology of intuitive judgement* (pp. 49–81). Cambridge Cambridge University Press; doi:10.1017/CBO9780511808098.004

Kahneman, D., & Tversky, A. (1979). Prospect Theory: An Analysis of Decision under Risk. *Econometrica*, *47*(2), 263–291. doi:10.2307/1914185

Neys, W. D. (2006). Dual Processing in Reasoning: Two Systems but One Reasoner. *Psychological Science*, *17*(5), 428–433. doi:10.1111/j.1467-9280.2006.01723.x PMID:16683931

O'brien, D., & Manfrinati, A. (2010). The mental logic theory of conditional proposition. In *Cognition and Conditionals*. Probability and Logic in Human Thinking; doi:10.1093/acprof:oso/9780199233298.003.0002

Seland, D. (2017). Why (and How) We Choose. *Quality*. Retrieved from http://search.ebscohost.com/login.aspx?direct=true&db=bth&AN=121986065&site=eds-live

Stanovich, K. E. (1999). *Who is rational?: Studies of individual differences in reasoning*. Lawrence Erlbaum Associates Publishers. doi:10.4324/9781410603432

Stanovich, K. E. (2004). *The robot's rebellion: Finding meaning the age of Darwin Chicago*. Chicago University Press. doi:10.7208/chicago/9780226771199.001.0001

Turnbull, O. H., Evans, C. E., Bunce, A., Carzolio, B., & O'Connor, J. (2005). Emotion-based learning and central executive resources: An investigation of intuition and the Iowa Gambling Task. *Brain and Cognition*, *57*(3), 244–247. doi:10.1016/j.bandc.2004.08.053 PMID:15780457

Woods, S. (2009). *Digital Body Language*. New Year Publishing.

Zhang, K. Z., Zhao, S. J., Cheung, C. M., & Lee, M. K. (2014). Examining the influence of online reviews on consumers' decision-making: A heuristic–systematic model. *Decision Support Systems*, *67*, 78–89. doi:10.1016/j.dss.2014.08.005

KEY TERMS AND DEFINITIONS

Central Route: Is taken when one is motivated to generate thoughts in response to substantive content (a shopper wishes to compare the prices of similar products) and has the ability to do so (is not mentally tired).

Classic Economic: A theory that describes consumers as rational economic actors that select an alternative only after considering all the relevant information.

Emotion-Based Learning (Intuition): We are born with an automatic mechanism that memorizes our emotional reaction whenever we face a new experience. These emotional reactions, positive or negative, are stored in our memory. When we face a similar situation in the future, those stored memories will be expressed as a "hunch" to guide our decisions. For example, if a child is bitten by a dog, the next time he sees a dog he will "intuitively" know how it feels from a representation of the feelings stored in his memory. Intuition is how one learns to approach or avoid new situations and interactions based on the emotional memory of past events without having to consciously process them again.

Emotional Process (System 1): The emotional process is generally automatic, affective and heuristic-based. It quickly proposes intuitive answers to problems as they arise. This operates below the surface of consciousness, transfers messages through biological channels such as skin conductivity and sweat glands, and automatically makes many of our decisions.

Peripheral Route: Is taken when one is unable or unwilling to execute the cognitive assignment (no matter how much a shopper wishes to dig into the details of a specific product, he is just too mentally exhausted to do so).

Purchase Decision: The level of dominance of each process at a particular time is the key determinant of purchasing decisions. Visitors are more likely to add a product to their cart when the emotional process takes control, as they are directed by "how it feels" and not "is it worth it."

Rational Process (System 2): The rational process is slow, effortful, conscious and rule based. It is the one that generates the logical and rational response.

Section 3
Identity

Chapter 11
How Bollywood Filmdom Operates in India and in the International Arena:
Consumption of Bollywood

Nandini Sen
https://orcid.org/0000-0002-2844-6456
Heriot Watt University, UK

ABSTRACT

The chapter discusses the influence and impact of product placement of Bollywood cinema. It examines the different strategies adopted in Bollywood movies for promotional purposes in India and internationally. It does an evaluation of the effectiveness of this type of communications, including deciding about travel destinations and concentrates on the viewer's recall on the consumption of the product and its impact on improving brand image. The chapter is also to understand the consumer buying behaviour in terms of Bollywood. It assesses the product placement of Bollywood in India based on its popularity and the diversity in the types of placements and was analysed using ethnography as a method tool. From the study it was observed that the importance of Bollywood movies on masses is evident in India and internationally. Consumers feel that the advertisements should be entertaining and the same should be conjoined with the storyline in order to convey the brand message in the best possible way. The chapter tries to locate the solutions and recommendations of the Bollywood film crisis.

INTRODUCTION

The chapter will include influence of celebrities in establishing a brand. It is a commonly used trend which was evident even in yester years. Movies are noticeable medium for entertainment in India, commonly the Bollywood cinema is a speciality for lot of things such as colourful outfits, interesting destinations and singing and dancing sequences (Dwyer & Patel, 2002). The movies do not alone focus the Indian audience, but also non-resident Indians. The movies communicate many things to the audience such as

DOI: 10.4018/978-1-7998-3115-0.ch011

Copyright © 2020, IGI Global. Copying or distributing in print or electronic forms without written permission of IGI Global is prohibited.

storyline, grooming, fashion and about latest trends. The spectators of the Bollywood cinema would be considering the movie as a make-believe fact and will be emotionally occupied by the actors and the incidents of the movie especially on dressing, behaving etc. Product placement in Bollywood cinema was started in early 2000 in the form of in-film advertisement where many iconic brands sponsored film promotions. Similarly, Bollywood films also promote other movies along with a contest in the product package to attract the mass. This draws in money.

Each section in this chapter will focus on the product placement in Bollywood. Bollywood cinema branding was started in early 2000 in the form of in-film advertisement. It will briefly discuss the background of the Bollywood films. The chapter in the initial stage will set the focus. It will traverse through a path of literature review, the controversies and problems in the subject of Bollywood consumption, and a brief ethnography. It will give a direction to the future research. The conclusion will draw the results and summarise the whole chapter.

BACKGROUND

To begin, it is necessary to comment on my use of the term Bollywood. I use it, as has now to the Hindi-language commercial cinema of India based primarily in Mumbai (previously

Bombay). Despite common misconceptions it constitutes only *one* industry and/or cinemas. These include several regional commercial cinemas as well as the art cinema of India known as Parallel Cinema or New (Wave) Indian cinema. Of India's many cinematic traditions, however, it is Bollywood that has attained a global reach and a considerable measure of international commercial success characterized the term Bollywood as derogatory, arguing that it maintains Hollywood as its standard of reference and that, by implication, it positions Indian cinema as a stepchild of Hollywood. Commonly believed to have emerged only in about the past decade, originating as a term used in some English language Indian trade journals in a slightly jokey, self-deprecating way, Rajadhyaksha (2003) describes the term Bollywood as having become an expression of the outsider's fascination with a slightly surreal practice that nevertheless appears to possess the claim to be a genuinely popular art form (2003:29). It is arguable whether the (even if one accepts that it was ever primarily that), and whether any Bollywood fan would art form. Regardless of such debates, the term Bollywood has achieved widespread currency industrial practice and a distinctive aesthetic. The term Bollywood connotes a characteristic set of stylistic conventions, the prominence of song-and-dance sequences, recognizable themes and genre categories, Indian cultural values, and an overall entertainment ethos.

The term also encompasses a manifestation of the star system that includes primarily actors but also producers, directors, playback singers, lyricists, musical composers/directors and choreographers. Moreover, both audiences and producers appear to be able to reconcile Bollywood's ideological investment in a conservative Hindu nationalism — which often positions itself narratively in opposition to Western values and to Muslims — with its paradoxical but ubiquitous appropriation of Western locations and modes of dress and dance. Additionally, Bollywood also happily counts a half dozen Khans among its major male stars, including Shahrukh Khan, the darling of diasporic audiences, and Aamir Khan of *Lagaan* fame.

Rajadhyaksha (2003:27) convincingly asserts arguing that: Bollywood admittedly occupies a space analogous to the film industry, but might best be seen as a more diffuse cultural conglomeration involving a range of distribution and consumption activities from websites to music cassettes, from cable to radio.

If so, the film industry itself — determined here solely in terms of its box office turnover and sales of print and music rights, all that actually comes back to the producer — can by definition constitute only a part, and perhaps even an *alarmingly small* part, of the overall culture industry that is currently being created and marketed.

It must be emphasized, however, that Bollywood's appeal outside of the Indian subcontinent is not limited to the Indian *diasporic* populations in the United States, Canada, UK, Middle East, southern and East Africa, the Caribbean and elsewhere. Indian cinema's (primarily Bollywood's) presence in many African countries is not only a long-established one, as media anthropologist Brian Larkin (2002, audiences in northern Nigeria, but its popularity has also been consolidated in the *absence* of an Indian diasporic population with the importation.

Rapid developments in information and communication technology have given rise to an increasingly globalized film industry. The Internet represents a powerful marketing tool that is nearly universally accessible. Prior to 1998, the sources of funding for film production were not always entirely above board. In fact, links were commonly made between organized crime and money laundering and the Indian film industry. Since 1998, however, funding sources have become more diversified, encompassing bank loans, direct foreign investment (DFI) and other legal means (Dubey, 2010). For example, 100% DFI is allowed for products and services related to film production, distribution, marketing and exhibition (Dubey, 2010). Not surprisingly, many of the American majors have expressed an interest in the Indian film industry.

Recently, companies like Emami, Audi, Aircel, etc. had effectively used this strategy to sponsor and benefitting to a large extent. Even song sequences are being ushered with money to highlight commercial products. The placement of the product was done in one famous songs sequence where they are choreographed in front of an emami stall where there is a lot of crowd buying Navaratna oil (Padmanabhan and Jena, 2013). a product of emami. The writers (2013) also say product placement has been a trademark of emami's marketing strategy over the years. Nowadays the product placement is a million-dollar business satisfying the film producers for reducing production cost and to market. The advertising agency could understand the behavior of the movie and identify areas or sequences for product placement by making suitable changes on situations, if required. Thus, in films, advertisements are significant parts of marketing budgets for corporates.

Literature Review

Bollywood is apparently trapped in some sort of purgatory of global cultural expectations; at any given time, it's too Indian to be accessible to Western audiences, too north Indian-centric for the rest of South Asia, too imitative of Hollywood to be appreciated as authentic Indian cinema among North Americans seeking something exotic, too potent of an imposition of an Indian version of modernity on other traditional societies, or too low culture to qualify as real art for snobs of all national origins. (Lal 2004). Bollywood is no longer inaccessible to Western audiences.

Bollywood films are making waves across the international stage, not only with their perfectly synchronized dancing, but also in their depiction of Indian travel behaviors. This industry is one of the largest film industries in the world, producing over 1,000 movies every year. It is a $72 billion industry selling six billion tickets annually (Desai, 2005; Lovgren, 2004; Minocha & Stonehouse, 2006). Its commercial size grew at the robust rate of 58% in the five-year period between 2001 and 2005 (Lorenzen & Täube, 2008). Film exports also expanded 30–50% year on year during the same period and were forecast to increase by a further 20% to 2010 (2008). A large chunk of this movie output from India comes from the city of Mumbai, formerly known as Bombay. Hence, the moniker of *Bollywood* was given to the Indian film Industry. As a rapidly developing country, India has seen tremendous growth in its 300 million strong middle class (Rempel, 2007) and their purchasing power in the past two decades. This growth boom has impacted all sectors of the Indian economy, including outbound international tourism. The combination of these forces has created an opportunity for growth in overseas tourism destinations, often influenced by Indians' perception of Bollywood films. A noteworthy piece of evidence of the Indian market potential is the recent surge of Indian tourists to

Spain after the release of the Bollywood film – *Zindagi Na Milegi Dobara*, set against a Spanish backdrop (Harjani, 2011). Six months after its showing, the Spanish tourism board saw a 32% upswing of visitors from India to Spain (Harjani, 2011). Similarly, Mr. Yash Chopra, a major producer/director of Bollywood movies, idealized Switzerland as a romantic destination in his films and subsequently caused an increase in outbound travel from India to Switzerland, increasing the outbound travel from India by 30% (Dubey, 2008). With then proliferating number of consumers of Bollywood films, destination marketers are eager to capitalize on this crown jewel of the Asian market.

Evoking positive perceptions of the destination through image presentations has become an effective way to catapult the target destination into the tourist's consideration set. Images of film locations affect the audience's selection of one destination over another and their subsequent behaviors in the destination (Bandyopadhyay, 2008; Han & Lee, 2008; Young & Young, 200,. Kim & O'Connor, 2011). Not surprisingly, the tourists who travel to a place depicted in a movie arrive with expectations and images about the location like what is shown on screen (Butler, 2011). The images of the film thus affect some destination image components and heighten tourists' interest in visiting (Kim & Richardson, 2003). Beverley and Niki (2009) suggested that media induced tourism helps tourists fulfill fantasies of being in the films via the vicarious experience of traveling to the sites where they were filmed.

Hudson and Ritchie (2006) have pointed out that some films are more successful than others in inducing tourism. They have also identified some critical factors that contribute to destination promotion. If the story line and the site are inter-linked, the audience is more likely to be emotionally involved with the film (Tooke & Baker, 1996). The box-office success of a film can be a good predictor of movie-induced tourism (Grihault, 2003).

In the list of too somethings mentioned above, South Africa appears to be an exception in several instances. Bollywood is no longer inaccessible to Western audiences Most South Africans coming from Tamil- and Telegu-speaking (i.e. South Indian) backgrounds seem eagerly to consume vocal South Indian dissident view. Any perceived imitativeness of Hollywood does not its South African fans; on the contrary, most cite its wholesomeness (usually referring to Bollywood's lack of explicit sex and excessive violence) as being distinctive from Hollywood. North Americans may deem Bollywood a so-called authenticity. In fact, criticisms of Bollywood's lack of authenticity appear to reside primarily in the argument that its construction of India is unrealistic; arguably, it is this very lack of realism that constitutes its primary appeal (Ebrahim, 2008).

Thus, began a general research interest in Bollywood which has, in the interim, seen steadily growing scholarly attention and a corpus of academic publications, emerging primarily from the United Kingdom and the United States. This sudden increase of publications about Bollywood has occurred much to the chagrin of those scholars within India who have been engaging in academic research of not only Bollywood but also other Indian cinemas. Scholarship on Bollywood, emanating from both Western scholars and NRI scholars domiciled in the West, demonstrates the hegemony of the production and publication.

Sudha Rajagopalan (2005) has documented a taste for Indian cinema in post-aid to have something of a cult status in Japan.

The October 2006 issue of the North American journal *South Asian popular culture* is dedicated to the study of Indian cinema's global reach. Seeking to decenter Hollywood in debates on cinema and globalization, it includes articles and anecdotal accounts of Indian cinema in countries as diverse as Spain, Romania, Bulgaria, Egypt, Greece, Israel, the former Yugoslavia, Italy and Turkey, among others — by non-NRIs. Other Peru and China.

In South Africa, there exists an established (2004:212) notes that [i]t was not long after their appearance in South Africa and that as early as 1936, the Indian government appealed to the South African government. The appeal was appearing to be purely a money-making matter and not for the education of the Indian community (Board of Censors 1939, cited in Jagarnath 2004). although the segregationist policies of the South African government limited its exposure and appeal beyond the Indian population.

MAIN FOCUS OF THE CHAPTER

This chapter discusses several contemporary factors with focus on how the Bollywood market is operating. The Bollywood film is a cultural form that combines several aesthetic styles, from within India and from the outside. With its formal heterogeneity and as a product of one of India's largest cities, Mumbai Bollywood has had an ongoing fascination with arrival, that is, with India's status as a contemporary nation-state. While some Bollywood films seem to celebrate fantasy scenarios of India's arrival on the global scene, at the same time they express anxiety about affective possibilities within a new Bollywood of higher production values and larger global reach, an India of mobile borders and attenuated historical context.

In the 1950s, 1960s, and 1970s, romantic sequences in Indian films were primarily shot in the mountainous region of Kashmir in India, widely regarded as heaven on earth. Bollywood directors were mesmerized by the beauty of Kashmir, so much so that the mountains in Kashmir became synonymous with romance in Bollywood. However, when the terrorism threats of the late 1980s made the region difficult to reach, and later inaccessible, Bollywood directors began seeking substitute locations overseas (Macionis, 2004; Macionis & Sparks, 2008). Fascination with foreign locations within Bollywood began in the mid- 1960s when Raj Kapoor (Bollywood Producer/Director/Actor) shot his first color film, titled *Sangam,* in Italy, France, and Switzerland. This started the foreign locations trend in Indian cinema. The trend accelerated in the 1970s to 1990s when actors were transported to striking foreign locations like the Swiss Alps and Britain's Summer Isles, which were the primary backdrops of many Yash Chopra productions (Shah, 2012). More than 200 Bollywood titles have been shot in Switzerland over the past two decades alone (Bollywood drives…, 2008).

Most of the Swiss sequences are dream scenes in which lovers dance or romp on Alpine meadows strewn with flowers or roll in the snow in unlikely flimsy Indian garb on wintry slopes (Tagliabue, 2010). Many Indians flock annually to Swiss locations in which popular Bollywood films were shot to recreate and relive scenes from their favorite films (Tagliabue, 2010).

Veteran Bollywood director Mr. Yash Chopra, noted as one of the greatest filmmakers in the history of Indian cinema, singlehandedly boosted tourism in Switzerland by regularly featuring the country's lakes, misty valleys, and snowcapped mountains as the backdrop for his song and dance sequences during his career spanning 53 years (Dubey, 2008). So grateful was the Swiss Tourism Authority that they named a lake after him. The director also played a part in promoting Britain as a glamorous destination. His classic film *Lamhe* (1991) was shot in London and the Lake District. When he produced *Mujhse Dosti Karoge* a decade later, Chopra again returned to England's Lake District to film aboard one of the steamers which ply between Glen Ridding and Pooley Bridge, reveling in the twisting lake, rolling hills, and winding roads of the national park (Macionis, 2004; Macionis & Sparks, 2009).

Some of the biggest blockbusters of Bollywood, shot in Western Europe, that impacted Indian Bollywood viewers are *An Evening in Paris (*France and Switzerland*) Chandani, Lamhe, Dilwale Dulhaniya Le Jayenge* (UK, mainly Switzerland), *Bachna Ae Haseno* (Italy & Switzerland), *Taal* (Britain), *Kabhi Khushi Kabhi Gham, (UK), Tal* (UK), *Namastey London* (UK), *Cheeni Kum* (UK), *and Zindagi Na Milegi Dobara* (Spain). Many articles in the popular press have reported that Indian audiences and even non-Indian audiences who watch Bollywood movies on a regular basis visit the destinations shown in the movies (Taglibue, 2010; Munshi, 2012; Lovgren, 2004; Padmanabhan, 2010). To capitalize on this film-induced tourism, destination marketers must creatively advertise to these Bollywood viewers.

Major attraction and integral part of Bollywood movies are the elaborate song sequences. Almost every Bollywood movie has song sequences and dance numbers contributing to its earnings/profit, fashion-style in dress industries and these elaborate numbers are often a major deciding factor in determining whether the movie will be a hit or a flop. Often, movie songs are shot at a scenic destination outside India, even though the rest of the movie is filmed within India. This creates an exotic appeal within the movies and plays a major role in attracting viewers. Movie soundtracks, music videos, and even remixed versions of songs of the Bollywood movies released in India and abroad are major pull factors to attract viewers to the theater (Padmanabhan, 2010).

Controversies

While Bollywood films enjoyed popularity in Soviet Union, the Middle East, and Africa for decades, there has been a push for a more marketable form of popular Indian cinema in the West. In a global marketplace, Western consumption of India's cultural products — whether books, beauty queens, or movies — has become an important sign of India's claim to modernity. Although Mumbai's (formerly Bombay) popular Hindi-language cinema has usually been associated in the West with strange and outrageous musical films and plots derived from Hollywood and Western directors.

Danny Boyle (Slumdog Millionaire) have incorporated the Bollywood idiom in their films as a type of kitschy cool and formal innovation. Having won a suite of awards, including the Oscars for Best Picture, Director, and Song, the British production, Slumdog Millionaire, is socio-realistic fantasy shot on location in Mumbai with an Indian cast and crew. India's Bollywood success story in the West is, after all, not quite a Bollywood film, or even an Indian film. Could an Indian have made Slumdog? has been a refrain in commentaries about Slumdog's success in the U.S. and in England. If Slumdog is not a Bollywood film, the story behind Slumdog's production — a British director with little funding and lots of guts goes to India to make a film with a cast of unknowns.

It is the plotline of Rakesh Omprakash Mehra's popular 2006 film, Rang de Basanti (Color it Saffron). In this fantasy of a British woman making a Bollywood film about colonial India, Rang de Basanti seems to ask: Does it take a Western perspective to make Bollywood cinema truly modern? In Rang de Basanti, Indian elite youth have gone global, taking on a cool urbanized disaffection. A young British woman arrives in India with a desire to make a film about the struggles of famous Indian revolutionaries (Bhagat Singh, Chandresekhar Azad, Rajguru, Ramprasad Bismal, Ashfaqullah Khan) against colonial rule as depicted in her grandfather's diaries of the early 1930s. A group of Delhi college students must be retrained in the history of revolution as the British woman attempts to recreate in them the authentic fervor from India's colonial past in order to act successfully in her film. In this way the acting out of British colonial nostalgia reinvigorates dissident political energies in the young. With an aesthetic interplay between the colonial romance and the contemporary youth film, Mehra attempts to make the trauma of colonial history new, youthful, and exciting. By contrasting scenes of the increasing dissident youth in present day India with scenes of the young protagonists playing revolutionaries in Rang de Basanti, the film envisions a particular brand of more violent anti-colonial protest as the carrier of modernity.

Findings in this study indicate that engagement with Bollywood movies does have a positive impact on foreign travel involvement of Indians. Thus, it can be inferred that respondents noting higher levels of engagement also were more likely to indicate higher levels for both hedonic and utilitarian involvement in foreign travel. Results also indicate that utilitarian foreign travel involvement impacts destination awareness. The more involved a Bollywood movie viewer is with the utilitarian aspects of foreign travel, the more aware that the viewer is of a specific destination. It is then critical for destination marketers to target viewers who indicate higher levels of foreign travel involvement and are thusly, more aware of the destination being featured in films. Media does matter, and images portrayed in the media can deeply influence a Bollywood film viewer's awareness of a foreign destination (Bollywood gives a boost to tourism in Britain, 2008). As noted earlier, it is Bollywood movies that have brought the world to Indians.

Though featured in past Bollywood films, countries such as Greece, Austria, and the Netherlands have yet to be featured within a successful Bollywood blockbuster, or have failed to be identified as the correct country. For example, *Silsila*, directed by the famous Yash Chopra, was not a box office success, but since has risen to cult status among Bollywood viewers (Jha, 2011). Filmed partially in the Netherlands, the scenes of the Keukenhof Tulip Gardens are intertwined with mountains covered in snow with the main characters running about, potentially confusing the audience with images similar to those shot in Switzerland. Likely due to the confusion of country identity, the Netherlands has a high prevalence of Indian Bollywood viewers rating 'no opinion/image'. Similarly, multiple Bollywood films have featured Grecian backdrops, including *Chalte Chalte, Tashan,* and *Wanted,* though only one was commercially successful – *Wanted* reached blockbuster status as the highest grossing film in Bollywood in 2009. It is likely that the limited exposure of Greece in films has contributed to the lack of image among Indian viewers.

Problems

Though the presence of Bollywood is being felt in India and internationally, a major challenge in the form of pirated CDs exists in the way of tapping the Indian and international market in a profitable manner. Therefore, better coordination is needed at the governmental level so that the trade and distribution of pirated CDs can be prevented. Next, the Bollywood-led cultural engagement should be a two-way process. The growing influence of Bollywood and the limited capacity of indigenous movie production can generate discontent among locals and native artists and the issue could be politicized (Singh, 2008).

Chrisafis (2002) reported that more than US$210 million dollars is spent each year by more than 200,000 Indian tourists traveling and is growing at 13% annually. The author quoted a statement by Subramaniam (British Tourist Authority, BTA manager) '... for Indian film enthusiasts, visiting British locations where Indian stars have made films is akin to a pilgrimage' and mentions that 'visitors from India want to follow a Bollywood trail'. With the global reach of Bollywood, it is evident that not only

Indians could be attracted to these destinations but so could people from many different countries where Bollywood movies are watched. Kishwar (2004) reported that TV channels in Indonesia, Singapore, Thailand, Malaysia, Egypt, Algeria, Morocco, and many other African and Asian countries show almost half-a-dozen Hindi films a day.

Another major attraction and integral part of Bollywood movies are songs. Almost every movie in Bollywood has song sequences and dance numbers that have a major contribution to its earnings/profit and are the major deciding factors in determining whether the movie will be a hit or a flop. In most movies, songs are shot at a scenic destination abroad even though the rest of the parts are filmed in India. This creates an appeal to the movies and plays a major role in attracting viewers. The movie sound track CDs, music videos, and even remixed versions of songs of the movies released in India as well as abroad are major pull factors to attract viewers to the theater (Padmanabhan, 2010). Activity behaviors positively influence consumption behaviors at a destination. Perhaps this is because consumers are likely drawn to a location for nonconsumption purposes such as the scenery or the culture, and then once at a destination, viewers enhance their experience with the destination through consumption behaviors.

Overall, this study has successfully predicted the causal relationships among movie engagement, involvement, destination awareness, and tourist activity and consumption behaviors. These findings further suggest a need to determine acceptable marketing techniques and approaches to prominently feature foreign destinations in Bollywood movies. Bollywood films are viewed by millions in India and across the world and are a powerful source of information. However, to date, the power of Bollywood films as a source of travel motivation has been understudied in the tourism marketing field.

This research provides justification to destination marketers and media organizations to utilize the full potential of Bollywood movies to reach billions of people. Because tourism-related behaviors vary among individuals, movie engagement and involvement with travel can be viewed as critical measures for analyzing consumer behavior in relation to tourism. These findings may not be generalizable to the study population because the sample was restricted to a convenience sample in one city in India. Future studies should be expanded to include multiple cities and should seek to obtain a much larger sample, using random sampling techniques. Additionally, future studies could ask respondents more specific questions that could be used to verify media influence on their actual purchase and activity behavior.

India should, therefore, provide enough room for the cultural sentiments of India in its cultural diplomacy. It could opt for organizing combined and specific film festivals for Indian independent and Bollywood movies. Though Bollywood is gaining ground in the cultural arena of Southeast Asia, efforts need to be made to transform Bolllywood's soft power engagement into a well-crafted Indian policy of cultural diplomacy in Southeast Asia (Singh 2008).

SOLUTIONS AND RECOMMENDATIONS

Always the positive audience ratings should be highlighted. Repeat screenings can be done to reflect the public demands. Bollywood films will constitute both national and international cultural phenomenon that will go beyond the films it produces. Bollywood films should be included in the national and international feature film screening channels time slots so that it can rub off its ghettoized nature. Bollywood films' style, art and culture should remain in the national and international viewers' consciousness, living spaces and performing arts. The consumption of Bollywood films, music, celebrity gossips and fashion should grow inside the minds of the viewers. The countries must make provisions for international cooperation in film related areas, including coproduction, distribution, festivals and cultural programmes, and information exchange. The business should encourage strategies for exhibition of the films in the partner countries of India. Desai (2004) notes that though earlier Bollywood was rarely registered in diaspora but now the Bollywood filmic imagination has gone down deeply inside the diasporic audience's heart and mind. They have discovered their own experiences in these Bollywood films. Thus, cultural product of Bollywood has been drawn inside the lucrative market of diaspora.

ETHNOGRAPHY

When I returned to India after long periods of postgraduate study and PhD in the United Kingdom and Germany, I felt surprised as Bollywood being screened in some mainstream venues and were subtitled in English. My curiosity as associated with my childhood evoked memories of sitting through what seemed like dialogues in a language I understood — all relieved by the song-and dance sequences which left both me and other spectators humming as we left the cinema.

Souraj Dutta (PhD scholar, Film Studies, University of St Andrews, 22 September 2019) said that he got interested in Bollywood very naturally. According to him Bollywood is part of Indian culture. The youth of India get exposure to Bollywood through T.V., cinema halls. Souraj was fascinated by the star-centric Bollywood cinemas. Shahrukh Khan's presence and Sunday movies were a major influence in his life after his parents. He has even chosen Bollywood films, its contemporary values in intertextual and self-referential practices as his PhD topic. The realm of Bollywood films (Pardes, Dilwale Dulhania Le Jayange, Dil to Pagal Hai) prepared his world of fantasy, moral values and imagination. He modeled his world around the 1970's and 80's Rajesh Khanna and Amitabh Bachchan films. The stars' presences and their entertaining performative appeals built up part of his world. Though his topic of PhD is Bollywood but his under graduation and Masters are in English Literature. He started to watch European films. He learned how to distinguish art house films from Bollywood films. He has differentiated Indian films in terms of era. He said historically after 1980's mainstream Hindi films produced from Bombay can be called Bollywood. To understand the Bollywood consumption pattern, we can track the evolution of Bollywood. It is coming out of big budgets to small budget. Unlike earlier times the small budget films are doing well in the market and making good profit. Producers can find out that one house cannot possibly produce a big budget film anymore. The multi-corporate house productions are producing the films together. Thus, they are sharing the film cost. They are dividing the cost in terms of labour, set, costumes, music direction, actor's cost. The revenue rights, satellite, and global distribution are being divided among the big corporate houses.

He cited a concrete example of Bollywood consumption and Bollywood audience. The film 'Andhadhun' catered to a narrower audience whereas 'Om Shanti Om' was for the broader audience. This division of narrow audience and broad audience determine the budget of the film. He emphasized on the patterns of the cinema consumption, the emergence of the multiplex and the audience demography. These are all related to Bollywood economics, export cost and the specificity of the market.

Souraj and his fraternity community said that the Bollywood consumption and distribution have revolutionized with the entrance of the Netflix, Amazon Prime, streaming, pirated videos. The elites who avoided the Bollywood films are nowadays watching films like 'Andhadhun', 'Gangs of Wasepur'. Crowd funding, digital streaming, parallel films without the usual songs and dances are giving multiplex businesses. After a couple of months, the Bollywood films are going for the structured, legitimate and organized streaming through Netflix and other similar websites. I can only reiterate that these multiplex models, legitimate website streaming have increased the exhibition spaces for Bollywood consumption.

There are film scholars like Sanghita Sen (PhD Scholar, Film Studies, University of St Andrews) who finds Bollywood consumption as non-adorable. She doesn't like the aesthetics of Bollywood. Her position is very clear. She is not at all comfortable with the objectification of women in Bollywood. The question here arises that why producers are not taking steps towards this crude and crass objectification women in Bollywood films. As a film studies scholar she is bound to watch Bollywood films but not based on principles. She declares that she considers piracy streaming as a method of watching Bollywood consumption. She is apprehensive that under the current BJP Government there might be difficulty to sustain the quality and liberal ambience of the Bollywood film industry. Nationalism can enter the filmdom which will hamper the good film-making both in Bollywood and parallel cinema. It will affect the Bollywood cinema consumption. Snaghita's words can be validated. Even as increasing attention has been given the phenomenon of Mumbai cinema as global, scholars such as Sumita S. Chakravarty, Tejaswini Ganti, Vijay Mishra, M. Madhava Prasad, Ashish Rajadhyaksha, and Jyotika Virdi have highlighted the constructions of various nationalisms produced by the industry from post-independence, that repeatedly reassert an imaginary unified India. However, within the larger framework of film culture in India, popular Indian cinema or Bollywood-style, has historically been a negligible form of low culture as considered by elite Indian critics vis-à-vis Western forms of film. Although Bollywood films include a pastiche of cultural and historical styles and consistently quote Hollywood and other plots, these conventions have more often been seen as propagating bad, frivolous, or unintentionally kitschy copies of source material, rather than working within an innovative or postmodern aesthetics as described by Fredric Jameson and others. While today there is a greater celebration of Bollywood aesthetics as representing authentic Indian culture and national identity, modernity in Indian film is still marked by realistic aesthetic. Indeed, the marketing of Rang de Basanti as a realistic film signals its contemporeinity and modernity (Aggarwal 2010).

The film-critic and film-maker Dr Piyush Roy (University of Edinburgh) is very hopeful about the development and evolution of the Bollywood industry. There will always be a large audience in India and abroad for watching and relishing the advut rasa or the genres of awe, love, fear and happiness on the big screen showcasing Bollywood films. He has even compared the Bollywood consumption with watching the other craze that is cricket. Dr Roy unlike Souraj reflects that Bollywood consumption is universally consumed in India. Bollywood films are made for family consumption and Bollywood gets on your nerves and becomes your habit. Indian audience has no other option and they enjoy this pleasant habit. Dr Roy has divided Bollywood in three sections- Raj Kapoor took the industry to East Europe and more specifically to Soviet Block. Amitabh Bachchan fulfilled the mission (stardom) of Bollywood in a very successful manner. He took it to Middle East. Shahrukh Khan's glory through Bollywood romantic films touched the Western world.

According to film critic Dr Piyush Roy (2019) Bollywood has touched more than 100 countries. It's an illuminating point that China is the biggest market of Bollywood films. Films like 3 Idiots, Dangal and Secret Superstar are superhits in China. His colleague, Stephen Horne a film editor and film colourist from Edinburgh was overwhelmed after watching 'Kuch Kuch Hota Hai' in 2003. He explained that he had not watched a film like this before. He said,"It was something which I never watched. Everything, all emotions, colours were so heightened. After that I only watched Bollywood films for the next six months. Bollywood caters me unrealistic films which seem to me as realistic. I am a big-serious fan of Bollywood films. I didn't know what Bollywood was. Afterward I realised that Bollywood is a continuous film festival not only across India but also among diaspora and Western audience. The fantasy allows the subject to objectify himself/herself, and therefore make himself anew.

Stephen Horne (Film critic, film maker and colourist, Edinburgh, 2019) said that corporate funding is very common to build up the film and to develop the market. In the West immigration of Indian diaspora forming South Asian communities composed the market. Small cinema halls, pirated videos, satellite TV, Indian radio stations are creating a stable market and more awareness about the major Bollywood releases. Stephen's intriguing answer about the Bollywood market has really enriched the concepts Bollywood consumption. There exists a huge potential market for the Bollywood in Southeast Asia given the large Indian Diaspora and limited production capacity of local film industries. Moreover, Indian movies are also becoming popular among the indigenous and non-Indian origin population. "The popularity of Indian movies is moving beyond the Little India in Singapore and three big names of Indian cinema, popularly known as the three Khans - Shahrukh Khan, Amir Khan and Salman Khan - have been very popular in the Malay world - Malaysia and Indonesia. Telecasts of Indian movies in Indonesia have become almost a daily affair and Indian movies are also being released with the regional language subtitles in some Southeast Asian countries." Singh (2008, p-2).

FUTURE RESEARCH DIRECTION

Nowadays the product placement is a million-dollar business satisfying the film producers for reducing production cost and to market well. This type of advertising was started in India by Leo Entertainment by Leo Burnets. The advertising agency could understand the behavior of the movie and identify areas or sequences for product placement by making suitable changes on situations, if required. Thus, in film advertisements are significant parts of marketing budgets for corporates (Padmanavan and Jena, 2013). Future researches can happen based on the statistical tests how Bollywood movies use and integrate product placement into their storylines, verbal reference by characters in the movies. Researches should not overlook about how far these products can be appropriate for the movie scenes. They should require actor's endorsement. Future research may investigate the brands from Bollywood industry which were primarily presented in a positive context and were mainly associated with the primary movie characters.

Almost all the products were featured in such a way that their brand names or logos are to be shown their other functional or aesthetic qualities as well. This study was exploratory and descriptive. Future studies should use a more sophisticated empirical design, providing for deeper understanding of the phenomenon. Future studies could use a longitudinal design to look at how perceptions of destination image vary over the years as more and more Bollywood movies are filmed abroad. Additionally, the study design can be adapted for use in other Asian countries to see how Bollywood films influence the destination perceptions of other Asian populations and compare the effects to the results identified in this research. Furthermore, the scope of the study can be expanded to analyze the perception of worldwide destinations featured in Bollywood movies, including the United States, Malaysia, Australia, and New Zealand. As increasing numbers of Indians travel worldwide, future studies can examine if Bollywood movies play a lesser or greater role in motivating Indians to travel to specific destinations. As movie producers shift location shooting to Spain, Portugal, and other countries, the country rankings found in this study will certainly change. For example, the impact of one movie as a motivation to visit Spain is likely to fade over time. Future studies can examine these issues. if Bollywood movies play a lesser or greater role in motivating Indians to travel to specific destinations. As movie producers shift location shooting to Spain, Portugal, and other countries, the country rankings found in this study will certainly change. For example, the impact of one movie as a motivation to visit Spain is likely to fade over time. Future studies can examine these issues.

CONCLUSION

Though the presence of Bollywood is being felt in India and abroad, a major challenge remains in the form of pirated CDs exists in the way of tapping the international market in a profitable manner. Therefore, better coordination is needed at the governmental level so that the trade and distribution of pirated CDs can be prevented. Next, the Bollywood-led cultural engagement should be a two-way process. The growing influence of Bollywood and the limited capacity of indigenous movie production can generate discontent among locals and native artists and the issue could be politicized (Singh 2008).

If Bollywood films are to progress in terms of their exposure in the West they need to drastically improve their accessibility of their own cinema after they are being released in the cinema halls meaning they need better and more widely released DVDs, Blu-Rays, cable channels, they need much more widely release on Netflix, Amazon Prime and they need of much better quality than they currently are. Bollywood films are fantastic in quality when they are first released but when they are out of cinemas they are neglected, they deteriorate, they are not restored, they are not maintained. They just rot and rot and rot. You can't see these films after they are out of cinemas. If I want to watch Bollywood films, I cannot watch them comfortably. Whereas if I want to watch a Hollywood film on Netflix, I can watch it quite comfortably. The quality is beautiful. If I want to watch 'Mother India' or 'Sholay' I can't watch it as the picture quality is so bad. If it has to reach a broader audience in the West Bollywood needs to improve its quality (Horne, interview by the researcher 2019).

According to Scala and Maynard (2006), product placement of Bollywood films is a marketing plan which will be used by an advertiser to place his product/products in a movie. The companies will generally be interested in placing its brand rather than a particular product in movies. For example, when coca cola advertises, it emphasizes that as a brand and not as any other soft drink. Generally, Bollywood films portray the culture of the nation-state, products and practices endorsed by the regional stars or iconic brands who can have an impact on the movie goers. The rapid growth of urban middle class has led to an increase in multiplex theatres in the country and subsequently increased the audience strength moving to theatres. Compared to Hollywood and Bollywood movies, the brands can get longer visibility in regional/independent films. Bollywood can build up its empire based on the same model. The popular brand placement studies measure the degree of efficiency of product placements on the basis of the remembrance of the brand. A study conducted in India reveals that participants were significantly positive with respect to brand placement and the preference for such placements were positive than that of other types of television advertisements.

Commercialism has been an integral part of all forms of mass media that have been in existence since the nineteenth century. There is no better way to reach the audience than to place a product in the hands of stars, who the audience views with dreamy eyes and who possess an incredible power to influence consumer behavior. The concept of product placement in the movies has been an engaging and exciting research topic for mass communication scholars for many years now. For Bollywood filmmakers the practice of product placement is an established concept.

Bollywood movies not only reflect the day-to day life of ordinary Indians, but, as in America, have also become a part of Indian life. As a result, the Indian audience, instead of thinking of a movie as a make-believe phenomenon, can relate to it and become emotionally involved with the actors working in it. They look to Bollywood to tell them how to dress fashionably, how to talk impressively, and how to behave in social settings (Dwyer & Patel, 2002). For a long time, screen stars have served as idols for Indian audiences. As a result, Bollywood has become a huge marketplace for promoting goods and services (Kripalani, 2006).

There were a few Hindi films before the 1990s that featured identifiable brands in some of the scenes. However, those brand placements were on a very limited scale and generally went unnoticed by the audience. The first highly noticed product placement was Coca-Cola in the box office hit movie *Taal* (The Rhythm) in 1999 (Kripalani, 2006).

Coca-Cola appears more than once in *Taal* as a prominent drink accompanying the stars in various emotional situations such as love, friendship, and nostalgia (Kripalani, 2006). Since then, product placement has become common in Hindi films.

A large sample was obtained, this study utilized a convenience sample to gather data. Thus, the findings of this study may not be generalizable to the entire Indian population. Future studies should utilize a random sampling procedure to gather a sample more representative of the entire population. Additionally, no verification procedures were utilized to check perceptions or travel behavior; the survey simply asked respondents to specify personal perceptions, intentions, and behavior, which could have been exaggerated, understated, or incorrectly recorded. Adding more specific questions in future data collection could aid in the verification of the influences of media on travel intentions and image perceptions. Overall, this study has successfully predicted the causal relationships among movie engagement, involvement, destination awareness, and tourist activity and consumption behaviors.

These findings further suggest a need to determine acceptable marketing techniques and approaches to prominently feature foreign destinations in Bollywood movies. Bollywood films are viewed by millions in India and across the world and are a powerful source of information. date, the power of Bollywood films as a source of travel motivation has been understudied in the tourism marketing field. This research provides justification to destination marketers and media organizations to utilize the full potential of Bollywood movies to reach billions of people. Because tourism-related behaviors vary among individuals, movie engagement and involvement with travel can be viewed as critical measures for analyzing consumer behavior in relation to tourism.

REFERENCES

Bandyopadhyay, R. (2008). Nostalgia, identity and tourism: Bollywood in the Indian Diaspora. *Journal of Tourism and Cultural Change*, *6*(2), 79–100. doi:10.1080/14766820802140463

Butler, R.W. (2011). It's only make believe: the implications of fictional and authentic locations in films. *Worldwide Hospitality & Tourism Themes, 3*(2), 91 – 101.

Chrisafis, A. (2002, May 6). Tourism on standby for Bollywood boom. *The Guardian*, p. 3.

Desai, J. (2004). *Beyond Bollywood: The cultural politics of South Asian diasporic film*. New York: Routledge. doi:10.4324/9780203643952

Desai, J. (2004). *Beyond Bollywood: The cultural politics of South Asian diasporic film*. New York: Routledge.

Dubey, B. (2008, Oct. 18). Bollywood, pied piper for tourists. *Times of India*.

Dwyer & Patel. (2002). *Cinema India: The visual culture of Hindi film*. Rutgers University Press.

Ebrahim, H. (2008). *From Ghetto to Mainstream: Bollywood in South Africa*. Taylor and Francis, Unisa Press.

Grihault, N. (2003). Film tourism - The global picture. *Travel & Tourism Analyst*, *5*, 1–22.

Han, H., & Lee, J. (2008). A Study on the KBS TV drama winter sonata and its impact on Korea's Hallyu tourism development. *Journal of Travel & Tourism Marketing*, *24*(2-3), 115–126. doi:10.1080/10548400802092593

Harjani, P. (2011). India's tourists flock to Spain. *CNN.com*. Retrieved from http://www.cnngo.com/mumbai/life/indian-movie-boostsspanish-tourism-694426

Hudson, S., & Ritchie, B. (2006a). Promoting destinations via film tourism: An empirical identification of supporting marketing initiatives. *Journal of Travel Research*, *44*(4), 387–396. doi:10.1177/0047287506286720

Hudson, S., & Ritchie, J. R. B. (2006). Film tourism and destination marketing: The case of Captain Corelli's Mandolin. *Journal of Vacation Marketing*, *12*(3), 256–268. doi:10.1177/1356766706064619

Jagarnath, V. (2004). The politics of urban segregation and Indian cinema in Durban. In P. Kaarsholm (Ed.), *City flicks: Indian cinema and the urban experience*. Calcutta: Seagull Books.

Jha, S. K. (2011). *Silsila, Lamhe are my Favourites: Yash Chopra*. Retrieved from: http://articles.timesofindia.indiatimes.com/2011-06-27/news-interviews/29708368_1_yash-chopra-dhool-ka-phool-veer-zaara

Kim, S., & O'Connor, N. (2011). A cross-cultural study of screen-tourists' profiles. *Worldwide Hospitality and Tourism Themes*, *3*(2), 141–158. doi:10.1108/17554211111123005

Kishwar, M. (Ed.). (2004). *Manushi. India Together- Revised Version of a Presentation at the Conference of India*. Retrieved from: http://www.indiatogether. org/manushi/issue139/idea.htm

Kripalani. (2007). Trendsetting and product placement in Bollywood film: Consumerism through consumption Top of Form, New Cinemas: *Journal of Contemporary Film, 4*(3), 197-215.

Lal, P. (2004). *Bollywood ain't world cinema*. http://www.greencine.com/article?action=view&articleID=125

Larkin, B. (2002). Indian flms and Nigerian lovers: media and the creation of parallel modernity. In *The anthropology of globalization: A reader*. Malden: Blackwell Publishing.

Lorenzen, M., & Täube, F. A. (2008). Breakout from Bollywood? The roles of social networks and regulation in the evolution of Indian film industry. *Journal of International Management*, *14*(3), 286–299. doi:10.1016/j.intman.2008.01.004

Lovgren, S. (2004, January 21). Bollywood: Indian films splice Bombay, Hollywood. *National Geographic News*. Retrieved online from http://news.nationalgeographic.com/news/2004/01/0121_040121_bollywoodfilms.html

Macionis, N. (2004). Understanding the film-induced tourist. In *International Tourism and Media Conference Proceedings*. Melbourne, Australia: Tourism Research Unit, Monash University.

Macionis, N., & O'Connor, N. (2011). How can the film-induced tourism phenomenon be sustainably managed? *Worldwide Hospitality and Tourism Themes*, *3*(2), 173–178. doi:10.1108/17554211111123032

Macionis, N., & Sparks, B. (2009). Film-induced tourism: An incidental experience. *Tourism Review International*, *13*(2), 93–101. doi:10.3727/154427209789604598

Minocha, S., & Stonehouse, G. (2006). The "learning trap": A Bollywood frame from strategic learning. *Management Decision*, *44*(10), 1344–1362. doi:10.1108/00251740610715687

Munshi, N. (2012). *Spain's starring role in Bollywood movie a boon to tourism*. Retrieved February 11, 2013 from: http://adage.com/article/globalnews/ spain-s-starring-role-bollywood-movie-a-boon-tourism/232511/

Padmanabhan, G. (2010). Jive to the beat. *The Hindu*.

Rajadhyaksha, A. (2003). The "Bollywoodization" of the Indian cinema: Cultural nationalism in a global arena. *Inter-Asia Cultural Studies*, *4*(1), 25–39. doi:10.1080/1464937032000060195

Rajagopalan, S. (2005). *A taste for Indian films: negotiating cultural boundaries in post- Stalinist Soviet society* (PhD thesis). Indiana University.

Rempel, S. (2007, Mar. 8). Now it's the Indian dream; middle class drives economy expected by IMF to surpass the U.S. by 2050. *The Toronto Star*.

Shah, G. R. (2012). The man who sparked Bollywood's love of foreign locales. *The New York Times Global Edition: India*. Retrieved online from: http://india.blogs.nytimes.com/2012/10/23/the-man-who-sparkedbollywoods- love-of-exotic-locales/

Singh, K., & Best, G. (2004). Film-induced tourism: motivations of visitors to the Hobbiton movies set as featured in the lord of the rings. In *International tourism and media conference proceedings*. Tourism Research Unit, Monash University.

Tagliabue, J. (2010). A beloved Bollywood extra draws Indians. *The New York Times*. Retrieved from: https://www.nytimes.com/2010/07/12/world/europe/12swiss.html?_r=0

Tooke, N., & Baker, M. (1996). Seeing is believing: The effect of film on visitor numbers to screened locations. *Tourism Management*, *17*(2), 87–94. doi:10.1016/0261-5177(95)00111-5

Young, A., & Young, R. (2008). Measuring the effects of film and television on tourism to screen locations: A theoretical and empirical perspective. *Journal of Travel & Tourism Marketing*, *24*(2-3), 195–212. doi:10.1080/10548400802092742

KEY TERMS AND DEFINITIONS

Bollywood Advertisement: An agency for sponsoring and branding a film in the market. It encourages people and producers and distributors to buy the tickets or the film copies. It also draws attention of the market to the specific film for the consumption by packaging the product inside its ideas and services of developing fashion industries depending on the fashion and style used in the film.

Bollywood Consumption: A measurement for calculating profit share in India and abroad. It can also be reflected from the density of distribution of the film often handled by different distributors depending on territory, with each negotiating a different deal with the producer. It also depends on the big named actors or stars, the name of the producers, etc.

Bollywood Film Audience: A specific group of people who are interested to watch Bollywood films in public cinemas and other venues. They also consume films via alternative platforms such as videos, DVDs, home cinemas and television channels. From its beginning Bollywood consumers are mainly influenced by their choice of films in the context of their catharsis, moral fabric, anxieties, happiness and sadness.

Bollywood Films: A large body of commercial films produced after Indian independence. They are made in Hindi and other languages like Urdu. Bollywood films are highly popular in Indian subcontinent, Asia, Russia, Middle East. It is also popular among Indian diasporas in South Africa, the Caribbean, the US, and Europe. These films are mainly produced from a city called Bombay and hence the name is Bollywood films. These films typically incorporate a mixture of genres, with music, melodrama, romance, action, mythologies and social dramas.

Bollywood Industry/Market: A place where Bollywood cinemas are sold. The amount of money a film takes during theatrical release. The market figures often used in the popular and trade press. It is used as indicators of film's profitability/ success. Each of these films will have its own specific deal.

Bollywood Product Placement: It is a cost-effective means of gaining global media. It is a unique way to familiarise consumer with brand and product and connect to audience with added benefit of association with the popular Bollywood films. It is important because it gives clues that why should we not ignore other revenue streams of the Bollywood films. Theatrical release of a film only generates a minor proportion of the revenue collection, with the major percent coming from ancillary markets such as DVDs, musical CDs and nowadays how film-corporate markets like Netflix, Amazon Prime absorb them including broadcasting through major TV channels and other licenses like computer games, merchandise, theme parks, etc.

Bollywood Travel Destination: The popular Bollywood films plays a major role in audience's mind by influencing them to choose a travel destination which has been used in the specific film. Film shooting spots in Bollywood films create imaginative and luxurious travel frames and destinations in audience's mind. The link between travel destination/tourism and Bollywood films has been long recognized and nowadays it has been strengthened and globalized as essential elements and effects of Bollywood films.

Chapter 12
Not a "Coke and Chips" Holiday: Museums in Danish Coastal Tourism

Barbora Gulisova
https://orcid.org/0000-0002-8562-4714
University of Southern Denmark, Denmark

Lulu Anne Hansen
Museum of Southwest Jutland, Denmark

ABSTRACT

This chapter, from a historical anthropological perspective, discusses the role of heritage museums in Danish coastal tourism. It is argued that the museum experience is highly contextual making it necessary to understand how place specific heritage interacts with tourist holiday motivations and museums understanding of their role as heritage suppliers. The interplay of these factors must be understood to create better bonds between museums and visitors especially in a tourism context. In order to do this, new questions must be asked, and research should move away from binary understandings of demand and supply.

INTRODUCTION

The aim and purpose of this chapter is to offer some empirically and conceptually founded observations on the specific activity of visiting museums in the context of coastal tourism on the Danish west coast. The paper argues that the distinction between cultural tourists and other forms of tourists constitutes an unhelpful blurring of concepts, at best. It is based on a static concept of of museum visits as holiday activity, to be dealt with as a general phenomenon, when it is rather highly contextual and must be understood as such.

The aim of the paper is to challenge the general perceptions within academic literature of what museums are and, as such, argue that no one size fits all model exists, when it comes to museum's way og engaging with their audiences. This goes particularly in a tourism context (Chhabra 2010). Several functions of museums have been mentioned such as the aim to educate, collect and conserve objects

DOI: 10.4018/978-1-7998-3115-0.ch012

Copyright © 2020, IGI Global. Copying or distributing in print or electronic forms without written permission of IGI Global is prohibited.

(Alexander 1996; McLean 1994), provide entertainment and serve as institutions of knowledge and research. However, the main claim of this article is, that although museums do serve all these functions the historical roots of the museum culture and popular perceptions of the museums role in society differs somewhat depending on which kinds of museums are the focus of discussion.

For this reason, it makes sense to approach the topic from a point of departure that does not only look at museums from a consumer perspective but to also include perspectives dealing with ways in which museums interact with society and how this affects the cultural contexts in which museums are understood. The attempt is to move away from the traditionally demand and supply driven binary perceptions of museums as attractions (Hannam and Knox 2010). This is particularly interesting in a tourism context since museums are often considered potential drivers in tourism development.

BACKGROUND

In 2016(a) a report from VisitDenmark acknowledged that German tourists do not know much about Danish history and culture, and that there is a need to attract them to the cultural offer already existing. At the same time, the report proposed connecting culture to nature and the wide beaches, which are what the tourists love about Denmark. Another study found that the number of tourists actually using cultural offers during their holiday is higher than the number of tourists stating culture as their motivation for visiting the country (VisitDenmark, 2016b). Such numbers can, although perhaps not surprising, seem puzzling. It constitutes a contradiction between travel motivation and holiday choice of activities.

The mentioned report stated that there are more overnight stays in coastal Denmark than Copenhagen, but 57% of the tourists in Copenhagen can be defined as cultural tourists, while this is the case for only 24-39% of the visitors in the rest of the country. Moreover, in the capital region 56% of museum visitors are international, while only 8% and 4% of the museum visitors in Midtjylland and Nordjylland, respectively, are international. There are big differences between the museums, depending on their marketing and displays. According to the report by VisitDenmark (2016a), 22% of the international nights taken in Denmark in 2014 were on the West coast, where Ringkøbing-Skjern museum and Sydvestjyske museer have a high proportion of international visitors, mostly thanks to Bork Vikingehavn (83%; part of the Ringkøbing Skjern Museum) and Ribes Vikinger (55%; part of the Sydvestjyske Museer), respectively. Also, VisitDenmark (2016b)'s report states that while the coastal and natural tourists belong to the non-cultural category, not motivated by learning about culture and history many museums in the area have a high number of international visitors. They therefore advocate that the museums could play an important role when tourists are in the area and need to find activities to do, some experiences to have. The intention here is, therefore, to gain a better understanding of the question at hand. An historical and anthropological approach was chosen to shed light on previously unrecognized aspects of the role of museums in Danish Coastal destination.

MAIN FOCUS OF THE CHAPTER

Using Denmark as a case, the authors first present an historical analysis of the museum as cultural institution and present at typology based both on the aims, themes and geographical focuses of individual museums. Furthermore, this typology will be used to single out two main forms of museums outside of

Danish urban centers: The themed and the local and regional museum. Focusing on these two forms of museums the chapter will discuss how these as the most common forms of museums outside of urban centres can be understood in the context of coastal tourism, a form of tourism that, in a Danish context, is usually motivated by love of nature and not cultural attractions. By combining the emic perspective of the visitors of museums as a cultural activity with knowledge of how the museums have traditionally defined themselves, the relational aspect of meaning making with regards to museums in a tourism context becomes clearer and hence, so does the possibility of establishing a more equal dialog between visitor and museum.

This paper is based on historical records and the data collected for the research project "Kulturarvsformidling og kystturisme – et umage par?", supported by the Museernes Udviklingspulje, as part of the Culture Plus (Slots- og Kulturstyrelsen, 2016). The purpose of the project was to establish knowledge and ground for action to develop the role of heritage museums in coastal tourism.

Methodology

Guided by the constructivist approach (Denzin & Lincoln, 2011), this study first used desk research and archival studies to understand the role and perceptions of museums in society as well as semi-structured interviews for data collection on tourists' views (Hansen 2013). Regarding visitors' perspectives this gave the interviewees the freedom to talk more about the aspects they chose as most relevant while covering the topics of research, bringing more detailed opinions, valuable information and better understanding of the phenomena studied (Jennings, 2010). Seeing the interviews through Kvale (20007)'s 'traveler metaphor', the interviewer tried to reach a common understanding with the interviewees of the phenomena researched, by exploring the meanings and narratives of the interviewees together with them, asking questions and encouraging their story telling. In this postmodern approach, the interview is a site of interchange of opinions between the interviewer and the interviewee, talking about a common theme, making the interview a 'construction site of knowledge' (Kvale, 2007).

For this study, two interview guides were used. One applied in the museums, where the guests were interviewed after their visit, with questions mostly relating to the actual museum visit, and to a lesser degree to the holiday experience as a whole. The other guide was applied to interview tourists in other locations than museums. A question related to photographs was incorporated to better understand the tourists' views of their holiday in the area. Using visual methods allows for the creation and access of knowledge about aspects that are not easily accessible only by using traditional non-visual methods (Rakic & Chambers, 2012). For this study, photo-elicitation of secondary source visuals, and in some cases, participants' own photos, was used to obtain data in the context of the interviews (Jenkins, 1999; Andersson Cederholm, 2004). Participants spoke more openly while talking about the photos, and often some taken-for-granted aspects were mentioned during this part of the interview, that were not talked about otherwise.

Purposive sampling was used in which Danish and German tourists to the area were approached for an interview, as these are the main visitors here according to VisitDenmark (2016c). The interviews took place in 3 different museums in the area, as well as a shop/cafeteria in a popular part of a holiday island and a camping site in another popular destination. The sampling stopped when information redundancy was reached (Jennings, 2010), and maximum variation sample (Tracy, 2013) was applied by the inclusion of both tourists who actively sought out heritage attractions and those who did not. The final sample of interviews used for the analysis was 66, these were transcribed in the original language, coded, and analysed in relation to the theories, categorizations and reports treated below.

Heritage and Heritage Tourism

In order to understand the meaning of historical heritage attractions in a coastal tourism context heritage tourism as a concept must be understood. Heritage has been defined and described in several ways by a number of researchers, resulting in various "interpretations and descriptions" of it (Timothy & Boyd, 2006, p. 2). The definition by Ashworth (2003) and Graham et al. (2000) as heritage being "the present-day use of the past" (Timothy & Boyd, 2006, p. 2) is among the most accepted ones among the scholars. Knudsen & Greer (2008, p. 20) specify," heritage is a set of ideas, symbols and events that establishes and reinforces the social cohesion and identity, real or imagined, of a group of individuals." However, they caution against simply equating heritage with history, citing Edson (2004, p. 338) in saying, "Heritage has greater symbolic meaning than the object, time or place that is the historical reference".

Visiting sites of historical importance, such as urban and other built areas, ancient settlements and monuments, agricultural and rural landscapes, and places where historical events happened, but also locations with significant and particularly attractive culture, all form part of the phenomenon called heritage tourism, which belongs to the most significant types of tourism (Timothy & Boyd, 2006). Richards (2000) agrees but also states that "heritage can cover many elements of living culture as well as the cultural and natural past" (p. 10). He also refers to Yale (1991) who noted that "heritage tourism is 'centered on what we have inherited, which can mean anything from historical building to art works, to beautiful scenery'." (Richards, 2000, p. 9). Also, the definition of heritage adopted in the World Heritage Convention by UNESCO (1972) reflects that broad view of the issue (Richards, 2000, p. 9).

Timothy and Boyd (2006) talk about "a major unrepresentative imbalance in the heritage industry" (p. 7) as most of the attractions have at their core artefacts related to the elites or royalty (castles, cities, mansions, cathedrals, etc.), while the ordinary people's heritage, based on their day-to-day lifestyles is unrepresented (farms, houses, fishing boats, factories, schools, cultural landscapes, etc.) although this is changing (Timothy & Boyd, 2006). McKercher and du Cros (2005: 211-212) adopt a more marketing oriented definition of cultural tourism as "a form of tourism that relies on a destination's cultural heritage assets and transforms them into products that can be consumed by tourists." ICOMOS (1999) defined heritage broadly as including tangible (cultural and natural environments, landscapes, historic sites, places and built environments) and intangible (collections, living experiences, and past and continuing cultural practice and knowledge) assets, but the definition has been expanded to include contemporary and heritage arts expressing something unique about a certain worldview. According to Kirshenblatt-Gimblett (2004) the intangible and the tangible heritage are linked together, as the tangible often obtains meaning from the intangible, which is expressed in the tangible.

Jamal & Kim (2005) state that heritage is related to the historical past, and they argue that heritage tourism essentially is about existence, belonging, life, and change from the past through the present into the future. To interpret the present, but also one's belonging and identity, it is important to reckon on the past. Earmarking, interpreting and communicating parts of the past by use of performances, artefacts, sites and texts are involved in heritage tourism. Heritage is not simply represented or displayed, but it involves negotiation, contestation, personification and performativity.

Heritage tourism and cultural tourism seem similar. Accordingly, cultural tourism refers to those who want to learn about the destination's history and culture, demanding authentic and unique experiences, and it includes heritage, lifestyle, creative industries, contemporary art and popular culture. In the report, VisitDenmark (2016a) defines three groups of cultural tourists: cultural deniers, culture users, and culture experts.

Cultural and heritage tourism are closely related, as culture often forms part of heritage tourism (Timothy & Boyd, 2006; Richard, 2000), and heritage attractions are often part of cultural tourism (Boyd, 2002; DuCross & McKercher, 2015). Assets such as museums, monuments, historical sites etc. are included both under heritage and cultural tourism (Timothy & Boyd, 2006; Richard, 2000; Boyd, 2002; DuCross & McKercher, 2015; VisitDenmark, 2016a).

Museums in Coastal Tourism

According to Richards (2000), heritage tourism development in different countries shows variations in heritage concepts. He gives examples of the Scandinavian open-air museums from the turn of the 20th century, which developed due to loss of traditional cultural handicrafts and rural ways of life. To interpret local culture, Ecomuseums developed in France, in Netherlands the preservation of landscapes as a whole was emphasized, while in Japan and Australia theme parks focused on either local or foreign cultural heritage. Nevertheless, as Bonn et al. (2007) write, "each type of attraction has its own unique combination of benefits and advantages; some focus more on the historical aspect, some on the cultural, and others mix geographic and heritage elements" (p. 346). Smith (2003) writes that "history has a dynamic quality to it and will vary according to our perceptions and interpretation of it within the present" (p. 83), and Schouten (1995) emphasized the importance and the meaning of interpretation for understanding and enlivening history.

The roots of the historical museums can be found in the renaissance treasure rooms of European kings and princes dating as far back as to the 12the century (Lewis 1992). The treasures kept in such collections were characterized by their qualities of exoticism and rarity. They were constituted by gifts given to the sovereigns by allies and subjects who would have acquired them during their travels or connections to e.g. colonies and were early on available to be viewed by the public. During the 19th century public consciousness and engagement in articulating and supporting ideas of a collective past as the foundation of nations states became more pronounced. This led to two developments. First, the royal and privileged collections mentioned above were re-thought in a new context focusing on their meaning of prestige for the whole nation (Lewis 1992). Although to a certain extent also spurred by a transnational quest for scientific use of collections (Randsborg 2000), in the national mindset symbols of the scope and reach of the nation state were important reminders of the value og nations states. Secondly, an interest in the roots of the nation resulted in an increased interest in ancient times making the profession of archaeology and later also history founding professions in legitimizing the nation state. Both themes produced an immense amount of objects to be displayed and kept as a reservoir of collective memory for the growing nation states and their publics. This is perhaps best illustrated in the formulation of the national museum as a state institution putting objects on display to be viewed and appropriated with proper respect and veneration.

However, while the nation state developed its power and grasp of its populations, another complex of ideas caused the development of another kind of museum institution. The local museum. Local museums grew out of regionalism as this began to develop in the course of the late 19th to early 20th century. Nationalism and regionalism were not necessarily contradictory forces (Storm 2003). Part of knowing and appropriating the nation was also to know and appreciate its different regions. And within these regions a desire for acknowledgement and recognition drove the enthusiasm of creating reservoirs of local and regional memory, traditions, specificities, and crafts slowly becoming a part of the past.

Both kinds of museums grew out a veneration for roots and a glorious past. As time grew by another kind of museum developed as well. This kind the authors have chosen to name the themed museum although it encompasses several different kinds of museums from the open-air history museums to museums commemorating particular industries or crafts. Such museums seem, with few exceptions, to have been a post war phenomenon hugely spurred on by the mechanization of agriculture and later the mechanization of hard industry. As it has previously been pointed out, the decline in significant professions or industries seem to spur on the museological veneration for sites and objects relating to such activities.

Finally, during the 1980s, a real explosion in the amount of historic sites and smaller museums dedicated to built and themed heritage sites took place. This development has been well documented in literature and was paralleled by an equally impressive rise in the consumption of what one might call the heritage industry (Lowenthal 1998). In this period the growth in museum visitors is arguably the largest one ever seen.

Nowadays museums serve a great deal of other purposes. In particular, museums have been the focus of much attention, when it comes to reinvigorating peripheral and agricultural regions through tourism development (Richards 2005; P Courtney, G Hill, D Roberts 2006).

On the Danish West Coast such developments can also be observed. Here, already in the late 1960s the themed museums of the Danish fisheries and maritime activities was established in Esbjerg, the so called capital of the West Coast, generating 250.000 visitors at its highest in the 1990s. Also, the 1980s saw the beginning of a new museum theme in the form of the so called "Bunker Museums" build around the negative heritage of the Second World war and the remains of the German built Atlantic Wall (Hansen & Jensen 2013). Similarly, in the 1990s the themed Viking museums became established with the most successful examples in Ribe Vikingcentre (1992), Ribe Vikingemuseum (1992) and Bork Vikingehavn (2000).

Along with such museums a long series of local museums coexist. By now many have fused with larger museum units, but they often have in common that they were established in the early decades of the 20th century and they represent the characteristics of local communities. Examples can be found in the west coast island of Fanø, an extremely popular tourist spot where two museums in the main town of Nordby were established. Finally, the west coast is inhabited by the town museums of the larger towns which tell the history of local towns and their development. For many years they have had a very similar set up and display. They are now, as then, situated in areas that have, during the same period, become coastal destinations of both national and international tourists.

Coastal Tourism: Nature and Heritage

Landscape is an important aspect of Danish tourism, as mentioned in the introduction, and most of the overnight stays take place on the coast. The concept of coastal tourism, as defined by Hall & Page (2006, p. 292), "embraces the full range of tourism, leisure and recreationally oriented activities that take place in the coastal zone and the offshore coastal waters" including the supporting infrastructure and activities, and the coastal tourism facilities. They point out the three components, as identified by Pearce & Kirk (1986), that form "the coastal environment: the hinterland (where accommodation and services are provided), the transit zone (i.e. dunes) and the recreational activity zone (beach and sea)" (Hall & Page, 2006, p. 291).

The development of Danish coastal tourism began in the late 19th century, when people from larger urban areas "discovered the recreational value of the small fishing villages close to the coast" (Tress, 2002, p. 111). It was sparked by artists, who looked for unspoiled landscape, small villages with simple life, and real natural experiences instead of spas and seaside resorts. The artists' environment and the natural scenery of the coast attracted urbanites to move there for summer holidays. The houses they stayed in were built on small hills and the windy side of dunes, because "people wanted to experience seascape, landscape and nature" (Dahlkild, 1991; referred to in Tress, 2002, p. 113). The coastal areas also attracted many Germans living in big cities, as a vacation in a rented second home allowed for recreational activities, such as bathing, walking on the beach or in the dunes, fishing, cycling through the countryside, and experiencing the coastal landscape (Schultz, 1988; referred to in Tress, 2002).

According to Andersen (2015) the holiday home tourism is the most dominating one in the coastal zone of Denmark. It is in the places of the largest natural attractiveness, and the lowest commercial facilities that it takes place. Here, the holiday home tourists do not spend much on events and attractions, but prefer to have their experiences in the holiday home or its nearby environment. Based on a study of holiday home tourists on Bornholm, Andersen (2015) found that the tourists mainly wanted to spend time together and relax. The factors that influenced their choice of accommodation were, among others, the atmosphere, the sea and the closeness to nature.

Landscape and Heritage

Aplin (2007) considers the role landscapes have as an important part of our heritage. Landscapes that endure and are easy to recognize provide us with a 'sense of place' (p. 430). They are cultural landscapes, since they, to various degrees, developed due to the interaction of people through their spiritual, economic, and cultural systems, and the nature. Aplin (2007) refers to Davis (2005), who based on the concept of place, the interaction between culture and places, and the resulting local distinctiveness point to the Ecomuseum as a means of creating a sense of place for, a wider population. Richards (2001, p. 12) writes, "the meanings of landscapes draw on the cultural codes of the society for which they were made. Specific landscapes are the product of particular cultural practices."

Knudsen and Greer (2008) acknowledge the fact that heritage tourism, as all other kinds of tourism, takes place in landscape, which, to varying degrees, always is a product of culture. To understand heritage tourism, it is necessary to understand the process by which ordinary cultural landscapes become symbolic, how these become guardians of historical content, why and how they are preserved and become tourism attractions. This is also the case for coastal landscapes. Some cultural landscapes transform their ordinariness, signifying aspects of local, regional and national culture as symbolic landscapes (Meinig 1979, pp. 164-165).

Knudsen and Greer (2008), in their study of the (then) proposed national park Thy, describe how the landscape of the area became the symbol of Danish countryside, mostly thanks to painters, musicians and writers of the 18th century, who presented it in their work. This was important in creating the symbolic landscape nowadays sought out by tourists who come to see and experience the landscape that is shown and described in the well-known paintings and the novels. Krauss (2005) in his case study of Northern Friesland also points out the interaction and connection between nature and the human process forming the landscape.

In another study of Thy, Knudsen (2012) looked at the different views of the landscape from the "insider" and the "outsider" perspective (Lowenthal, 1972; Tuan 1972; 1974a&b). The difference between insider and outsider is in the lived experiences with the specific landscape. And since the experiences of people differ, so will their views of the landscape in question do. A detailed knowledge of history and culture is required to interpret landscape in any full or rich way. One must realize this in explanations of tourism and this in turn means that cultural/heritage tourism has limits – limits that are bounded more by acculturation than by tourism policy or infrastructural expenditure" (p. 119). Furthermore, he writes that meaning is not given in tourism, but contested through discourse and carefully negotiated, and that "in the absence of 'insider' meaning, 'outsider' meanings are constructed for what one gazes upon by making reference to available concepts (p. 119).

Daugstad's (2008) study shows that "nature and culture are appreciated for their experiential qualities" (p.410), engaging in activities such as fishing or riding. The emphasis on traditional or old features is reinforced by promoting selected cultural heritage, e.g. staying in a listed building, or visiting a nationally important, traditional cultural landscape. She noted, "there is a growing trend for tourists to move away from the traditional outside perspective of merely passing through a landscape and experiencing it only through their eyes. The modern tourist wants the personal experience of tasting, feeling, and hearing stories about the landscape, and to experience it first-hand" (p. 413).

Du Cross & McKercher (2015) define cultural landscapes as integrating natural and cultural values, and being a cultural asset illustrating how people by doing certain activities, change the environment. It is in this interaction that tourists use and interpret heritage.

Use of Heritage

Often, tourists do not perceive themselves as cultural tourists, although they do cultural activities, such as visiting museums and churches, looking at typical, old architecture, eating at traditional restaurants etc., while on holiday (Schouten, 2007). Selby (2010) refers to Bagnall's (2003) study that showed that heritage is used actively; the visitors apply their memories and personal histories to verify or challenge the interpretation of exhibits. Selby (2010, p. 44) points out that even Urry (2002), known for his 'tourist gaze', has developed a concept of 'sense-scapes', and also talked about a sixth sense, 'Kinaesthetics', related to how the body relates to space.

Ashworth (2000) writes that tourists use various heritages in various ways, and he gives four characteristics of the resources used in heritage tourism: (1) the variety of heritage services and goods consumed by tourists; (2) heritage is an omnipresent resource, because, although some might be more eminent, all places and people have a past and a heritage, even though it might not necessarily be interpreted as distinctive; (3) the heritage resources are used for other purposes and by other people than tourists, and (4) based on the previous, tourism mostly uses resources that were not produced for a tourism market and "which are currently owned and managed by those who are unaware of, indifferent to or even hostile towards that use (Borg, et al., 1996)". Ashworth (2000) also talks about the 'place specific tourism' (p. 23) where everyday environments and locales of the destinations are used as a generalized heritage to characterize and identify experience of a given place. The peculiar historical heritage and the characteristically local factors, which show society's values and norms, form the identity of places. He also acknowledges that the proportion of the tourism market attracted to heritage during their holiday is growing, as the definition of it has broadened to include the daily-life heritage of regular people and a wider range of heritage products is offered: "tourists consuming heritage (in the form of historical architecture, artefacts collections, folk traditions and craft souvenirs) may be merely continuing their everyday activities and their consumption behaviour is often indistinguishable from that of residents." (p. 24). Poria (2010) argues that not all visitors to a heritage site come because of actual interest in what is represented. For him a heritage site is not necessarily equal to a historic site - what matters is the visitors' sense and feeling of it being a part of their personal heritage, meaning. This means that the same site will mean different things to different people. This relates to the relative authenticity (Timothy & Boyd, 2006) – the impression being subjective, depending on one's own social education, and therefore varying among different people. Timothy and Boyd (2006) write that the meaning of heritage does not stem directly from the site or relic itself, but it is a combination of how the item is displayed and interpreted and the visitor's background. They also conclude, that "instead of seeking reality, most tourists simply want a holiday experience that is entertaining, enjoyable and memorable" (p. 5).

Poria (2010) talks about different categories of visitors to heritage sites. One of them is Chen's (1998), who categorized the visitors according to two main motives - personal benefits, such as recreation, relaxation, and sightseeing; and gaining knowledge. The question is if and how uses of heritage changes in different tourism contexts.

Rural vs. Urban Heritage

In her work on cities, Smith (2007) emphasizes the importance of distinctive place identity for the places to be able to differentiate themselves from others and to attract visitors. But, she points out that tourists will assess their perceptions of the place in relation to their home. She discusses the issue of 'placelessness' as a 'could be anywhere' (p. 99) feeling, often experienced in leisure centres, theme parks, etc., also giving the example of resorts, that combine familiar elements to make the tourists feel like 'at home'. But "these elements are displaced or misplaced, local heritage has often been eroded to make way for them, and the result is a kind of nowhere land, home to no one". (Smith, 2007, p. 99) Further, she points out that participants of mass tourism generally like the reassurance of familiarity, and therefore the placeless enclaves appeal to them, while she in another study (Smith, 2003) says that e.g. cultural tourists seek authenticity, cultural diversity and difference.

Du Cross and McKercher (2015) talk about the importance the physical location of a cultural heritage asset has on its visitation and use. The location is also linked to the time a tourist is willing to spend on cultural tourism, where especially those for whom culture is only a secondary part of a trip will prioritize their time among various competing uses of it. At the same time, cultural heritage tourism is often a time-consuming activity.

However, in looking at the issue from an historical perspective the dichotomy between heritage and culture seems less clear cut. As described above the sea and the coastal landscape became symbolic in a Danish context drawing in artists, poets and writers who took inspiration from describing the power of nature and the sea (Hansen 2018). At the same time the first coastal tourists became fascinated with the unspoiled nature of local communities. In the context of the Danish coast the idea of a specific maritime culture became a dominant theme as artists and poets popularized the areas. In the same way as the early dwellers leaving the urban centers to find health and rest in agricultural areas were looking for a combination of nature, history and original communities (Boegh 1993), so was the mental landscape of the coastal tourists shaped by more than a simple search for nature and health. It was also shaped by a search for the authentic, the original and educative in the form of – amongst other things – heritage sites such as churches, memorials and symbols of maritime culture. In the context of the Danish West

Coast Nature and culture were in this way inherently connected in the context of coastal tourism. In this research we particularly interested in what role heritage and education played for tourist today based on the historically founded presumption that the two are not opposites in the form of education vs. relaxation but that they can constitute integrated forms of being in the coastal landscape. Below, we will look at the perception of heritage museums in the Danish coastal context.

Sun, Sea and Museums?

There are tourists who purposefully visit museums during their holiday, others that almost coincidentally enter some, and still others who will avoid them. Therefore, it is important to look at why those who do visit museums choose to do so, while others choose to stay away. The interviewees in this research had different reasons to visit. There were examples of Falk & Dierking (2013)'s category of explorers saying that they visit museums because of their interests in general. The facilitators, for whom it was important that the whole family would have a good experience were represented by several visiting a museum because they wanted to show it to friends and relatives. While the explorers are generally interested in museums or history, the professionals or hobbyists with specific interests were also found here and some examples contained several categories. For instance, one visitor had visited the book print museum in the town of Esbjerg, because there was a history of book printing in the family, while going to the Maritime Museum in the same town, because her family wanted to go.

It could also be discussed whether Falk and Dierking (2013)'s categorization does not cover the whole range of the possible museum visitor's motivation. With regards to interests, their categories either cover those generally interested in history and museums, or those with specific interests related to their hobby or job. But the people specifically interested in one part of the past (e.g. Vikings, the Middle Ages, or WWII), not the history in general, do not fall into any of these categories.

Here, the question is whether the museums in this area just do not attract the rechargers. Could this be because the definition of the category, that talks about museum being a retreat from daily life, is based on museumgoers in general, while here the interviewees were all tourists, for whom the whole holiday already was an escape from daily life? Would there have been more rechargers if local visitors were also included? And if not, then does it mean that the museums in this area just do not attract the rechargers, which would seem somewhat surprising given the coastal context. Perhaps this is because the understanding of rechargers does not make sense in a non-urban context?

A few of the tourists could be seen as respectful pilgrims with relation to the Second WWII bunkers, without thinking about it in that way. They might not have come to visit the bunkers with the sole purpose of honoring the memory of those who were affected by the history of WWII, but for example, one said that he found the history of a former soldier whose bunker was discovered many years after the war, and who could revisit it, and found that it was as he left it, fascinating. Corresponding to the VisitDenmark (2016a; 2016b) and Wonderful Copenhagen's (2015) reports, there were no experience seekers who hurries from one museum or site to another, to see as much as possible on the holiday with regards to heritage sites found among the sample of this study. As the interviews show the tourists came to enjoy the peaceful natural environments, relax and spend time with their families. Many pointed out the difference between the stressed Germans and the calm and quiet Danes. For some, museums were more associated with education than relaxing holiday activity. Also, the Danish tourists in the area wanted a relaxing holiday, enjoying nature, and, if they visited the museums, it was to learn something about the area (Danes in particular), or to have an experience with their kids. Generally, it could also be said that, of those interviewed in other places than museums, many started out by saying that they do not visit them, or were not interested in heritage, although while talking about their holidays, it became clear that they actually did visit museums perhaps not reflecting over the activity as such. It could also be argued, that although the tourists did not see museums as an important part of their holiday, there were some who did or planned to visit The Maritime Museum in Esbjerg, or the Viking museum in Ribe or Bork, and even some who did it regularly, though they mostly talked about the entertaining part of the visits. In this way they saw museums more as other types of leisure activities than serious learning places (Falk and Dierking, 2013).

Nevertheless, several of the respondents saw it as a matter of course to visit museums and other heritage attractions when visiting European capitals for instance. A very typical facilitator/explorer view opposed to experience seeker was expressed by one visitor who said that they visited the Maritime Museum in Esbjerg, and Naturkundemuseum in Blåvand, because it was also interesting for their grandson, while at the same time ruling out that they went on holiday to visit museums.

Museums and Education

Museums are places of displaying and communicating heritage and history, and the educational part of the museum experience was mentioned by several of the interviewees, whether they were talking about a museum recently visited or museums in general, confirming Falk & Dierking (2013)'s definition of heritage sites. It was important for parents and grandparents alike that children learned something about the past. While the Danes were most interested in showing their children the past in general (the development of society), the main emphasis for the Germans with regards to learning was often related to the history of the Second World War when Germany had occupied Denmark. For example, one German tourist, when asked about the reason for visiting a bunker, answered that they wanted to explain its history to their children. Another emphasized the importance of showing children the war history, and how much damage war can cause. He then moved on to say that showing the general development of the country to the kids was also important. At home, for instance, they usually visited different museums beginning with town museums to show the history of local community to their children. Generally, several Germans were interested in learning of the history of the war.

Education - implicit or explicit - was not only relevant for children, though, but also for the general public, and it also took place at other sites than museums. One Danish visitor spoke a lot about the tough life at the coast (with the powers of nature, the fishing trade, etc.), but was less interested in the history of WWII.

The apparent divergence regarding which part of the past people found most interesting or important to learn about - whether the general development, or the specific war history - can be understood in different ways. The fact that the Danes mostly wanted to learn more about the hard life at the coast in general, while the Germans mostly emphasized WWII history, can be interpreted by Jamal & Kim (2005)'s concept of micro-local vs. macro-social and global perspectives. Here the micro-local is represented by the Danes, for whom the specific hard life on the coast due to the natural conditions etc. was most interesting, while the macro-social and global is represented by the Germans, who were more interested in the common history that they could also relate to, i.e. WWII.

The topic of the bunkers and the war history could evoke strong feelings especially among some of the German interviewees, confirming Smith (2003)'s findings about individual sensibilities with regards to dissonant aspects of heritage. This could be found to the extent where some did not even want to talk about the War. Based on this, a reason for many others to talk about the importance of learning about the war-history in the area could be that they found it important to mention it to the interviewer as a duty in recognizing their own dark heritage.

Another reason can be that they do not learn much about this part of history at home, or only learn it from a certain perspective, corresponding to Poria (2010)’s view of usually showing only the winner’s history, while they, while in Denmark, have the opportunity to see it from more perspectives. This was exemplified by one visitor, who visited an exhibition about the allied bombings during WWII. The theme surprised the interviewee, who was used to being told that only the Germans were the bad ones in the war. The fact that people wanted to learn and pass the knowledge to children support two of the five most important reasons that Poria et al. (2006) identified in heritage tourists. Another one was leisure pursuit (enjoy nature, the family, relax), which was mentioned by most of the interviewees here as well, also confirming the reports from VisitDenmark (2016a; 2016b), as well as supporting Timothy & Boyd (2006)’s theory of tourists mostly just wanting enjoyable experiences. This could be discussed in the view of Falk & Dierking (2013)’s statement, that there is no sharp boundary between education and entertainment, and that most people accept that museums fulfill both needs. In this way the coastal tourists do not seem to differ from a more general picture. This is not new. However, the research indicated that the themed museums are perceived as something other than the town museum when it comes to visitors framing and meaning making in the experience.

Also, the research did indicate some difference when it comes to visiting heritage museums in the coastal context. One set of parents said that they all had learned something while also enjoying the visit together. While another, even though they usually visited the same three museums when they were on holiday in the area, said that that was enough, because “we want to be here on holiday and not for education.” This example shows that for some there is a sharp boundary between the serious museums experience of learning, and the entertaining or relaxing part of the holiday. This again challenges Falk and Dierking (2013)’s theory that visitors integrate the two. This is further supported by another visitor who emphasized the need to just have fun and not constantly having to ask oneself “What have I learned from this?”

While views like this confirm Du Cross and McKercher (2015)’s view of tourists not wanting deeper learning, there were also examples of people generally wanting to learn about the places and people of the area visited (Richards, 2007). One family said that they always visited museums, because their holiday was more than “Coke and chips”,

Those interviewees that actively searched for, and used heritage sites in the form of museums can be seen as the ‘multicultural audience’ as defined by Poria (2010). They wanted an enriching experience, where they learned something and were maybe even challenged by their heritage encounters. This also questions Falk and Dierking (2013)’s statements that a visit to a museum is “reinforcing or highlighting what you already now”. This was true for only a few of the interviewees, while for most there were new things to discover.

When it came to reflecting on heritage encountered at the museums, it was mostly the Danes who reflected on their own background, especially when seeing displays of something they personally could relate to. The Germans also kept a personal distance from the themes encountered, which could again be explained by Jamal and Kim (2005)’s micro-local vs. macro-global concept, where for the Danes the displays represented part of their personal/identity heritage, while it was something foreign for the Germans.

The research indicated that coastal tourists in the Danish context are generally interested in learning something new, or seeing things from other perspectives, both something specific to the area, but also something common, something they somehow can relate to. At the same time, the edutainment, combining fun and some learning seemed important, and this could be achieved by presenting lighter parts of the common history and development, rather than only the tragical WWII history. Furthermore, while the local museums have a larger connection with the nation state and in this way tell narratives related to national and local interests and history, the themed museums seem to fit in better with the macro-global perspectives of the German visitors, who seemed more engaged with the history involving their own heritage.

SOLUTIONS AND RECOMMENDATIONS

Based on the literature review and the analysis, this section includes the following recommendations about how museums in coastal areas and in interaction with other sites and facilities can make historical heritage experiences more attractive for tourists.

Clearly, the museums cannot compete with capitals about cultural tourism as explained above, and neither should they, but once tourists are in coastal areas it is important to understand the complex interplay between museum, tourists and heritage interpretation. Here it is first important to make local and regional heritage visible and accessible for them. This could be done by bringing interpretation out in nature. This could overcome the first hurdle of many tourists perceived gap between education (Falk and Dierking, 2013) and relaxation, fun, enjoyment, and entertainment (VisitDenmark 2016) for the edutainment aspect (McPherson, 2006). This also affects marketing and cooperation.

Many of those interviewed at the museums said they visited because they happened to notice it when they drove by, they saw an advertisement for it in a brochure, or lacked something to do that day and looked around for some activity. None said that they had the visit planned from home. This raises the issue of creating opportunities for interest and it might well be worth looking at Hall & Page's (2006) idea of zones as different ways of engaging with and raising awareness of heritage related activities.

Interpretation, education and performativity also emerge as highly relevant issues to address. First, knowledge of the relation between place specific heritage and tourists' way of engaging with this heritage must be of interest to museums. Knowledge of audiences and understanding of ways of engaging with them, while still being loyal to professional considerations of interpretation should be subjected to well thought out strategies. For example, the Germans have other feelings about the bunkers, and different knowledge about the fishing and trade history of the area, than the Danes do. But there should be place for negotiation and dialogue about what tourists know in relation to their heritage encounters (Jamal and Kim, 2005). Facilitation performativity – the opportunity of hands-on experiences, and the possibility for negotiation and personification of the heritage experiences will allow the visitors for better understanding of the connection between the past, the present, and the future.

FUTURE RESEARCH DIRECTIONS

Much literature on museum visitors and marketing focus on how to market and package the heritage experience as a product for consumption by visitors. In the same way models have been developed for heritage organisations and destinations to edge out what their particular narrative and followingly interesting selling points are.

This study, however, showed a complex pattern which in this relative limited case study of the Danish West coast pointed to differences in perceptions of heritage depending on differing nationalities, on views and uses of history and heritage in private life, on holiday - and not least on the narratives that can act as hooks to grab the interests of the visitors.

Future studies in visitor behaviour might gain from considering these perspectives in specific context as the way the different elements weigh against each other will rarely be the same from one museum to the next. For this reason, future attempts at creating models on heritage consumption should to a greater extent take into account the place specific and context related understanding of different tourists' relation to local heritage.

CONCLUSION

In this chapter, an attempt has been made to understand tourism and museum culture by using historically anthropological approaches to asking questions and gain empirical knowledge. The aim was to find similarities and meeting points between museums and visitors rather than seeing them as mutually independent pillars. It was argued that the themed and local museums in the case studied in Denmark have very different aims and hence resources for addressing and engaging with visitors. In the rural and coastal areas, themed museums often have a history of coming into being as attractions and hence have different ways of engaging with audiences. At the same time local museums historically have had a focus on the nation state or the role of the local in the national – often with far less resources to spent on exhibitions and engaging visitors. Here already certain differences in visitor expectations and possibilities and scope of museum's heritage interpretation become clear.

Furthermore, the empirical study showed that, although there is a clear difference in travel motivations between tourists visiting urban centers and more rural or coastal regions, it might not be because museums as heritage sites are less relevant in a non-urban context. Although the numbers from VisitDenmark presented above have already indicated this, the present study has pointed to some of the reasons why this might be. First, historically an idea has developed within academic literature, that coastal holidays were different from the educative purpose of much early form of travel. However, historically the culture of coastal tourism has drawn on both nature and culture. For tourists interested in history and heritage therefore, there seems to be what could be called a "syllabus" of heritage belonging to the coast. Although the content seemed to differ somewhat between Danish and German visitors. Maritime culture, building culture and, as something newer, the remains of the Atlantic Wall are elements contained in this syllabus.

But, for other visitors, without this interest in history and heritage, a museum visit might not seem relevant on a coastal holiday. Only in this aspect entertainment becomes the focus of the experience. Here the educative element must be down played as a museum visit to some might be perceived as in direct opposition to the purpose of the holiday, which is to relax.

ACKNOWLEDGMENT

The project *Heritage interpretation and coastal tourism – a mismatched couple?* was funded by Grants for Development of Museums by "The Danish Agency for Culture and Palaces" (380,000 Danish kroner.). The authors would also like to thank organizational partners in the project. They were: Museum Sønderjylland, Ringkøbing Skjern Museum, Varde Museum, and Centre for Tourism, Innovation and Culture (TIC), University of Southern Denmark.

REFERENCES

Andersen, L. F. (2015). The spatial and experiential dimensions of coastal zone tourism in Denmark. In A. Lorentzen, K. T. Larsen, & L. Schrøder (Eds.), *Spatial Dynamics in the Experience Economy* (pp. 174–190). Abingdon: Routledge.

Andersson Cederholm, E. (2004). The Use of Photo-elicitation in Tourism Research: Framing the Backpacker Experience. *Scandinavian Journal of Hospitality and Tourism*, *4*(3), 225–241. doi:10.1080/15022250410003870

Aplin, G. (2007). World Heritage Cultural Landscapes. *International Journal of Heritage Studies*, *13*(6), 427–446. doi:10.1080/13527250701570515

Ashworth, G. J. (2000). Heritage, Tourism and Places: A Review. *Tourism Recreation Research*, *25*(1), 19–28. doi:10.1080/02508281.2000.11014897

Ashworth, G. J. (2003). Heritage, identity and places: For tourists and host communities. In S. Singh, D. J. Timothy, & R. K. Dowling (Eds.), *Tourism in Destination Communities* (pp. 79–97). Wallingford: CABI. doi:10.1079/9780851996110.0079

Bagnall, G. (2003). Performance and Performativity at Heritage Sites. *Museum & Society*, *1*(2), 87–103. doi:10.29311/mas.v1i2.17

Bonn, M. A., Joseph-Mathews, S. M., Dai, M., Hayes, S., & Cave, J. (2007). Heritage/Cultural Attraction Atmospherics: Creating the Right Environment for the Heritage/Cultural Visitor. *Journal of Travel Research*, *45*(3), 345–354. doi:10.1177/0047287506295947

Borg, J., Costa, P., & Gotti, G. (1996). Tourism in European heritage cities. *Annals of Tourism Research*, *23*(2), 306–321. doi:10.1016/0160-7383(95)00065-8

Boyd, S. (2002). Cultural and Heritage Tourism in Canada: Opportunities, Principles and Challenges. *Tourism and Hospitality Research*, *3*(February), 211–233. doi:10.1177/146735840200300303

Chen, I. S. (1998). Travel Motivation of Heritage Tourists. *Tourism Analysis*, *2*, 213–215.

Dahlkild, N. (1991). *Fra sommervilla til feriehytte: Om århundredskiftets og mellemkrigstidens fritidsbebyggelser. Byplanhistoriske Noter (23)*. København: Dansk Byplanlaboratorium.

Daugstad, K. (2008). Negotiating Landscape in Rural Tourism. *Annals of Tourism Research*, *35*(2), 402–426. doi:10.1016/j.annals.2007.10.001

Davis, P. (2005). Places, "Cultural Touchstones" and the Ecomuseum. In G. Corsane (Ed.), *Heritage, Museums and Galleries*. Abingdon: Routledge. doi:10.4324/9780203326350_chapter_28

Denzin, N. K., & Lincoln, Y. S. (2011). *The SAGE Handbook of Qualitative Research*. SAGE Publications Inc.

Du Cros, H., & McKercher, B. (2015). *Cultural Tourism* (2nd ed.). Routledge.

Edson, G. (2004). Heritage: Pride or passion, product or service? *International Journal of Heritage Studies*, *10*(4), 333–348. doi:10.1080/1352725042000257366

Graham, B., Ashworth, G. J., & Tunbridge, J. E. (2000). *A Geography of Heritage: Power, Culture and Economy*. London: Arnold.

Hall, M. C., & Page, S. J. (2006). Coastal and Marine Recreation and Tourism. In M. C. Hall & S. J. Page (Eds.), *The Geography of Tourism and Recreation: Environment, place and space* (3rd ed., pp. 291–314). Abingdon: Routledge. doi:10.4324/9780203420249

Hansen, L. A. (2014). *"All is data" – the ontological status of empirical material in tourism. In Tourism Methodologies - New Perspectives, Practices and Procedures*. CBS Press.

Hansen, L. A., & Jensen, M. B. (2014). To be demolished or protected – bunkers from concrete blocks to cultural heritage. In Bunkers – Atlantvoldens perspektiver i Danmark. Odense.

Hird, J., & Kvistgaard, P. (2010). *Oplevelsesrum: Turisme, kulturarv og oplevelser - et krydsfelt*. Århus, Denmark: Forfatterne og Academica.

Icomos. (1999). https://www.icomos.org/charters/tourism_e.pdf

Jamal, T., & Kim, H. (2005). Bridging the interdisciplinary divide: Towards an integrated framework for heritage tourism research. *Tourist Studies*, *5*(1), 55–83. doi:10.1177/1468797605062715

Jenkins, O. H. (1999). Understanding and Measuring Tourist Destination Images. *International Journal of Tourism Research*, *1*(1), 1–15. doi:10.1002/(SICI)1522-1970(199901/02)1:1<1::AID-JTR143>3.0.CO;2-L

Jennings, G. (2010). *Tourism Research*. Milton, Queensland, Australia: John Wiley & Sons Australia Ltd.

Kirshenblatt-GimbletT, B. (2004). Intangible heritage as metacultural production. *Museum International*, *56*(1/2), 52–65. doi:10.1111/j.1350-0775.2004.00458.x

Knudsen, D. C. (2012). Insiders and Outsiders in Thy. In A. K. Soper, C. E. Greer, & M. M. Metro-Roland (Eds.), Landscape, Tourism, and Meaning (p. 109-119). Ashgate.

Knudsen, D. C., & Greer, C. E. (2008). Heritage Tourism, Heritage Landscapes and Wilderness Preservation: The Case of National Park Thy. *Journal of Heritage Tourism*, *3*(1), 18–35. doi:10.1080/1743873X.2008.9701248

Kruse, R. J. II. (2005). The Beatles as place makers: Narrated landscapes in Liverpool, England. *Journal of Cultural Geography*, *22*(2), 87–114. doi:10.1080/08873630509478240

Kulturstyrelsen; Udvikling Fyn; VisitAalborg; VisitDenmark; VisitAarhus; Wonderful Copenhagen. (2014). slks.dk/fileadmin/user_upload/Projektbeskrivelse_godkendt_17_december_2014.pdf

Kvale, S. (2007). *Doing Interviews*. London, UK: SAGE Publications Ltd. doi:10.4135/9781849208963

Kvistgaard & Hird. (2016). *kvistgaardoghird.dk*. Accessed 5. 6. 2016 at http://kvistgaardoghird.dk/#home-section-forsking

Lewis, G. (1992). Musseums and their precursors: A Brief Wold Survey. Manual of Curaorship, 2, 1-26.

Lowenthal, D. (1972). *Geography, Experience, and Imagination. In Tourism Business Frontiers: Consumers, Products and Industry* (pp. 211–219). Butterworth-Heinemann.

Meining, D. W. (1979). *Symbolic landscapes. I D. W. Meinig, The Interpretation of Ordinary Landscapes* (pp. 164–192). Oxford: Oxford University Press.

Museer, S. (2014). *sydvestjyskemuseer.dk*. Accessed 10. 7. 2016 at https://www.sydvestjyskemuseer.dk/da/besoeg-museerne/museet-ribes-vikinger/

Museer, S. (2015). Projectdescription - pulje til udvikling af museumsområdet og museernes opgavevaretagelse. Kulturarvsformidling og kystturisme - et umage par? Esbjerg, Denmark.

Museet for Varde By og omegn. (2016). http://sargaanja.wix.com/vamhjemmeside

Olwig, K. F. (2004). Ecotourism and authenticity [Comment]. *Current Anthropology*, *45*(4), 491–492.

Palmer, C. (2002). Christianity, Englishness and the southern English countryside: A study of the work of H.J.Massingham. *Social & Cultural Geography*, *3*(1), 25–38. doi:10.1080/14649360120114125

Pearce, D. G., & Kirk, D. (1986). Carrying capacities for coastal tourism. *Industry and Environment*, *9*(1), 3–6.

Poria, Y. (2010). *The Story behind the Picture: Preferences for the Visual Display at Heritage Sites. In Culture, Heritage and Representation*. Surrey, UK: Ashgate Publishing Limited.

Poria, Y., Butler, R., & Airey, D. (2003). The Core of Heritage Tourism. *Annals of Tourism Research*, *30*(1), 238–254. doi:10.1016/S0160-7383(02)00064-6

Rakic, T., & Chambers, D. (2012). Introducing visual methods to tourism studies. In T. Rakic & D. Chambers (Eds.), *An introduction to visual research methods in tourism* (pp. 4–14). Abingdon, UK: Routledge.

Randsborg, K. (2000). National History, Non-national Archaeology: The Case of Denmark. Oxford Journal of Archaeology, 19(2), 211–22.

Richards, G. (2000). Tourism and the World of Culture and Heritage. *Tourism Recreation Research*, *25*(1), 9–17. doi:10.1080/02508281.2000.11014896

Richards, G. (2001). *Cultural Attractions and European Tourism*. Wallingford: CAB International. doi:10.1079/9780851994406.0000

Richards, G. (2001). *The Development of Cultural Tourism in Europe. I G. Richards, Cultural Attractions and European Tourism*. Wallingford: CABI Publishing. doi:10.1079/9780851994406.0000

Ringkøbing-SKJERN Museum. (2016). *levendehistorie.dk*. Accessed 10. 7. 2016 at http://levendehistorie.dk/Forside-11

Scarles, C. (2012). Eliciting embodied knowledge and response: Respondent-led photography and visual autoethnography. In T. Rakic & D. Chambers (Eds.), *An introduction to visual research methods in tourism* (pp. 70–91). Abingdon, UK: Routledge.

Schouten, F. F. (1995). *Heritage as historical reality. In Heritage, Tourism and Society* (pp. 21–31). London: Mansell.

Schouten, F. F. (2007). Cultural Tourism: Between Authenticity and Globalization. In G. Richards (Ed.), *Cultural Tourism: Global and Local Perspectives*. Binghamton, NY: Haworth Hospitality Press.

Selby, M. (2010). People-Place-Past: The Visitor Experience of Cultural Heritage. In E. Waterton & S. Watson (Eds.), *Culture, Heritage and Representation*. Surrey, UK: Ashgate Publishing Limited.

Slots- og Kulturstyrelsen. (2016). *slks.dk*. Accessed 30. 5. 2016 at https://slks.dk/presse-nyt/pressemeddelelser/2016/kulturturister-vil-ogsaa-have-strand-shopping-og-storbyliv/

Smith, M. (2007). Space, Place, and Placelessness in the Culturally Regenerated City. In G. Richards (Ed.), *Cultural Tourism: Global and Local Perspectives*. Binghamton, NY: Haworth Hospitality Press.

Smith, M. K. (2003). *Issues in Cultural Tourism Studies*. London: Routledge. doi:10.4324/9780203402825

Storm, E. (2003). Regionalism in History. *European History Quarterly*, *33*(2), 251–265. doi:10.1177/02656914030332005

Strand, H. (2016). *hvidbjerg.dk*. Accessed 10. 7. 2016 at http://www.hvidbjerg.dk

Timothy, D. J., & Boyd, S. W. (2006). Heritage Tourism in the 21st Century: Valued Traditions and New Perspectives. *Journal of Heritage Tourism*, *1*(1), 1–14. doi:10.1080/17438730608668462

Tracy, S. J. (2013). *Qualitative research methods: collecting evidence, crafting analysis, communicating impact*. Chichester, UK: Wiley-Blackwell.

Tress, G. (2002). Development of Second-Home Tourism in Denmark. *Scandinavian Journal of Hospitality and Tourism*, *2*(2), 109–122. doi:10.1080/15022250216289

Tuan, Y. F. (1972). *Topophilia: Personal Encounters with the Landscape. In Man, Space, and Environment*. Oxford: Oxford University Press.

Tuan, Y. F. (1974a). Space and Place: Humanistic Perspective. *Progress in Geography*, *6*, 233–246.

Tuan, Y. F. (1974b). *Topophilia: A Study of Environmental Perception, Attitudes, and Values*. Englewood Cliffs, NJ: Prentice-Hall, Inc.

UNESCO. (1972). *Convention Concerning the Protection of the World Cultural and Natural Heritage*. Paris: UNESCO.

Urry, J. (1990). *The tourist gaze*. London: Sage.

Urry, J. (2002). *The Tourist Gaze: The New Edition*. London: Sage Publications.

Victoria's Palace. (2016). *victoriaspalace.dk*. Accessed 10. 7. 2016 at http://www.victoriaspalace.dk/shop/frontpage.html

VisitDenmark, Videncenter for Kystturisme, & Region Syddanmark. (2014). *Ferie i Kystdanmark - warum nicht?* TNS Gallup.

VisitDenmark. (2016a). *Kulturturisme i Danmark: Kyst- og naturturister & Storbyturister*. København: VisitDenmark.

VisitDenmark. (2016b). *International markedsføring af Danmark som rejsemål - Notat med fokus på kulturoplevelser. VisitDenmark*. København: VisitDenmark.

VisitDenmark. (2016c). https://www.visitdenmark.dk/sites/default/files/vdk_images/PDF-and-other-files/Analyser/2016/status_paa_turisternes_overnatninger_i_danmark-2015.pdf

Yale, P. (1991). *From Tourist Attractions to Heritage Tourism*. Huntingdon: Elm.

KEY TERMS AND DEFINITIONS

Coastal Tourism: Tourist activities that geographically take place within a coastal zone.

Education: The activity of learning or adding to personal knowledge and skills.

Heritage: What is being perceived as important and valuable historical knowledge by different communities.

Heritage Tourism: tourism where interest in heritage and heritage sites is a travel motive.

Interpretation: The activity of disseminating knowledge about history and heritage to the public by museum professionals.

Landscape: The visible features of a land whether untouched by man or created by and in interaction with man.

Museum: A public or private institution dedicated to a goal of collecting historical objects, knowledge creation and knowledge dissemination. It includes both public and privately funded activities.

Chapter 13
"Consumption" of Past to Define Ethnic Identity in Real Time and Space:
The Case of Turkish Georgians in Turkey and Germany

Nino Okrostsvaridze
Ilia State University, Georgia

Elisabed Bzhalava
Ivane-Javakhishvili State University, Georgia

ABSTRACT

This research examines the strength of the Turkish Georgians ethnic identity in Turkey and Germany, issues of socialization with German society, and perception of "home" and "consumption" of the past to define ethnic identity. Consumption is not only a way of behaving, but it is also part of a way of life, which is defined by ethnic and religious identity, which itself defines consumer behaviour. A perception of self-identification, linkage with forefathers, and a search for a long-lost past are particularly necessary in foreign countries, and different reminders regarding the past and origin are considered to be the best means. Consumption of "past" and (re)construction of memories form a tight-knit ethnic unit in a foreign country, and institutionalization of own culture is so strong that many of the ethnic participants feel as if they were living in their own country. Ethnic "retailers" (communities, membership groups) provide the "emotional glue" that sticks ethnic participants together giving them a sense of identity.

DOI: 10.4018/978-1-7998-3115-0.ch013

Copyright © 2020, IGI Global. Copying or distributing in print or electronic forms without written permission of IGI Global is prohibited.

INTRODUCTION

And yet, if everything is moving where is here? Doreen Massey

The contemporary world has been facing legal and illegal migrancy due to social, economic, political, and religious problems, or a combination of these. The number of migrants is growing every day. Mostly they are moving from the East to the West or to Europe. Movement includes not only the physical activity, but also the displacement of culture, traditions, and customs from one ethnical space to another. During migration, two different cultures – Eastern and Western – cross each other, as people take with them a part of the their culture. On the new soil they encounter unfamiliar culture and a new reality where the past and the present clash. This could be the reason for the migrants' dual existence, dissatisfaction with the new reality and reluctance to accept it, which prompts them to lock themselves into traditions in order to protect their identity.

On the other hand, this new reality may win migrants over and create "new" people, "free from past". However, before this happens, they may be overwhelmed with the following questions: Who am I? What is home? Is it the place where I was born? Or where I grew up? Where do I locate my community? Is home a geographical space, a historical space, or an emotional and sensory space? And when does it become my fortress, a strategic space I could call home? These questions are essential and meaningful in their lives.

Migration consists of three important and general issues: maintenance sense of identity, adaptation/(re)socialization and assimilation. Our work addresses the migration of Turkish Georgians from Georgia to Turkey (Village Hayriye) and then to Germany (Gummersbach /Bergneustadt) in the 1960s. Three different cultural elements – Georgian, Turkish and German – influence their mode of life and affect their everyday perceptions of reality. The authors aim to study- Turkish Georgians as "consumers" of past and to answer the following questions: why and how they "consume" past in real time and space. However, before their present lifestyle is discussed, the past events must be briefly remembered. As Reshmi Dutt-Ballerstadt writes, "in order to intuitively and physically understand the trajectory of migrancy, the old route must be travelled" (Ballerstadt, 2010, p. xi)

BACKGROUND

Throughout career and especially since 2009 it has been the privilege and challenge to work toward contributing to study Turkish Georgians` identity and their ethnic, cultural memory. Field sites were Inegol (Turkey) and Bergneustadt/Gummersbach (Germany). The researches were conducted by experienced field workers, who studied migrants and migration problems in second and third countries.

The work is interdisciplinary and is based on the patterns from "immersion fieldwork", "participant observation" since 2009 in Turkey and 2012 and 2019 in Germany. "Immersion fieldwork" means being there to observe and to learn, to be part of the community, family (which is not easy), to be integrated into kinship system with its network of obligations and reciprocity, to value the idea of "walking a mile in the shoes" (Madden, 2010) of others and attempt to gain insight by being in the same social space as the subject of research and to conduct typically face-to-face, direct research.

The intimacy of interaction and ease of communication would hardly be possible for non-Georgian researchers in Turkey and Germany. Because being Georgian for Turkish Georgians, is much more than just a trust. Issues of obligation, reciprocity, and the formation of friendship, impose serious responsibilities. The research is based on long-term process of "gradual building up of trust". (O`Reilly, 2009, p. 175) During the field works the researchers used: questionnaires, full field notes, jottings, and diaries. It should be noted that, "science of anthropology owns not a little to the art of photography", (Tylor, 1876, p. 184) during the field trips an impressive number of audio, video files, photo and documentary materials were recorded and compiled. Nowadays it is very popular cyber ethnography (external observe) which was very helpful during research process too.

Back to the Past: 1. Muhajirs in Hayriye

Muhajirat was a complex phenomenon. During the Russo-Turkish War in 1877-78, on the basis of the Berlin treaty, Achara and other historical provinces of Georgia were attached to the Russian Empire. One part of the Georgian population came under Russian rule; the other part immigrated as "Muhajirs" to Ottoman Turkey. As a result of living in culturally and traditionally different countries (Russia, Ottoman Empire), the lifestyles of the Georgian Muslim communities began to diverge, influencing their mentality and family economic-cultural mode of life. "Muhajirat" was not only a Georgian problem; it concerned the Caucasus too. Georgian Muhajirs, leaving their homelands, were subjected to Turkish political, economic, and cultural influence. They either intentionally or unintentionally absorbed "new traditions", but in spite of the natural process of assimilation, they tried to maintain self-identity, traditions, and customs, which were reflected in different ways. Due to Russian and Ottoman policy, Georgian Muslims had to leave their dwellings to find shelter on new soil. Some of them could not reach their "desired heaven" and died on the way. But those who survived went to the mountain and coastal regions of Turkey. One of these places was the village Hayriye ("Small Moscow", "Machakhela"), established by Imam Haci Mehmed Efendi between 1880 and 1888. About two hundred and fifty Georgian muhajirs left their villages near Artvin by some sources villages of Machakhela: Chukuneti, Chkhutuneti, Kirkiteti, Khinkileti, Kirnati to find a "new hope" in Turkey. According to villagers, their ancestors constructed Hayriye in accordance with their previous residence in Georgia. Georgians call the central part "Ortamahalle" the district of Khinkiladze. There are a school, mosque, shop, tea-house, cooperative society, and administrative building there. In the Eastern part, there are the districts of Cambazoğlu and Kirkitadze. In the Southern part of the village, there is an upper district "Yukari mahalle" (in Turkish) i.e. "Sikaleti". In front of it, in the Western part, there is a district of "Vakielebi" i.e. "karşımahalle". Hayriye derives from the word *"hayir"*, which means *"happiness, welfare, and good"*. But there are several existing versions of the story behind the village name: Georgian liked the place so much that they shouted "Hayırdır inşallah!" (May God give us good). Some attribute this name to the Circassians. Ethnic Georgians call the village "Machakhela", because their forefathers emigrated from Machakhela villages. The village has a nickname "küçük Moskova" (small Moscow) given by the residents of nearby ethnic Georgian villages. The success and welfare of the village earned it this nickname. After migration to Germany in the 1960s to the 1970s, Turkish Georgians gained European experience and used it for the sake of the village. European culture had a great influence on them. Hayriye became a very successful village with a well-established infrastructure. Because they lived by European experience and not by religious dogmas, they became "Communists" to neighboring villagers for forgetting their traditions and customs. As for the nickname "Small Moscow", it became an expression of success and material prosperity.

Back to the Past: 2. Muhajirs in Germany/Bergneustadt

The issue of belonging among Turkish individuals in Germany needs to be considered in the context of social, political, historical, local, national, transnational and global influences, which play a role in the construction of complex individual patchwork identities. Werner Schiffauer

In the 1960s, due to high levels of unemployment in Turkey and the need for inexpensive labour in the expanding economies of Europe, Turkey concluded a bilateral agreement to supply workers to Germany. Approximately one million Turks crossed the border until 1974, hoping to get rich fast. Europe was attractive to them due to its high living standards. The majority of migrants with rural backgrounds and primary school educations could not gain higher positions in Germany. They began working in fields of the metal processing industry, taking positions of low occupational hierarchy. But later, the branches in which they were employed diversified to include the service sector, food production and technology. The oil crisis in 1973 stopped the following recruitment of foreign labour (Anwerbestopp für Ausländer) and accelerated the decision-making process for emigrants. It resulted in growing numbers of arriving family members in Germany, exceeding the number of returnees at the end of the 1970s. The growing numbers of "foreign elements" created difficulties for Germany. Thus the stop of foreign labor recruitment became a barrier for incoming laborers, but a boon for those already living in Germany. However, in the 1980s, the Federal Republic of Germany approved a sanction to prevent family reunification by limiting the arrival of family members and decreasing the maximum age of arrival for immigrants' children to sixteen years. In 1983, the Kohl Government passed the so called "Voluntary Repatriation Encouragement Act which offered migrants financial incentives (Starthilfe) to return to the homeland. The act offered a grant of 10.500 Mark per adult and 1.500 Mark per child, which resulted in return of 100.388 Turkish migrants in 1983" (Bozkurt, 2009, p. 33) However for the majority of them this decision proved to be disadvantageous, causing financial retrogression in Turkey due to ill-judged investments and unemployment problems. This greatly influenced their relatives in Germany and slowed down the process of returning to their homeland. Moreover, the social-political tension in Turkey, especially after the military coup and Kurdish movement in the 1980s motivated most Turks to reconsider their return. The migration continued in the 1980s "with arriving children, spouses, asylum seekers, students, as well as birth to Turkish families in Germany and reached a population of 2.6 million residents in 2005 that is expected to exceed three millions in 2030" (Bozkurt, 2009, p. 33) Such a wave of migration was not expected by the receiving country; the Turks were considered temporary guest workers (Gastarbeiter) who would return to their homeland after a few years. But the German Republic "made a mistake" in planning to get off cheap. Turks were offered lower positions with modest salaries, which would never be convenient for an ordinary German. At the outset, such "unpretentious" laborers seemed very attractive to the government; they could not foresee that in years to come, guest workers would not return to Turkey but rather their numbers would grow, furthered by the birth rate and advantage of living in Europe.

A small but steady stream of Hayriye villagers immigrated to Germany in the 1960s for better employment and living opportunities. Due to the high level of unemployment in Hayriye, Ahmed-Ozkan Melashvili[1], an architect, and Faik Ertan a teacher, interpreted the Turkish Government's announcement[2] as a wonderful opportunity for Hayriye. They prepared the "Village Development Cooperative" (VDC) charter and filled out the necessary government forms. Once Turkey approved their application, the Hayriye men went via the VDC to West Germany, where most got jobs in manufacturing industries. But unfortunately, this migration emptied the village. Since the 1960s, Turkish Georgians (from Hayriye village) have been living in Gummersbach (Bergneustadt, Derschlag, Apfelbaum, Börnchen). Turkish Georgians also reside in Heidelberg, Halle, Eppelhaim, etc.

Bergneustadt, a part of the Berg region, is located 50 kilometers east of Cologne, in North Rhine-Westphalia (Germany). This small town resembles Hayriye with its beautiful nature, forest and water. When Georgian Muhajirs went to Turkey, they chose the land to mirror their homeland (with rich natural resources). About five hundred to six hundred villagers from Hayriye reside in Bergneustadt. The population has continued to grow since the 1960s. In 1996, they had the idea to create an organization "Hayriye köy yardımlaşma derneği" (village charity/development society). Before the society was established, the villagers could hardly collect any money for Hayriye infrastructure. At that time only two hundred and fifty to three hundred villagers lived in Bergneustadt. The majority of them were working in the car industry (in Turkey they were workers with rural backgrounds, cutting and cultivating the wood. This activity could not be useful in Germany). In 2005, the villagers from Hayriye established the "Kafkas Club"[3] (Caucasian Club) society in Bergneustadt. The aim of this organization was to gather ethnic Georgians and Caucasians (Circassians, Abkhazians) residing in Bergneustadt. Every year ethnic Georgians hold Hayriye days, when they gather, make Georgian foods, and play accordion. They think that such gatherings are very important for being together, because a foreign place and setting will make them foreigners to one another in the course of a decade.

"Campsite" or "Home"?

Homelessness is coming to be the destiny of the world

Martin Heidegger

The movement and migration from one place to another and the drastic change of dwelling involve a complex "transformation and transmutation of self, psyche, language and the experience of citizenship" (Ballerstadt, 2010, p. 135) Muslim Georgians in Inegol (Turkey) could maintain their identity with the help of an illusionary homeland and dwelling. However, since the 1960s, the second movement of Turkish Georgians to Germany (as a country of third culture) has changed their identity, moreover dualized their existence. A new physical reality (European reality), unlike Eastern-Caucasian, invaded them and has had a great influence on the second and third generations. Permanent migration made them nomads and the sense of a "dwelling as one's fortress" devaluated. The landscape of home became a temporary "campsite" (Carter, 1992) devoid of any roots or promises of permanent stay. Such interpretation of home with the Georgian migrants makes it evident that a meaningful and indispensable dwelling did not exist for them. There are several words in the Turkish language that refer to home, but the most prevalent ones are "ev" and "yurt", which have domestic connotations and refer to a house in which a family resides. The equivalents of homeland are "memleket", "vatan", "yurt", "anavatan", "anayurt", and "ülke". The most frequently used expression is "vatan", which has roots in Arabic and means "the place of residence and home" (Sözlük, 2007) Similar to "vatan", "yurt" is used to refer to the place of birth and dwelling. Other widely used expressions are "memleket" and "ülke", which refer to the place of birth, ancestral home, and the motherland (Atalay, 1999) and (Püsküllüoğlu, 2007). But we should add that "ülke" has strong territorial references and is closer to "vatan", whereas "memleket" has emotional connotation and implies attachment to one's home town (Doğan, 1995) Turkish Georgians, when talking about their forefathers, use the word "memleket", which implies their ethnic belonging to "Gürcistan" (Georgia).

In the German language, home translates as "das Haus", "das Heim", "das zuhause", "die Heimat", and "die Wohnstätte", but most commonly "das Heim" and "die Heimat". Unfortunately, Turkish Georgians (the second and third generations) living in Bergneustadt (Germany) have lost the perception of both "memleket" and "Heimat", leaving these words now to be used only as lexicological definitions. For them, neither Turkey nor Germany is their homeland. Twofold migration has made both home and homeland an illusion. Home is not seen "as a sanctuary and nucleus of identity" (Morley, 2000, p. 51) any more. It has only practical functions: be comfortable, equipped, and just for living. All ethnic Georgians living in Bergneustadt have houses in Hayriye or in Inegol, which were (re)built or repaired with money earned in Germany. Despite the fact that most of them are not going to live in these houses, they spend money for their reconstruction. In this case, a house is not only a dwelling, but also an association with the past. They repair houses in villages that they do not even intend to live in, but do so for the sake of a hope and stimulus to return there someday. This is not a guaranteed return, but something of a pledge to return. The above-mentioned condition was the reason for dual existence, when a person is physically in one nation but psychically in another, as if he/she loses his own roots and lives between two worlds: a lost past and an unacceptable present. He/she becomes a nowhere creature. Parallels can be drawn with the plurality of life-worlds as discussed by Peter L. Berger, Brigitte Berger and Hansfried Kellner in *The Homeless Mind* (Berger, P. Berger, B. and Kellner, H., 1974) Meena Alexander, in her work "The Shock of Arrival: Reflections on Postcolonial Experience", quite aptly says that the questions we ask are "not necessarily new: Where am I? Who am I? And hardest of all, when am I?" (Alexander, 1996, p. 142) A dual existence appears when the ethnic mentality, formed throughout centuries, clashes with "new traditions". Dual existence is estrangement from one's ethnic origin and the new reality. It is difficult to define who you really are and where your home is. You can neither move forward nor backward. But this condition could be the reason for self-determination. Reshmi Dutt-Ballerstadt, in her work "The Postcolonial Citizen the Intellectual Migrant", says, "as a naturalized citizen of the United States, the question of return has a double emphasis now. Every time I go back to India I say "I am going home." Days before leaving India to return to Oregon, I say "my holidays have ended. I am returning home again" (Ballerstadt, 2010, p. 131) Turkish Georgians living in Bergneustadt, face the same difficulties. When they go to Hayriye (mostly in summer) they say "we are going home", but days before leaving Turkey, they say, "we are going back home". The concept of "home" is still empty and vague for them. They cannot determine its location and continue to live at an illusionary "home", situated at the crossroads of two different traditions and cultures. Since the 1960s, three generations of Turkish Georgians have lived in Bergneustadt. The first generation had to learn the new language and culture, as well as cope with the torture of being separated from their homeland. They often encountered resentment and hostility from the host population, as unwelcome guests in a "new land". The Germans, considered to be lovers of national culture, expressed resentment, irritation, dissatisfaction, and anti-Turkish sentiment resulting from the migrants' long term stay, citizenship, birth rate, and the growth in number of restaurants and mosques. Here should be added that according to Turkish Georgians, there was neither religious nor ethnic conflict in Bergneustadt. But some women mentioned that they encountered religious and ethnic discrimination. (Some of them were denied permission to work because of wearing shawl.) The Germans gave the following nicknames to their unwelcome guests, and later the citizens: "Kanake" (the same as in English "Nigger", often used in songs), "Kanaken camp", "sons of Gastarbeita", "Kanaks with brain", "Asiatic warriors", "Islamic force", etc. These terms express the attitudes towards Turks, which gradually led to estrangement. The opposite concept of "Heimat" is "Fremd", "Ausländisch", and "Entfremdung". "Heimat" is associated with security and belonging whereas "Fremd" evokes a feeling of alienation and isolation (Morley, D. and Robins, K., 1995) and is synonymous with hardship and a loss of a sense of belonging.

When a member of one ethnic group settles down on a new land and becomes its citizen, he/she is engaged in making this country his rightful homeland. Self-affirmation is a part of this process. When German Americans in the United States tried to make a "new land" their rightful homeland, the motto was: "wir sind keine Fremden in diesem Lande" (we are not strangers in this country) (Meyer, 1890, 54. Am 6. Oktober) The same motto can be used for Turks residing in Germany. Besides, they are German citizens protected by a constitution, but the question is whether they consider themselves to be a part of this country or not. As mentioned above, the Turks are still "unwanted" citizens who exceeded the limit of their stay long before. Feeling isolation and separation, they experience alienation. We raise the question of when exactly the feeling of isolation and alienation appears. Eva Hoffman, a Polish emigrant to Canada and the author of several books, thinks that a movement from one country to another is not solely a geographical movement, but also a cultural one characterized by confrontations with new values. "I think every immigrant becomes a kind of amateur anthropologist, you do notice things about culture or the world that you come into, that people who grew up in it, who are very embedded in it, simply do not notice. I think we all know it from going to a foreign place. At first you notice the surface things, the surface differences. And gradually you start noticing the deeper differences. And gradually you start with understanding the inner life of the culture, the life of those both large and very intimate values" (Stroinska, M. and Cecchetto, V., 2003, p. 104). These very cultural and religious differences and values became the main reason for alienation. Despite the fact that the second or third generation of Turks was born in Germany and go to schools with Germans, their lives are different from the lives of their German peers. They are perceived as strangers, because they do not fit into the (fictive) ideal type of the standard German in terms of social and physiological characteristics (Mecheril, P. Teo, T (Hrsg)., 1997) all non-ethnic Germans are perceived as foreigners. This difference is shown even in schools. According to Turkish Georgians, their children are always considered second class people, however well they play football. The stress of otherness as a social stigma made many of them criminals, which can be considered a manifestation of self-protection, an instinct of self-preservation. Many Turkish Georgians in Bergneustadt were drug users and sellers, but the "Kafkas Club" community saved their lives. The change in immigrants' status from ordinary countrymen to "Ausländers" deepened the perception of emptiness and alienation. They became second-class people who were not able to live in well-off districts. Despite the fact that they gained capital, they could not increase their social status. The Turks and Turkish Georgians distance themselves from Germans due to the differences in culture, traditions and religion. While Germans portray immigrants as backwards, the Muslim minority associates the host culture with corruption and moral degradation. The Muslim family mode of life is based on religious dogmas; in this case, European and Eastern values and cultures clash. Islam, like Christianity, forbids sexual freedom that characterizes European and Western society. So in this "corrupted environment", Islamic families try to maintain religious traditions and protect their children against outside influence. But the children, who find themselves in a difficult situation, sometimes protest. An adult who has German friends wants to be like them, even in having a sexual partner. That is why parents who are "old fashioned" and socialized in a different socio-cultural context do everything not to "lose" their children. The paradox is that alienation has positive effects. This stigma made Turks more religious, as Islam became a shelter. Some of them began wearing shawls. Unlike parents, they understood the meaning and importance of it. So "traditional Islam" was replaced with "real Islam". Moving to a new country is a difficult experience, and religion may help immigrants to cope with acculturative stressors and the anxiety of separation from the home country. Religion is important for "Muslim Meskhetian[4] families too but many reported that after moving to America their religious ties became even stronger….they often learn to read the Quran and understand its contents. As a result of increased religiosity, Muslim Meskhetian women who formally did not wear head-coverings when they lived in Krasnodar, now wear a headscarf, often engaging in namaz (prayer) five times a day. (Pirtskalava, 2019, p. 51)

Estrangement and isolation increased the importance of the family and ascribed new meaning and function to it, releasing them from emptiness. They united against an "enemy" and focused on main values, which set them apart from others. Not only family members, but also villagers were unified by the "stress on otherness". It is important for them to have people around who are from the same country or village (ethnic Georgians), and who share the same traditions and culture. They meet together at home or within their community, where there are familiar smells and tastes of a domestic atmosphere. They talk about politics and past, watch Turkish channels (sometimes Georgian channels), listen to Turkish music, play Gandagana and Kolsama on the accordion, and tell stories and anecdotes about Hoca Nasred in with a cup of tea and "narghile". This process of collective imagination is a kind of illusion that satisfies the need of "home". Individual or collective reconstruction of the past is based on ethnic identification and memories, which are stored in their minds and continue to affect their everyday perceptions and interpretations of reality. They are like archaeologists, trying to move further back into the past to form the whole image by way of mere fragments of memories and a "ritual of remembering". It is "from the past that we are able to perceive, create and give life to our ritual. It is from this that we derive strength, that we can recognize our existence as human beings" (Rivera, 1979, p. 21). These processes of collective imagination and home-making give them the strength to survive in an insensitive world. The state of foreignness and the stress on otherness are painful not only in Germany but in Turkey too. The Turks in Germany have a negative attitude toward the researchers from Turkey and refused to be interviewed because researchers use the term "Türkiyeli" (the one from Turkey) but Turks who live in Germany are called in Turkey "Almanyalı" (one from Germany), "Almancı"(Germanized), "diluted Turks" or "Deutschländer" with a mostly negative connotations. Alienation and distance between "Germanized Turks" and Turks living in Turkey are based on financial and mental disparity.

(Re) Construction of Memory and "Consumption" of Past to Define Identity

Greatest number of memories comes back to us when our parents, our friends, or other persons recall them to us.

M. Halbwachs

The idea of consumption itself has to be set back into the social process, not merely looked upon as a result or objective of work

The World of Goods

Multi-disciplinary studies of consumption have proliferated in the last two decades. There is widespread agreement about the importance of consumption in the contemporary world. Some argue that it is a principal driving force behind social and economic development, others that it is the core preoccupation of populations across much of the world. We have seen an exponentially grown interest in consumption and consumerism not only in social sciences, but also in arts and humanities and popular discourse alike. In this process the focus of the topic has dispersed, and contemporary theories of consumer culture and consumer society appear more or less fragmented. In the 1990's, consumer practices were most often seen as matters of style, identity and culture. Recently, however, a growing number of writings have started to analyse consumption as economically rooted, politically divisive, socially cohesive or mundane and routine matter.

Consumption is the meaningful use people make of the objects that are associated with them. The use can be mental or material; the objects can be things, food, ideas or relationships, culture-specific product, even traditions, culture and language. The first and important step in consumption is considered to be appropriation, establishing a mental association with the objects to be consumed. Once appropriated, people can use the objects to define their place, identity, status in different social units. For example, the clothes one wears can be important for defining one's gender, social rank, ethnic identity. Consumption is not only a way of behaving, it is part of a way of life, which is defined by ethnic and religious identity, which itself defines consumer`s behavior. It is well-known that ethnic identity not only significantly influences consumption behavior but also has a considerable impact on the socialization of individuals.

The important question is how Turkish Georgians in Turkey and Germany manage to survive as group and why these kinds of people still strive to maintain their sense of identity or retain their cultural memory. We place the concept of **identity and culture** as the most complex and powerful influence on consumer (Turkish Georgians) behavior at the heart of the analysis. It should be highlighted that "Consumption" of past and (re)construction of memory became some kind of driving force for Turkish Georgians to survive in culturally/traditionally different countries (Turkey and Germany).

Identity is modern conceptual construct, used in social and behavioral sciences to refer to people`s sense of themselves and distinct individuals in the context of community. Identity refers to people`s socially determined sense of who they are –like a social statement of who one is. (Woodward, 2007) It also can be viewed as a process of self-identification whereby individuals define themselves and others into specific groups using different labels. (Barth, 1969), (Cuellar, I. Nyberg, B. and Maldonado, M, 1997), (Rossiter, J. R. and Chan, A. M., 1998), (Tajfel, 1981)

In the 1880s, when Turkish Georgians immigrated to Turkey, they initially tried to **choose lands that reminded them of Georgia**, creating the association and illusion of their homeland. Some villages in Turkey were named after Georgian villages they emigrated from. After settlement, they began to **build their dwellings** and constructed the villages in accordance with their previous residence in Georgia.

Dwelling is very important in person`s life. Being among the most salient expressions of traditional world-view and culture, a dwelling, first of all, can be seen as a pure and sacred material phenomenon and secondly, as a temple created by one's ancestors, as a "material complex of practical value, and as an ideal object of symbolic value. We can see its economic and social aspects and analyze its import in social life … [and in] formation of a social and economic model…" (Buxrashvili, 2005, p. 111) It is a capital source of information, also creating the mood of inner space, which helps a person to form a sense of self-identity. It is focal point of people`s lives-both physically and emotionally, "it embodies elements of being both highly personal and strongly social, such that it encompasses private and public meanings". (Gaston, 1994 (1958), p. 155) Dwelling is a place of memory and dreams "the place where things and relations, materials and bodies, fantasy and facts can be dominated and domesticated, governed and articulated" (Chamber, 2001, p. 161). It is our corner of the world, our first universe, a real cosmos in every sense of the word. It comes to signify not only a personal space of belonging and sheltering that is protected against others, but expresses also a collective imaginary placement that divides us from the other, who have their own mentality maps, boundaries, social and political references and spatial projection on territories." (Bozkurt, 2009, p. 14) Turkish Georgians established communities and lived together; forming one social organism and determined it to be a solely Georgian space. By building the houses, they drew a line between "we" and "others", "inner" and "Outward", that is, the micro and the macro worlds from the ethnical as well as individual point of view. United two worlds "symbolic and real."

After setting up their dwellings, it was very important for them to **maintain the memory of their origin** and be in touch with the past. An empty house did not provide relevant reminders for the reconstruction of memories stored in their minds and affecting their daily perceptions and interpretations of reality. A building alone cannot fully ensure a connection with one's past and ancestors. A perception of self-identification, linkage with forefathers, and a search for a long lost past are particularly necessary in foreign countries, and **different reminders regarding the past and origin** are considered to be the best means.

Object/reminders are symbols that can tell researcher who people are, who they have been and who they wish to become. Objects can play a very important role in establishing social and personal identities. Visually identifying an object within someone`s possession, can tell us much about a person. The psychologist William James asserts, that the self- "who I am is understood not just to be "me", as in my body and my thoughts, but also what is "mine"….it means that external things, objects become associated with selfhood, "we feel and act about certain things that are ours very much as we feel and act about ourselves". (James, 1988, p. 140) If we ask a question- do material things/reminders/objects exist without us, apart? No, because they are social and at the same time individual, which "reveal" "themselves" (importance and meaning) in perception of identity. Objects are part of a live information system, one of the basic insights of recent conceptualisation of material culture studies, has been the idea that objects have "social lives" or biographies". (Appadurai, 1986) Therefore Turkish Georgians used to bring to their dwellings various things, domestic objects with ethnic elements, associated with their homeland to perceive an ethnic space. For example boxes (with Georgian symbols), cradles for child, agricultural weapons, and family things with Georgian names, for example, "Godori"-(it is a large wicker basket of cylindrical form without handles used for the gathering grapes, fruit, and etc.) Even nowadays these things are kept. During ethnological field works we have found many culture-specific things, brought by first Muhajirs to Turkey, they have lost their practical significance and are no longer used, but with these "sacred ones" Turkish Georgians define ethnic identity, (re)construct past, ethnic memory and in this way are connected with their forefathers. As American retailing analyst named Victor Lebow proclaims, we convert the use of goods into **rituals**, that we seek our **spiritual satisfaction**, our ego satisfaction in consumption... (Lebow, 1955, p. 7) With "these ethnic elements" empty buildings turned into dwelling places and were filled with ethnic "spirit", which made Muhajirs feel comfortable and satisfied. Touching them, one was closely connected to the past and could remember one's origin and separate "I" from "others". In this way, the distinct concepts of "Chveneburi",[5] "hısım",[6] "Gürcü",[7] and "all the others" were formed by Muhajirs. Important part of Turkish Georgians` self-identification could be also considered emotional significance and value that one attaches to membership of a particular group (Tajfel, 1981) In other words; a person's ethnic identity involves one's sense of belonging to a group.

On the second stage, it was important to maintain this ethnic space and to follow rules that were supposed to become dogmatic for the future generation, too. In order to **protect this ethnic space**, it was important to avoid the invasion of "outsiders", i.e. non-Georgians, who could cause the diffusion of other ethnic traditions and customs, putting their ethnical identity in danger and causing degradation.

That is why Turkish Georgians used a "protective shield" – they never sold land to outsiders, in order to avoid assimilation with foreigners and foreign traditions, which was facilitated by Turkish policy.[8]

Turkish Georgians not only protected territory, but also their genetic heritage against contamination. They were strongly endogamic and preferred to marry within their own tribes. It is well-known in science that marriage is not only a social but also a biological event. Muhajirs were aware that in the mixture of blood, accompanied by "characteristically new traditions", the Georgian space would be violated and devalued. Thus, on the basis of the following components – 1. Dwelling as the place where the past and the present cross each other, creating spiritual linkage with ancestors; 2. "Territorial borders", defining "I" and "others", "one of ours", and "the outsider"; 3. Protection of inner space from other ethnic groups by a) not selling the land to outsiders, and b) unmixed marriage – Turkish Georgians maintained their ethnicity and survived themselves and the future generations.

Ethnic identity implies many dimensions including "a sense of common customs, language, religion, values, morality, and etiquette". (Webster, Effects of Ethnic Identification on Marital Rols in the Purchase Decision Process, 1994, p. 321) **Culture-specific** foods (products) could be added to Webster`s "list". In recent years, culture has become even more important and has been recognized as a vital factor that has an impact on all facets of consumer behavior (Quester, P.G. and Wendt-Eccles, J.V., 2002) It is defined as "learned and shared symbols, values, attitudes, knowledge and behavior" (Gronhaug, K. Gilly, M. and Penazola, L., 1993, p. 279) Members of a particular culture acquire common behavior patterns that shape and influence them in many aspects of their lives (Wallendorf, M. and Reilly, M. D., 1983) Relationship between ethnic identity and ethnic (culture-specific) food consumption is particularly important, because ethnic foods reflect the shared values, attitudes, beliefs, and behaviors of a certain culture and symbolize the cultural traditions, heritage, and norms of the native country (Carrus, G. A. and Caddeo, P., 2008). Accordingly, food can become a powerful way of showing a relationship to and identification with a particular ethnic group (Carrus, G. A. and Caddeo, P., 2008). The preparation of Georgian foods and consumption of various Georgian sorts of fruits, still known with Georgian names (for example, "Barakai Mskhali", "katsistavai Msxkhali", "Diderai Mskhali", "Seserai Mskhali", "Boshorvai Mskhali", "Jave Vashli", "Shavi Fkhali", "Kindzi", "Boravo", "Tsotsolai", "Jolo", "Adesa", "Metrovela", "Fkhal Lobia", "Barbunie Lobio", "Chadi", Fkhal Lobia", "Charxlis Shechamandi", "Korkoti", Khmeli Lobiao", "Akhali Lobio", "Doshorva", "Kalajo", "Jave Lobio", Nigoziani", Kerchkhi Lobiai", "Khavitsa", "Tkemali", "Chrekhela", "Chanchurai Fafa", and etc) strengthen the collective identity of Turkish Georgians in Turkey and Germany by connecting them to the homeland ("Memleket" in Turkish).

It is very interesting that consumption of food is cultural behavior pattern and value, manifested in through ethnic identity. Perhaps the most powerful example is offered by the In-Group Bias Theory (Brewer, 1979) which posits that members of a certain group are predisposed to think that their own group as well as its products is superior to other groups and their products. (In this process consumer ethnocentrism (CET) plays an important role). According to Cleveland and colleagues "[t]he food habits of minorities tend to be highly resistant to change "because they are practical or symbolically meaningful behaviors for a given culture." (Cleveland, M. Laroche, M. Pons, F. and Kastoun, R., 2009, pp. 198-199) By contrast, dress and entertainment are fundamentally different in the sense that they are more publicly displayed and may, therefore, require social approval.

Stayman and Deshpande (Stayman, D. and Deshpande, R., 1989) introduced the construct of "felt ethnicity," namely the idea that ethnicity is not only subjectively determined but also that it changes from time to time in response to situational factors such as whether an individual is in the presence of in-group or out-group members. In their seminal study, Stayman and Deshpande discovered that Asian,

Hispanic, and Anglo American subjects chose not to consume ethnically relevant food when in an ethnically diverse social setting such as a business lunch. According to Stayman and Deshpande, "social science research supports the view that situations likely influence the effects of ethnicity on behavior and that the relevant construct to focus on is not self-designated ethnicity as an individual trait but felt ethnicity as a situationally determined state" (Stayman, D. and Deshpande, R., 1989, p. 362) Under this view, "one's cultural identity is not stable but dynamic." (Zmud, J. and Arce, C., 1992, p. 449) For example, Turkish Georgians are more likely to consume Georgian foods than German food when they are together or celebrating village day in Germany "in-group", but when they are with Turks or Germans they prefer Turkish (in Turkey) and German (in Germany) food. They experience "mixed emotions or ambivalence" (Otnes, C. lowery, T. and Shrum, M., 1997) at a given time, or "multiple and co-existing identities" (see for example, (Stayman, D. and Deshpande, R., 1989) As Oswald argued "in consumer culture, ethnic identity can be bought, sold and worn like a loose garment" (Oswald, 1999, p. 304)

Ethnic identity could be viewed as a **complex psychological process** that involves perceptions, cognition, affect and knowledge structures about how a person thinks and feels about himself/herself and others in the society (Cuellar, I. Nyberg, B. and Maldonado, M, 1997), (Tajfel, 1981), (Webster, Attitudes Towards Marketing Practices: The Effects of ethnic Identification., 1991) The brilliant patterns of consumption of "past" and perception of ethnic identity, we have found on the gravestones of Turkish Georgians in Turkey and Germany. The inscriptions with: 1. Georgian surnames (in Georgian language), 2. The place of birth or 3. The place of birth with "Li" suffix (in Turkish language suffix –Li [4] gives the sense of belonging to somewhere) for example, "Batum" or "Batumlu" –(means that a person was from Batumi (region of Georgia) Gravestone inscriptions are important "live" not "dead" like "Being there and here", sources of information, expressed by language.

Psychological theories of motivation can shed light on why people come to desire certain things. One frequently used categorization breaks down human perceived needs into five categories: 1. Physiological needs, such as hunger and thirst. 2. Safety needs, for security and protection. 3. Social needs, for a sense of belonging and love. 4. Esteem needs, for self-esteem, recognition, and status. 5. Self-actualization needs, for self-development and realization. At present in the professional literature on consumption, there is a tendency to suppose that people use goods for two or three restricted purposes: material welfare, psychic welfare, and display. The patterns of **"display", "status" or "recognition"** could be viewed also furniture brands in Inegol with Georgian or semi Georgian names-"Vardi", (roze), "Modi" (come), "Sinatle" (light), "Tetri home" (white home), "Didi Koltuk" (big armchair). Using Georgian names, symbols and etc. is an attempt to satisfy spiritual needs and ego. Psychologists have noted that the degree to which people perceive a need is clearly related to two important factors: our own past experience, and the experience of groups to which we compare ourselves. These create reference groups and membership groups. Membership groups are groups to which the person belongs, such as families, communities, and groups. **Membership groups** are important sources of information and also sources of pressure to conform to group practices and norms. Past, as experience for Turkish Georgians is essential part of their every day perception of reality. They could be belonged to "membership group" which dictates norms and recalls past to them.

Language is the most fundamental form of communication, serving as a catalyst around which activities, histories, and interpretations coalesce; language is the mirror of culture (Czinkota, M. and Ronkainen, I., 1995) As described by Brown "a language is a part of culture and a culture is a part of language; the two are intricately interwoven so that one cannot separate the two without losing the significance of either language or culture" (Brown, 1994, p. 165) Language forms convey shared and unique meanings because culture is more expansive than language (Nida, 1998)

As we have mentioned above in Turkish "memleket" has emotional connotation and implies attachment to one's home town, Turkish Georgians, when talking about their forefathers, use the concept "memleket", which implies their ethnic belonging to "Gürcistan" (Georgia). Why do Turkish Georgians use "Memleket" and not other Turkish words expressing "homeland"? This is the question which is related to ethnic consciousness of Turkish Georgians. "Consuming" this concept, they underline their ethnic identity and ancestral background. In order for a nation to exist, in addition to the belief in existence of "people", there must be also a belief in the existence of specific territory which is believed to be in some way "appropriate" for "having a special affinity with", or "belonging" to only that people. (Hertz, 1944) Turkish Georgians had and have special affinity with Georgia- ancestral land. "Memleket" مَلَكَ) - Arabic word and means to appropriate, take possession of, accupy, take over, capture, take or get as one's own, come into possession or control of ;مَمْلَكَةٌ - kingdom, regality) (Al-Mawrid, 2010) In Turkish (Genel Türkçe Sözlük, TDK) "memleket" has the following meanings – 1."Bir devletin egemenliği altında bulunan toprakların bütünü, ülke. (the country, teritories united under the sovereignty of state) 2. Bir kimsenin doğup büyüdüğü yer, şehir, yurt (The place of birth) The meanings could be understood as 1. Homeland, the defined place where the nation inhabits and dwells and 2. The teritory belonged to family. (Kurtoğlu, 2005) For example in Turkish there is such form of question "Memleketin neresi?" (Where are you from? or where is your homeland?) Consequently for Turkish Georgians "Memleket" is Georgia and emotionally are connected to the place of their ancestors` birth.

SOLUTIONS AND RECOMMENDATIONS

And yet, if everything is moving, definition of "home" has become vague for migrants in foreign countries. But migration has positive sides. Consumption of culture-specific food is always in great demand. Turkish local markets and restaurants in Germany offer culture-specific products to migrants to make them feel their homeland; exactly this "emotional glue" creates illusion of something very native and sacred. "Host" countries are able to get benefit from such restaurants and markets, control them and get information of migrants` ethno-psychology. All these elements could be helpful for governments and ethnic minorities to conduct cultural dialogue and avoid racial, ethnical and religious clash, which unfortunately takes place in many European countries.

FUTURE RESEARCH DIRECTIONS

The authors plan to study Turkish Georgians` communities and restaurants in Turkey, their behavior in "own/ private space", where they dominate and outside the community as ethnic minority. In semi private and semi-public space people feel free –because it is their inner, ethnic space, where they are able to express their point of views, (the researchers focused on the same issue when studied Turks living in Georgia. Turks felt more comfortable and confident in their community-restaurant, than outside) It is important for migrants to have people around who are from the same country, share the same traditions and culture. They meet together at restaurants, which have domestic atmosphere with familiar smells and tastes. Hypothesis: Public space is heavily influenced by dominant norms and values. Majority defines and effects ethnic minority in public spaces but not in semi-public or semi private spaces -like communities and restaurants, owned by them.

CONCLUSION

Displacement, as a movement of something from its initial place or position, has influenced many people's cultural and ethnic identity. Nomadism is becoming more and more poignant, which could be the reason behind identity crises and loss of self. "Home" becomes a past tense, replaced by a temporary "campsite". Life in a new country and becoming an immigrant are often connected with a number of problems, and newly arrived immigrants often need to discover their own strategies to solve them. Scholars who study adaptation expect that the longer a refugee is away from their homeland, the more likely their cultural values, traditions, and lifestyles will change. Yet, Turkish Georgians/Twofold Muhajirs at the crossroads of three cultures, with neither a real nor permanent home, strangers in a foreign and "native" land, torn apart by two sets of memories and two opposing ways of the present and the past, are an interesting example of a society that has preserved many of their cultural traditions in the face of multiple forced migrations and displacement experiences. Consumption of "past" and (re)construction of memories have formed a tight-knit ethnic unit. Institutionalization of Georgian culture is so strong that many of Turkish Georgians feel as if they were living in their "own" country. Ethnic "retailers" (communities, membership groups) provide the 'emotional glue' that sticks ethnic participants together giving them a sense of identity. Ethnocentrism also has great impact on the "membership groups" as it is "the universal proclivity for people to view their own group as the center of the universe, to interpret other social units from the perspective of their own group, and to reject persons who are culturally dissimilar while blindly accepting those who are culturally like themselves" (Shimp, T. and Sharma, S., 1987, p. 280) And also "when people speak a similar language, have a common history or ancestry, and a similar ethnic origin, they will automatically behave in the same way that is the same, but different from other groups" (Minor-Cooley, D. and Brice, J., 2007, p. 2)

We are defined as people not only by what we think and say, but by what material things we possess, surround us. As Lan Woodward admits all of them help to establish, mediate and assist us in the performance of our personal and social identities. (Woodward, 2007) Domestic objects, (reminders) "consumed" by Turkish Georgians and their narrativization play important role in social performance; because they are related to Turkish Georgians` life history (past) and also have influence over their current life. Turkish Georgians use objects as aids to developing and managing their identity.

Turkish Georgians struggle to make a new beginning by fitting in with the new "motherland" (Germany), and at the same time to maintain their own ethnic culture, space and identity, upholding their self-imposed endogamy. But the following question crops up: how long will it last?

ACKNOWLEDGMENT

This study is based on two fellowships- Coimbra Universities Group Scholarship and Shota Rustaveli National foundation and DAAD-German Academic Exchange Scholarship, (interviews were conducted by researchers Prof. Elisbed Bzhalava and Dr. Nino Okrostsvaridze in Turkey and Germany) We are grateful for Turkish Georgians` constant support through our fieldworks.

REFERENCES

Al-Mawrid, B. (2010). *A Modern Arabic-English Dictionary*. Beirut, Lebanon: Dar El-IlmLilmalayin.

Alexander, M. (1996). *The Shock of Arrival: Reflections on Postcolonial Experience*. Boston: South End Press.

Appadurai, A. (1986). Introduction: Commodities and the Politics of Value. In The Social Life of Things: Commodities in Cultural Perspective. Melbourne: Cambridge University Press.

Atalay, H. (1999). *Inglizce-Türkçe Sözlük*. Ankara: Türk Dili Kurumu.

Ballerstadt, R. (2010). *The postcolonial Citizen, the Intellectual Migrant*. New York: Peter Lang Publishing, Inc. doi:10.3726/978-1-4539-0057-4

Barth, F. (1969). *Ethnic Groups and Boundaries*. Boston: Little Brown.

Berger, P., Berger, B., & Kellner, H. (1974). *The Homeless Mind*. New York: Vintage books.

Bozkurt, E. (2009). *Conseptualising "Home". The Question of belonging among Turkish Families in Germany*. Frankfurt, New York: Campus Verlag.

Brewer, M. B. (1979). In-group bias in the Minimal Intergroup Situation: A Cognitive-Motivational Analysis. *Psychological Bulletin*, *86*(2), 307–324. doi:10.1037/0033-2909.86.2.307

Brown, H. D. (1994). *Principles of Language Learning and Teaching*. Englewood Cliffs, NJ: Prentice-Hall.

Buxrashvili, P. (2005). *Dwelling in the Life and Culture of Ancient Georgia*. Tbilisi.

Carrus, G. A., & Caddeo, P. (2008). *Science Direct*. Retrieved 5 2, 2018, from The Role of Ethnic Identity and Perceived Ethnic Norms in Purchase of Ethnic Food Products: http://www.sciencedirect.com

Carter, P. (1992). *Living in New Country, History, Travelling and Language*. London: Faber and Faber.

Chamber, L. (2001). *Culture After Humanism: History, Culture, Subjectivity*. New York: Routledge.

Cleveland, M., Laroche, M., Pons, F., & Kastoun, R. (2009). Acculturation and Consumption: Textures of Cultural Adaptation. *International Journal of Intercultural Relations*, *33*(3), 196–212. doi:10.1016/j.ijintrel.2008.12.008

Cuellar, I., Nyberg, B., Maldonado, M., & Roberts, R. E. (1997). Ethnic Identity and Acculturation in a Young Adult Mexican-Origin Population. *Journal of Community Psychology*, *25*(6), 535–549. doi:10.1002/(SICI)1520-6629(199711)25:6<535::AID-JCOP4>3.0.CO;2-O

Czinkota, M., & Ronkainen, I. (1995). *International Marketing*. The Dryden Press.

Doğan, A. (1995). *Osmanlıca Türkçe sözlük*. Ankara: Akcag Yayınları.

Gaston, B. (1994). *The poetics of Space*. Boston: Beacon Press. (Original work published 1958)

Gronhaug, K., Gilly, M., & Penazola, L. (1993). Barriers and Incentives in Consumer Acculturation. *European Advances in Consumer Research*, *1*, 278–286.

Halbwachs, M. (1992). *On Collective Memory*. Chicago: Academic Press.

Hertz, F. (1944). *Nationality in History and politics*. London: Kegan Paul Trench, Trubner and Co.

James, W. (1988). Possessions and extended self. *The Journal of Consumer Research*, 139–165.

Kurtoğlu, A. (2005). Mekansal Bir Olgu Olarak Hemlşehrilik ve Bir Hemşehrilik Mekanı Olarak Dernekler. *European Journal of Turkish Studies*. https://journals.openedition.org/ejts/375

Madden, R. (2010). *Being Ethnographic*. London: Sage.

Mary Douglas and Baron Isherwood. (1979). *The World of Goods*. Routledge.

Mecheril, P., & Teo, T. (Eds.). (1997). Rassismuserfahrungen von Anderen Deutschen-eine Einzelfall-betrachtung. Psychologie und Rassismus, 175-201.

Meyer, G. (1890, Oct. 6). Die Deutschamerikaner. Festschrift zur Feier des Deutschamerikanischen Tages in Milwauke. Winsconsin.

Minor-Cooley, D., & Brice, J. (2007). The Problems with Ethnic Identification and Its Potential in Cross-Cultural Marketing. *Academy of Marketing Science Review*, *11*(9), 1–9.

Morley, D. (2000). *Home, Territories, Media, Mobility and Identity*. London: Routledge.

Morley, D., & Robins, K. (1995). *Spaces of Identity: Global Media, Electronic Landscapes and Cultural Boundaries*. London: Routledge.

Nida, E. (1998). Language, Culture and Translation. Foreign language Journal, 29-33.

O'Reilly, K. (2009). *Key Concepts in Ethnography*. London: Sage.

Oswald, R. L. (1999). Culture Swapping: Consumption and the Ethnogenesis of Middle-Class Haitian Immigrants. *The Journal of Consumer Research*, *25*(4), 303–318. doi:10.1086/209541

Otnes, C., Lowrey, T. M., & Shrum, L. J. (1997). Toward and Understanding of Consumer Ambivalence. *The Journal of Consumer Research*, *24*(1), 80–93. doi:10.1086/209495

Pirtskalava, E. (2019). Being here and there: a case study of Muslim Meskhetians` identity and belonging, formation and reconstruction in the United States. Caucasus Survey, 7(7), 44-59.

Püsküllüoğlu, A. (2007). *Türkçe Sözlük*. İstanbul: Can Yayınları.

Quester, P. G., & Wendt-Eccles, J. V. (2002). The Influence of Perceived Cultural Differences on Marketing Managers' strategic Decision making. An Explorary Study. *Journal of Asia-Pacific Marketing*, *1*(2), 47–62.

Rivera, T. (1979). Chicago literature: Fiesta of the Living, The Identification and Analysis of Chicago Literature. *Bilingual P/Editional Bilinguo*, 19-36.

Rossiter, J. R., & Chan, A. M. (1998). Etnicity in Business and Consumer Behavior. *Journal of Business Research*, *42*(2), 127–134. doi:10.1016/S0148-2963(97)00113-6

Schiffauer, W. (1997). *Die Ehre in der Türkischen Kultur*. Berlin: Die Ausländerbeauftragte des Senats.

Shimp, T., & Sharma, S. (1987). Consumer Ethnocentrism: Construction and Validation of the CETSCALE. *Journal of Marketing*, *25*(8), 280–289. doi:10.1177/002224378702400304

Sözlük, T. (2007). *Türk Dil Kurumu*. Retrieved 12 10, 2012, from www.tdk.gov.tr: www.tdk.gov.tr

Stayman, D., & Deshpande, R. (1989). Siatuational Ethnicity and Consumer Behavior. *The Journal of Consumer Research*, *16*(3), 361–371. doi:10.1086/209222

Stroinska, M., & Cecchetto, V. (2003). *Exile, Language and Identity. The Role of Language in the Reconstruction in Exile*. Frankfurt am Main: Peter Lang.

Tajfel, H. (1981). *Human Groups and Social Categories: Studies in Social Psychology*. Cambridge: Cambridge University Press.

Türkçe Sözlük. (1998). Ankara: Türk Dili Kurumu.

Tylor, E. (1876, Jan. 6). Dammann`s Race-photographs. *Nature*.

Wallendorf, M., & Reilly, M. D. (1983). Ethnic Migration, Assimilation and Consumption. *The Journal of Consumer Research*, *10*(3), 292–302. doi:10.1086/208968

Webster, C. (1991). Attitudes Towards Marketing Practices: The Effects of ethnic Identification. *Journal of Applied Business Research*, *7*(2), 107–116. doi:10.19030/jabr.v7i2.6251

Webster, C. (1994). Effects of Ethnic Identification on Marital Rols in the Purchase Decision Process. *The Journal of Consumer Research*, *21*(2), 319–331. doi:10.1086/209400

Woodward, L. (2007). *Understanding Material Culture*. London: Sage. doi:10.4135/9781446278987

Zmud, J., & Arce, C. (1992). The Ethnical and Consumption Relationship. *Advances in Consumer Research. Association for Consumer Research (U. S.)*, *19*, 443–449.

KEY TERMS AND DEFINITIONS

Consumption of Past: Using "things" or "objects" in real time and space to create emotional connection with ancestors, to build new "home" on the base of past and to define ethnic identity.

Culture-Specific Reminders: Foods, products, objects, etc. to make us feel ethnic identity.

Ethnic Identity: Domination of ethnic self.

Ethnic Memory: Genetic /historical memory passed down from generation to generation.

Illusionary Perception of Home: Attempts to create and define positive connotation of comfort.

Turkish Georgians: "Muhajirs" (Muslim Georgians) migrated from Georgia (Adjara region) to Turkey in 19th century.

ENDNOTES

1 He popularized Georgian culture in Turkey. He was killed in Bursa on July 5, 1980.

2 The idea of promoting rural development through cooperatives. In 1964 when Turkey's Ministry of Village Affairs was formed, the ministry devised a plan to utilize the earnings of migrant workers to improve village conditions. It encouraged residents of poor villages to organize village development cooperatives (VDCs).

3 This society is subordinated to the Turkish consulate in Cologne. There are about ten organizations established by migrants from Turkey.

4 In 1944, as a result of Stalin's social policy to clean the southern border of the Soviet Union of "undesirable peoples", a Muslim population, primordially comprised of Turkish-speaking Meskhetians, was deported from Georgia to Central Asian republics. After ethnic conflict in Uzbekistan in 1989, a part of this population and the informants for this research, relocated to Russia and from there to the US.

5 The Georgian word "Chveneburi", used by Turkish Georgians, means "one of ours".

6 Hısım is a Turkish word for "related by blood". See Türkçe Sözlük, 1998.

7 Gürcü" is Turkish for "Georgian".

8 "One of them was a compulsory military service, which channeled Georgians and other ethnic minorities into a unified stream of Turkish society; besides, by the constitution of Turkey, Chapter Four "Political Rights and Duties", Article 66, "everyone bound to the Turkish state through the bond of citizenship is a Turk."

Chapter 14
Dwelling and Cult in the Life and Culture of the Ancient Georgians

Paata Bukhrashvili
Ilia state University, Georgia

ABSTRACT

As a consequence of long-term organic integration with their homeland, a characteristic lifestyle developed among the Georgians. This is particularly evident in the richly variegated customs, traditions, and norms of everyday behavior. To a significant degree they are conditioned by thousands of years of adaptation to the environment, and its associated biocultural and socio-economic forms. From the earliest times these complexes of economic-cultural relations implied the possession of the land by social units – families – on the basis of juridical norms founded upon blood relationship. Such relations were firmly grounded upon common tribal shrines, through which was acknowledged the tribal territory's chief patron and regulator. It follows that each land-owning family of the tribe, on the basis of vassalage to the shrine, was directly responsible before the shrine, and, accordingly, the moral comportment of each tribal member was marked by deep and honest respect for the deity.

INTRODUCTION

The material and intellectual culture of the Georgians (and of the Caucasian peoples overall) has been studied for well over a century. A rich scholarly heritage has come down to us, due to the selfless and tireless labor of our predecessors. A particularly important stage in Georgian historiography began in the 1930's, formed in the political and ideological context of the times, from which stemmed a series of stereotypical models, which formed the background for the study of the history and culture of the Georgian people (or of peoples in general). Since the late 1980's, when the Georgians once again took up the task of self-realization and reform, much of the work which had been accepted without question came under new scrutiny.

DOI: 10.4018/978-1-7998-3115-0.ch014

Copyright © 2020, IGI Global. Copying or distributing in print or electronic forms without written permission of IGI Global is prohibited.

It is well known that in such conditions creative energy appears with renewed force, as is reflected in the lives of contemporary Georgians. It is precisely these circumstances which inspired us to take up once again the question of ancient dwellings, against the background of the Georgian scholarly heritage (Bukhrashvili, 2005).

Proceeding from what was stated above, the primary object of the present work is to analyze the phenomenon of the dwelling on the basis of ethnographic and archaeological data, and situate it in stadially arranged social formations, according to their level of development; to address the question of the dwelling as reflective of spatial perception, and demonstrate the perspicacity of such an approach; to the extent that it is possible, to highlight the role of the dwelling in everyday life, taking into consideration those geographic and social-economic factors specific to the peoples of the Caucasus, especially those of its central region.

From the perspective of stadial development we will seek to outline the pathway from domestic religious practice ("hearth") to that of the tribal shrine ("sanctuary"), and thus determine the role played by spiritual factors in Georgian traditional life.

In effect, our approach to the concrete cultural phenomenon of the dwelling is based on that worked out by Acad. G. Chitaia in the field of Georgian historical research, drawing upon the intensive and multidisciplinary study of phenomena in their spatial setting - an approach rendered possible by the rich assemblage of materials already gathered.

As for the thematic orientation of our research, we consider appropriate the use of the term paleoethnology. This term might seem more suited to the study of ethnic unities already vanished from the historical scene (Bukhrashvili, 2003), but we believe it also appropriate to the investigation of the Kartvelians (Carling et al., 2019) and other Caucasian peoples, who have occupied their present territories for millennia.

BACKGROUND

As a consequence of long-term organic integration with their homeland, a characteristic lifestyle developed among the Georgians. This is particularly evident in the richly variegated customs, traditions and norms of everyday behavior. To a significant degree they are conditioned by thousands of years of adaptation to the environment, and its associated biocultural and socio-economic forms. From the earliest times these complexes of economic-cultural relations implied the possession of the land by social units – families – on the basis of juridical norms founded upon blood relationship. Such relations were firmly grounded upon common tribal shrines, through which was acknowledged the tribal territory's chief patron and regulator. It follows that each land-owning family of the tribe, on the basis of vassalage to the shrine, was directly responsible before the shrine, and, accordingly, the moral comportment of each tribal member was marked by deep and honest respect for the deity. There formed, accordingly, such moral and spiritual principles, that to act against the collective's system of values was tantamount to opposition to the divine patron itself. The gravest punishment for insult to the deity and the tribe was expulsion, which meant permanent separation from one's flesh and blood, one's family. From this it follows that the highest goal of each tribal member was service to one's own tribe and village, and therefore to one's homeland, motivated by awe of the divinity. It was precisely this fear of God that grounded the highest form of love, upon which developed the entire diverse spectrum of pan-Georgian or intra-regional customs, traditions and practices, many of which are continued to the present day.

The ethnic group is a specific unity of individuals, which depends not only on common genetic origins and spiritual-cultural unity, but also a shared historical fate.

Each culture fosters among the individuals who grow up within its womb a distinctive "cognitive screen", upon which they project and represent their perceptions of the external world. It is precisely in the nature of these cognitive screens that ancient and contemporary peoples differ from each other, in terms of the content and structure of their perceptions of reality.

There is one other essential difference between the habitual thought of ancient and modern peoples: Ancient peoples inhabited a universe of absolute veracity. They had clear and final responses to all cardinal questions: How the universe, their land and their ethnic group were created, what fate awaits them after death, etc. In ancient social thought, as a rule, there reigned a unity of belief, and individuals had little occasion to doubt general values; they had no need to choose among them. Contemporary people must be content with approximate, temporary and changeable responses to the same questions, which is clearly a very different situation from that which dominated the everyday lives of the ancients.

Ancient peoples' relation to objects and knowledge was different as well. Now we often hear that contemporary people are excessively materialistic and focussed on things, but it must be pointed out that nonetheless, their relation is fleeting and superficial. Today people discard things as soon as something better or more modern comes along. In ancient times individuals and their possessions – house, land, tools and utensils, even the seemingly most insignificant – were bound by a deep, one might say, personal relation. Each object, created by an ancestor and passed down over generations, had its own fate, force, name; and it was only with great pain that the ancients parted with these artefacts. Anciently, possessors were tied by relations difficult for us to conceive to the land, the homestead, the loss of which was felt as a tragedy. In early societies possession represented one of the chief forms by which individuals "extended" themselves beyond their bodies.

Ancient societies were characterized by an orientation toward the past and the old. Ancient peoples were psychologically turned toward the past. If, for contemporary people, looking toward the past meant looking backward, for the ancients looking toward the past meant looking forward, whereas the future was behind their backs. This spatial metaphor underlies the Georgian word "ts'inap'ari" - literally "forebears" - in which it is clear that for ancient Georgians their flesh and blood, their children, were primary, and, in the perception of the living, those who passed away were not placed behind their backs but rather imagined as preceding the living on their life's path like a lit candle. For traditional peoples the past is clear, visible; whereas the future is unknown and unseen. The ancestors light the path toward where the living go. Orthodox Christians perceive the space in similar terms, whom the saints (exemplary for theirfaith, ideas and kindness) lead on the path of earthly existence. We recall Vaxtang Kotetishvili's words with regard to the mountains: "It is very difficult to go to the mountains. Up their things are experienced differently, there are distinctive ideas and desires. There life takes a different form and death seems if anything easier. There is sort of panthcon, whcrc thc treasure of departed souls is preserved like Tamar's grave". The distinguished scholar understood correctly the need to maximally establish contact with the context in which he conducted his research, and its mode of experience.

It must be pointed out, that at present certain forces are attempting to disrupt the faith, confessional beliefs and theistic perception of traditional societies. They are striving to uproot their orientation toward the past, toward traditions, and it could even be said, toward their ethnic self-conception; and in exchange turn their gaze toward an unknown and uncertain future. In fact, this future, although portrayed in dazzling, glittering colors, is no different in essence from the "happy communist future", whose taste post-Soviet society has yet to digest. As we indicated, in order to bring about the reorientation of traditional societies and peoples toward this supra-ethnic happy unity, it is in the first place necessary to make those societies possessing an ethnic self-conception forget their own identities. To this end, these forces do battle with ethnic, national awareness, which they deem to be synonymous with backwardness and ignorance, and designate with such terms as "provincial fascism". In fact, these are those forces, for which love, kindness, enlightenment and ethnic world-view and belief are no more than excess baggage.

In conclusion, we wish to point out, that before beginning discussion of specific questions we deemed it necessary to lay out for our readers our views on social-historical processes, so that they might more clearly understand our thoughts on the problems of ethnic history, since Martin Luther said in 1521 "*hier stehe ich, ich kann nicht anders* (Here I stand, I can do no other)" (Leaver, 2019).

MAIN FOCUS OF THE CHAPTER

On the Interrelation of Ethnic Culture and the Phenomenon of the Dwelling Place

We interpret the dwelling to be one of the most salient expressions of traditional (hence, ethnic) world-view and culture. Insofar as the dwelling is, in the first place, a purely material phenomenon, and, secondly, a sort of temple created by early people, it is a capital source of information (Figure 1).

The dwelling, doubtless, is a reflection of its builders' ethnically-conditioned cognition of the world, which evolved as a consequence of their blood- and seed-linked relation to their environment and homeland. It is also without a doubt that this materialization and formation in relation to the home environment, anointed by the blood and bones of the ancestors and crowned by the heavenly spirits, was a lengthy process (Ingold, 2019). Finally, the dynamic interaction with the permanent features of the environment led to the formation of the ethnic group's "cultural visage" by Nicholas Yakovlevich Marr, characterized by resistance to change despite the vicissitudes of the passing centuries (Buchraschwili, 2014; Simon, 2018).

The centuries-long existence of the ethnic group is conditioned by the heritability of language and cultural traditions and practices. The formation of the ethnic society is conditioned by the direct relationships among its members, which is only possible when they reside on the same territory. On that same territory occurs the consolidation of the associated cultural unity within the ethnic community. It is precisely here, in one specific locality, that it evolves into a complete, durable sociocultural unit, which enables its permanence across time and place, and its capacity to give and receive something of value.

During the study of cultural-historical and ethnic relations, the investigator is confronted by numerous difficulties. Among them is increasingly narrow specialization (the tempo of which has been increasing in recent times) conditions the collection and analysis of factual materials. In itself this tendency is inevitable and progressive, but unfortunately, the actual degree of cooperation among scholars often lags behind. One of the chief obstacles to the successful investigation of ethnic processes, one which in fact hinders mutual comprehension among the relevant disciplines, is the weakness of the theoretical groundwork.

It is probably true that there is no justification for the study of ethnic phenomena from a single disciplinary perspective, without the cooperation of others. Unfortunately, such situations all too frequently occurred among us. Each individual discipline, which took the ethnic group as its object of study, examined it from its particular point of view. This led to a curious state of affairs: These disciplines did not so much serve to study the ethnic group (as research object), as, on the contrary, ethnic research came to

Figure 1. Forms of residential buildings in ancient Georgia

serve their compartmental interests. This sort of stance toward concrete, multifaceted dynamic phenomena created the circumstances within which ethnography, archaeology, cultural history, historiography, linguistics and adjoining disciplines interpret, each in their particular manner, the objective phenomenon of the ethnic unity. Needless to say, such circumstances are incompatible to the extent that the ethnic group (people) is a whole, concretely-existing entity, and therefore it is inadmissible that such a unified phenomenon be studied in fragmentary fashion, carved up according to sectarian academic interests. Otherwise, each discipline in the process of investigation would divide up the object of study according to its particular norms and logic, which is likely to lead to paradoxical results. The study of the ethnic group must be of a multidisciplinary nature. Each discipline, which participates in the investigational process, must take into account the conclusions, methodology and observations which have resulted from the study of the ethnic group as research object. In this collaborative process, the multifaceted object of study is examined by taking into consideration each other's conclusions.

In the investigation of ethnogenetic phenomena, a multidisciplinary stance implies the broad and methodologically correct utilization of ethnogenetic data; and their connection with other types of historical materials and those supplied by adjacent fields of study (such as certain ones concerned with natural phenomena: ethnobotany, ethnozoology, etc.). The multidisciplinary approach, in the first place, takes account of the variegated nature of the relevant facts: their anthropological, archaeological, folkloristic, historical, linguistic, ethnological, onomastic and other characteristics (Buchraschwili, 2011; Hu, 2013; Tuite, 2017).

Unfortunately, despite certain efforts, the multidisciplinary approach to the study of ethnogenetic questions has not yet become totally accepted, due, probably, to its great difficulty and the various unresolved methodological issues.

In the past, one of the most useful attainments of investigation of this question can be considered the establishment of the temporal parameters of the ethnogenetic process, and of its broadly-comparative methodology.

It is believed that ethnogenesis as a historical process begins with the first form of ethnic unity, with the consolidation of the tribe (Zakhariuk, 1977).

It is also acknowledged that physical-anthropological types were consolidated during Neolithic times. Archaeologists associate the Neolithic with the final formation of tribal organizations (Hodder, 2018). On the basis of lexicostatistic methods, it is believed that the principal language families now existing consolidated in the Neolithic (Rama, 2013). On this basis, it is appropriate to situate the beginning of the ethnogenetic process in the Neolithic. Of course, it is impossible that the chronological study of the ethnogenesis of each of the world's peoples should begin in the same period; but it is clear that such processes are to be situated stadially in prehistoric times.

Experience teaches us that it is methodological feasible to carry out research of ethnogenetic character both within a particular ethnic group, as well as within a defined territory. In the first instance, the field-ethnographic study of the contemporary ethnic community has particular importance, which then enables one on the basis of scientific procedure to work back from the contemporary situation toward the past; in the second instance, we undertake the investigation of the problem from the earliest cultural vestiges found on the territory under study, and then move forward in time toward the present. We believe that it is necessary, in the process of studying any given ethnic formation, that investigation take place in both directions, so that to data from the deepest layers of archaeological investigation are juxtaposed the results obtained from the ethnographic analysis of materials ready-to-hand from living populations. That is to say, it is possible to maximally profit from interdisciplinary research. This is all the more the case, in that such a stance appears to us completely justified with regard to a region such as the Caucasus, where the autochthonicity of the Ibero-Caucasian peoples stands out in clear relief. To that extent, the seeking of parallels among chronologically-separated cultures of common origin, once the methodological mechanism is worked out, should not be totally unjustified. We will add that the earliest conditioner of cultures of common origin is, in our belief, the durable and long-lasting cultural-agricultural complex developed in the given region as a consequence of adaptation. This complex serves as the primary axis for the evolution of such cultures.

In the sphere of material culture, the indicators of ethnic identity (which are conditioned by adaptation to the sphere of everyday life) are fairly numerous as concerns settlement types, insofar as the latter formed and evolved in accordance with the topography of a given place. As a consequence of their study the specificities of settlement organization can be determined – placement with regard to the central square, the sanctuary, etc. (Buchraschwili, 2013)

From the standpoint of ethnic specificity, the dwelling is particularly informative, in that this specificity might manifest itself as basic construction (underground dwelling, half-underground, placement of rooms, roofing ...), orientation with regard to outbuildings, and the like. The deployment of internal space can be considered an ethnic marker: placement of the hearth, form of the hearth, function of rooms and their position, location of sacred corner or shrine, orientation of entrance, position of chimney or ventilation-hole (Geo.: ერდო), etc. An entire series of specificities characterize the domestic furnishings, food, agricultural equipment, etc.

In eastern Georgia, according to ethnographic materials, in the context of a historically-evolved sedentary population, the individual familial homestead represented the basic dwelling type in village settlements. The individual familial homestead, for its part, in its essential structure, is reflective of the cultural-agricultural lifestyle of the population of a given micro-region, as well as being one its constituent components.

In Georgian village settlements of the 1920's, in one form or another, traces of their original social and economic lifestyles were still preserved. It is precisely for this reason, that, in the investigation of social and agricultural forms, the settlement is an important primary source of data. In Georgian villages of all various forms, in the placement of homesteads within the village, the tradition of settlement according to monogenetic blood-related groups is attested. The monogenetic settlement is a firm and historically enduring tradition. Settlement by monogenetic neighborhoods, as characteristic of ancient lifestyles, was maintained in the morphology of village layout for many centuries. Therefore, in the analysis of the cultural-agricultural nature of a studied settlement as a result of archaeological investigation, the study of the ethnographically-established settlement forms is especially informative. The morphology of the settlement of a historically-evolved sedentary population, in view of its conservative nature, was relatively unaffected by the passage of time. It is thus justified to assume that, in our region, settlement forms retained their earlier forms relatively unchanged.

The village in central Kartli was composed of monogenetic groups distributed by neighborhood (or quarter). Precisely this region was the cradle of the crowned-ventilation-shaft or "darbazi" (დარბაზი) -style house. Archaeological and ethnological data show that not only was the "darbazi"-style house preserved for a long period, but also the form of settlement. It is well-known that the topographical relief constrained the placement of settlements. It conditioned its external form, but not its type. The settlement type was based on the cultural-agricultural lifestyle developed within the population (Buchraschwili, 2013).

With respect to the "darbazi", as one of the domestic structural types widespread in central Transcaucasia, we believe a few words about its morphology are appropriate.

At the first stage of the evolution of the dwelling, the principal typological features of the darbazi were: a large undivided space (occupied by a 3 or 4-generation family group); darbazi morphology; open hearth and hearth-chain (ojinjali - ოჯინჯალი); poor quality of internal lighting (coming through the ventilation-shaft, through which the smoke exited); stamped-earth floor (soxane - სოხანე); porch at ground level (p'armaghi - პარმაღი); expansion of the floor-plan depthwise; three-beam roofing system; wide single door with wooden hinges and bolt; low furniture, and correspondingly low horizon of domestic activities; house dug into the ground; wood-working principally done with adzes and axes without use of saws; crowned roofing, slightly sloped roof-terrace; thick stone walls with niches for storage; oak as primary type of wood material (Buchraschwili, 2013).

We think that the materials presented above make it quite clear that, in the Caucasus - and specifically on the territory of today's eastern Georgia -, traces of continuity of lifestyle can be revealed from the earliest times almost without interruption, as a result of archaeological and ethnological research. The earliest settlements have been detected and investigated, and many forms of dwelling have been examined. Therefore, we think, that it is entirely justified and indeed desirable to trace the evolution and development of the dwelling phenomenon from earliest times to the present on the basis of variegated materials. Its representation in this manner along the vertical axis will portray for us the desired panoramic representation according to ethnogenetic processes taking place on the designated territory. To the extent that the dwelling phenomenon, as a consequence of adaptation of ethnic elements to the inhabited environment, is one of the component elements of ethnic culture, it is likewise a clear reflection of the same element's insertion into the occupied environment as a distinctive "biocene".

At the same time, the examination of the inhabited complex along the vertical axis is clearly justified insofar as it represents a method for the dynamic analysis of the most characteristic elements of ethnic culture. In this circumstance, its presentation along the vertical axis (retrospectively) presents us with a means to establish not only the recent stages in its development, but also a means to see the complex process of the relation between traditional elements and innovation.

When we discuss the dwelling and its phenomenon in any given traditional society, in the first place, perhaps, we must attempt, to the extent it is possible, to reveal the principles of the functional mechanism of the appropriation of the external environment by humans (Descola, 2017). In other words, those principles must be established, according to which the transformation took place in human cognition from "nature" to "culture", from "unappropriated" to "appropriated". At the same time, the specificities of the traditional model of domestication and appropriation of space, which evolved in concrete ethnic modes of life, are very interesting and worthy of attention in the research process (Ingold, 2019; Pollard, 2019).

It is clear from all of the above that in the study of the dwelling, as characteristic complex of ethnic culture, a series of puzzles present themselves before the researcher, each of them inseparably connected to the others. Without their analysis in length and breadth it is almost unimaginable how one is to distinguish, in the complex structure of a people's intellectual history, the nucleus without which it is impossible to understand even approximately the nuances of ethnic history.

The dwelling will be the primary theme of the present study; more precisely, we will attempt to lay out what role this phenomenon played in general in ethnic lifestyle and culture; to what degree it reflects the unique unity of a people (ethnic group) as evolved through blood-linked genetic relations; the gentle and yet directed process of their incorporation into a "biocene" with their homeland and divinely-granted territory.

By dwelling, first of all, we intend the primary residential structure within which is situated a specific microsocial unit: the family. In parallel we will discuss its orientation toward other elements of the inhabited complex (such as the yard, auxiliary agricultural structures, cultivated fields, etc.), and we will attempt to delimit its place in the formation and evolution of the family; in the consolidation of the cognition of interior and external space; in the formation and working-out of "genotheism", as the family's ideological foundation.

And finally, we will indicate once again, that in the following chapters of the chapter we will attempt to analysis the existing archaeological and ethnographic materials available to us concerning the dwelling in the Kartvelian world and especially the central region of its contemporary territory, according to the above-mentioned markers, in the following sequence:

i) The dwelling and spatial perception;
ii) The dwelling and domestic religion;
iii) The dwelling and clan-tribe social organization.

House and Shrine in Ancient Georgia.

The Role of the Dwelling Phenomenon in the Formative Process of Opposed Spatial Concepts – "Inside" and "Outside", "Domestic" and "Wild"

From the earliest period the dwelling, as a type of artificial micro-environment separated from the natural ambient environment, played a key role in humans' self-conception, in their appropriation of their own place in Mother Nature. To each one of us it is clear, that the residential building, house, in general, is of capital importance in the evolution of the worldview of the individual and also of the collectivity living under one roof, by one hearth, "under the wings of their guardian angel". People themselves attributed the most complex function to the dwelling – to be a sort of inspiration that conditions and constrains its own creators' (humans') spatial cognition and other forms of habitual thought.

As people built their own homes, they thereby segmented themselves off from the environment. The home became a place of spiritual repose and peace. It is there, within their own homes, that people feel themselves to be lords and masters, since they deem themselves to be the founders and creators of this micro-space. All things contained within this micro-space – created and used by their hands – are products of their intelligence; from this stems their individual and social consciousness. They too breathed a "soul" into these things, brought them to life. As the home was built, its ceiling became the sky, whereas the floor symbolized the earth. The walls thereupon acquired a delimiting function, and the hearth became a sacred place; thereupon the central pillar became the residence of the "angel of the foundation" (pudzis angelozi - ფუძის ანგელოზი).

The home separated people from the cosmos, stood between them, and thereby acquired a complex of interrelated traits. On the one hand, the home belongs to people, manifests their material universe. On the other hand, the home links people to the exterior world, represents, in significant part, that same world reduced to human parameters. Inside it, people coexist with the world. It is precisely thus that, as so often occurs, the codes of human body parts, cosmic elements and components of the dwelling are superimposed (Baiburin, 1983).

It is also worthy of note that the thus-modeled features and markers are attributed to those objects also, to which early humans assigned a function at the center of their world. The understanding of concepts of our ancient ancestors was filled and permeated with such meanings, such as city, temple, sanctuary; to their number we can also add the home. If within the temple the face of the universe was consciously (intentionally) perceived, within the dwelling the world-form was perceived unconsciously. This property is of special significance for understanding this phenomenon from both a material and spiritual point of view. The structure of the home – dwelling - in significant part parallels the structure of the universe in the sense that it has its own center, "periphery", etc. On the basis of rich archaeological and ethnographic data we can speak of the homogeneity of the structure of the house and the settlement; we can use this point of view especially in the case of circular-shaped settlements, in which the residences are distributed around a distinctly central place.

As we already pointed out, the dwelling plays a major role in the formation and transformation of people's spatial cognition. The home had a determining influence on the formation of such spatial oppositions as "inside" and "outside". In human consciousness, the binary division of the environmental surroundings into the categories of "inside" and "outside" entailed the corresponding binary division of the component elements within that space into "internal" (or "domestic") and "external" (or "savage, wild"). Whatever or whoever came "inside" became "domestic", whereas those of the "outside" were "wild".

Thus, the division of the universe into two parts correspondingly evoked two "sub-universes" in human cognition. The "inside" universe, created by humans, necessitated a base or foundation around which spatial conception (and subsequently, social conception) was formed. This base is the center around which the components of the "interior" are united; it gathered around itself humans' "inside" universe, and became the anchoring point for this space. This center and cornerstone is the hearth. It is that chief component of the dwelling around which all is centered; one could say that it is itself the symbol of the home, it is its foundation. If the hearth were to be extinguished, the family would die out also; as long as the home flourishes, the hearth is lit. The hearth was that chief point and center, around which the entire "inside" universe turned.

The division of space into "inside" and "outside" universes would have occurred in the earliest times, more exactly, when the social group took possession of its food-producing territory. Therefore, we can assert that the formation of "inside" and "outside", as categories of spatial perception, corresponded to the appearance and formation of early-agricultural cultures among the tribes inhabited central Transcaucasia. It is at this time that people consciously took possession of their territory, their homeland.

The Dwelling as "Family Temple"

The dwelling, as the materialized reflection of the culture of a distinct social organism, namely the family, along with many other functions, fulfilled the very important role of religious center for the unit's ideological whole, the family. From the distant past, the family's most holy relics, and various objects fulfilling sacred functions, were kept in the home; there, in the hearth, burnt the "sacred" flame; there stood the mother pillar, as a symbol of family unity; there were stored various idols.

Traces of domestic cultic practice can be found on the territory of contemporary eastern Georgia; in archaeological sites, it is attested as early as the Eneolithic. From the point of view, the "ritual" hearths excavated at site of "Khramis Didi Gora" are of special interest; within them, besides ashes, were found bones of sacrificed animals (sheep), miniature weapons, clay oval "bread-loaves", and – a find which is particularly noteworthy –, anthropomorphic statues (Figure 2).

These figurines represent for the most part female-gendered divinities, which at this distant time, in the consciousness of our ancestors, seem to us to have depicted goddesses serving as guardian angels of the home. In the Kartvelian world, the female gender of the protective divinities of the home is also attested in mythology. "The angel of the home was female. She was invisible, but she could appear in dreams in the guise of a neighbor's girl. No one may see the guardian angel in her true form. The guardian angel dwells in the family in the form of a young, spotless virgin. No one may see her, but she can take on the appearance of a neighbor's daughter" (Tuite, 2017).

Since the family angel appeared as a spotless virgin, it is possible that it is from here that the tradition stems, that when guests, regarded as a blessing come from God came to the family, the family had their virgin daughter serve them, as their most valuable and purest representation of the guardian angel. She would serve the guests and even bathe their feet, bring them food and lay out the bedding. By respecting the purity of their host's daughter, guests – perceived to be sent from God – brought divine goodness into the household. It may well be that this sort of conception of external persons entering the "interior" space underlay the institution of "anti-marriage" (ts'ats'loba), which in earlier times would not have been restricted to the east Georgian highlands, and would have been of common Georgian (or even Caucasian) distribution (Tuite, 2007).

It can be clearly seen, on the basis of numerous examples from Georgian ethnic culture, that the hearth represented the nucleus of the dwelling, its fundamental component. It is at the place of the hearth that the family's protective deity is displayed, its guardian angel. The hearth is the connective link between the family members and the guardian angel; it is the bridge that permits contact and relation between them. It is precisely at the hearth that patron deities (*ghvtishvilni* "children of God") manifest themselves, and take possession of the space as their shrine. Thus the hearth is the symbol of the family. The fire burning in the hearth is the family's immortality. When the elders would travel far from the village, they would tell the remaining family members: "do not betray the hearth, do not let the hearth-flame die out". An intruding enemy would first attempt to overturn the hearth, as the gravest insult to the family.

Thus the hearth represents the center, the heart of the family, which unites and ties it together, forges a bond among the social unit that is the family bound by common blood and property. The hearth is the visible reflection of family unity; it symbolizes the whole, undivided family unit.

It follows that it appears to us fully justified to point out with the appearance of the hearth, which in its part implies the formation of the dwelling and of the family, there also appeared domestic religion – "genotheism" – as a phenomenon linked to the consolidation of the family as social organization. Therefore, we can assume that the formation of domestic religion ("genotheism") in the Caucasus – and in particular in its southwestern region – dates back to the Neolithic, when there appear the first systematic settlements (Manning, 2008). This phenomenon achieves its completed form in the Eneolithic period, as we believe is reflected in materials from eastern Transcaucasian sites of the Shulavera-Shomu-Tepe Culture. It can also be assumed domestic deities would have appeared at the same time as objects of family cultic activities, since the dwellings of this period were of monogenetic composition. In later periods, however, the social collective was organized around the deity of fertility.

"Home" and "Shrine" in Ancient Georgia

The interrelation of the domestic cult and the tribal cult is of especial interest. The relevant data from Georgian ethnography is, we believe, rich and capable of telling us much. As the same time it should be noted that the ancient Near Eastern world has been well-studied from this angle, which enables us to examine Georgian data from a comparative standpoint.

Figure 2. Anthropomorphic figures from the monuments of the Eneolithic age discovered on the territory of Georgia

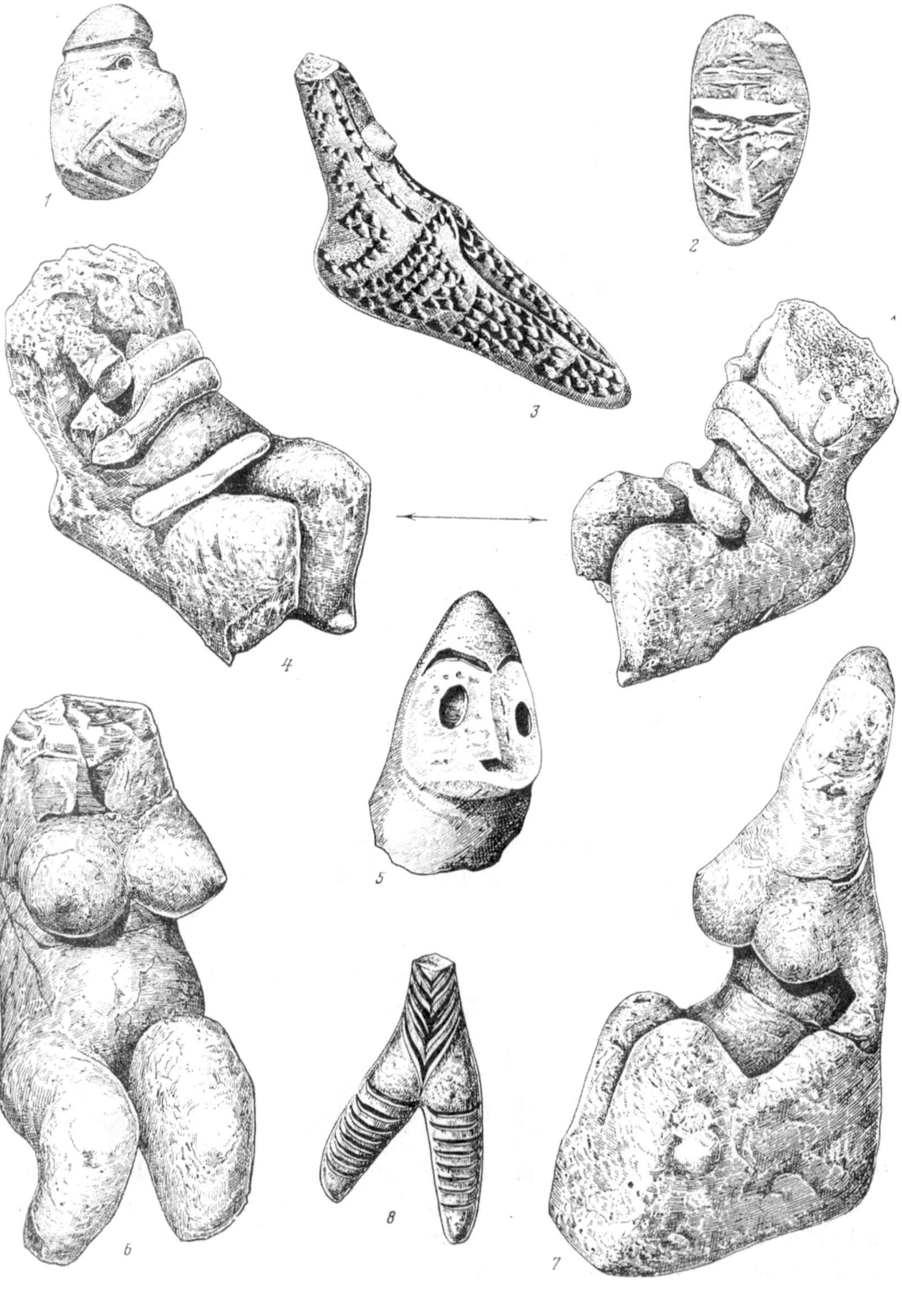

It is of particular importance to note the materials concerning the Hattic civilization, since some scholars have linked the Hattic language to the Northwest Caucasian family, and the Hattic ethnic group to the peoples of the Caucasus. The Hattic ethnic group would have existed in central Anatolia from the end of the 3rd millennium or the beginning of the 2nd millennium BC. It has been acknowledging that Hittite religion, a quite original and distinctive phenomenon, represented the synthesis of the religions of the Hittites and those peoples with whom they had been in contact. As a consequence, the Hittite pantheon contained not only the gods of the Indo-European tribes (Nesites, Luvians, Palaites) who had appeared relatively recently in central Asia Minor, but also those of the aboriginal peoples of central Anatolia, including the Hattians or Pre-Hittites. As many now acknowledge, the Hittite people resulted from the mixture and consolidation of Hattic and Indo-European tribes in the beginning of the 2nd millennium BC. Hittite religion was polytheistic, showing no traces of monotheism. It was oriented toward assuring, first of all, that people did not lose their relationship with nature, and fostering belief and awe in the face of supernatural powers. Each clan, even if it comprised only a small settlement, had its own divinity. In the temples of larger settlements and regional centers were images of several, sometimes dozens, of gods, which indicates the coexistence of these divinities. These idols "lived" primarily in temples, or else were set up in open-air cultic sites. An entire series of religious festivals was performed in the temples: monthly or annual, New-Year's, autumn or other types of ceremonies. The king and queen participated in these ceremonies, along with their chief retainers and temple officials. Besides local divinities, the Hittites also had "state gods".

A similar hierarchical arrangement of deities (neighborhood, village, clan, entire valley ...) appears in the highland Georgian (and pan-Caucasian) pre-Christian religious system. Each settlement or clan had its patron deity, its own sanctuary, as is confirmed, we believe, by Georgian archaeological and ethnographic data. Sites dating from the 15th-7th centuries BC have been found, which are extremely significant for the study of the spiritual culture of the ancient societies of eastern Georgia. Among them are the sanctuaries found at the settlements of Natsargora, Qatlanikhevi and Khovlagora, and the sanctuaries situated apart from the settlements at Melaani and Meli-Ghele, which have been described in detail by Acad. K. Pitskhelauri in his monographs (Pitskhelauri, 1973). In these chapter the author notes correctly that sanctuaries of similar structure are found in today's eastern Georgian highlands, with an elevated area in the center of which is situated the shrine. It can be said with confidence that despite the passage of three thousand years, the materials referred to above, along with ethnographic data, indicate spiritual and cultural continuity among the populations of this region.

A similar structure can be detected in the western Caucasian highlands. For example, according to ethnographic materials from Svaneti, each cultic building, which now bears the name of a saint introduced during the comparatively recent spread of Christianity to this region, was dedicated to the divine patron of a Svanetian clan composed of one or more lineages. The members of the clan, for their part, referred to themselves as the clan patron's "men" (*maral*).

In this respect the Upper Svanetian festival observed by us in the village Hadish in 1980 and 1984 (Svanetian multidisciplinary expedition, dir. Mikheil Chartolani) is of interest. Of the festivals celebrated in Hadish, that of Lichenish is the most important – for this reason, Svans refer to it typically as "Hadishoba". The festival is in honor of the male children born in the village each year, to assure their health and prosperity, and is expressed through the worship of "Hat-wearing St.George", and the presentation of new vassals into his service (Bukhrashvili, 2014). Families without sons also participate in the festival, in order to petition the shrine for the birth of male heirs. On the whole, the phenomenon of the shrine of

Lichenish is a clear example of the syncretism typical of Caucasian cultures in general, since along with the function of assuring fertility (in male children), the divinity is the patron of domestic and wild animals.

As a structural analogy to the Svan clan and its shrine, we can mention the Khevsur clan and its institution of shrine "vassalage" (*jvarisq'moba*). According to ethnographic data, each male Khevsur undergoes the "sac'uleoba" ritual, representing the "adoption" of the newborn male child (up to one-year-old) by the shrine deity. The naked baby is rolled under the banner (*drosha*) of the shrine three times. Only those who had undergone the "sac'uleoba" ritual could become full-fledged vassals, and possess a homestead on the clan lands under the patronage of the shrine.

We know that in the eastern Georgian highlands, each shrine deity or "child of God" has its own community of vassals (*saq'mo*), by which is meant the society grounded in unbroken tradition which has a common shrine with its divine patron. The vassals have a common legal code and foundation myth (*andrezi*); it follows from this that they have a common vision of their past, united by identical customs and norms of behavior. The community of vassals (*sa-q'm-o* < *q'ma* "vassal") has a designation similar to that of a brotherhood (*sa-dzm-o* < *dzma* "brother"); the morphology parallels their common semantics (Mamulia, 1979). Thus the shrine represents the symbol of the unity of the brotherhood as social unit founded on mythic and religious concepts.

The terms for "shrine" in the eastern Georgian highlands – *jvari* (lit. "cross") and *khat'i* (lit. "icon") – designate the patron deities of a given clan or tribe, as well as their earthly residence. It follows from this that the shrines are centers of local theocratic administration, with developed temple economies, including lands possessed by the shrines in the lowlands.

For example, of the twelve communes in the Aragvi valley which composed the traditional tribe of Pshavi, each has its own clan sanctuary with its complex of buildings and shrine lands, which represented the social and cultic centers of the commune. Besides clan shrines, each village in the commune had one or more local shrines, one of which was dedicated to the "place mother" (*adgilis-deda*) or "mother of God".

Alongside the commune sanctuaries there also existed shrines at which all Pshavians worshipped: Lasharis-Jvari at Khmelgora, the shrine to Tamar at Ghele, the K'viria shrine, and the Damast'e shrine by the Matura Valley.

From the examples just mentioned there can be deduced the entire hierarchical architectonics of the shrines of Pshavi. On the lowest, most local level are village-internal shrines, representing the unity of the village. On the next higher level are the communal shrines, and at the crown of the pyramid are the shrines common to the "Pshavian nest" (*bude pshavi*), the traditional homeland of the Pshavians.

SOLUTIONS AND RECOMMENDATIONS

The author believes it is possible to determine certain homologies between the hierarchical architectonics of the shrines of Svaneti and those of Pshavi. This will allow us to discuss similarities between the theocratic administrative systems of these two regions. It has also be established that family religion (genotheism), in the form of the cult of the "place mother" or the "angel of the foundation" in each family, was the foundation upon which evolved such relations. As for other regions in the eastern Georgian highlands, for example Mtiuleti, it had been demonstrated that here too, the village – as unit of settlement – is mostly composed of families from one lineage. This led to typical patronymic settlements, which evolved as a consequence of the segmentation of earlier family-based clans. Many such patronymic settlements possess a common defense tower, in which the inventory of the family cult was kept, and where common family festivals were celebrated. What is important is that common agricultural and economic interests, as expressed through the common ownership of different types of land. Mtiuleti and the valleys adjoining it, from the point of view of settlement structure, present the same sort of picture as do other Georgian regions.

FUTURE RESEARCH DIRECTIONS

It is worthy of special attention that, as is clarified by the analysis of archaeological and ethnographic materials, the given structure along the whole belt of Abkhazeti-Svaneti-Racha-Pshav-Khevsureti-Chechnia-Daghestan and a common religious-social structure characterizes this belt. This got its source from the familial cult, from "genotheism", which in the common Caucasian region is already established from the Eneolithic-Early Bronze period.

CONCLUSION

Within the designated location, the analysis of archaeological and ethnographic material collected on the territory of the central Transcaucasus (contemporary Eastern Georgia) has given us the possibility of making the following conclusions:

1. We consider it to be sufficient to warrant the supposition that at the dawn of world civilization, in human cognition, the hierarchical disposition of internal (domesticated) and external spaces, correspond to one another and on the basis of the unity of spatial differences of both occurred the sense of a single psychic background. Precisely this psychic background, this perception of these theo-psychic streams must have become subsequently the basis of religious world-view and general cosmology.

As we touch on the phenomenon of habitation and the perception of the spatial universe, we want once again to note, that the dividing of space into 'internal' and 'external' universes must have happened in ancient times, precisely in the period, when a social group took possession of its own agricultural and habitational territory. On the territory of the central Transcaucasus this stage must have happened in the period of germination and development of early agricultural culture. As is it considered that in this period the achieved level of productive forces aided the permanent dwelling in one spot and the increase in population.

Following from this we must conclude, that in the consciousness of tribes dwelling on the territory of the central Transcaucasus, the final formation of spatial division of the universe into two main parts, into the notions of 'interior' and 'exterior', chronologically, belongs to the end of the 6th millennium BCE and the beginning of the 5th millennium BCE.

2. In the habitation the hearth represents the center, heart, of the family, which unites by blood relation and by communal possessions the family as a social unit. The family, is one such totality united by material possessions and kinship relations, but the hearth is a visible, tangible representation of this unity; a united, indivisible symbol of the family.

We consider there to be warrant to suppose that as soon as there appeared the hearth, which in itself means the formation of the habitation and the family, familial religion appeared, genotheism; as a fully formed phenomenon of a social organism (the family). Already from the Neolithic period, when the first systematic settlements appear, in Caucasia we must suppose the formation of familial religion, genotheism. This phenomenon acquires a fully formed appearance in the Eneolithic period, which we think clearly is depicted in materials coming from the studied remains of settlements in the Eastern Transcaucasus ("Shulaveri-Shomuthepe" Culture).

The level of development of productive forces of the Patriarchal-Clan arrangement conditions the size of the family community. The naturally increased community (temi) gradually undergoes segmentation, is divided into a series of smaller familial communities, which time and again grow and in their turn again are divided up. The big [i.e. extended] family historically is a universal phenomenon. It is characteristic of almost every people and not only at a low level of development, but also later. Precisely in such a social unity, in the extended family, began from the earliest stage of development the formation of familial religion – "Genotheism"; more precisely its development began together with and alongside the development of the extended family, as a social organism and the development of familial religion ("Genotheism") began as the ideological basis of familial unity.

It is especially worthy of note that, as is clarified by the analysis of archaeological and ethnographic materials, the given structure along the whole belt of Abkhazeti-Svaneti-Racha-Pshav-Khevsureti-Chechnia-Daghestan and a common religious-social structure characterizes this belt. This got its source from the Familial cult, from "Genotheism", which in the common Caucasian region is attested already

3. If we consider the studied structure on the basis of ethnographic data of the family, we can suppose, that already in the period of the spread of the Kura-Araxes culture the extended ('big') family is in appearance by its dwellings, by its type of agricultural territory and settlement. In the following periods, almost up to today, the big family is attested in the life of the Caucasian peoples. We are far away from the contention, that the big family of the Kura-Araxes Cultural period is the direct ancestor of the big family studied in ethnographic life, but we think, that this primary social and kinship structure, which thereafter became a foundation for the social entity studied by ethnographer in the central Transcaucasus, in the period of the spread of Kura-Araxes culture already appears to have been worked out and fully developed.

REFERENCES

Baiburin, A. (1983). *Jhilishche v obrjadakh i predstavleniax vostochnix slavjan* [Dwelling in rites and performances of Eastern Slavs]. Leningrad: Nauka.

Buchraschwili, P. (2014). *Nicholas Marr – 150*. Tbilisi: Amirani.

Bukhrashvili, P. (2001). *Kartli and Kakheti in the last quarter of the 18th and beginning of the 19th centuries*. Tbilisi: Amirani.

Bukhrashvili, P. (2003). *For a delimitation of the place of the phenomenon of dwellings in the daily life and culture of the Georgian people in the past (An attempt at Paleo Ethnological study)*. Tbilisi: Amirani.

Bukhrashvili, P. (2005). *Sacxovrisi qartveli eris yofasa da kulturashi zvelad* [Dweling in the life and culture of the ancient Geirgians]. Tbilisi: Amirani.

Bukhrashvili, P. (2013)., House" in ancient Georgia. In *Proceedings of III international congress of Caucasiologists* (pp. 27-28). Tbilissi: Iv. Javakhishvili Tbilisi State University.

Bukhrashvili, P. (2014). *Saint George the great Knight*. Tbilisi: Amirani.

Carling, G., Cronhamn, S., Farren, R., Aliyev, E., & Frid, J. (2019). The causality of borrowing: Lexical loans in Eurasian languages. *PLoS One*, *14*(10), 1–33. doi:10.1371/journal.pone.0223588 PMID:31665148

Descola, P. (2017). ¿Humano, demasiado humano? / Human, Too Human? *Desacatos*, (54), 16–27. doi:10.29340/54.1737

Hodder, I. (2018). Things and the Slow Neolithic: The Middle Eastern Transformation. *Journal of Archaeological Method and Theory*, *25*(1), 155–177. doi:10.100710816-017-9336-0

Hu, D. (2013). Approaches to the Archaeology of Ethnogenesis: Past and Emergent Perspectives. *Journal of Archaeological Research*, *21*(4), 371–402. doi:10.100710814-013-9066-0

Ingold, T. (2019). Art and anthropology for a sustainable world. *Journal of the Royal Anthropological Institute*, *25*(4), 659–675. doi:10.1111/1467-9655.13125

Leaver, R. A. (2019). Die Lieder by Martin Luther [review]. *Notes*, *75*(4), 701–704. doi:10.1353/not.2019.0053

Mamulia, G. (1979). *Klasobrivi sazogadoebisa da saxelmcopos chamokalibeba Qartlshi* [The Emergence of Ckass Society and State in ancient Kartli (Iberia)]. Tbilisi: Mecniereba.

Manning, P. (2008). Materiality and Cosmology: Old Georgian Churches as Sacred, Sublime, and Secular Objects. *Ethnos: Journal of Anthropology*, *73*(3), 327–360. doi:10.1080/00141840802324011

Pitskhelauri, K. A. (1973). *Agmosavlet saqartvelos tomta istoriis ziritadi problemebi dzv. c XV-VII s.s* [Main issues of the history of tribes of Eastern Georgia (BC XV-VII cc)]. Tbilisi: Mecniereba.

Pollard, J. (2019). *The use and reuse of stone circles: fieldwork at five Scottish monuments and its implications*. Archaeological Journal; doi:10.1080/00665983.2019.1596354

Rama, T. (2013). Phonotactic Diversity Predicts the Time Depth of the World's Language Families. *PLoS One*, *8*(5), 1–9. doi:10.1371/journal.pone.0063238 PMID:23691003

Simon, Z. B. (2018). (The impossibility of) acting upon a story that we can believe. *Rethinking History*, *22*(1), 105–125. doi:10.1080/13642529.2017.1419445

Tsanava, A. (1992). *Qartuli Mitologia* [Georgian Mythology]. Tbilisi: Merani.

Tuite, K. (1999). On the etymology and earliest social significance of ts'ats'loba", Amirani. *Journal of the International Caucasologigal Research Institute*, *I*, 13–19.

Tuite, K. (2007). Dialect Change: Convergence and Divergence in European Languages/How New Languages Emerge. *Journal of Linguistic Anthropology*, *17*(2), 314–316. doi:10.1525/jlin.2007.17.2.314

Tuite, K. (2017). Love stories: Language, private love, and public romance in Georgia. *Journal of the Royal Anthropological Institute*, *23*(1), 216–217. doi:10.1111/1467-9655.12576

Zakhariuk, O. (1977). O ponjatii, fact" v arxeologicheskoi hauke [On the concept of "fact" in archaeological science]. *Sovetskaja Arkheologia.*, *4*, 21–27.

KEY TERMS AND DEFINITIONS

Genotheism: Phenomenon linked to the consolidation of the family as social organization.

Georgiy Spiridonovich Chitaya: (Georgian გიორგი ჩიტაია; 10 [23] November 1890, Poti —1986, Tbilisi. Georgia) Georgian ethnographer, academician of the Academy of Sciences of the Georgian SSR (1969), founder of the Tbilisi Ethnographic Open-Air Museum. He studied the ethnogenesis, material and spiritual culture of Georgians and other peoples of the Caucasus.

Mtiuleti: (Georgian: მთიულეთი; literally, "the land of mountains") is a historical province in eastern Georgia, on the southern slopes of the Greater Caucasus Mountains. It primarily comprises the White Aragvi Valley, and is bordered by Gudamakari on the east, Khando on the south, Tskhrazma on the west, and Khevi on the north.

Nicholas Yakovlevich Marr: (Russian: Никола́й Яковлевич Марр, Nikolay Yakovlevich Marr; Georgian: ნიკოლოზ იაკობის ძე მარი, Nikoloz Iak'obis dze Mari; 6 January 1865 [O.S. 25 December 1864] – 20 December 1934) was a Georgia-born historian and linguist who gained a reputation as a scholar of the Caucasus during the 1910s before embarking on his "Japhetic theory" on the origin of language (from 1924), now considered as pseudo-scientific, and related speculative linguistic hypotheses.

Pshavi: (Georgian: ფშავი) is a small historic region of northern Georgia, nowadays part of the Mtskheta-Mtianeti mkhare, ("region"), and lying chiefly among the southern foothills of the Greater Caucasus mountains along the Pshavis Aragvi River and the upper reaches of the Iori River in the neighbouring region of Tianeti to the south-east.

Svaneti or Svanetia: (Suania in ancient sources; Georgian: სვანეთი Svaneti) is a historic province of Georgia, in the northwestern part of the country. It is inhabited by the Svans, an ethnic subgroup of Georgians.

Tamar the Great: (Georgian: თამარ მეფე) (c. 1160 – 18 January 1213) reigned as the Queen of Georgia from 1184 to 1213, presiding over the apex of the Georgian Golden Age. A member of the Bagrationi dynasty, her position as the first woman to rule Georgia in her own right was emphasized by the title mepe ("king"), afforded to Tamar in the medieval Georgian sources.

Vakhtang Ilyich Kotetishvili: (Georgian. ვახტანგ ილიას ძე კოტეტიშვილი, October 24, 1893, Georgia - January 17, 1937) folklorist, essayist, literary critic, critic, historian, artist, scholar, sculptur journalist and public figure. Ancestor of Georgian folklore.

Chapter 15
Housing Consumption:
A Territorial Analysis of Housing Market Drivers

Joao Lourenço Marques
https://orcid.org/0000-0003-0472-2767
GOVCOPP, DCSPT, University of Aveiro, Portugal

Paulo Batista
https://orcid.org/0000-0001-5544-298X
GOVCOPP, DCSPT, University of Aveiro, Portugal

Eduardo Anselmo Castro
https://orcid.org/0000-0001-9017-5098
GOVCOPP, DCSPT, University of Aveiro, Portugal

Arnab Bhattacharjee
Heriot-Watt University, UK

ABSTRACT

Housing is more than a living space; it represents a social status capable of promoting several forms and levels of socialization and segregation. Housing is characterized by a set of attributes and functions that are valued differently, in which the consumption of "good housing" is made considering the preferences of their attributes, perceived tangibly/intangibly by the consumers. The reciprocal relation between housing and space, and the lack of structured information capable of apprising the key drivers of such dimensions increase the complexity of understanding the rational mechanisms of evaluating the real housing value. Despite the challenges associated with the modelling of housing markets, urban studies and spatial econometric literature provide a broad (but unfinished) theoretical framework and practical tools that are able to describe, understand, and predict households' housing consumption. Thus, the aim of this chapter is to present concepts and techniques to rationally capture individual and collective housing preferences, and the way in which they interact.

DOI: 10.4018/978-1-7998-3115-0.ch015

Copyright © 2020, IGI Global. Copying or distributing in print or electronic forms without written permission of IGI Global is prohibited.

INTRODUCTION

As an economic good, housing can be clearly distinguished from other goods and services. There are two main sources of this uniqueness. First, housing is both a consumption and an investment good (Henderson & Ioannides, 1983; Arrondel & Lefebvre, 2001). Broadly speaking, the literature in this area emphasizes that, absent institutional constraints and frictions, the difference between the investment demand for housing and the consumption demand explains decisions to purchase houses for owner occupation and for renting out. In this chapter, we focus on housing consumption only and therefore abstract from this issue.

Second, houses embed important territorial characteristics that make them an important proxy for understanding consumer preferences and the way in which spatial structures are organized. This is the central issue we focus on. Then, this chapter analyses the role of an econometric framework applied to housing consumption analysis to provide useful insights about individual behaviours that lead to the emergence of complex territorial structures, both in terms of spatial patterns and spatial interdependence.

Different methodologies and techniques used to assess how households choose their residential locations, and which are the most valuable housing attributes that, in turn, affect house prices. Two main perspectives are typically adopted, stated and revealed preferences: the former, are based on surveys, while the latter, use spatial econometric methods to infer the weights of each attribute for the price formation. The literature points out advantages and disadvantages of using each of these strategies, and the option depends on the purpose of the work (Marques et al, 2010). If the availability of data is not a major constraint, the use of hedonic price models, which is very popular in urban economics domain to analyse the value of residential properties and their determinants (environmental aspects, infrastructures, services accessibility aspects, neighbourhood factors, etc.), has a strong potential for use, mainly to describe and understand potential drivers of spatial diffusion of housing consumption.

Hedonic methods are based on the principle that goods are not homogeneous and differ in numerous characteristics, and in the case of housing, a huge set of attributes can be considered as relevant information. However, the application of standard hedonic models suffers from some constraints, particularly because, the residuals, when applied in the context of housing market, contain systematic spatial information that is not captured by the regression model. To overcome some of these constraints, a variety of spatial econometric techniques has been developed with the aim of capturing the spatial structure of housing prices, in addition to the use of spatial variables. This chapter intends to systematise both the major theoretical challenges of modelling the housing market dynamics, focusing on the relevance of space in that context, and the more technical and analytical perspective, where methodological progresses in the spatial econometric literature to capture the role of space in housing market, are not accompanied by the theoretical developments in urban studies literature. Presenting the link between the conceptual and the empirical approach is assumed as a major challenge of this work. In short, this chapter allows a global understanding of: i) the role of market mechanisms in housing consumption; ii) the importance of econometric tools to identify consumption and territorial behaviour patterns; and iii) the multiple dimensions of the phenomena, described by a set of standard econometric approaches.

HOUSING CONSUMPTION AND THE MARKET

Housing plays an important role in developed countries with significant impacts in the overall economy and society; its significant multiplier effects (on employment, prices and consumption), its noteworthy impact on the growth of urban systems, and its impacts on household expenditures (representing the most valuable single asset owned by most individuals), are three reasons to justify the importance of the housing sector as a key driver of quality of life in modern societies (Marques, 2012; Streimikiene, 2015). As an economic good, housing consumption expenses represents 18% of the total final consumption expenditures of households in the EU and housing contributes about 30% to the EU's 2013 GDP (Gerstberger & Yaneva, 2013).

The process of choosing and moving to a residence to live is a relevant moment for households, strictly dependent on the needs associated with special life-cycle circumstances, such as: marriage, birth of children, divorce, death of a partner, entering or finishing stages in education or income changes, among other factors (Clark & Onaka, 1983). Thus, changes in the life conditions of the individual are determinant in housing consumption patterns.

In Western societies, and in Europe in particular, a consensus is established about important market failures that shapes the housing market mechanism, explaining the prevalent state interventions, at a level that Bourne (1981) describes as "*a large and increasing role in almost all aspects of housing production and consumption*". In fact, as the author argues, "*...governments act as financiers, insurers, regulators, speculators, administrators, builders, landlords, and frequently destroyers*" but, despite their apparently pervasive role, government interventions are usually pointed to as supportive of the efficient housing (ideal/free) market system rather than designed to substitute it. In fact, the more direct state interventions, such as the direct provision of houses (and social housing in particular) was reduced to minimum levels in recently years. In fact, Arnott (1987) concludes that in most contexts, the housing market acts essentially as a competitive market and the adoption of classical economics frameworks prevails as the key tools to analyse the housing market drivers that guide the decision-making processes, both of individuals and institutions. As a result, classical economics frameworks using econometrics techniques are widespread across the studies of housing consumption drivers, which justifies the adoption of this line of research and debate in the work presented here.

However, current research also acknowledges that housing markets are complex. Rather than being defined by a single combination of a quantity and a price, the market equilibrium for a heterogeneous good such as a house is given by the combination of a vector of hedonic characteristics with a vector of hedonic prices (Lancaster, 1966; Rothenberg et al., 1991). Hence, we generally have the coexistence of several submarkets, each corresponding to a different market equilibrium (Rothenberg et al., 1991) underlined by the spatial distribution of hedonic characteristics and hedonic prices. This heterogeneity, driven by supply rigidities and transaction costs, shapes the territory as landscapes of submarkets (Bhattacharjee et al., 2016).

Consumption and the Market Mechanism

A market, as pointed out by Stark & Clippinger (1999) and Thévenot (2001), can be described as a collective device that allows compromises to be reached, not only on the nature of the goods to produce and distribute, but also on the value to be given to them; this argument justifies why market prices and the mechanisms that ensure price formation behind different housing market conditions (housing price drivers) have been a well disseminated empirical effort in housing studies.

The conditions by which the exchanges (transactions) of goods and services between different individuals occur are usually assumed as a result of (individual) preferences. The key models of classic economics (namely the conception of a market of perfect competition, with its associated postulates) (re-)emerges today, as an unwavering reference framework. These core models are based on a set of postulates about the "*psychosocial*" characteristics of the agents (selfish, rational, totally informed), a behaviour guided by an exercise of maximisation of the individual benefits (utility), defined through its participation in market exchange. Following this theoretical framework, the free-market mechanism, despite its possible distortions, failures and externalities is viewed as a process of auto-regularization of consumption and production. The value assigned by each individual is used in the exchange process, in which, assuming an instantaneous mechanism of information flow - low or zero transaction costs (North, 1984), translated on a equilibrium value accomplished to the exchange.

Value concept plays an important role to understand the consumption drivers of a good. Brown (1984) identifies value as resulting from a multi-dimensional notion. First, the author highlights that value arises from a conceptual realm that translates the preferences for specific "*physical*" qualities of the commodities, which match abstract, moral and immaterial conceptions. Second, a circumstantial aspect arises as a relational realm: since value is assigned in specific contexts (including specific spatial locations), the subject is aware of the existence of the commodity within a set of possibilities. Finally, the objective realm of value emerges from the confrontation, in a given context, of the commodity in the face of a set of constraints: its utility, its eventual scarcity and the individual's budget constraints.

Housing Value and the Economics Framework

The previous reference to the concept of value and the definition of the market, as well as to the focus of the economic analysis in the study of its mechanisms, serves here to underline the role of the market price as a reference of the value of the housing consumption in contemporary societies.

The refinement of classical economic models has been assumed as a major framework for (empirical) studies on housing consumption drivers. New analytical techniques, as will be detailed later, allow us to easily obtain i) the identification of the elements (attributes) that drive housing consumption, and ii) the relevance (weights) of those elements, as they are codified in the market and can be recovered from a market analysis perspective.

Moreover, most recent modelling advances fix the housing market specificities, as we see later, and are mostly concerned with the leading role of territorial attributes as major drivers of housing prices, making modern economic models on housing drivers more reliable through the analysis of market prices.

Two major frameworks are usually followed in empirical attempts: a macro and a microeconomic approach; here, the emphasis will be on the microeconomic strategy, as it focuses on the individual agents' behaviours and thus it will be more suited to answer research questions about the individuals' drivers of housing consumption.

Behind this microeconomic approach are mostly the theoretical ideas of the "*marginalist school*" (Lengwiler, 2009) of economics, which introduced postulates about the general individual's behaviour (the "homo economicus") with economic reasoning grounded in mathematical modelling and a "*mechanistic*" and "*deterministic*" quantitative approach to the market analysis (Waterman, 2003). This theoretical background combined with the dominant philosophical approach to scientific research (positivist, reductionist) constituted the necessary ingredients for the origin of empirical benchmarks based on mathematical formalism, the econometrics approach.

The development of econometric tools applied to microeconomics (the phenomena related with the individuals' behaviour), led to two empirical approaches: i) structural models and ii) the models in their reduced form (Sims, 1986) which are used to analyse the value assigned through a conceptual market mechanism. As mentioned by the author, the two approaches are methodological variations that allow the different research issues and the availability of resources to be accommodated (data or computational capacity, for example). They differ in the greater or lesser detail with which the socio-economic mechanisms are described through mathematical language. Therefore, here the more flexible and widespread *reduced form* framework will be followed.

Being based on the definition of a wide set of theoretical propositions about the market conditions, rules and agent behaviours, makes it less demanding on both data and mathematical devices. After all, the framework focuses on the selection of a representative set of determining factors in the formation of market prices (general drivers, from both demand and supply) as well as general mathematical specification about the relation between these set of elements and the transaction price. However, models in their reduced form have their own limitations and do not help, unequivocally, to specify the individual's interaction mechanisms themselves, since they are established on a theoretical and aggregated (agent) level; moreover the price drivers are mostly recovered through statistical summarization of market data (Timmins & Schlenker, 2011). Another point highlighted by the authors is the possible source of errors that arise from erroneous assumptions on the connection between the theory; for example, the theoretical choice of relevant drivers of market prices) and the model specification (how they will be measured in empirical applications).

Following the usefulness of reduced form modelling frameworks, most of the technical limitations have been partially overcome with recent efforts. In fact, the selection and specification of the relevant attributes are not only crucial to the reliability of the models but they are also the basis for understanding housing consumption preferences; as will be addressed in section 3, a remaining major challenge on this is related to the role of space in housing market drivers, for which a contribution to the debate will be presented.

The Characteristics of Housing as a (Market) Good

Housing can be defined as "(...) *the stock of houses, apartments, and other shelters that provide the usual residences of persons, families, and households*" (Adams et al., 2008), but it is much more than this; it is: i) a social or collective good, in which a certain minimum standard of housing is needed and should be available for all families, regardless of their ability to pay; ii) a package of services, which is related to its location (accessibility of jobs and amenities) and neighbourhood (parks, schools and social environmental) attributes; and iii) an economic good and sector, which is exchanged in a market, is part of the fixed capital stock and produces benefit and utility (Bourne, 1981).

As an economic good, housing can be clearly distinguished from other goods and services. Five major differences make houses somewhat special and different from other goods (Costa, Dentinho, & Nijkamp, 2010): the first is its durability; a building can last for many decades or even centuries and the land where the house is placed is permanent; the second is that being an expensive investment (the only good that is both a consumption good and an investment) it is the greatest asset of a lifetime for most individuals (many of them have to request bank financing in which the availability of credit and interest rates are important aspects helping to define the potential demand); the third important distinction is related to immobility, both location and intrinsic attributes are consumed jointly with the housing itself in a spatial fixity; fourth, when the location is taken into account, no two houses are exactly equal in terms of cost, space, location, and neighbourhood and thus the inhomogeneity caused by its multi-dimensionality is another specific housing characteristic; the fifth particular characteristic is the policy overlay, meaning that housing is subjected to several institutional regulations imposed by government at various levels; and finally, vi) housing is an economic good where the interlink of spatial externality effects and its valorisation plays an important role. There are of course goods on the market with some of these characteristics; however, housing is unique in its combination of them all (Batista, 2019; Marques, 2012).

Both characteristics and functions of houses are, directly or indirectly, closely associated with the notion of space and its distinct aspects – spatial heterogeneity, spatial dependences and spatial scale. Because qualitative differences in housing (use value), as well as quantitative price differences (transaction value), are not constant over space (where each location provides specific urban amenities), the relation between the housing market and how space is organised, both in terms of spatial patterns and spatial interactions, is a very important issue. These aspects (territorial expression and housing market) are reciprocally interlinked, in the sense that housing outcomes not only reflect but also shape social, economic and territorial differences. The acknowledgement that housing stock is impossible to detach from its location and neighbourhood context is clearly emphasised by Bourne (1981), who mentions that the relationships between housing and space are circular and cumulative, that is, housing is both cause and effect. Fingleton (2003) argues that characteristics of houses can be defined through the prism of space, namely: houses are a durable good in a fixed location: accordingly, houses within the same neighbourhood capture the value of shared amenities (the surroundings of houses). Different forms of spatial segmentation (spatial clusters) are easy observable, for example, houses within a neighbourhood tend to have similar structural characteristics (because they are usually built at the same time), which reinforces the homogeneity of locational context

Space has a strict influence on housing and vice versa, underlined in the following five points: i) no two houses are identical, particularly when location is taken into account; ii) each housing location provides specific urban amenities; iii) the value of housing depends on location (at the micro and macro scale) and this dependency changes over time; iv) mobility potential depends on housing location and on the accessibility to leisure and work places; and v) the way housing shows status depends on its internal characteristics and on its specific location. Stull (1975) proposed a taxonomy of housing attributes that combine physical properties with three major spatial-territorial elements: i) environmental and neighbourhood features (combining the surrounding morphological components with land uses patterns and socioeconomic aspects of neighbourhood residents) ii) proximity to locational amenities (usually translated as accessibility of the housing, measured by distance, travel time or costs, to a specific facility or land use, whether desirable or undesirable) and iii) provision of public services and characteristics (which includes the links to basic services such as water, electricity or collective transport networks and its costs). Following that, empirical microeconomic attempts to model agent behaviours in housing markets quickly shift to initial theoretical-quantitative approaches, where spatial-territorial dimensions are weakly represented, to a focus on modelling strategies where territoriality plays a major role in housing market price models (Barlow & Duncan, 1992). In fact, modelling housing prices through econometrics frameworks was one of the first branches of studies on "spatial econometrics" (Paelinck & Klaassen, 1979).

The role of housing in the economy (at the macro and micro level) and the importance of space (location) in the housing market, thus, justify a theoretical and methodological approach in which the most important and essential aspects of these interdependences are emphasized.

ANALYSIS OF THE MAJOR DRIVERS OF HOUSING CONSUMPTION

Housing is a heterogeneous good, the price of which depends on the valuation of several factors that vary in space and time and depend on preferences of individuals, as highlighted in the previous section. The multiplicity of factors involved ([(in)direct, (in)tangible, (sub)objective, short or medium term] and the interactions that occur between those factors require the development of analytical approaches able to describe and understand the dynamic of housing consumptions. Due to the lack of high-quality information and adequate tools to support decision-making, the housing market is considered imperfect and not fully transparent. The complex and multidisciplinary nature of the housing market thus justify the importance of data and models, either to understand the theoretical background of the mechanisms that determine the functioning of the market and its dynamics, or to provide the basis for the development of decision support tools and policy formulation and assessment.

Notwithstanding the enormous developments in analytical techniques and, in particular, in spatial econometrics techniques, there is great potential for progress both in the techniques and their application to the housing market analysis, more specifically on the drivers that determine their performance, where the behaviour of individuals and households has a crucial rule (Anselin, 2010; Pollakowski, 1995). It is relatively consensual that any kind of technical approach should follow an interdisciplinary perspective and an integrated structure capable of dealing with: (i) (un)available information; ii) the multidimensionality of the phenomena; iii) the high uncertainty to which the evolution of behaviours are subject; iv) the need to combine objective and subjective information; and v) the dynamics of collective perceptions, expectations and preferences, which are interdependent of exogenous factors (see spatial dependence and spatial heterogeneity below).

Regarding the information, or simple data, produced and used by the various actors directly or indirectly involved in the housing market, it can be divided into three categories: i) objective information of the demand (number of households, their disposable income and household structure); ii) objective information about the supply (quantitative and qualitative data of the existing housing stock and financial constraints); and iii) subjective information about the demand, corresponding to buyers' preferences, consumptions and expectations (Marques, 2012).

The more objective statistical information about general conditions of the housing market, the quantity and the quality of dwellings are typically provided by national institutes of statistics or by any other organism of public administration. Real estate agencies (individually or organized in groups) used to have their own housing database resulting from their business; however, the number and types of properties do not necessarily reflect housing stock. The (objective) information gathered by loan associations and mortgage banks can also be useful for the purpose of housing analyses.

Imagine that it was possible to present an exhaustive list of sources for housing (market) information, the conclusion would be the same as that which can now be drawn from the sample of sources presented above; almost all of the various types of sources suffer from a lack of information which, according Pollakowski (1995), can diverge in the following types of features: i) measure of property value (transition price, asking price or estimated values); ii) quality of housing characteristics (number of data items:

structural characteristics, seller and buyer characteristics, financing, and length of time on market); iii) location details (address, census track, city, suburban or rural); iv) completeness; v) representativeness (sample size); and vi) length of time covered and frequency (time series to analyse the housing market dynamic).

Regarding the more subjective data, two major strategies to collect and analyse housing consumption behaviour through econometric tools can be considered, classified as revealed preference and stated preference strategy (Timmermans et al., 1994). The former is based on the collection of real market data, where consumers reveal their appreciation of the various attributes associated with housing, through directed observation of each effective act of purchasing, the market price and the characteristics of house transacted. The latter, stated preference method, is based on a simulation of the market in a way that the fictitious consumers will accurately and truthfully state their willingness to pay for additional units of the commodity. This strategy uses surveys on individuals (or a sample of it) to assess the preferences for various attributes that characterize a house. Also called contingent valuation methods, this type of approach simulates market scenarios rather than actual situations; therefore, they record stated or intended measures of willingness to pay under hypothetical conditions.

However, several other formal and informal models can be found in the literature which are able to describe, understand and predict housing market behaviour, in its various dimensions.

Based on Power (2008) and Holsapple (2008) a taxonomy of decision support systems (DSS) is proposed, following efforts of authors in other works (Marques et al., 2018), which covers the various dimensions and requirements mentioned above. In a highly simplified way, three types or levels can be assumed, depending on the information they use and the type of answers that can be obtained: i) situational (diagnostic); ii) forecast (projection); and iii) interactive (foresight).

- [Level 1] Situational or Diagnostic DSSs – these aim to gather and systematize a set of variables, translated into socio-economic and territorial indicators to capture the dynamics of a specific phenomenon. Many models could be included in this category, but in the context of housing consumption, hedonic models have been assumed as a powerful method of estimating the demand for a good and more specifically to understand, in a logic of revealed preferences, which attributes are relevant in explaining housing prices, as well as their spatial distribution and interactions.
- [Level 2] Forecast or Projection DSSs – these are based on rigorous analytical formalisms that allow anticipation of decisions that respond to the evolution of an expected future. This category includes time series extrapolation models, in which their feasibility depends on the availability of information about the past (sufficiently long and representative time series) and the assumption that this evolution is subordinated to a pattern that can be extrapolated to the future (parameters are constant or have a constant evolutionary trend) and there are no exogenous variables capable of significantly changing the evolution of the time series.
- [Level 3] Interactive or Foresight DSSs – these have a more complex and interdisciplinary nature. The models developed here provide a systematic mechanism for dealing with the interdependence and subjectivity of information, thus contributing to the formulation of policies where the integration of multidisciplinary activities is of vital importance – multiple-criteria decision analysis is an example of a technique that can be used to capture decision maker's stated preferences.

The models presented in this section, the econometric hedonic models plus their spatial counterparts (spatial econometric models (Paelinck & Klaassen, 1979), are included in the first category (DSS Level 1), and typically are able to capture the subjectivity of housing consumption preferences (revealed), and their patterns and interdependence across the territory. The origin of hedonic models, associated with composite goods analysis, goes back to Lancaster's (1966) theory of consumption; they were first applied to the housing market by Rosen (1974) to assess the determinants of housing prices. Hedonic pricing model continue to be actively used in housing studies and the literature at this level is quite diverse (see Batista, 2019; Marques, 2012 as examples where different applications of hedonic models were developed). The major challenge to this framework is the integration of territorial attributes (Freeman, 1979; Straszheim 1974) .

General Challenges of Housing Market Analysis

The standard motivation of spatial econometric hedonic models is to show a credible causal relationship between housing prices and a set of attributes observed in the market, expressing the best explanatory power of the value of a dwelling, given by the following formulation:

$$Y = f(X, \beta) + \varepsilon \qquad (1)$$

Where: Y is a vector of the housing value (euros per m^2); β are vectors of hedonic prices, reflecting the weight of attributes in housing price explanation, X is the matrix that quantifies the attributes of dwellings (related to their intrinsic and their location characteristics); and ε is the vector that represents the stochastic component. This model specification relies on the observation of market outputs (market transaction prices) and their relation to a set of attributes, describing the individual good itself and the willingness to pay for a specific set of attributes. Several specifications to model the relationship between selling (or rent) price and the characteristics of dwellings can be found in the literature, from additive (linear form) to multiplicative (logarithmic form). Theory provides no clear guidance for the selection of a specific model; however, following Bhattacharjee et al. (2012), it is reasonable to assume a small modification to the semi-log form, where logarithm of price per square metre of living space is regressed on the logarithm of house area, constrained by several other hedonic housing characteristics.

The inclusion of relevant variables in the model is crucial; nevertheless, even if all the tangible housing characteristics are considered, the model may have problems of specification when the spatial dimension is ignored or not modelled properly. Typically, spatial effects are represented by location attributes (such as neighbourhood characteristics) or distances to any kind of urban amenities, but also may arise from a combination of spatial heterogeneity and spatial dependence (Anselin, 1988).

The reasoning behind the model, expressed by equation 1 above, is that the mechanisms to explain the housing prices are homogeneous over space and do not interact with each other; however, this assumption is far from true. Across different neighbourhoods, housing attributes are valued in diverse manners by consumers and externalities (positive or negative) may occur on the housing (hedonic) price formulation. In short, spatial heterogeneity in housing market analysis is justified because is fair to assume that there is a declining pattern of prices with distance from the centre (consumers prefer to be close to the major centralities) and there is a spatial variation of some dwelling characteristics reflecting any kind of supply constraint (size for instance); and spatial dependence or spatial autocorrelation, implies that (hedonic) prices of nearby houses or spatial units tend to be similar than houses located further away – a kind of spatial spillover or a form of contagion effect. Both, spatial heterogeneity and autocorrelation are issues of bias and loss of efficiency addressed in the estimation of hedonic models. The use of spatial econometric models to address these two types of spatial effect is becoming increasingly standard and at the same time is challenging.

Spatial Housing Market Preferences and Housing Consumption

Statistics have a long history as a tool to describe patterns of geographic data. The origins of quantitative approaches in different social sciences (and even natural sciences, such as epidemiology) go back the mid-19th century, in the seminal study of the spread of cholera in London. Combining statistics with geography allowed it to be concluded that the mechanism of spread of the cholera disease was not explained by air transportation of microorganisms (the explanation advanced by scientific dominant theory at that time), but by the ingestion of contaminated water. That conjecture was sustained by the observation of the spatial structure of data, namely the analysis the location of infected individuals and the locations of drinking water wells, suggesting a close relation between these two dimensions. This kind of geographical analysis provided accurate explanations of different phenomena and led to the development of the subfield of spatial statistics.

These quantitative efforts were concerned mostly with the development of measures of spatial dependence, focusing on the statistical relations between georeferenced objects in the geographic space. One of the most recognized results was presented as the Moran's I statistic, later updated by Getis & Ord (1992) – both can be considered important contribution to spatial analysis and are extensively used today. Univariate statistical (spatial) measurements of dependence are useful, but not a sufficient effort to understand spatial dynamics. In the late '60s, accompanying the increasing availability of microdata (and georeferenced data at small geographic scales), econometricians collected evidence that an increasing amount of data did not, if spatial properties of data are ignored, lead to increased efficiency of the standard econometric models. Following that hypothesis, Paelinck & Klaassen (1979) defended an approach which draws upon spatial theory for various branches of economy and geography; these efforts to explicitly incorporate spatial processes in econometrics are usually considered as the foundation of a new sub-field of applied economy, called spatial econometrics. This new discipline emerged with the aim of incorporating theoretical insights into specifying spatial structures in econometrics analysis.

Recent research (Batista, 2019; Corrado & Fingleton, 2012; LeSage & Pace, 2014; Marques, 2012) highlights the crucial role of space in housing market analyses and its relevance to understanding households' preferences and decisions; however, space itself is very complex to model, both spatial heterogeneity and spatial dependence.

1. Spatial heterogeneity

Spatial homogeneity, as mentioned before, is a strong assumption in the hedonic housing price context; if not analysed conveniently, it can be a potential source of specification errors. Spatial heterogeneity occurs when a territorial segmentation exists in the housing market and, therefore, hedonic prices associated with different attributes are not constant over space (Basu & Thibodeau, 1998). In the context of the model expressed in equation 1, spatial heterogeneity implies that the vector of regression coefficients remains stable within specified subareas but varies across different subareas (i).

$$Y_i = f(X_i, \beta_i) + \varepsilon_i \tag{2}$$

The recognition of housing segmentation and the argument that caution should be exercised when interpreting the results of standard hedonic models was identified early in the literature [e.g. (Duncan Maclennan, 1977)]. Five reasons emphasise the importance of the defining housing sub-markets or housing preferences segmentation in house price modelling: i) as already mentioned, it increases the prediction accuracy of the prediction of the statistical hedonic models, avoiding bias and errors in standard estimations; ii) it enables researchers to better understand the spatial variation in housing prices; iii) it improves lenders' and investors' abilities to price the risk associated with financing homeownership; iv) it reduces search costs to housing consumers; and finally, v) in many cases adequate treatment of spatial heterogeneity could considerably reduce the presence of spatial dependence effects, even though the two problems are theoretically distinct.

Housing is by its nature a heterogeneous good, characterized by a diverse set of attributes, in which no two houses are exactly the same; however, it is possible to find dwelling units in a specific territory that can be viewed (more or less) as perfect substitutes by the households, in which households can be satisfied by a set of different dwellings with similar attributes (both intrinsic and extrinsic). In this case dwellings compete with one another as alternatives for the demanders of housing space (Galster, 1996; Pryce, 2013). This argument places the concept of substitutability of housing units in line with spatial heterogeneity.

Despite the argument that housing submarkets should be adopted as a working framework, some ambiguity remains about how to deal with this issue. The early empirical works on submarkets tended to be segmented into two major perspectives: i) those studies that adopt a *supply side determinant*, focusing on the similarity of structural internal dwelling attributes and the neighbourhood characteristics (Maclennan & Tu, 1996; Watkins, 2001); and ii) those that focus on *demand side determinants*, such as on household incomes or other demographic and socioeconomic characteristics that result in distinct subgroups of demand (Allen, Springer, & Waller, 1995). The combination of these two perspectives reflects a territorial segmentation of willingness to pay for different housing attributes (tastes and preferences), hedonic price vector (β i).

In which condition are these approaches equivalent? The answer is, not always. It is possible to envisage situations where: i) homogeneity in hedonic characteristics does not imply a close substitutability, for example, in the situation where two locations with similar houses, inhabited by two different social groups (young qualified professionals and middle-aged middle classes), it is expected that different tastes and different responses to fashion will generate a local branding effect; and ii) heterogeneity in hedonic characteristics can imply a close substitutability; for example, in a situation where two houses with very different hedonic characteristics can be good substitutes – a flat in the centre or a house on the outskirts (Bhattacharjee et al., 2016).

Thus, as the housing market is segmented and structured by a complex spatial pattern, different social groups with specific interests, preferences and economic capabilities tend be organized into distinct territorial clusters. The literature points to two economic reasons to justify the formation of submarkets: i) the weak competition, resulting from the inelasticity of housing demand and supply across different locations; and ii) a general demand spatial discontinuity pattern, where individuals reveal different preferences in different locations, while remaining within the same spatial submarket.

Housing segmentation or spatial heterogeneity can also be classified into discrete heterogeneity and continuous heterogeneity. The former consists of a pre-specified set of spatially distinct units, between which model coefficients and other parameters are allowed to vary. This type of specification will be easily performed assuming that spatial units can be defined *a priori* following specific methodologies, for instance, the use of traditional administrative boundaries, or expert knowledge. An alternative specification, to avoid the uncertainty of geographic boundaries, is grounded on statistical models which address a continuous heterogeneity specification. In this approach, the regression coefficients are allowed to change over the geographic space in a continuous model specification which combines the regression model with a model for spatial regimes in its parameters. In this case, a set of multivariate techniques (regression, ANOVA, factorial and cluster analysis) can be applied to aggregate units with similar characteristics in order to find groups where the principle of substitutability can arise. For a detailed review of the attempts between the use of econometric frameworks to analyse housing markets and the need to ensure the multi-dimensionality of space, see Batista (2019) and Marques (2012) for a further discussion.

2. Spatial Dependence

Spatial dependence was observed and analysed early in housing market studies (Can, 1990; Cubbin, 1970; Kain & Quigley, 1975). In a broader sense it emerges by the degree to which objects at some location in geographic space are similar in some way to other objects or activities located nearby. In the context of the housing market, this occurs when the value of a dwelling and the preferences for a set of housing attributes are influenced by neighbourhood characteristics. Extending the arguments of equation 1, the price *Y* is not only explained by its own associated housing characteristics (X), but also by the characteristics of neighbouring properties. The weight matrix (W) represents the way in which the influence of the neighbourhood is considered (Anselin, 1988, 1995).

$$Y= \rho W_1 Y+\beta X+ \lambda W_2 \varepsilon+ \mu$$

$$\text{with } \mu \sim N(0, \sigma^2 I) \qquad (3)$$

The sources of observed spatial dependence can be provided by four major explanations:

- … it is a part of the observed agglomeration structures in the geographic space; specifically, in a housing development process, it is well known that a great number of housing development projects occur at the same time at specific locations, which leads to housing characteristics being highly correlated.
- … it can arise from the geometric and dimensional framework used to measure it; the standard Euclidian geometrical reference to analyse spatial data can result in modelling bias, caused by a spatial heterogeneity which is not well fixed. Moreover, specifying a true spatial dependence structure potentially means considering another geometrical and dimensional framework or an approach which minimizes that assumption.
- … it can result from a model misspecification or the lack of precision of georeferentiation; missing important variables, an unsuitable functional form and the spatial aggregation of data samples are major examples of this drawback which leads to spatial autocorrelation.
- … it also arises from the valuation process, as the transaction price agreed between buyers and sellers will affect the price of the surrounding area; especially where a comparison method is used – which is very common in the residential real estate industry.

The first two points recall the previous discussion on spatial heterogeneity, that is, the importance of the adopted a geometric reference framework. Following the general interpretation of Tobler's first law [of geography] – TFL – (Sui, 2004; Tobler, 2004), houses that are close in some geometric reference are likely to have similar attributes and prices; a high spatial autocorrelation will then be an intrinsic characteristic of that data. Recognizing this phenomenon (Chudik et al., 2011) define it as strong spatial dependence and show that it can be fixed through the expansion of standard models with spatial-specific regressors [see Arnab Bhattacharjee & Holly, 2013 for further discussion of the conceptual distinction between strong and weak dependence and their link with the spatial weights matrix].

Part of the specification challenges described above can be partially solved considering dummy variables (Wooldridge, 2008) as additional repressors using: i) binary dummy variables, describing whether an observation will be inside or outside of a previously defined spatial-territorial unit, which should be interpreted as a proxy to fix the effects of all (hidden) characteristics of the agglomerative structure; or ii) slope dummy variables, combining the information of the spatial unit and the value of the other attributes in the model, giving a more accurate model specification of heterogeneity [this was the framework adopted, for example, by Batista (2019) and Marques (2012)]. These auxiliary spatial variables not only provide an integrated framework to specify the spatial heterogeneity (and submarkets) in the same equation model setting, but will also potentially mitigate the strong spatial dependence usually found within the homogenous spatial structures.

As mentioned before, the spatial weights matrix plays a crucial role in capturing spatial dependence. Typically, spatial models are defined as functions of arbitrary topological (first order) geographic space, determined *a priori* by the researcher. Different measurements of spatial weights can be assumed, spatial contiguity and geographic distances, as represented in Figures 1.

Figure 1. Topological spatial relations used in standard W specifications: contiguity and distances

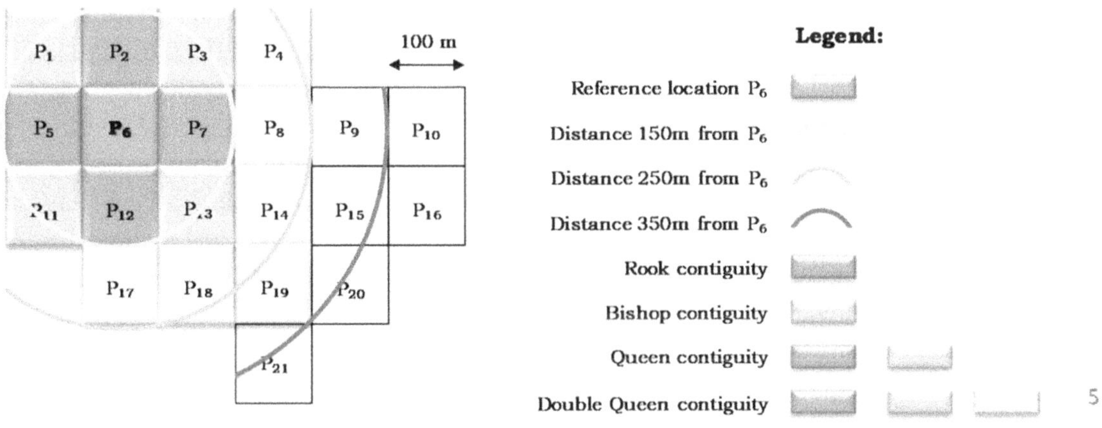

Holding for now the specification of W and assuming that all heterogeneity effects are fixed (plus that time dependence effects are also fixed), an *a priori* strategy for specific spatial dependence follows different economic interpretations. It is possible to consider effects on all model components: on dependent, independent or even on the unobservable stochastic component of the econometrics model; see Elhorst (2014) for a detailed analysis of all possibilities (see Figure 2).

Figure 2. Specifications of spatial dependence models (Adapted from Elhorst, 2014)

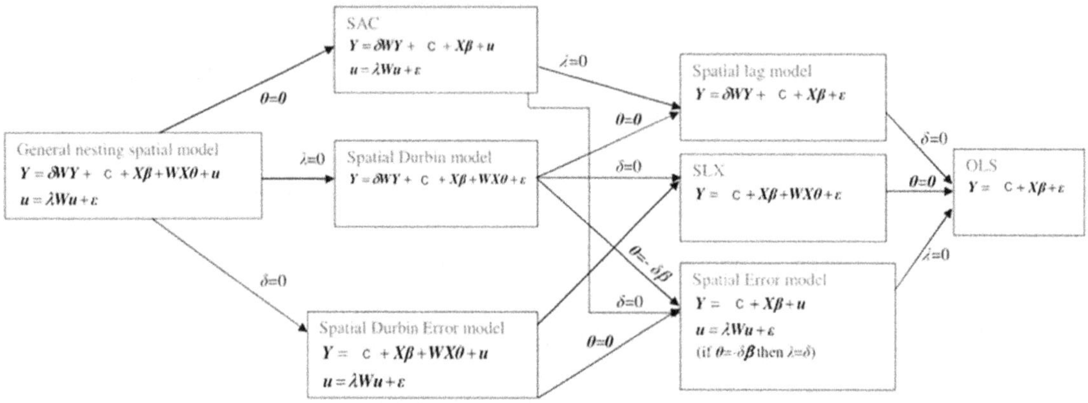

Each kind of possibility described in the previous figure arises from specific economic theoretical interpretations. Although there is some conceptual confusion and a lack of guidelines, the debate within spatial econometrics focuses on three major types of interaction effects. Elhorst (2014) describes its mathematical-statistical model specification in a cross-section data framework, plus some examples about its economic interpretation.

As noted by Anselin (1999, 2002) the usual debate of econometricians has been focused on a choice between spatial lag or spatial error models, but statistical inference efforts to guide this choice are very few; in fact, these specification choices are concerned mostly with theoretical assumptions. The choice of a spatial lag model setting usually assumes that spatial interactions are explicitly revealed by market mechanisms: the (average) outcome (housing price) for a territorial unit j is achieved through its relationship with the outcome observed in all other territorial units. This interpretation restricts territorial interactions to some kind of invisible hand economic mechanism which governs the territorial system. On the other hand, the spatial error model is concerned with an understanding of spatial dependence as a proxy to an underlying mechanism. In the literature, these kinds of phenomena are usually described as shocks – exogenous (to the market) mechanisms which may not be only economically driven, but a proxy between economic phenomena with social, environmental or, in general, territorial dimensions.

LeSage (2014) examines the usual specification choice challenges within regional economic empirical efforts and argues that researchers should focus on two specification alternatives: the spatial Durbin model, advocated for theoretical assumptions related with a global spillover mechanism behind spatial issues or the spatial Durbin error model advocated for the assumption of local spillover mechanisms.

The different types of spillovers are somewhat artificial. Indeed, the author suggests that the global spillover specification is usually chosen when the focus is mainly on economic behaviour, where economic adjustments are assumed following a well-known spatial structure: its effects are incorporated directly in market drivers. Local spillovers embrace economic relations which are imposed by a specific geographic structure as they "*involve only neighbours, but not higher-order neighbours (…) [nothing] that neighbours need not be defined as only regions in close physical proximity*" (LeSage, 2014,). This implicitly assumes that the "local" is the proxy to an assumption of a spatial structure which is exogenous to market determinants: the definition of proximity follows the generic definition of the TFL of geography – assuming the geographic space is an exogenous container of economic phenomena. In conclusion, the spatial Durbin error model specification is oriented to an economic model which is highly sensible to the spatial structure behind it: it assumes economic phenomena take place in a spatial-territorial structure eventually defined by non-economic drivers, which justifies the inclusion of the spatial error model specification in addition to the spatial lag of independent variables. Jointly, all of these insights support the choice of a spatial error model to investigate the nature of space that overlaps standard econometric models.

Despite its usually low interest from a mathematical-econometric perspective, the specification of the geometrical properties of interactions is very relevant for researchers: it is the most important assumption to understand the spatial phenomena incorporated in the different specification spatial econometric models.

Two main problems, related to the geographic nature of the problem, are identified by Arnott (1987): i) the underlying geographic processes are frequently non-stationary and have complex spatial dependence structures; ii) datasets frequently contain relatively few observations, with only one realization of the process, complicated by acute boundary effects.

In fact, a close look at the nature of W raises an important question: what are the drivers of the spatial interaction structure (W)? Usually W is defined *a priori* (Figure 1), focusing on answering econometrics and statistical problems to ensure the consistency of model estimations, for instance, to achieve stationary conditions of all parameter estimators, obtained through standard techniques (Elhorst, 2014).

The choice of W in econometrics is usually driven by model specification issues, trying to reach to a desirable predictive capacity or the improvement of the estimation power of the model. In fact, they do not have a primary interest in the role of the spatial configuration of territoriality. But it is important to notice that, according LeSage (2014), the idea that the inferences of parameters are sensitive to the use of a particular weight matrix "*is perhaps the biggest myth about spatial regression models*". As demonstrated by the authors, "*most variants of W would likely share common elements, and this often makes the results from the various W more similar than different. If the estimates and inferences are not all that sensitive to the specific weight matrix used, it is difficult to see how current economic theory can shed light on a specific "ideal" weight matrix*". One important source of the myth behind the key role of W in model sensitiveness is empirical works focused on observation-level approaches and the inferences from spatial regression models. LeSage & Pace (2009) argue against these approaches in order to analyse the role of W; the standard regression model and its interpretation is to summarize measures of the direct, indirect and total average effects on the dependent variables – which is usually the point of econometricians, rather than to fine tune guided by goodness-of-fit strategies. In fact, the exogenous effects on disturbances are usually oriented to guarantee low signal-to-noise settings, instead of interest in an exogenous (to the economic phenomena under study) mechanism of spatial dependence expected by economic theory.

However, there is usually very little formal evidence supporting such choices (Anselin, 2002), and wrong conclusions may be drawn, mainly because interaction between objects (dwelling or spatial units) often cannot be explained by observed measures of distance and thus, fixed and arbitrary spatial weights matrices might not be an adequate procedure. Spatial structures (spatial interactions and also spatial patterns) are driven by tangible and intangible factors, and thus, do not necessarily conform to physical concepts of distance or contiguity. Space is potentially anisotropic, heterogeneous and multidimensional, where objects tend to deform space and change the action of the field of forces, extending, shrinking or even annihilating distances. Therefore, the choice of methodologies based purely on bi-dimensional Euclidean space and based on fixed structures appears to be questionable.

Given the ambiguities regarding measurement of spatial weights, and in line with the notion of multidimensional non-Euclidean space, potentially driven by factors which are different from geographic distance or contiguity, the spatial weights matrix (W) can be considered as an unknown, and under certain assumptions is possible to be estimated (Batista, 2019; Bhattacharjee et al., 2012; Marques, 2012) where new methodologies to assess spatial spillovers were developed and applied to the urban housing market of Aveiro.

The most important argument behind the distinction between the notion of two-bi-dimensional Euclidean and multidimensional non-Euclidean space (and somewhat responsible for it) is the way that space is structured and analysed. And in line with Henri Poincare (1895) space is characterised as a rigid and immutable structure; the objects (individual or collective agents acting in the territory) are precisely distributed and organised based on pre-assumed logic and a well-known metric. The space can be reduced to the essence of bi-dimensional Euclidean geometry, fitting with our geometric perception of space. The latter refers to a more complex representation of space, where the location of objects is responsible for producing and transforming space itself. Lefebvre (1991), among several other philosophers, sociologists and geographers (Harvey, 2006), produced seminal works underlying the importance of symbolic meanings and lived space, which emerged in opposition to the pure notion of the geometry of space.

For instance, Marques (2012) demonstrated that by not assuming any fixed and known pattern of spatial interactions it is possible to capture significant spatial spillovers (positive and negative interactions that are meaningful in the specific spatial context), not detected by current traditional approaches or any of the several standard specifications of distances and contiguity.

This concern suggests that the notion of neighbourhood and the consumption of space, and consequently the definition of a spatial weight matrix, seem to be more complex than the consideration of a physical space. The adoption of an unknown dimensionality and geometry of spatial-territoriality calls for a more flexible approach, with a focus on multidisciplinary debates on the notions of space and how to understand it.

CONCLUSION

In recent decades, the housing market has undergone profound transformations in societies. The demographic and social change of the population has led to new housing demands and requirements. Thus, to improve housing supply, urban policy makers, planners, economists and local tax appraisers, among other housing market agents, are expected to expend considerable effort in understanding the nature and characteristics of these changes, which require an effective knowledge of a complex set of phenomena, which involves a vast diversity of tangible and intangible tastes and consequently, different patterns of consumption.

The methodologies presented in this chapter are focused on the hedonic pricing model, where it is possible to capture the importance (preferences) of housing attributes (intrinsic characteristics, as well as characteristics associated with the external environment of a house) in the explanation of the house price value. In turn, both the hedonic prices of attributes (households' preferences) and the stochastic error affect the overall value of each house and each of them depends on its location. This necessarily implies that space configures the housing market in a multifaceted and complex way.

Thus, focusing on housing spatial structures, this chapter contributes to an analysis of the behaviour of the housing market, reflected by the household preferences for a set of housing attributes, where the understanding of spatial urban structures assumes particular relevance, both in terms of absolute location, reflecting the distances to various urban amenities (green areas, services, facilities, etc.), and relative location, considering the influence of the neighbourhoods (not necessarily measured by physical distances). The former capture how households assess the importance of various urban amenities in the context of the bundle of housing characteristics, while the latter allows an understanding of the way that different spaces (housing submarkets) are characterized and connected in a broader urban context.

Despite the complexity and difficulties of analysing space, in the context of housing markets, location is very important in determining the value of a property, having positive and negative externality effects. Two important features of the notion of space are highlighted in the spatial econometric and urban studies literature: i) spatial heterogeneity (patterns) and ii) spatial dependence (interaction or spillovers). A third distinct (but linked) aspect of spatial analysis, not mentioned in this work, but crucial in the analysis of urban spatial structure is the scale where these two phenomena occur. One spatial configuration at a certain scale is not necessarily the same as at another, leading to the so called "ecological fallacy". The challenges emphasised throughout this chapter call for trans- and multidisciplinary approaches.

ACKNOWLEDGMENT

This work is based on research covered by the research project: DRIVIT-UP – DRIVIng forces of urban Transformation: assessing pUblic Policies (POCI-01-0145-FEDER-031905). This work was financially supported by the research unit on Governance, Competitiveness and Public Policy (UID/CPO/04058/2019), funded by national funds through FCT - Fundação para a Ciência e a Tecnologia.

REFERENCES

Adams, D., Watkins, C., & White, M. (2008). *Planning, public policy and property markets* (Vol. 21). John Wiley & Sons.

Allen, M., Springer, T., & Waller, N. (1995). Implicit Pricing Across Residential Rental Submarkets. *The Journal of Real Estate Finance and Economics, 11*(2), 137–151. doi:10.1007/BF01098658

Anselin, L. (1988). *Spatial Econometrics: Methods and Models*. Boston: Kluwer. doi:10.1007/978-94-015-7799-1

Anselin, L. (2002). Under the Hood: Issues in the Specification and Interpretation of Spatial Regression Models. *Agricultural Economics, 27*(3), 247–267. doi:10.1111/j.1574-0862.2002.tb00120.x

Anselin, L. (2010). Thirty years of spatial econometrics. *Papers in Regional Science, 89*(1), 3–25. doi:10.1111/j.1435-5957.2010.00279.x

Arnott, R. (1987). Economic theory and housing. In G. Duranton, V. Henderson, & W. Strange (Eds.), Handbook of regional and urban economics (vol. 2). Elsevier Science Publishers.

Arrondel, L., & Lefebvre, B. (2001). Consumption and investment motives in housing wealth accumulation: A French study. *Journal of Urban Economics, 50*(1), 112–137. doi:10.1006/juec.2000.2209

Barlow, J., & Duncan, S. (1992). Markets, states and housing provision: Four European growth regions compared. *Progress in Planning*, *38*, 93–177. doi:10.1016/0305-9006(92)90006-2

Basu, S., & Thibodeau, T. G. (1998). Analysis of spatial autocorrelation in house prices. *The Journal of Real Estate Finance and Economics*, *17*(1), 61–85. doi:10.1023/A:1007703229507

Batista, P. (2019). *The interaction structure of e-territorial systems: territory, housing market and spatial econometrics / A estrutura de interação de um sistema e-territorial. Território, mercado de habitação e econometria espacial*. Universidade de Aveiro.

Bhattacharjee, A., Castro, E., Maiti, T., & Marques, J. (2016). Endogenous Spatial Regression and Delineation of Submarkets: A New Framework with Application to Housing Markets. *Journal of Applied Econometrics*, *31*(1), 32–57. doi:10.1002/jae.2478

Bhattacharjee, A., Castro, E., & Marques, J. (2012). Spatial Interactions in Hedonic Pricing Models: The Urban Housing Market of Aveiro, Portugal. *Spatial Economic Analysis*, *7*(1), 133–167. doi:10.1080/17421772.2011.647058

Bhattacharjee, A., & Holly, S. (2013). Understanding interactions in social networks and committees. *Spatial Economic Analysis*, *8*(1), 23–53. doi:10.1080/17421772.2012.722669

Bourne, L. S. (1981). *The geography of housing*. London, UK: Edward Arnold.

Brown, T. C. (1984). The Concept of Value in Resource Allocation. *Land Economics*, *60*(3), 231–246. doi:10.2307/3146184

Can, A. (1990). The Measurement of Neighbourhood Dynamics in Urban House Prices. *Economic Geography*, *66*(3), 254. doi:10.2307/143400

Chudik, A., Pesaran, M. H., & Tosetti, E. (2011). Weak and strong cross-section dependence and estimation of large panels. *The Econometrics Journal*, *14*(1), C45–C90. doi:10.1111/j.1368-423X.2010.00330.x

Clark, W. A. V., & Onaka, J. L. (1983). Life Cycle and Housing Adjustment as Explanations of Residential Mobility. *Urban Studies (Edinburgh, Scotland)*, *20*(1), 47–57. doi:10.1080/713703176

Corrado, L., & Fingleton, B. (2012). Where is the economics in spatial econometrics? *Journal of Regional Science*, *52*(2), 210–239. doi:10.1111/j.1467-9787.2011.00726.x

Costa, J., Dentinho, T., & Nijkamp, P. (2010). *Mercado Fundiário e Habitação. Compêndio de Economia Regional: Teoria, Temática e Políticas (1)*. Principia.

Cubbin, J. (1970). *A hedonic approach to some aspects of the Coventry housing market*. Coventry, UK: University of Warwick, Department of Economics.

Elhorst, J. P. (2014). *Spatial Econometrics: From Cross-Sectional Data to Spatial Panels*. Berlin, Germany: Springer. doi:10.1007/978-3-642-40340-8

Fingleton, B. (2003). Externalities, Economic Geography, and Spatial Econometrics: Conceptual and Modeling Developments. *International Regional Science Review*, *26*(2), 197–207. doi:10.1177/0160017602250976

Freeman, A. M. (1979). The hedonic price approach to measuring demand for neighbourhood characteristics. In D. Segal (Ed.), *The economics of neighbourhood*. Cambridge, MA: Elsevier. doi:10.1016/B978-0-12-636250-3.50015-5

Galster, G. (1996). William Grigsby and the Analysis of Housing Sub-markets and Filtering. *Urban Studies (Edinburgh, Scotland)*, *33*(10), 1797–1805. doi:10.1080/0042098966376

Gerstberger, C., & Yaneva, D. (2013). *Statistics in focus 2/2013 - Analysis of EU-27 household final consumption expenditure*. Eurostat.

Getis, A., & Ord, J. K. (1992). The Analysis of Spatial Association by Use of Distance Statistics. *Geographical Analysis*, *24*(3), 189–206. doi:10.1111/j.1538-4632.1992.tb00261.x

Harvey, D. (2006). Space as a Keyword. In N. Castree & D. Gregory (Eds.), *David Harvey: A Critical Reader*. Oxford, UK: Blackwell Publishing Ltd. doi:10.1002/9780470773581.ch14

Henderson, J. V., & Ioannides, Y. M. (1983). A model of housing tenure choice. *The American Economic Review*, *73*(1), 98–113.

Holsapple, C. (2008). *DSS Architecture and Types. In Handbook on Decision Support Systems*. Berlin: Springer Berlin Heidelberg.

Kain, J., & Quigley, J. M. (1975). A Theory of Urban Housing Markets and Spatial Structure. *Housing Markets and Racial Discrimination: A Microeconomic Analysis* (1), 9–55.

Lancaster, K. J. (1966). A new approach to consumer theory. *Journal of Political Economy*, *74*(2), 132–157. doi:10.1086/259131

Lefebvre, H. (1991). *The production of space*. Oxford, UK: John Wiley & Sons Ltd.

Lengwiler, Y. (2009). *The Origins of Expected Utility Theory. In Vinzenz Bronzin's Option Pricing Models*. Berlin: Springer Berlin Heidelberg.

LeSage, J., & Pace, R. (2009). *Introduction to Spatial Econometrics* (1st ed.). Boca Raton, FL: Chapman & Hall/CRC. doi:10.1201/9781420064254

LeSage, J. P. (2014). What Regional Scientists Need to Know about Spatial Econometrics. *The Review of Regional Studies*, *44*(1), 13–32. doi:10.2139srn.2420725

LeSage, J. P., & Pace, R. K. (2014). The biggest myth in spatial econometrics. *Econometrics*, *2*(4), 217–249. doi:10.3390/econometrics2040217

Maclennan, D. (1977). Some Thoughts on the Nature and Purpose of House Price Studies. *Urban Studies (Edinburgh, Scotland)*, *14*(1), 59–71. doi:10.1080/00420987720080061

Maclennan, D., & Tu, Y. (1996). Economic Perspectives on the Structure of Local Housing Systems. *Housing Studies*, *11*(3), 387–406. doi:10.1080/02673039608720864

Marques, J. (2012). *The notion of space in urban housing markets* (PhD thesis). Universidade de Aveiro.

Marques, J., Castro, E., & Bhattacharjee, A. (2012). Methods and models for analysis of the urban housing market. In Emerging Challenges for Regional Development and Evolving Infrastructure Networks and Space. Edward Elgar.

Marques, J., Wolf, J., & Borges, M. (2018). Modelling the urban transformation at local scale. *Rivista Urbanistica Informazioni*, 80–83.

North, D. C. (1984). Transaction Costs, Institutions, and Economic History. *Journal of Institutional and Theoretical Economics*, 7–17.

Paelinck, J., & Klaassen, L. (1979). *Spatial Econometrics*. Farnborough, UK: Saxon House.

Pollakowski, H. (1995). Data Sources for Measuring House Price Changes. *Journal of Housing Research*, *6*(3), 377–387.

Power, D. J. (2008). *Decision Support Systems: A Historical Overview. In Handbook on Decision Support Systems 1*. Berlin: Springer Berlin Heidelberg.

Pryce, G. (2013). Housing Submarkets and the Lattice of Substitution. *Urban Studies (Edinburgh, Scotland)*, *50*(13), 2682–2699. doi:10.1177/0042098013482502

Rosen, S. (1974). Hedonic Prices and Implicit Markets: Product Differentiation in Pure Competition. *Journal of Political Economy*, *82*(1), 35–55. doi:10.1086/260169

Rothenberg, J., Galster, G., Butler, R. V., & Pitkin, J. K. (1991). *The Maze of Urban Housing Markets: Theory, Evidence and Policy*. Chicago, IL: University of Chicago Press.

Sims, C. A. (1986, Winter). Are forecasting models usable for policy analysis? *Quarterly Review of the Federal Reserve Bank of Minneapolis*, 2–16.

Stark, D., & Clippinger, J. (1999). Heterarchy: Distributing Intelligence and Organizing Diversity. In J. Clippinger (Ed.), *The Biology of Business: Decoding the Natural Laws of Enterprise*. San Francisco, CA: Jossey-Bass.

Straszheim, M. (1974). Hedonic estimation of housing market prices: A further comment. *The Review of Economics and Statistics*, *56*(3), 404–406. doi:10.2307/1923985

Streimikiene, D. (2015). Quality of life and housing. *International Journal of Information and Education Technology (IJIET)*, *5*(2), 140–145. doi:10.7763/IJIET.2015.V5.491

Stull, W. J. (1975). Community environment, zoning, and the market value of single-family homes. *The Journal of Law & Economics*, *18*(2), 535–557. doi:10.1086/466822

Sui, D. Z. (2004). Tobler's first law of geography: A big idea for a small world? *Annals of the Association of American Geographers*, *94*(2), 269–277. doi:10.1111/j.1467-8306.2004.09402003.x

Thévenot, L. (2001). Organized Complexity. *European Journal of Social Theory*, *4*(4), 405–425. doi:10.1177/13684310122225235

Timmermans, H., Molin, E., & Noortwijk, L. (1994). Housing choice processes: Stated versus revealed modelling approaches. *Netherlands Journal of Housing and the Built Environment*, *9*(3), 215–227. doi:10.1007/BF02496997

Timmins, C., & Schlenker, W. (2011). Reduced-Form Versus Structural Modeling in Environmental and Resource Economics. *Annual Review of Resource Economics*, *1*(1), 351–380. doi:10.1146/annurev.resource.050708.144119

Tobler, W. (2004). On the First Law of Geography: A Reply. *Annals of the Association of American Geographers*, *94*(2), 304–310. doi:10.1111/j.1467-8306.2004.09402009.x

Waterman, A. M. C. (2003). Mathematical Modeling as an Exegetical Tool: Rational Reconstruction. In *A Companion to the History of Economic Thought*. Malden, MA: Blackwell Publishing Ltd. doi:10.1002/9780470999059.ch37

Watkins, C. (2001). The Definition and Identification of Housing Submarket. *Environment & Planning*, *33*(12), 2235–2253. doi:10.1068/a34162

Wooldridge, J. (2008). *Introductory econometrics: A modern approach* (4th ed.). Mason, OH: Cengage Learning.

KEY TERMS AND DEFINITIONS

Housing Market: Refers to the supply and demand for houses in a particular territory (country, region, or neighbourhood).

Housing Preferences: Refer to certain features any consumer wants to have in a housing (intrinsic attributes or structural characteristics of the property and extrinsic attributes or location characteristics of the property).

Spatial Dependence: When housing values or preferences in a specific location are influenced or correlated by other observations located in the neighbourhood.

Spatial Econometric Analysis: Collection of statistical techniques that deal with the particularities of space (heterogeneity and dependence), in this context, useful for accurately describing housing preferences of households.

Spatial Heterogeneity: Occurs when there is a territorial segmentation in the housing market and, therefore, either the preferences associated with different attributes, or the characteristics of the dwellings, are not constant throughout the territory.

Chapter 16
Alpaca Meat:
Constraints and Reinforcements on Consumption

Yezelia Danira Caceres
https://orcid.org/0000-0002-5027-8081
Universidad Nacional de San Agustín de Arequipa, Peru

Sara Gonzalez
ISCSP-Universidade de Lisboa, Portugal

Juan Rivera Medina
https://orcid.org/0000-0003-0627-7871
Universidad Nacional de San Agustín de Arequipa, Peru

ABSTRACT

The chapter analyses alpaca (Vicugna pacos) meat production and consumption in Peru. The analysis highlights what affects alpaca meat consumption, drawing from exploratory studies in the Andean high zone of Arequipa, Puno, and Cusco. The reasons that are behind alpaca meat consumption decisions are anthropological aspects related to historical and cultural processes, as well as the commercial channels and the presentation of the product. In this sense, the authors link the theoretical approach on consumption, emphasizing the influence of the consumer in the market and vice versa. Nevertheless, it is interesting to note that even in the current conditions of the market there is a growth in the demand for alpaca meat resulting from the increase in tourism flows, not only of foreigners but also Peruvians.

INTRODUCTION

For a long time, Anthropology focused on the study of the economic aspect of societies. From Malinowski *Argonauts of the Western Pacific* (1922), where Kula worked as system of exchange of bracelets and necklaces connected with political authority; to Marcell Mauss (1925) with the potlatch, an indigenous community practice in Pacific Northwest Coast of Canada where this practice reflected the leader wealth

DOI: 10.4018/978-1-7998-3115-0.ch016

Copyright © 2020, IGI Global. Copying or distributing in print or electronic forms without written permission of IGI Global is prohibited.

and power at the same time the reaffirmation of family, clan and the connection with the supernatural. Economic Anthropology has focused on three types of society: non-market, market and transitional and for a long time there were two main approaches. The first, the formalist approach, perceived economic behavior has resulted from rational choices with the purpose of competition and maximizing the income. Substantives, the second approach, defended that in non-commercial societies economy is embedded in institutions/practices which are plural in terms of objectives and nature. In this sense, these two theoretical positions look to economy beyond capitalism and mercantilism, privileging the substantives components of economy. Another theoretical frame that marked anthropology was Marxist analyses where class relations were the main focus. In particular, French neo-Marxist economic anthropologists were interested in exploring the traditional modes of production by capitalism. A clear example is Godelier (1977) and Meillasoux (1975) work. In this sense, anthropology escapes from a vision of *homo economicus* criticizing that only economic reason or practical reason are the conditions for buying or consume goods. In the 70´s, 80´s and 90´s a new paradigm was established mainly in cultural material but also in consumption. This new approach focused on the importance of understanding the influence of consumers in the markets moving from the studies connected with production to consumption and seeing people as economic agents (Falk & Campbell, 1997). With this shift, social sciences could focus on the appropriation and attribution of social meaning of goods and their circulation in the different contexts and everyday life.

In this logic, this chapter focuses on Peru alpaca meat consumption as a way to understand the cultural aspects that condition consumption. Peru is the world number one alpaca producer and has 87% of the South American camelid population (Ministerio de Agricultura y Riego [MINAGRI] 2016). The alpaca habitat is found in the Andean high zone of Peru, Bolivia, Argentine and Chile, with Peru having the highest population of alpacas with 3,685,516 (Instituto Nacional de Estadistica e Informática del Perú [INEI], 2012). The information of the present chapter corresponds to the analysis of the alpaca meat consumption with emphasis in the southern Peruvian departments of Arequipa, Puno and Cusco, which have the biggest populations of South American camelids. Alpaca is valued for its high fineness in its fiber and the extraordinary attributes of its meat, however the income earned by alpaca breeders places it as the poorest and most economically marginalized in Peru.

This chapter synthesizes information from the author's development consulting work – *Desarrollo sostenible de comunidades vulnerables en 3 provincias altoandinas de Arequipa y Puno* (Rivera & Caceres, Línea de Base del Proyecto: Desarrollo sostenible de comunidades vulnerables en 3 provincias altoandinas de Arequipa y Puno, 2016) and *Análisis del sistema de valor de carne del sub sector de carne de alpaca y llama for the aspects of comercialization* (Caceres, 2002) - and from two theses – *Estudio de la comercialización de carne de alpaca. Mercados y Fuentes* (Caceres, 1998) about the study of the commercial channel of alpaca meat considering the demand and supply relationships in each intermediation and the value chain.

The methodology is qualitative and quantitative by combining data obtained through in-depth interviews aimed at consumer analysis, and surveys directed at intermediaries in commercial channels and observation, also to southamerican camel's producers in different periods of time according to the mentioned studies.

We start with a description of camelid breeding and production activity in Peru, including the socio-economic context and the use of resources – water and land – for production. The second part is divided in two. First, we characterize the commodity chain for alpaca products, focusing on meat and wool. The second part deals with this cultural aspect. We engage with theories of food as a component of cultural behavior and examine the development of a taboo that constrains alpaca meat consumption. The final section, third part, examines possibilities for change, including (mostly ineffective) attempts by government and NGOs to promote alpaca consumption by touting its health benefits and supporting infrastructures to increase selling of alpaca meat. We also analyze why these measures did not succeed in dispelling the negative opinions and social taboo surrounding alpaca meat.

ANALYZING THE COMMODITY CHAIN OF ALPACA PRODUCTION AND THE INCOME / LIVELIHOODS OF PRODUCERS

The presence of camelids in Peru were essential to the development on agriculture since they were used as pack animals allowing the development of knowledge and technology as well the increase of a more diverse food and diet. One of the main causes for this change was the domestication of camelids, mainly the *guanaco* (*Lama guanicoe*) which is the origin of llama and *vicunã* (*Vicugna vicugn*) the origin of alpaca. Peru has 3 685,516 alpacas (INEI, 2012), of which 99% belong to small breeders and 1% in diverse forms of breeding (medium and big size companies, cooperatives, associations, peasant communities, etc.). The alpaca population is distributed in the departments of Puno (1,459,903), Cusco (545,454) and Arequipa (468,392); Huancavelica (308,586); Ayacucho (230,910) and other regions. There are two breeds of alpaca: Huacava (80%), Suri (12%), and hybrids of the two (9%). Exploring the commercial potential of this product is important because of its direct contribution to the livelihoods of *alpaqueros* – people who breed alpacas - whose incomes from alpaca can reach approximately US$1700 annually (DESCOSUR, 2016). Income varies with herd size, from US$1642 per year for small producers to US$2025 for medium producers (Antonini, Cristofanelli, Polidori & Renieri, 2006).

With the regard of the feeding of alpaca, they eat from the natural pasture conformed by different types of vegetation: grasslands, *puna* grass, *bofedales* and *tolares*. Most alpaca grazing takes place around or above 3800 meters above sea level, in areas where farming is not possible (INEI, 2012).

It is important to point, that the breeding of alpaca and llama is joint as well the usufruct of its derivatives. Generally the meat and leather are sold from llama and the fiber, meat and lather are sold from alpaca. In the process of selling the meat, llama meat has a higher income because of the bigger size when compared to alpaca. We would like to acknowledge that the meat from llama is not sold as "llama meat" but under the name of "alpaca meat". Although no reason is attributed to justify this, one possible explanation may be the fact that llama meat has a bigger prejudice than alpaca meat. In consequence, it´s extremely difficult to separate what is alpaca and llama meat consumption so the study refers to alpaca meat although the results of the questions correspond to appreciations of alpaca and llama meat.

The breeding of camelids is extensive and requires large tracts of land shared among families, which are referred to as "condominiums," where families remain at different periods of the year and also have residences in nearby small towns. Families go to the local markets weekly or biweekly to buy supplies and sell alpaca products. Given the rural setting, there is limited mobile telephone and television coverage, and almost non-existent connection to the internet. The use of mobile cell phones is important because it allows coordination of daily matters that were previously resolved by radio announcements. Radio is still the most important means of communication because it works even when there is excessive rainfall, hail and storms. Case studies show radio have been used to disseminate information on breeding and husbandry measures, resulting in improved productivity (Caceres, 2012).

It is possible that for the *alpaquero* family the breeding of camelids is a way of life in which the market elements and income are important but these are not the only considerations. Women play an important role in camelid breeding and husbandry. In some seasons of the year the men travel to cities or work in temporary construction in nearby towns, leaving the women and children in the camp to take care of the alpaca breeding activities. The heads of the household average 50 years of age, the women 40 years. Alpaca breeding and production knowledge is transmitted from parents to children. As the children get older they usually migrate to larger towns and cities. (Rivera & Caceres, 2016).

The productive activities during the year differs in periods for the parturition, reproduction, shearing, sanitation and killing although the breeding process is made and known by the alpacas producers have not yet been developed techniques with a higher level of effectiveness. About the infrastructure practices that families do there is the construction of irrigation channels, pasture fertilization, the construction of stone fences and wires built on cooperation between neighbors. The area is affected with greater recurrence due to droughts, frosts and climatic variations causing health problems for families and their livelihoods. Blockages in the roads restrain the possibility of mobility and sometimes provoke mortality and effect the animal health; food and water shortage; and the devastation of natural pasture. In the data collection of 2008 the number of sick and dead animals increased from 10% in a normal year to 25% in Cusco and 45% in Arequipa resulting in a lost in the livestock capital (Unidad de coordinación de emergencias y rehabilitaciòn de emergencias de FAO Peru, 2008)

In the commercial transactions is very important the bonds of friendship, familiarity and trust between collectors and producers that exchange loans of money and / or delivery of products that are made under the promise of payment. The markets are a very important space for the camelid producers as they not only serve to do transactions but also to contact and fulfill social ties.

The commercial circuit of alpaca fiber is traditional and in result has created bigger allowances for the processing industry compared to the alpaca producers. So in the case of alpaca fiber, the commercialization chain is divided into two options. The first is directed towards the fiber collection center that is organized by the alpaca producers themselves with the support of institutions and the government, which then proceeds to classify it and sell it to the traditional circuit or export. The second option follows the traditional circuit that consists of delivering the fiber to the intermediary where it is sold to the processing industry. The first option has been implemented since 2008 and emerged as a response to the low fiber prices paid to the producer on which credits granted by Agrobanco depend. This system has proven to have increased the profit margins of *alpaquero* producers. With regard to the leather commercialization, the distinction is made between offspring and older animals. The small animals or offspring are sold at local markets for the elaboration of handcrafts and have a larger commercial value than leathers from adult animals which are sold in a smaller proportion than the offspring. In the animal species llamas are preferred over alpacas because of their larger size and low price. It should be mentioned that in the process of selling leather from alpacas, as it happens in the case of llama meat, it´s identified as from llamas and given the name of *llamos*.

THE COMMERCIALIZATION OF ALPACA MEAT

It is estimated that yearly consumption reaches at least 300.000 heads of alpaca and 100.000 of llama, which is equivalent to at least 8 million kg of meat per year (Finland Futures Research Centre, 2019). These results are confirmed by the percentage of separation of the animals for slaughtering, whereby a family with a possession of 100 animals at least allocates 10 animals for the slaughter per year. However, several investigations suggest that this data is growing due to various factors including reports from La Raya Research and Production Center in Puno, on alpaca's production rate, report a 20.8% for the *Huacaya* breed.

The production of alpaca and the first phases of its commercialization are carried out in rural areas and the sale to the final consumer in urban areas, representing a constraint on transportation and meat presentation in the markets and stores. This situation is caused by the slaughtering process: producers are located in remote areas of populated centers giving them two options of transportation in which one of them, the animal, is killed on the farms and later transported in buses or public transportation and the other, the producers carry the animal alive to be killed in the slaughtering house and later sold in the market. The cost of transportation from the producer's home to the markets is expensive because the distance is very long and because small producers only kill and sell alpaca meat 1-3 times a year making the gains slightly outweigh costs.

In the market, the largest meat supply and sale is between April and June, the price being influenced by seasonality and by the other red meat. In relation to intermediaries, price penalty is applied to the bad carcass and they´re transported (without refrigeration) in the local transport services for the cities. It can be seen that the demand of the tourism sector is higher between June and October.

It should be mentioned that the *Norma Técnica Peruana 201.043* points out that the alpaca meat should be obtained from healthy animals, killed and skinned in inspected and authorized slaughter-houses (Instituto Nacional de Defensa de la Competencia y de la protección de la Propiedad Intelectual [INDECOPI], 2005). It adds too that the alpacas should not have antibiotics, conservatives, tenderizer residuals or substances that by their nature threaten the health of the consumer. The appropriate provision of infrastructure and sanitary control in the slaughterhouses of the area requires relevant economic investments, which due to the economic conditions of the producers, cannot be assumed by a single supplier requiring the contribution of the State. This not only imply the slaughterhouses conditions but also training and establishing good practices that would have a chain effect for management knowledge and technological development in the area.

For this reason, slaughtering hygiene and health conditions are crucial for the presentation of the product. The National Agricultural Health Service in Peru has so far provided the sanitary authorization for operation for less than 5 slaughter houses nationwide (Servicio Nacional de Sanidad Agraria [SENASA], 2020), so it is possible that most of the meat sold has not been properly killed and do not have the sanitary evaluation stamps that indicate the final result of the veterinary evaluation. Consequently the limited supply of slaughters implies that it cannot be sold in traditional markets or in supermarkets; likewise, the technological regulation of meat for the corresponding sealing is not implemented being understood as clandestine market. This situation contributes to the fact that commercialization is not very visible and in points of sale little is known.

Figure 1. Commercial chain of products derived from alpaca

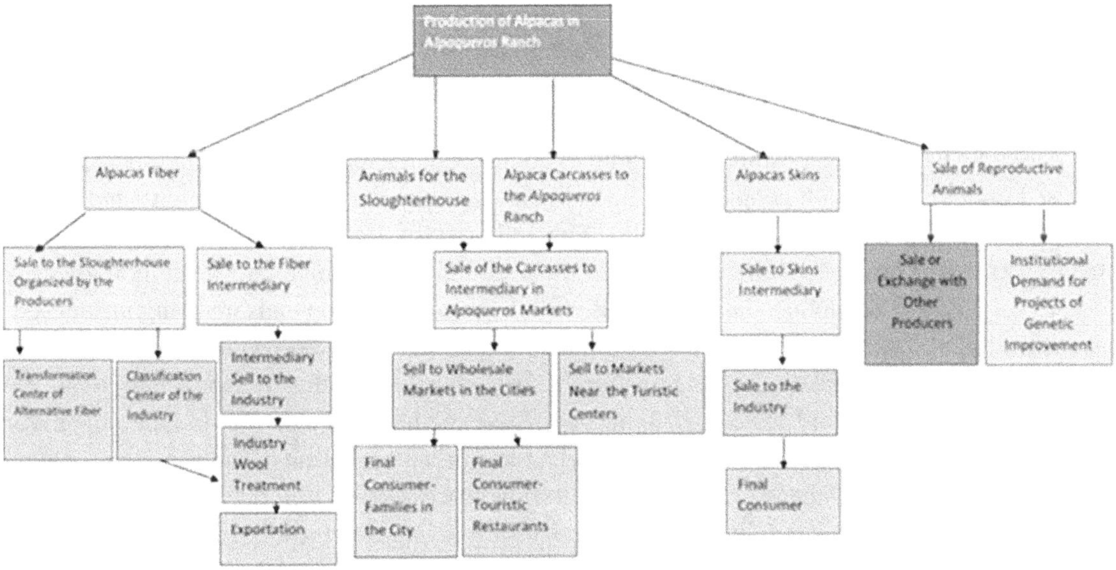

ALPACA MEAT CONSUMPTION

Consumption is a reflex of social and cultural constraints and decisions. We can add three components to consumption: it´s a system of meaning and has the purpose to abolish symbolic necessity; second, consumption is a "code" in which are translated social relationships and produce in itself subjectivity, in turn, a classification system of goods, people, products and others is created. (Rocha & Barros, 2006). In this sense rituals belong to the structure of culture and they have an important role in the consumption process, involving goods and services which construct cognitive schema and scripts (Luna & Gupta, 2001). Therefore, symbols express cultural values and throw consumption rituals, consumer goods become symbols of cultural values (Luna & Gupta, 2001).

In this scenario, food is expected to be an indispensable component to culture, containing in itself meanings and processes whereby identities are constructed connecting with the symbolic and aspects of representation and meaning (Salazar, 2001). Consequently, it is the individual and group classifications that characterize what food is and what is not from historically derived cultural materials that influence social learning (Mintz, 2001). In this regard, it is the ideas associated with meat and the symbolic meaning that determine the value to society (Fiddes, 1991). In the case of alpaca meat the association and incentive of the negative symbolism makes consumption inexistent or when bought, not acknowledged. The consumption outlines are specific in a sense that exist a generational gap: consumers that on average are 50 years old and don´t admit the consumption and a younger minority group, mainly concentrated in the tourism sector which admits the consumption based on the nutritional properties. In this sense, we can differentiate three types of consumers: the frequent native consumer motivated by price and habit; the consumer who is motivated by health aspects and the tourist restaurants.

Peruvian society built and maintained a taboo that constrains or even prevents alpaca meat consumption. Taboos can have different purposes: they can protect against health risks, or guarantee the spiritual state of individuals; rationing or the monopolizing natural resources etc. Therefore, majority of cases of food taboos affects all of society and can be periodically suspended or reinforced (Meyer-Rochow, 2009).

The alpaca meat taboo is an aspect that reveals the understanding of the dynamics of the Peruvian society which connects with ethnicity, colonialism and migration. It is worth mentioning that this perception is also visible in the llama meat consumption in Bolivia, Chile and Argentina. In work developed in La Paz regarding llama meat consumption, Sammels connects llama meat, ethnicity and socioeconomic class based on interviews with people from the indigenous community living in the city and *mestizos* from middle and upper class (Sammels, 1998). The author starts from the point of view that taboos related to llama meat are not governed but part of the negotiation of ethnicity between individuals and the context of race and economic class (Sammels, 1998). This negotiation ends up being influenced in what was the Spanish colonial power and later postcolonial context led by the white elite which marked social relations through racial distinctions that feed a socio-racial hierarchy (Wilson, 2010).

To this connotation the word *cholo* is attributed. *Cholo* is explained in the period after the end of World War II when Peru had a process of urbanization and a rural-urban migration of indigenous people who later identified as *cholos* (Quijano, 2003). This migration process was based on the search for a better education and work thereby withdrawing the power that *sierras* had over the city and thus creating a difference between the andean peasants and urban *cholos* (Thorp & Paredes, 2010). It is worth mentioning that the term is currently used in two contexts: in the urban areas of the capital and the main Peruvian cities to refer to the one coming from the mountains, characterized as being shy, unknown, dumb and out of touch; and in some areas of the mountains as is the case of Cusco refers to a person with love: *cholito*.

To this description of *cholo* another justification for not eating alpaca is supported by a rhetoric that quantifies it with diseases. As mentioned before, due to the non-existence of health conditions, the presence of *sarcociystiosis* found in carcasses is often found in alpaca meat. S*arcocystiosis* is a parasitic disease that does not affect people but alters its acceptability by generating an unpleasant appearance on the product. It can be confused by other parasitoids of high zoonotic potential. *Macrocysts* and *microcysts* being the first, not detected visually and mostly found in the heart and diaphragm as well as in skeletal muscles; and the second, which is the size of a grain of rice, can be detected with the eye, and is mostly found in the esophagus and neck and to a lesser extent in any skeletal muscle. This parasitoid is generally confused with *cysticercosis* which constitutes a real danger to man and presents similar clinical signs (cysts). In addition to this, stories and myths are perpetuated that may have begun with the association of epidemic diseases in contact with European animals that polluted the cattle of alpacas and llamas and that in the 19th century were perpetuated by mohair traders to deny the competition of the alpaca fiber industry (Markowitz, 2012). As a result of this component, alpaca meat is associated first, with the indigenous community that sells it and also with the *cholos* that consume it, interconnecting with the idea of dirt and disease. Douglas, when talking about the concepts of dirt and taboo affirms that the idea of pollution depends on the variables of each context (Douglas, [1966] 2001) since dirt is associated with disorder and therefore there is a need to clean it to organize the environment (Douglas, [1966] 2001).

In this scenario alpaca meat is associated with a community that lives in the edge of society connecting them with dirt, unsanitary constructing the image of danger that is controlled by the taboo that prevents the possible transgression of the moral code. Aviles said: "*Peru is organized in such a way that people are educated in discrimination. It's something you learn in school, in families. It is something "normal" and happens everywhere, including the provinces. My dad, for example, was from the mountains, that is cholo. And for him the peasants were Indians, "cholos" who could not sit at the table to eat with the rest. If you educate yourself a little, if you go to university, you realize that (discrimination) is not right and you learn to silence it or moderate it a little. But it's still inside, isn't it?*" (Pighi, 2017, para. 8).

Consequently, in the urban context, traditional foods are associated with poverty and lowest social status - in particular Andean goods are considered inferior - and when migrants earn higher incomes their consumption of traditional products drops (Smith & Trivelli, 2001). Eating more expensive meat is considered a privilege that conveys an idea of social mobility contrary to alpaca meat which is cheap and denigrating. Even when there is consumption of alpaca meat it is normal for people cover it up or simply do not admit that they consume it. This situation is also due to the colonial process that Peru stifled in which there was a control and prohibition of the cultivation of certain products and ritual acts associated with the agricultural cycle and devaluation of certain indigenous foods - as is the example of *kiwicha* or *maca*. (Ministerio de la Cultura, 2011). But this process is not linear in a sense that indigenous communities developed a strategy of assimilation and reproduction of their own cultural standards. Despite this, the elite began to nationalize the food – especially after its independence - combining different cultural aspects that had presence in Peru such as Spanish, African, French, Japanese cultures among others (Ministerio de la Cultura, 2011). We can say that behind this taboo on alpaca meat there is not a rational relation but a culturally and historical one (Fiddes, 1994) with the purpose to maintain the identity, affection and meaning of belonging to a group (Meyer-Rochow, 2009; Mintz & Dubois, 2002).

Novo-Andean Cuisine is a clear example of how the valorization of Peruvian food had an impact on the public sphere and consequent internationalization. A process of reappropriation of local elements removing them from their context initiated by the urban upper class that combined, selected and transmitted knowledge to obtain social distinction and economic success (Matta, 2013). According to Matta (2013) it can be translated into an "*elite movement of gastronomic exploration, consisting in selecting a set of indigenous food and ingredients to make a new ethnic offering in the global gastronomic market*" (para. 41).

As the tourist flow to Peru increases, it is more common to find dishes prepared based on alpaca meat and sold in tourist and gourmet restaurants from Arequipa, Puno, Cusco and Lima. The most recognized Peruvian chefs have made dishes based on alpaca meat and have preparations at the most important exhibitions and gastronomic fairs in Peru. However, consumers in this segment usually attribute their consumption to the curiosity and eccentricity of the dish, that is, they are mostly consumers for the first time. This leads one to think that it is possible that the attributes or rejections change as the decision of the consumption in the younger generations is made since the meaning of alpaca meat may have some changes as societies and individuals change (McCraken, 1986). It is even possible that, through advertising and consumption rituals, the value of alpaca meat is transferred as a gourmet good and that as a consequence, increased value in foreign societies and implied incentives for Peruvians to value and generate new consumption rituals. Howes proposes that goods acquire new values and uses in accordance with local reality, eventually building cultural schemes locally (Howes, 1996). However, in this contextualization process where alpaca meat is revalued due to the demand of tourism elements such as the provision of meat for segments afford high prices cannot afford to be jeopardized.

EXAMINING POSSIBILITIES FOR CHANGE, INCLUDING (MOSTLY INEFFECTIVE) ATTEMPTS TO PROMOTE ALPACA CONSUMPTION

In the last 30 years the Peruvian state, non-governmental organizations and international cooperation have invested a large quantity of money to promote the consumption of alpaca meat based on the fact that these efforts contribute to the improvement of the income of *alpaqueros* producers. The actions have been diverse and very little coordinated or linked to a common strategy for product positioning in a group of consumers. While there were initiatives to sell it to the medium high stratum waiting for higher prices there were also a campaign to the low economic stratum trying to convince them to revalue their consumption. To date it is appreciated that Peruvians mostly know that it is a healthy meat but that they do not incorporate it into their diet.

For example, in 1997 - 1998 the Institutional Coordinator of the *Alpaquero* Sector (CISA) - NGO, in agreement with the Association of Exporters, the international cooperation invested in the promotion of the product in the low economic income strata which already consumed. The strategy covered two components: the first aimed at providing information on the nutritional characteristics of the product under the slogan "Healthy Meat" reinforce the nutritional properties to increase consumption; and the second component, aimed at the improvement in the conditions of sale of the product providing the sellers of implements and refrigeration modules for the conservation of the product. It is worth mentioning that in this period Peru was going through an inflationary process increasing unemployment and low income levels so consumption of alpaca meat could be sustained in the low prices of the product compared to the other red meats. It should also be noted that there are NGOs who have given training on the adequate killing of animals and implemented rural slaughterhouses in some farms

On the other hand, with the financing of the Spanish Agency for International Cooperation and the NGO Desco, was installed a modern and large slaughterhouse plant and transformation of meat products in Chivay district which had serious problems in the management of supply, demand and prices. After a short time the plan did not work mainly because of the transportation of animals which implied higher transport costs generating sustainability risk in the supply. On the other hand, the distribution of meat in cuts to supermarkets and restaurants implied logistical limitations and promotion in the Lima market as well as the incipient development in the alpaca meat-based pork line.

An alternative to the consumption of fresh alpaca meat is the elaboration of alpaca sausages. The commercial process of sausages is based on the loss of its intrinsic characteristics of low cholesterol and nutrition. Sausage formulas add higher percentages of products derived from pork to alpaca, for example for the elaboration of alpaca bologna according to the recommendation of development of products with alpaca meat from FAO project, have an added 34% of alpaca meat and 21% of pork and 20% of loin bacon, with similar compositions in the rest of the sausages so the use of alpaca meat for sausage production loses its comparative advantage based on being a low calorie product. And its production is justified in the possibility of sale avoiding the use of its possibilities of generating competitive advantages based on its intrinsic properties, and looking for the benefits of commercial in the short term. (Organización de las Naciones Unidas para la Agricultura y la Alimentación Oficina Regional para América Latina y el Caribe, 2005). Another processing option may be the production of charqui where the intrinsic characteristics of the product are not lost. However, this possibility may be unfeasible if you think about selling to the local market since the demand is small and the charqui of other meats is preferred. Collazos et al. (1996) points out that Charqui contains on average 58% protein, 26% moisture, 4% fat and 12% ash. Also, according to the regulation of the Peruvian technical standard NTP 201.059 (Instituto Nacional de Defensa de la Competencia y de la Protección de la Propiedad Intelectual [INDECOPI], 2006) it considers a minimum content of 45% protein, 12% fat, maximum content of 20% moisture.

There are even experiences of organization of producers concerned with improving their management processes, hygiene conditions which have carried out joint marketing processes. As the years have passed private business initiatives have arisen selling alpaca meat in butchers that are distinguished by the best presentation in relation to those sold in market stalls some located in large markets such as the New Hope Market in the largest market in the Peruvian south "El Avelino" and others nationwide with better characteristics of meat sales.

Between 2013 and 2016 there were activities to promote consumption carried out by the Ministry of Agriculture and Irrigation of Peru through *Sierra Exportadora* program that promoted consumption, highlighting the nutritional qualities without a segmentation strategy focusing on informing and carrying out tasting activities of dishes based on alpaca meat in universities and others establishments. It also invested in the construction of animal slaughterhouse plants. Is necessary to remark that an information campaign is needed on the real effects of *sarcosistiosis* on human health which is a limitation in product purchasing decisions.

The process of revaluation of the consumption of alpaca meat could increase the income of the *alpaqueros* but negatively affect local consumers implying a loss of value and use of a valuable local resource for food security, as seen in experiences of other products such as quinoa, which was not consumed locally because it was considered food for chickens and that after advertising campaigns and growing external demand has seen its prices rise and thus has limited access to local people.

RECOMMENDATIONS

In this section we are going to show a more practical vision and solution related with the problems presented above. One of the biggest problems in selling alpaca meat is the presentation and inappropriate marketing channels. The effort to implement public measures to ensure a secure and healthy production, sale and consumption has not been efficient to increase the incentive of alpaca meat consumption. The main problem is related with the lack of coordination of public politics with all the agents that are part of the alpaca meat marketing chain which includes: *alpaqueros*, intermediate buyers from markets, and industry and consumers.

There is not a general and a broad vision of the interconnectivity within this particular sector which is imbibed to the cultural and social constraints. In this sense it is necessary to support the formalization and application of public politics in the reality of Peru and in this sector as well the coordination with the different agent's public and private institutions in the local and state institutions. At the same time, it is necessary that public policies for the *alpaquerss* subsidize this sector due to the situation of the poverty of producers and the environmental benefices that *alpaqueros* bring to the surrounding small towns.

From the experience of the construction of streets by international cooperations, it is a lesson learned that in order to establish public slaughterhouses it is necessary to consider the way of life and traditions of *alpaquero* family. This sector is mainly composed with small and medium-sized producers and therefore the location and operation of the slaughter plants are affected by the viability of gathering animals and their transportation. This aspect is very important since there are collectors who go to the *alpaqueros* houses on motorized vehicles, implying high transportation costs that increase as they move farther away from the markets.

In general, it is necessary to follow pending elements: development of road infrastructure and product mobility, logistics and cold chain available at distribution points; development of government inspection capacity to ensure product quality, sale of meat classified and valued by cuts; and development of packaging that follows the requirements for supermarket sales. In particular, for good quality and prices higher than those of the market, vertical integration strategy can be an advantage because of the constant improvement in each of the production processes.

Also, the good nutritional properties of alpaca meat should be included in the strategy to strengthen the food security of Peruvians because it brings several health benefits (protein, iron content, low fat and cholesterol) and can be included in a balanced diet, considering that in Peru the proportion of undernourished people increases, overweight and obesity affect all age groups in men and women and constitutes a public health problem. In this perspective it is necessary to encourage a more dynamic vision of the alpaca meat market. Besides this benefits, the comparative nutritional characteristics of alpaca and llama meat from male animals of the same age would produce greater quantity of high quality meat being the chemical composition similar for both meats (Antonini, Torres, Cristofanelli, Polidori, & Renieri, 2006). Therefore, it is suggested that the State should promote productive specialization with compatible activities and processes for specialized breeding for meat purposes. In addition, it is important to improve and value fiber and meat productive specialization which means a different knowledge implementation, breeding, and killing.

It should be mentioned that the *Norma Técnica Peruana 201.043* (INDECOPI, 2005) point that the alpaca meat would be obtained from healthy animals, killed and skinned in inspected and authorized slaughterhouses and shouldn't have any antibiotics, conservatives, tenderizer residuals or substances. The appropriate provision of infrastructure and sanitary control in the slaughterhouses requires relevant economic investments which due to the economic conditions of the producers cannot be assumed by a single supplier requiring the contribution of the State not only by the provision of infrastructure but also for training and establish good practices that would have a chain effect for management knowledge and technological development in the area.

Finally, in relation to a better understanding of the consumer position and vision constructionist perspective may be a tool to better understand the possibilities to increase alpaca meat consumption because of the privileges of the social context that frame consumer's perception on a micro cultural level (Mansori, Sambasivan & Md-Sidin, 2015). Marketing has an important role to engage people in alpaca meat acceptance and purchasing because marketer´s actions can transfer cultural meaning to consuming goods (Luna & Gupta, 2001). It is necessary to perceive alpaca meat, in a constant flow and movement, in relation to its understanding in society (McCraken, 1986). It is necessary to have a broad vision of alpaca meat market combining a macro view - related to the constitution of infrastructure - and a micro view - related to consumers.

FUTURE RESEARCH DIRECTIONS

This chapter provided an inside of the general situation of alpaca meat production, commercialization and consumption. Because we are dealing with a complex theme and situation it is necessary to gather more information, details and the way they interconnect.

In this regard, it is important to understand with more detail the gender differentiations in alpaca breeding; this focus may allow the comprehension of the labour and domestic labour division to easily and effectively implement measures that could increase the alpacas breeding (in relation with the infrastructure, material and knowledge). Is also necessary to consider the migration process from the rural area to the cities and the impact on ecosystem services.

Besides this perspective and in relation with *alpaqueros* and their communities it is necessary to comprehend the new dynamics of consumption in the different classes and tourist sector. It is important to improve research of food habits and food related consumption habits/patterns of low class, high class and tourist consumers. Especially of local products, the scoop analyses should be redirected to the process of purchase and the reasons of the consumption from the individuals and groups that buy this type of meat. This could answer some questions of when alpaca meat is bought; who takes care of the purchase; which places and areas they shop; and the price of the alpaca meat, etc.

In relation to these guidelines it is necessary to accomplish a comparative study with different countries where consumption of camelids meat are condemned. In this chapter we have seen that in Bolivia llama meat has a similar status as alpaca meat in Peru. In this sense a generic study with the different camelids breeders in Ecuator, Bolivia, Chile and Argentina would show the similarities and possibly show similar problems. Also it is important to see in the particular case of Australia, where there has been a growing production of alpaca, positioning alpaca meat as a very high quality product and where consumption of the same is considered sophisticated increasing prices than other "exotic" meats such as crocodile, elk and others. Perhaps this factor has some impact on the local market and the international market and could open an opportunity for the export of Peruvian alpaca meat. With these three possible directions we are trying to underline the necessity of a macro and micro study that can connect different perspectives from two types of lenses to a more complete understanding of alpaca meat consumption.

Finally, it is important to consider that there are limitations of information: for example, in the quantitative aspects of alpaca population data due to the increase recurrence of ice storm and cold phenomena alpaca cattle suffered infections and deaths reported in the emergency communications. However, it is possible that the data contained in the emergency reports are somehow exaggerated. In the same situation, data from slaughter houses are scarce and limited and there is no statistical information on the volumes of sale as well. Likewise, the reports of the Ministry of Agriculture on animals are not consistent with the data of the census, in the same way the price reports of the National Statistics Institute are not consistent with the market prices. In this situation and besides field and market constrains, it is urgent to development a better quantitative data collection combining in-depth interviews for the analysis of the demand since many consumers hide their consumption.

CONCLUSION

Peru is the world number one alpaca producer which makes this economic sector an income to numerous indigenous families that live in the countryside/*sierra* and small towns Although the importance to the economic system and exchange of primary products – which is the case of fiber – the killing and commercialization conditions of alpaca meat are very precarious and usually don´t follow the health regulations. On another level, we have seen that besides the structural problems lies the cultural constraints fed by historical background and social stratification. In this sense, alpaca meat belongs to a ritual consumption that in turn become the origin of culture and consequently part of the classification of the world (Douglas & Isherwood, 1996). What we wanted to focus is the market conditions influence in consumption as well culture as an arbiter of taste and consumption. We show that consumption is not about individual decision but rather, perceived form cultural relationships that establish decisions and basic choices (Campbell & Falk, 1997) in which alpaca meat contributes to the construction and maintenance of *cholos* identity in opposition of non-cholos through symbolic meaning.

But besides this, we are talking about power too. We have to take into account cultural and historical processes which Peru suffered especially with the colonization that changed the structure of society and in consequence cultural aspects of food practices. In this sense, food is a component that helps the construction and maintenance of different groups but also the identity of a country. Consumers use product symbolism to define social reality and maintain specific behavior patterns associated with social roles (Solomon, 1983). The rejection and even public shaming of meat consumption is connected with the well presented colonial social structure that harasses indigenous and *cholo* people that buy this type of meat and consequently social prejudices are built. Power is a component that ables the understanding of goods and attraction, affirmation of consumer's negotiation of purchase (Grafton-Small, 1987). A clear reflection of this situation, is the double standard that alpaca meat has when bought in the market or in the restaurants, or more specific, when the preparation into a dish is made by the finest restaurant or at home, by a regular family.

Despite this negative scenario, NGO´S have been doing work to improve the health conditions of alpaca killing and sales channel, especially the traditional marketing channels, but until this moment there has not been a substantial improvement in the commercialization of alpaca meat that would increase the consumption. In the same context, public measures sponsored by the Peruvian state have not reached the proposed objectives, mainly because there is no public policies of contact with the breeders communities and their economic reality. There is not a coordinate action in the country between the different organizations and public institutions that include breeder's communities and alpaca meat buyers and sellers. We made evident that alpaca meat selling is class oriented in a sense that low class people usually buy in the markets where presentation and health conditions are not given importance contrary to butcher stores, where meat presentation is mainly used to attract consumers. This is evident when the government promotes two types of programs specific for middle class and the other to low class. The only sector where alpaca meat doesn't have a negative impact is in touristic sectors and services where it is seen as an eccentric and Peruvian product, complemented by curiosity and the desire to have different experiences of life and food. We can conclude that the problem has resulted from the lack of interest and investigation of cultural perspective of alpaca meat in Peruvian society and communities.

REFERENCES

Ansaloni, F., Claros, A., Marquina, R., Pyszny, F., Quispe, J., & Zapata, J. (2006). Análisis del ingreso agricola proveniente de la producción de carne de camélidos sudamericanos en los paises latinoamericanos: resultados preliminares de una comparación de estudios de caso. In C. Renieri, E. Frank, & O. Toro (Eds.), *Camélidos Sudamericanos Domésticos: investigaciones recientes* (pp. 313–333). Lima, Peru: DESCO.

Antonini, M., Torres, D., Cristofanelli, S., Polidori, P., & Renieri, C. (2006). Calidad de la carne y carcasa de la llama (Lama glama) y la alpaca (Lama pacos) peruanas. In C. Renieri, E. Frank, & O. Toro (Eds.), *Camelidos sudamericanos domésticos. Investigaciones recientes* (pp. 113–123). Lima, Peru: DESCO.

Aviles, M. (2016). *De donde venimos los cholos*. Lima, Peru: Seis Barral.

Caceres Cabana, Y. (1998). *Estudio de la comercialización de carne de alpaca. Mercados y Fuentes* (Unpublished master dissertation). Universidad nacional de San Agustin de Arequipa, Arequipa, Peru.

Caceres Cabana, Y. (2002). *Análisis del sistema de valor de carne del sub sector de carne de alpaca y llama* (Unpublished doctoral dissertation). Universidad Nacional Agraria La Molina, Lima, Perú.

Caceres Cabana, Y. (2012). El Uso de la Radio para Mejorar la Respuesta Local a la Variabilidad Climática: el Caso de los Criadores de Alpacas de la Región Andina del Perú. Manchester, Reino Unido: Nexus for ICTS, Climate Change and Development (NICCD).

Caceres Cabana, Y. (2019). Aspectos cualitativos que influyen en el consumo de carne de alpaca en el sector turismo. Papper presented at Seminario nacional: Carne de camélidos: potencialidades, politicas y consume, Arequipa, Perú.

CRISE. (2007). *Fluid Identities Exploring Ethnicity in Peru*. Oxford, UK: Maritza Paredes.

CRISE. (2010). *Ethnicity and the Persistence of Inequality*. Oxford, UK: Rosemary Thorp & Maritza Paredes.

Cristofanelli, S., Antonini, M., Torres, D., & Polid. (2004). Meat and Carcass quality from Peruvian llama (Lama glama) and alpaca (Lama pacos). *Meat Science*, 589-593. doi:10.1016/S0309-1740(03)00174-8

DESCOSUR. (2016). *Linea Base Proandino*. Arequipa, Peru: DESCOSUR.

Douglas, M. (2001). *Purity and Danger*. New York, NY: Routdledge. (Original work published 1966)

Douglas, M., & Isherwod, B. (1996). *The World of Goods towards an anthropology of consumption*. New York, NY: Routledge.

Falk, P., & Campbell, C. (1997). *The Shooping Experience*. London, UK: Sage Publications.

Fiddes, N. (1991). *Meat: a natural symbol*. London, UK: Routledge.

Fiddes, N. (1994). Social Aspects of Meat Eating. *The Proceedings of the Nutrition Society*, *53*(2), 271–280. doi:10.1079/PNS19940032 PMID:7972141

Finland Futures Research Centre. (2019). *A Scenario for the future of the peruvian agri - food sector 2030, focusing on andean native crops*. Turku, Finland: Author.

Gade, D. W. (2013). Llamas and Alpacas as "Sheep" in the Colonial Andes: Zoogeography Meets Eurocentrism. *Journal of Latin American Geography*, *12*(2), 221–243. doi:10.1353/lag.2013.0009

Gainer, B. (1995). Ritual and Relationships: Interpersonal Influences on Shared Consumption. *Journal of Business Research*, *32*(3), 253–260. doi:10.1016/0148-2963(94)00050-O

Gallegos, R. (2013). Indice productivos de alpacas del Centro de Investigación y Producción La Raya. *Journal of High Andean Research*, *15*(02), 255–262. doi:10.18271/ria.2013.8

Grafton-Small, R. (1987). Marketing, or the anthropology of consumption. *European Journal of Marketing*, *21*(9), 66–71. doi:10.1108/EUM0000000004717

Instituto Nacional de Defensa de la Competencia y de la Protección de la Propiedad Intelectual. (2006). *Norma Técnica Peruana 201.059: 2006. Carne y productos cárnicos. Charqui. Requisitos*. Lima, Peru: INDECOPI.

Instituto Nacional de Defensa de la Competencia y de la protección de la Propiedad Intelectual. (2005). *Carne y productos cárnicos. Definiciones, requisitos y clasificación de las carcasas y carne de alpacas y llamas*. Lima, Peru: INDECOPI.

Instituto Nacional de Estadística e Informática. (2012). *IV Censo Nacional Agropecuario*. Lima, Peru: INEI.

Luna, D., & Gupta, S. F. (2001). An integrative framework for cross-cultural consumer behavior. *International Marketing Review*, *18*(1), 45–69. doi:10.1108/02651330110381998

Mansori, S., Sambasivan, M., & Md-Sidin, S. (2015). Acceptance of novel products: The role of religiosity, ethnicity and values. *Marketing Intelligence & Planning*, *33*(1), 39–65. doi:10.1108/MIP-03-2013-0050

Markowitz, L. (2012). Highland Haute Cuisine: The Transformation of Alpaca Meat. In E. Elizabeth Finnis (Ed.), *Reimagining Marginalized Foods*. Tucson, AZ: The University of Arizona Press. doi:10.2307/j.ctt1814g4b.5

Matta, R. (2013). Native Eating: The Modern Roosts of Peruvian Food Heritage. *Anthropology of Food*, *8*(S8). doi:10.4000/aof.7361

McCracken, G. (1986). Culture and Consumption: A theoretical account of the structure and movement of the cultural meaning of consumer goods. *The Journal of Consumer Research*, *13*(1), 71–84. doi:10.1086/209048

Meyer-Rochow, V. B. (2009). Food taboos: Their origins and purposes. *Journal of Ethnobiology and Ethnomedicine*, *5*(18). PMID:19563636

Ministerio de Agricultura y Riego. (n.d.). *Hoy se celebra el Dia Nacional de la Alpaca*. Lima, Peru: MINAGRI.

Ministerio de la Cultura. (2011). *Lima, Cocina e identidad La culinaria peruana como patrimonio cultural inmaterial*. Lima, Peru: Government Printing Office.

Mintz, S. W. (2001). Comida e Antropologia – uma breve revisão. *Revista Brasileira de Ciências Sociais*, *16*(47), 31–41. doi:10.1590/S0102-69092001000300002

Mintz, S. W., & Du Bois, C. M. (2002). The Anthropology of Food and Eating. *Annual Review of Anthropology*, *31*(1), 99–119. doi:10.1146/annurev.anthro.32.032702.131011

Organización de las Naciones Unidas para la Alimentación y la agricultura. (2005). *Desarrollo de productos con carne de alpaca*. Lima, Peru: FAO.

Pighi, P. (2017, January 18). Por qué a muchos peruanos les cuesta reconocerse como cholos. *BBC News Mundo*. Retrieved from https://www.bbc.com/mundo/noticias-america-latina-37489332

Quijano, A. (2003). Notas sobre raza y democracia en los países andinos. *Revista Venezolana de Economía y Ciencias Sociales*, *9*(1), 53–59.

Rivera Medina, J., & Caceres Cabana, Y. (2016). *Línea de Base del Proyecto: Desarrollo sostenible de comunidades vulnerables en 3 provincias altoandinas de Arequipa y Puno*. Arequipa, Peru: DESCOSUR.

Salazar, R. D. (2001). Comida y Cultura: Identidad y significado en el mundo Contemporâneo. *Estudios de Asia y Africa*, *36*(1), 83–108.

Sammells, C. (1998). Folkore, food, and national identity: Urban legends of llama meat in La Paz, Bolivia. *Contemporary Legend*, *1*, 21–54.

Servicio Nacional de Sanidad Agraria. (2020). *Estado Situacional de los mataderos con respecto a la autorización sanitaria*. Lima, Peru: SENASA.

Servicio Nacional de Sanidad Agraria. (n.d.). *Estado Situacional de los mataderos con respecto a la autorización sanitaria*. Lima, Peru: SENASA.

Smith, S. M. & Trivelli, C. (2001). *El Consumo Urbano de Alimentos Andinos Tradicionales*. Lima, Peru: Coleccion Minima 40.

Solomon, M. R. (1983). The role of products as social stimuli: A symbolic interactionism perspective. *The Journal of Consumer Research*, *10*(3), 319–329. doi:10.1086/208971

Tuesta, A. V. (2013). *La riqueza exportadora de nuestra Sierra*. Lima, Peru: Sierra Exportadora.

Unidad de coordinación de emergencias y rehabilitaciòn. (2008). *¿Cuál ha sido el Impacto en 2008 de las Bajas Temperaturas en la Agricultura y Ganadería Altoandina?* Lima, Peru: Organización de las Naciones Unidas para la agricultura y la alimentación FAO en el Perú.

Weismantel, M. J. (1988). *Food, Gender, and Poverty in the Ecuadorian Andes*. Philadelphia, PA: University of Pennsylvania Press.

Wilson, F. (2010). Indians and Mestizos: Identity and Urban Popular Culture in Andean Peru. *Journal of Southern African Studies*, *26*(2), 239–253. doi:10.1080/03057070050010093

ADDITIONAL READING

Instituto Nacional de Estadística e Informática del Perú INEI. (2012). IV Censo Nacional Agropecuario. Recuperado el 13 de 11 de 2019, de http://censos.inei.gob.pe/Cenagro/redatam/?id=CensosNacionales#

Organización de las Naciones Unidas para la alimentación y agricultura. (2019). http://www.fao.org/peru/noticias/detail-events/es/c/319827/. Recuperado el 13 de 11 de 2019, de http://www.fao.org/peru/noticias/detail-events/es/c/319827/

KEY TERMS AND DEFINITIONS

Alpaca: Scientific name is *Vicugna pacos*. A species of South American camelid.

Alpaca Meat: Is the soft substance (muscles) that covers the bones of alpaca.

Alpaqueros: Community or people that breed lamas and alpacas.

Cholo: Connotation given to the mountains rage migrants that installed in the city after World War II in Peru, creating a difference between the Andean peasants and urban cholos. Currently, this word is also use in two contexts: in the urban areas of the capital and the main Peruvian cities to refer to the one coming from the mountains, characterized as being shy, unknown, dumb and out of touch; and in some areas of the mountains as is the case of Cusco refers to a person with love, cholito.

Consumption Ritual: Process in which consumer goods transforms in symbols of cultural value.

Taboo: Social mechanism that can be reinforced or suspended in different context to prevent possible transgression of the moral code.

Chapter 17 The Portuguese Luxury Wine Market: A Study on the Perceptions of Wine Brand Managers

Nuno Metello de Nápoles
University of Porto, Portugal

Helena Nobre
University of Aveiro, Portugal

Raquel Meneses
University of Porto, Portugal

ABSTRACT

Wine has been a part of human history for thousands of years, serving both social and religious roles. Just a few centuries ago, it became possible to store wine in good conditions, allowing it to be bottled and aged, which created a luxury product, consumed as a token of prestige. This study aimed to analyse wine brand managers' perceptions on the motivations behind luxury wine consumption. Given the exploratory nature of the study, eight interviews with Portuguese luxury wine producers and distributors' managers have been undertaken. The content analysis of the interviews seems to indicate that, overall, there is a strong understanding of the consumers' motivations. Yet, there are certain more specific aspects with the potential to be explored in order to raise the efficiency of the strategies being employed.

INTRODUCTION

Luxury wine has been gaining increasing importance in the global market, in which there is an increase in the demand and consumption of luxury wine brands (Wolf, Morrish, & Fountain, 2016). The research was carried out on the Portuguese wine market, characterized by small wine producers and a proliferation of private wine brands, generally lacking international recognition. Most Portuguese wine brands

DOI: 10.4018/978-1-7998-3115-0.ch017

Copyright © 2020, IGI Global. Copying or distributing in print or electronic forms without written permission of IGI Global is prohibited.

belong to a small group of medium/large companies that control the distribution channels domestically and abroad. Portugal represents an interesting research setting as it is the country with the highest annual per capita consumption of wine, according to 2017 data from the International Organisation of Vine and Wine (OIV), but, on the other hand, the luxury wine sector is still underrepresented.

The notion of luxury has always existed throughout human history, although it might not have been formally defined since the beginning, and interpreted in different ways, such as in Ancient Greece. Mc-Cants (2007) mentions that, upon the XVIIth century, the supply of more valuable and sumptuous goods has led to a greater separation between social classes. From this perspective, a luxury good is presented as something unique, exclusive and accessible to only a small fraction of the population (Cristini, Kauppinen-Raisanen, Barthod-Prothade, & Woodside, 2017). In the last decades, we have seen a shift in the luxury consumption, from the excellence of handcrafted goods, an essential element of real luxury, to the massification of goods that maintain their logos and conspicuous function that confers social status (Amaldoss & Jain, 2005; Vigneron & Johnson, 1999).

This chapter aims to understand managers' perceptions on the motivations of the consumers to acquire luxury wines, a topic that, according to Kim and Johnson (2015), deserves further deepening. Besides the existing studies in the literature aimed to understand the evolution of the concept of luxury in the wine sector, from the consumers' point of view (Boncinelli, Dominici, Gerini, & Marone, 2019; Bruwer, Saliba, & Miller, 2011; Wolf et al., 2016), or from the producer/brand (Thach, Charters, & Cogan-Marie, 2018), accordingly to Bruwer et al. (2011), few articles aimed to examine the contrast between what the brands have sought to offer to the consumers and what the consumers actually search for in a luxury wine. Through in-depth interviews, information was collected from a group of wine brand managers and producers on their opinions and knowledge about the real motivations of wine consumers, particularly luxury wine consumers. Such information was subsequently compared with the results published in academic literature regarding the behaviour of wine brand consumers. The study also aimed at analysing the Portuguese world of producing companies and private brands in this market and elaborate a set of management recommendations in order to reach a standard for domestic luxury wine in line with the international panorama.

BACKGROUND

The Consumption of Luxury Goods and Brands

The historical debate between philosophers, economists and several authors on the meaning of luxury shows that its definition in absolute terms is not possible at all (Mortelmans, 2005). The so many different interpretations, concepts and attributes that the consumers associate with luxury goods are various and complex (Sjostrom, Corsi, & Lockshin, 2016). Typically, high cost is considered the critical factor directly associated with premium products by most consumers (Keller, 2009), when compared with lower-range products (Dubois, Laurent, & Czellar, 2001). However, one might argument that high cost is only an inevitable consequence of the combination of all the product's attributes (Wiedmann, Hennigs, & Siebels, 2009). The concept of luxury is understood to aggregate a set of attributes (Sjostrom et al., 2016), in which the products are classified as belonging to the luxury category for having the highest standards in a series of requisites (Atwal & Williams, 2009). Within the luxury attributes, there are four attributes that stand out: quality, authenticity, exclusivity and price (Atwal & Williams, 2009; Mortelmans, 2005).

Quality, or excellence, is one of the most important attributes as far as luxury is concerned (Dubois et al., 2001). High quality is the expectation that luxury brands offer to the consumers when compared with other brands, for which it is unlikely that the image of luxury remains associated with the brand when quality is lower (Seo & Buchanan-Oliver, 2015). When the quality of the product is perceived as low, a high cost will be disproportional and the product is no more than a bad imitation, a false luxury (Mortelmans, 2005). When a high level of quality is perceived, a price premium is justifiable. The mental association between quality and luxury is so intense that the two terms are almost synonyms (Mundel, Huddleston, & Vodermeier, 2017). Quality also encompasses several other related attributes: technology, engineering, design, sophistication and artisanal manufacture (Vigneron & Johnson, 2004).

Authenticity may be associated with several terms, such as origin, production methods, credibility, moral values, purity, tradition, aura (since it demonstrates natural evolution and history) or even self-expression (Beverland, 2005; Morhart, Malar, Guevremont, Girardin, & Grohmann, 2015). Concerning wine in particular, authenticity is closely related to the cellar history, production philosophy and processes (Wolf et al., 2016). In this regard, authenticity contains all the elements that concern the product itself, the production processes, the connection to history and the "myths" created by the market, the consumers, and even the brand itself. Brand authenticity may be verified on a real basis through information about the brand, original labels, age, ingredients or performance. Nonetheless, it is also an interpretation of the consumers, that is, a projection of expectations, beliefs and perspectives (Morhart et al., 2015). Authenticity demands a balance between the production, distribution and marketing components and the managers' will to maintain the tradition of production methods, product stylization, values and location, the taste for excellence production and the commitment to keep the label away from modern industrialization and commercial motivations, which aim for maximal profitability and mass sales. The combination of all these real and perceived factors favours the creation of an aura around the luxury brand that differentiates it from widely consumed brands (Beverland, 2005, 2006).

Scarcity, rarity or exclusivity are deeply rooted aspects in human life and an essential requisite for human behaviour (Lynn, 1991). Luxury brands must keep a high notoriety level, but also control the scarcity level, through limited production and selective distribution (Phau & Prendergast, 2000). Otherwise, and if sales were massified, the brand would lose its exclusivity status and, consequently, its appearance of magnificence (Mortelmans, 2005). Such search for uniqueness is based on the assumption that the perceptions of exclusivity and rarity increase the desire for the brand, particularly if the article is expensive (Lynn, 1991; Verhallen & Robben, 1994). The sensations of exclusivity and rarity also increase the price of the articles (Vigneron & Johnson, 2004). Regarding wines and spirit drinks, consumers understand that the quantity may vary and may be limited due to, for instance, the weather conditions during the year (Catry, 2003). Although this is true, this perception of scarcity and rarity may also be created by the brands, in order to make the products more desirable and appreciated (Verhallen & Robben, 1994). In this sense, production is limited so as to create a myth. Nevertheless, while factual rarity is somewhat boring and insufficient if the components surrounding it are not perceived as desirable, qualitative rarity involving modern luxury is the brands' answer to contradict current industrial mass production processes. Such qualitative rarity may be created, for instance, by incorporating a manual process into a mechanized one (Kapferer, 2012).

Luxury brand managers must pursue limited distribution (Hennigs et al., 2012; Keller, 2009; Seo & Buchanan-Oliver, 2015). Total control of distribution must be regarded as an essential principle of a luxury business model, in which brands control the image of rarity by having few points of sale, in appropriate places (Kapferer & Valette-Florence, 2016). Therefore, distribution of luxury items must be operated directly by the brands, or through specialized stores, dedicated solely to the brand (Kumagai & Nagasawa, 2017). The retailing of luxury goods relates to experience, in which the moment of consumption is exclusive itself (Kapferer, 1997).

High cost is an inevitable consequence (Wiedmann et al., 2009) of the conjunction of all combined attributes. According to Sjostrom et al. (2016), luxury products should only be made available to the consumers who perceive quality and limited quantity and, as such, who are willing to pay a premium price. Such high cost is partially explained by the high production costs associated with quality products, which are perceived by the consumers as a plausible explanation for the price (Lim, Brun, Runyan, & Kim, 2013; Mundel et al., 2017), and by the singularities made by the intangible elements, such as heritage, tradition, history, country of origin, famous clients, and an imaginary lifestyle (Kapferer & Valette-Florence, 2016). There is even the need to establish high prices for luxury products, and it is not advisable for the brands to leave the consumers in any doubt about the merits inherent in buying these products (Keller, 2009). Also, it is necessary to distinguish that, rather than their absolute price, the differential price between luxury products and products with comparable functionality is what is relevant in this attribute (Kapferer, 1997).

Motivations for Luxury Consumption

The motivation mechanisms underlying the purchase of a luxury good are often impulsive, emotional or extravagant. Whoever buys a luxury article is, in fact, buying a dream (Dubois & Paternault, 1995). The motivation for buying luxury articles is primarily due to the pursuance of status and appearance (Atwal & Williams, 2009), which are not basic needs. Consumers assess products differently as they seek to satisfy more basic needs, such as eating, drinking and being safe (Maslow, Frager, Fadiman, McReynolds, & Cox, 1970). Status is a shallower need that appears once those more basic needs are met (Mundel et al., 2017). The association of luxury with a higher status occurs because luxury is both the intrinsic quality of a product or experience and the immaterial quality provided by the brand in question (Nueno & Quelch, 1998). However, the perception of the value of luxury by the consumer is not only related to the set of social aspects such as ostentation, status, distinction or the desire to impress others. It is also dependent on the financial, functional and utility components. The financial, functional, personal and social dimensions are on the basis of the basic motivations underlying luxury consumption (Hennigs et al., 2012). The relative importance of these dimensions varies according to culture. Therefore, understanding consumers' behaviour implies understanding the value that consumers allocate to possession or consumption. In a conscious or unconscious way, intentionally or not, each one perceives his possessions as part of himself (Belk, 1988).

The Levels of Luxury

For centuries, luxury was restricted to few people, such as aristocrats and elites (Wolf et al., 2016). It was a lifestyle reserved for the most powerful, such as pharaohs, kings, queens and their courts and, later on, merchants and manufacturers. It was used to express exquisite taste and impress crowds, pleasing the most influent circles of consumers (Kapferer, 2014). While, traditionally, luxury items were consumed by the economically most powerful circles as a form of ostentation and social status, its origin is still latent among consumers (Kapferer, 2014). Nevertheless, in recent years, there has been a "luxury democratization" (Mundel et al., 2017; Silverstein & Fiske, 2003). The brands' focus has thus shifted from a group of extraordinary people to an ordinary group, who the brands however make believe to be extraordinary (Kapferer, 2014).

With respect to wine, the study by Mundel et al. (2017) refers that, among other items, wine and spirit drinks are fairly high regarding the threshold between affordable luxury and traditional luxury, which means that there is an opportunity to market wine as a traditional luxury product. While this opportunity actually exists, it should be considered that there is also a strategy in the opposite direction, since the brands that were dedicated to consumers with more economic power only are now also dedicated to new product lines or extensions and new brands, in order to reach middle class consumers (Silverstein & Fiske, 2003; Vigneron & Johnson, 2004). Silverstein and Fiske (2003) name such luxury democratization as "Mass Prestige" or "Masstige". With these terms, the authors refer to items that occupy a very particular position between massification and prestige. Although there are now concepts, within the scope of luxury, that differ from the traditional concept, with various levels and different consumers identified, luxury brands must take into account some rules in order to avoid the brand's wear, since one of the basic principles of luxury is exclusivity or scarcity. As awareness raises, a brand may increase its sales and profits, but this can discourage purchases from its original consumers. To counter this, brands may choose to increase their sales by appealing to a broader group of consumers, though with a lower profitability than the original, using different rarity and exclusivity tactics, creating several sublevels within the same brand, each placed at a different price level, with distinct distribution patterns (Kapferer & Valette-Florence, 2018). Thus, brands become social bookmarks of stratification, in which the only obstacle to access the desired item is the financial limit of the individual himself (Mundel et al., 2017).

From the affordable luxury consumers' point of view, the consumption of products and services takes place for reasons that differ from those of the traditional elite consumers (Silverstein & Fiske, 2003). Truong, McColl, and Kitchen (2009) refer that there is a desire to simulate the lifestyle of the wealthiest, or that of the social class immediately above theirs. Current luxury means dignity, belonging, and symbolizes the pursuance for status (Kastanakis & Balabanis, 2012), implying that luxury serves self-interests, with desire for material possession and conspicuous utilization (Cristini et al., 2017). While the concept of traditional luxury was already not simple, such luxury popularization caused even more confusion (Kapferer, 2012; Kastanakis & Balabanis, 2012), further fragmenting its meaning (Cristini et al., 2017). The new luxury consumers are younger than the traditional luxury customers used to be, more numerous, obtain money more quickly, and are more flexible in financing and inconstant in their choices (Truong et al., 2009). Luxury brands quickly understood this and, as such, they compete for their attention and try not only to sell symbolism and power to a broader market (Kapferer, 2012), but also to establish meaningful relationships between the consumer and the brand (Nobre & Simões, 2019). Depending on the context, consumers may perceive, as luxury, products, services and brands that do not meet the traditional notion of symbolic and luxurious consumption. For instance, water may be seen either as a basic need or as a luxury item, depending on the situation and location (De Barnier, Falcy, & Valette-Florence, 2012).

The Luxury Wine Market

There is little understanding about the nature of the luxury wine market (Beverland, 2004), especially about the marketing strategies to be used in luxury wines in order to reach consumers (Thach et al., 2018). Wine has been part of the human history for more than six thousand years, serving social and religious functions. Its modern expression, with quality improvement and increased shelf life, has begun around the XVIIth century (Soleas, Diamandis, & Goldberg, 1997). Wine used to be consumed only by the aristocracy and other elites, the only social groups with economic power to buy and store wine in good condition. After, through several developments and innovations, it was possible to decreased wine oxidation, facilitating shipping, storage and, consequently, the possibility of adding aromatic features in the bottle, which were, until then, eliminated by the defective condition in which the wine reached the consumer. This allowed wine to be consumed and appreciated by emerging classes. Wine became a differentiating good, consumed conspicuously as a mark of distinction in public places, increasing its value owing to its evolving and ephemeral qualities (Howland, 2013).

With the increase in quality, luxury wines have emerged, from which the Bordeaux Premier Cru are possibly among the world's most famous. Such original brand identification was as initiative of the French Government in 1855, while searching to provide a structure for wine production in Bordeaux. Being classified meant obtaining prestige, with this honourable classification being kept until today (Reyneke, Pitt, & Berthon, 2011). Currently, luxury wines provide important knowledge for the brands in all sectors of this segment, since they represent some of the oldest brands still in activity. These brands have gone through price wars, with competitors selling at very low prices, wars, scandals, inconstant phases such as periods of crisis and changes in taste and, still, many have survived (Beverland, 2005).

Regarding the specific Portuguese scenario, wine has always been part of the country's history, closely connected to multiple generations of producers and farmers. In 1994, the Porter report has confirmed this, placing wine as one of the country's foundations for economic growth. Through the strategies advocated in this report, it was possible to achieve, more than 20 years later, significant improvements in wine, with increased quality (Gonçalves, Ribeiro Mendes, Sardinha, & Rodrigues, 2015).

The wine market has drastically changed in most countries over recent centuries, with its consumption having been democratized (Rössel & Pape, 2016). Such evolution is due to the higher number of appreciators, which, in turn, made the producers focus their strategy and production on the use of simpler and accessible grape varieties, allowing the less connoisseur consumers to learn about wine complexity. This brought more and less connoisseur consumers, with more or less experience and knowledge, closer, taking part and participating in the opinions on the different wines (Howland, 2013). Hence, wine has become common in people's daily lives, purchased and consumed as a necessary good in a household context, though its purchase has a special nature (Ritchie, 2009). Nevertheless, such democratization also causes a paradox. Wine becomes no more than an ordinary consumption good, no longer being relevant for the construction and maintenance of the identity of whoever consumes it. With the dissemination of mass consumption, its purchase and consumption have led to a democratization that caused a decrease in the production and consumption of great wines in the European wine-producing countries. Still, wine's per capita consumption has increased and invaded people's taste and preferences, thus reaching a broader market (Rössel & Pape, 2016).

Characterization of Luxury Wine

Wine is a complex product category (Wolf et al., 2016). Considering the notion of the different levels of luxury, it is possible to place the best wine brands as an affordable luxury article, similarly to other product categories, such as spirit drinks and fragrances, since there is a high proportion of consumers who are able to reach the top of these categories more easily than other categories more expensive in general (Sjostrom et al., 2016). In fact, if one of the requisites to be considered a traditional luxury item is the expensive price (Keller, 2009), even the "best" wines cannot be considered as such, given that less than five per cent are sold at a price above 100 dollars (Sjostrom et al., 2016), and even the wines sold above 50 dollars per bottle are typically rather scarce and acquired by consumers who are true connoisseurs. Wines classified as "icons" are consistent with the luxury status; however, these wines represent approximately one per cent of the global wine market (Beverland, 2004).

Rather than absolute price, one should consider the differential price between luxury products and products with comparable functionality (Kapferer, 1997), with the product category being directly related to the association with luxury (De Barnier et al., 2012). Although wine may be considered an affordable luxury, mainly due to its accessible price, luxury wine features are interconnected with the characteristics identified for luxury items in general. Heritage and pedigree, aesthetic consistence, commitment to quality, the relationship with the place, the production method and the relativization of purely commercial motivations represent luxury wine characteristics (Beverland, 2006).

Therefore, a high-quality wine may age for decades, reflecting its high quality. Its quality may also depend on the vineyard's location, or have a designation synonymous with quality, such as *Vintage*, which may also have an impact on quality, since this qualification is only assigned in exceptional years (Thach et al., 2018). Regarding consumption, experience is important, and it is not possible to limit the importance of consumption to the physical features of the product. The way how the bottle is opened and how the wine is poured into a glass are fundamental aspects that allow the maximization of all the consumer's sensations.

In turn, authenticity may be observed with the *Champagne* example. By understanding the importance of the development of symbols connected with nature, and in order to move producers away from an excessively industrialized process, a criterion of respect for tradition was developed in France to identify the best *Champagnes*, thereby creating a strategy that proved to be critical for the creation of authenticity in the production method (Beverland, 2005). Similarly, in other wines, oenologists focus on producing with authenticity, emphasizing what nature and the harvest provided for that particular year. As a complement, they do not disregard the production methods and practices, such as the care with destemming and the purchase of high-quality barrels (Thach et al., 2018). In turn, rarity, as far as wines are concerned, is achievable by putting limits on the vineyard, or by keeping production low. If harvests have low quality, the wine is usually disqualified and is not sold that year. Even efficient selective distribution may be achieved in luxury wines through exclusive outlets, restaurants, events, or even certain clubs. The price is required to be high enough; otherwise, the wine risks losing its conspicuous appeal to consumers (Hall, 2016).

METHODS

The study followed a qualitative methodology, through in-depth interviews to eight managers of luxury brands of still and fortified wines, operating in Portugal and selling in the national and foreign markets. In-depth interviews are one of the most common and powerful techniques to understand human behaviour without imposing an *a priori* categorization that limits the data collection process (Fontana & H. Frey, 1995). The use of such methodology aimed at the comprehension of managers' perceptions on the luxury wine consumers' motivations in Portugal. Therefore, through a qualitative study, it was possible to deeply analyse the opinions and strategies used by managers. The aim of qualitative research is to explore and describe poorly studied areas, and develop theory, thereby enabling the generation of knowledge in a particular area (Morse, 1991).

The data collected from through in-depth, semi-structured interviews, allowed the consistent exploitation of a set of relevant data for the topic under study, given the exploratory nature of the research (Fontana & H. Frey, 1995). The interviews aimed at getting information on managers' opinions and perceptions on the motivations of luxury wine consumers. The interview script contained an initial familiar question to the participant (Whiting, 2008), in order to grasp his previous experience; a question to define what he understands by luxury wines; several questions on brand strategy and on the perceptions on the consumers and their motivations; and a final question to understand his opinion regarding the sector's evolution in Portugal. There were also auxiliary sub-questions to facilitate the answer, in case the participants did not deepen the main questions being asked. The conclusion of the interview, which according to Whiting (2008) deserves due attention, took place only when the interviewer and the interviewee considered it comfortable and that all the topics had been appropriately addressed.

The Participants

The participants in the research study are managers who deal with a great diversity of wine, from rosé to white, verde, red and Port wines. The companies they work for produce and/or distribute wines from several wine-growing regions in Portugal and also abroad. Most managers do not deal with luxury wines only, which allows them to distinguish what motivates consumers when they search for luxury wines from when search for wines from the other ranges. In order to keep their privacy, the managers were identified by their initials.

All the participants except one (IR) have higher education levels. Their age is between 23 (BLX) and 51 years old (AS). Regarding their experience, the range is very wide, between 9 months (BLX) and 28 years (AS). AS and PM are international Area Managers working for the same company for 28 and 9 years, respectively. They work for a Portuguese company established more than 50 years ago that produces fine wines, Port wines, and has vineyards abroad. VG is Key Account Manager and BLX and MO are Brand Managers of recognized brands in Douro, Dão, Alentejo, Vinhos Verdes, Lisboa and Port Wines. They work in a wine distribution company with approximately 25 years. BM is Brand Manager in a wine producer company of fine wines in Douro's region and Port wines. IR has 25 years of experience in this area. She works in a wine distribution company since its establishment in 2013. She is responsible for a private wine club with members that are wine connoisseurs with high income. She only works with premium wines, from all over the world, Port wines and premium destilates, such as whisky and gin. JPM has been a manager for 15 years in a wine producing company with vineyards in five countries across 3 continents.

Analysis of the Interviews

From the content analysis of interviews, it was possible to identify 16 consumer motivations for purchasing luxury wines, according to managers' perceptions:

- **Authenticity:** Authenticity reflects the brand's aura and the fundamental values on which it is based. The creation of authenticity involves a great deal of paradoxes. For example, the brand wishes to remain true for its fundamental basis while remaining relevant (Beverland, 2005). Authenticity was only mentioned 5 times by 2 of the interviewees.
- **Self-satisfaction:** Self-satisfaction relates to hedonism, since the consumer looks for personal rewards and satisfaction, which he obtains through products that are assessed according to subjective emotional benefits and through satisfactory intrinsic properties, rather than by considering only functional benefits (Vigneron & Johnson, 2004).
- **Exclusivity:** A limited number of consumers who possess or have conditions to acquire the brand and who project such image of exclusivity onto a limited number of privileged people (Phau & Prendergast, 2000).
- **Distribution control:** The controlled use of distribution, instead of mass distribution channels, is made through sales in exclusive outlets, restaurants, events or certain clubs (Hall, 2016). This is a requisite for exclusivity and prestige, ensuring that channel selection and control are in line with the brand's promise (Keller, 2009).
- **Scarcity and rarity:** Scarcity affects consumers' reactions to products. It increases the value of any possessable good. Thus, the scarcer a product is, the higher its value and desirability will be. Scarcity, or rarity, are determined by the limited quantity available or by the limited number of points of sale, which limit the possession of a given product (Verhallen & Robben, 1994).
- **Consumption experience and occasion:** Experience is the purchase of a series of memorable events for a service or good, which are provided in specific and different moments, depending on the context and situation, aiming at the interaction with the consumer in a more personal and intimate way. Beginning with the product's essence, it is amplified through a set of tangible, physical and interactive experiences (Atwal & Williams, 2009).
- **Importance of image:** The first test is, almost always, done with the eyes. The extrinsic aspects of the product provide the consumer social and aesthetic utility, which end up strongly influencing his sensory perceptions and, hence, his expectations (Mueller & Lockshin, 2008).
- **Packaging:** Package design involves several considerations, ranging from content protection to the impression of the communication that is desired by the brand. Therefore, it has two essential functions: the functional attribute (ergonomics, durability, recycling) and the visual impact (Orth & Malkewitz, 2008).
- **Conspicuousness and status:** The purchase of products that satisfy not only material needs, but also social needs, such as prestige. It is the ratio between price and utility that serves as a purchase motivator and reflects customer self-image into others (Amaldoss & Jain, 2005; Heine, Atwal, Crener-Ricard, & Phan, 2018; Taylor, 2016).
- **Brand sharing and recognition:** The appeal to the consumers' perception of the product and brand value, which is closely interconnected with the consumer's orientation and identification with the symbolic brand's appeal (Kwon, Seo, & Ko, 2016).

- **Storytelling:** Stories are a form of written or oral literature in which meanings, forms and functions are placed in cultural contexts, scenes and/or events that give meaning to action. Stories may be analysed by using conventional techniques, categorization, content encoding and concept construction (Cohen, Manion, & Morrison, 2002).
- **Trends:** Cultural, social and external contributions that determine brands' meaning and influence their consumption (Seo & Buchanan-Oliver, 2015).
- **Expensiveness:** Expensive price as an element that allows to infer quality and value (Bagwell & Bernheim, 1996; Lim et al., 2013; Mundel et al., 2017).
- **Premium quality:** The mental association between luxury and quality is so strong that these words are almost synonymous (Dubois et al., 2001). Premium quality is the expectation that luxury brands offer in contrast to non-luxury brands (Seo & Buchanan-Oliver, 2015).
- **Properties:** Quality assignment to wine may depend on intrinsic attributes, namely on their physical and chemical properties, such as colour, degree of alcohol and flavour, which are specific to each product and cannot be altered without changing the product itself (Boncinelli et al., 2019).
- **Wine's age:** Wine's importance for the consumer is not only associated with the brand, but also with the fact that it is Vintage and with the year of harvest (Blair, Atanasova, Pitt, Chan, & Wallstrom, 2017). Some Vintage wines are assigned better scores from critics than other years (Thach et al., 2018).

Table 1. Analysis of the results of the qualitative study

Motivation for purchasing	Interviewees who mentioned the motivation	Number of times that the motivation was mentioned
Authenticity	2	5
Self-satisfaction	7	25
Exclusivity	8	34
Distribution control	7	18
Scarcity and rarity	7	20
Consumption experience and occasion	8	46
Importance of image	4	8
Packaging	3	5
Conspicuousness and status	8	56
Brand sharing and recognition	8	48
Storytelling	3	5
Trends	1	3
Expensiveness	8	26
Premium quality	7	15
Properties	5	10
Wine's age	3	5

As table 1 presents, there are five motivations all the participants mentioned and agreed to be crucial regarding luxury wines. Thus, it is not strange that these motivations were also the ones mentioned the most times along the interviews. According to the participants, these motivations are the most important in the process of buying a luxury wine and were also identified in the literature review which gave a specific approach for all of them. About conspicuousness and status, AS was the participant that mentioned it the most, and in his opinion most people don't know what they are drinking but if they have money, they like to show it. This opinion is corroborated by Atwal and Williams (2009) when they say that the motivation for buying luxury articles is primarily due to the pursuance of status and appearance. Brand sharing and recognition was another motivation mentioned several times along the interviews. About this motivation, JPM states that: "Information is abundant everywhere, in the internet and in specialized magazines. A young consumer can get information with extreme readiness." VG agrees with this opinion by saying that the democratization of information allowed more consumers to have greater access to these wines, so they consume more. However, there is a clear risk as awareness raises. A brand may increase its sales and profits, but this can discourage purchases from its original consumers (Kapferer & Valette-Florence, 2018). The consuming experience and occasion was another motivation that in the opinion of the participants deserves attention as it is not possible to limit the importance of consumption to the physical features of the product. When asked about what takes the consumers to drink luxury wines, MO answers: "The experience, the moment and the pleasure". About exclusivity, it increases the desire for the brand, particularly if the product is expensive (Lynn, 1991; Verhallen & Robben, 1994). All the participants referred exclusivity, mentioning it 34 times. Quoting BM: "Instead of talking about 60% of the population, we are talking to one per cent or less of the population that has access to these wines.". Expensiveness is the last motivation mentioned by all the participants and it was also the less often mentioned. However, it is essential when referring to luxury wines, because the mental association between quality and luxury is so intense that the two terms are almost synonyms (Mundel et al., 2017). Like IR says: "In these cases, the price works the other way around. The more expensive the wine, the rarer it is, so it makes it more desirable.". However, the price is always related with other motivations, as BM says: "If it was all about the price you could grab any wine and say that the price it's six thousand euros. Nobody is going to pay that amount and you are not creating luxury.".

SOLUTIONS AND RECOMMENDATIONS

Regarding motivations for luxury wine consumption, as mentioned by Beverland (2006), they are very similar to those of the majority of other luxury items. Thus, from the studies of several authors, thirteen essential motivations have been identified: image, status, use occasion, quality, authenticity, pleasure, scarcity, price, function, experience, symbolism, trends and rewards. According to different authors, these are the consumers' motivational factors that must be taken into account by managers and by wine companies, under penalty of not acting on the basis of what is demanded by the market, particularly in a market that is increasingly characterized by luxury democratization (Wolf et al., 2016), which, through means such as magazines and the internet, enables the exacerbated display of all wine's features (Howland, 2013).

The study also allowed to better understand the current profile of premium and luxury wine consumers, which meets the notion of "luxury experience" (Nobre & Simões, 2019), giving room to consumers who look for a holistic experience, rather than just a transactional relationship with wine brands (Atwal

& Williams, 2009). In fact, the current consumer, even though looking for conspicuousness, also seeks for an hedonic experience (Vigneron & Johnson, 2004). This way, we propose that consumers are currently divided into three big categories:

Table 2. Types of consumer and their motivations for purchasing

Types of client		Exhibitionists	Self-conscious	Wine connoisseurs
Motivations for purchasing luxury wine	Authenticity			X
	Self-satisfaction		X	X
	Exclusivity	X		X
	Distribution control	X		X
	Scarcity and rarity	X		X
	Use experience and occasion	X	X	X
	Importance of image	X		
	Packaging	X		
	Conspicuousness and status	X		
	Brand sharing and recognition	X		X
	Storytelling			X
	Trends	X		
	High cost	X		X
	Premium quality	X	X	X
	Features		X	X
	Wine's age		X	X

- **The "Exhibitionists":** look for social recognition, prestige and status in wine. The motivation for purchasing is others' esteem, which is only reached if the manifestation of wealth is evident (the Veblen effect). There is a signalling of ostentation, which derives from a balance relationship between price and status (Amaldoss & Jain, 2005; Bagwell & Bernheim, 1996; Heine et al., 2018; Taylor, 2016). Many individuals desire status and devote their energy to its achievement. Status is a form of power, consists of others' respect, consideration and jealousy, represents the objectives of a culture. Expensive price is, for these consumers, a prestige and status aspect conveyed by the brand (Eastman & Goldsmith, 1999). The importance assigned to the choice of wine is also different according to the occasion of use. Wine encompasses a symbolic value and is considered a social bookmark depending on its range. For this reason, in public situations where important reference groups meet, or when wine is offered as a gift, opting for a luxury wine distinguishes them and entails a high symbolic meaning (Ritchie, 2009).

- **The "Self-conscious":** have a more individualist background, in which consumption occurs for hedonic reasons. The brand and its symbology are less relevant and there are needs, desires and the search for new experiences (Atwal & Williams, 2009; Heine et al., 2018). These consumers relate more with sensory perception, fantasy, emotional aspects and the experience with the product itself. Such consumers look for personal rewards and satisfaction, which they obtain by consuming and purchasing sumptuous products (Vigneron & Johnson, 2004), for their subjective and intangible benefits (Dubois et al., 2001).
- **The "Connoisseurs":** are the consumers with a hedonist and perfectionist profile (Vigneron & Johnson, 1999). They are more interested in the pleasures offered by wine, place less emphasis on price and more on wine quality, characteristics and performance.

From table 2, it becomes evident that there are motivations that are shared by the three groups. Another reasonable conclusion is that "Exhibitionists" and "Wine connoisseurs" share several motivations between them and that the "Self-conscious" have motivations that are more similar to those of the "Wine connoisseurs".

There are two motivations that are common to all three groups: use experience and occasion and premium quality. While quality is a general motivation as far as luxury products are concerned, use experience and occasion may have different meanings for each group. For the "Exhibitionists", such experience must be shared in public occasions, where they can exhibit the wines purchased in order to obtain recognition and status. Since the main objective is the exhibition of these wines to reference groups, where "Connoisseurs" or "Self-conscious" can be found, the wine has to show high quality standard, under penalty of being disapproved by the other groups. For the "Self-conscious", motivation is related to the experience provided by wine, to pleasure and enjoying the moment. Thus, they may consume these wines more privately, for the sheer pleasure of it. If they share, it will tendentially be with people with whom they are intimate and to whom they wish to provide a pleasant moment. In turn, for the "Connoisseurs", the experience consists of tasting a wine that they already know or want to know. They look for these wines for private occasions and special public occasions.

"Exhibitionists" and "Connoisseurs" share between them some motivations for purchasing; nevertheless, some of them have different meanings for each group. Exclusivity, distribution control, scarcity and rarity, brand sharing and recognition and expensiveness are motivations shared by both groups. Concerning exclusivity, "Exhibitionists" look for certain limited quantity wines because they know that only a small percentage of the population is able to obtain them. This confers them status before their peers. In turn, "Connoisseurs" actually believe that there is a trade-off between the existing quantity of wine and its quality. Regarding brand sharing and recognition, "exhibitionists" are more interested in accessing the information disclosed, which influences them to purchase the wine. In other words, they look for opinions, either professional or amateur, leading them to an opinion-based decision. "Connoisseurs" search for the recognition of the brand and wine, since it identifies the style and its placement, which they know to be of quality. As far as expensive price is concerned, for "Exhibitionists" this is a crucial motivation, especially in situations of greater public exposure, since price confers status. For instance, in a restaurant, they may order the most expensive wine on the list, disregarding all other factors. In turn, for "Wine connoisseurs", high cost is considered a mere consequence of all its features and symbology, making it mandatory, since it is a luxury item.

Table 3. Study hypotheses for future research

H1	Selective distribution positively influences the exclusivity perceptions of a premium wine brand.
H2	Exclusivity has a positive effect on the recognition of the premium wine brand.
H3	Brand recognition has a positive effect on the attitude towards the premium wine brand.
H4	Expensive price positively influences the luxury image associated with the premium wine brand.
H5	The perception of authenticity has a positive effect on the attitude towards the premium brand.
H6	The association of a luxury image with a wine brand has a positive effect on the quality perceived by the consumer regarding that brand.
H7	Quality has a positive effect on the consumer's attitude towards that premium wine brand.
H8	The experience with a luxury wine brand positively influences perceived hedonism.
H9	Perceived hedonism positively influences the attitude towards the premium wine brand.
H10	The positive attitude towards the luxury wine brand has a positive effect on the consumer's purchase intention.

The "Self-conscious" and "Connoisseurs" show more similarities. Besides use experience and occasion and premium quality, common to all groups, self-satisfaction, wine properties and age are the motivations in common between both groups. Regarding self-satisfaction, the "Self-conscious" feel comfortable with a product with which they identify themselves and for the pleasure of enjoying, alone or in group, a luxury wine. For "Wine connoisseurs", self-satisfaction is the result of the opportunity to have a different and enriching experience regarding their knowledge of the world of wine. That is the case, for instance, of the oenophiles and world of wine passionates. Wine features and age are important for the "self-conscious" because they want to taste different wines. Rather than being worried about wine tannins, acidity, sugar and lightness, they look for wines that provide them a different experience. They want to understand what a wine of a certain age is, experience that evolution and figure out what those wines provide them in comparison with lower-range wines. In turn, "Wine connoisseurs" may find it important to taste a given wine for its organoleptic properties, since they are savvy consumers. And, for this very reason, wine's age, year of harvest and the fact that it is Vintage is fundamental to them. When they have to choose a wine, they choose accordingly to the brand and year, because their knowledge allows them to know that that particular year was a quality harvest.

The experiential component with wine had a particular emphasis throughout this study and, according to what is reported by several authors, wine consumption is a set of experience-related practices (Beverland, 2005). By providing significant experiences, brands create and keep bonds with the consumers, enabling engagement (Nowak, Thach, & Olsen, 2006). This search for relevant experiences (Nobre & Simões, 2019) may also be framed with the managers' quest for brand promotion through social networks. Exposure on social networks may be considered as a search for social status and focus on conspicuousness, more related to celebration, expression and creativity (Atwal & Williams, 2009). Therefore, an interesting strategy to be analysed by managers is the endorsement of important events, such as weddings and relevant parties. Sponsoring events by supplying wines from a brand will allow all guests in the celebration to immerge themselves in the experience (Peterson, 2005). Such strategy also enables product placement in a real context since, by posting photos on social networks and by mentioning the wine brand, it is possible to increase the brand awareness and recognition with no relativization of the quality perceived and of the brand's placement (Quelch, 1987).

FUTURE RESEARCH DIRECTIONS

Based on literature review and the analysis of in-depth interviews, a set of study hypotheses, representing a starting point for future studies, was formulated (see Table 3). Thus, a quantitative study, through a survey by questionnaire to luxury wine consumers, is recommended in order to validate some of the information obtained from qualitative data and, more specifically, to test the hypotheses presented.

Hypothesis One: Selective distribution positively influences the exclusivity perceptions of a premium wine brand.

This hypothesis attempts to confirm that selective distribution seeks to control brands' scarcity level, through limited production (Phau & Prendergast, 2000), and, as such, avoiding mass sales and the loss of the brand's exclusivity status (Mortelmans, 2005). Hennigs et al. (2012) underline the importance of limited distribution, stating that managers must pursue it. This meets the expectations of luxury brand consumers (Kapferer & Valette-Florence, 2016).

Hypothesis Two: Exclusivity has a positive effect on the recognition of the premium wine brand.

This hypothesis attempts to confirm that exclusivity increases desire, incrementing the brand awareness (Lynn, 1991; Verhallen & Robben, 1994). Phau and Prendergast (2000) argue that luxury brands should maintain a high level of awareness through the scarcity level, limited production and selective distribution.

Hypothesis Three: Brand recognition has a positive effect on the attitude towards the premium wine brand.

With this hypothesis, it is intended to confirm that luxury brands with a high awareness level (Phau & Prendergast, 2000) become social stratification bookmarks (Mundel et al., 2017). The motivation for purchasing is primarily due to the search for status and recognition (Atwal & Williams, 2009). Such association between luxury and status occurs, according to Nueno and Quelch (1998), because luxury is both the intrinsic quality of a product or experience and the intangible quality provided by the brand in question.

Hypothesis Four: Expensive price positively influences the luxury image associated with the premium wine brand.

The intention of this hypothesis is to confirm that the price of the luxury wine is an element that is raised in order to avoid risking the loss of its conspicuous appeal to consumers (Hall, 2016). According to Keller (2009), there is the need to establish high prices for luxury products, so that the brands do not leave the consumers in any doubt about the merits associated with the purchase of these products.

Hypothesis Five: The perception of authenticity has a positive effect on the attitude towards the premium brand.

This hypothesis aims to confirm that consumers seek for authenticity in a different way, maintaining the brand's essence (Beverland, 2005), without relativizing perceived quality and wine's placement (Quelch, 1987). According to Wolf et al. (2016), authenticity is closely related to the cellar history, production philosophy and processes.

Hypothesis Six: The association of a luxury image with a wine brand has a positive effect on the quality perceived by the consumer regarding that brand.

This hypothesis aims to confirm that the mental association between quality and luxury is so intense that the two terms are almost synonyms (Mundel et al., 2017). Such high quality is the expectation that luxury brands offer to the consumers when compared with other brands, for which it is unlikely that the image of luxury remains associated with the brand when quality decreases (Seo & Buchanan-Oliver, 2015).

Hypothesis Seven: Quality has a positive effect on the consumer's attitude towards that premium wine brand.

Quality, or excellence, arises as one of the main attributes as far as luxury is concerned (Dubois et al., 2001). This hypothesis attempts to confirm that consumers associate quality with luxury, with the two terms being almost synonymous (Mundel et al., 2017), and that such association increases the attitude towards the brand.

Hypothesis Eight: The experience with a luxury wine brand positively influences perceived hedonism.

This hypothesis aims to confirm that luxury wine provides the consumer with an experience that is a source of immediate and individual pleasure (Sheth, Newman, & Gross, 1991). This reinforces the shift from "have in order to be" to "possess in order to experiment" (Cristini et al., 2017). According to Christodoulides, Michaelidou, and Li (2009), the focus is on the consumption mode and how it is perceived, since experience is associated with the desire to consume products that provide sensory pleasure and satisfy intrinsic needs.

Hypothesis Nine: Perceived hedonism positively influences the attitude towards the premium wine brand.

As a source of immediate and individual pleasure (Sheth et al., 1991), a luxury wine gains a positive attitude from consumers, providing them with personal rewards and satisfaction. These consumers are more interested in the pleasures offered by wine, placing less emphasis on price and more on the quality that derives from wine characteristics and performance (Wolf et al., 2016).

Hypothesis Ten: The positive attitude towards the luxury wine brand has a positive effect on the consumer's purchase intention.

This hypothesis aims to confirm that the positive attitude towards the brand influences the motivation for purchasing luxury items (Atwal & Williams, 2009). A positive attitude increases the intention of whoever buys a luxury item and who is actually purchasing a dream (Dubois & Paternault, 1995). According to the occasion for consumption, either private or public and depending on the context, consumers acquire wines in different places and with specific aims. Such perception of the occasion is intimately related to the purchase decision, in a conscious or subconscious way, also depending on the consumer's degree of engagement (Ritchie, 2009).

CONCLUSION

The present work has some limitations. First of all, the small amount of companies with luxury wines in Portugal restricts the market to a very limited number of players, which do not intend to reveal their strategies for these products. Such limitation is also generated by the market. In Portugal, most consumers don't look for luxury wines and, in foreign markets, the Portuguese luxury wine has little expression. All these factors explain why there is few research dedicated to Portuguese luxury wine market. Also, more interviews with people from different, more operational areas and front-office, would allow a more comprehensive perception of the market. The sample was chosen for convenience, according to the researchers' acquaintances in the sector and in the companies of the wine business, which may contribute to some bias in the results obtained. In order to allow face-to-face interviews, only companies in the Northern region were considered, although these are represented in different producing regions in the country. The semi-structured interview method may also be seen as a limitation itself. If, on one hand, it allows for the deepening of topics that arise along the dialogue with the participant, but, on the other hand, for interviewers with limited experience, it may lead to subjects with little relevance for the study or to the under exploitation of topics that could arise and be further deepened. To inquire directly consumers' perceptions would complement results from the interviews with managers and test if all relevant motivations for purchasing were identified, and if there is some evolving purchase-motivating trend that deserves the attention of wine brand companies and managers.

REFERENCES

Amaldoss, W., & Jain, S. (2005). Conspicuous consumption and sophisticated thinking. *Management Science*, *51*(10), 1449–1466. doi:10.1287/mnsc.1050.0399

Atwal, G., & Williams, A. (2009). Luxury brand marketing – The experience is everything! *Journal of Brand Management*, *16*(5), 338–346. doi:10.1057/bm.2008.48

Bagwell, L. S., & Bernheim, B. D. (1996). Veblen effects in a theory of conspicuous consumption. *The American Economic Review*, *86*(3), 349–373.

Belk, R. W. (1988). Possessions and the extended self. *The Journal of Consumer Research*, *15*(2), 139–168. doi:10.1086/209154

Beverland, M. (2004). Uncovering "theories-in-use": Building luxury wine brands. *European Journal of Marketing*, *38*(3/4), 446–466. doi:10.1108/03090560410518648

Beverland, M. (2005). Crafting brand authenticity: The case of luxury wines. *Journal of Management Studies*, *42*(5), 1003–1029. doi:10.1111/j.1467-6486.2005.00530.x

Beverland, M. (2006). The 'real thing': Branding authenticity in the luxury wine trade. *Journal of Business Research, 59*(2), 251–258. doi:10.1016/j.jbusres.2005.04.007

Blair, A. J., Atanasova, C., Pitt, L., Chan, A., & Wallstrom, Å. (2017). Assessing brand equity in the luxury wine market by exploiting tastemaker scores. *Journal of Product and Brand Management, 26*(5), 447–452. doi:10.1108/JPBM-06-2016-1214

Boncinelli, F., Dominici, A., Gerini, F., & Marone, E. (2019). Consumers wine preferences according to purchase occasion: Personal consumption and gift-giving. *Food Quality and Preference, 71*, 270–278. doi:10.1016/j.foodqual.2018.07.013

Bruwer, J., Saliba, A., & Miller, B. (2011). Consumer behaviour and sensory preference differences: Implications for wine product marketing. *Journal of Consumer Marketing, 28*(1), 5–18. doi:10.1108/07363761111101903

Catry, B. (2003). The great pretenders: The magic of luxury goods. *Business Strategy Review, 14*(3), 10. doi:10.1111/1467-8616.00267

Christodoulides, G., Michaelidou, N., & Li, C. H. (2009). Measuring perceived brand luxury: An evaluation of the BLI scale. *Journal of Brand Management, 16*(5-6), 395–405. doi:10.1057/bm.2008.49

Cohen, L., Manion, L., & Morrison, K. (2002). *Research methods in education*. Routledge.

Cristini, H., Kauppinen-Raisanen, H., Barthod-Prothade, M., & Woodside, A. (2017). Toward a general theory of luxury: Advancing from workbench definitions and theoretical transformations. *Journal of Business Research, 70*, 101–107. doi:10.1016/j.jbusres.2016.07.001

De Barnier, V., Falcy, S., & Valette-Florence, P. (2012). Do consumers perceive three levels of luxury? A comparison of accessible, intermediate and inaccessible luxury brands. *Journal of Brand Management, 19*(7), 623–636. doi:10.1057/bm.2012.11

Dubois, B., Laurent, G., & Czellar, S. (2001). *Consumer rapport to luxury: Analyzing complex and ambivalent attitudes*. Academic Press.

Dubois, B., & Paternault, C. (1995). Observations - Understanding the world of international luxury brands - The dream formula. *Journal of Advertising Research, 35*(4), 69–76.

Eastman, J. K., & Goldsmith, R. E. (1999). Status Consumption in Consumer Behavior: Scale Development and Validation. *Journal of Marketing Theory and Practice, 7*(3), 41.

Fontana, A., & H. Frey, J. (1995). *Interviewing: The art of science*. Academic Press.

Gonçalves, V. C., Ribeiro Mendes, F., Sardinha, I. D., & Rodrigues, R. (2015). Twenty years after the Porter Report for Portugal. *Competitiveness Review, 25*(5), 540–554.

Hall. (2016). Exploring wine knowledge, aesthetics and ephemerality: clustering consumers. *International Journal of Wine Business Research, 28*(2), 134-153. doi:10.1108/IJWBR-09-2015-0044

Heine, K., Atwal, G., Crener-Ricard, S., & Phan, M. (2018). Personality-driven luxury brand management. *Journal of Brand Management, 25*(5), 474–487. doi:10.105741262-018-0090-8

Hennigs, N., Wiedmann, K. P., Klarmann, C., Strehlau, S., Godey, B., Pederzoli, D., ... Oh, H. (2012). What is the Value of Luxury? A Cross-Cultural Consumer Perspective. *Psychology and Marketing*, *29*(12), 1018–1034. doi:10.1002/mar.20583

Howland, P. J. (2013). Distinction by proxy: The democratization of fine wine. *Journal of Sociology (Melbourne, Vic.)*, *49*(2-3), 325–340. doi:10.1177/1440783313481746

Kapferer, J. N. (1997). Managing luxury brands. *Journal of Brand Management*, *4*(4), 251–259. doi:10.1057/bm.1997.4

Kapferer, J. N. (2012). Abundant rarity: The key to luxury growth. *Business Horizons*, *55*(5), 453–462. doi:10.1016/j.bushor.2012.04.002

Kapferer, J. N. (2014). The artification of luxury: From artisans to artists. *Business Horizons*, *57*(3), 371–380. doi:10.1016/j.bushor.2013.12.007

Kapferer, J. N., & Valette-Florence, P. (2016). Beyond rarity: The paths of luxury desire. How luxury brands grow yet remain desirable. *Journal of Product and Brand Management*, *25*(2), 120–133. doi:10.1108/jpbm-09-2015-0988

Kapferer, J. N., & Valette-Florence, P. (2018). The impact of brand penetration and awareness on luxury brand desirability: A cross country analysis of the relevance of the rarity principle. *Journal of Business Research*, *83*, 38–50. doi:10.1016/j.jbusres.2017.09.025

Kastanakis, M. N., & Balabanis, G. (2012). Between the mass and the class: Antecedents of the "bandwagon" luxury consumption behavior. *Journal of Business Research*, *65*(10), 1399–1407. doi:10.1016/j.jbusres.2011.10.005

Keller, K. L. (2009). Managing the growth tradeoff: Challenges and opportunities in luxury branding. *Journal of Brand Management*, *16*(5-6), 290–301. doi:10.1057/bm.2008.47

Kim, J., & Johnson, K. K. (2015). Brand luxury index: A reconsideration and revision. *Journal of Fashion Marketing and Management*, *19*(4), 430–444. doi:10.1108/JFMM-05-2015-0043

Kumagai, K., & Nagasawa, S. (2017). The effect of selective store location strategy and self-congruity on consumers' apparel brand attitudes toward luxury vs. non-luxury. *Journal of Global Fashion Marketing*, *8*(4), 266–282. doi:10.1080/20932685.2017.1348241

Kwon, J., Seo, Y., & Ko, D. (2016). Effective Luxury-Brand Advertising: The ES-IF Matching (Entity-Symbolic Versus Incremental-Functional) Model. *Journal of Advertising*, *45*(4), 459–471. doi:10.1080/00913367.2016.1226995

Lim, C. M., Brun, A., Runyan, R., & Kim, Y.-K. (2013). Segmenting luxe-bargain shoppers using a fuzzy clustering method. *International Journal of Retail & Distribution Management*, *41*(11/12), 848–868. doi:10.1108/ijrdm-01-2013-0012

Lynn, M. (1991). Scarcity effects on value: A quantitative review of the commodity theory literature. *Psychology and Marketing*, *8*(1), 43–57. doi:10.1002/mar.4220080105

Maslow, A. H., Frager, R., Fadiman, J., McReynolds, C., & Cox, R. (1970). Motivation and personality (Vol. 2). Harper & Row.

McCants, A. E. C. (2007). Exotic goods, popular consumption, and the standard of living: Thinking about globalization in the early modern world. *Journal of World History, 18*(4), 433. doi:10.1353/jwh.2008.0008

Morhart, F., Malar, L., Guevremont, A., Girardin, F., & Grohmann, B. (2015). Brand authenticity: An integrative framework and measurement scale. *Journal of Consumer Psychology*, *25*(2), 200–218. doi:10.1016/j.jcps.2014.11.006

Morse, J. M. (1991). Evaluating Qualitative Research. *Qualitative Health Research*, *1*(3), 283–286. doi:10.1177/104973239100100301

Mortelmans, D. (2005). Sign values in processes of distinction: The concept of luxury. *Semiotica*, *157*(1-4), 497–520.

Mueller, S., & Lockshin, L. (2008). *How important is wine packaging for consumers? On the reliability of measuring attribute importance with direct vebal versus indirect visual methods*. Academic Press.

Mundel, J., Huddleston, P., & Vodermeier, M. (2017). An exploratory study of consumers' perceptions: What are affordable luxuries? *Journal of Retailing and Consumer Services*, *35*, 68–75. doi:10.1016/j.jretconser.2016.12.004

Nobre, H., & Simões, C. (2019). NewLux Brand Relationship Scale: Capturing the scope of mass-consumed luxury brand relationships. *Journal of Business Research*. doi:10.1016/j.jbusres.2019.01.047

Nowak, L., Thach, L., & Olsen, J. E. (2006). Wowing the millennials: Creating brand equity in the wine industry. *Journal of Product and Brand Management*, *15*(5), 316–323.

Nueno, J. L., & Quelch, J. A. (1998). The mass marketing of luxury. *Business Horizons*, *41*(6), 61.

Orth, U. R., & Malkewitz, K. (2008). Holistic package design and consumer brand impressions. *Journal of Marketing*, *72*(3), 64–81. doi:10.1509/jmkg.72.3.64

Peterson, R. A. (2005). In search of authenticity. *Journal of Management Studies*, *42*(5), 1083–1098. doi:10.1111/j.1467-6486.2005.00533.x

Phau, I., & Prendergast, G. (2000). Consuming luxury brands: The relevance of the 'Rarity Principle'. *Journal of Brand Management*, *8*(2), 122–138. doi:10.1057/palgrave.bm.2540013

Quelch, J. A. (1987). Marketing the premium product. *Business Horizons*, *30*(3), 38–45.

Reyneke, M., Pitt, L., & Berthon, P. R. (2011). Luxury wine brand visibility in social media: An exploratory study. *International Journal of Wine Business Research*, *23*(1), 21–35. doi:10.1108/17511061111121380

Ritchie, C. (2009). The culture of wine buying in the UK off-trade. *International Journal of Wine Business Research*, *21*(3), 194–211.

Rössel, J., & Pape, S. (2016). Who has a wine-identity? Consumption practices between distinction and democratization. *Journal of Consumer Culture*, *16*(2), 614–632. doi:10.1177/1469540514536192

Seo, Y., & Buchanan-Oliver, M. (2015). Luxury branding: The industry, trends, and future conceptualisations. *Asia Pacific Journal of Marketing and Logistics*, *27*(1), 82–98. doi:10.1108/apjml-10-2014-0148

Sheth, J. N., Newman, B. I., & Gross, B. L. (1991). Why we buy what we buy: A theory of consumption values. *Journal of Business Research*, *22*(2), 159–170.

Silverstein, M. J., & Fiske, N. (2003). Luxury for the masses. *Harvard Business Review, 81*(4), 48.

Sjostrom, T., Corsi, A. M., & Lockshin, L. (2016). What characterises luxury products? A study across three product categories. *International Journal of Wine Business Research*, *28*(1), 76–95. doi:10.1108/ijwbr-05-2015-0017

Soleas, G. J., Diamandis, E. P., & Goldberg, D. M. (1997). Wine as a biological fluid: History, production, and role in disease prevention. *Journal of Clinical Laboratory Analysis*, *11*(5), 287–313. doi:10.1002/(sici)1098-2825(1997)11:5<287:Aid-jcla6>3.0.Co;2-4 PMID:9292395

Taylor, C., & Barber, N. A. (2016). How will my wine purchase decision be viewed by others? *Journal of Wine Research*, *27*(3), 202–225. doi:10.1080/09571264.2016.1173533

Thach, L., Charters, S., & Cogan-Marie, L. (2018). Core tensions in luxury wine marketing: The case of Burgundian wineries. *International Journal of Wine Business Research*, *30*(3), 343–365. doi:10.1108/IJWBR-04-2017-0025

Truong, Y., McColl, R., & Kitchen, P. J. (2009). New luxury brand positioning and the emergence of Masstige brands. *Journal of Brand Management*, *16*(5/6), 375–382. doi:10.1057/bm.2009.1

Verhallen, T. M. M., & Robben, H. S. J. (1994). Scarcity and preference - An experiment on unavailability and product evaluation. *Journal of Economic Psychology*, *15*(2), 315–331. doi:10.1016/0167-4870(94)90007-8

Vigneron, F., & Johnson, L. (2004). Measuring perceptions of brand luxury. *Journal of Brand Management, 11*(6), 484-506.

Vigneron, F., & Johnson, L. W. (1999). A review and a conceptual framework of prestige-seeking consumer behavior. *Academy of Marketing Science Review*, *1*(1), 1–15.

Whiting, L. S. (2008). Semi-structured interviews: Guidance for novice researchers. *Nursing Standard*, *22*(23), 35–40. doi:10.7748/ns2008.02.22.23.35.c6420 PMID:18323051

Wiedmann, K. P., Hennigs, N., & Siebels, A. (2009). Value-Based Segmentation of Luxury Consumption Behavior. *Psychology and Marketing*, *26*(7), 625–651. doi:10.1002/mar.20292

Wolf, H. L., Morrish, S. C., & Fountain, J. (2016). A conceptualization of the perceptions and motivators that drive luxury wine consumption. *International Journal of Wine Business Research*, *28*(2), 120–133. doi:10.1108/ijwbr-09-2015-0038

KEY TERMS AND DEFINITIONS

Authenticity: Made in the traditional way, or in a way that truly resembles an original.
Connoisseur: An expert judge in matters of taste.
Democratization: The action of making something accessible to everyone.
Hedonism: The devotion to pleasure as a way of life.
Massification: The practice of making luxury products available to the mass market.
Social Status: Relative rank that an individual holds in a social hierarchy based upon prestige.
Vintage: The year and place in which high quality wine was produced.

Chapter 18
The Consumer Role for Sustainable Development:
How Consumers Contribute Sustainable Development Goals

Seda Yildirim
Tekirdag Namık Kemal University, Turkey

ABSTRACT

The term sustainable consumption is not only a behavior type in marketing and a just consumption behavior, it is more than this. Sustainable or responsible consumption behavior can change the world. Sustainable consumption concept has been investigated widely in the literature and factors that effecting sustainable consumption or being a green consumer has been investigated recently, too. But the relationship between sustainable development and consumer behavior isn't investigated sufficiently. After 2030 Sustainable Development Goals set up, responsibilities and roles have been an important issue to achieve sustainable development in the long term. In this point, this study aims to investigate the consumer role for sustainable development goals through sustainable consumption patterns and trends.

INTRODUCTION

Sustainable development approach forces world leaders to make a balance between economic, social and environmental elements when achieving economic development. Both of developed and developing countries have been aware of climate change, global warming, environmental pollution and fast exhaustion of natural resources for a long time (Yıldırım et.al., 2016). Current economic models, current production and consumption patterns should be change into green economic approach, green production technologies and sustainable consumption patterns to leave more habitable world for the next generation. Accordingly, it can be said that the rise of sustainable consumption is mostly related with sustainable development term. After the United Nations determined the importance of environmental sustainability and warned the world about limited natural resources, economies understood that they were on the wrong scent. The

DOI: 10.4018/978-1-7998-3115-0.ch018

Copyright © 2020, IGI Global. Copying or distributing in print or electronic forms without written permission of IGI Global is prohibited.

history of sustainable development began in 1960s but 2000s gave life to sustainability. In 1962, Rachel Carson explained the relationship between toxicology, ecology and epidemiology in her book and said that maintaining human health and animal species were all based on clear agricultural methods (International Institute for Sustainable Development, 2012). Then year of 1972 brought two main events for sustainable development. Club of Rome published Limits to Growth and presented a report for the impacts of economic development on natural environment. UN Conference on the Human Environment was held in Stockholm by 1972 and UNEP was established. It can be said that sustainable development gained its international recognition in 1972 (Sustainable Development Commission, n.d.). The Brundtland Report defined the term of sustainable development formally and introduced this term to the whole world in 1987 (Klarin, 2018). By the United Nations Conference on Environment and Development (1992), fist action plans and strategies were set for sustainable development. UN Conference on Environment and Development (1992) which was called as the Earth Summit, provided "the Rio Declaration, the Forest Principles, Agenda 21, the Convention on Biological Diversity and the Framework Convention on Climate Change" as basic outcomes (Whitfield, 2015). In 2012, UN Conference on Sustainable Development (Rio+20) set first sustainable development goals that were called as the Millennium Development Goals (Sustainable Development Goals Knowledge Platform, n.d.). The Millennium Development Goals were transformed into 2030 Sustainable Development Goals by the UN Sustainable Development Summit in 2015. Today, the world aims to achieve 2030 Sustainable Development Goals till 2030. The brief history of sustainable development shows that the world has begun to change into sustainable world by governmental and institutional partnerships (Yıldırım and Yıldırım, 2020).

Households and individuals are worried about the future because of the increased environmental issues and problems (Bostancı and Yıldırım, 2020). Transforming consumption patterns and also production system have become one of the most important change movements to achieve sustainable development. Sustainable consumption and production take strength from each other. Sustainable production is based on green marketing approach. Green marketing approach aims to protect environment when producing goods and services to meet consumer needs and wants. So, consumers can find eco-friendly products in the market easily (Yeng and Yazdanifard, 2015). Although buying green products involves half of the sustainable consumption, buying second hand products or reducing consumption are also important patterns in sustainable consumption. Excessive consumption causes many negative environmental and psychological outcomes that responsible consumers prefer to buy green products or they keep other sustainable consumption patterns (Jastrzebska, 2017). The Commission on Sustainable Development formally set the term of sustainable consumption as a consumption type as the usage of services and related products which respond to basic needs and bring a better quality of life while minimizing the usage of natural resources and toxic materials as well as the emissions of waste and pollutants over the life cycle so as not to jeopardize the needs of future generations (Allaway,2012).

This study aims to explain the contribution of consumers for sustainable development. In this context this study will investigate the relationship between sustainable consumption patterns and 2030 Sustainable Development Goals (SDGs). The study employs qualitative research method and uses secondary data to determine the importance of sustainable consumption patterns to achieve 2030 SDGs. Accordingly, this chapter will study on these questions:

- What are the sustainable consumption patterns?
- What is the main role and responsibility of consumers for sustainable development?
- How can consumers contribute sustainable development goals?
- What is the link between sustainable consumption and 2030 Sustainable Development Goals?

TRANSFORMING CONSUMPTION PATTERNS INTO SUSTAINABLE CONSUMPTION

The consumption is thought as a final step of economic activities. The capital evaluates and distributes natural resources, businesses produce goods and services and then people buy these goods and services. Usage of resources will determine the next consumption level (Goodwin et.al., 2008). Economists determined consumption behavior based on "Utility Theory" in the past. But consumer behavior is not always rational, psychological factors also influence human behavior and buying decision (Sheth et.al.,1991).

Traditional economy said that consumers meet their wants and needs through material products. Max-Neef's study showed that consumers meet their wants and needs through material and non-material elements. In addition, economic growth did not always provide happiness as traditional economy thought. Max-Neef determined that economic growth provided specific welfare but it was not permanent forever. Because exhaustion of natural resources, pollution and socially-inequalities all influence the degree of welfare (Mont, 2004:138). In other words, current consumption patterns have threatened the socio-economic system for a long time (WBCSD, 2011).

Consumption patterns and production approaches cause environmental changes such as global warming, biodiversity loss, mass of waste etc. These environmental changes have been pointed out by the United Nations (UN) since 1992 Earth Summit. With 2002 World Summit on Sustainable Development, 10-year framework of programs for sustainable consumption and production was set up (Ferrara and Serret, 2008). The world has accepted the importance of sustainable consumption for a long time but reports show that sustainable consumption patterns are not so usual or common consumption patterns for consumers. However, everybody knows about sustainable consumption term. To prevent unsustainable consumption patterns, society must be informed better or new alternative production and consumption approaches (Mont, 2004:151).

Sustainable consumption aims to live within the Earth's carrying capacity and providing present and future consumers' needs (The Federal Government, 9). Oslo Symposium in 1994 defined sustainable consumption as " the use of services and products that meeting basic needs and providing better life quality while minimizing the use of natural resources and reducing toxic materials, waste and carbon emission etc. to protect the needs of next generations". According to this definition, it can be said that sustainable consumption includes both of social dimension and environmental dimension at the same time. Economic dimension includes being a consumer-centered business that financial profitability is less important than consumer satisfaction. As Guideline 49 of the United Nations determination, sustainable consumption aims "*meeting present and next generations' needs through sufficient goods and services that are economically, socially and environmentally sustainable*" (UN, 2019).

Hobson (2008:123) discussed the position of sustainable development whether it is close to well-being or economic growth. He said that the term of sustainable consumption could be defined as an alternative consumption pattern and also it presented a value type. Environment, economy and society which are three main dimensions of sustainable development, can expect different means from sustain-

Table 1. Three Basic Perspectives for Sustainable Consumption

Perspectives	Meanings
Environmental	It focuses on reducing consumption levels and usage of sources between 50% to 90%. Also it expects consumers to change their usual consumption pattern into sustainable consumption pattern through buying organic products or recycling packaged products to be less harmful for the environment.
Economic	It focuses on production and consumption patterns and it aims to change production technologies into more sustainable methods and consumption patterns into green consumption approach as consuming less or re-use and repair.
Social	It focuses on social justice and community vitality. It aims to reduce inequalities between global and national consumption patterns. In this point, everybody should have equal access to basic needs through sustainable livelihood sources.

Source: compiled by author from Hobson, 2008:123-124

able consumption. Table 1 shows different meanings for sustainable consumption in the context of environmental, social and economic perspectives.

Changing consumption patterns aren't so easy in the short term and consumers may not understand the importance and need of sustainable consumption quickly. In this point, transforming consumption patterns into sustainable consumption needs support from main four groups as "governments and regulators, consumers, businesses and civil societies" (WBCSD, 2011). WBCSD (2011) determined that consumers were responsible for accepting and sharing environmental values. Consumers take a responsibility when they give a buying decision. On the other side, sustainable production plays a critical role in the market to encourage sustainable consumption patterns. If businesses do not produce green products with sufficient quantities and quality, consumers can not fill up their needs or wants without harming environment. Consumption patterns are driven by some important factors such as economic forces, technology, politics, culture, value, lifestyle etc. Like as the drivers of consumption patterns, some drivers are based on governments, institutes or businesses and some of them are based on consumers. OECD (2008) studied on promoting sustainable consumption and production and determined some basic drivers for promoting sustainable consumption and production. In this point, table 2 explains the drivers of promoting sustainable consumption and production:

As seen in table 2, many implications or tools encourage consumers to have sustainable consumption patterns. It can be said that consumers can be transformed into green consumers or citizens successfully when they are informed and educated well. Information access, campaigns, labels and education will increase awareness of sustainable development and consumers will be more sensitive for the environment.

Literature showed many studies that investigating green consumers and sustainable consumption patterns. For example, some studies indicated that higher-educated people mostly preferred to buy green products and they mostly paid higher cost for green products (Van Liere and Dunlap 1981; Diamantopoulos et al.,2003; Young et.al., 2010; Zhang and Wu, 2012; Zhao et.al., 2014; Yıldırım and Candan, 2015). Some researchers determined that green product buyers mostly felt responsible for the environment. So, values, feelings or psychological factors were seen as the most effective drivers for buying green products (Chan, 2000; Pinto et.al.,2011; Yıldırım and Candan, 2015;). Sustainable consumption behavior mostly includes buying green products but sustainable consumption behavior means much more than buying green products. In this point, there is a growing trend for 3R (reduce-reuse-recycle) adoption in the market (Yan and Yusniza, 2016). To achieve sustainability, consumers can keep 3R principle in their usual consumption patterns (Abeliotis et.al., 2010; Yang et.al.,2014; Widyaningsih et.al., 2015; Musso

Table 2. The Drivers of Promoting Sustainable Consumption and Production

Drivers	General Implementations *
Standards and Mandatory Labels	- Reducing energy usage in household appliances or fuel usage are both important standards. - Mandatory labeling on consumer products for health reasons is so common implications such as warning on cigarettes - Nutritional labeling such as food content and GMO (Genetically modified organism) are so common in many OECD countries and EU countries.
Taxes and Charges	- Taxes and charges can influence consumer buying behavior. Taxes are more effective tools than regulations that households and consumers make a buying decision based on tax and charge factor. For example, reducing car emissions, household energy consumption, water use and household waste are related to taxes and tax level can limit usage of energy consumption, water consumption and car emission etc. Shortly, higher consumption of energy or water will cost higher. - Also taxes and charges on polluting products such as batteries, plastic bags, tires, disposable cameras can limit the usage of these items. - Many countries have deposit schemes that consumers are charged when they buy product. When product is returned, consumer can have a refund.
Subsidies and Incentives	- Many OECD governments try to encourage consumers to transform sustainable consumption. In this point, monetary grants, donations of goods and fiscal incentives and tax reductions are prior tools to encourage consumers. - When the price gap is sufficient enough, consumers will prefer sustainable products or sustainable usage. With buying sustainable products or having sustainable usage, consumers can make a profitable decision. - To promote sustainable transport, many countries support vehicles with less CO_2 emissions or riding bicycle. - To promote household energy efficiency, subsidies and fiscal incentives are so effective tools. Many countries support household to invest sustainable energy systems such as equipment such as boilers, energy-efficient windows, insulation, water and space heats, solar heating installations etc.
Communications campaigns	- Information and awareness-raising programs for sustainable consumption is an important tool to encourage consumers. - With the help of marketing and advertising campaigns, consumers can get more idea for sustainable products. - Government campaigns aim to support sustainable consumption behavior in the long term. - Communication campaigns should include socially-conscious consumption and ethical consumption. - Consumers should be warned about food consumption.
Education	- Many OECD countries employ teaching programs for sustainable development. - The UN's 10-year-programmes for Sustainable Consumption is also effective tool to transform society into sustainable society. - Sustainable schools are good project for teaching sustainable development (for example; Italy and the United Kingdom). Also, governments encourage "eco-schools" in a country. - If there is not any eco-school in a country, government can sponsor environmental education at primary, secondary and tertiary levels.
Voluntary Labeling	- Voluntary labeling has been mostly used, recently. These labels point out environmental and social claims and they are verified by governments of non-governmental organizations. - Organic cotton, dolphin-safe tuna or sustainable forestry are prior samples of multi-criteria labels. The aim of these labels is to compare products with others and give an information to consumer. - Some countries give more importance to voluntary labels. For example, "German Blue Angel" and "Nordic Swan" are the most known labels. - Eco-labeling can be supported by governments in a country. - "The Fairtrade Label" determined ethical goods or services and this label is based on not-for-profit international Fair Trade Labelling Organization (FLO). In some countries, this label is so important for consumers. - "Rainforest Alliance" is also important tool to influence consumer choices. - New labels are also help consumers to make a sustainable choice.
Corporate reporting	- Companies used corporate sustainability reporting to give information about their social and environmental practices. Companies usually report their practices such as *corporate governance, environmental performance, health and safe of employees, community contributions and supply chain management.* By these reports, consumers can get information about environmental and social conditions of production process. However, consumers should be careful about information's reality which is come from companies. - Most of OECD countries, corporate sustainability reporting is voluntary. On the other side, some countries *(Belgium, Denmark, France, the Netherlands, Norway),* corporate sustainability reporting is a legal obligation.
Advertising	- Tools of advertising commercial are always a strong driver to persuade consumers or inform them about products or services. In this point, commercial advertising can promote sustainable consumption behavior. - In OECD countries, consumers are protected by regulations that including fair trading legislation and policies. - Companies have been careful about concerning environmental protection or social equality and welfare conditions that commercial advertising tools point out environmental or social sustainability elements as much as product or brand. For example, automobile companies used features about climate change in their advertising campaigns. Some brands point out human rights, animal rights or labor rights in their commercial campaigns.
Public procurement	- Governments are the most effective power to transform markets into sustainable and green markets and they have a power to change citizens into green citizens. - Most OECD countries has transformed usual trading policies into sustainable and environmentally-friendly practices. - *Austria, Denmark, Finland, Germany, the Netherlands, Sweden and the United Kingdom* are called as "deep green" countries that including green procurement. - Green procurements generally includes products as *paper items (recycled, chlorine-free), heating appliances, information technology equipment, cleaning products, packaging, furniture, motor vehicles, energy and waste services.* - Sustainable procurement is also includes working with international organizations as *the multilateral development banks (World Bank, Inter-American Development Bank, Asian Development Bank) or UN agencies (such as Environmentally and Socially Responsible Procurement Working Group)*
Understanding consumer Behavior	- Promoting sustainable consumption needs detailed analyses of consumer behavior. In this point, detailed survey and researches can be helpful to understand consumer behavior towards green products or sustainable consumption patterns. - According to survey results from OECD countries, it can be said that price and income influence sustainable consumption. Age, gender, personal biases are also important factors that influencing sustainable consumption. For example, women are more close to buying green products. Young people focus on environmental protection when they consume. Labeling, branding and design can influence consumer choice that consumer want to be known through their consumption style.
Combining Policy Instruments	- Governments should make a decision on which policy instruments can influence promoting sustainable consumption. - Governments usually implement policies on energy, waste, transport, food and tourism to promote sustainable consumption. For example, energy efficiency is an important area for countries that taxes, labeling and charges can be used to promote sustainable energy consumption. Successful waste management can reduce environmental pollution that governments support household to reduce waste or water waste. To reduce CO_2 emission, governments implements policies or taxes on vehicles. Promoting fair trade agricultural products, healthy products and nutrition are important tools to support food sustainability.
Institutionalizing Sustainable Consumption	- Sustainable consumption concept needs to be institutionalized through legal policies, special programs on sustainable consumption, sustainable development strategies.
*Some implications are employed by specific country. The author prefer to summarize all of them with general implications	

Source: compiled by author from OECD, 2008

and Palmeira, 2017). For example, households can reduce consumption of electricity usage or water in their house. Also, they can reduce the amount of organic and inorganic waste (Widyaningsih et.al., 2015).

THE LINK BETWEEN 2030 SUSTAINABLE DEVELOPMENT GOALS and SUSTAINABLE CONSUMPTION PATTERNS

To create sustainable world, developed and developing countries should recognize and accept sustainable development goals at the same time. First sustainable development goals were called as Millennium Development Goals (MDGs) which included 8 main themes to be achieved by 2015. The world leaders worked on sustainable goals as "ending poverty and hunger, achieving equal education and empowerment, reducing child mortality, improving health, ending HIV/AIDS and other diseases, achieving environmental sustainability and developing global partnership" through Millennium Development Goals (UNPD, n.d.). Unfortunately, MDGs didn't provide expected improvements in the world. Especially, focusing on ending poverty in developing countries since 2000s misguided the world that environmental problems have increased. Water scarcity climate changes, ecosystem loss, ocean acidification and other environmental deteriorations are the real threatens for humanity that sustainable development goals should improve both of environmental and economic life together (Griggs et.al., 2013).

By September 2015, the UN adopted 2030 Development Agenda and set up 17 goals and 169 subgoals. (MDGMONITOR, n.d.). 2030 Sustainable Development Goals guide to people, organizations and countries to reach sustainable development degree through its 17 main goals. It can be said that 2030 SDGs are expanded version of MDGs. In this point, the main titles of 2030 SDGs are similar to MDGs (ICLEI- Local Governments for Sustainability, 2015). According to the 2030 Agenda for sustainable Development, 17 sustainable development goals can be explain as below (UN, 2015):

- *Goal 1- No poverty:* It aims to reduce poverty for all people in the world by 2030.
- *Goal 2- Zero Hunger:* Like as poverty, hunger is one of the biggest problem in the world. Goal 2 aims to end hunger and provide food security. Reducing the number of hunger people by 2030 and maintaining the diversity of seeds, plants and animals is so important for the sustainable world.
- *Goal 3- Good health and Well-Being:* Goal 3 aims to reduce the maternal mortality ratio in the world at first and it aims to end fatal diseases. To maintain human well-being, healthcare system should be improved both in developed and developing countries.
- *Goal 4- Quality Education:* Equal and quality education should be accessible for every girls and women as much as boys and men in the world. By 2030, it is aimed to reduce the number of uneducated girls and women in the world.
- *Goal 5- Gender Equality*: It is aimed to end every types of discrimination against women and girls in the world.
- *Goal 6- Clean Water and Sanitation:* There are still many people that can not access drinkable water or clean water in the world. By 2030, achieving universal water security and equitable access to clean water is so important goal.
- *Goal 7- Affordable and Clean Energy:* By 2030, goal 7 aims to achieve accessible and affordable energy for everybody in the world. Especially, sustainable energy resources and systems should be increased by 2030.

- *Goal 8- Decent Work and Economic Growth:* It is important to achieve sustainable development in the long term. Everybody can be able to have a job by 2030. Less developed countries and developing countries should be supported by developed countries.
- *Goal 9- Industry, Innovation and Infrastructure:* New technologies that supporting sustainable development goals and not harmful for the nature should be increased.
- *Goal 10- Reduced Inequalities*: Goal 10 aims to achieve economic development for human well-being in less developed and developing countries as well as developed countries. There should be new economic and social policies to end inequalities in the society.
- *Goal 11- Sustainable Cities and Communities*: By 2030, it is an important goal to achieve adequate, safe and affordable housing services for every people in the world. Urban planning should be re-designed by sustainable approaches.
- *Goal 12- Responsible Consumption and Production:* By 2030, the number of sustainable consumer or green consumer should be increased and sustainable consumption behavior should be expanded globally. Waste management should be planned by sustainability principles.
- *Goal 13- Climate Action:* The impacts of climate change on earth should be analyzed to prevent deadly outcomes.
- *Goal 14- Life Below Water:* Pollution in seas, marines and oceans should be decreased till 2030. Actions that destroying biodiversity under water such as overfishing and illegal fishing should be ended.
- *Goal 15- Life on Land*: Biodiversity on land should be protected. Ecosystem of land has been destroyed for a long time.
- Goal 16- *Peace, Justice and Strong Institutions:* The structure of institutes should be strengthened. Violence and death rates should be decreased. Effectiveness of the law and legal rules should be improved in less developed and developing countries.
- Goal 17- Partnerships for the goals: 2030 SDGs can be achieved globally by global partnership that developed countries should support less developed countries. The partnerships between developing countries and developed countries should be increased.

2030 Sustainable development goals cannot be achieved by just government or organizations. Different roles and responsibilities should be coordinated for the common goals by people. Table 3 summarizes these roles and responsibilities.

It is fact that people are responsible for sustainable development as a consumer and citizen (see table 1). While governments, institutes or businesses are transforming, the contribution of consumers and citizens has been ignored for a long time. As seen in Millennium Development Goals, individual impact for sustainability was ignored. By 2030 SDGs, the world recognized the individual impact on sustainable development. In this point, consumers can learn how they can contribute sustainable development or they can understand the responsibility for sustainable future through Goal-12 (SCP).

The Contribution of Consumers through Goal-12 (SCP)

Consumers have a vital role to play in achieving sustainable world by 2050 (WBCSD, 2011). Accordingly, consumers are responsible to protect environment and support social life in the context of sustainable development. Sustainable consumption patterns will support sustainable development in the

Table 3. Roles and Responsibilities in 2030 Sustainable Development Goals

Who	Roles	Responsibilities
Institutions	Governments	Countries which adopted 2030 Sustainable Development Goals, needed to reorganize their state administrations in line with these objectives. In particular, the first role in ending poverty and hunger belongs to the state administration. In order to prevent hunger, the state should give the necessary importance to agricultural development. It is important to support the farmers in the country, to support domestic agriculture and to promote organic agriculture. Community health is also one of the first public services that the state administration will be interested in. It is important for countries to make plans for protection and improvement of public health, to ensure that the necessary vaccines are completed in childhood, and to provide the necessary medicines and treatments in the country. In this context, it can be said that the first three 2030 SDGs are directly related to state administration.
	Local governments	Local governments (cities, villages, towns and other local governments) are also expected to act in support of the state administration. Municipalities play an important role in setting a sustainable city and urban life. Within the 2030 SDGs, Goal 11 is directly under the responsibility of local governments.
	Schools	Goal 4 is directly related to schools in countries. It is important that girls and boys are able to exercise their right to equal education. High quality pre-university education and training is also an important goal in schools.
	Hospitals	Hospitals should fulfill their duties in terms of sustainability of public health. According to Goal-3, hospitals and medical personnel are both responsible to improve public health and well-being of people in a country or city.
	Universities	Universities should provide the necessary support for the development of sustainable technology and related education. It is important to include the concept of sustainability in university education and to provide education to students.
Private Sector	Manufacturer/ Business	Within the target of sustainable consumption and production, manufacturers should develop and market products that use harmless or limited resources to the environment, human and animal health, or with minimum harm. Producers also have a great responsibility. Energy use, clean use of water resources and minimal damage to the natural environment are also important stages of the production process. As a result of the wrong production policies and plans of the enterprises, natural life in the world has been rapidly disrupted.
Person	Citizens/ Consumers	In society, people often stand out with their consumer identities. The shape and structure of consumption behavior directly affects sustainable life. At this point, consumers take a great responsibility and behave in accordance with green- or sustainable consumption behavior. In order to achieve sustainable development in the long term, it is imperative that individuals should change their consumption behavior in a way that is more sustainable. In addition, citizens can support sustainable environment through preferring bicycles or electric vehicles instead of diesel vehicles, cleaning in public spaces, paying attention to energy saving and water cleaning.

Source: adapted from Yıldırım, 2018

long term. In this point, 2030 Sustainable Development Goals determine the importance of sustainable consumption through Goal-12. Transition towards Goal 12- Sustainable Consumption and Production is a key element for achieving sustainable development in the long term. By Rio Earth Summit (1992), the participation of consumers/citizens into sustainable development goals was recognized formally. Consumers or citizens causes environmental pollution and destruction through the consumption of energy, water or other natural resources and leaving waste too much (UNEP,2015). The positive participation of consumers /citizens will accelerate the transition of sustainable development. However, there are differences between consumers / citizens from developed and developing countries. For example, UNEP (2009:4) determined that there were differences for sustainable consumption approach between developed countries and developing countries as below:

- Most of people still have troubles to meet their basic needs because of insufficient accessible resources such as energy, clean water etc. that sustainable consumption should provide sustainable solutions to meet consumers' energy or clean water needs in developing countries. In this point, sustainable consumption approach suggests developing countries to adapt renewable energy sources and sustainable technologies to provide social well-being for people.
- Sustainable consumption patterns are more related with consumers from developed countries. With high consumption of resources in developed countries, consumers are responsible from environmental destruction. Accordingly, consumers should adapt sustainable and green consumption behavior to consume less or buy green products to be less harmful for the environment.

According to Goal 12, Sustainable Consumption and Production aims to adapt all level of the lifecycle of products and services (from production to delivering) into sustainable system to be less harmful for the environment (Oneplanetwork, n.d.a). Until 2030 SDGs, sustainable consumption and production wasn't a prior goal to be achieved. However, the importance of sustainable consumption and production has been always recognized by the history. In web site of Oneplanetwork, the history of sustainable consumption and production in important events were summarized as below (Oneplanetwork, n.d.b):

- The first mention of sustainable consumption and production was belonged to "Limits to Growth" in 1972,
- By UN World Commission on Environment and Development- 1987, it was determined that the consumption standards should support ecological environment,
- In 1992 UN Conference on Environment and Development, unsustainable consumption and production was found as the biggest guilty to destroy the ecological environment,
- World Summitt on Sustainable Development-2002 determined the importance of promoting and accelerating sustainable consumption and production.
- With Launch of the Marrakech Process on SCP, countries which had to decide on promoting sustainable consumption and production, establish a coalition in 2003.
- The Marrakech Process 10-Year Framework of Programs (10YFP) was adopted by 2012- UN Conference on Sustainable Development,
- Finally, 2030 Sustainable Development Goals adopted *"Goal 12- Ensure sustainable consumption and production"* in 2015.

Sustainable consumption issue includes both of under-consumption and over-consumption at the same time. For example, people from less developed countries are suffering from not consuming well enough to meet their needs or wants. On the other side, there is rising consumer class from developing countries that is consuming excessively (UNEP, 2015). Accordingly, it can be said that sustainable consumption is not just a green consumption behavior in the context of sustainable development. The goal of sustainable consumption also includes social equality in consumption patterns. In this point, sustainable consumption is thought to be related with many sustainable development goals. Table 4 helps to understand the relationship between MDGs and Sustainable Consumption.

Table 4. The Relationship between MDGs and Sustainable Consumption (SC)

MDGs	The relationship with SC	Expectation
Goal 1: Eradicate extreme poverty and hunger	When there is an efficient resource use in the process of goods and services production, the productivity will increase and the costs will decrease. With the help of higher demand of green products, the number of green enterprises will increase in the market. Then, new market areas and job opportunities will improve the economy through green economy approach. This result is expected help reducing poor people who earn money less than $1 a day. In addition, better resource planning and better management of agricultural areas will bring more sustainable farming and it will increase the availability of food.	Sustainable consumption can reduce poverty and hunger
Goal 4: Reduce child mortality *Goal 5:Improve maternal health*	The health status is so important for human well-being. Better and improved health status will bring better life standards in physical and psychological degree of people.	Sustainable consumption can bring better health status.
Goal 7: Ensure environmental sustainability	By 2015, it aims to reduce the proportion of people who can not access to safe drinking water. So, better water treatment infrastructure, new programmes for preventing pollution will help to increase the clean water availability.	Sustainable consumption patterns can help preventing water pollution in the long term.

Source: adapted from UNEP, 2009:7

To protect environmental life and maintain humanity, consumption and production patterns should be changed as soon as possible. In this point, the active participation of consumers to this change movement is so important to achieve sustainable development goals. Goal-12 aims to reduce the proportion of waste at business and consumer level and also improve waste management in production process through 10-year programs (UNCTAD, 2017).

According to UNEP (2015), sustainable consumption and production (Goal 12) can be effective tool to reduce poverty or achieve Goal 1. For example;

- When the demand for natural resources decrease, the availability of them will increase,
- When negative impacts on climate change is reduced, the livelihood from nature such as agriculture, fishery etc. can be maintain longer,
- With the help of cleaner air, water and land, the health status will be improved,
- Poor people can afford many goods and services when the efficiency is improved in production systems
- New production systems and new market opportunities will create new job areas (UNEP, 2015:36).

Essentially, Goal-12 is linked to almost every 2030 SDGs (Especially, Goal-2, Goal-3, Goal-4, Goal-8, Goal-9, Goal-13, Goal-14 and Goal-15) and this is the most cost-efficient way to achieve economic development with reducing negative impacts on environment and social life. Goal-12 presents the aim of Sustainable Consumption and Production (SCP) but this goal supports other goals of 2030 SDGs directly and indirectly. For example, energy efficiency, efficiency in usage of natural resources and water sources, reducing CO_2 emission and waste are all linked with achieving Goal-12. Transforming private enterprises/businesses into green enterprises/businesses is so important to achieve 2030 SDGs. To main-

Table 5. The relationship between responsible consumer attitudes and 2030 SDGs

Responsible consumption type	Consumer behavior	Link to SDGs
No waste	Limiting consumption of material goods and services, Keeping planned buying behavior, Using reusable products, Re-using object for new aims and sharing used objects with other consumers	Goal 2 and Goal 11
To avoid from artificial needs	Stopping excessive buying, Avoiding fashion and advertisements impact, Using current products for a long time as soon as it works, Ensuring economical use	Goal 10 and Goal 11
Being green consumer	Limiting consumption of products which are not eco-friendly, Preferring recycling products, Preferring eco-labeled products, Buying products with ecological farming, Buying regional or local products, Buying unpackaged products or reusable packaged products, Re-using products as possible as it.	Goal 3, Goal 6, Goal 7, Goal 13, Goal 14 and Goal 15
Being ethical consumer	Avoiding from products that produced by slave, children or low-paid labor, Buying traditional products, Buying products from social economy implementation, Preferring products from disadvantaged manufacturers as handicapped or unemployed co-operatives	Goal 1, Goal 3, Goal 4, Goal 5, Goal 8, Goal 9, Goal 10 and Goal 11
Being political consumer	Preferring products from family businesses or local manufacturers, Avoiding from businesses that keeps negative and tyrant management. Not buying products from countries with oppressive political system	Goal 7, Goal 10, Goal 16 and Goal 17

Source: adapted from Jastrzebska, 2017:202-203

tain sustainable economic growth, economy should keep environmentally-friendly models and policies that this issue is linked with Goal-12. Achieving protection of forestry, oceans and seas, reducing waste and CO_2 emission and environmental pollution, limiting usage of natural resources and having energy saving usage models are mostly based on sustainable consumption and production patterns (HLPF, 2018).

SOLUTIONS AND RECOMMENDATIONS

This study shows that the role of consumers is so important to achieve 2030 Sustainable Development Goals in the long term. The contribution of consumers for sustainable development can be seen by table 5. The consumption patterns influence environmental, economic and social life so deeply. When transforming current consumption patterns into sustainable patterns (usage of 3R principle, sustainable consumption, responsible consumption or ethical consumption etc.), the balance between environmental, social and economic life can be favorable with regard to sustainable development.

When meeting needs and wants, consumers can make green choices and they can support sustainable development. Consumers play an important role in sustainable development because the Earth's resources are limited and natural environment needs to be protected for the future. Excessive consumption behavior causes excessive waste in the environment. Governments has been aware of the danger that come from excessive consumption and production patterns and they keep new regulations and policies to promote sustainable consumption and production patterns. If consumers want to contribute sustainable development, they can keep sustainable consumption patterns as soon as possible.

FUTURE RESEARCH DIRECTIONS

The study provides a brief framework for the link between sustainable consumption patterns and sustainable development. The results of this study suggest that consumers are responsible for sustainable development goals. This study focuses on how consumers can contribute 2030 Sustainable Development Goals (SDGs), currently. In the context of theoretical approach, we can suggest that consumers should join the movement of sustainable development and they take a real responsibility to achieve sustainable development goals. We can suggest the below list for future research directions:

- Future studies can analyze the link sustainable consumption patterns and the impact of sustainable consumption on the achievement of 2030 SDGs through empirical researches. The significant empirical findings can prove the significant relationship between sustainable consumption patterns and the achievement of 2030 SDGs.
- Future studies can focus on specific sustainable consumption patterns to explain its impact on sustainable development
- Analyzing the relationship between sustainable consumption patterns and the achievement of 2030 SDGs can help setting future sustainable development goals.

CONCLUSION

Being sustainability is not only belonged to institutes' responsibilities. Consumers and citizens should join sustainable movement and take a responsibility, too. At individual level of being sustainable is mostly based on governmental policy or institutional incentives. The prior studies have showed that there was a big gap between actual buying green products and attitude towards green products. Probably, consumers accept social norms on the survey but they do not purchase green products in real life (Vermeir and Verbeke, 2006; Terlau and Hirsch, 2015). Dobson (2007) suggested that green consumers or green citizens should be encouraged by sustainable policies and implications. When businesses produce or promote green products, consumers will buy more. Sustainable consumption behavior usually needs encouragement and information (Csutora, 2012; Thogersen and Schrader, 2012; Terlau and Hirsch, 2015). It is known that sustainable consumption behavior contributes sustainable development. Accordingly, sustainable consumption behavior studies should be re-designed or researches should investigate right point in buying green products or preferring green products. Unfortunately, prior studies focused on superficial indicators for sustainable consumption behavior (Nguyen et.al., 2018). Recent knowledge show that governments and institutes should participate in sustainable consumption process through providing information, support or prohibitions (Jackson and Michaelis, 2003; OECD, 2008; Csutore, 2012; Qu et.al., 2015; Terlau and Hirsch,2015; Nguyen et.al.,2018).

To achieve 2030 Sustainable Development Goals, the direct partnerships of consumer and citizen are needed. Goal-12 which aims to promote sustainable consumption also encourages consumers to be more responsible to protect natural environment as much as producers. When the demand of green products is higher, the availability of green products will be higher. On the other side, consumers can contribute to achieve Goal 6, Goal 13, Goal 14 and Goal 15 through responsible consumption behavior in the long term. Protection of forest areas, oceans and seas, cleanness of water resources and preventing climate change and global warming can be achieved by responsible consumers. In addition, Goal 11 aims to achieve green citizen in a sustainable city that consumption behavior of citizens is also crucial for sustainability. As a result, it can be said that the role of consumers (and citizens) shouldn't be ignored and consumers (and citizens) should be encouraged and promoted by governments.

REFERENCES

Abeliotis, K., Koniari, C., & Sardianou, E. (2010). The profile of the green consumer in Greece. *International Journal of Consumer Studies*, *34*(2), 153–160. doi:10.1111/j.1470-6431.2009.00833.x

Allaway, D. (2012). *Briefing Paper: Sustainable Consumption and Waste Prevention.* Retrieved January 10, 2020 from https://www.oregon.gov/deq/FilterDocs/2050-SustConsumpWastePrevention.pdf

Bostancı, S. & Yıldırım, S. (2020). A Conceptual Study on Sustainable Communities and Ecological Citizenship. *IGDIR University Journal of Social Sciences*, (5), 203-218.

Chan, K. (2000). Market Segmentation of Green Consumers in Hong Kong. *Journal of International Consumer Marketing*, *12*(2), 7–24. doi:10.1300/J046v12n02_02

Csutora, M. (2012). One more awareness gap? The behaviour-impact-gap problem. *Journal of Consumer Policy*, *35*(1), 145–163. doi:10.100710603-012-9187-8

Diamantopoulos, A., Schlegelmilch, B. B., Sinkovics, R. R., & Bohlen, G. M. (2003). Can socio-demographics still play a role in profiling green consumers? A review of the evidence and an empirical investigation. *Journal of Business Research*, *56*(6), 465–480. doi:10.1016/S0148-2963(01)00241-7

Dopson, A. (2007). Environmental Citizenship: Towards Sustainable Development. *Sustainable Development*, *15*(5), 276–285. doi:10.1002d.344

Ferrara, I. & Serret, Y. (2008). Introduction. *OECD Journal: General Papers, Special Issue: Household Behaviour and the Environment, 2008*(2), 5-18.

FuiYeng, W. & Yazdanifard, R. (2015). Green Marketing: A Study of Consumers' Buying Behavior in Relation to Green Products. *Global Journal of Management and Business Research: E Marketing, 15*(5).

Goodwin, N., Nelson, J. A., Ackerman, F., & Weisskopf, T. (2008). *Consumption and the Consumer Society. Instructor's Notes And Exam Questions. GDAE Teaching Modules on Social and Environmental Issues in Economics*. Medford, MA: Global Development And Environment Institute Tufts University.

Griggs, D., Stafford-Smith, M., Gaffney, O., Rockström, J., Öhman, M. C., Shyamsundar, P., ... Noble, I. (2013). Sustainable development goals for people and planet. *Nature*, *495*(7441), 305–307. doi:10.1038/495305a PMID:23518546

HLPF. (2018). *2018 HLPF Review of SDGs implementation: SDG 12 - Ensure sustainable consumption and production patterns.* Retrieved November 10, 2019 from https://sustainabledevelopment.un.org/content/documents/196532018backgroundnotesSDG12.pdf

Hobson, K. (2008). Sustainable Consumption in the United Kingdom: The "Responsible" Consumer and Government at "Arm's Length". *Journal of Environment & Development, 13*(2), 121–139. doi:10.1177/1070496504265013

ICLEI- Local Governments for Sustainability. (2015). *From MDGs to SDGs: What are the Sustainable Development Goals.* ICLEI BRIEFING SHEET - Urban Issues, No. 01

International Institute for Sustainable Development. (2012). *Sustainable Development Timeline.* Retrieved November 10, 2019 from https://www.iisd.org/pdf/2012/sd_timeline_2012.pdf

Jackson, T., & Michaelis, L. (2003). *Policies for Sustainable Consumption. Sustainable Development Commission.* Retrieved November 10, 2019 from https://pdfs.semanticscholar.org/b5f9/70330c8b0d02044a00b665a4e27f613a131d.pdf

Jastrzebska, E. (2017). The Responsible Consumer As An Answer To New Sustainable Development Challenges. *Ekonomia I Środowisko, 1*(60), 198-206.

Klarin, T. (2018). The Concept of Sustainable Development: From its Beginning to the Contemporary Issues. *Zagreb International Review of Economics & Business, 21*(1), 67–94. doi:10.2478/zireb-2018-0005

MDGMONITOR. (n.d.). *Category: Sustainable Development Goals.* Retrieved November 10, 2019 from https://www.mdgmonitor.org/sustainable-development-goals/

Mont, O. (2004). Institutionalisation of sustainable consumption patterns based on shared use. *Ecological Economics, 50*(1-2), 135–153. doi:10.1016/j.ecolecon.2004.03.030

Musso, F. & Palmeira, M. (2017). *3Rs of Sustainability and the impact on consumer behaviour and people's values.* 24th Recent Advances in Retailing & Services Science Conference - EIRASS 2017.

Nguyen, H. V., Nguyen, C. H., & Hoang, T. T. B. (2018). Green consumption: Closing the intention-behavior gap. *Sustainable Development, 27*(1), 118–129. doi:10.1002d.1875

OECD. (2008). Promoting Sustainable Consumption. Good Practices In OECD Countries. OECD Publications.

Oneplanetwork. (n.d.a). *Sustainable Consumption and Production: an operational approach to sustainability.* Retrieved November 10, 2019 from https://www.oneplanetnetwork.org/sites/default/files/briefings_on_scp.pdf

Oneplanetwork. (n.d.b). *What is SCP?* Retrieved November 10, 2019 from https://www.oneplanetnetwork.org/about/what-scp

Pinto, D.C., Nique, W.M. & da Silva Anana, E. (2011). Green consumer values: how do personal values influence environmentally responsible water consumption? *International Journal of Soncumer Studies, 35*(2), 122-131.

Qu, Y., Li, M., Jia, H., & Gua, L. (2015). Developing More Insights on Sustainable Consumption in China Based on Q Methodology. *Sustainability*, *7*(10), 14211–14229. doi:10.3390u71014211

Sheth, J. N., Newman, B. I., & Gross, B. L. (1991a). *Consumption Values and Market Choices: Theory and Applications*. Cincinnati, OH: South-Western Publishing Co.

Sustainable Development Commission. (n.d.). *History of SD*. Retrieved November 10, 2019 from http://www.sd-commission.org.uk/pages/history_sd.html

Sustainable Development Goals Knowledge Platform. (n.d.). *United Nations Conference on Sustainable Development, Rio+20*. Retrieved November 10, 2019 from https://sustainabledevelopment.un.org/rio20

Terlau, W., & Hirsch, D. (2015). Sustainable Consumption and the Attitude-Behaviour-Gap Phenomenon - Causes and Measurements towards a Sustainable Development. *International Journal on Food System Dynamics*, *6*(3), 159–174.

The Federal Government. (2018). National Programme on sustainable Consumption, From Sustainable Lifestyles towards Social Change. Federal Ministry for the Environment, Nature Conservation, Building and Nuclear Safety, Bonn, Germany.

Thidell, A. (n.d.). *Sustainable Consumption And Green Lifestyles Definitions And Concepts*. https://mst.dk/media/mst/68633/Background%20paper%20A%20-%20Session%201.pdf

Thogersen, J., & Schrader, U. (2012). From Knowledge to Action—New Paths Towards Sustainable Consumption. *Journal of Consumer Policy*, *35*(1), 1–5. doi:10.100710603-012-9188-7

UN (United Nations). (2015). *Transforming Our World: The 2030 Agenda For Sustainable Development*. A/RES/70/1. Retrieved November 10, 2019 from https://sustainabledevelopment.un.org/content/documents/21252030%20Agenda%20for%20Sustainable%20Development%20web.pdf

UN (United Nations). (2019). *The contribution of consumer protection to sustainable consumption*. TD/B/C.I/CPLP/17. Trade and Development Board, Trade and Development Commission, Intergovernmental Group of Experts on Consumer Protection Law and Policy, Fourth session, Geneva, 8 and 9 July 2019, Item 3 (a) of the provisional agend.a

UNCTAD. (2017). *Achieving the Sustainable Development Goals through Consumer Protection*. UNCTAD/DITC/CPLP/2017/2.

UNEP. (2009). *Mainstreaming Sustainable Consumption and Production and Resource Efficiency into Development Planning*. DTI/1235/PA.

UNEP (United Nations Environment Programme). (2015). *Sustainable Consumption and Production*. Global edition. Author.

UNPD. (n.d.). *Millennium Development Goals*. Retrieved November 10, 2019 from https://www.undp.org/content/undp/en/home/sdgoverview/mdg_goals.html

Van Liere, K. D., & Dunlap, R. E. (1981). Environmental concern: Does it make a difference? How it's measured? *Environment and Behavior*, *13*(6), 651–676. doi:10.1177/0013916581136001

Vermeir, I., & Verbeke, W. J. (2006). Sustainable Food Consumption: Exploring the Consumer "Attitude – Behavioral Intention" Gap. *Journal of Agricultural & Environmental Ethics*, *19*(2), 169–194. doi:10.100710806-005-5485-3

WBCSD (World Business Council for Sustainable Development). (2011). *A vision for sustainable consumption, Innovation, collaboration, and the management of choice*. Retrieved November 10, 2019 from http://docs.wbcsd.org/2011/10/AVisionForSustainableConsumption.pdf

Whitfield, K. (2015). *Quick Guide to Sustainable Development: History and Concepts*. Retrieved November 10, 2019 from http://www.assembly.wales/research%20documents/qg15-003%20-%20sustainable%20development%20history%20and%20concepts/qg15-003.pdf

Widyaningsiha, N., Tjiptoherijantob, P., Widanarkob, S., & Seda, F. (2015). Linkage model between sustainable consumption and household waste management. *Procedia Environmental Sciences*, *28*, 195–203. doi:10.1016/j.proenv.2015.07.026

Yan, G. R., & Yusniza, K. (2016). Moving Towards Sustainable Consumption: A Study of Reduce, Reuse and Recycle (3Rs) Adoption among Malaysians. *"Marketing to the Bottom of the Pyramid in Emerging Markets" - Vol. 3 IBAICM-2016: Third International Conference on Marketing*.

Yang, Q.Z., Zhou, J. & Xu, K. (2014). A 3R Implementation Framework to Enable Circular Consumption in Community, *International Journal of Environmental Science and Development*, *5*(2).

Yıldırım, S. (2018). Roles And Responsibilities In Sustainable Development Goals. *International Congress of Management, Economy and Policy, 201*, 425-433

Yıldırım, S., & Candan, B. (2015). Segmentation of Green Product Buyers Based on Their Personal Values and Consumption Values. *Environmental Values*, *24*(5), 641–661. doi:10.3197/096327115X14384223590212

Yıldırım, S., & Yıldırım, D. Ç. (2020). *Achieving Sustainable Development Through a Green Economy Approach. In Advanced Integrated Approaches to Environmental Economics and Policy: Emerging Research and Opportunities* (pp. 1–22). IGI Global Pub.

Yıldırım, S., Yıldırım, D. Ç., & Gedikli, A. (2016). Sustainable Consumption Trends in the World in the Context of Green Economy and Sustainability. In M. M. Erdoğdu, T. Arun, & I. H. Ahmad (Eds.), *Handbook of Research on Green Economic Development Initiatives and Strategies* (pp. 66–84). IGI Global. doi:10.4018/978-1-5225-0440-5.ch004

Young, W., Hwang, K., McDonald, S., & Oates, C. J. (2010). Sustainable Consumption: Green Consumer Behaviour When Purchasing Products. *Sustainable Development*, *18*, 20–31.

Zhang, L., & Wu, Y. (2012, December). Market segmentation and willingness to pay for green electricity among urban residents in China: The case of Jiangsu Province. *Energy Policy*, *51*, 514–523. doi:10.1016/j.enpol.2012.08.053

Zhao, H. H., Gao, Q., Wu, Y. P., Wang, Y., & Zu, X. D. (2014, January 15). What affects green consumer behavior in China? A case study from Qingdao. *Journal of Cleaner Production*, *63*, 143–151. doi:10.1016/j.jclepro.2013.05.021

KEY TERMS AND DEFINITIONS

2030 Sustainable Development Goals: Seventeen sustainable goals that are expected to be achieved by 2030.

Consumption: The usage of products and services to meet needs or wants.

Consumption Pattern: A model that presenting one type of consumption.

Green Consumer: A consumer that is sensitive for protection environment when he/she makes a buying decision.

Green Product: A product type that is less harmful for the environment.

Sustainable Consumption: Consumers prefer green products to be less harmful for the environment or they consume less.

Sustainable Development: A development model that aims to achieve economic development through protecting natural environment and keeping social welfare.

Sustainable Production: Enterprises keeps environmentally-friendly production technologies to protect natural environment and use efficient energy and natural resources at the same time.

Section 4
Tendencies

Chapter 19
Automotive Sector Moving Towards Mobility Companies:
The New Mobility Landscape

Marlene Almeida
ICHEC Brussels Management School, Belgium

ABSTRACT

The global automotive industry is both vast in its complexity and vital to the lifestyles of many residents in the industrialized world. Cars not only make transportation easier, but are associated with a sense of freedom and economic accomplishment. A better understanding of people's lifestyles, values, and mobility needs has led the automakers to redefine their long-term strategies as a base to a new development of products/services to support the new mobility. This chapter highlights the challenges and the main disrupting factors for the automotive sector to move towards mobility companies. This chapter gives a close look to understand how the industry has been influenced by different trends in an evolving society and what technologies have been playing a key role for the future mobility companies. Case studies of leading companies are given as examples for a future vision. This chapter is addressed to academics and professionals interested in mobility and in understanding how automotive sector landscapes are changing in a changing society.

INTRODUCTION

The automotive industry is a critically important stakeholder influencing the sustainability of passenger transport (Sovacool et all., 2019). Also, the automotive industry is inherently innovative and has the third highest industry rating for Research and Development (R&D), accounting for 15.5% of global research and development spending in 2017 (Statista, 2017).

Giving the importance of the automotive sector, this chapter will underline the profound transformation that the industry has been subjected to in the past years, and how it has been responding to the different challenges in a fast-changing society.

DOI: 10.4018/978-1-7998-3115-0.ch019

Copyright © 2020, IGI Global. Copying or distributing in print or electronic forms without written permission of IGI Global is prohibited.

The first point of this chapter will highlight how automotive industry is changing towards mobility companies. Next, what are the trends supporting this new mobility era, followed by a short explanation of how new technologies and innovation play a role as key drivers for this change. Two examples of concepts coming from the automotive industry will be explained: Toyota e-palette and Renault EZ line-up. With some examples coming from new players in this new landscape: Navya Autonom, Easymile EZ10 shuttle. As a conclusion, some key points will be underlined on the future of mobility in coming years and upcoming challenges.

This chapter will highlight the disruption between the past and the future and how car manufacturers are responding to these challenges. Within the new trends, 3 have been identified in this chapter as the most relevant to support the new Mobility Landscape. The first would be electrification. As observed, most of car manufacturers have started electrifying their current line-up of vehicles. The electrification in automotive sector was a first reaction of the rising environmental concerns, in this case specifically looking into the CO2 and NOX emissions in major cities. Problems with smog and health issues have been rising within population living in urban areas. The third is Smart Cities. They are a result of an ever-growing digitalisation of services within people's daily lives. Digitalisation has led to increasing number of digital services, e-commerce, and others, supported by different technologies that needed to be integrated and are also part of the vehicles used today.

Technology plays as major enabler for different service models. As an example, from Digital Platforms to Internet of Things and Big Data, the services will be in future one of the biggest sources of revenue for many industries, including automotive. The information and data generated will enable more and more personalised services. This is where car manufacturers will, not only deliver the right product but also the right services to satisfy people growing needs.

Also, from Product and Service point of view, Automotive sector is not only changing on Powertrain technology, moving from Internal Combustion Engines (ICE) to Electric power, but also moving towards mobility companies (e.g. Mobility as a Service (MaaS) companies (Israel, 2018)).

In this chapter, two case studies of leading companies are explained. First example is from the Japanese giant Toyota Motor Corporation. The second, from the French, Groupe Renault. In both cases, both manufacturers have presented concepts with a people-centred approach thinking of future mobility services and tackling the issues of goods deliveries in a new mobility offer.

In parallel, the traditional Original Equipment Manufacturers (OEM's), have new competitors, smaller start-ups bringing new mobility solutions, making the mobility market more competitive than ever. This chapter will present two examples of companies competing in this arena: Navya and Easymile.

At the end of this article, some conclusions and recommendations highlighting new requirements from Governance and Regulators as drivers of change (a more top down approach) and the increasing demand by people for more green, flexible and safe type of mobility, a consumer-people-centric approach to mobility (a more bottom up approach). A set of ideas for future research are also described as part of the conclusion of this article.

THE FUTURE OF MOBILITY

Mobility now has a different meaning. The main goal is to build a-mobility for all, a mobility that is accessible to everyone, at any place, at any time. It's mobility on demand when it's needed to be, when it aids in solving daily struggles, when it responds to spontaneous needs. Look into mobility not only has a need for a product, but as a product that is associated with a service. An ecosystem is built around products and services that respond to future mobility challenges.

To better understand what those challenges are, there is a need to understand the way society and urban areas have evolved.

At the end of the 19th century, the Industrial Revolution (also known as the first Industrial Revolution) was a key turning point to how cities and people evolved, and how the needs in mobility have significantly changed. The Industrial Revolution significantly changed the layout of cities, and urban centres struggled to accommodate the huge migration flows (people looking for better working opportunities within the cities). Cities expansion and commuting movements played a major role in the mobility that started to develop, from public transport to private usage of a car. In the early 20th century, with established new manufacturing processes, the cars became widely available. Baby boomers (generation has borne between 1946 and 1964) were the first consumer generation. They purchased cars, making societies more and more car-oriented. Within this booming society, the car takes also the role of status representation within society and a sign of wealth. At the same time, cars start to create heavy traffic and contributing to overall pollution, especially within big urban centres (creating high levels of pollution and smog). Also, and in parallel, they also contributed to breaking up communities and disrupting social life.

The inefficiencies with the use of a car start to be more obvious. The car stands still, unused for more than 90% of the time and carries an average of 1 and a half people (stated in a briefing from a study from Transport & Environment, June 2017, ITF OECD 2016 and BEUC 2016). The same report states that "each car occupies 150m2 of urban land". Another big problem is the costs generated by congestion. In the EU economy, it represents €100Bn annually (ref. Urban Mobility, European Commission). As mentioned in the same report, "the convenience that made the car a 20th-century icon has been eroded by its popularity".

People happiness was impacted. Oil crises, pollution, traffic and huge congestion. Reaching a point saturation, there was a need for disruption, for change. Being cities the most affected by this saturation, city representatives started to act: mobility needed a shift. These factors created opportunities for new modes of mobility with the potential to provide a more sustainable and optimized commuting experience. The point is to shift from a car-oriented approach to a more human social approach and to respond to people needs. What we call "people-centric mobility" (ref. Report from Arcadis organisation). This is key to ensure the quality of life of the people in urban environments.

First actions were to increase public transport network, but in most city structures, this action was not enough. Investments in public network not always have the return on investment needed to justify it. So, what started to make more sense, was to combine the different modes of transportation available. From public modes (bus, train, tram, others) with adapted new means of transport (car-sharing, ride-sharing, others), and the rise of micro-mobility modes (scooters, bicycles, others), to ultimately providers of tailored services to the users.

At the same time, public authorities started to impose measures and implement restrictive policies for private car usage within urban areas. Ultimately some cities started to ban cars within certain urban zones, especially within historical centres, where the use of a car would not make sense anymore. Also, slow speed areas started to appear, the increase of pedestrian areas, to make cities more friendly for pedestrians, make neighbourhoods more pleasant and healthier. Such changes are happening at fast speed in some cities. A real car-free movement that is set to become a trend in the future.

This movement is spreading, and cities are all embracing car-free living. Some expect that the inventory of vehicles, in Europe will decline to 25% by 2030. For the US, the forecast is a reduction of 22%

(ref. PWC report, five trends transforming the Automotive Industry). To cope with this trend, urban mobility needs to be re-invented. Urban planners started to study more profoundly how they could re-invent their urban spaces, creating more multimodal options, looking into re-defining their own streets: multi space for trams, buses, cars, bicycle lanes and pedestrians' areas. The car is no longer the main urban mobility option giving place to new service-based solutions.

A good example is the city of Milan, in Italy Europe. A chapter from Eltis – The Urban Mobility Observatory, indicates "every day, 850,000 people enter Milan and 270,000 exits the city – resulting in a total of 5.3 million trips per day. Although most people use public transport to get around Milan (57% of all trips are taken by public transport, 30% by cars, 7% by motorbike and 6% by bicycle), the city still has one of the highest European rates of car ownership (50.5 cars every 100 inhabitants compared to London 31, Berlin 29, Paris 25) and one of the highest concentrations of particulate matter among large European cities". Within this context, another study (www.transportenvironment.org) on the city of Milan showed that "30, 000 fewer private cars were purchased since car-sharing debuted in the city and 42% used the service in combination with public transport suggesting car sharing is part of multimodality" (ref. Does Sharing cars really reduce car use? Report from Transport & Environment, June 2017).

For reference, the average car occupancy rate for BlaBlaCar is 2.8 person per car in the US, compared to Europe's average of 1.7 person (as already mentioned in average a private car is occupied by 1 and a half person).

In a wider spectrum a US study "indicates the global car fleet could be reduced by a third if sharing schemes were widely adopted." (ref. *Three Revolutions in Urban Transportation*, UC Davis, May 2017). A study by McKinsey & Company (ref. "How Shared Mobility will change the Automotive Industry", published chapter in April 2017), estimates that "despite the current value of shared mobility services in Europe is estimated to be €5.1 billion which is forecast to grow to more than €100 billion by 2025". Car manufacturing companies have started to expand their offering to include more mobility services. So, it is expected in the future to have specific mobility needs covered by a variety of product and services.

A whole ecosystem will bring solutions to the people to respond to everyone's daily struggles. Cities are also re-thinking mobility accesses. In big urbanised areas, city centres have always been mostly used by masses of people. In Europe, most cities are built around historical centres, with narrow streets, paved stone streets, limited-access roads, a precious heritage from the medieval times. With the car banned policies, these historical points of interest have been converted into pedestrian areas with more space for leisure activities. As cities are becoming increasingly walkable, car ownership is declining. So, while car bans, pedestrian and bike lanes are expanding bringing great benefits to people: cleaner air, more social interaction leading to a better quality of life within big urban centres are rising.

We could easily imagine that commuters that come to the city for their work, could be using an electric vehicle (EV), hybrid vehicle (HV), Fuel Cell vehicle (FCV) type of vehicle. For the last mile, for example to reach work, commuters could use a public mean of transport or rent a micro-mobility solution (e.g. Lime, City Bike, or others). A mother with his child, could be using an on-demand service with a community-based vehicle that has single purpose to take kids safely to school (Madslien, 2017). A disabled or elderly could also benefit from new mobility services more adapted to their condition, given that current public transportation offer is not always adapted to their needs (Cirella et al., 2019; Whittle et al., 2019).

A better understanding of people's lifestyles, values and mobility needs, as led the automakers to re-define their long term strategies as a base to new development of products / services, to support the Mobility as a Service (MaaS) approach (Israel, 2018; Hilton, 2018; Lane, 2019; Pitt, 2019).

AUTOMOTIVE SECTOR MOVING TOWARDS MOBILITY COMPANIES

Trends Supporting the New Mobility Era

From observing different leading companies and new players in the automotive market, three main trends supporting the new mobility era have been identified: Electrification, Environment and Smart cities (sensor-based society). These trends are supported by authority's regulations that looking into improving urban environments, making them more appealing for people to live in. The focus will be in urban areas where the highest concentration of challenges can be observed, like congestion, pollution, long commuting time, others. Another supporting Trend is the increasing awareness on environmental issues, like Climate Change, focus on Planet A (there is no Planet B), recycling and other related environmental concerns, supported by UN sustainable goals. Digitalisation and the rise of a sensor-based society have been key for Smart Cities' development.

1. **Electrification:** It is now a hot topic (Noel et al., 2018; World Economic Forum, 2018; PWC, 2018; Kanger et al., 2019; Giampieri et al., 2020). After the legacy of the Dieselgate scandal (started with Volkswagen group), only in European Union's roads there are 35.8 million polluting Euro 5 and 6 diesel cars and vans (ref. 2017 May - Transport & Environment press report). These number of vehicles were sold between 2011 and 2016 and exceed the nitrogen oxides (NOx) limits. It was now clear that car manufacturers needed to find a quick alternative with an alternative powertrain, cleaner, to be competitive in this new arena of a "clean vehicle approach". A big disrupter was the Tesla Inc. with CEO Elon Musk. The introduction of Tesla model S (introduced in 2012) and Tesla model X (introduced in 2015), the brand proved that premium cars, with an appropriate product and leasing plan, could turn on the flame for electric vehicles (EV) on higher segment category. In Europe, the big sponsors of EV were mainly the Nordic countries. They have played a major leading role in the introduction of EVs. If we look at the case of Norway, with the right incentives, low cost of energy and a network in place, this Nordic country is today the leader with more than 50% of their cars on the road being electrified (EV, PHEV, HV combined). The increase concerns for the environment and the right incentives made possible the change, from traditional Internal Combustion Engines (ICE) engines, to alternative cleaner powertrains to be introduced into the market. Because of the current actions to make air cleaner within big urban areas and restrictions put in place by cities (ban ICE engines from cities) to reduce pollution levels, it was clear that any new mobility solution brought to the cities would need to be clean energy-based. In the public sector, more buses are introduced based on fuel cell (FC) and electric (EV), with new technologies for recharge e.g. fast charging, induction charging. Thinking about the street speed restrictions within the major cities (especially in Europe), EV seems to be the natural choice.
2. **Environmental concerns**: It's a topic that nobody is indifferent to these days (Günther, 2020). Many specialists in the field defend that the planet is changing. Temperature is rising and with it, the impact in people's everyday life. We face more and more extreme weather events, with "heat waves" during the summer (what we call urban heats within cities) and more extreme storms. This awareness has created many reactions from different public and private institutions, but also created big waves of protest based in citizen initiatives, as the most known case today: the 'Greta effect' and consequently the need to focus on Climate Change. City restrictions are the result of the will of many politicians, which acknowledge the need to act, if they want their cities to become more

liveable again. By promoting restrictive accesses, it relieves the cities from its major congestion issues. On the other hand, it created more challenges for commuters to come in and out of the cities. Also, the goods deliveries and logistic flows have become a big problem. How to manage big trucks, delivery van's that is also a big congestion source within urban areas (Saidan et al., 2018). The expansion of car-based transport over the last half-century has brought a wide range of ecological and social impacts, such as noise, congestion, accidents, air and water pollution, climate change and resource depletion (Graedel and Allenby, 1998; Mayyas et al., 2012). The automotive industry is facing on-going challenges to improve the sustainability of its manufacturing processes and vehicle emissions due to economic, environmental, marketability and policy concerns (Stoycheva et al., 2018; Giampieri et al., 2020).

3. **Smart cities:** Digitalisation is a key driver for Smart Cities to evolve (Sturges, 2016). We are heading into a sensor-based society where everybody is connected. Today, even without knowing, we can be traced. Sensors have become an important source of information. The definition of Smart Cities is necessarily linked to IoT, everything is connected, things are communicating between them without even action from a human (World Economic Forum, 2015). Digitalisation has brought an enormous complexity within the way things work (Boano et all., 2016; SMMT, 2017). Decision-makers should make the best use of the information at their disposal to provide the best decision-making actions. Smart, connected, and automated vehicles will have a significant impact on the safety, efficiency, and convenience of future transportation and mobility (Baunach et all., 2018). Smart Mobility is considered one of the 10 most disruptive technologies with a revolutionary impact on people' lives, the society and the economy throughout the coming decades (Gomes et all., 2017; McKinsey, 2013).

Innovative Technologies as Key Driver

New technologies and innovation are key drivers of new mobility solutions today (Modi, 2018; Bartnik et al., 2018). They play as major enablers for different business models translated into services for all.

Technology integrated into the vehicles, as autonomous driving, alternative powertrains like electric or fuel cell vehicles are important to sustain new business models and can support the cleaner cities approach within big urban areas, affecting positively the quality of life of people. Technologies of support of services, as "trace-and-track" services, digital platforms, data communication devices play a supporting role to implement different services not only for people that are using the mobility solutions available but also support the goods delivery. The key word today is Optimization.

But to achieve optimization, it needs to have the right supporting tools: Mobility as a Service (MaaS) solutions, Shared Mobility, Big Data linked with in-vehicle services and Connected Car (Sell et al., 2019) are the main contributors for future mobility optimisation.

Major cities struggle with congestion. One of the first priorities is to open those flows of mobility that create pollution not only in terms of CO2 or NOX emissions, but also traffic noise. Autonomous driving can be a way to achieve traffic optimization and improve passenger safety.

Internet of Things (IoT) transforms a vehicle into a Connected Car, it opens into many services linked with Vehicle to Infrastructure (V2I) communication but also the possibility for vehicles to communicate among each other like Vehicle to Vehicle (V2V) communication. It can be easily imagined the use of infotainment systems in vehicles opens many opportunities for in-vehicle services.

Predictive analytics can make use of the information shared and stored by vehicles. With Big Data it will be much easier for users or fleet managers companies to be informed when their vehicles need, for example, maintenance, winter tyres or other services alike. Also, public authorities' managers of the road infrastructure can make use of Data especially for managing Public Transport networks.

Shared mobility also opens windows of opportunity for on-demand services. They can be linked with many different solutions: from car-sharing, ride-hailing, peer to peer schemes to micro-mobility sharing opportunities, like bike-sharing and smaller mobility solutions (e.g. Lime, City Bike, or others) and other new micro-electric powered solutions.

Multimodality has become more interesting in this new mobility landscape. MaaS solutions (multi-modal platforms) have been created for a more efficient route planning, especially within cities. Digitalisation has made possible the creation of this kind of platforms and will be massively used in the future specially thinking on city restrictions to vehicles (max speed 30km/h or 50km/h or even complete banning of cars in city centres).

Examples of Concepts (e.g. Toyota e-Palette, Renault EZ line-up, ...)

The examples that will be given are not only targeting the problems of mobility of people but also tackle the problem of the goods delivery. People and Goods are the two key pillars of the current concept offer. Below examples give a prelude of how mobility could look like within the near future.

1. **e-Palette:** The first example is Toyota's e-palette concept, presented in CES Las Vegas in 2018 (ref. President of Toyota Motor Corporation, Akio Toyoda's speech). The company has presented not only a vehicle (hardware product) but also the different user scenes examples on how it could work. A full ecosystem of vehicles, which will continuously move to provide and support the different needs of the people and goods delivery. As mentioned by the president of Toyota Motor Corporation, the company is on transition "from an automobile company to a mobility company". To achieve this, the company no longer relies on just software but is developing a platform to support future services. This platform will be "the backbone for mobility as a service, for autonomy, for car-sharing" and other services they want to make possible to realise. It is the company intention that customers take benefit of this platform by creating a bridge between their own devices (phone, computer and other devices) and the vehicle. The car to become a seamless extension of customer's personal devices. The car will be "a personal assistant on wheels, able to anticipate people's needs through predictive artificial intelligence".

As mentioned by Akio Toyoda, "In the future, much of the mobility on demand, or mobility as a service will be powered by autonomy". On the other hand, autonomy as such will be also supported by electrification. Akio Toyoda also confirmed during this event (CES Las Vegas 2018) the plan of electrification of the company, with a target to achieve "by 2025, every model in the Lexus and Toyota line up will either be electric or will have an electrified option".

The foundation for future mobility is designed. Electrification, combined with Mobility Services Platform, and Autonomous Technology, are the key components in the company's vision of future mobility services and mobility commerce (Akio Toyoda Speech, Press Conference, CES Las Vegas event, January 2018).

Within this context, the e-Palette was presented as one of the concepts that meet this new generation of mobility services. This vehicle will make the best profit from the "flexible platform that can be easily adapted to support a range of uses including ride-sharing, delivery and retail". As also mentioned by Akio Toyoda, "Today, you have to travel to the store. In the future, with e-Palette, the store will come to you!"

This concept vehicle will provide services that cover from ride sharing, delivery and retail, to specific needs like becoming a moving restaurant (e.g. Pizza Hut), a Fab Lab and others. Services can go from medical support to entertainment, and each e-Palette can be "re-configured" to a specific need. The focus is on efficiency with a 24/7 and On-Demand, services to serve the people's needs. This multi-functionality and flexibility are just in line with what are the new Society goals. e-Palette fits into a new "business ecosystem" to respond to the future mobility services and e-commerce needs. During the presentation at CES Las Vegas 2018, the brand presented some user scenes (potential ideas for the usage of this vehicle):

- "Real e-commerce"- On-Demand retail experience. E.g. People wanting to buy a pair of shoes, specific models can be easily selected by an e-commerce application. After selection of a few models, the vehicle will come to the person with the selected pair of shoes. The person can then try them out and purchase if they would like to. This is possible using a platform that allows people to order on-line and where recognition technologies (e.g. face recognition) will allow access to the vehicle to make a choice and shopping experience possible.
- "Multi-purpose moving Space"- "meaning of transportation may change". E.g. Fab Lab: while a person moves from the office to meet clients, make best use of commuting time while preparing a demo/meeting to your customer. It's all about making the best use of time, even if it is commuting time.
- "Mobile Personal Shops"- "personal mobile market place". E.g. Items can be sold (e.g. second hand, craftsman products, others) without the presence of the owner. The moving market place will go and be visited by people that are interested in those specific items. The use of recognition technologies (e.g. face recognition, digital identification, others) are essential to make this new way of e-commerce work.
- "On Demand City" – for events where several services are required (e.g. in a concert place), several e-palettes can be used to serve the community (moving restaurants, entertainment, and others), while everyone is assisting to a concert.

Alike Toyota, the automotive sector has understood they will not be able to think only as a vehicle provider. Automotive is moving towards a mobility company, where new solutions in terms of mobility services will be imposed.

New services have been created in the last years, to respond to people's needs for more flexibility. OEM's merge services to become more competitive. For example, BMW and Daimler created a Joint Venture "Your Now". The two big players merge ecosystems to deliver on-demand mobility: Car-Sharing, Ride-Sharing, Parking, Charging Infrastructure and Multimodality (1 Billion€ joint investment).

2. **EZ line up**: The Groupe Renault has been taking a leading role in the promotion of EV vehicles. In 2018 the company had already presented 5 electric models in the line-up and has been very active in car-sharing collaborations and in the promotion of robot-vehicles in open roads. The French Group has been actively presenting interesting concepts under their new EZ line up.

At the press event in Paris Motor Show 2018, the Chief Operating Officer (CEO) of Groupe Renault, Thierry Bolloré presented 3 different concept vehicles, targeting different needs for people and goods deliveries. As part of Renault's "2017 – 2022 Strategic Plan", these vehicles fit a vision of a new mobility landscape, with solutions for people usage and goods delivery in an urban environment. The first concept is "EZ-Go", a concept car targeting shared urban mobility. It's a robo-taxi like (autonomous, connected and electric). The second is "EZ-Pro" a concept for urban last-mile delivery, specially designed to "offer an optimum solution both for professional and the end customer". As mentioned by the company CEO Thierry Bolloré, with this vehicle "we are proposing a customisable offer, which means that the users can choose, how, where and when the packages can be delivered". And the 3rd concept was a newly unveiled vehicle in the show named "EZ-Ultimo". It's a concept for premium shared mobility services, a luxury robo-vehicle.

Inspired by the EZ-GO and EZ-PRO concept-cars unveiled in 2018, the Groupe Renault continues to explore new mobility options. EZ-POD is a small robo-vehicle (autonomous, connected and electric) designed to transport people but also to carry goods over short distances. Given the small size of the vehicle we can easily imagine this vehicle as a complement to first and last mile usage, as indicated in the press release (Renault EZ-Pod, an explorative vehicle for the first and last mile, May 16, 2019).

One of the last reveals of the brand under the EZ range was the EZ-FLEX. Revealed in the "Viva Technology show" in Paris from May 16 to 18, 2019, the EZ-Flex is an experimental, electric and connected light commercial vehicle. It's a compact size vehicle that features a modular rear design for easy adaptation of the different package's transportation. A collaboration with La Poste (French national post-office) is expected. The aim is to "analyse the vehicle data and feedback from postal staff will serve for a greater understanding of the day-to-day realities of last-mile deliveries", as mentioned in the press release (*Renault EZ-Flex and La Poste: Trial for Last Mile Deliveries*, May 16, 2019).

The different concepts presented by the Groupe Renault shows the new mobility intentions to respond to the society needs.

OEM's have understood the importance of meeting people demands and expectations. In a connected society, businesses need to re-invent themselves to face the society needs. A more People-centred approach is essential and a clearer understanding of the inefficiencies in society will need to be tackled by everyone (from public institutions, private citizens and big corporations). Only by working together it's possible to continue to improve and achieve a more sustainable lifestyle, and ultimately improve the quality of Life. Automotive OEM's are seeing this opportunity rise and are working in creating new models of mobility and testing them, to provide the most efficient mean of transportation for all.

New Players in the Mobility Landscape (e.g. Navya Autonom, Easymile EZ10 Shuttle)

Other big players in the mobility arena are also making their appearance. A new Start-up culture is rising, especially bringing new services and products to the automotive sector, competing with the traditional Original Equipment Manufacturers (OEM's).

1. **Autonom**: Navya is a company that was established in 2014 and has developed the "Autonom" range. They have equipped their current 3 vehicles with a high level of autonomous driving capability. As the brand indicates in their website (https://www.navya-corp.com/index.php/en/), they are provider of "autonomous, shared and electric" mobility. The" Autonom Shuttle", its Navya's

first development dedicated to first and last-mile transportation. This vehicle can carry up to 15 people. It's a vehicle that can be remotely monitored. It can drive autonomously within a specific path and has been used in several pilots in Europe and the US. Also, part of the Navya's Line up its "Autonom Cab". This vehicle is what we can qualify of a Robo-taxi. As mentioned by the brand, this vehicle "provides an intelligent transport service for individual trips in urban centres". Maximum capacity is of 6 passengers. The Autonom Cab "is a fluid, continuous and effective solution that answers user expectations in terms of service before, during and after their trip. The cab was designed from the outset to be autonomous, meaning that there is no cockpit, steering wheel nor pedals". The Autonom Tract it's the third developed vehicle by Navya and it's expected to start its first road tests in the year 2020. This vehicle will be dedicated to goods transport.

2. **EZ10:** The French company is rivalled by EasyMile with the vehicle EZ10. Like the Autonom Shuttle from Navya, it is meant for First and Last Mile commuting. The company was also founded in 2014 and started as a high-tech start-up specialized in providing both software powering autonomous vehicles and the last mile smart mobility solutions. They are specialists in the development of the necessary technologies to support autonomous driving capabilities but also future services: as mentioned in their website (https://easymile.com) they are looking into Multi-sensors localization techniques; Obstacle detection and avoidance; navigation, path planning and control; Connectivity (V2V, V2I); Fleet management; Safety and cybersecurity.

Many other start-ups are also appearing in this new mobility arena with different propositions to serve people and goods delivery, ultimately to provide better future on-demand services.

SOLUTIONS AND RECOMMENDATIONS

Looking into a more top-bottom approach, Governments recognise the strategic importance of the automotive industry for the economic development. In a report from the European Commission ("Cars 21 High Level Group Final Report 2012"), "Car Industry is responsible for 12 million jobs, €92bn trade balance and €30bn investment in R&D". This would be a sector that given its importance to society will not be disregarded by authorities.

Innovation is one of the key factors and a market driver for this industry. The industry has already revealed some very innovative concepts as the ones presented in this chapter (e.g. Toyota and Renault). Research is needed to further develop better connected vehicles, achieving Zero emission and the Safety requirements needed.

Technology developments in terms of powertrains (EV, Fuel Cell …) will be essential to achieve a Zero emission vehicle and impact positively the environment. Also, the automotive sector needs to make sure that these new systems will be manufactured in the cleanest way possible. Many people concerned about battery manufacturing process, especially for EV and are concerned that a recyclability process is in place, to face this ever growing EV market.

From a more bottom-up approach, this new Mobility Landscape (MaaS and Smart Mobility for the people) will take a more people-centric and consumer- focus approach. Mobility will need to respond to ever changing consumer habits and needs for a new type of mobility. Given this perspective, the car manufacturers will certainly change their models of business. It can be easily imagined that the entire chain will be affected, from production to retailers, from products offered to new services. Production manufacturing will need to become more flexible to accommodate a higher growing demand for personalisation. Also, with 3D printing technology becoming more affordable today, people could build their car or at least personalised it at their taste or even own daily desires. Retailers will no longer have the same role as today. They will need to be re-invented to attract people again. Could be that showrooms become places like transition hubs supporting communities, where people will be looking into changing modes of transport depending on their travel needs (leisure, holiday or simply for commuting to work).

FUTURE RESEARCH DIRECTIONS

For future research studies, it would be important to understand the impact of laws and regulations in this new landscape of mobility. Regulations are becoming stricter, and the sector needs to adapt more and more to the ever-growing demands of the regulators.

What type of new mobility needs in cities, given all restrictions happening already today in terms of accessibility (higher number of pedestrian zones in cities); speed (speed reduction in certain areas to as low as 10km/h); banning of ICE engine vehicles. Also, thinking of future digital societies, how will Cities regulate the sharing/ ride-hailing schemes? Autonomous Driving introduction who will be liable in case of an accident (Men or Machine?).

Also, how to make sure that automotive will offer mobility solutions for all people in society, looking into a more inclusive approach, supporting the group of people that face the greatest difficulties, like disabled or elderly that will become one of the biggest issues in society as we are facing an ever-elderly society.

More in-depth studies will certainly be useful to understand how people lives will be ultimately affected, and how will automotive adapt to all new requirements from Governance and Regulators (top-down approach) and the increasing demand by people for more green, flexible and safe type of mobility (bottom-up movement).

CONCLUSION

The automotive industry is changing their mindset providing to current product the vision of valuable services and from pure automotive to a mobility company. They are studying and looking into people needs and using the new trends and technologies that support this change, to reflect them into the product and service development.

During this Chapter, it was highlighted the evolution of the Automotive Industry through time, starting from the first Industrial revolution and how cars became a mass product, used by everyone. Soon enough, the high number of vehicles on the road started to become a real problem and a big challenge to solve by Public authorities. Also, for People, especially in big urbanised areas, started to face the consequences of pollution, smog, affecting their health seriously. Another issue was congestion, long commuting times started to become a real issue and influencing negatively the quality of life of people.

A need for change started to rise and was heavily supported by different trends that affected mobility overall. In what concerns the automotive Industry, in this chapter, three trends have been identified as playing a major role to support the rise of a new Mobility Landscape: Electrification (Electric Vehicles);

Environment (Low to Zero-emission vehicles, city Car Banning policies) and Digital transformation (Smart Cities, connected objects and a sensor-based Society bringing new digitalised services).

New technologies and innovation supported by these new trends are key drivers for new mobility solutions. Advanced technologies re-design completely the new vehicle offers (e.g. autonomous driving, digital or face recognition technologies, in-car digital services, trace and track technologies and many others). New user scenes can easily be imagined.

Some of these technologies are reflected in the concepts presented by the two major automotive case studies presented in this chapter. From Toyota Motor Corporation, the e-Palette Concept is bringing new concepts of travel. As mentioned by Akio Toyoda, "In the future, much of the mobility on demand, or mobility as a service will be powered by autonomy". He also mentioned, "Today, you have to travel to the store. In the future, with e-Palette, the store will come to you!". From Groupe Renault, on the concept proposed for Goods delivery, company CEO Thierry Bolloré mentioned, with this vehicle "we are proposing a customisable offer, which means that the users can choose, how, where and when the packages can be delivered". The mentioned examples only highlight how disruptive it can be future mobility.

The same approach can be seen with Navya's Autonom Line-up and Easymile solutions especially focusing on first and last-mile mobility solutions.

The future will be focused on delivering a truly personalized customer experience. Current trends and technologies support the development of Products and Services to sustain this new lifestyle and ultimately influence the future consumer behaviour.

The automotive sector is making efforts in meeting the new consumer expectation. They are committed to exploring new forms of business by proving Product and Services in a sustainable and responsible way, with a stronger People-Centric approach. This will be the key to improve people's quality of life, in the future.

REFERENCES

Arcadis (EURONEXT: ARCAD), Global Design & Consultancy. (2019). *People-centric mobility is key to the future success of cities.* https://www.arcadis.com/en/global/news/latest-news/2019/06/people-centric-mobility-is-key-for-the-future-success-of-cities/

Bartnik, R., Wilhelm, M., & Fujimoto, T. (2018). Introduction to innovation in the East Asian automotive industry: Exploring the interplay between product architectures, firm strategies, and national innovation systems. *Technovation, 70–71*, 1–6.

Baunach, M., Martins Gomes, R., Malenko, M., Mauroner, F., Batista Ribeiro, L., & Scheipel, T. (2018). Smart mobility of the future – a challenge for embedded automotive systems. *Elektrotech. Inftech., 135*(4-5), 304–308. doi:10.100700502-018-0623-6

Boano, C., Römer, K., Bloem, R., Witrisal, K., Baunach, M., & Horn, M. (2016). Dependability for the Internet of things: From dependable networking in harsh environments to a holistic view on dependability. *E&I Elektrotechnik und Informationstechnik, 133*(7), 304–309. doi:10.100700502-016-0436-4

CES Las Vegas. (2018). *Toyota Motor Corporation, President Akio Toyoda - Speech.* Press event presentation. https://global.toyota/en/album/videos/20566886

Cirella, G. T., Bąk, M., Kozlak, A., Pawłowska, B., & Borkowski, P. (2019). Transport innovations for elderly people. *Research in Transportation Business & Management, 30*. doi:10.1016/j.rtbm.2019.100381

Easymile. (n.d.). https://www.easymile.com

Eltis – The Urban Mobility Observatory. (n.d.). https://www.eltis.org/discover/case-studies/shared-mobility-enabling-maas-milans-sump European Commission (2012) Cars 21 High Level Group Final Report 2012 ec.europa.eu/growth/content/vision-2020-recommendations-help-car-industry-reach-new-heights-0_en

European Commission. (2019). *Mobility and Transport*. https://ec.europa.eu/transport/themes/urban/urban_mobility_en

Giampieri, A., Ling-Chin, J., Ma, Z., Smallbone, A., & Roskilly, A. P. (2020). A review of the current automotive manufacturing practice from an energy perspective. *Applied Energy*, *261*, 114074. doi:10.1016/j.apenergy.2019.114074

Gomes, R. M., Baunach, M., Malenko, M., Ribeiro, L. B., & Mauroner, F. (2017): A co-designed RTOS and MCU concept for dynamically composed embedded systems. OSPERT'17.

Graedel, T., & Allenby, B. (1998). *Industry ecology and Automobile*. Prentice Hall.

Groupe Renault. (2019). *EZ-Flex and La Poste: Trial for Last Mile Deliveries*. Press Release. Retrieved from https://media.group.renault.com/global/en-gb/groupe-renault/media/pressreleases/21225825/renault-ez-flex-une-premiere-experimentation-avec-la-poste

Günther, M., Kacperski, C., & Krems, J. F. (2020). Can electric vehicle drivers be persuaded to eco-drive? A field study of feedback, gamification and financial rewards in Germany. *Energy Research & Social Science*, *63*, 101407. doi:10.1016/j.erss.2019.101407

Hilton, J. (2018). Transforming the way we access and use transportation and mobility services. *Automotive Industries*. Retrieved from http://search.ebscohost.com/login.aspx?direct=true&db=bth&AN=138283403&site=eds-live

Israel, R. (2018). Mobility-as-a-service: The coming transportation revolution. *FS Private Wealth: Journal of Family Office Investment*. Retrieved from http://search.ebscohost.com/login.aspx?direct=true&db=bth&AN=135702114&site=eds-live

Kanger, L., Geels, F. W., Sovacool, B., & Schot, J. (2019). Technological diffusion as a process of societal embedding: Lessons from historical automobile transitions for future electric mobility. *Transportation Research Part D, Transport and Environment*, *71*, 47–66. doi:10.1016/j.trd.2018.11.012

Lane, B. W. (2019). Revisiting 'An unpopular essay on transportation:' The outcomes of old myths and the implications of new technologies for the sustainability of transport. *Journal of Transport Geography*, *81*, 102535. doi:10.1016/j.jtrangeo.2019.102535

Madslien, J. (2017). Intelligent mobility. *Professional Engineering*. Retrieved from http://search.ebscohost.com/login.aspx?direct=true&db=bth&AN=123453640&site=eds-live

Mayyas, A., Qattawi, A., Omar, M., & Shan, D. (2012). Design for sustainability in automotive industry: A comprehensive review. *Renewable & Sustainable Energy Reviews*, *16*(4), 1845–1862. doi:10.1016/j.rser.2012.01.012

McKinsey. (2013). *Disruptive technologies: advances that will transform life, business, and the global economy*. https://www.mckinsey.com/insights/business_technology/disruptive_technologies

McKinsey & Company. (2017). *How Shared Mobility will change the Automotive Industry April 2017 chapter*. https://www.mckinsey.com/industries/automotive-and-assembly/our-insights/how-shared-mobility-will-change-the-automotive-industry

Modi, S., Spulber, A., & Jin, J. (2018). Impact of automated, connected, electric, and shared (ACES) vehicles on design, materials, manufacturing and business models.

Navya. https://www.navya-corp.com/index.php/en/

Noel, L., Zarazua de Rubens, G., Kester, J., & Sovacool, B. K. (2018). Beyond emissions and economics: Rethinking the co-benefits of electric vehicles (EVs) and vehicle-to-grid (V2G). *Transport Policy*, *71*, 130–137. doi:10.1016/j.tranpol.2018.08.004

Paris Motor Show. (2018). *Groupe Renault – Company's CEO Thierry Bolloré - Speech*. Press event presentation.

Pitt, J. (2019). Transparent Ownership of Mobility-as-a-Service [Editorial]. *IEEE Technology and Society Magazine*, *38*(2), 5–8. doi:10.1109/MTS.2019.2913064

PWC. (2018). *Five Trends transforming the Automotive Industry*. https://eu-smartcities.eu/sites/default/files/2018-03/pwc-five-trends-transforming-the-automotive-industry.compressed.pdf

PWC. (2018). *Five trends transforming the automotive industry*. Available from: https://www.pwc.at/de/publikationen/branchen-und-wirtschaftsstudien/eascy-five-trends-transforming-the-automotive-industry_2018.pdf

Saidani, M., Yannou, B., Leroy, Y., & Cluzel, F. (2018). Heavy vehicles on the road towards the circular economy: Analysis and comparison with the automotive industry. *Resources, Conservation and Recycling*, *135*, 108–122. doi:10.1016/j.resconrec.2017.06.017

Sell, R., Rassõlkin, A., Wang, R., & Otto, T. (2019). Integration of autonomous vehicles and Industry 4.0. *Proceedings of the Estonian Academy of Sciences*, *68*(4), 389–394. doi:10.3176/proc.2019.4.07

SMMT. (2017). *The digitalisation of the UK automotive industry*. Academic Press.

Sovacool, B., & Brossmann, B. (2014). The rhetorical fantasy of energy transitions: Implications for energy policy and analysis. *Technology Analysis and Strategic Management*, *26*(7), 837–854. doi:10.1080/09537325.2014.905674

Sovacool, B. K., Rogge, J.-C., Saleta, C., & Masterson-Cox, E. (2019). Transformative versus conservative automotive innovation styles: Contrasting the electric vehicle manufacturing strategies for the BMW i3 and Fiat 500e. *Environmental Innovation and Societal Transitions*, *33*, 45–60. doi:10.1016/j.eist.2019.02.004

Statista. (2017). *Percentage of Global Research and Development Spending in 2017, by Industry*. Available at: https://www.statista.com/statistics/270233/percentage-of-global-rundd-spending-by-industry/

Stoycheva, S., Marchese, D., Paul, C., Padoan, S., Juhmani, A., & Linkov, I. (2018). Multi-criteria decision analysis framework for sustainable manufacturing in automotive industry. *Journal of Cleaner Production*, *187*, 257–272. doi:10.1016/j.jclepro.2018.03.133

Sturges, D. (2016). Rethinking the City. *Automotive Design & Production*. Retrieved from http://search.ebscohost.com/login.aspx?direct=true&db=bth&AN=115873558&site=eds-live

Transport & Environment. (2016). *Dieselgate: Who? What? How? (Study report September 2016)*. Author. https://www.transportenvironment.org/publications/dieselgate-who-what-how

Transport & Environment. (2017). *Does Sharing cars really reduce car use? - June 2017 - Transport & Environment Brief Report (ITF OECD, 2016; BEUC, 2016)*. https://www.transportenvironment.org/sites/te/files/publications/Does-sharing-cars-really-reduce-car-use-June%202017.pdf

Transport & Environment Brief Report. (2017). *Does Sharing cars really reduce car use?* https://www.transportenvironment.org/sites/te/files/publications/Does-sharing-cars-really-reduce-car-use-June%20 2017.pdf

Transport & Environment Press Report. (2017). *35 million dirty diesels are driving on Europe's roads today, new research finds*. https://www.transportenvironment.org/press/35-million-dirty-diesels-are-driving-europe%E2%80%99s-roads-today-new-research-finds

Transport & Environment Press Report. (2017). *Fixing Dieselgate in Europe (Briefing report May 2015)*. https://www.transportenvironment.org/sites/te/files/publications /2017_05_Fixing_Dieselgate_in_Europe.pdf

UC Davis / ITDP. (2017). *Three Revolutions in Urban Transportation May 2017 – report*. https://steps.ucdavis.edu/wp-content/uploads/2017/05/STEPS_ITDP-3R-Report-5-10-2017-2.pdf

Whittle, C., Whitmarsh, L., Haggar, P., Morgan, P., & Parkhurst, G. (2019). User decision-making in transitions to electrified, autonomous, shared or reduced mobility. *Transportation Research Part D, Transport and Environment*, *71*, 302–319. doi:10.1016/j.trd.2018.12.014

World Economic Forum. (2015). *Is this the future of the internet of things?* https://www.weforum.org/agenda/2015/11/is-this-future-of-the-internet-of-things/

World Economic Forum. (2018). *Electric vehicles for smarter cities: the future of energy and mobility*. http://www3.weforum.org/docs/WEF_2018_%20Electric_For_Smarter_Cities.pdf

KEY TERMS AND DEFINITIONS

Car-Sharing: App-based and point to point station-based systems (e.g., Cambio); free-floating car sharing such as Car2Go or Zen Car (using only electric cars).

MaaS: Mobility as a service.

Multi-Modal: Use of different modes of transport from Public transport (train, bus, tram, others) to car, bike, or other sharing schemes including walking.

On-Demand Services: Providing goods and services is almost instant or in minimal time. The service request to destination is performed using an app.

People-Centric Mobility: Mobility solutions thinking on people-first approach.

Ride-Sharing: App-based short-distance ride-sharing services (e.g., Uber); and long-distance ride-sharing (e.g., BlaBlaCar).

Robo-Taxi: Taxi completely autonomous used for on demand services.

Chapter 20
The Roles of Time Orientation and Innate Innovativeness on Intentioned Adoption of an AI Innovation:
The Study of Millennial Consumers in London, UK

Giorgi Antadze
https://orcid.org/0000-0003-3106-1415
London South Bank University, UK

ABSTRACT

Innovation adoption is a widely understudied area. However, there has been a substantial amount of arguments concerned with the extent to which personality traits affect innovative behavior. Thus, the purpose of this study is to examine the extent to which personality traits, namely time orientation and innate innovativeness, influence intentioned adoption of the specific innovation – the virtual nurse assistant. The organisation of the chapter is as follows: The first part of the chapter introduces the study to the reader and starts with the research background, followed by the research problem, rationale of the study, and research objectives. The second part consists of literature review, critically evaluating the relevant secondary sources to derive the research hypothesis. The third part represents the results and findings of the study, followed by the conclusion and recommendations as the closing part of this chapter.

INTRODUCTION

Today it is impossible to imagine humanity evolving without artificial intelligence (AI) (Lowe et al., 2019; Miller, 2019). Smart cities, self-driving cars and humanoid robots are the evidence of the ability of AI to further revolutionise industries and alter the consumption patterns (Bundy, 2017). Healthcare

DOI: 10.4018/978-1-7998-3115-0.ch020

Copyright © 2020, IGI Global. Copying or distributing in print or electronic forms without written permission of IGI Global is prohibited.

is one of the sectors where AI has already brought huge opportunities (Jiang, F et al., 2017). A report by Accenture (Fu et al., 2017) defines AI in healthcare as "a collection of multiple technologies, which enable machines to sense, comprehend, act and learn, so they perform clinical healthcare functions."

Virtual nurse assistant (VNA) is one of the innovations in the healthcare market inspired by AI. This is an advanced technology in mobile health (m-Health) services, namely a concept of healthcare practices provided through tablets and cell phones (Zhao et al., 2018). AI-powered virtual nurse avatar provides medical services through the mobile application aiming to reduce unnecessary visits to the practitioner. At present, the VNA can assess symptoms and give limited medical advice during a verbal or text message communication with the consumer (Figure 1). Additionally, this innovation can continuously monitor the consumer's health through wearable technology and update personal medical data as well as alert medical professionals if necessary (Ram, 2018). However, the biggest advantage and the future potential of this innovation is in self-learning and the prediction of a patient's health condition based on the input medical data, which further enriches every time consumers interact with the technology (Ram, 2018). Therefore, VNA have a realistic potential to outperform human doctors in setting official diagnosis and even offer sophisticated treatment recommendations where the self-care is applicable. The appearance of such advanced VNA in the marketplace depends on healthcare regulations rather than practical capabilities for its development in the next couple of years (Olson, 2018).

Inventors of the innovation believe that advanced VNA will change consumption patterns within the medical market (CognitionX, 2018). However, the success of the innovation is depended on the consumers' decision, whether to adopt or reject it. The decision itself is influenced by many different variables, one of them exists within the consumer itself – personality traits. Thus, the purpose of this chapter is to define the extent at which personality traits, namely Innate Innovativeness (II) and Time Orientation (TO) influence consumers' cognitive processing in regards of intentions to adopt the innovation in question.

BACKGROUND

Innovation Adoption

The innovation adoption process has been conceptualised as sequential with the consumer journey starting from the initial awareness of the innovation and passing through different stages until reaching the adoption decision (Rogers, 2003). The definition of innovation itself varies within existing literature (Baregheh et al., 2009). Nevertheless, the most widely used is by Rogers (2003) standing for "any idea, practice, or material artefact perceived to be new by the relevant unit of adoption". In relation to products, Garcia & Calantone (2002) subsequently added that the product can only be deemed as innovative if it provides the value and is diffused to other parties beyond the innovator.

The failure rate of new product diffusion in social systems is relatively high, resulting in marketers' restless effort to identify customer segments with favourable dispositions towards a novelty (Ho & Wu, 2011). Consumers who are open to new experiences are to be the first to adopt innovations and with their behaviour motivate others to imitate them (Hoffmann & Soyez, 2010). Researchers argue that understanding consumer characteristics plays a vital role in identifying these type of consumers (Gatignon & Robertson, 1985). This led to an intense examination of consumer psychographics in relation to new product adoption behaviour (NPA), wherein one of the most interesting concepts for marketers is consumer innovativeness (d'Hauteville et al., 1998). Consumer innovativeness is the individual's predisposition to purchase new and unfamiliar products/brands rather than remaining with previous choices and consumption patterns (Steenkamp & Gielens, 2003).

Figure 1. Example of the Narrative of the VNA

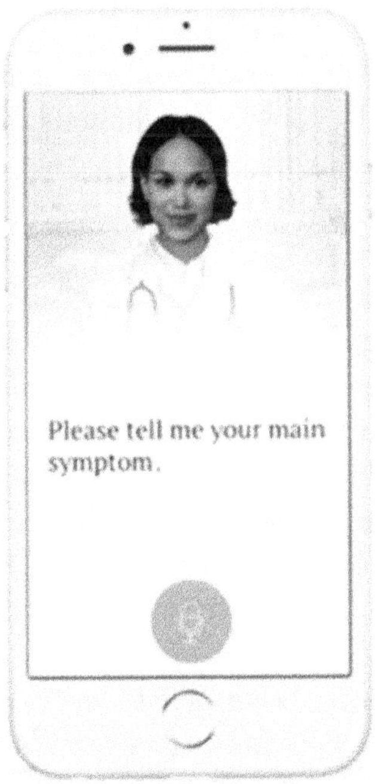

Let me introduce you with Molly, she is virtual nurse powered by artificial intelligence which enables her to operate just like human practitioner, however only virtually (she is an online robot). Molly enables consumers to treat themselves without using human doctor for minor health issues (cough, temperature, muscle pains etc.) by providing them with medical recommendations after checking their symptoms and setting diagnosis during the virtual appointment.

In addition, more personal information she possesses on a consumer, better personalized healthcare service she can deliver them. Molly also provides users with information related to medications or illnesses and continuously monitors their health through wearable technology.

Several studies demonstrate that consumer innovativeness plays an important role in new product acceptance (Chao et al., 2012; Im et al., 2007; Midgley & Dowling, 1993). Furthermore, researchers had focused on identification of antecedents and factors influencing consumer innovativeness, which in turn also affect the acceptance of innovation (Bartels & Reinders, 2011). Consumer innovativeness is positively correlated with personal values such as independence, tolerance to ambiguity, hedonism, stimulation and negatively with conservatism, dogmatism and a need for structure (Venkatraman & Price, 1990; Foxall et al., 1995; Lassar et al., 2005). Personality traits were strongly related to values, representing the core of consumers' cognitive structure (Bilsky & Schwartz, 1994). The personal values demonstrated above are closely associated with the consumers' personality trait known as a TO. This psychological dimension refers to individual's cognitive involvement on his/her psychological past, present or future time frames, representing fundamental aspects of consumers' attitudes and behaviour (Shipp et al., 2009). Individuals with diverse TO dimensions, who also differ in terms of prioritised personal values, which in turn are correlated either negatively or positively with the consumer innovativeness (Zimbardo & Boyed, 1999). Some theories point in the direction of possible cause and effect relationship between mentioned psychological dimensions of TO, personal values and consumer innovativeness (Bilsky & Schwartz, 1994; Zimbardo & Boyed, 1999). Since the latter is the key psychological dimension within the innovative behaviour, the next section proposes to overview studies examining consumer innovativeness from different angels and identify the gap in the knowledge within this area of interest.

Gap in the Knowledge

Researchers identify three perspectives within consumer innovativeness: global (trait), domain-specific and behavioural (Goldsmith & Foxall, 2003). Hirschman (1980) had earlier stated that behavioural or actualised innovativeness involves an earlier acquisition of new information by an individual compared to other members of society. The scholar further divides this concept into adoptive innovativeness (information adoption through the direct experience - product acquisition) and vicarious innovativeness (information adoption through the indirect experience – without product purchase). Due to marketers' interest in adoptive innovativeness, various scales were developed for studying the role of global also known as innate (II) and domain-specific innovativeness (DSI) within actualised behaviour (Roehrich, 2004).

II is the personality trait of the consumer, responsible for the individual's reactions towards newness, whereas DSI refers to the tendency of the consumer to acquire information and new products within a specific domain (Hirunyawipada & Paswan, 2006). The DSI is mainly the result of strong personal interests related to particular product category (Roerich et al., 2002). Therefore, it is not surprising that the majority of studies found a strong correlation between innovative behaviour and high scores of DSI (Klink & Athaide, 2010; d'Hauteville et al., 1998; Goldsmith & Foxall, 2003). However, there is disagreement among scholars concerned with the link between II and adoptive behaviour: some researchers demonstrated significant positive relationship between these two variables (Limayem & Khalifa, 2000, Wood & Swait, 2002; Foxall et al., 1995), whereas others came out with the different results (Lassar et al., 2005). Im et al. (2007) suggest that the inconsistency around the topic might be the result of ignorance of other intervening variables. For this reason, Leicht et al. (2018) have recently examined innovativeness as the moderating variable influencing the relationship between performance and effort expectancy and the intention to adopt autonomous cars. The scholars claimed that II only indirectly (thorough moderation of perceived performance expectancy) affected consumers' intentions to accept the innovation. In consideration of the relationship between consumer innovativeness and actualised behaviour, TO is an underexplored antecedent of these two variables (Karande & Merchant, 2012). This proposes further research in the area, which is addressed by this chapter.

Existing literature demonstrates several studies concerned with antecedents of II and actualised behaviour: Clark & Goldsmith (2006) examined the role of interpersonal influence on II and adoptive behaviour; Handa & Gupta (2009) later studied the influence of demographic variables on II and e-commerce adoption. Only one study has examined the impact of time orientation on consumer innovativeness so far (Merchant et al., 2014). However, this research does not demonstrate the effects of these personality traits on the intentioned or actualised behaviour. Moreover, there was no study found examining effects of TO and II on consumer perceptions related to the innovation attributes that in turn directly affect the intended adoption of the VNA in the UK market. Therefore, this study intends to shed more light on some crucial aspects of consumer behaviour by applying demonstrated concepts of TO and II to a specific context: the intentioned adoption of the virtual nurse assistant.

Rationale of the Chapter

The study focuses on an AI-powered VNA that intends to provide full healthcare service to the consumer in terms of health-related issues, which can be treated without necessary intervention of a human practitioner. Thus, this chapter aims to provide consumer insights related to the intentioned acceptance of the innovation in question.

The study examines Behavioural Intention (BI) rather than actual behaviour as the innovation is still in its development stages. Although intention might differ from actual behaviour, the former is a key determinant factor for the adoption of innovation within the pre-introduction stage of the product lifecycle (Holak & Lehmann, 1990). On the other hand, personality traits play a crucial role in NPA (Arts et al., 2011). Therefore, author measure the extent to which personality traits, such as TO and II influence the intended receptiveness of the innovation. Thus, determining the value these variables possess in developing marketing strategies specifically for the VNA adoption. The focus of the study is on II rather than on DSI, as the former refers to personality trait on which existing literature demonstrates counter arguing findings in relation to NPA.

Im et al. (2007) suggest that in order to further define the roles of personality traits within BI, it is necessary to consider other intervening factors affecting innovation acceptance. Hence, author also analyses the effects of TO and II on consumer perceptions related to innovation attributes. To accurately determine the role of personality traits on individuals' perceptions, it is necessary to minimise preconceived subjective ideas that alter consumer perceptions (Svendsen et al., 2013). Due to this reason, the only selected participants with no prior knowledge of the VNA, whereas the innovation was initially introduced to the respondents with the description included in the questionnaire.

The value of the research is in its contribution to general academic knowledge on consumer behaviour by understanding the role of TO in BI to adopt an innovation. Also, the study provides valuable consumer insights for marketers within the healthcare industry, especially for those working on the development of AI nurse assistants in the UK.

FOCUS OF THE STUDY

The overall aim of this chapter is to examine the roles of TO and consumer innovativeness within cognitive processing of a consumer leading to intentioned adoption of the virtual nurse assistant. The objectives are as follows:

- To examine consumer perceptions related to the VNA attributes and determine their roles in intentioned adoption of the innovation;
- To assess the roles of TO and II on consumer perceptions related to the innovation attributes;
- To critically evaluate the effects of TO on consumer II and assess their overall roles within the consumers' intentions to adopt the VNA.

Perceived Attributes of Innovation

Individuals' behaviours correspond to their perceptions of reality, which is the matter of subjective interpretation of things in the objective circumstances (Schiffman & Wisenblit, 2015). Therefore, consumers' subjective perceptions concerned with attributes of new products represent important explanations in the adoption or rejection of innovations and there is a specific instrument for studying innovation acceptance (Moore & Benbasat, 1991). The items included in the instrument explicitly emphasise the importance of measuring perceptions related to innovation use rather than the innovation itself (Koul & Eydgahi, 2017). Other predictive theories widely used in innovation adoption literature are theory of reasoned action, theory of planned behaviour (Ajzen, 1985), technology acceptance model (Davis, 1989) and unified theory of acceptance and use of technology (Venkatesh et al., 2003). All these models heavily rely on consumer perceptions concerned with Product Attributes (PA) in foreseeing individuals' expected actions towards an innovation (Kapoor et al., 2015).

Studies examining m-Health technology adoption show that strength of influence of innovation attributes influencing consumer decision varies depended on the numerous variables (Karahoca et al., 2018). However, perceived relative advantage (RA) and perceived risk (PR) have been demonstrated as one of the most important factors when examining the roles of innovation attributes within consumer intentions of innovation adoption. Thus, this chapter focuses on the roles of RA and PR - as the key directly influential variables - on intentioned adoption of innovations close to the VNA concept:

Hypothesis 1: PR negatively affects BI;
Hypothesis 2: Perceived RA positively affects BI;

Role of Personality Traits on Consumer Perceptions and Innovation Adoption.

Every individual has different perceptions in regards to the same stimuli under the same condition (Verneau & Griffith, 2016) and perception is the unique process, whereby an individual cognitively selects, organises and interprets stimuli into coherent and meaningful portray of the world (Schiffman & Wisenblit, 2015). Perception is the result of a combination of two inputs: physical stimuli, received by human sensors from the external environment and internal inputs such as values, expectations, past experiences and motives. Thus, interpretation of external stimuli influenced by the internal input, produces unique and subjective perception (Solomon, 2018). Barnett et al. (2015) claim that personality traits strongly affect human behaviour, cognition, and beliefs. Personality traits are psychological dimensions of individual differences in tendencies to demonstrate consistent patterns of feelings, thoughts and actions (Allen, 2006). As a cluster, traits represent personality and are inherent or acquired from the external environment, with the tendency to further develop as the result of personal evolution (McCrae et al., 2000).

Traits play an essential role in the decision making to engage in a behaviour by affecting beliefs related to an action and their subjective evaluation process, that subsequently lead to an intention and finalise with the specific action/inaction (Figure 2). In relation to product purchase or adoption, the behaviour would lead to certain outcome are largely determined by the perceived PA (Schiffman & Wisenblit, 2015). On the other hand, psychologists agree that personality traits are linked to behaviours though a cognitive process, altering human perception and influencing the decisions (James, 1890). This means that PA have unique, subjective mental representation within every individuals' minds. Subsequently the stronger favourable attitude of extroverts compared to introverts towards a product appealing for extraversion trait (e.g. social technology) could be the result of stronger positive evaluation of its perceived usefulness by the extrovert individuals (Svendsen et al., 2013). Thus, the relationship between personality traits and BI cannot be homogenous when the products in question differ. That is why, there is a strong relationship between personality traits and consumer perceptions related to attributes of the technology introduced in their study (Devaraj et al., 2008).

Figure 2. Theory of reasoned action (adopted from Ajzen et al., 1980)

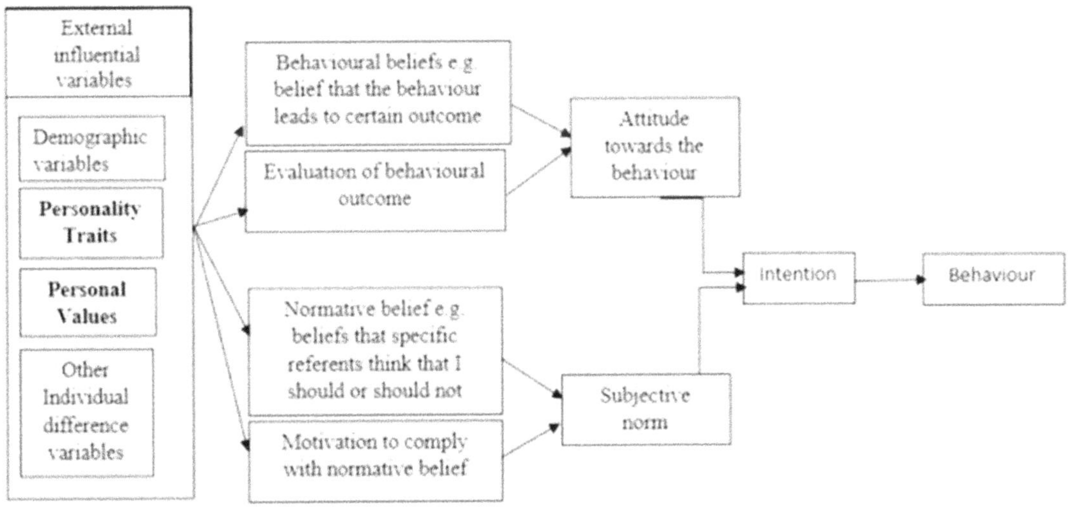

Prayoga & Abraham (2016) oppose the theories that justify the involvement of personality traits within the adoptive behaviour, revealing no significant correlation with any of personality traits with perceived usefulness and BI to adopt healthcare wearable technology. Difference was explained by stating that the participants' BI was affected by the perceived usefulness of the technology that assumingly was based on the product description provided prior to the study and its alignment with the personal needs. The conclusion was that the examined perceptions were not mediating the effects of personality traits to the BI. Interestingly, earlier research by Svendsen et al. (2013) demonstrated different results, while examining the role of personality traits within participants' beliefs and BI related to a hypothetical software technology that was also initially introduced to the research participants' during the study. The research revealed significant correlations between personality traits and constructs of Technology Acceptance Model (TAM).

Trait relationship with intentional or actual behaviour can also be explained by linking traits to the personal values (Bilsky & Schwartz, 1994). Is defined as the guiding principles of conscious behaviour that are cognitive representations of individuals' end state of being and mode of conduct (De Mooij, 2010). The individual's personality traits give rise to the specific corresponding or compensatory values, depending on the person's satisfying needs of growth or deficiency (Caprara et al., 2006). For instance, individual with an excitement-seeking trait is likely to devalue security and develop corresponding value stimulation (growth need). On the other side, individual characterised with anxiety is likely to develop compensatory value security (deficiency need), opposing stimulation value within the wheel of value theory (Bilsky & Schwartz, 1994). There is a significant positive correlation between personal values and personality traits (Roccas et al., 2002) and tradition, as the personal value negatively affected NPA in China (Wang et al., 2008).

The above-mentioned determine strong relationships between personality traits and human behaviour, whereas the former is connected with the latter by altering consumer's cognitive processes and perceptions. Based on the identified theories, the linkage between consumer II as a personality trait and BI to adopt an innovation becomes clear and logical. Due to the fact, subsequent section critically examines literature related to this relationship.

Innate Innovativeness and Innovative Behaviour

II has been defined as an individual's generalised unobservable trait reflecting inherently innovative personality, predisposition and cognitive style (Im et al., 2007). Some researchers had earlier stated that consumers' innovative cognitive style plays a significant role in NPA, as these types of consumers are one of the first to adopt innovations (Midgley & Dowling, 1993). Also an innovative consumer is associated with high stimulation level, tolerance to ambiguity, independence, impulsivity, inner-directed, capacity for status, extraversion, flexibility and risk-taking characteristics (Steenkamp & Gielens, 2003). Highly innovative consumers, also known as innovators make decisions independently, have high interests in novelty and strong desire to seek experiences stimulating their cognition and/or sensory. Thus, these types of individuals aspire to understand the technical information related to new products (Venkatraman & Price, 1990). Subsequently, Ho & Wu (2011) indicated that innovators were associated with opinion leadership in regards of new products, as they want to be the audience from whom peers seek information to maintain their social status. Besides, they are confident in their ideas and decisions, but due to the quick decision-making process, they are associated with impulse buying behaviour. Furthermore, innovators are less conforming to established rules as their inner nature demands risk-taking, uncertainty and imprecision from them.

Empirical studies looking at the relationship between II and NPA counter argue the findings, despite characteristics ascribed to innovative consumers (Im et al., 2007). The issue is the result of an indirect relationship between II and intentioned or actual NPA, which is greatly influenced by other intervening variables. There is a positive effect of II on the intentioned NPA (Steenkamp & Gielens, 2003). However, the moderating role of external factors (such as marketing input) within this relationship and stated that in some cases it might be strong enough that no evidence could be found for significant linkage between II and NPA. Im et al. (2003) also stressed that only II could weakly determine NPA, which encouraged to introduce other variables into their research, whereas the stronger link between II and NPA was identified by integration of demographic variables such as income and age. Subsequent to these findings, some academicians have designed research models examining direct and indirect effects of II on BI (Oliveira et al., 2016; Yi et al., 2006). Indirect effect explains the influence of II on mediating variables, which in turn greatly affect BI. On the other hand, direct link scenario is meant to capture possible effects of II on BI directly, without taking into account different mediator variables between the relationship (Limayem et al., 2000).

The impact of consumer innovativeness on BI mediated through perceptions related to ease of use and usefulness of the technology and the most proximate influence on cognitive interpretations of the stimuli are factors related to an individual's psychology. Thus, the positive relationship between innovativeness and the TAM constructs is supported, but the direct link between innovativeness and BI is insignificant (Lu et al., 2005). Also consumers scoring high on II scored low on PR scale compared to other participant's low on II dimension, whereas innovators were also found to easily envision benefits of the innovation (He et al., 2018) and there is a positive moderating effects of II in the relationship between perceived RA and BI and only weak direct linkage between II and BI (Ho & Wu, 2011) .

Although the direct association of II does not predict specific BI or actual behaviour, it is obvious that the trait plays an important role within consumer psychology, influencing cognitive process, perceptions and behaviours (Kim et al., 2011):

Hypothesis 3: II positively affects RA (a) and negatively PR (b);

Time Orientation and Innovative Consumer

Several researchers studied different personality traits along with personal values, which positively or negatively correlated with II (Ali, 2019; Steenkamp & Gielens, 2003). TO represents one of such psychological dimensions, overlapping with the characteristics ascribed to high or low levels of consumer innovativeness (Karande & Merchant, 2012). Thus, this section reviews this personality trait and identifies its relationship with II.

The psychological interpretation of time shapes the way individuals experience the world (Kant, 1999). Time perception as a crucial aspect of human psychology (James, 1890), whereas later scholars coined the term TO and focused on individuals' time perspective and its influence on human behaviour (Zimbardo & Boyed, 1999). Earlier, Lewin (1951) conceptualised time perspective as "the totality of individual's views of his/her psychological past and future existing at a given time" and explains that it is the process by which the flow of personal experiences is automatically partitioned within psychological past, present and future time frames. It is subconsciously practiced by every individual and utilised with varying degrees in different situations to lead to optimal decisions. However, when a tendency develops within an individual's psychology to overemphasise one of the time frames, the idealised mental framework gets distorted, and the individual becomes specific temporal frame oriented (Zimbardo & Boyed, 1999). The distortion is mainly the result of behavioural and/or cognitive learning of things acquired from culture, family, education, social group and religion (Stolarski et al., 2015). Chronically elicited specific TO within psychology can be referred to a personality trait, which largely determines an individual's lifestyle (Philipp, 1992). Indeed, it is urged that psychological emphasis on past and/or future events have significant influence on present behaviour to the extent that these events are actually present on the cognitive level of behavioural functioning (Nuttin, 2014). A study by Begradaa (1990) revealed that consumers are mainly past, present or future oriented. However, the research also identified individuals with a combination of two of those temporal dimensions (e.g. past and future). In their famous study, Zimbardo & Boyed (1999) describe different characteristics of TO dimensions, overlapping or contradicting with the values and characteristics ascribed to the innovative individuals. The extent to which consumer is past, present or future oriented, affects his/her perceptions related to new product evaluation (Karande & Merchant, 2012). Thus, it is necessary to consider further literature review related to TO in order to identify how this dimension relates to II, distorts consumer perceptions and influences behaviours.

Past orientation has been associated with a tendency to think about the past and connect present actions and events to the emotions and experiences from the past (Karande & Merchant, 2012). This dimension is based on nostalgia, referenced to a longing for the past experiences and preference of objects similar to the ones common in past days with positive attitudes towards the past negatively affect general evaluations concerned with future. Consumers prone to nostalgia show greater favourable predispositions towards the products associated with past compared to consumers with less nostalgic feelings. This shows that predominantly past oriented individuals are risk aversive and prone to structured situations where they feel more secured (Holbrook & Schindler, 1994). The decision-making processes of these types of consumers are greatly influenced by their past experiences, they are not attracted by novelty, do not take chances and tend to be conservative (D'Alessio et al., 2003). Also, compared to others, past oriented individuals are the most distrustful of anything and anyone different. These people have a stable sense of self through years, and their present life is affected by their positive or negative experience from the past (Zimbardo & Boyed, 1999).

Present orientation implies an individual's cognitive focus on current events, whereas concerns related to future consequences or attachment to bygone days is diminished (Harber et al., 2003). These individuals embrace the thrill of the moment, tend to be hedonistic and risk-taking, thus focusing on short-term gratification (Murrell & Mingrone, 1994). Consumers with this psychological dimension are characterised with low self-control and high stimulation level (Hodgins & Engel, 2002). Therefore, they are inclined to impulse buying behaviour (Lennings & Burns, 1998). Besides, present oriented individuals seek for the ways simplifying their life (Davies, 1994). Therefore, these types of consumers prefer novelty and variety during their shopping behaviour (Karande & Merchant, 2012). Present orientated individuals were identified to have the tendency to take things as they are in life, be open to changes and avoid setting high expectations (Cotte et al., 2004) and practical attitudes towards a given reality, making the most of joys and getting personal benefits out of it (Makri & Schlegelmilch, 2017).

Future orientation refers to a consumer's general preoccupation with the future and future events (Strathman et al., 1994) and decisions of future oriented person is largely influenced by evaluations of future consequences, gains and losses as the result of their actions (Harber et al., 2003). These types of consumers are achievement driven, and their future goals represent crucial aspects of their life. Thus, they are greatly resistant to today's gratification in favour of a better tomorrow (Karande & Merchant, 2012). Besides, they are characterised with less risk-taking actions and more self-control compared to present oriented consumers. Although the former takes less joy from the present, they tend to make steady progress towards their future goals by putting effort into their work and sticking to their planned schedules (D'Alessio et al., 2003). Future oriented consumers are reported to be motivated by their aspiration to become more efficient in terms of achieving their goals simultaneously (Cotte et al., 2004) and less sensitive towards novelty than present oriented consumers, they show interests in innovative products, but only after careful consideration and detection of a match between a new product and their personal objective (Karande & Merchant, 2012). Future oriented individuals are greatly adaptable of traditions to new circumstances and live with the idea that the most important events in life will occur in the future (Van Everdingen & Waarts, 2003). Besides, these individuals love to structure the future and set certain expectations to shed light on their future (Kooij et al. 2018). This goes in line with the earlier findings by Begradaa (1990), whose results revealed that the future-oriented consumers were attracted by new experiences in terms of holidays, which were extensively planned by them prior the event occurrence. The research by Park et al. (2017) shows that the future orientation has a significant positive correlation with conscientiousness and insignificant relationship with openness to change traits. The opposite pattern is demonstrated in terms of present orientated individuals.

Numerous studies demonstrate role of TO within different aspects of an individual's life, proving evidence of its crucial role within consumer behaviour (Park et al., 2017). Merchant et al. (2014) examined the influence of TO on II and due to the limited studies in this area, called for further research. Therefore, this chapter examines the impact of these variables on consumer perceptions that mediate effect on BI to adopt the specific innovation in question:

Hypothesis 4: Past orientation negatively affects RA (a) and positively PR (b);
Hypothesis 5: Present orientation positively affects RA (a) and negatively PR (b);
Hypothesis 6: Future orientation positively affects RA (a) and negatively PR (b);
Hypothesis 7: Past orientation negatively affects II;
Hypothesis 8: Present orientation positively affects II;
Hypothesis 9: Future orientation negatively affects II;

Conceptual Model

The critical review of the relevant literature in the previous parts of the chapter explained and justified relationships between personality traits, consumer perceptions and behaviour. Based on reviewed theories the conceptual framework (Figure 3) of the study and reiterates hypothesis by relating them to the research objectives:

Figure 3. Conceptual model

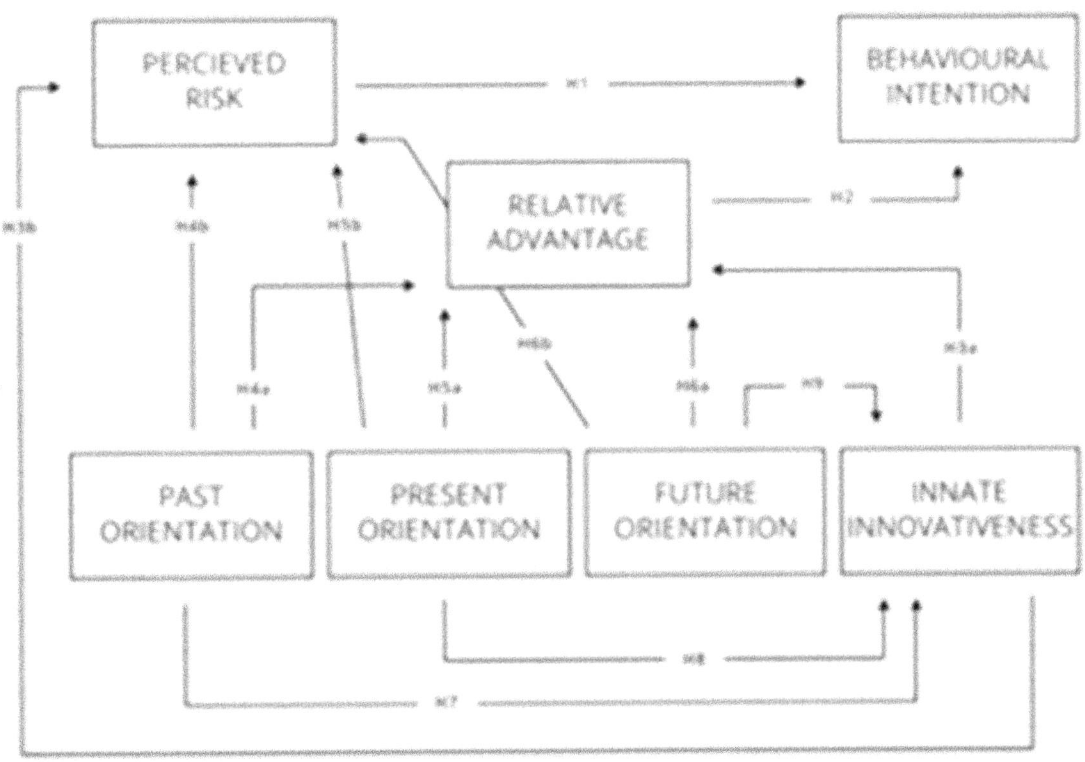

Methodology

The targeted audience of the research are millennial consumers living in London, UK. The rationale for focusing on this audience is as follows: At first, reports indicate that consumers within this age group are emerging users of the present VNA in the UK market (Iacobucci, 2018), thus estimating their receptiveness of the advanced VNA carries an important value. Secondly, millennials are a tech-savvy generation, inclined to new experiences (Chkoniya et al., 2019). In order to reveal the influence of personality traits on consumer perceptions, it was decided to only survey respondents who had no prior knowledge of the VNA. Therefore, their initial awareness and perceptions were developed after reading the narrative demonstrated within the questionnaire (Figure 1).

The self-administered quantitative questionnaire comprises of four sections, whereas the last two are further dived into sub-sections:

1. **Screening questions** collect factual data with two questions: "have you ever heard about virtual nurse assistant?" and "do you suffer from any major illnesses?" To avoid bias and minimise preconceived subjective ideas that alter consumer perceptions, respondents answering "yes" to one of these questions are not able to proceed with the questionnaire.
2. **Demographic set of questions** collect factual data with the list and category types of questions concerned with age, sex, education level and income. The purpose of this data is to ensure sample homogeneity, which in turn validates the accuracy of the results.
3. **Questions related to the VNA**

Description of the VNA– the research instrument includes the small narrative of the VNA, due to respondents no prior awareness of the innovation (Figure 1).

Questions related to perceptions collect opinion data for examining the extent to which participants perceive the use of the VNA risky or advantageous due to its attributes. This data is crucial in measuring mediated effects of personality traits on BI. Items included within the scales of RA and PR were developed by the researcher according to the guidance provided by Saunders et al. (2012). Constructed questions were further benchmarked with the similar items used in Kapoor et al.'s (2015) study. This section of the research instrument employs 5-point Likert rating style questions, as a less confusing and reliable way for obtaining the required data (Nunnally, 1975). The scales of RA and PR comprise of three and two items respectively, whereas each investigative question measures specific attribute related to risks or RAs of the VNA identified in the appendix III.

BI scale comprises with two items collecting behavioural data on intentioned adoption of the VNA. The first item examines general willingness to adopt the innovation, whereas second item measures participant's intentions specifically concerned with a substitution of a human practitioner with the VNA. These items were also developed by the researcher employing a similar procedure used for building the scales of PR and RA.

4. **Personality trait questions** collect opinion and behavioural data with the purpose of identifying specific scores on personality trait scales, representing participants' level on TO and II dimensions. The scale for measuring II has been adopted from the study by Pallister & Foxall (1998), who claimed internal reliability and discriminant validity of the shortened version of original II scale developed by Hurt et al. (1977). Latter stated that the instrument items measure consum-

ers' broad innovative trait related to creativity, willingness to change and openness to newness in general, which in turn predict the receptiveness of innovations. Scales for measuring dimensions of TO have been adopted from the study by Merchant et al. (2014), who claimed high validity and reliability of the inventory. All the scales within this section make use of 5-point Likert questions were adopted only II scale consists of 10 items, past orientation – 5 items, present orientation – 7 and future with 9. Data has been collected in 2018 from 250 subjects and analysed using SPSS.

Results Discussion

The findings from the descriptive statistical analysis revealed that the majority of respondents foresee RA of the VNA, and only small percent considers the innovation as risky to use. Despite these positive evaluations of the innovation, significant high number of respondents were uncertain about its adoption even for its general use and only 35% expressed acceptance of the VNA. However, further analysis demonstrated that the risk represents a little barrier for the millennial consumers to adopt the innovation, in case they foresee the RA of the new product. Thus, considering theory of reasoned action, it can be conceptualised that evaluations of risk related attributes receive less importance from millennial consumers compared to advantageous attributes, which come out to be stronger driving force of BI on overall. In addition, considering that the VNA was initially introduced to the respondents with a small narrative during the research, it is more reasonable to deduce that millennials who are uncertain about innovation's acceptance will incline towards its adoption once more information about the product usage is communicated in the market.

Examination of effects of personality dimensions on the respondents' perceptions confirmed that II altered consumers' cognitive process. Namely, the results determined that II had much greater effects on reducing risk perceptions than positive impact on envisioning RAs of the innovation. This means that consumers with higher II dimension perceive less risk from new and unfamiliar products compared to the ones with low on this dimension. Also, although weak, but still there is a statistically significant difference between these types of consumers in envisioning benefits provided by innovations. These results coincide with the findings by He et al. (2018). On the other hand, dimensions of TO were not found to make any differences within respondents' perceptions concerned with the specific attributes of the VNA. This does not mean that these personality traits do not affect consumer's cognitive process. However, the finding indicates that their roles within examined perceptions are insignificant in this case, which goes against the idea of generalising the impact of personality traits on every aspect of human behaviour.

Interesting patterns were revealed while examining relationships between TO dimensions and II. Past orientation has been found to negatively influence II, whereas the relationship became more obvious when analysing extremely past oriented respondents' results on the innovativeness scale. This result supports, that past orientation negatively influences consumers' innovativeness as a trait (Karande & Merchant, 2012; Merchant et al., 2014). This means that consumers who are greatly past oriented, either stand against the personal values and characteristics ascribed to the II dimension or possess these variables with the lesser degrees than innovative consumers. The finding also automatically confirms the inverse relationship, that innovative consumers cannot be conservatives or traditionalists, at least not with the same degrees as extremely past oriented individuals. This indicates that preferences, behaviour and cognitive process of innovative and past oriented consumers diverge from one another. However, this does not mean that their behaviour would always be non-homogenous. For instance, previous studies showed that past oriented people were found to reduce PR by purchasing familiar and well-experienced products

(Wang et al., 2008). However, frequency analysis conducted by this chapter on extremely past oriented participants' responses on the items of PR scale demonstrated non-homogenous predispositions. These results prove that in order to predict overt behaviour it is necessary to take a wider look on numerous forces - other than personality traits - that might be also influencing human behaviour.

Present and future orientations did not determine statistically significant relationships with II. This opposes the findings by Merchant et al. (2014), who identified positive and negative relationships between these two respective TO dimensions and II within US consumers. Interestingly, this study's results from the correlation analysis of future orientation and II determined significance level (.069) close to the acceptable margin (0.05), whereas the correlation coefficient (as expected) indicated to the negative relationship of the variables. Thus, this result along with findings by Merchant et al. (2014) might indicate that the relationship between TO dimensions and II is moderated by other variables, reasonably other psychological dimensions or some sort of other external stimuli, which in turn altered the results of these two related studies.

The overall role of TO within intentioned adoption of the VNA can be considered as insignificant if not taken into account its effects on II, which in turn distorts the consumer perceptions, whereas the latter only influenced the BI to some extent. Thus, the findings of this chapter do not mean that the examined personality dimensions are insignificant in innovation adoption concept. However, the results do imply that in this case these dimensions were not identified as crucial. Overall, it is determined that the perceived RA is the main influence factor of BI to adopt the VNA among all other variables measured during the study. Thus, segmenting the market based on the consumer motives would better yield desirable outcome in terms of accelerating the adoption of the VNA. The Table 1 summarises the results and showcases rejected/accepted hypothesis.

Table 1. Summary of tested hypothesis

	Objective 1	**Status**
Hypothesis 1	Perceived risk negatively affects behavioural intention	Accepted
Hypothesis 2	Perceived risk advantage positively affects behavioural intention	Accepted
	Objective 2	
Hypothesis 3	Innate innovativeness positively affects RA(a) and negatively PR (b)	Accepted
Hypothesis 4	Past orientation negatively affects RA(a) and positively PR (b)	Rejected
Hypothesis 5	Present orientation positively affects RA(a) and negatively PR (b)	Rejected
Hypothesis 6	Future orientation positively affects RA(a) and negatively PR (b)	Rejected
	Objective 3	
Hypothesis 7	Past orientation negatively affects innate innovativeness	Accepted
Hypothesis 8	Present orientation positevely affects innate innovativeness	Rejected
Hypothesis 9	Future orientation negatively affects innate innovativeness	Rejected

SOLUTIONS AND RECOMMENDATIONS

Were revealed relevant consumer insights that can be deployed within marketing strategy for accelerating the innovation's adoption rate once the advanced VNA enters the introductory stage of its product life cycle:

1. Millennial consumers evaluate the VNA quite positively, however to accelerate its adoption rate consumers should be further educated regarding the technology in question. Although this might be the least challenge for the start-ups developing the innovation in cooperation with the NHS, several points must be taken into consideration to engage millennial consumers efficiently. Rather than trying to reduce PR, greater focus should be dedicated to promoting the RA of the innovation. This is due to millennial consumers being more influenced with perceived advantage provided by the VNA rather than PR while intending to adopt the innovation. However, these consumers seem to envision the overall value proposition of the innovation, lower value is allocated to the medical recommendations given by the AI nurse. This indicates to the possible challenge where the innovation can be adopted and used for the "secondary" purposes (e.g. getting instant medical information or monitoring health condition) rather than substituting human practitioners for the specific medical cases. Thus, it is necessary to explicitly communicate the benefits of consulting with AI nurse/doctor.
2. Examination of II effect on millennial consumers' perceptions related to the innovation attributes revealed that the former was only moderately altering the latter. Considering that the consumer decision is also influenced by numerous other variables, it can be stated that the market segmentation according to the personality dimensions during the advanced VNA's market entry stage would be less effective. However, since the study empirically confirmed the influence of personality trait influence on the cognitive process, intelligence can be effectively applied to the consumer retention strategy. Namely, in case the inventors enable VNA to build psychological prototypes of individual user (e.g. using psychological tests, similar to the ones used in the study), the AI nurse would have ability to engage and communicate with the consumer on the psychological level, which in turn will greatly increase consumers' engagement and life time value.
3. There are negative and positive correlations between some of the personality traits, which in turn also correlate with the specific personal values. The intelligence in this field enables to gain deep consumer insights by identifying just several personality dimensions/personal values possessed by a consumer. Utilising this intelligence within marketing strategies will help to design marketing campaigns on the individual level, which in turn will greatly reduce unnecessary marketing costs not just for the VNA, but also for every innovation engaging with the consumers on an individual level.

FUTURE RESEARCH DIRECTIONS

The study revealed interesting findings and some unexpected patterns within the results. This has led to several suggestions for further research:

1. The results showed that the relationship between future orientation and II was insignificantly negative, however close to the acceptable statistical significance level. The previous study by Merchant et al. (2014) identified the same relationship as significantly negative. This leads to the reasonable assumption that there are moderator variables in this relationship, which apparently have varied across these two studies. If this hypothesis is true, then these moderator variables should also be affecting consumer decision making process. Thus, further research is suggested in this area.
2. The findings revealed that perceptions related to risks and RA only partly affected intentioned adoption of the innovation. This means that there are other specific factors which also influence consumer intentions to adopt this innovation. Therefore, qualitative research is suggested to shed more light on this area.
3. Lastly, further research is called for replicating this study with the bigger sample size and with the original version of TO scale across different cultures. This will thoroughly re-examine emergence of diversified patterns within the findings of the same study in different markets.

CONCLUSION

The research aimed to examine the roles of TO and II within consumer intentions to adopt the virtual nurse assistant. The objectives of the study followed the rationale provided by the theory of reasoned action, explaining that the personality traits are linked to actual behaviour through the cognitive processing, altering consumer perceptions and evaluation process concerned with the behaviour in question.

The purpose of the first objective was to examine consumer perceptions and determine their roles within the intentions to adopt the innovation. The results showed that PR do not represent strong barriers for the millennial consumers to adopt an innovation in case they foresee RA of a new product. Overall, it was determined that millennial consumers are open to accept the VNA. However, they require more information prior the actual behaviour.

The second objective of the chapter was to measure the effects of personality dimensions within consumer perceptions. Out of the examined personality traits, only II has been identified as a directly influential force on consumer perceptions during this study. Namely, the results revealed that II had greater effect on reducing risk perceptions than positive impact on envisioning RAs of the innovation. On the other hand, TO dimensions did not demonstrate any significant relationships with the consumer perceptions in this case.

The final objective was to examine relationships between TO dimensions and II, and in conjunction with the predecessor results of the study, determine the overall roles of these dimensions within BI and past orientation was found to be negatively influencing II. However, other dimensions failed to prove their relationships with innovativeness. Considering all findings of the study, overall roles of examined personality dimensions within intentions to adopt the VNA were identified as weak.

Results confirm that II as a key psychographic variable within innovation adoption concept, only weakly influences BI. However, compared to other studies, this research precisely explained the reason of this weak relationship by examining the role of II within perceptions that directly affect BI and estimated its importance in causality of perceptions. Overall, while the results of this study confirmed that psychological dimensions affect consumer cognition, they also emphasized that personality traits not always have their expression in overt behaviour during all relevant occasions.

REFERENCES

Ajzen, I. (1985). From intentions to actions: A theory of planned behavior. In *From intentions to actions: A theory of planned behavior* (pp. 11–39). Springer. doi:10.1007/978-3-642-69746-3_2

Ajzen, I., Heilbroner, R. L., Fishbein, M., & Thurow, L. C. (1980). *Understanding Attitudes and Predicting Social Behaviour*. Prentice Hall PTR.

Ali, I. (2019). Personality traits, individual innovativeness and satisfaction with life. *Journal of Innovation & Knowledge*, *4*(1), 38–46. doi:10.1016/j.jik.2017.11.002

Allen, B. P. (2006). Personality theories: development, growth, & diversity (5th ed.). London: Routledge.

Arts, J. W. C., Frambach, R. T., & Bijmolt, T. H. A. (2011). Generalizations on consumer innovation adoption: A meta-analysis on drivers of intention & behavior. *International Journal of Research in Marketing*, *28*(2), 134–144. doi:10.1016/j.ijresmar.2010.11.002

Baregheh, A., Rowley, J., & Sambrook, S. (2009). Towards a multidisciplinary definition of innovation. *Management Decision*, *47*(8), 1323–1339. doi:10.1108/00251740910984578

Barnett, T., Pearson, A. W., Pearson, R., & Kellermanns, F. W. (2015). Five-factor model personality traits as predictors of perceived & actual usage of technology. *European Journal of Information Systems*, *24*(4), 374–390. doi:10.1057/ejis.2014.10

Bartels, J., & Reinders, M. J. (2011). Consumer innovativeness & its correlates: A propositional inventory for future research. *Journal of Business Research*, *64*(6), 601–609. doi:10.1016/j.jbusres.2010.05.002

Bilsky, W., & Schwartz, S. H. (1994). Values & personality. *European Journal of Personality*, *8*(3), 163–181. doi:10.1002/per.2410080303

Bundy, A. (2017). Preparing for the future of Artificial Intelligence. *AI & Society*, *32*(2), 285–287. doi:10.100700146-016-0685-0

Caprara, G. V., Schwartz, S., Capanna, C., Vecchione, M., & Barbaranelli, C. (2006). Personality & Politics: Values, Traits, & Political Choice. *Political Psychology*, *27*(1), 1–28. doi:10.1111/j.1467-9221.2006.00447.x

Cassell, J. (2019). Artificial intelligence for a social world: The underlying mission is to better understand social interaction and to build machines that work more collaboratively and effectively with humans. *Issues in Science and Technology VO*, *35*(4), 29.

Chao, C., Reid, M., & Mavondo, F. T. (2012). Consumer innovativeness influence on really new product adoption. *Australasian Marketing Journal*, *20*(3), 211–217. doi:10.1016/j.ausmj.2012.02.001

Chkoniya, V., Madsen, A. O., & Coelho, T. (2019). The impact of information and communication technologies in fish consumption in Portugal: Building a support for the coming generations. *Economia Agro-Alimentare*, *21*(3), 855–872. doi:10.3280/ECAG2019-003016

Clark, R. A., & Goldsmith, R. E. (2006). Interpersonal influence & consumer innovativeness. *International Journal of Consumer Studies*, *30*(1), 34–43. doi:10.1111/j.1470-6431.2005.00435.x

Cognition, X. (2018). *CogX 2018 - Pre Primary Care.* Retriever from: https://www.youtube.com/watch?v=T_qslD7rAWs

Cotte, J., Ratneshwar, S., & Mick, D. G. (2004). The times of their lives: Phenomenological & metaphorical characteristics of consumer timestyles. *The Journal of Consumer Research, 31*(2), 333–345. doi:10.1086/422112

D'Alessio, M., De Pascalis, V., Guarino, A., & Zimbardo, P. G. (2003). Testing Zimbardo's Stanford Time Perspective Inventory (STPI) - Short Form: An Italian Study. *Time & Society, 12*(2-3), 333–347. doi:10.1177/0961463X030122010

d'Hauteville, F., Goldsmith, R. E., & Flynn, L. R. (1998). Theory & measurement of consumer innovativeness. *European Journal of Marketing, 32*(3), 340.

Davies, G. (1994). What Should Time Be? *European Journal of Marketing, 28*(8), 100–113. doi:10.1108/03090569410067604

Davis, F. D. (1989). Perceived usefulness, perceived ease of use, & user acceptance of information technology. *Management Information Systems Quarterly, 13*(3), 319–340. doi:10.2307/249008

De Mooij, M. K. (2010). *Global marketing & advertising: underst&ing cultural paradoxes.* Los Angeles: Sage.

Devaraj, S., Easley, R. F., & Crant, J. M. (2008). How Does Personality Matter? Relating the Five-Factor Model to Technology Acceptance & Use. *Information Systems Research, 19*(1), 93–105. doi:10.1287/isre.1070.0153

Foxall, G., Bhate, S., Pallister, J., Szmigin, I., Bagozzi, R. G., & Maddock, S. (1995). Consumer innovativeness & cognitive style. *European Journal of Marketing, 29*(5), 6.

Fu, R., Collier, M., Yin, L., & Christiansen, P. (2017). *Artificial Intelligence: Healthcare's New Nervous System.* Accenture.

Garcia, R., & Calantone, R. (2002). A critical look at technological innovation typology & innovativeness terminology: A literature review. *Journal of Product Innovation Management, 19*(2), 110–132. doi:10.1111/1540-5885.1920110

Gatignon, H., & Robertson, T. S. (1985). A Propositional Inventory for New Diffusion Research. *The Journal of Consumer Research, 11*(4), 849–867. doi:10.1086/209021

Goldsmith, R. E., & Foxall, G. R. (2003). The measurement of innovativeness. In *The measurement of innovativeness* (pp. 321–330). Elsevier. doi:10.1016/B978-008044198-6/50022-X

Handa, M., & Gupta, N. (2009). Gender Influence on the Innovativeness of Young Urban Indian Online Shoppers. *Vision: The Journal of Business Perspective, 13*(2), 25–32. doi:10.1177/097226290901300203

Harber, K. D., Zimbardo, P. G., & Boyd, J. N. (2003). Participant Self-Selection Biases as a Function of Individual Differences in Time Perspective. *Basic and Applied Social Psychology, 25*(3), 255–264. doi:10.1207/S15324834BASP2503_08

He, X., Zhan, W., & Hu, Y. (2018). Consumer purchase intention of electric vehicles in China: The roles of perception & personality. *Journal of Cleaner Production, 204*, 1060–1069. doi:10.1016/j.jclepro.2018.08.260

Hirschman, E. C. (1980). Innovativeness, Novelty Seeking, & Consumer Creativity. *The Journal of Consumer Research, 7*(3), 283–295. doi:10.1086/208816

Hirunyawipada, T., & Paswan, A. K. (2006). Consumer innovativeness & perceived risk: Implications for high technology product adoption. *Journal of Consumer Marketing, 23*(4), 182–198. doi:10.1108/07363760610674310

Hodgins, D. C., & Engel, A. (2002). Future time perspective in pathological gamblers. *The Journal of Nervous and Mental Disease, 190*(11), 775–780. doi:10.1097/00005053-200211000-00008 PMID:12436018

Hoffmann, S., & Soyez, K. (2010). A cognitive model to predict domain-specific consumer innovativeness. *Journal of Business Research, 63*(7), 778–785. doi:10.1016/j.jbusres.2009.06.007

Holak, S. L., & Lehmann, D. R. (1990). Purchase Intentions & the Dimensions of Innovation: An Exploratory Model. *Journal of Product Innovation Management, 7*(1), 59–73. doi:10.1111/1540-5885.710059

Holbrook, M. B., & Schindler, R. M. (1994). Age, Sex, & Attitude Toward the Past as Predictors of Consumers' Aesthetic Tastes for Cultural Products. *JMR, Journal of Marketing Research, 31*(3), 412–422.

Hurt, H. T., Joseph, K., & Cook, C. D. (1977). Scales for the measurement of innovativeness. *Human Communication Research, 4*(1), 58–65. doi:10.1111/j.1468-2958.1977.tb00597.x

Iacobucci, G. (2018). Babylon app increases CCG's costs. *BMJ (Clinical Research Ed.), 360*(8137), k221. doi:10.1136/bmj.k221 PMID:29339378

Im, S., Mason, C. H., & Houston, M. B. (2007). Does innate consumer innovativeness relate to new product/ service adoption behavior? The intervening role of social learning via vicarious innovativeness. *Journal of the Academy of Marketing Science, 35*(1), 63–75. doi:10.100711747-006-0007-z

James, W. (1890). The Principles of. *Psychology, 2*, 94.

Jiang, F., Jiang, Y., Zhi, H., Dong, Y., Dong, Q., & Li, H. (2017). Artificial intelligence in healthcare: Past, present & future. *Stroke and Vascular Neurology, 2*(4), 230–243. doi:10.1136vn-2017-000101 PMID:29507784

Kant, I. (1999). *Critique of pure reason*. Cambridge University Press.

Kapoor, K. K., Dwivedi, Y. K., & Williams, M. D. (2015). Empirical Examination of the Role of Three Sets of Innovation Attributes for Determining Adoption of IRCTC Mobile Ticketing Service. *Information Systems Management, 32*(2), 153–173. doi:10.1080/10580530.2015.1018776

Karahoca, A., Karahoca, D., & Aksoez, M. (2018). Examining intention to adopt to internet of things in healthcare technology products. *Kybernetes, 47*(4), 742–770. doi:10.1108/K-02-2017-0045

Karande, K., & Merchant, A. (2012). The Impact of Time & Planning Orientation on an Individual's Recreational Shopper Identity & Shopping Behavior. *Journal of Marketing Theory and Practice, 20*(1), 59–72. doi:10.2753/MTP1069-6679200104

Kim, W., Anthony Di Benedetto, C., & Lancioni, R. A. (2011). The effects of country & gender differences on consumer innovativeness & decision processes in a highly globalized high-tech product market. *Asia Pacific Journal of Marketing and Logistics*, *23*(5), 714–744. doi:10.1108/13555851111183101

Klink, R. R., & Athaide, G. A. (2010). Consumer Innovativeness & the Use of New versus Extended Br& Names for New Products. *Journal of Product Innovation Management*, *27*(1), 23–32. doi:10.1111/j.1540-5885.2009.00697.x

Kooij, D., Kanfer, R., Betts, M., & Rudolph, C. W. (2018). Future Time Perspective: A Systematic Review & Meta-Analysis. *The Journal of Applied Psychology*, *103*(8), 867–893. doi:10.1037/apl0000306 PMID:29683685

Koul, S., & Eydgahi, A. (2017). A systematic review of technology adoption frameworks & their applications. *Journal of Technology Management & Innovation*, *12*(4), 106–112. doi:10.4067/S0718-27242017000400011

Kurzweil, R. (2010). *The Singularity Is Near: When Humans Transcend Biology*. Prelude Books.

Lassar, W. M., Manolis, C., & Lassar, S. S. (2005). The relationship between consumer innovativeness, personal characteristics, & online banking adoption. *International Journal of Bank Marketing*, *23*(2), 176–199. doi:10.1108/02652320510584403

Leicht, T., Chtourou, A., & Ben Youssef, K. (2018). Consumer innovativeness & intentioned autonomous car adoption. *The Journal of High Technology Management Research*, *29*(1), 1–11. doi:10.1016/j.hitech.2018.04.001

Lennings, C. J., & Burns, A. M. (1998). Time perspective: Temporal extension, time estimation, & impulsivity. *The Journal of Psychology*, *132*(4), 367–380. doi:10.1080/00223989809599271 PMID:9637020

Lewin, K. (1951). Field Theory of Social Science: Selected Theoretical Chapters. *The Annals of the American Academy of Political and Social Science*, *276*(1), 146–147. doi:10.1177/000271625127600135

Limayem, M., Khalifa, M., & Frini, A. (2000). What Makes Consumers Buy from Internet? A Longitudinal Study of Online Shopping, *IEEE Transactions on Systems. Man & Cybernetics: Part A*, *30*(4), 421–432. doi:10.1109/3468.852436

Lowe, B., Dwivedi, Y. K., & d'Alessandro, S. (2019). Consumers and technology in a changing world. *European Journal of Marketing*, *53*(6).

Lu, J., Yao, J. E., & Yu, C. (2005). Personal innovativeness, social influences & adoption of wireless Internet services via mobile technology. *The Journal of Strategic Information Systems*, *14*(3), 245–268. doi:10.1016/j.jsis.2005.07.003

Makri, K., & Schlegelmilch, B. B. (2017). Time orientation & engagement with social networking sites: A cross-cultural study in Austria, China & Uruguay. *Journal of Business Research*, *80*, 155–163. doi:10.1016/j.jbusres.2017.05.016

McCrae, R. R., Costa, P. T. J., Ostendorf, F., Angleitner, A., Hrebícková, M., Avia, M. D., ... Smith, P. B. (2000). Nature over nurture: Temperament, personality, & life span development. *Journal of Personality and Social Psychology*, *78*(1), 173–186. doi:10.1037/0022-3514.78.1.173 PMID:10653513

Merchant, A., Rose, G., & Rose, M. (2014). The Impact of Time Orientation on Consumer Innovativeness in the United States and India. *Journal of Marketing Theory and Practice*, *22*(3), 325–338. doi:10.2753/MTP1069-6679220307

Midgley, D. F., & Dowling, G. R. (1993). A Longitudinal Study of Product Form Innovation: The Interaction between Predispositions & Social Messages. *The Journal of Consumer Research*, *19*(4), 611–625. doi:10.1086/209326

Miller, A. (2019). The intrinsically linked future for human and Artificial Intelligence interaction. *Journal of Big Data*, *6*(1), 38. doi:10.118640537-019-0202-7

Moore, G. C., & Benbasat, I. (1991). Development of an Instrument to Measure the Perceptions of Adopting an Information Technology Innovation. *Information Systems Research*, *2*(3), 192–222. doi:10.1287/isre.2.3.192

Murrell, A. & Mingrone, M. (1994). Correlates of temporal perspective. *Perceptual & Motor Skills,* 78 (3), 1331-1334.

Nunnally, J. C. (1975). Psychometric theory—25 years ago & now. *Educational Researcher*, *4*(10), 7–21.

Nuttin, J. (2014). *Future time perspective & motivation: Theory & research method.* Psychology Press. doi:10.4324/9781315802244

Oliveira, T., Thomas, M., Baptista, G., & Campos, F. (2016). Full length article: Mobile payment: Underst&ing the determinants of customer adoption & intention to recommend the technology. *Computers in Human Behavior*, *61*, 404–414. doi:10.1016/j.chb.2016.03.030

Pallister, J. G., & Foxall, G. R. (1998). Psychometric properties of the Hurt-Joseph-Cook scales for the measurement of innovativeness. *Technovation*, *18*(11), 663–675. doi:10.1016/S0166-4972(98)00070-4

Park, G., Schwartz, H. A., Sap, M., Kern, M. L., Weingarten, E., Eichstaedt, J. C., & Seligman, M. E. P. (2017). Living in the Past, Present, and Future: Measuring Temporal Orientation With Language. *Journal of Personality*, *85*(2), 270–280. doi:10.1111/jopy.12239 PMID:26710321

Park, G., Schwartz, H. A., Sap, M., Kern, M. L., Weingarten, E., Eichstaedt, J. C., ... Seligman, M. E. P. (2017). Living in the Past, Present, and Future: Measuring Temporal Orientation with Language. *Journal of Personality*, *85*(2), 270–280. doi:10.1111/jopy.12239 PMID:26710321

Philipp, S. F. (1992). Time orientation & participation in leisure activities. *Perceptual and Motor Skills*, *75*(2), 659–664. doi:10.2466/pms.1992.75.2.659 PMID:1594428

Prayoga, T., & Abraham, J. (2016). *Behavioral Intention to Use IoT Health Device: The Role of Perceived Usefulness*. Facilitated Appropriation, Big Five Personality Traits, & Cultural Value Orientations.

Ram, A. (2018). *Babylon signs digital health deal with Samsung*. Retrieved from https://search.proquest.com/docview/2072565216

Roccas, S., Sagiv, L., Schwartz, S. H., & Knafo, A. (2002). The big five personality factors & personal values. *Personality and Social Psychology Bulletin*, *28*(6), 789–801. doi:10.1177/0146167202289008

Roehrich, G. (2004). Consumer innovativeness: Concepts & measurements. *Journal of Business Research, 57*(6), 671–677. doi:10.1016/S0148-2963(02)00311-9

Rogers, E. M. (2003). *Diffusion of innovations* (5th ed.). New York: Free Press.

Saunders, M. N. K., Lewis, P., & Thornhill, A. (2012). *Research methods for business students* (6th ed.). Harlow, UK: Pearson.

Schiffman, L. G., & Wisenblit, J. (2015). Consumer behavior (11th ed.). Harlow: Pearson.

Shipp, A. J., Edwards, J. R., & Lambert, L. S. (2009). Conceptualization & measurement of temporal focus: The subjective experience of the past, present, & future. *Organizational Behavior and Human Decision Processes, 110*(1), 1–22. doi:10.1016/j.obhdp.2009.05.001

Solomon, M. R. (2018). Consumer behavior: buying, having, & being (12th ed.). Harlow, UK: Pearson.

Steenkamp, J. E. M., & Gielens, K. (2003). Consumer & Market Drivers of the Trial Probability of New Consumer Packaged Goods. *The Journal of Consumer Research, 30*(3), 368–384. doi:10.1086/378615

Stolarski, M., Fieulaine, N., & van Beek, W. (2015). *Time perspective theory; Review, research, & application*. Cham: Springer International. doi:10.1007/978-3-319-07368-2

Strathman, A., Gleicher, F., Boninger, D. S., & Edwards, C. S. (1994). The consideration of future consequences: Weighing immediate & distant outcomes of behavior. *Journal of Personality and Social Psychology, 66*(4), 742–752. doi:10.1037/0022-3514.66.4.742

Svendsen, G. B., Johnsen, J. K., Almas-Sorensen, L., & Vitterso, J. (2013). Personality & technology acceptance: The influence of personality factors on the core constructs of the Technology Acceptance Model. *Behaviour & Information Technology, 32*(4), 323–334. doi:10.1080/0144929X.2011.553740

Van Everdingen, Y. M., & Waarts, E. (2003). The Effect of National Culture on the Adoption of Innovations. *Marketing Letters, 14*(3), 217–232. doi:10.1023/A:1027452919403

Venkatesh, V., Morris, M. G., Davis, G. B., & Davis, F. D. (2003). User Acceptance of Information Technology: Toward a Unified View. *Management Information Systems Quarterly, 27*(3), 425–478. doi:10.2307/30036540

Venkatraman, M. P., & Price, L. L. (1990a). Differentiating Between Cognitive & Sensory Innovativeness: Concepts, Measurement, & Implications. *Journal of Business Research, 20*(4), 293–315. doi:10.1016/0148-2963(90)90008-2

Verneau, F., & Griffith, C. J. (2016). *Consumer behaviour in a changing world: food, culture & society*. Bradford, UK: Emerald.

Wang, G., Dou, W., & Zhou, N. (2008). Consumption attitudes & adoption of new consumer products: A contingency approach. *European Journal of Marketing, 42*(1), 238–254. doi:10.1108/03090560810840998

Wood, S. L. & Swait, J. (2002). Psychological Indicators of Innovation Adoption: Cross-Classification Based on Need for Cognition & Need for Change. *Journal of Consumer Psychology, 12*(1), 1-13.

Yi, M. Y., Jackson, J. D., Park, J. S., & Probst, J. C. (2006). Understanding information technology acceptance by individual professionals: Toward an integrative view. *Information & Management*, *43*(3), 350–363. doi:10.1016/j.im.2005.08.006

Zhao, Y., Ni, Q., & Zhou, R. (2018a). Review: What factors influence the mobile health service adoption? A meta-analysis & the moderating role of age. *International Journal of Information Management*, *43*, 342–350. doi:10.1016/j.ijinfomgt.2017.08.006

Zimbardo, P. G., & Boyd, J. N. (1999). Putting Time in Perspective: A Valid, Reliable Individual-Differences Metric. *Journal of Personality and Social Psychology*, *77*(6), 1271–1288. doi:10.1037/0022-3514.77.6.1271

KEY TERMS AND DEFINITIONS

Artificial Intelligence (AI): Artificially created system that enables machines to learn and act just like humans.

Behavioural Intention (BI): Decision to act in a particular way, that is yet to be actualised.

Domain-Specific Innovativeness (DSI): The tendency of the consumer to acquire information and new products within a specific product domain.

Innate Innovativeness (II): Individual's generalised unobservable trait reflecting inherently innovative personality, predisposition and cognitive style.

Mobile Health (m-Health): A concept of healthcare practices provided through tablets and cell phones.

New Product Adoption (NPA): Acceptance and continues usage of a new product by a consumer.

Perceived Risk (PR): Consumer's subjective risk perception attributable to a product usage.

Product Attributes (PA): Product's tangible (e.g., size, colour) and intangible (e.g., reliability, brand equity) characteristics.

Relative Advantage (RA): In this chapter perceived relative advantage is defined as consumer's subjective advantageous perception attributable to a product usage.

Time Orientation (TO): Individual's psychological predisposition towards mentally being to his/her perceived past, present or future time frames.

Virtual Nurse Assistant (VNA): m-health technology powered by AI intended to provide healthcare services that are applicable without necessary intervention of human practitioners.

Chapter 21
Decision Making as a Socio-Cognitive Process

Monique Borges
https://orcid.org/0000-0002-9820-4591
GOVCOPP, DCSPT, University of Aveiro, Portugal

João Lourenço Marques
https://orcid.org/0000-0003-0472-2767
GOVCOPP, DCSPT, University of Aveiro, Portugal

Eduardo Anselmo Castro
https://orcid.org/0000-0001-9017-5098
GOVCOPP, DCSPT, University of Aveiro, Portugal

ABSTRACT

Researchers from multidisciplinary scientific fields have been puzzled by human behaviour in dynamic and complex decision-making contexts. Since the seventeenth century, several theoretical, conceptual, and empirical contributions have emerged. These contributions evidence the need to critically assess the rational foundations of decision theories, stemming from the cognitive basis for human heuristics and bias. This chapter focuses on how socio-cognitive theories have been introduced as analytic tools to explain individual and collective behaviours, decision rules, and cognitive mechanisms. In particular, the authors advance some arguments explaining its importance and the underlying challenges of social representations as part of the decision-making process. They propose a methodological script that stresses the social representations approach and encounters more functional and operational settings.

INTRODUCTION

There is a large amount of literature providing insights on the subject of decision-making and the overall process. It goes back to the seventeenth century with solid and formal studies and reached a point of maturity in the mid and late 1940s grounded on mathematical foundations and quantitative methods (Doyle

DOI: 10.4018/978-1-7998-3115-0.ch021

Copyright © 2020, IGI Global. Copying or distributing in print or electronic forms without written permission of IGI Global is prohibited.

and Thomason, 1999). Decision theory has been useful in explaining how individuals make choices by following certain axioms. Real life decisions, however, uncover some flaws in the application of these axioms, as they require multidisciplinary examination. New emerging theories of decision-making acknowledge that it is essential to add more layers, which are able to deal with the complexity of cognitive bias and other issues in social sciences. Every decision encounters trade-offs with challenges for both sides: who designs the decision process and who has to choose, and to whom those decisions are directed. The complex exercise during problem formulation and alternative design is related to the way expectations, preferences and uncertainty are dealt with. Otherwise, the outputs, besides being useless, are nothing less than grave (and irreversible) mistakes. Every model is an attempt at simplification, grounded on assumptions that outline the understanding and application of the results. Regarding decision models, names such as Nicholas Bernoulli, John von Neumann, and Oskar Morgenstern, Herbert Simon, Daniel Kahneman and Amos Tversky are great contributors to this question, ranging from rational foundations to a cognitive basis for human heuristics and bias. In the 1950s, in order to bridge some of the gaps in the decision literature, because human behaviour cannot be simply explained by classic economic models, some authors called for debate on the influence of motivation, conflict, cognitive limits to rationality, and planning and innovation (Arnott and Gao, 2019a; Hoch, Kunreuther, and Gunther, 2001; Jodelet, 2008; Moscovici, 1988; Simon and Newell, 1971; Tversky and Kahneman, 1974, 1981).

Hoch et al., (2001) present a systematic compilation based on evidence-based experiences from four perspectives: personal, managerial, negotiator, and consumer. The direction goes towards simulation models, optimization tools, behavioural approaches, anchoring and adjustment strategies. However, even though integrated approaches are assumed to be important and some guidelines include such concern, other aspects continue uncovered by the literature. As in many other decision-making domains, consumer behaviour clearly draws on economic and psychological factors. Besides expected means-ends objectives, understanding consumption patterns involves a complex interrelation of subjective dimensions of the (socio) cognitive structure. Indeed, with a strong contribution of the overall cognitive framework, Reynolds and Olson (2001) share evidence on how behaviour is determined by the characteristics of the choice situation, evoking beliefs and (unconscious) motivations. Many decision-making models have been used as a reference for marketing strategies over the past decades, with particular focus on behavioural decision theory. Stankevich (2017) shows how these theories have challenged predictions from economic theory and assumptions about rationality. Using the official definition of consumer behaviour, recalled by Stankevich, means the processes used by individuals, groups, or organizations are at the basis of analysis, as well as the impacts that these processes have on the consumer and society. About this, Gupta (2009) structures the importance of this notion according to possible applications, beyond marketing purposes, namely in the spectrum of policy. The implications for public policy should not be understated. First, because consumer decisions or behaviours reveal preferences for specific goods and services, and consequently because "the way in which other people behave and the internal motivations that influence consumer choices are just as likely to bias and override individual preferences as the cognitive short-cuts" (Policy Studies Institute, 2006; p. 42).

The way individuals and groups take decisions in practice challenges the methods and techniques of decision-making, and mostly its formalizations. The baseline of this research is that decision-making processes have to be successful in matching and ensuring a balance between descriptive assumptions and rationalist components, in order to encounter the elements which influence how decisions are taken (social and psychological aspects) and the form in which a decision maker is expected to decide (rational and logical shortcuts).

The discussion of a framework based on the interlink of these conceptual approaches intends to move the research on decision-making processes forward. Special attention is paid to the importance of (socio) cognitive models. First, decisions result from mental representations, either from individual actors or from groups, often using more or less sophisticated methods to aggregate choices. Then, one must not forget that these choices represent preferences, are context dependent and highly grounded on perceptions. Brewer and Hewstone (2004) explain how these mental representations are a product of the way people hold their social world. Past-experience and learning processes interact in a complex manner, assigning elementary importance to the representative and anchoring heuristics. Individually, each one carries out personal filters revealing and clarifying the existence of subjective evaluations of objective events. When this individual behaviour extends to group processes, other challenges emerge.

The background framework of this chapter includes: i) the main challenges and traps assigned to the decision-making process; ii) the complex process of formation of preferences and choices; and iii) the inclusion of socio-cognitive drivers, to support further explanations of the heuristics of judgment. The chapter then focuses on how these aspects, with particular concern given to representativeness, anchoring and other socially embedded factors, have been part of the development and application of decision support systems. The contribution of this work relies on a methodological script explaining how the theoretical pieces developed throughout the chapter challenge a housing policy decision process. The housing policy decision process covers multiple consumer perspectives, starting by acknowledging housing as a basic product to be satisfied. These decisions, subject to consumer preferences and choices, provide the range of products available on the market for purchase and usage.

BACKGROUND

The Cognitive Process of Decisions: Decision-Making and Social Representations

A) Lost in Decision Theory

Decision-making is one of the basic cognitive processes of human behaviour (Y. Wang and Ruhe, 2007), whereby choices are based on preferences, expectations, motivations, beliefs, utility principles, and other criteria. Depending on the specific decision context, decision strategies might require additional schemas to deal with the multiplicity of perspectives of a group of decision makers. The importance of applying models and methods to clarify the values of each agent, their goals and preferences becomes evident. Along the process, successive steps involve processes of information gathering, judgment and evaluation, followed by post-decision processes, which help people adapt to (Ranyard, Crozier, and Svenson, 1997). While acknowledging that decisions are made within a social context, the authors admit that it is perhaps this social and economic significance of decisions that has resulted in considerable influence on psychological approaches to the study of decision-making in various scientific areas. Indeed, the concepts of utility and subjective probability and the theories that explain their integration have shaped psychological research and influenced research paradigms in this domain.

Subjective expected utility theory emerges as one of the basic models for explaining rationality of behaviour, which assumes that decisions are obtained by summing the set of alternatives and their utility weighted by the subjective probability of their occurrence. However, the value of maximizing utility as a normative choice principle has been widely criticized, for example, by Simon and Newell, (1971), who argued that people adapt to the context in which they are making decisions by identifying appropriate actions to goals. They proposed an alternative principle, arguing that its application was dependent on discrimination and evaluation, and on competencies that human beings lack (Simon & Newell, 1971). Thus, they support the argument on the concept of limited rationality, which incorporates the basic assumption that rationality is relative to the decision maker's information processing capabilities. These are some examples of the early approaches explored to consolidate and understand the behavioural mechanisms of each individual in order to overcome the errors and biases of reasoning. Models based on subjective expected utility theory or prospect theory tend to assume that decision-making is a mechanical process. In particular, these models assume that the rules for combining probabilities and values are constant in different contexts. However, research in this area points to alternative approaches where decision makers apply a range of decision-making strategies. These depend on decision rules to deal with the complexity of the decision context (Pligt, 1999); so, instead of sophisticated information-processing strategies, people rely on intuitive heuristic rules that reduce the complexity of this process, such as the limitations in anticipating or understanding the direct impact and the consequences of choices (Betsch and Haberstroh, 2005; A. Kruglanski and Ajzen, 1983; Simon and Newell, 1971; Tversky and Kahneman, 1974). The individual's behaviour, routines, preferences and motivations will define the strategy or decision shortcuts. Gowda and Fox (2002) argue there is an effort in understanding how people's choices operate under conditions of high uncertainty and risk and conclude that the answer is to use systematic logics to organize their judgments and choices (see also Dohmen, Falk, Huffman, and Sunde, 2018). Moreover, they consider that this systematic pattern does not conform to the rational decision-making process advocated and used by economists, because people seem to follow certain heuristics or rule systems that help them make judgments in conditions of uncertainty and low levels of information (see also: Kruglanski and Ajzen, 1983; Tversky and Kahneman, 1974). Some trends in the area of cognitive psychology, which involves the link between cognitive and social psychology, can be useful in explaining the strategies and arguments adopted by individuals or groups (Kruglanski and Ajzen, 1983; Ranyard et al., 1997; Surel, 2000).

B) From preferences to choices

Now is discussed the way people interact and make decisions in contexts with specific information systems, behaviours and organizational structures. Groups are particularly important in the context of decision-making, as decision-making involves the need to create synergies and articulate knowledge and information, often dispersed across diverse individuals. In this context, not only is it important to understand how individuals act within each decision group, but also how communication can influence the process and its outcomes. This analysis naturally arises the question of how decision makers deal with interdependence and uncertainty, which results in structural factors that determine the levels of trust between and within groups. Another question that immediately arises is how individuals consider themselves or others and how the group shapes individual preferences, strengthening an overall logic. In this regard, we highlight the cognitive characteristics of individuals, the social structure and dominant values, and also the organization of institutional and economic structures.

Political culture is used as an example, which Almond and Verba (1963) define by a diversity of dimensions, centred on values and norms, that explain the political action confined to the specific contexts in which this political action takes place. In other words, this stems from the process of socialization, in which people shape their attitudes according to their experiences throughout their lives. These socialization processes delimit a set of factors that assume greater or lesser influence on individual's (electoral) preferences, for example, the area of residence, ethnicity, or the (electoral) behaviour of the group of individuals of which they are part. This example is an illustration of the normative dimension, as an activity where values are assigned to a society.

The decision-making process involves a dynamic interaction with the environment, including cycles of actions and reactions to any changes that may occur in this context. Thus, social psychology can be placed in this debate. Social representations, objectification and anchoring processes are some of the concepts and theoretical approaches that become important to understand how cognition and decision match, and shed light on the process of formation of preferences. These aspects will be carefully analysed in the following section.

Since Von-Neumann and Morgenstern, who proposed the expected utility theorem, many other studies followed to counterargument as some consistency axioms, such as completeness, transitivity and continuity, define a blind vision in search of rational and mechanical behaviour that does not comply with reality (see D. Arnott and Gao, 2019; Tversky and Kahneman, 1974). In fact, research on judgment, behavioural decision-making and social cognition find applications in many fields. Specifically discussing goals, policies, preferences and actions, Markman and Brendl (2005) focus on consumer behaviour to explain how choice strategies and information processing are constituents of preference and action. Yet, they recognize it is difficult to provide evidence between goals and motivations, because these key aspects are not consciously accessible. The authors debate on the difficulty of predicting future preferences, as these often diverge from the actual preference (in the moment they are questioned). The authors recall a study of Kruglanski et al. (2002) about people's ability to generate sensible explanations, where they conclude different choice patterns according to the cognitive closure level. This means that people who typically need to complete their decisions tend to systematically choose a certain option. A certain mechanical mental rule can be applied, because instead of real preferences they are stating a biased answer, placing the easy solution as the correct option. The authors conclude that in these cases the explanation given for the answer suggests that they were unaware of the factors that were actually affecting their choice. Despite Markman and Brendl (2005) using several studies to explain goals are often active without people being consciously aware of their activation, illustrate the importance of framing strategies, or what the authors further call semantic network, to shape the cognitive structure.

The understanding of the preference formation process aims to support the individual-collective transition, where multiple social dilemmas and collective traps come cross (the prisoner's dilemma or the tragedy of the commons), and other mathematical properties are raised (as Condorcet's classic paradox or Arrow's impossibility theorem). However, the literature presents a functional perspective on groups and decisions, namely by mobilizing social decision schemes (see: Forsyth, 2010). The mix of benefits and liabilities are based on the assumption that groups have greater informational resources and capacity to process that information and, therefore, the collective knowledge provides better conditions to detect errors in reasoning. But, if not planned carefully, a group decision process may end in failure. There are group discussion pitfalls that mess up the consensus-building decision process. Forsyth (2010) lists some of those, including, among others, responsibility denial, muddling through, or shared information bias. These pitfalls reflects the effect of individual psychological and interpersonal needs for the group. Group decision support systems are recommended to deal with the cognitive limitations that lead to these negative effects. So, in addition to motivations and conflictual interests, there are technical constraints that must be thought through in order to gather and combine preferences, choices and decisions. On this matter, some axioms of rational decision-making must be discussed or, at least, their extent has to be acknowledged. These axioms illustrate the complexity of decision rules, evidencing that decision frameworks are more than effective mathematical combinations as they derive from individual intelligence, knowledge and experience. If a certain simplicity is assumed in choosing between two alternatives, when these preferences are set for a larger amount of options or are subject to societal issues, such simplicity is questioned. Individual or collective exercises in this field will guide to alternatives, where some are dominant while others are disposable. But, along the process, transitiveness issues can arise, and the preference value assigned to the first two pair of alternatives can be completely changed; this can be a tricky decision parameter to deal with. To overcome the problems of intransitivity, what social psychologists (such as Kahneman and Tversky) have shown is that the outcome (conscious or not) can be easily manipulated or biased if the overall preference patterns are known, or if the alternative list is short. As Gonzalez (2017), we also underline that these studies are often led by the fields of economics or psychology which results in a certain divide between different understandings of rationality or conflicting decision-making mechanisms. The challenge, then, remains in designing a preference (and decision aiding) model that simultaneously establishes overall priorities representative of the perceptions and identity appropriation process, and somehow deals with the consequences of decisions (e.g. scenario building). This debate in continued in the following section.

Decisions and Their Socio-Cognitive Basis

In this section, other approaches are discussed for analysing and considering the formation of preferences and choices. In particular, our concern relies on how to deal with cognitive and behavioural biases, how social representations determine preference patterns and how are these brought into the decision-making context.

As discussed throughout this work, the behavioural standards for alternative evaluation, preference stating and ordering have been widely studied within rational guidelines. Doyle and Thomason (1999) highlight a list of works dealing with direct logics of preference. Among them is the research by Wellman and Doyle (1991) on preferential semantics for goals, the conclusions of which point to the heuristic advantages, stemming from the way decision-planners use them to encode both preferential and intentional information. The authors believe that framing strategies allow for presenting a simpler decision problem without necessarily sacrificing decision-theoretic accountability. Nonetheless, despite the new paths opened by logics as mentioned above, framing schemes have to be carefully applied, as their formulation impacts on the mental structure and, therefore influences judgments (Tversky and Kahneman, 1974). On this matter, Beratšová, Krchová, Gažová, and Jirásek (2018) claim that besides framing issues there are additional factors with significant impact for the decision process and outcomes, such as previous experience or knowledge, and the individual's engagement with a topic. When dealing with this [socio-cognitive] subjective dimension, there is no clear manual to ensure a de-biasing effect on decision makers. The literature review on framing and bias conducted by the authors explains that the framing influence is preference-driven, according to the attractiveness of the options. The way the problem is both formulated and presented arouses (unconscious) motivations and interests. Some of these aspects are dealt with in the prospect theory, where impressions, perceptions and memories play a central role for decision-making. Based on the four groups of factors influencing framing presented by Beratšová et al. (2018), it is possible to identify a more objective dimension related with the decision situation setup (information and options) and other subjective-related one, defined by experience and demographics. To this analysis, adds further discussions on the importance and influence of beliefs, values, and behaviour in the decision-making process (see: Cahill, Duveen, and Lloyd, 1990; Higgins and Bargh, 1987; Oliveira, 2007).

Contributions from the field of social psychology, in particular, rely on the assumption that human knowledge and intelligence are built through a continuous process that involves the assimilation and accommodation of the various elements combined and transformed into cognitive structures (Moscovici, 1988; Smith and Semin, 2007). In the study of these processes, the concept of social representations can take a prominent place, given the importance of shared meanings, as well as its socio-cognitive function in the assimilation of new ideas and practices in order to guide communication and individual behaviour (Maury, 2007; Moscovici, 1988), especially through the processes of objectification and anchoring (Vala and Castro, 2013).

A) Social Representations

Social representations theory is a theory about the intervention of social regulations in cognitive functioning (Doise, 1993). It is thus a privileged conceptual tool to understand lay knowledge and decision-making processes. As noted by Moscovici (2001), actual knowledge within a social context is driven by memory, perception, information gathering and dissonance. But, he goes further in recognizing the major importance to other dimensions, based on values, histories, conventions and symbols. The theory of social representation is framed here as an analytic lens to study the social knowledge phenomena as, in his words, "thinking consists for the larger part of looking for exchange and agreement" (Moscovici, 2001, p. 14). Two interdependent processes are proposed to understand social representations: objectification – the process of knowledge creation about the social object – and anchoring – integration of this knowledge in individuals' reality (see for example Bordarie and Gaymard, 2015; Wagner et al., 1999; Laroche, 1995; Cahill et al., 1990; Moscovici, 1988). Rather than discussing recurrent approaches, as those based on the epistemology of the rationality of an isolated individual, it is expected to argue its importance and underline crucial implications of including social representations as part of the decision-making process.

To our knowledge, there are currently few research contributions where social representations approach supports both analytical and empirical inputs for (and based on) the practice of collective decision-making (find evidence on the works presented by Lorenzi-Cioldi and Alain Clémence 2004; Marková 2017; Maury 2007; Rubira-García, Puebla-Martínez, and Gelado-Marcos 2018; Santos 2007; Voelklein and Howarth 2005). Despite its potential to explain learning and the instructional processes, behaviourism, cognitivism and social constructionism are within the three main theoretical paradigms that have dominated this type of research (Chaib, 2015). While discussing similarities shared by these theories, two main aspects are advanced by the author: they are formulated for and within mono-cultural contexts (neglecting more complex contexts often conducted by multidisciplinary and interrelated environments); and group communication and interaction are not explicitly taken into account as explanatory elements.

Understanding social representations is more than associating two meanings (representation and social). The notion of social representation reveals a barrier between what is the "outside objective reality" and what is mental or symbolic, or in other words, it matches the social phenomena to the so-called objective and economic phenomena. Identity appears as something assigning meaning to the representation shared by a group, community or institutions, and it acts as a social system (establishing values, rights, duties, sense of belonging) and moves people to act together or accordingly.

Carugati (1990) introduces another contribution to the symbolic construction of shared reality, which constitutes the 'objective knowledge' of both social groups and individuals. In particular, he refers to intelligence as social representations and recalls the scientific approaches of Sternberg (in the '80s) stressing that intelligent behaviour is largely defined by the socio-cultural context in which it occurs, for which specific structures and mechanisms are applied. The conceptions of intelligence are viewed in a complex environment and are context-dependent. Thus, as decisions and behaviours are embedded in particular socio-economic and political dynamics, knowledge and reactions are assumed to depend on different world-views that derive from the dynamic relationships between actor and environment. Carugati (1990) frames this interaction with the engagement in problem-solving and goal-directed activities. In fact, he presents social representations "as socio-cognitive principles, which are activated in decision-making situations and by specific social positions" (Carugati, 1990, p. 134). The author corroborates the conception of Moscovici about the way groups and individuals act as social actors, contributing to a broad construction of experiences and shared meanings to justify attitudes and actions. Furthermore, Carugati explains that these socio-cognitive constructions are dynamic, and new social representations are transformed by the way individuals or groups encounter new experiences linked to new social positions. Communication and information (or knowledge) play a key role in this process, as they provide particular kinds of structures.

B) Group decisions and heuristics

The premise of social representation has its roots in the research of Emile Durkheim, who distinguished individual representations as those which were not shared in opposition to the collective representations formed from the communication of thoughts, in words, images and symbols. Groups might share different social representations in comparison to others. According to Lorenzi-Cioldi and Clémence (2004), the transformation of abstract information into concrete meaning is a process of amalgamation of many individual normative rules grounded in ideas, values and beliefs. Knowledge is anchored (or positioned by) the perspective of the group, which demands a link between the individual and social levels. Even though, the interaction between and within groups does not lead only to consensual arrangements, as they often produce dissensus or contradiction (Marková, 2017), which implies that different and incompatible cognitive styles and forms of knowledge can co-exist within one social group (Voelklein and Howarth, 2005). These statements give theoretical support for a link between social representations theory and decision-making models.

So far, socio-cognitive theories have been introduced as analytic tools to explain behaviour, decision rules or shortcuts, cognitive mechanisms. The ways people gather, process and share information and interpret their surrounding environments are frequently used as key research problems (Oliveira, 2007). From here, the debate is narrowed down to group decision-making, as it happens in the formulation of public policies. In this context, Ostrom (1998) assumes that individuals act instrumentally and institutions provide a sense of identity, shape preferences and goals; thus, the institutional design frames decision-making in challenging and uncertain contexts and motivational complexity. Complementary to this idea, other authors affirm that decisions and outcomes reflect the interaction between individual behaviour and institutional structures, and thus individuals and organizations seek power, status and economic advantages, as well as their means and ends to respond to their interests but both are dependent on the institutional logics (Thornton and Ocasio, 2008; Wrona, Ladwig, and Gunnesch, 2013). There are a set of interrelated issues leading to collective identity, such as specific mechanisms used by institutions to exert their effects on individuals and organizations, towards collective identities of institutionalized groups, organizations, professions or populations. Thus, collective identity is the cognitive, normative and emotional connection experienced by members of a group – based on characteristics like those of other members of that group – and it emerges from social interactions and communication. Each individual or organization can be part of several groups simultaneously, for which a set of rules, norms and prescriptions are assumed, with the concern of protecting the collective interests.

In practice, several attempts have been made to explain and improve group decision-making, and somehow have sustained the idea that groups allow for identifying and integrating individual view-points through participation (Brodbeck, Kerchreiter, Mojzisch, and Schulz-Hardt, 2007; Forsyth, 2010; Moorhead, Ference, and Neck, 1991). Different conceptions of knowledge, as discussed, have an operative meaning in real-context decision-making processes and important heuristics come into the debate – availability, anchoring and adjustment, and representativeness. Many researchers have provided sound research on this matter by discussing the cognitive and the psychological determinants of choice to explain the relation between decision values and experience (see for example D. Arnott and Gao, 2019; Kahneman, Slovic, and Tversky, 1982; Tversky and Kahneman, 1974, 1981, 1986). In particular, anchoring and adjustment bias have been used to explain how judgments tend to be excessively influenced by an initial impression, perspective, or value (Epley and Gilovich, 2006). According to the authors, this is used to explain preference reversals, the hindsight bias, subadditivity in likelihood judgment, social comparison and egocentric biases. They also suggest that adjustment behaviours have cognitive-load manipulations. In other words, information and knowledge are subject to judgmental heuristics and cognitive bias. Some theorists use schemata, heuristics and bias as important pieces of cognitive models (namely in attribution theory), even though they have failed to establish a hierarchy among them, or to translate it to general theories of decision-making (David H. Silvera and Laufer, 2005; Oliveira, 2007). The complexity of the decision-making process increases when these issues overlap with the process-related pitfalls, such as procrastination, bolstering, denying responsibility, muddling through, satisficing or trivializing the discussion (for more complete details see Brodbeck et al. (2007); Lu, Zhang, Ruan, and Wu, 2007). The impact of shared cognitions on group process has been studied to a certain extent and information-processing issues evidence these pitfalls (Hogg and Tindale, 2001), namely throughout groups with different characteristics (Brodbeck et al., 2007).

The abovementioned aspects seem to be interrelated, but persist as loose contributions. In this debate contributes with some arguments on how socio-cognitive dimensions are integrated into decision-making approaches.

MAIN FOCUS OF THE PAPER

Decision-Making in Practice

The state of the art on decision analysis describes the main barriers and contributions for decision-making theory and its application to real world contexts. As discussed throughout this chapter, major contributions rely on both knowledge-dependent issues and the cognitive system of human behaviour. Endless layers could be added to explain the complexity of decision-making (the following aspects are the result of a compilation of some research in this field – see for example, (A. W. Kruglanski and Higgins, 2007; Marques et al., 2019; Parnell, et. al, 2013; Russo and Schoemaker, 1990; Tversky and Kahneman, 1974):

- content-related aspects (available information, different sources of knowledge ranging from more objective to opinions and expertise);
- path dependency and contextual set-ups (involving levels of uncertainty and (un)defined value-hierarchy with many dependencies and conflicts;
- mental representations, impulse or adjustment processes, shared beliefs or familiarity;
- group decision-making traps or pitfalls.

Decision support methods have many features that appear adequate to specific decision contexts. Therefore, the concept of decision support systems (DSS) has evolved quickly, with applications in the most diverse contexts (Arnott and Gao, 2019b; Arnott and Pervan, 2005; Eom and Lee, 1990; McCosh and Correa-Perez, 2006). The research and empirical experience developed under real-world decision environments (involving different governance arrangements, social actors, sectorial approaches and spatial contexts), has motivated contributions for a taxonomic framework that sheds light on key characteristics of the decision process and models, type of information and main outcomes (Marques et al., 2019). The context delimitation has a strong analytic approach, including many techniques to organize, gather and process information. Forecasting and prospective decision approaches balance quantitative methods often used to anticipate or predict evolutions that follow expected patterns and qualitative (or mixed) methods that enable decision makers to deal with more complex, interdependent and subjective contexts. Participation and interactive techniques are an active part of all decision contexts and echo the socio-cognitive dimensions discussed throughout this chapter.

Independently of the context in which DSS are applied, they should follow an interdisciplinary perspective and an integrated structure, to deal with i) information constraints; ii) the multidimensionality of the decision context; and iii) the perceptions, expectations and preferences of decision makers and the overall community. Indeed, the search for a taxonomy of DSS has been broadly outlined, including conceptual focus, empirical approaches, type of data and collection methods, or technical and organizational specificities (see, for example, Arnott and Gao, 2019; Arnott and Pervan, 2005; Elsawah, Guillaume, Filatova, Rook, and Jakeman, 2015; Gachet and Haettenschwiler, 2003; Power, 2008). An interesting perspective shared by Teng and Ramamurthy (1993) is based on the assumption that group decision-making includes the collective availability of knowledge. For these authors, the taxonomy deals with both the process and the content support dimensions. The conceptualization of the levels within each dimension includes references to decision-analysis-oriented models, such as many multiple criteria decision-making procedures and algorithms, Delphi techniques and knowledge-based components providing intelligent support. These examples evidence scientific and empirical efforts towards a functional taxonomy of decision support systems.

Socio-Cognitive and Model-Based Approaches

During the decision process, decision makers, stakeholders and experts struggle in many ways, while sharing information and knowledge, communicating and interpreting results. System-based frameworks are often used to deal with the adaptive properties of decision contexts.

Processing and analysing information is of major importance in supporting decisions. As previously discussed, mathematics, statistical analysis and modelling are commonly used to activate and improve data collection, analysis and interpretation. However, it is important to note that existing information may not be enough, that it is not always possible to combine and organize (objective and subjective) information, and that decisions are subject to contexts of high uncertainty. Thus, decision theorists and cognitive psychologists have introduced the concepts of risk and preference, in assessing multiple alternatives, while recognizing the role of communication and perception, rules and access to information (Andrews, 2007; Betsch and Haberstroh, 2005; Dohmen et al., 2018).

Different decision strategies are expected to require different selection criteria. A wide variety of decision-making strategies developed in the field of decision theory must therefore be considered and complemented with cognitive science. In this regard, Y. Wang and Ruhe (2007) present a taxonomy for the different strategies and their decision-making criteria. The proposed classification falls into four categories: i) intuitive, ii) empirical, iii) heuristic and iv) rational. The first two are in line with cognitive psychology and human behaviour, and there is no specific rational model to explain these decision processes. There are a set of decisions that fall into these categories because they are based on arbitrary choices and preferences justified by personal propensity, expectations, and/or common meanings. Then, the last two are rationally-based and are either static or dynamic. The first defines the set of decisions whose environment changes are independent of the decision makers' activities. In addition, different decision strategies can be selected for the same situation or context based on the decision makers' values and attitudes toward risk and their ability to predict future outcomes. Here, the heuristic category plays an important role for communication and individual behaviours, as it results from the individual system of value and principles (social representations and shared social meanings). On the other hand, dynamic decision contexts occur whenever the decision maker's activities and strategies cause changes in the environment. Despite the clear distinction of categories presented by the authors, there are endless studies and applications of mechanisms and methodologies to deal with the complexity of decision-making processes.

In the last 10 years, few works have focused on the link between socio-cognitive aspects and decision-making, suggesting that the prospect of an integrated cohesive science has not materialized over time (Núñez et al., 2019). However some studies deserve attention: see, for example, Alexandre, Navarro, Reynaud, and Osiurak, 2019; Cairney and Weible, 2017; Chatzidakis, Kastanakis, and Stathopoulou, 2014; Dohmen et al., 2018; Gorbunov, Rauterberg, and Barakova, 2019; Kuehnhanss, 2019. These works are important scientific contributions as they share many experimental findings deriving from behavioural heuristics. They provide modelling frameworks to deal with the interactive dimension of the group decision process; thus, methodological guidelines are often grounded on assumptions from the cognitive science of choice and reflect attempts at adjusting-to-context of multiple economic, behavioural and cognitive theories. Others shed light on theories of situated cognition, social cognition and flow to clarify the influence of these characteristics on the process of learning and decision-making (Goel, Junglas, Ives, and Johnson, 2012). Simultaneously, considerable attention in the scientific literature accounts for the use of information and communication technology (computerised systems), as it provides strong support for real-time decision-making. The three categories established by Ringberg and Reihlen (2008) can be used to structure these socio-cognitive models and conceptual approaches, as they organize the social mechanisms according to cultural and private models (cognitive context), their reflectively and/or categorically application (cognitive process), and adaptive capacity through social context (environmental feedback). The figure presented below illustrates the complexity of the socio-cognitive system and its categorization for modelling purposes.

Figure 1. Socio-cognitive determinants and process outcomes (adapted from Chatzidakis et al., 2014; Ringberg & Reihlen, 2008)

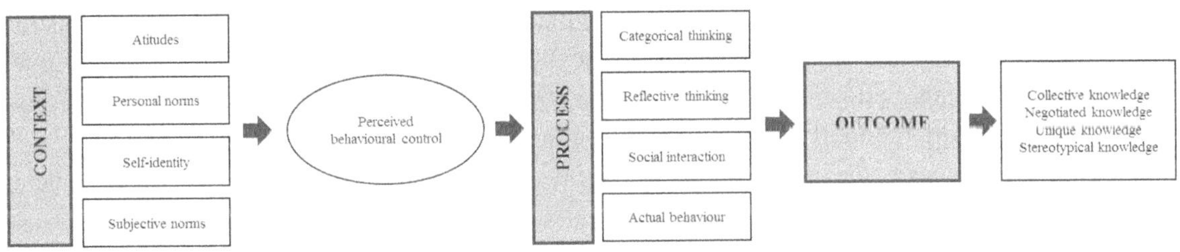

It remains unclear how these cognitive maps and mental representations can be integrated into decision support models, producing effective outputs. They rely on methodological assumptions and experiments and therefore provide robust conceptual approaches and consistent model frameworks. However, these are not designed to deal with real-world decision contexts. Moreover, managing complex decisions encounters multi-actor, multi-scale, and dynamic decision-making processes (Ayeni, 2003; Elsawah et al., 2015; Marques et al., 2019). According to J.-J. Wang, et al. (2009) all dimensions of decisions have an internal impact and weights are assigned to indicate their relative importance. In this sense, different weights directly influence the results of the alternatives that make up the system under analysis. As a corollary of this complexity, the need arises to articulate the components of rationality and subjectivity of decisions (materialized in the criteria weights). Indeed, the authors suggest that the methods can be classified into i) subjective weighting methods, ii) objective weighting methods and iii) mixed weighting methods. In the case of (i) subjective weighting, the weights depend only on the preference of the decision makers (not including articulation with the quantitatively measured data); in contrast, (ii) objective weights are obtained by structured methods (more rigorous models based on modelling or other mathematical formalisms) based on the analysis of the initial data. There are limitations within these approaches, either because they are mostly grounded on the knowledge system each individual holds, ignoring other structural elements, or because they are too focused on objective information, which lacks on detail to ensure the quality of the decision. The (iii) integrated methods attempt to address these limitations. Other weighting mechanisms can be used to describe and aggregate decision preferences. For instance, multi-criteria methods have been successfully used, as they generally comprise five components which are: goal, criteria, decision maker's preferences, alternatives, and outcomes (Kumar et al., 2017; Sabaei, Erkoyuncu, and Roy, 2015). Decision support systems have proven to be suitable in addressing such complexity and multi-criteria methods (MCDA) are often used as a reference framework in many contexts (see Marques et al., 2019; Marques et al., 2018; Wolf et al., 2019). Regarding the use of multi-criteria methods there is indeed a lack of integration of the cognitive aspects in this type of analysis. Contributions in this field are placed by Carneiro et al. (2016), where well known MCDA outputs (using methods as AHP, TOPSIS and MACBETH) are compared with the application of a cognitive analytic process. Besides the configuration of criteria and alternatives, the added layer of this method concerns to the definition of decision makers' behaviour style, expertise level and credibility of other decision makers. Even though this work sheds light on the incorporation of some subjective dimensions of decision makers' interests by enabling an individual expression on how they would face the decision process, a critical assessment goes towards the bias that this evaluation (made by the decision maker) brings into the outputs. First, the reasoning schemas are framed by individual preferences and judgments, which are socially constructed. Second, these preferences tend to be adjusted to each context, leading to some distance between intentions and actions. Third, using a satisfaction metric based on the perception of decision makers about the quality of output (chosen alternatives) can be a fragile assumption. This said, notwithstanding the advances in the design and application of DSS (health, water supply, energy, investment, strategic planning, policymaking, …) a critical assessment goes towards the lack of an integrated framework dealing with the individual-collective cognitive and behavioural biases.

A final comment goes to the inclusion of social representations in decision tools. Intelligence, design and choice seem to be attached through a complex web of theories, methods and effects driven by social and behavioural sciences (Arnott and Gao, 2019b). Despite the lack of research evidence on this approach in the past few years, some authors have evidenced the disappearance of specific orientations in this matter, after a period of emergence, consolidation and development (Jodelet, 2008; Rubira-García et al., 2018). Contributions in the domain of social psychology have evidenced paradigmatic orientations on social cognition; collective beliefs, ideologies and social representations; and identity and its impact group processes (Jodelet, 2008; Vala and Costa-Lopes, 2012). Somehow, these dimensions are reflected in some of the studies mentioned above, particularly addressing information processing strategies, collective beliefs and shared representations, or intra and inter-group relations.

SOLUTIONS AND RECOMMENDATIONS

The notion of social representations has been placed as a core socio-cognitive dimension along this chapter and its interdisciplinary application is acknowledged. Rubira-García et al. (2018), reaffirm its use over other scientific fields because of the heuristic potential that it offers. Hitherto, was argued on how theory and practice used social representations as a holistic framework for understanding the behaviours of and within communities and groups of individuals in particular contexts. A stream of experimental research divides theoretical proposals from attempts of framing the notion into particular scientific contexts, orientations and debates; while this happens, “fundamental concepts are neglected or forgotten, and alternative sub-models emerge, sometimes without true dialogue” (Jodelet, 2008, p. 414; cf. also Valentim, 2013).

The contribution of this work relies on a methodological script explaining how the theoretical pieces developed throughout the chapter challenge a housing policy decision process. The choice of housing policy is related to how easy it seems to illustrate the different sides of the socio-cognitive perspective during the decision-making process, while implicitly suggesting a useful reflection for decision strategies with application to consumer behaviour. Indeed, social representations in the context of housing have been used to understand the relationship between residents and their homes, often through application of surveys and socio-economic analysis (see, for example, Santos, 2007). However, to our knowledge, there are no explicit cases where these representations have been used as inputs for the decision outcome.

In Portugal, local decision makers have recently been challenged to formulate local housing strategies, within a *New Generation of Housing Policies* embedding a set of objectives that provide adequate housing (for more detail see República Portuguesa, 2018; UN-Habitat, 2017).

As expected, there is an interplay of different knowledge sources or information providers for decision-making: categorized here as technical advisors, local decision makers [politicians], key players (or stakeholders). The link with the premises of social knowledge derive from the interdependent stages of decision process, where these actors interact, participating in a continuous process of assimilation

Figure 2. Methodological script overview

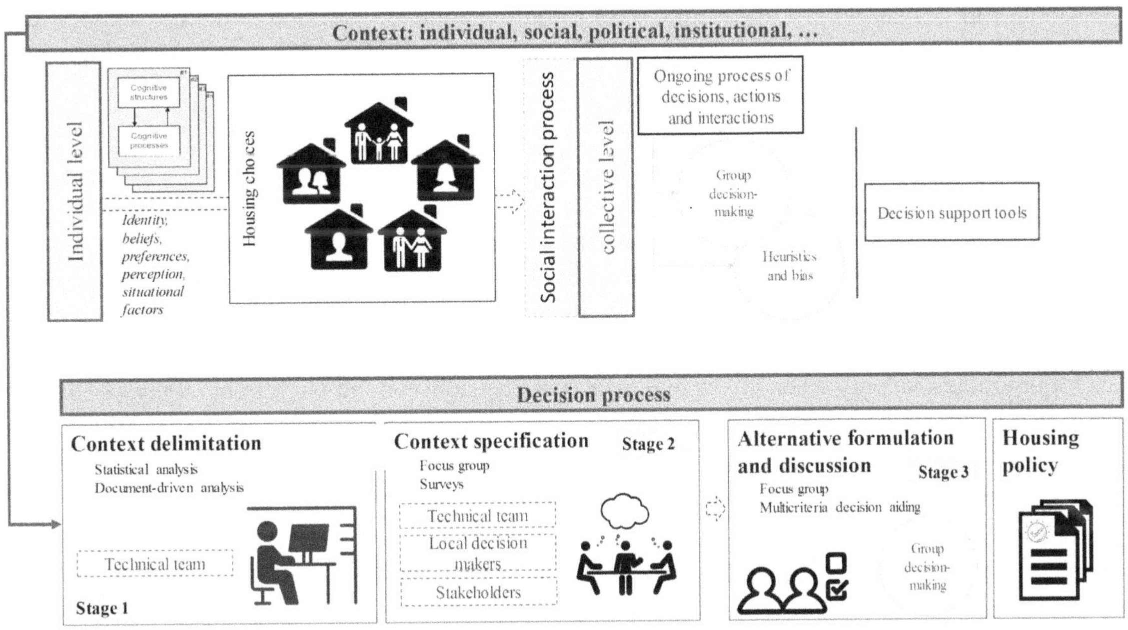

and accommodation of information, opinions and experiences; therefore transforming social/collective knowledge into cognitive structures (see Figure 2).

The decision process, in general, involves two stages: gathering and analysing objective information, which is available in statistical databases or other documental sources; and sharing and updating such context delimitation with *in situ* specificities, built on subjective and dispersed information. When opinions are used to complement research work (as happens in stage 2) process and outcome biases begin, as individuals assess topics according to our daily life, characteristics of our environment, the information that circulates in it and the people of our near or distant environment (Rubira-García et al., 2018). The triple lens of social representation (social subject, the individual subject and the object) require methodological efforts. These dimensions are not explicitly present in the illustration, because they are not typically addressed in any decision phase. However, at the risk of this comparison resembling common sense, as it is often referred to in the critical analysis on this subject, social representations are assumed to be direct and indirectly driven in this framework.

Focus groups (stages 2 and 3), in this context, bring together decision makers representing key policy areas or activities. So, besides individual bias and different social representations, they inevitably transpose institutional values into the process: school principals or mayors have different perspectives on the collective needs and address housing problems following different (sometimes contradictory) standards. A mismatch is often evidenced between the formulation of strategic action plans and their implementation. As decisions are context-dependent, some misalignment can be justified (e.g. exogenous dynamics, unexpected restrictions, political leadership). However, some failures stem from the inadequacy of the actions to the real-context needs: they were badly defined from the beginning. In the context of housing policy formulation, minority ethnic groups, old-age people and people in a situation of economic vulnerability are among the target groups. Either by knowledge (allowing understanding and explaining reality closely linked to social interaction), identity (individual or group characteristics) or behavioural patterns (cognitively oriented), these individuals present different conceptions of housing. If these representations diverge, in an extreme way, from what is collectively decided (indirectly incorporating social representations, as mentioned above) the plan may be doomed to failure.

FUTURE RESEARCH DIRECTIONS

The decision-making process faces similar challenges as those discussed above, related to cognitive abilities and limitations (e.g. information processing, knowledge diversity, context effects). The methodological script sheds light on this debate and enables a shift from the mainstream social psychological research towards more functional and operational settings. Its relevance goes beyond the formulation of sectoral policies, namely when analysing consumer decision-making from a social perspective (improving Kardes, Herr, and Nantel, 2005; Reynolds and Olson, 2001; Stankevich, 2017). For example, Zinkhan and Braunsberger (2004) apply the notion of cognitive complexity, explaining its relevance to understand consumer behaviour and the difficulty to design measure rules. The cognitive complexity consists on the strategies used to organize and store cognitive content, including mental representations, knowledge and beliefs, perception on real-world objects and their attributes, context-specific experience (Bartels & Johnson, 2015; Zinkhan & Braunsberger, 2004).

Future research goes toward the application of the guiding principles of this methodology, to identify social representations and its impact on collective decision-making outcomes.

CONCLUSIONS

This chapter compiles key readings on the evolution of decision theories given the need to understand human social behaviour and its impact on group decision-making. A conceptual framework is provided, stemming from a narrow definition of rational behaviour to explain how normative values and social frameworks structure the processes of choice, shaped by individual expectations, beliefs, social contexts and symbolic representations of the world (Hoch et al., 2001; Scott, 2001).

Individual and collective decision-making has been a research subject involving multidisciplinary perspectives and scientific domains. Major contributions stem from empirical-analytic or theoretical-methodological studies. On the one hand, there are works that systematize the evolution of decision theories and demonstrate recent trends evidencing how decision support systems have dealt with (collective) preferences and choices. A remarkable compilation is presented by Arnott and Gao, (2019) and Arnott and Pervan, (2005), who show how decisions have embodied social psychology, group behaviour, expert systems, knowledge-management, optimization and simulation models or computer-based systems. Contributions in these fields are quite consolidated and their empirical evidence relies on the implementation strategies in case studies and real-life decision contexts. On the other hand, the role of social cognition in decision-making has been mostly confined to a theoretical approach, where social representations are not held. A certain misalignment between theory and practice has contributed to general definitions of basic assumptions and principles.

This chapter analyses the evolution of decision theories and discussed the importance of social representations as a core socio-cognitive mechanism. This reflection echoes an attempt to change the way decision-making processes are being designed, accounting for important methodological and scientific advances by placing cognitive leaning aspects and social psychological frameworks (e.g. social representations) at the core of the decision-making process. Given the fragmented contributions from multidisciplinary fields, it is not possible to establish consolidated orientations on methods or techniques that ensure accurate analysis and the incorporation of the social representations dimensions in the process. However, it seems clear that its integration should occur at both levels, the explanatory level (social positions, outputs, choices, preferences, cognitive structures and contexts) and the operative level (seeking to inform decision makers of possible deviations consistent with the social representations and, therefore, shaping the plan of alternatives). To conclude, it is desirable to combine diversified methodologies (quantitative, qualitative and mixed models) to accommodate the complexity phenomena under study (Jodelet, 2008; Nascimento-Schulze and Carmago, 2000).

ACKNOWLEDGMENT

This work is based on the PhD thesis in progress (SFRH/BD/118478/2016), funded by FCT (Fundação para a Ciência e a Tecnologia) and COMPETE 2020-POCI. It is as well a contribution for the research project: DRIVIT-UP – DRIVIng forces of urban Trnsformation: assessing pUblic Policies (POCI-01-0145-FEDER-031905). This work was financially supported by the research unit on Governance, Competitiveness and Public Policy (UID/CPO/04058/2019), funded by national funds through FCT.

REFERENCES

Alexandre, B., Navarro, J., Reynaud, E., & Osiurak, F. (2019). Which cognitive tools do we prefer to use, and is that preference rational? *Cognition*, *186*(February), 108–114. doi:10.1016/j.cognition.2019.02.005 PMID:30771701

Almond, G. A., & Verba, S. (1963). *The Civic Culture: Political Attitudes and Democracy in Five Nations*. SAGE Publications. doi:10.1515/9781400874569

Andrews, C. J. (2007). Rationality in Policy Decision Making. In F. Fischer, G. Miller, & M. Sidney (Eds.), Handbook of Public Policy Analysis: Theory, Politics and Methods (pp. 161–172). Taylor & Francis.

Arnott, D., & Gao, S. (2019a). Behavioral economics for decision support systems researchers. *Decision Support Systems*, *122*(February), 113063. doi:10.1016/j.dss.2019.05.003

Arnott, D., & Pervan, G. (2005). A Critical Analysis of Decision Support Systems Research. *Journal of Information Technology*, *20*(2), 67–87. doi:10.1057/palgrave.jit.2000035

Ayeni, B. (2003). The design of spatial decision support systems in urban and regional planning (pp. 20–33). Academic Press.

Bartels, D. M., & Johnson, E. J. (2015). Connecting cognition and consumer choice. *Cognition*, *135*, 47–51. doi:10.1016/j.cognition.2014.11.024 PMID:25527275

Beratšová, A., Krchová, K., Gažová, N., & Jirásek, M. (2018). Framing and Bias: A Literature Review of Recent Findings. *Central European Journal of Management*, *3*(2), 23–32. doi:10.5817/CEJM2016-2-2

Betsch, T., & Haberstroh, S. (2005). *The routines of decision making* (T. Betsch & S. Haberstroh, Eds.). Lawrence Erlbaum Associates.

Bordarie, J., & Gaymard, S. (2015). Social Representations and Public Policy: Influence of the Distance from the Object on Representational Valence. *Open Journal of Social Sciences*, *03*(09), 300–305. doi:10.4236/jss.2015.39038

Brewer, M. B., & Hewstone, M. (2004). *Social cognition*. Blackwell Publishing Ltd.

Brodbeck, F. C., Kerchreiter, R., Mojzisch, A., & Schulz-Hardt, S. (2007). Group decision making under conditions of distributed knowledge: The information asymmetries model. *Academy of Management Review*, *32*(2), 459–479. doi:10.5465/amr.2007.24351441

Cahill, S. E., Duveen, G., & Lloyd, B. (1990). *Social Representations and The Development of Knowledge* (Vol. 20). Academic Press.

Cairney, P., & Weible, C. M. (2017). The new policy sciences: Combining the cognitive science of choice, multiple theories of context, and basic and applied analysis. *Policy Sciences*, *50*(4), 619–627. doi:10.100711077-017-9304-2

Carneiro, J., Conceição, L., Martinho, D., Marreiros, G., & Novais, P. (2016). Including cognitive aspects in multiple criteria decision analysis. *Annals of Operations Research*.

Carugati, F. F. (1990). From social cognition to social representations in the study of intelligence. In Social Representations and The Development of Knowledge (pp. 126–143). doi:10.1017/CBO9780511659874.008

Chaib, M. (2015). Social representations, subjectivity and learning. *Cadernos de Pesquisa*, *45*(156), 359–371.

Chatzidakis, A., Kastanakis, M., & Stathopoulou, A. (2014). Socio-Cognitive Determinants of Consumers' Support for the Fair Trade Movement. *Journal of Business Ethics*, *133*(1), 95–109. doi:10.100710551-014-2347-9

Dohmen, T., Falk, A., Huffman, D., & Sunde, U. (2018). On the relationship between cognitive ability and risk preference. *The Journal of Economic Perspectives*, *32*(2), 115–134. doi:10.1257/jep.32.2.115 PMID:30203932

Doyle, J., & Thomason, R. H. (1999). Background to Qualitative Decision Theory. *AI Magazine*, *20*(2), 55–68.

Elsawah, S., Guillaume, J. H. A., Filatova, T., Rook, J., & Jakeman, A. J. (2015). A methodology for eliciting, representing, and analysing stakeholder knowledge for decision making on complex socio-ecological systems: From cognitive maps to agent-based models. *Journal of Environmental Management*, *151*, 500–516. doi:10.1016/j.jenvman.2014.11.028 PMID:25622296

Eom, H. B., & Lee, S. M. (1990). A Survey of Decision Support System Applications (1971–April 1988). *Interfaces*, *20*(3), 65–79. doi:10.1287/inte.20.3.65

Epley, N., & Gilovich, T. (2006). The anchoring-and-adjustment heuristic : Why the adjustments are insufficient. *Psychological Science*, *17*(4), 311–318. doi:10.1111/j.1467-9280.2006.01704.x PMID:16623688

Forsyth, D. R. (2010). *Group Dynamics*. Cengage Learning.

Gachet, A., & Haettenschwiler, P. (2003). *Developing Intelligent Decision Support Systems: A Bipartite Approach*. Berlin: Springer.

Goel, L., Junglas, I., Ives, B., & Johnson, N. (2012). Decision-making in-socio and in-situ: Facilitation in virtual worlds. *Decision Support Systems*, *52*(2), 342–352. doi:10.1016/j.dss.2011.09.001

Gonzalez, C. (2017). Decision-Making: A Cognitive Science Perspective. In S. E. F. Chipman (Ed.), *The Oxford Handbook of Cognitive Science* (pp. 264–270). Elsevier.

Gorbunov, R. D., Rauterberg, M., & Barakova, E. I. (2019). A cognitive model of social preferences in group interactions. *Integrated Computer-Aided Engineering*, *26*(2), 185–196. doi:10.3233/ICA-180590

Gowda, R., & Fox, J. (2002). *Judgments, Decisions, and Public Policy* (R. Gowda & J. C. Fox, Eds.). https://ebooks.cambridge.org/ref/id/CBO9780511584206retrieved

Gupta, S. (2009). *Branding and Advertising*. Global India Publications.

Higgins, E. T., & Bargh, J. A. (1987). Social Cognition and social perception. *Annual Review of Psychology*, *38*(1), 369–425. doi:10.1146/annurev.ps.38.020187.002101 PMID:3548576

Hoch, S. J., Kunreuther, H. C., & Gunther, R. E. (Eds.). (2001). *Wharton on making decision*. John Wiley & Sons, Inc.

Hogg, M. A., & Tindale, R. S. (2001). *Group Processes*. In Blackwell Handbook of Social Psychology. Blackwell Publishing Ltd.

Jodelet, D. (2008). Social representations: The beautiful invention. *Journal for the Theory of Social Behaviour*, *38*(4), 411–430. doi:10.1111/j.1468-5914.2008.00383.x

Kahneman, D., Slovic, P., & Tversky, A. (1982). *Judgment under uncertainty: heuristics and biases*. Cambridge University Press. doi:10.1017/CBO9780511809477

Kardes, F. R., Herr, P. M., & Nantel, J. (2005). *Applying social cognition to consumer-focused strategy* (F. R. Kardes, P. M. Herr, & J. Nantel, Eds.). Lawrence Erlbaum Associates.

Kruglanski, A., & Higgins, E. T. (2007). *Social Psychology: Handbook of Basic Principles. Political Psychology* (Vol. 29). The Guilford Press.

Kruglanski, A., & Ajzen, I. (1983). Bias and error in human judgment. *European Journal of Social Phsycologysycology*, *13*(1), 1–44. doi:10.1002/ejsp.2420130102

Kruglanski, A., Shah, J. Y., Fishbach, A., Friedman, R., Chun, W. Y., & Sleeth-Keppler, D. (2002). A theory of goal systems. *Advances in Experimental Social Psychology*, *34*, 331–372. doi:10.1016/S0065-2601(02)80008-9

Kuehnhanss, C. R. (2019). The challenges of behavioural insights for effective policy design. *Policy and Society*, *38*(1), 14–40. doi:10.1080/14494035.2018.1511188

Kumar, A., Sah, B., Singh, A. R., Deng, Y., He, X., Kumar, P., & Bansal, R. C. (2017). A review of multi criteria decision making (MCDM) towards sustainable renewable energy development. *Renewable and Sustainable Energy Reviews, 69*, 596–609. . doi:10.1016/j.rser.2016.11.191retrieved

Lorenzi-Cioldi, F., & Clémence, A. (2004). Group processes and the construction of social representations. In M. B. Brewer & M. Hewstone (Eds.), *Social cognition* (pp. 298–320). Academic Press.

Lu, J., Zhang, G., Ruan, D., & Wu, F. (2007). *Multi-Objective Group Decision Making* (Vol. 6). https://www.worldscientific.com/worldscibooks/10.1142/p505retrieved

Markman, A. B., & Brendl, C. M. (2005). Goals, Policies, Preferences, and Actions. In F. R. Kardes, P. M. Herr, & J. Nantel (Eds.), *Applying social cognition to consumer-focused strategy* (pp. 183–199). Lawrence Erlbaum Associates.

Marková, I. (2017). The making of the theory of social representations. *Cadernos de Pesquisa, 47*(163), 358–374.

Marques, J., Borges, M., Batista, P., Gonçalves, C., & Wolf, J. (2019). Drivers and models to support policies of territorial transformation. *Conference Proceedings on the 4th International Conference on CHANGING CITIES: Spatial, Design, Landscape & Socio-economic Dimensions.*

Marques, J., Wolf, J., & Borges, M. (2018). Modelling the urban transformation at local scale. Rivista Urbanistica Informazioni, dall'Istituto nazionale di Urbanistica, 80–83.

Maury, C. (2007). *Social representations: A tool box Literature review.* Report for the Project n° 0288848-2 co funded by the European Commission within the Sixth Framework Progra.

McCosh, A. M., & Correa-Perez, B. A. (2006). *The optimization of what? Intelligent decision-making support systems.* London: Springer.

Moorhead, G., Ference, R., & Neck, C. P. (1991). Group Decision Fiascoes Continue: Space Shuttle Challenger and a Revised Groupthink Framework. *Human Relations, 44*(6), 539–550. doi:10.1177/001872679104400601

Moscovici, S. (1988). *Notes towards a description of Social Representations.* Academic Press.

Moscovici, S. (2001). Why a Theory of Social Representation? In K. Deaux & G. Philogène (Eds.), *Representations of the social: Bridging theoretical traditions* (pp. 8–35). Oxford: Blackwell.

Nascimento-Schulze, C. M., & Carmago, B. V. (2000). Psicologia social, representações sociais e métodos. *Temas em psicologia social, 8*(3), 287–299.

Núñez, R., Allen, M., Gao, R., Miller Rigoli, C., Relaford-Doyle, J., & Semenuks, A. (2019). What happened to cognitive science? *Nature Human Behaviour.* PMID:31182794

Oliveira, A. (2007). A Discussion of Rational and Psychological Decision-Making Theories and Models: The Search for a Cultural-Ethical Decision-Making Model. *Electronic Journal of Business Ethics and Organization Studies Scenarios, 12*(2), 12–17. http://ejbo.jyu.fi/pdf/ejbo_vol15_no1.pdfretrieved. Retrieved from http://ejbo.jyu.fi/pdf/ejbo_vol15_no1.pdf

Ostrom, E. (1998). Theory of Collective Action A Behavioral Approach to the Rational Choice Presidential Address, American Political Science Association. *The American Political Science Review*, *92*(1), 1–22. doi:10.2307/2585925

Parnell, G. S., Bresnick, T., Tani, S. N., & Johnson, E. R. (2013). *Handbook of Decision Analysis*. Wiley. doi:10.1002/9781118515853

Pligt, J. (1999). Decision making. In A. Manstead & M. Hewstone (Eds.), *The Blackwell encyclopedia of social psychology*. Oxford: Blackwell.

Policy Studies Institute. (2006). *Designing policy to influence consumers: Consumer behaviour relating to the purchasing of environmentally preferable goods*. Project under the Framework contract for economic analysis ENV.G.1/FRA/2006/0073 – 2nd.

Portuguesa, R. (2018). *Para uma nova geração de políticas de habitação*. Academic Press.

Power, D. J. (2008). Decision support systems: a historical overview. In *Handbook on decision support systems 1* (pp. 121–140). Springer. doi:10.1007/978-3-540-48713-5_7

Ranyard, R., Crozier, R., & Svenson, O. (1997). *Decision making. Cognitive models and explanations*. Taylor & Francis.

Reynolds, T. J., & Olson, J. C. (2001). *Understanding consumer decision making: The means-end approach to marketing and advertising strategy*. Academic Press.

Ringberg, T., & Reihlen, M. (2008). Towards a socio-cognitive approach to knowledge transfer. *Journal of Management Studies*, *45*(5), 912–935. doi:10.1111/j.1467-6486.2007.00757.x

Rubira-García, R., Puebla-Martínez, B., & Gelado-Marcos, R. (2018). Social representations in studying information, knowledge, and mediations: A critical review. *Social Sciences*, *7*(12), 256. doi:10.3390ocsci7120256

Russo, J. E., & Schoemaker, P. J. H. (1990). *Decision traps : ten barriers to brilliant decision-making and how to overcome them*. Simon & Schuster.

Sabaei, D., Erkoyuncu, J., & Roy, R. (2015). A review of multi-criteria decision making methods for enhanced maintenance delivery. *Procedia CIRP*, *37*, 30–35. doi:10.1016/j.procir.2015.08.086

Santos, M. C. de O. (2007). A Representação Social da Moradia [The Social Representation of the Housing]. *Estudos e Pesquisas em Psicologia, 7*(2), 336–341. pepsic.bvsalud.org/pdf/epp/v7n2/v7n2a18.pdf

Scott, R. (2001). *Institutions and organizations*. Thousand Oaks: Sage.

Silvera, D. H., & Laufer, D. (2005). Recent Developments in Attribution Research and Their Implications for Consumer Judgments and Behavior. In F. R. Kardes, P. M. Herr, & J. Nantel (Eds.), Applying social cognition to consumer-focused strategy (pp. 53–77). Lawrence Erlbaum Associates.

Simon, H. A., & Newell, A. (1971). Human problem solving: The state of the theory in 1970. *The American Psychologist*, *26*(2), 145–159. doi:10.1037/h0030806

Smith, E. R., & Semin, G. R. (2007). Situated Social Cognition. *Current Directions in Psychological Science, 16*(3), 132–135. doi:10.1111/j.1467-8721.2007.00490.x

Stankevich, A. (2017). Explaining the Consumer Decision-Making Process: Critical Literature Review. *Journal of International Business Research and Marketing, 2*(6), 7–14. doi:10.18775/jibrm.1849-8558.2015.26.3001

Surel, Y. (2000). The role of cognitive and normative frames in policy-making. *Journal of European Public Policy, 7*(4), 495–512. doi:10.1080/13501760050165334

Teng, J. T. C., & Ramamurthy, K. (1993). Group Decision Support Systems: Clarifying The Concept And Establishing A Functional Taxonomy. *INFOR, 31*(3), 166–185. doi:10.1080/03155986.1993.11732225

Thornton, P. H., & Ocasio, W. (2008). Institutional Logics. In R. Greenwood, C. Oliver, R. Suddaby, & K. Sahlin-Andersson (Eds.), *The sage handbook of organizational institutionalism* (pp. 99–129). SAGE Publications. doi:10.4135/9781849200387.n4

Tversky, A., & Kahneman, D. (1974). Judgment under Uncertainty: Heuristics and Biases. *Science, 185*(4157), 1124–1131. doi:10.1126cience.185.4157.1124 PMID:17835457

Tversky, A., & Kahneman, D. (1981). The Psychology of Preferences tend to follow regular patterns that can be described mathematically. *Scientific American, 246*, 160–173.

Tversky, A., & Kahneman, D. (1986). Rational Choice and the Framing of Decisions. *The Behavioral Foundations of Economic Theory, 59*(4), 251–278. doi:10.1086/296365

United Nations Human Settlements Programme (UN-Habitat). (2017). *Human Rights in Cities Human Rights in Cities*. Author.

Vala, J. (2012). Dynamics and dilemmas in social psychology: Social relations, identities and cognition. *Portuguese Journal of Social Science, 11*(1), 3–14. doi:10.1386/pjss.11.1.3_1

Vala, J., & Castro, P. (2013). Pensamento social e representações sociais e psciologia social do conhecimento quotidiano. In J. Vala & M. B. Monteiro (Eds.), *Psicologia Social*. Fundação Calouste Gulbenkian.

Voelklein, C., & Howarth, C. (2005). A review of controversies about social representations theory: A British debate. *Culture and Psychology, 11*(4), 431–454. doi:10.1177/1354067X05058586

Wang, J.-J., Jing, Y.-Y., Zhang, C.-F., & Zhao, J.-H. (2009). Review on multi-criteria decision analysis aid in sustainable energy decision-making. *Renewable & Sustainable Energy Reviews, 13*(9), 2263–2278. doi:10.1016/j.rser.2009.06.021

Wang, Y., & Ruhe, G. (2007). The Cognitive Process of Decision Making. *Journal of Cognitive Informatics and Natural Intelligence, 1*(2), 73–85.

Wellman, M. P., & Doyle, J. (1991). Preferential Semantics for Goals. *Proceedings of the 9th National Conference in Artificial Intelligence*, 698–703.

Wolf, J., Borges, M., Marques, J. L., & Castro, E. (2019). Smarter Decisions for Smarter Cities: Lessons Learned from Strategic Plans. In C. Rego & M. I. Sánchez-hernández (Eds.), *New Paths of Entrepreneurship Development: The Role of Education, Smart Cities and Social Factors* (pp. 7–30). Springer. doi:10.1007/978-3-319-96032-6_2

Wrona, T., Ladwig, T., & Gunnesch, M. (2013). Socio-cognitive processes in strategy formation - A conceptual framework. *European Management Journal*, *31*(6), 697–705. doi:10.1016/j.emj.2013.07.005

Zinkhan, G. M., & Braunsberger, K. (2004). The complexity of consumers' cognitive structures and its relevance to consumer behavior. *Journal of Business Research*, *57*(6), 575–582. doi:10.1016/S0148-2963(02)00396-X

KEY TERMS AND DEFINITIONS

Decision Heuristics: The rational and logical shortcuts used as decision rules while assessing aspects of complex problems during decision-making processes.

Social Representations: Shared knowledge resulting from the intervention of social regulations in cognitive functioning.

Socio-Cognitive Structures: The organization of cognitive frameworks, which explains the integration of individual perceptions into more complex networks embedded in social and collective contexts.

Chapter 22
Neuromarketing as an Environmental Awareness Tool:
The Sustainable Consumption

Alexandre Silva de Quevedo
Universidade Federal do Rio Grande do Sul, Brazil

Daniela Müller Quevedo
Feevale University, Brazil

Paola Schmitt Figueiró
Feevale University, Brazil

Elissa Kerli Fernandes
Universidade Federal do Rio Grande do Sul, Brazil

ABSTRACT

One of the greatest concerns of the last century is that human activities can extinguish the living conditions on the planet. In order for the technological and business advancement to be rational and environmentally sustainable in all areas of human knowledge, changes in paradigms must be made. To understand where these habits/paradigms originate from, how they are established, and how they can be altered, the field of neuroscience may be an excellent ally. Neuromarketing is a branch of neuroscience research still under development, using technologies already applied in neuroscience to product marketing. Therefore, the present study aims to conceptualize neuromarketing as a possible tool for sustainable consumption. In summary, this chapter presents a critical review of the main studies conducted by researchers in the last decade related to the theme of sustainable consumption associated with neuromarketing. The present findings may help to identify priority areas related to conscious consumption and neuromarketing.

DOI: 10.4018/978-1-7998-3115-0.ch022

Copyright © 2020, IGI Global. Copying or distributing in print or electronic forms without written permission of IGI Global is prohibited.

INTRODUCTION

In general, the growing social and ecological awareness of society is influencing citizens, as consumers, to understand the relevance of environmental management and sustainability actions. There is a need to transform consumption into an attitude that is perceived as an engagement in preserving the planet's sustainability and environmental quality. This engagement results in a better quality of life for all people and the planet at large.

In this scenario, for a better acceptance of a product at all levels, in addition to the product quality, the companies must show an attitude towards environmental responsibility, which is necessary to achieve consumers' growing ecological awareness (Bauer, 2011). Currently, transparency and concrete attitudes are considered relevant when consumers evaluate a company. These factors indicate that companies do not just have "green marketing propaganda" and are not greenwashed. In this regard, actions aiming at understanding the behavior and perception of this new green consumer are essential. Those new postures may guide market strategies for the company and, also, for its disclosure as a socially engaged company integrated with the communities in which it operates. Furthermore, those companies can be seen as having a sustainable development and the well-being of all.

In order to understand the green consumer behavior, few studies have been conducted using neuroscience techniques (Lee, 2014; Oliveira, 2014; Balconi, 2019). A large amount of data showing brain areas activated when subjects are exposed to goods (e.g., food and clothing) and leisure activities, instead, studies evaluating cerebral activation in the presence of environmental elements, and their assessments are exiguous. In this line of study, Khaw et al. (2015) evaluated how people would evaluate environmental factors compared to other products assessment. Given that the environment has no market price, the authors evaluated which brain regions are activated when subjects were required to evaluate environmental resources or consumer goods. Data showed that there is no brain activation at environmental valuation, unlike other goods, even if one were willing to pay more for environmental goods than for consumer goods. This study demonstrated that the mechanisms used to value natural goods might differ from those that value other market goods. Therefore, these results indicated the importance of conducting studies relating to marketing and neuroscience, also called neuromarketing, to better understand human consumption behavior (Silva, 2019).

Neuromarketing is a branch of neuroscience research that is still under development and use technologies, already applied in neuroscience, to product marketing. In this interdisciplinary field, it has been sought to understand and investigate consumer behavior through the study of the brain (BERCEA, 2013). Employing qualitative and quantitative approaches, neuromarketing aims to address some limitations of conventional marketing studies (BERCEA, 2013), such as low accuracy and behavioral biases (GREEN; SRINIVASAN, 1990).

It is believed that consumers do not directly express their preferences for marketed products. Thus, the use of neuromarketing can help to identify feelings, afflictions and conflicts present during evaluations and decision-making regarding a product. Through brain activity, areas and even cortical / subcortical circuits can be identified. Part of the human brain has already been mapped, so the triggering of neuronal activity during product exposure or the need to decide which one to acquire (i.e. green vs. regular product) may indicate the types of thoughts that guide human behavior (ARIELY; BERNS, 2010).

Willingness-to-pay reflects the measure of financial resources that the consumer is willing to give for an object for sale (MATTOS; MATTOS, 2004). But how does our brain compute this value?

Using functional magnetic resonance imaging (fMRI), it is possible to observe the correlation between activity levels in the medial orbitofrontal cortex (mOFC) and the dorsolateral prefrontal cortex (DLPFC) with the amount that consumers are willing to pay for a given object. This decision considers the benefits that it can generate. The mOFC receives extensive sensory information (REMPEL-CLOWER, 2007) and is involved with emotional aspects of behavior and DLPFC has a central integrative function for motor control and behavior (LU; PRESTON; STRICK, 1994). The connectivity of these regions suggests that economic values can be computed first in mOFC for evaluation, and then passed to DLPFC to influence motor commands (PLASSMANN; O'DOHERTY; RANGEL, 2007).

By associating neuroimaging tools with methods such as eye tracking, it is possible to study human behavior, perceptions and attitudes towards green products, based on the environmental sustainability concepts. In this way, would it be possible to predict and even stimulate certain attitudes related to more conscious consumption using neuromarketing strategies? To answer this research question, this study, through a systematic review, selected scientific articles that focused on neuromarketing and sustainable consumption research. Therefore, the present article aimed to identify and assess neuroscience tools applied to marketing that can be associated with sustainable consumption, and the development of consumer awareness strategies towards environmental sustainability. The term environmental sustainability was inserted in the research because its concept defines the way people act in the use of natural resources and provides solutions to his needs, and others, so as not to harm the natural environment and ensure its use for future generations. This chapter is structured to present a literature review covering the key concepts of neuromarketing, sustainable consumption, and green consumers, the research methods used for the study, followed by the analysis and discussion of the main articles listed.

MAIN FOCUS OF THE CHAPTER

Environmental Sustainability

From the large conferences held by the United Nations (UN) on the environment since the 1970s, when environmental problems grew in scale, much has evolved on the theme, starting with conceptual definitions considered fundamental for alignment and understandings about sustainable development. The term "Sustainable Development" emerged in 1980 and was consecrated in 1987 by the World Commission on Environment and Development in the Brundtland Report, also known as Our Common Future, published in 1988. This report was characterized by its definition and the principles that underlie it. The best-known concepts of sustainable development are present in the report, published by the UN (1988):

I) This is a new type of development, that is able to maintain human progress not only in some regions and for some years, but all over the planet and even the distant future;

II) It is one that meets the needs of the present without compromising the ability of future generations to meet their own needs;

III) In summary, sustainable development is a process of transformation in which the exploitation of resources, the direction of investments, the orientation of technological development and institutional change are in harmony and reinforce the present and future potential in order to meet the needs and aspirations.

Therefore, sustainable development is a process of transformation in which the exploitation of resources, the direction of investments, the orientation of technological development, and institutional changes harmonize and strengthen the present and future potential to meet future needs and aspirations. Sustainable development can be seen in various discussions and optical, being guided by three major scientific paradigms that guide the philosophical basis of the discussions: Technocentrism, Ecocentrism and Sustencentrismo (GLADWIN et al., 1995).

The first step towards achieving sustainable development is to recognize that natural resources are finite, generating the ideal use of natural goods, with discretion and planning. From this idea, it is possible to trace a new model of economic development for humanity. At present, development is still confused with economic growth. Development depends on the increasing consumption of energy and natural resources, where economic activities and consumption behavior are encouraged to the detriment of natural resource depletion. In contrast, sustainable development is related to quality rather than quantity, with the reduction of the use of raw materials and products. This implies changes in consumption patterns and the level of environmental awareness of the population. Dobson (2007) states that considerations of environmental citizenship can drive a change in behavior toward sustainable development. Environmental citizenship works at a deeper level, asking people to reflect on attitudes that demonstrate their behavior toward the environment. This change in behavior is the main objective of most environmental policies as a sustainable development strategy.

Sustainable Consumption and Green Consumer

Sustainable consumption, conscious consumption, responsible consumption, green consumption are all variants of the same concept. The issue of the environmental impact of consumption was initially defined within the limits of the notion of "green consumption," focusing a little later on the so-called "sustainable consumption." Sustainable consumption can be conceptualized as a mode of consumption capable of ensuring not only the satisfaction of the needs of present generations but also of future generations. This means opting for the consumption of goods produced with technology and materials less offensive to the environment, rational use of consumer goods, avoiding waste and excess, and after consumption, taking care that any residues do not cause degradation to the environment. Sustainable consumption is mainly associated with actions to review unsustainable consumption patterns and reduce social inequalities. Simple and everyday activities such as "shopping," basic goods or luxury items, began to be seen as behaviors and choices that affect the quality of the environment (PORTILHO, 2005). Conscious, well-informed, and concerned about environmental issues appear as a new strategy for changes towards a more sustainable society (HALKIER, 1999; PAAVOLA, 200).

Within the sustainability approach, the green consumer was broadly defined as one that, besides the quality/price variable, includes in its purchase choice, the environmental variable, preferring products that do not harm or are perceived as non-aggressive to the environment. Individual actions and choices motivated by environmental concerns have come to be seen as essential, and the consumer as the responsible, through their daily demands and choices, for changes in the energy and technological matrices of the production system (PORTILHO, 2005).

Ecological behaviors are undoubtedly complex and involve a variety of factors that influence purchasing behavior. These factors can be internal (e.g., attitudes, concerns, and values) and even external factors (PAÇO et al., 2018). Green consumption values are closely related to the appropriate use of environmental resources and personal property. Therefore, both the tendency to use financial resources prudently (frugality, value and price awareness, self-control of spending) and the tendency to consciously use physical resources (frugality, innovative use, product retention trend) positively correlate with the values of Green consumption. Greener consumers show not the only concern for environmental resources, but also personal resources, indicating the need to focus on personal aspects and the economic well-being of individuals. Understanding the impact of green consumption values on consumer behavior is therefore crucial, as an increasing number of companies focus on products and processes designed to minimize environmental damage. This concept can also be of high relevance to researchers and marketers interested in understanding how it shapes and impacts consumer responses to environmentally-based marketing campaigns and actions, including responses to green marketing communications (SHETH et al., 2011; HAWS et al., 2014; BAILEY et al., 2016; PAÇO et al., 2018).

In order to understand consumer behavior, neuromarketing appears as a new emerging and multidisciplinary method that encompasses neuroscience, psychology, and consumer behavior. Many companies have used neuromarketing to define marketing strategies, evaluating variables such as persuasion, novelty, and attention. In meanwhile, over the last decades, there has been a growing concern about the environment. Terms such as sustainability and sustainable development have become commonplace (SILVA, 2018). Businesses and governments have increasingly invested in environmental sustainability policies and strategies and how to convey this message to their audience. Nevertheless, there are still barriers related to these communication tools, making clear the need for further studies to better understand this green consumer interface and to identify the best ways to communicate with the population in order to implement an idea or concept.

The Neuromarketing

Neuromarketing is a branch of neuroscience research still under development that uses technologies already applied in the neuroscience field and now used to product marketing. Through both a qualitative and quantitative approach, one of the neuromarketing goals is to reduce the limitations of conventional marketing study methods, such as low precision and cognitive biases (BERCEA, 2013). Another important neuromarketing aim is to understand how the brain works during of decision-making. Neuromarketing studies are still very recent, according to Fisher et al. (2010), they were first reported in 2002, in a press release from an Atlanta company called BrightHouse, which announced the creation of a business unit using functional magnetic resonance imaging (fMRI) for marketing studies.

The knowledge in neuromarketing is useful to understand how consumers subjectively evaluate brands and products, not only for what they say but for what they feel. Because consumers, usually, do not fully express their preferences due to different factors (e.g. employee/employer relationship, politically correct issues), the use of neuromarketing can help to show hidden brain information that shows their true preferences. This information, theoretically, can be used to influence buying behavior (ARIELY; BERNS, 2010). For example, willingness-to-pay reflects the measure of financial resources the consumer is willing to give for an object for sale (MATTOS; MATTOS, 2004). Using fMRI, it is possible to observe the correlation between the activity levels in brain cognitive areas such as the medial orbitofrontal cortex (mOFC) and the dorsolateral prefrontal cortex (DLPFC) with the value that consumers are willing to pay for a given object considering the benefit that it can generate.

With the advancement of technology, such as neuroimaging techniques, it was possible to develop neuromarketing tests that are able to obtain "raw information" even before they become a perception/response. These imaging techniques can predict behavior and measure motivational (conscious and unconscious) and emotional information. Undoubtedly, imaging tests identify brain areas that are on (activated) or off (deactivated) in the presence of a given stimulus (e.g., jewelry), but the interpretation of these brain activity changes requires a human been (i.e., neuroscientist (COLAFERRO; CRESCITELLI, 2014).

The methods used in neuromarketing research can be divided into those that record the metabolic activity and those that record electrical activity in the brain, as follows:

The functional magnetic resonance imaging (fMRI): This neuroimaging technique is used to measure brain activity in response to different stimuli. It can be employed to identify activated areas and look for patterns as subjects experience marketing scenarios (BERCEA, 2013).

FMRI has a substantial advantage in resolving small and deep structures in the brain. However, some critical brain regions are affected by signal artifacts that may reduce the ability to obtain useful information (ARIELY; BERNS, 2010). This technique can be applied at different stages of marketing during the product development cycle. Firstly, analysis of activated brain regions can aid the design process itself, where neural responses can enhance the product before it is released. Secondly, fMRI can be used after the final product design, where neural responses are used in the advertising company to increase sales (ARIELY; BERNS, 2010).

Using the positron emission tomography (PET), Radioactive tracers (biological compound of interest labelled with a positron-emitting isotope) are administered to the subjects (BERCEA, 2013). Part of these radioactive isotopes will decay, and high-energy gamma-quants are formed. PET picks up these gamma-quants, and forms three-dimensional images, allowing examination of brain functions in vivo. This non-invasive technique may quantify cerebral blood flow, metabolism, and receptor binding. The spatial resolution by a PET scan is relatively high. However, it has a low temporal resolution (i.e., several minutes) (KENNING; PLASSMANN, 2005).

In the **Electroencephalography (EEG),** electrodes are placed on the scalp in certain areas to measure and record the electricity of superficial layers of the cortex. Through this technique, brain wave amplitudes are recorded, which correspond to certain mental states, such as wakefulness (beta waves), relaxation (alpha waves), calmness (theta waves) and sleep (delta waves) (BERCEA, 2013). The EEG has little sensitivity to deep brain structures (ARIELY; BERNS, 2010).

To apply the **Magnetoencephalography** (MEG), magnetic potentials are used to record brain activity at the scalp level. The magnetic field is not influenced by the type of tissue (blood, brain matter, bones); it can indicate the depth of localization in the brain with high spatial and temporal resolution. Compared to EEG, MEG is more sensitive to superficial cortical signals (mainly in the grooves) (ARIELY; BERNS, 2010).

The **transcranial magnetic stimulation** (TMS) utilizes magnetic induction to modulate the activity of specific brain areas located 1 to 2 centimeters inside without reaching the neocortex. The new TMS technology also allows the experimenter to reach lower brain areas. Furthermore, TMS can be easier to be applied because it is cheaper than PET or fMRI scanners. TMS discharges a magnetic field that passes through the brain, allowing to make changes to the neuronal tissues at specific locations. Using this mechanism, TMS is able to, temporarily, activate neurons (using high frequency) or disable neuronal activity (low frequency). TMS is able to highlight causal inferences by analyzing the subject exposed to a marketing stimulus, while some brain regions are deactivated, stimulated, or is not altered (BERCEA, 2013). As a research tool, TMS has been used to study the causal role of specific brain regions in different tasks, temporarily leaving them “offline” (i.e., deactivated) (ARIELY; BERNS, 2010).

The following methods can be used in association with the neuroimaging tools described above for more information and internal validation in the studies.

Eye Tracking allows to study behavior and cognition without measuring brain activity using different parameters. For example, using this method, the experimenter will be able to evaluate the spatial area where the subject is looking, for how long he is looking, the subject's path of vision, and changes in pupil dilation as the subject observes a given stimulus. It allows measuring the focus of attention and thus monitoring the types of behavior. Eye movements fall into two categories: fixations and saccades. Fixation occurs when eye movement pauses in one position, and the saccades are a change to another position. The resulting series of fixations and saccades is called the sweep path and is used in visual analysis perception, cognitive intent, interest, and context relevance. The Eye Tracking provides more accurate information than self-report, as research shows that the "claimed view" is not always the same as the "actually measured view."

The **response time measurement (RTM)** is the amount of time between stimulus appearance and response from the subject. This informs researchers about the complexity of the stimulus to an individual and how the subject relates to it. This inexpensive method can be used in recall studies or in measuring a subject's attitude toward certain stimuli.

Different Brain Information Techniques: The most efficient way to conduct neuromarketing studies is to use fMRI because of its ability to image changes in blood flow in the brain. While EEG, MEG, and other research methods reveal information about how the brain is functioning, measured outside the skull, fMRI reflects processes within the brain. MEG has excellent temporal resolution and better spatial resolution than EEG. However, MEG is limited to capturing activities on the surface of the brain. The fMRI modality is based on the use of an MRI scanner to image the changing blood flow in the brain. This procedure makes it possible to evaluate areas of the subject's brain that receive the most blood flow by experiencing a specific stimulus compared to rest time. FMRI has the great advantage that it can identify deep brain structures, especially those involved in emotional responses (Morin, 2011).

Heinonen (2018) reports a disadvantage of using fMRI to measure brain activity. According to him, participants can not stay long inside the magnetic resonance tube and, therefore, it is necessary to improve the methodology to shorten the research. Another disadvantage of fMRI that can be observed is the high cost of the equipment and its use.

According to Colaferro and Crescitelli (2014), the application of neuroscience in marketing investigations adds a new approach to marketing studies. The use of neuroscience offers the possibility of obtaining results from individuals' responses to positive and negative emotions, which can increase understanding of the unconscious and the mind, reducing uncertainties in the results of stated responses. Neuroscience can bring gains in its complementary use to other methods of collecting information, highlighting a new source that can bring different perspectives of information about the study of consumer behavior.

However, there is a need for further research on this subject, as it involves areas that have only recently been explored by science, that is, basic knowledge about brain functioning and its possible correlations with human behavior. Neuromarketing can be particularly beneficial for research where there is a disconnect between consumer knowledge and their real choice, such as green consumer behavior. Studying green consumer behavior can be considered problematic when using current research due to the difference between environmental perception and actual pro-environmental behavior (LEE et al., 2014).

In this case, Neuromarketing can contribute to the understanding of consumer behavior, making the difference between just a sustainable ideological positioning and genuinely sustainable consumption behavior. This understanding can help in creating more efficient pro-environmental marketing tools that also act as consumer environmental awareness.

Methodology of the Study

In this article, a qualitative research approach was used to analyze studies published in scientific journals that address the theme of Neuromarketing and sustainable consumption. This study applied the three-level methodological approach described by Zaman (2015), and these levels are described as Identification, Classification, and Evaluation. The study used as source the main databases available for the identification of relevant academic literature. The research listed the number of available literature for each defined keyword and the combination of these keywords. Then the available literature for the combination of keywords was initially critically evaluated by reading the abstract, followed by the complete content of the document.

A detailed description of the articles evaluated in this study is provided in Appendix 1.

Identification of studies in Neuromarketing, Sustainable Consumption and Environmental Sustainability

The study applied a screening procedure to identify relevant research papers in scientific journals focusing on neuromarketing and sustainable consumption. At this identification stage, the study used the Scopus and Scielo Databases as a search tool. Subsequently, given the limited number of scientific articles available on these bases for the crossover of keywords defined for the study, it was extended to Google Scholar. The study considered as keywords: Neuromarketing, Sustainable Consumption, and Environmental Sustainability.

The period considered for the research was from 2009 to 2019. To be considered for analysis, the articles should be published in scientific journals and resulting from a combination of the word Neuromarketing and, at least, one of the other words considered in the bibliographical search.

After compiling all results from the selected banks for screening and excluding repetitions, a total of 24 peer-reviewed journal publications were identified for classification and evaluation. Any publications other than articles published in scientific journals, publications in non-open journals, and articles in which the keywords were identified only in the bibliographic references were excluded from the selection.

Classification and evaluation of selected studies

The research identified the following six criteria for classifying selected studies: (1) date of publication, (2) geographic location of the study, (3) grouped keywords, (4) main research area, and (5) study extension regarding the concepts of Neuromarketing, Sustainable Consumption, and Environmental Sustainability.

The study assessed the relevance and scope of studies based on (1) only the use of neuromarketing and sustainable consumption terminology, (2) use of neuromarketing and sustainable consumption terminology without relationship, (3) use of neuromarketing and sustainable consumption terminology with a partial explanation, and (4) use of neuromarketing and sustainable consumption terminology, with a considerable amount of discussion and association.

The discussion regarding neuromarketing as a tool for sustainable consumption was held considering only the articles that used in their theme the three key words established in this research, and a broad analysis between the themes.

Results and Discussion

The present work shows results obtained through studies that address the theme of neuromarketing, sustainable consumption, and environmental sustainability. Moreover, other factors were evaluated such as date of publication, journals, authors' country of origin, a combination of keywords, and study extension concerning concepts of Neuromarketing, Environmental Sustainability and Sustainable Consumption and main area of research. The following sections present the main results of this review study, and a discussion using the articles that covered all the keywords listed, including broad discussion and establishment of relationships between the themes.

The Contextual Settings

The number of publications each year related to the proposed theme was evaluated from 2009 to 2019. During this period it is possible to identify that in the last 4 years there has been an increase of publications addressing the themes Neuromarketing, Environmental Sustainability, and Sustainable Consumption, with a highlight for 2015 with 21% (5) of the publications. Between 2015 and 2019 there are 71% of the publications of the last decade. These data highlights the innovation of this theme. Furthermore, the lack of information in this area is evidenced by the small number of publications found in the main databases and its concentration in the last years of analysis (Figure 1).

Figure 1. Distribution of papers by year

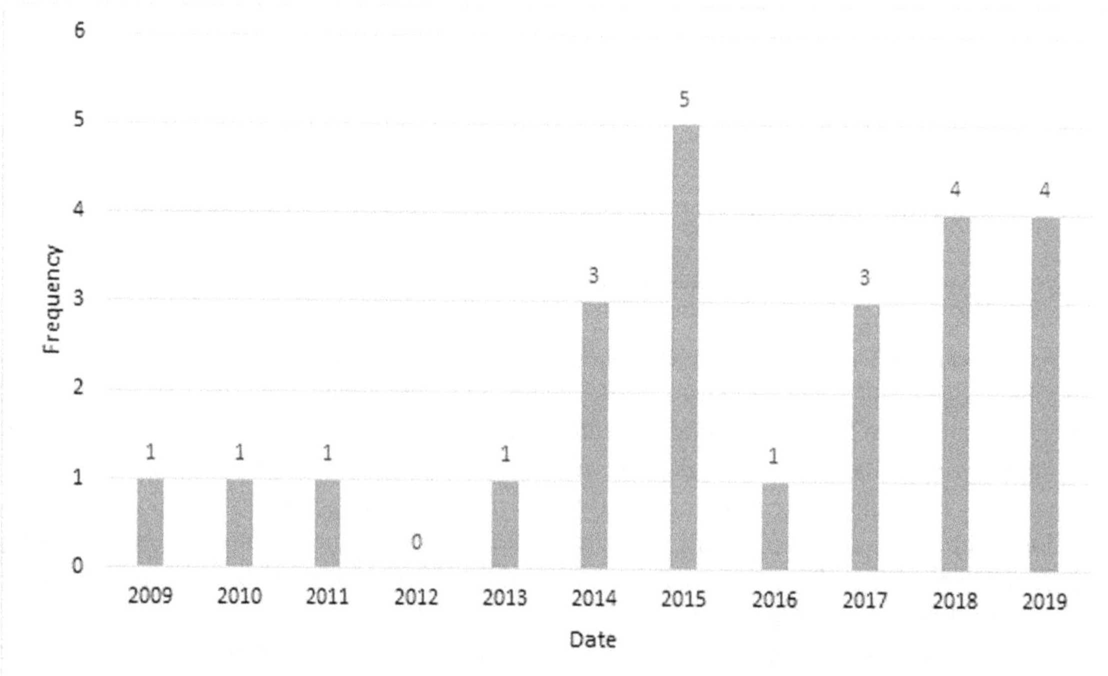

Table 1 presents the distribution of the number of publications among the journals. The studies on Neuromarketing, Environmental Sustainability and Sustainable Consumption have been published in a wide range of journals, not being possible to highlight one journal.

Table 1. Distribution of the number of publications among Periodicals

Journals	Frequency
AI & Society	1
Apettite	1
Bhavan's International Journal of Business	1
Brazilian Journal Science Technology	1
Designing Sustainable Technologies, Products and Policies	1
Ecological Indicators	1
European Journal of Business Science and Technology	1
Global Business and Management Research: an International Journal	1
Global Journal of Commerce & Menagement Perspective	1
Human Computation	1
IFAC	1
International Rev Public Nonprofit Mark	1
International Journal of Business Management	1
International Journal of Research in Marketing	1
Journal Business Ethics	2
Journal of Advertising Research	1
Journal of Retailing and Consumer Service	1
Journal of Research in Interactive Marketing	1
Latin American Journal Management for Sustainable Development	1
Philos. Technology	1
Physiology & Behavior	1
Problems of Sustainable Development	1
Sustainability	1
Total Geral	24

The theme of Neuromarketing and sustainable consumption is present in almost all continents. Figure 2 shows that the geographical distribution of publications covers 18 countries. The United States of America and Australia reported 5 and 4 studies related to the theme, respectively. These countries have more publications at this period, followed by India and Brazil, both with 3 studies. The American and European countries contributed most of the research in this area. These data indicate that studies using Neuromarketing as a tool for sustainable consumption have not yet been documented in a large number of countries around the world.

Figure 2. Geographical distribution

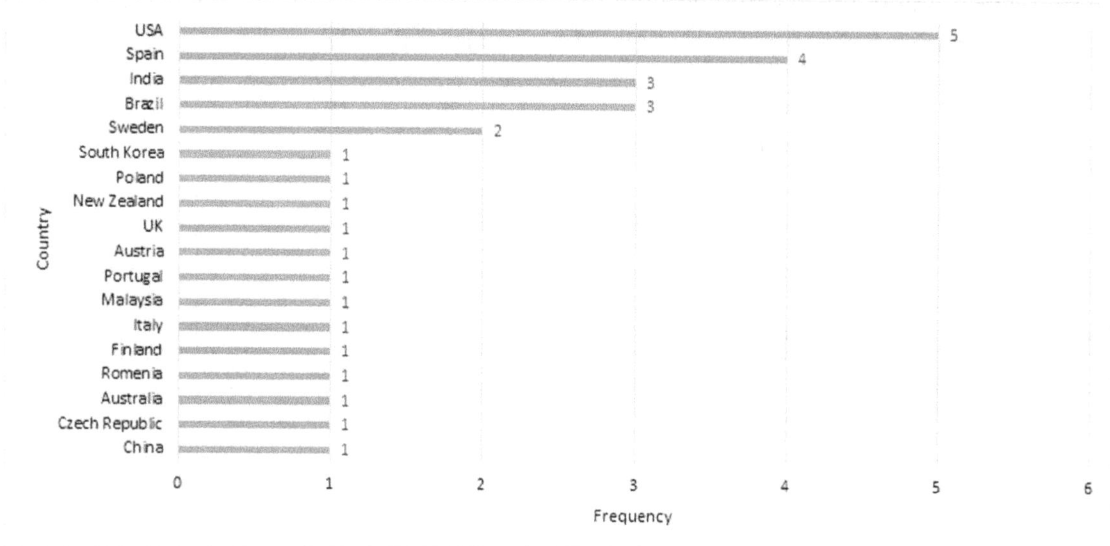

Table 2 presents the number of articles found with the keyword combinations established in the study methodology. Among the 24 papers selected, only 8 included, in their theme, the 3 established keywords. The lowest frequency observed was for the combination between Neuromarketing and sustainable consumption, with seven studies listed.

Table 2. Number of articles found with keyword combinations

Keyword Combination	Frequency
Neuromarketing and sustainable consumption (1)	7
Neuromarketing and Environmental Sustainability (2)	9
Neuromarketing and Environmental Sustainability and Sustainable Consumption (3)	8
Total	24

The articles were analyzed in relation to the extension of the study considering the concepts of Neuromarketing, Environmental Sustainability and Sustainable Consumption. Through the classification and evaluation step, it was possible to identify that only 25% (6) of these articles had a consistent discussion of neuromarketing as a tool for sustainable consumption, and not merely using the terminology and its descriptions (Figure 3). All six (6) articles considered in their theme the three key words established in this research, and will be discussed in more depth.

Figure 4 presents the distribution of articles by the year and by the extension of the study in relation to the concepts of Neuromarketing, Environmental Sustainability and sustainable consumption. It is identified that articles that use of terminology with broad discussion and relationship building (4) appear only from the year 2014. This demonstrates the advance of discussion and understanding of the theme over time and the possibility of using neuromarketing tools environmentally friendly.

Figure 3. Study scope

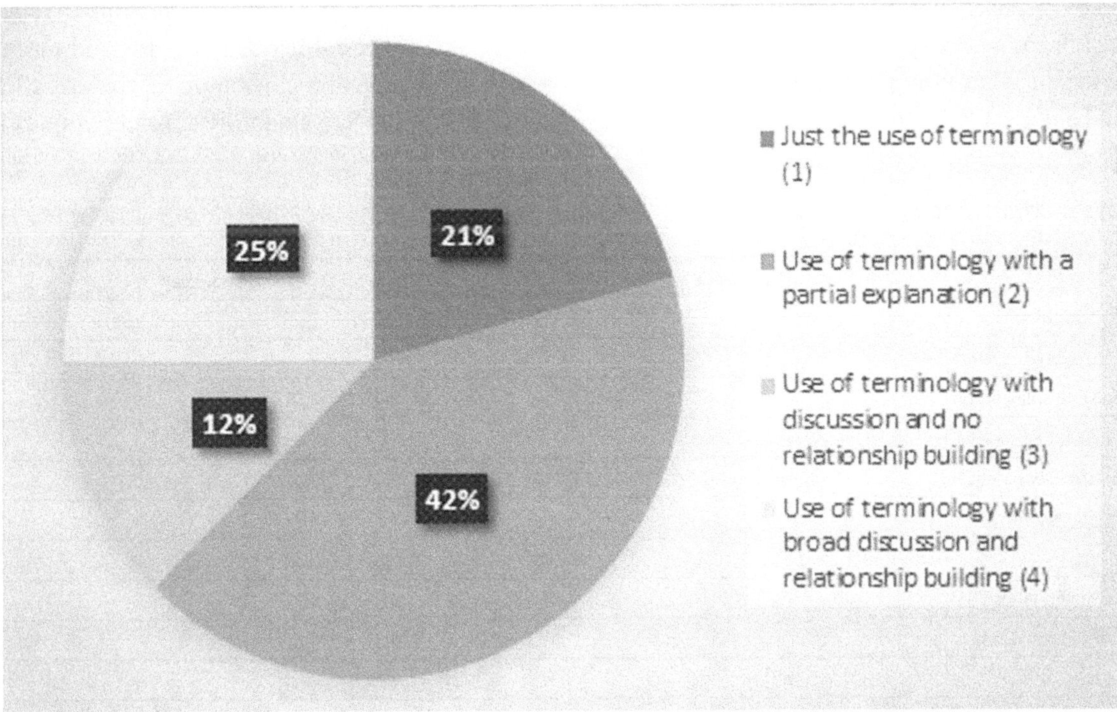

Figure 4. Distribution of articles by year and by study extension

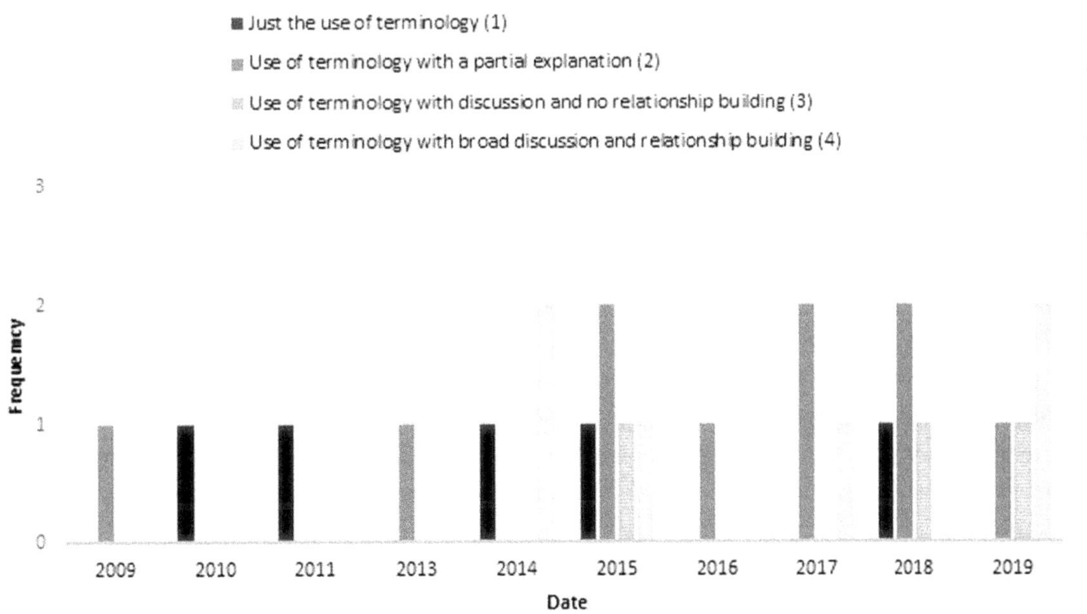

Through the data presented in table 3, it is possible to identify the concentration of the articles evaluated by research area. Food/drinks (5), Technology / Innovation (4), and Global Sustainability (3) stand out. For the seven (7) articles that used in their scope the three (3) established keywords and made a consistent relationship between neuromarketing as a tool for sustainable consumption, the areas that stand out are: Green consumers (2), Eco-friendly products (2), Global Sustainability (2) and Fashion (1).

Table 3. Main area of research

Main area of research	Frequency
Food / drinks	5
Technology/Inovation	4
Global Sustainability	3
Behavior and society	2
Eco-friendly products	2
Green consumers	2
Fashion	2
Consumer duties/Law	1
Ethics and consumer	1
Industry	1
Services	1
Total	24

Neuromarketing as a Tool for Sustainable Consumption

This chapter discusses the main tools and conclusions obtained in the articles where it was possible to identify in their scope the use of the three (3) keywords considered in this study and where a consistent relationship between neuromarketing as a tool for sustainable consumption is made. Through the 6 (six) articles that address Neuromarketing and Environmental Sustainability and Sustainable Consumption and that present a complete discussion relating these themes, it is possible to contextualize the advance of knowledge in the area. The studies discussed here were prepared by Lee et al. (2014), Fiestas et al. (2015), Balconi et al. (2019), Saczina (2019), Guyader et al. (2016) and Oliveira (2014).

Many sustainable consumption studies aim to identify consumer actions, emotions, and individual choices motivated by environmental concerns. As described by Lindstrom (2008), consumers can by no means express something that they really think consciously. Reactions and emotions are found in the brain in a short time and not consciously so that they can be translated into words described in a questionnaire. In this sense, Fiestas et al. (2015) present a study with a psychophysiological approach to measure the response to messages of how consumers emotionally process Green Advertising. Among the main results presented by the authors are: a) "Differences in the way people process emotions depend on the combination of elements used in the design of green advertising messages", b) "Messages designed with positive outcome (pleasurable outcome), and c) "a final-gain frame (emphasis on benefit versus cost) are more effective than those designed with negative valence and final-loss frame when trying to encourage environmentally friendly actions on the part of the consumer".

Fiestas et al. (2015) suggest further studies to help create advertising campaigns that encourage sustainable consumption. The authors suggest that this strategy is most effective by providing evidence on what type of stimulus is most effective in triggering emotions that inspire real behavioral changes. Figure 5 presents the methodological design used in the study by Fiestas et al. (2015).

Figure 5. Characteristics of the Designed Stimuli (Adapted from Fiestas et al, 2015)

Designed Stimuli	Positive/Gain Message ("PGM")	Negative/Loss Message ("NLM")	Neutral Message ("NM")
Valence	Positive	Negative	Neutral
End-State	Gain	Loss	
Objective	Intrinsic		
Assertiveness	Nonassertive Message		
Focus	Consequences for the receptor and for third parties		
Spatial Horizon	Distant and nearby problems		
Time Horizon	Future consequences		
Images	Images of nature and society		
Tone	Emotional		

According to the studies listed, it is possible to identify that emotion and affect influence decision making and may have high relevance in studies that require decision making with environmental bias. Neuromarketing supports existing theories by highlighting why human decisions are not always rational. In this way, it is possible to identify the potential of neuromarketing as a tool for sustainable decision making.

An example of a well-established relationship between neuromarketing and sustainable consumption is presented by Lee et al. (2014). Using Electroencephalogram (EEG), in this paper the authors propose a study to analyze how frontal brain area activations can identify the green consumer. EEG is an option for assessing brain electrical activity, with reduced cost compared to fMRI cited by Oliveira (2014). Lee et al. (2014) propose to answer the following research questions: Is there a pattern of EEG theta activities, particularly in the frontal cortex, which is associated with "green message processing" influencing purchasing behavior? Also, "Are the EEG signals of green consumers dependent on a task phase? Specifically, are green consumers' theta rhythms uniquely distinct only during the phase of green message processing, but not distinct during the phase of price information processing? "

Through a survey of 90 students, Lee et al. (2014) presented a neuromarketing study using the electroencephalogram (EEG), which directly records the distinctive activities of green consumers' front brain waves when processing green marketing messages. The subjects surveyed were taken to an EEG lab where they should sit in a comfortable chair made to place their chin on a chin rest. The experimental stimulus was presented on a computer monitor screen, located 30 centimeters from the interviewee's seat. The consumer product used in the experiment was a travel mug, featuring written descriptions without a visual representation, such as a text ad. Two versions of the ad were developed: one for green product option, and the other for standard product option. Respondents were given the task of reading the messages from both alternatives and selecting one of the products to purchase. Schemes of the experimental design are represented in figure 6.

Figure 6. Experiment EEG Scheme (Adapted from Lee et al, 2014)

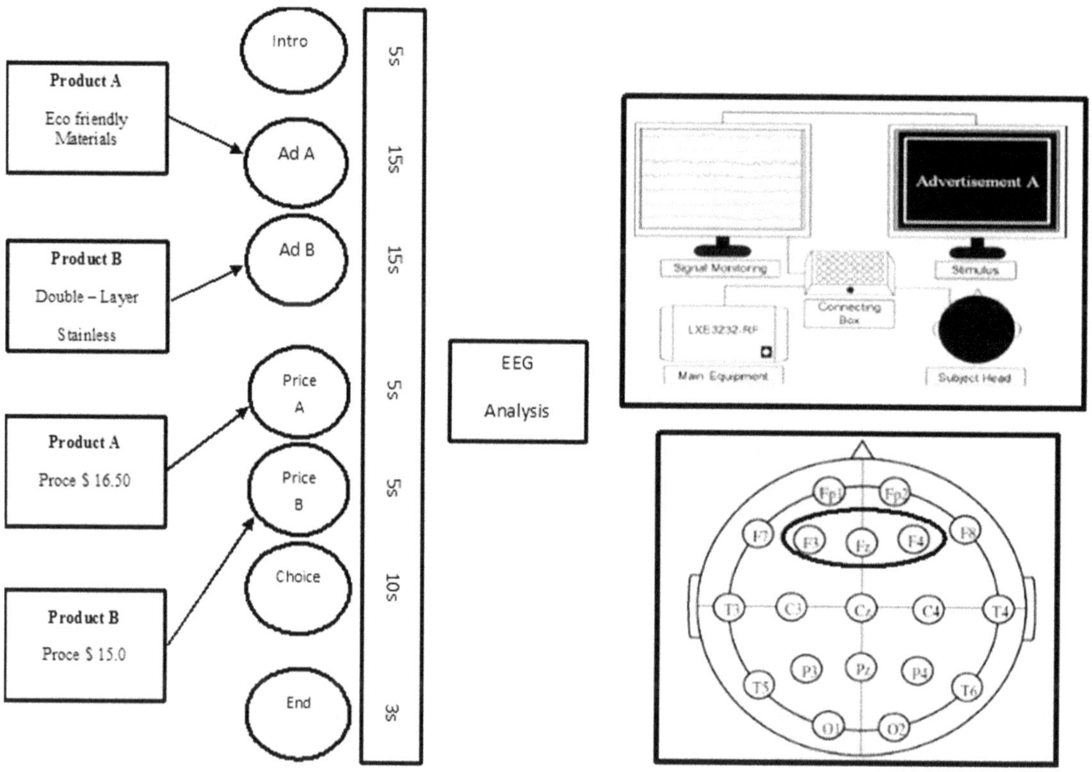

Lee et al. (2014) conclude that there is evidence that consumers who are governed by a high-order consumption goal called "green consumers" show distinct brainwave responses. "Green consumers" showed increased electrical activity in the frontal brain region in response to green products compared to non-green consumers. According to Silva (2018), in addition to these brain activity measurement techniques, it is possible to measure skin conductance, sweat rate, eye and pupillary movement, rate of neurotransmitters and hormones in the blood. The administration of these neurotransmitters also allows observing the changes generated. These methodologies make it possible to answer other questions of human behavior that do not have to go through brain processing directly.

Following the line of consumption patterns and EEG electroencephalogram changes the authors Balconi et al. (2019) present a study that aimed to deepen the understanding of luxury consumers' implicit intentions towards sustainability using a neuroscientific approach applied to the fashion domain luxurious. The authors also worked with a sample of individuals classified as "sustainable" and "unsustainable", where they were asked to observe a set of 10 stimuli representing environmental sustainability issues and then interact with a vendor while EEG recorded their cortical activity. Balconi et al. (2019)

observed higher levels of beta, delta, and theta waves in temporoparietal areas compared to fronto-central waves in sustainable consumers. However, unsustainable consumers had specific activation of the right temporoparietal theta band in similar situations. Khaw et al. (2015) in their environmental valuation study corroborates the results of Balconi et al. (2019), identifying that brain activation at environmental valuation is different from what occurs with other goods, even if the consumer is willing to pay more for environmental goods than for consumer goods. Through this green consumer behavior identified by the authors, it is possible to formulate communication strategies to review unsustainable consumption patterns. Conscious, well-informed, and concerned about environmental issues appear as a new idea for changes towards a more sustainable society (PAAVOLA, 2000).

Saczina (2019) presents a study focused on incorporating the findings made in the field of neuroscience in the design of mass communication messages to promote more effective environmental sustainability. The author, through bibliographic research, concludes that the future of sustainability efforts must be approached systemically and holistically, and neuromarketing can be an excellent alternative tool for environmental problems. Advances in neuroimaging technology have led to an explosion in the number of studies investigating the human brain and discoveries made in the field of neuroscience must be incorporated into the mass communication process.

Guyader et al. (2016) address the theme of this study, presenting research entitled "You can't buy what you can't see: Retailer practices to Increase the premium green." The study is part of an eye-tracking experiment used to analyze the visual attention of 66 participants. These demonstrate that retailers can attract consumer visual attention and increase eco-award through a variety of practices, such as providing relevant information, and guiding consumers within the store and offering an eco-friendly product as a rating. Another relevant result presented by the authors deals with management implications, such as the use of green price tags to signal environmentally friendly products. These actions might prevent greenwashed practices that can distract consumers from finding green products. In this scenario, Bauer (2011) reports that a better acceptance of a product at all levels requires an attitude of environmental responsibility of the company to meet the growing ecological awareness of consumers. It is considered relevant transparency and the disclosure of concrete able to reveal that a company not only has a "green marketing" speech.

According to the analyzed literature, it is possible to use neuromarketing as a tool to promote sustainable consumption. Although research in the field of neuroscience has made significant advances in recent years, the techniques used in this area of research are still costly and unavailable to less developed countries. Evidence of this can be provided by the dominance of studies found in the US and European countries. An alternative to higher-cost equipment may be the EEG, presented by Balconi et al. (2019) and Lee et al. (2014). Another tool that can be very useful is eye-tracking, according to Mansor and Isa (2018) and Guyader et al. (2016). Therefore, it is possible to show the potential of neuromarketing to support existing theories, demonstrating how it is possible to explain the results on sustainable consumption behavior and to show why human decisions are not always rational (SILVA, 2018).

In contrast to the studies that report the advantages of neuromarketing in the evaluation of actions, perceptions, and strategies for sustainable consumption, research in Neuromarketing may also present certain disadvantages. One of the disadvantages is associated with the fMRI measurement procedure, where participants cannot stay in the magnetic resonance tube for a long time, and another disadvantage that can be observed concerning research using fMRI is the high cost of the equipment and its use Heinonen (2018). Relatated to this, Oliveira (2014) presents a conceptual study aiming to define neuromarketing and identify its potential for sustainability studies. The author provides essential information that structuring a neuromarketing laboratory is expensive and requires high investment. Some devices are much less common in Latin America than in developed countries. For example, fMRI is one of the most expensive equipment used in this type of study, and they are not common in Latin America. These devices, when they exist, are usually allocated solely for diagnostic purposes without room for research.

In general, neuroscience tools applied to the marketing are successful in assessing the perception of individuals, which can increase understanding of the human unconscious and reduce uncertainty in outcomes. The most accurate tool for this, according to the studies, is fMRI, but it also has research limitations. For example, there are a small number of individuals that can be evaluated in a single round of experiments. This can be a problem for surveys that require large samples. In these situations, we can highlight the EEG method, according to the studies presented by Lee et al. (2014) and Balconi et al. (2019). The EEG method proved to be efficient in evaluating the activation of different brain areas in several situations of choice and perception.

Neuroscience can bring significant gains and advances in research that relates marketing and sustainable consumption, in its complementary use to other methods of collecting information. Thus, it is undeniable that these methodologies may bring different perspectives of information on the study of green consumer behavior. The articles listed in this study successfully present the use of Neuromarketing to evaluate the real behavior of green consumers. However, assessments of which actions would be most efficient as neuromarketing techniques in raising consumer awareness towards more sustainable consumption are not yet identified in these studies. There is a need to advance research addressing the neuromarketing techniques listed here and also new methods to minimize the identified weaknesses and the establishment of practical actions with the consumer.

FUTURE RESEARCH DIRECTIONS

The findings of this study are essential for researchers who wish to develop and extend their research in a multi and interdisciplinary way relating the areas of Marketing, Neuroscience, and Environmental Sustainability. This is an innovative theme, having identified the main gaps and trends in the current research scenario related to the keywords considered in this study. Through the analysis of the main authors listed in the research, we suggest further studies to help create advertising campaigns that encourage sustainable consumption. That strategy is most effective by providing evidence on what kind of stimulus is most effective in triggering emotions that inspire real behavioral changes.

Another option to study human behavior is proposed by Silva (2018). Currently, EEG and fMRI are widely used to identify activated regions during a specific behavior or task. However, it is often not possible to state whether a particularly active region is critical to generating such behavior or if it is only part of a parallel-activated circuitry. Therefore, Silva (2018) suggests the use of transcranial magnetic stimulation (TMS) to help investigate central nervous system physiology. TMS can disable or activate brain areas and can test the function of that specific region during a given task.

Also, another approach to follow is the use of animal models that may provide other types of techniques and studies that are not possible or ethically feasible to be performed in humans. These studies are essential to elucidate several underlying neurophysiological mechanisms involved, for example, in behaviors such as the reward and decision-making process.

CONCLUSION

Based on the literature review, this study concludes that it is possible to use neuromarketing as a sustainable consumption tool. This systematic review has attempted to incorporate relevant research in the field of neuromarketing and its use as a tool for sustainable consumption in the last decade. Through chronological analysis, it is evident that these data highlight the innovation of this theme. Furthermore, the lack of information in this area is evidenced by the small number of publications found in the main databases and its concentration in the last years of analysis.

Also, the present work has identified several tools that are being used in this research field, such as eye-tracking, EEG, and fMRI. The studies also emphasize the importance of research ethics for studies that address the understanding and conditioning of human behavior. For example, some research has addressed the management implications of effectively flagging environmentally friendly products. This can prevent Greenwashed practices that can distract consumers from finding green products seeking.

Despite the neuroscience research in presenting significant advances in recent years, the techniques used in this research area are still expensive and are not available to less developed countries. Evidence of this can be provided by the dominance of studies found in the US and European countries. An alternative to higher-cost equipment may be EEG or the use of psychophysiological tests. For initial studies on neuromarketing and green consumer behavior, psychophysiological tests can be efficient and used as a research methodology in the thematic area addressed in this research.

REFERENCES

ACCENTURE. (2014). *Circular advantage: innovative business models and technologies to create value in a world without limits to growth.* Available at: www.accenture.com/t20150523T053139__w__/ us en/_acnmedia/Accenture/Conversion Assets/DotCom/Documents/Global/PDF/Strategy_6/ Accenture-Circular-Advantage-Innovative-Business-Models-Technologies-Value-Growth.pdf

Ariely, D., & Berns, G. S. (2010). Neuromarketing: The hope and hype of neuroimaging in business. *Nature Reviews. Neuroscience*, *11*(4), 284–292. doi:10.1038/nrn2795 PMID:20197790

Armstrong, C. M., Niinimäki, K., Kujala, S., Karell, E., & Lang, C. (2015). Sustainable product-service systems for clothing: Exploring consumer perceptions of consumption alternatives in Finland. *Journal of Cleaner Production*, *97*(June), 30–39. doi:10.1016/j.jclepro.2014.01.046

Bailey, A., Mishra, A., & Tiamiyu, M. (2016). GREEN consumption values and Indian consumers' response to marketing communications. *Journal of Consumer Marketing*, *3*(7), 562–573. doi:10.1108/ JCM-12-2015-1632

Balconi, M., Sebastiani, R., & Agioletti, L. (2019). Sensory marketing: Perspectives on benefits consumers'grapple in choosing greener products. *Global Journal of Commerce & Menagement Perspective*, *11*, 1–14.

Bauer, M. M. (2013). *Estudo Sobre a Evidenciação Ambiental e Social Voluntárias das Empresas de Capital Aberto em Relatórios Anuais*. Tese de Doutorado. Universidade Feevale.

Bercea, M. D. (2013). *Quantitative versus qualitative in neuromarketing research*. MPRA Paper No. 44134.

Bulz, A. C., Stapleton, A., Lewoc, B., & Bulz, N. (2015). On a Master-plan Towards a Cognitive Science Networking Religion, Conflict and Peacebuilding and Technology, Culture and International Stability. *IFAC*, *48*(24), 183–188. doi:10.1016/j.ifacol.2015.12.080

Colaferro, C. A., & Crescitelli, E. (2014). A contribuição do Neuromarketing para o Estudo do Comportamento do Consumidor. *Brazilian Business Review*, *11*(3), 130–153. doi:10.15728/bbr.2014.11.3.6

Dobson, A. (2007). Environmental citizenship: Towards sustainable development. *Sustainable Development*, *15*(5), 276–285. doi:10.1002d.344

Eglash, R., Robert, L., Bennett, A., Robinson, K. P., Lachney, M., & Babbitt, W. (2019). Automation for the Artisanal Economy: Enhancing the Economic and Environmental Sustainability of Crafting Professions with Human-Machine Collaboration. *AI & Society*. doi:10.100700146-019-00915-w

Fiala, J., Toufarová, I., Mokrý, S., & Souček, M. (2016). Perception of local food labelling by generation z:an eye-tracking experimente. *European Journal of Business Science and Technology*, *2*(2), 152–159. doi:10.11118/ejobsat.v2i2.65

Fiestas, M. M., Viedma, M. I., Fernández, J. S., & Rios, F. J. M. (2015). A Psychophysiological Approach For Measuring Response to Messaging How Consumers Emotionally Process Green Advertising. *Journal of Advertising Research*.

Fisher, C. E., & … . (2010). *Defining neuromarketing: practices and professional challenges*. Harvard Review Psychiatry Perspective.

Goyal, A. P., Bansal, S., & Srivastava, S. (2018). Sensory marketing: Perspectives on benefits consumers'grapple in choosing greener products. *Sustainability*, *7*, 61–73.

Green, P. E., & Srinivasan, V. (1990). Conjoint analysis in marketing: New developments with implications for research and practice. *Journal of Marketing*, *54*(4), 3–19. doi:10.1177/002224299005400402

Guyader, H., Ottosson, M., & Witell, L. (2016). You can't buy what you can't see: Retailer practices to increase the green premium. *Journal of Retailing and Consumer Services*, *34*, 319–325. doi:10.1016/j.jretconser.2016.07.008

HALKIER. (1999). B. Consequences of the politicization of consumption: The example of environmentally friendly consumption practices. *Journal of Environmental Policy and Planning*, (1): 25–41.

Haws, K. L., Winterich, K. P., & Naylor, R. W. (2014). Seeing the world through GREEN-tintedglasses: Green consumption values and responses to environmentally friendly products. *Journal of Consumer Psychology*, *24*(3), 336–354. doi:10.1016/j.jcps.2013.11.002

Heinonen, J. (2018). Conjoint fMRI method for shortening analysis time. *Cogent Psychology*, *5*(1), 1446254. doi:10.1080/23311908.2018.1446254

Huang, R., Lee, S. H., Kim, H. J., & Evans, L. (2015). The impact of brand experiences on brand resonance in multi-channel fashion retailing. *Journal of Research in Interactive Marketing*, *9*(2), 129–147. doi:10.1108/JRIM-06-2014-0042

Kenning, P., & Plassmann, H. (2005). NeuroEconomics: An overview from an economic perspective. *Brain Research Bulletin*, *67*(5), 343–354. doi:10.1016/j.brainresbull.2005.07.006 PMID:16216680

Khaw, M. W., Grab, D. A., Livermore, M. A., Vossler, C. A., & Glimcher, P. W. (2015). The measurement of subjective values and its relation to contigent valuation and environmental public goods. *PLoS One*, *10*, 7.

Larsen, G., & Lawson, R. (2013). Consumer Rights: An Assessment of Justice. *Journal of Business Ethics*, *112*(3), 515–528. doi:10.100710551-012-1275-9

Lee, E. J., Kwon, G., Shin, H. J., Yang, S., Lee, S., & Suh, M. (2014). The Spell of Green: Can Frontal EEG Activations Identify Green Consumers? *Journal of Business Ethics*, *122*(3), 511–521. doi:10.100710551-013-1775-2

Leiva, F. M., & Carmona, D. G. (2019). Sparking interest in restaurant dishes? Cognitive and affective processes underlying dish design and ecological origin. An fMRI study. *Physiology & Behavior*. PMID:29908937

Lindstrom, M. (2008). *Buyology: truth and lies abaut why we buy*. New York: Doubleday.

Lu, M. T., Preston, J. B., & Strick, P. L. (1994). Interconnections between the prefrontal cortex and the premotor areas in the frontal lobe. *Research Systems Neuroscience*, *V341*(3), 375–392. doi:10.1002/cne.903410308 PMID:7515081

Mansor, A. A. A., & Isa, S. M. (2018). The Impact of Eye Tracking on Neuromarketing for Genuine Value-Added Applications. *Global Business and Management Research*, *10*, 1–11.

Mattos, K. M. C., & Mattos, A. (2004). Valoração econômica do meio ambiente: uma abordagem teórica e prática. São Carlos: Editora Rima.

Michelfelder, D. P. (2011). Dirty Hands, Speculative Minds, and Smart Machines. *Philosophy & Technology*, *24*(1), 55–68. doi:10.100713347-010-0009-0

Morin, C. (2011). Neuromarketing: The new science of consumer behavior. *Society*, *48*(2), 131–135. doi:10.100712115-010-9408-1

Naganna, N., & Pankajakshi, R. (2019). Globalization & Marketing with Environmental Sustainability: A Holistic Resource-Centric Analysis with Reference to Corporatization. Bhavan's International. *The Journal of Business*, *2*, 3–50.

Oliveira, J. H. C. (2014). Neuromarketing and sustainability: Challenges and opportunities for Latin America. *Latin American Journal Management for Sustainable Development*, *1*(1), 35–42. doi:10.1504/LAJMSD.2014.059779

ONU. (1988). *Relatório Brundtland "Nosso Futuro Comum"*. Assembleia Geral da ONU.

Paavola, J. (2001). Economics, ethics and green consumerism. In Exploring sustainable consumption: Environmental policy ant the social sciences. Oxford: Elsevier Science.

Paço, A., Shiel, C., & Alves, H. (2018). A New Model for Testing Green Consumer Behaviour. *Journal of Cleaner Production*. doi:10.1016/j.jclepro.2018.10.105

Plassmann, H., O'Doherty, J., & Rangel, A. (2007). Orbitofrontal cortex encodes willingness to pay in everyday economic transactions. *The Journal of Neuroscience: The Official Journal of the Society for Neuroscience, 27*(37), 9984–9988. doi:10.1523/JNEUROSCI.2131-07.2007 PMID:17855612

Portilho, F., (2005). Consumo sustentável: limites e possibilidades de ambientalização e politização das práticas de consumo. *Cadernos EBAPE.BR – Edição Temática – FGV, 3*(3), 1 – 12.

Puska, P., Kurki, S., Lähdesmäki, M., Siltaoja, M., & Luomala, H. (2018). Sweet taste of prosocial status signaling: When eating organic foods makes you happy and hopeful. *Apettite., 121*(1), 348–359. doi:10.1016/j.appet.2017.11.102 PMID:29180074

Rempel-Clower, N. L. (2007). Role of orbitofrontal cortex connections in emotion. *Annals of the New York Academy of Sciences, 1121*(1), 72–86. doi:10.1196/annals.1401.026 PMID:17846152

Saczina, M. (2019). Neuroscience in Linguistic Patterns of Communication Campaigns for Environmental Sustainability. Designing Sustainable Technologies. *Products and Policies, 14*(1), 109–118.

Santos, R.O.J., Oliveira, J.H.C., Moura, J., Giraldi, E., & Bruno, A.R. (2015). *Public policies and selective visual attention: The effectiveness of awareness messages among young people about the consumption of alcoholic beverages in Brazil.* Academic Press.

Sharma, S. (2017). Innovation in Marketing. *International Journal of Business and Management, 3*, 1897–1912.

Sheth, J. N., Sethia, N. K., & Srinivas, S. (2011). Mindful consumption: A customer centric approach to sustainability. *Journal of the Academy of Marketing Science, 39*(1), 21–39. doi:10.100711747-010-0216-3

Silva, A. C. S. (2019). *Potencial da Neuroeconomia para criação de estratégias de Implementação de marketing e políticas ambientais* (Dissertação, MBA em Gestão Ambiental). Universidade Federal do Paraná, Brasil.

Silva, C. G., Brito, R. M. M., Monteiro, A., Leal, J. A. F., Furtado, A., Andrade, N., ... Alconchel, M. P. (2014). SOCIENTIZE participatory experiments, dissemination and networking activities in perspective. *Human Computation, 2*(2), 119–135. doi:10.15346/hc.v1i2.4

Vargo, S. L., & Lusch, F. R. (2017). Service-dominant logic 2025. *International Journal of Research in Marketing, 34*(1), 46–67. doi:10.1016/j.ijresmar.2016.11.001

Zaman, A. U. (2015, March). A comprehensive review of the development of zero waste management: Lessons learned and guidelines. *Journal of Cleaner Production, 91*, 12–25. doi:10.1016/j.jclepro.2014.12.013

Zhao, R., & Zhong, S. (2015). Carbon labelling influences on consumers' behaviour: A system dynamics approach. *Ecological Indicators, 50*, 98–106. doi:10.1016/j.ecolind.2014.08.030

KEY TERMS AND DEFINITIONS

Brain Processing: Neurobiological mechanisms through which information (i.e., sensory, motor, memories) is handled by the brain.

EEG: Electrophysiological monitoring method that is used to record the electrical activity of the brain.

Environmental Sustainability: A systemic concept that involves a global development model incorporating aspects of a mass consumption system where the extraction of raw materials is considered a priority.

Eye Tracking: Process of measuring eye position (i.e., point of gaze) and movements (i.e., motion of eyes relative to the head).

fMRI: An imaging technique used to evaluate the activity in different areas of the central nervous system through the variation in local blood flow.

Green Consumer: Someone who has consumer attitudes towards preserving the environment.

Marketing: Business strategy that aims to optimize profits by adapting the production and offer of goods or services to the needs and preferences of consumers, using different parameters such as market research, design, advertising campaigns, and after-sales services.

MEG: A technique for mapping brain activity using the magnetic field produced by electrical currents that the brain naturally generates.

Neuroscience: The science that studies the nervous system based on molecular, anatomical, physiological, and cognitive principles.

TMS: A non-invasive diagnostic and therapeutic technique that uses magnetic fields to stimulate small brain regions.

RTM: Period of time between stimulus appearance and subject's response.

APPENDIX

Table 4.

n	Titulo	Authors	Periódico	Date	Country	Keyword Combination	[illegible]
1	Sweet taste of prosocial status signaling: When eating organic foods makes you happy and hopeful	Petteri Puska, Sami Kurki, Marja Lähdesmäki, Marjo Siltaoja, Harri Luomala	Appetite	2018	Finlandia	1	2
2	A Psychophysiological Approach For Measuring Response to Messaging How Consumers Emotionally Process Green Advertising	Myriam Martínez Fiestas, María Isabel Viedma, Juan Sánchez Fernández, Francisco J. Montoro Ríos	Journal of Advertising Research	2015	Spain	3	4
3	Sparking interest in restaurant dishes? Cognitive and affective processes underlying dish design and ecological origin. An fMRI study	Francisco Muñoz-Leiva, Diego Gómez-Carmona	Physiology & Behavior	2019	Spain	2	3
4	Service-dominant logic 2025	Stephen L. Vargo, Robert F. Lusch	International Journal of Research in Marketing	2017	EUA	2	2
5	On a Master-plan Towards a Cognitive Science Networking <<Religion, Conflict and Peacebuilding>> and<<Technology, Culture and International Stability>>	A.-C. Butz, A. Stapleton, B. Lewitz, N. Butz	IFAC	2015	Multi (USA, Australia	2	1
6	Carbon labelling influences on consumers' behaviour: A system dynamics approach	Rui Zhao, Shaozhuo Zhong	Ecological Indicators	2015	China	1	3
7	Perception of local food labelling by generation z: an eye-tracking experiment	Jan Fiala, Ivica Toufarová, Stanislav Mokrý, Martin Souček	European Journal of Business Science and Technology	2016	Czech Republic	2	2
8	Ethics and consumption: a difficult balance	Montserrat Díaz-Méndez	Int Rev Public Nonprofit Mark	2010	Spain	1	1
9	Neuromarketing and sustainability: challenges and opportunities for Latin America	Jorge Henrique Caldeira Oliveira	Latin American J. Management for Sustainable Development	2014	Brazil	3	4
10	Consumer Rights: An Assessment of Justice	Gretchen Larsen, Rob Lawson	J Bus Ethics	2013	Multi(UK and New Zealand)	3	2
11	The Spell of Green: Can Frontal EEG Activations Identify Green Consumers?	Eun-Ju Lee, Gusang Kwon, Hyun Jun Shin, Seungeun Yang, Sukhan Lee, Minah Suh	J Bus Ethics	2014	South Korea	3	4
12	Public policies and selective visual attention: the effectiveness of awareness messages among young people about the consumption of alcoholic beverages in Brazil	René de Oliveira Joaquim dos Santos, Jorge Henrique Caldeira de Oliveira, Janaína de Moura Engracia Giraldi 1, Adriano Rogério Bruno	Braz J Sci Technol	2015	Brazil	1	2
13	Sensory marketing: perspectives on benefits consumers grapple in choosing greener products	Aparna P. Goyal, Sanjeev Bansal & Sanjay Srivastava	Global Journal of Commerce & Management Perspective	2018	India	3	3
14	A Neuroscientific Approach to Explore Consumers' Intentions Towards Sustainability within the Luxury Fashion Industry	Michela Balconi 1, 2, Roberta Sebastiani 3 and Laura Angioletti	Sustainability	2019	Italy	3	4
15	The Impact of Eye Tracking on Neuromarketing for Genuine Value-Added Applications	Aida Azlina Mansor, Salmi Mohd Isa	Global Business and Management Research: An International Journal	2018	Malaysia	1	2
16	You can't buy what you can't see : retailer practices to increase the green premium	Hugo Guyader and Mikael Ottosson e Lars Witell	Journal of retailing and Consumer service	2017	Sweden	3	4
17	Innovation in Marketing	Shivanshu Sharma	International Journal of Business Management	2017	India	2	2
18	SOCIENTIZE participatory experiments, dissemination and networking activities in perspective	Cândida G. Silva, Rui M. M. Brito António Monteiro José A. Farias Leal, Adabriand Furtado, Nazareno Andrade, Francisco Paulo Gama Mota, Caroline Manahl, Teresa Holocher-Ertl, Manuel Pérez Alconchel	Human Computation	2014	Multi(Portugal, Brazil, Austria, Zaragoza)	2	1
19	Globalization & Marketing with Environmental Sustainability: A Holistic Resource-Centric Analysis with Reference to Corporatization	N. Naganna & R. Pankajakshi	Bhavan's International Journal of Business	2009	India	2	2
20	Implementation and Management of Life Cycle Approaches in Business—Challenges, Opportunities, Business Learnings and Best Practice	Lena Landström and Sara Palander	Designing Sustainable Technologies, Products and Policies	2018	Sweden	2	1
21	Neuroscience in Linguistic Patterns of Communication Campaigns for Environmental Sustainability	Magdalena Sadzyna	Problems of Sustainable Development	2019	Poland	3	4
22	Dirty Hands, Speculative Minds, and Smart Machines	Diane P. Michelfelder	Philos. Technol	2011	USA	1	1
23	Automation for the Artisanal Economy: Enhancing the Economic and Environmental Sustainability of Crafting Professions with Human-Machine Collaboration	Ron Eglash, Lionel Robert, Audrey Bennett, Kwame Porter Robinson, Michael Lachney, William Babbitt	AI & Society	2019	USA	2	2
24	The impact of brand experiences on brand resonance in multi-channel fashion retailing	Ran Huang, Stacy H. Lee, HaeJung Kim, Leslie Evans	Journal of Research in Intera	2015	USA	1	2

Chapter 23
Merging Explicit Declarations With Implicit Response Time to Better Predict Behavior

Rafal Ohme
Stellenbosch University, South Africa & NEUROHM, Poland

Michał Matukin
https://orcid.org/0000-0003-3579-1650
NEUROHM, Poland & Walnut Unlimited, UK

Paula Wicher
NEUROHM, Poland

ABSTRACT

Declarations and actions do not always overlap, and thus, predicting future behavior solely on the basis of self-reported measures seems to be ineffective. The authors propose a confidence index (CI): a measure based on Fazio's attitude accessibility model. CI integrates explicit and implicit perspectives and captures how long a person hesitates when stating an opinion. The more certain someone is the stronger the attitude-behavior link is likely to be. A study was conducted to uncover differences in attitudes between average- and top-performing sales agents from the automotive industry. The results for declarative data did not show any significant differences; however, the CI results yielded interesting significant differences between groups. Random decision forests analyses confirmed that merging explicit and implicit measures increases predictive power of the tool. The study provided actionable insights on how to improve sales team performance, which were then implemented and eventually validated by sales results.

DOI: 10.4018/978-1-7998-3115-0.ch023

Copyright © 2020, IGI Global. Copying or distributing in print or electronic forms without written permission of IGI Global is prohibited.

INTRODUCTION

Attitudes reflect people's experiences and perceptions. Most often they are defined as 'mental states regarding an object or issue' (Cooper, Blackman, & Keller, 2016). They provide a strategy for evaluating people or events, they involve a complex organization and guidance of evaluative beliefs, memories, and self-esteem. Attitudes are broadly applied and often used to analyze and interpret such phenomena as self-concepts, social influence, interpersonal attraction, social support, political and religious views or consumer and organizational behavior (Hussak & Cimpian, 2018; Prislin & Wood, 2005; Pornsakulvanich, 2017; Abdalla, Abdelal, & Soon, 2019; Alves, 2018; Alhawari, Verhoff, Ackermann, & Parzeller, 2019; Ajzen, 2008; Shamim, Cang, & Yu, 2019). Attitudes have also been associated with having the capacity to influence behavior (Fishbein & Ajzen, 1975; Ajzen, 1991; Ogunnaike, Kehinde, Omoyayi, Popoola & Amoruwa, 2017).

Researchers had already made the first attempts to structurally and systematically measure attitudes already in the early part of the 20th century. They did it by asking explicit questions and assigning numbers to the given answers in order to be able to compare them between respondents (Kruglanski & Stroebe, 2012, Cooper, Blackman, & Keller, 2016). Thurstone (1928) was the first author of an attitude scale measurement, which consisted of statements concerning a particular issue with a numerical value indicating how favorable or unfavorable it was judged to be. The respondents' task was to choose which statement they endorsed with the use of "agree" and disagree" answers. Likert (1932) suggested agreeing or disagreeing with the given statement at various strengths on the 5-point scale. Osgood (1962) proposed that attitude could be measured on a 7-point scale along three dimensions: evaluation (good/bad), potency (strong/weak), activity (active/passive). Attitudes were also measured with the use of semantic differential scales, which was a set of evaluative bipolar scales (Triandis & Fishbein, 1963).

One of the questions that emerged from a traditional or explicit approach to attitude questionnaires is how can researchers be certain that people declare their actual point of view? Thurstone himself stated that attitude scale usage should be limited to situations where researchers expected participants to tell the truth about their opinions (Thurstone, 1928). Tapping into real motives of human behavior has always been a challenge. Declarations and actions do not always overlap. A good example of such inconsistency one can be observed during political elections. People declare they will vote for a specific candidate, however, on the election day the results are not always in line with the ones predicted by the polls. This happens, because some motives of people's behaviors are not consciously accessible. In the last 50 years researchers have consistently shown that most of our cognitive processes take place outside of conscious awareness and control, nevertheless they do influence our perceptions, judgments and actions (Zajonc, 1968, 1980, 1984; Holender, 1986; Uleman & Bargh 1989; Bornstein 1989; Bornstein & Pittman 1992; Greenwald 1992; Murphy & Zajonc 1993; Murphy, Monahan & Zajonc 1995; Niedenthal & Kitayama, 1994; Bargh 1994, 1997; Ohme, 1997, 2001, 2009; Nosek, Hawkins, & Frazier, 2011; Ohme, Pochwatko & Blaszczak, 1999; Ohme & Boshoff, 2019; Matukin, & Ohme 2016, 2017). Especially in socially sensitive contexts, people may declare attitudes that are expected and approved. However, attitudes measured by explicit tools are based on rationally processed information, complying with social norms, evaluation apprehension or based upon "cost-benefit analysis" (Dovidio & Fazio, 1992).

Matukin and Ohme posited that a research predicting behavior solely on the basis of self-reported measures has been insufficient as it 'may not reflect ambiguous opinions or subtler differences in attitudes' (2016, 2017). Consumers might not have access to their opinion on a specific topic at the right moment or they simply do not want to share it. As a result, there might be a discrepancy between what they explicitly declare and what actually drives their behavior. Kraus (1995) carried out a meta-analysis study on the attitude-behavior link and showed a weak correlation r = .38 between declaratively expressed attitudes and behavior. If there is a discrepancy between what people declare and how they actually behave, then standard tools used to predict consumer behavior will have limited accuracy (op. cit.).

In business environment when decisions are based solely on tools that take into consideration only the explicit part of human attitudes various communication and managerial problems may emerge. The attitude-behavior gap may lead for instance to poor understanding of consumers' or employees' needs and expectations. This in turn may result in mismanagement, bad investments and low efficiency. On the other hand, application of a tool or an approach that will allow to reduce the attitude–behavior gap will help improve internal and external communication and eventually enhance satisfaction level and sales performance. In this chapter the authors will focus on implicit measurements that reach beyond declarative reports and seem most suitable and beneficial for business purposes.

IMPLICIT RESPONSE TIME BASED MEASURES OF ATTITUDES

As self-reported measures seem inadequate, other tools have been created to bridge the attitude-behavior gap. Today in consumer neuroscience there exist neuroimaging tools which use functional magnetic resonance or fMRI (Plassmann, O'Doherty, & Rangel, 2007; Izuma et al. 2017) and electroencephalogram or EEG (Ohme et al. 2009, 2010; Ariely & Berns, 2010; Maison, Oleksy, 2017) to better understand consumers emotions and what drives their actions. However, those tools are expansive, time consuming and invasive for the respondents. They also require a central location tests as the hardware needs to be supervised. Even less expensive techniques such as Galvanic Skin Response (GSR) measures (Ohme, Matukin, Pacula-Lesniak, 2011; Matukin, 2017) are imperfect as well as, due to their hardware requirements, they are hard to apply online. In the dynamic market environment in the digital disruption era time is crucial and the access to the emotional aspects of the consumers' choices and decisions need to be quick and effortless. Therefore, usage of these approaches, although valuable, will be rather limited. The question arises what method can be used to provide more accurate behavior predictions and at the same time be quick, cost effective and scalable, as these are obligatory features of any tool to be introduced to a business environment. The best solution may be brought about by rapidly growing field on implicit measures based on response time mechanisms that can be carried out online (Houben & Wiers, 2008).

RT As A Key Measure In Implicit Social Cognition

In the 1980's cognitive psychologists started pioneering research to identify traces of past experiences that unconsciously or implicitly influence our judgments, they called it implicit memory. Schacter described it as a type of long-term memory, which is acquired and used unconsciously and affects thoughts and behaviors (Schacter, 1987). One of the most well-known forms of implicit memory is procedural memory, which is used to recognize how to perform habits, skills, and automatic behaviors without conscious awareness. Jacoby and Witherspoon (1982) explored the link between memory and awareness in different contexts. They proved that remembering without awareness is also possible when it comes to episodic memory (personal facts and experience), but not with semantic ones (general facts and knowledge). For example, walking in a familiar area such as at home or in a workplace would involve implicit episodic memory. In the next decade, researchers gathered ample empirical evidence that social behavior operates on a similar principle. Greenwald and Banaji (1995) stated that earlier experience, even if people are unaware of it at that moment, influences opinions about others and the self. They integrated their observations into an implicit social cognition framework that focused on unconscious determinants of attitudes, self-esteem, and stereotypes. Moreover, they pointed out that self-reported measures are inadequate to capture implicit processes and to measure them more accurately indirect tools are required. Majority of such tools use respondents' response time (RT) or response latency or reaction time as a dependent variable reflecting implicit processes.

Mental chronometry, as a measure of the time course of mental operations in the human nervous system, had its beginnings in the late 1800s (Nicolas & Pins, 2014) and has been continuously developed since then. It is focused on measuring and comparing people's response time during various cognitive tasks. (Posner, 1978). Although mental chronometry has many variations and many analytic techniques have been applied within its domain (Meyer, Osman, Irwin, & Yantis, 1988), the majority of research efforts have relied on RT techniques. In the 19th century, the measurement of RT was made possible by a number of inventions including the chronoscope (Townslet & Trimble, 1935). However, it was Wilhelm Wundt who was the pioneer trying to understand human mental processes by measuring RTs in real situations and with his laboratory in Leipzig, he established a role model for scientific psychology laboratories. Wundt's heritage and his focus on precision of measurement had a tremendous impact on experimental psychology and influenced the design of experiments with the usage of RT for the following decades. However, the true renaissance of response time measurement was in the late 20th century, when computers that allow to precisely measure tasks in milliseconds became more accessible, and when the priming paradigm stormed the academic world (Rieber, 2013).

One of the popular paradigms to use RT to study unconscious information processing is a semantic priming. It refers to an exposure to one stimulus, which influences a response to the following stimulus, without conscious guidance or intention (Neely, 1991). For example, the word "student" is recognized more quickly (quicker RT) when following the word "school", because the two concepts are closely associated in the memory. Another popular approach is the Go/No-Go Association Task, which requires a participant to perform action 'Go' given certain stimuli (e.g. press a button) and inhibit the action 'No-Go' under a different set of stimuli (e.g. not press that same button). For instance, making fewer errors when conducting a task with pressing and not pressing the button in line with the instructions means improved response inhibition. It measures the strength of the association between a concept and the poles of an attribute dimension (Nosek & Banaji, 2001).

Implicit Association Test

The most popular and commonly used tool to measure implicit social cognition has been the Implicit Association Test or IAT. It was designed to detect the strength of an automatic association between mental representations of objects in the memory (Greenwald, McGhee, & Schwartz, 1998). It measures the time needed to make preferences or evaluative judgments. The main idea is that the pairs of categories that received faster responses have stronger associations than those receiving slower responses. One of the main advantages of the IAT is that it is less susceptible to response bias than explicit measures (Greenwald & Krieger, 2006) thus, it is more reliable. Moreover, its results are not changed by social desirability in socially sensitive domains (Greenwald, Poehlman, Uhlmann, & Banaji, 2009).

The IAT has reached its popularity also because of its online platform promoted by Project Implicit - a non-profit organization founded in 1998 by three scientists – Tony Greenwald, Mahzarin Banaji, and

Brian Nosek. Project Implicit popularized the online IAT test that can be taken by anyone on webpage (http://implicit.harvard.edu). They also provide consulting services, lectures, and workshops on implicit bias, promoting the whole concept of implicit (https://www.projectimplicit.net) The IAT test has many versions depending on the group and the studied topic. It can also be adjusted to meet various cognitive limitations by creating versions for different age groups (Thomas, Burton, & Ball, 2007) or groups with various mental impairments (Rüsch, Corrigan, Todd, & Bodenhausen, 2010). The IAT has been used in many disciplines, mainly to measure socially sensitive topics such as identities, prejudices, stereotypes, self-esteem, self-concept (Greenwald, Banaji, Rudman, Farnham, Nosek, & Mellott, 2002) or socially controversial attitudes. It was also proved that the IAT predicts a wide range of criterion measures such as interracial friendliness and voting or consumer choices (Greenwald et al., 2009).

The IAT has pushed forward the implicit measurement field, but it also met a critique. Brendl, Markman, and Messner (2001) argued that negative attitudes might be obtained not only from individuals, who actually hold pejorative beliefs toward the studied group but also from people, who have neutral or positive attitudes but are less favorable in their attitudes toward the second presented group. Secondly, in terms of reliability, the IAT demonstrates unsatisfactory internal consistency and its test-retest reliability stands at a relatively weak level (Nosek, Greenwald, & Banaji, 2005). Another criticism was that the response latencies depend on the familiarity of the presented stimuli (Kihlstrom, 2004). Finally, Greenwald and his colleagues conducted a meta-analysis study on IAT's predictive validity. The review included 122 research reports and found a weak average correlation r = .27 for prediction of behavioral judgment, and physiological measures (Greenwald et al. 2009).

A few more disadvantages are distinguished when one considers applying the IAT to a business environment. First of all, it allows the testing of only two phenomena at the same time, which could be inconvenient (Meissner, Grigutsch, Koranyi, Müller, & Rothermund, 2019) when taking into account market research needs that often require studying a few brands simultaneously. The IAT offers only a binary values study while business makes use of various evaluations, not only the dichotomous ones. The test requires numerous repetitions, which makes it time-consuming and tedious for non-academic respondents. It is especially problematic for online IAT studies when it is difficult to maintain respondents' attention while the test itself is already cognitively demanding. The study design is already complex, and less prepared participants might not understand what they need to do. Finally, the IAT provides solely implicit results and omits declarative data, which also provides relevant business insights. Taking into consideration the reasons above, business-oriented researchers turned towards alternative implicit measures.

Attitude Accessibility Approach

Russel Fazio was one of the first psychologists who carried out a series of studies and refer them to implicit measures. He claimed that attitudes can be activated spontaneously and do not need awareness or processing (Fazio, Sanbonmatsu, Powell, & Kardes, 1986). Attitudes have strong emotional components in nature, therefore it is not necessary to involve conscious consideration. Fazio, Powell, and Williams (1989) gave the proof that a response time paradigm might be an indicator for an attitude strength - the more quickly an attitude is expressed, the greater its strength. Moreover, the stronger the attitudes the more accessible they are and the higher confidence with which they are expressed. Thus, strong and highly accessible attitudes are more likely to guide behavior (Fazio & Williams, 1986; Fazio et al., 1989). In practice, the strength of an attitude refers to an individual's motivation, it generates the energy to act (Fabrigar, MacDonald, & Wegener, 2005). Accessibility indicates a frequency of attitude presence in conversations (Fabrigar et al., 2005). Current accessibility could depend on tiredness, being familiar with the topic or current experience (Fazio et al., 1989). Research showed that attitudes of consumers who were involved in product-related activities, were more accessible from memory - it was expressed by their higher confidence (faster response time) and greater likelihood to drive their behavior (Li, Cheng, Xiong, Ye, & Zhang, 2018).

Even if strength and accessibility seem to be similar and often will correspond with each other – they remain orthogonal phenomena (Fabrigar et al., 2005). In general, a strong attitude does not have to be accessible, even if it usually is. For example, an individual can have a strong attitude on some topic, but it is not easily accessible until someone asks about this specific issue. After being asked, the thoughts are more accessible and thus, more likely to influence the attitude and change the action (Glasman & Albarracin, 2006). On the other hand, it could be the other way round: a person may not be certain about the attitude toward something but has recently heard a lot about it and in effect, this attitude is highly accessible at this moment (Fabrigar et al., 2005). Fazio and Williams proved that strong and accessible attitudes are activated spontaneously when the attitude issue is presented (Fazio and Williams, 1986). They proved that the response time of the answers is an effective tool to measure attitude strength and accessibility. In one of their studies, they assessed a response time of respondents' declarations when they were rating candidates for the U.S. 1984 Presidential Elections. Four months later, one day after the elections, the respondents were asked if they had voted and for whom. Among voters with strong and highly accessible attitudes, 80 percent of the variance in voting behavior was explained by attitudes; on contrary, the attitudes of voters with weaker and less accessible attitudes were responsible for only 44 percent of the score. Thus, the measurement of accessibility and strength allowed to discover whether the respondents are confident about the expressed attitude and whether the attitude has the potential to drive them to action.

In the 21st century response time measurement went beyond academic settings and captured a lot of attention from business as it allowed the capture of specific aspects of psychological outcomes that were not caught by explicit measures (Gawronski & Hahn, 2019). Attitude Accessibility Tests identify unconscious representations such as emotions or needs that consumers rarely consciously think about or underestimate how relevant or instrumental they are for example, reactions toward pro-health warning labels on cigarette packages (Matukin & Ohme, 2016). Nowadays, such implicit measures aim to identify what is appealing for employers, shoppers or audiences and make business insights more reliable. For example, implicit measures enabled researchers to capture brand associations and attachments (Matukin & Ohme, 2016, 2017). TV ads may have an emotional impact on audiences and make them internalize positive product associations even if their declarative beliefs about the product seem unchanged (Strick, van Baaren, Holland, & van Knippenberg, 2009), which can be revealed by response time measurement (Matukin & Ohme, 2017). Clients might often not be fully conscious of affective facets of the consumer-brand link or they can be reluctant or feel constricted to explicitly talk about them (Dieckmann, Unfried, Schreder, & Kissel, 2018). Implicit measures enhance understanding of consumer responses such as brand attitude formation and product usage frequency especially when consumers are unable or unwilling to name the sources of influence on their behavior or opinion (Brunel, Tietje, & Greenwald, 2004; Matukin & Ohme, 2017).

The above findings have inspired the authors to conduct an empirical study held at an organizational setting. The goal was to uncover potential differences in pro-sales attitudes between average performing and top performing sales agents. In the study, the authors decided to integrate explicit and implicit measures in the attitude accessibility paradigm. They hypothesized that by doing so they will be in a better position to identify attitudinal differences between two behaviorally different groups of sales agents than if they relied to explicit measurements only.

HOW CONFIDENCE INDEX HELPED TO IDENTIFY SALES FORCE SKILL GAPS: A CASE STUDY

A medium-sized company from the automotive industry was facing a problem of low effectiveness in identifying sales force skills gaps that had been influencing their sales results. Thanks to operational data the company monitored the exact sales score of every team member, thus they knew that only 20% of the whole team was performing above expectations. However, whenever they have been administrating a traditional explicit questionnaire among their sales teams to understand the reasons behind their performance, the results had shown that most of the agents had a very high perception of their own skills, regardless of their actual sales effectiveness. This meant that there was a major discrepancy between questionnaire results (employee experience data) and actual sales (operational data, ie. sales records). Using traditional tools to measure attitudes and motives of the sales force seemed inadequate to identify differences between top and average salesmen. The company management started to look for a new tool that would minimize self-presentation bias.

The research goal was to indicate the competencies that differentiated the two groups of sales representatives: the above average-performing agents and the average ones. The two groups were identified thanks to the operational data (actual sales records) collected by the client. On a business note, with this research, the management wanted to understand why some of the sales representatives performed better than others and to eventually create a 'recipe' for a successful salesman. They also wanted to have a clear view of what competencies the company should focus on in planning a training program targeted to the representatives whose sales results were below expectations. The authors hypothesized that integrating explicit and implicit measures into a single index or Confidence Index would identify more attitudinal differences between two behaviorally different groups than explicit measurements alone.

Method

The response time method based on Fazio's attitude accessibility paradigm was applied. It measures the instinctive reactions of respondents and minimizes the influence of cognitive biases that might occur during traditional surveys and thus distort the final outcome (what actually occurred in the traditional explicit measures previously administered by the client). The response time method minimizes the biases typical for declarative questionnaires, such as social pressure or the so-called "sponsor effect". It also increases the ability to differentiate between groups, making the measurement more precise and suitable to identify attitudes related to actual behavior.

The Fazio response time method used in this study assesses the level of hesitation when providing a given answer delivers more accurate and actionable outcomes, than sole declarative answers. The values that are strong and accessible for the sales representatives are expressed with high confidence and indicated by faster response time whereas slower response time indicates weaker, less accessible attitudes expressed with hesitation. In this approach, the response time is assessed together with, and for every declarative answer provided, thus two types of data explicit and implicit are collected at the same time. The authors decided to merge it into a single number by multiplying declarative score and response time score into the Confidence Index.

The difference in the Confidence Index of the expressed attitudes between average- and above average-performing sales agents should indicate which of the features are instrumental for an effective sales agent. Because of the characteristic of the declarative data (percentage), a nonparametric chi-square for the independence of two variables test was applied to assess the differences between groups (average *vs* above the average agents) in the perception of a given statement. In the case of the Confidence Index built from declarative and response time data, a nonparametric Mann-Whitney test was applied due to imbalanced group sizes.

Moreover, to see whether the application of the response time measure and its merge with declarative scores into the Confidence Index really increases the predictive value, the Random Decision Forest (RDT) - machine learning statistics was applied. It supports the identification processes regarding the prediction of measurement values and their classification RDT is a tree-based classifying method with increased accuracy for both training and unseen data. The essence of the method is to develop large numbers of random decision trees analyzing sets of variables and to generalize their classification in complementary ways in order to improve classification accuracy. There are many variations of random forests and they are widely used for classification and regression tasks in machine learning and statistics. Random forests achieve competitive predictive performance and are computationally efficient to train and test, making them excellent candidates for real-world prediction tasks (Lakshminarayanan et al. 2014).

RDT is an appropriate tool to process data from imbalanced samples. The data set consisted of underrepresentation of above average-performing sales agents and overrepresentation of the average-performing sales agents, thus to create a valid model, the Synthetic Minority Oversampling Technique (SMOTE) was applied to re-balance the datasets (Chawla et al. 2002).

Procedure

A hundred and one sales representatives were asked to complete an online survey. The survey consisted of two parts – part one was the calibration phase – a tutorial that familiarizes respondents with how the survey works with a series of tasks that require proper button pressing and reading statements of different lengths. The second part consisted of a set of statements, presented one-by-one in a randomized order.

The statements describe important aspects of an effective salesperson, such as client-centered thinking, charisma, reliability, persistence, cooperation or motivation. They were selected based on the research on effective persuasion and influence in the sales environment (see: Sternthal, Phillips, & Dholakia, 1978; Milliman & Fugate, 1988; Zanna, Fazio, & Ross, 1994; Yukl, Kim, & Falbe, 1996). Then they were aligned them with feedback provided by professional coaches who train sales force agents or sales directors and eventually adjusted to the guidelines from the best in class experts (Ross & Tyler, 2011; Roberge, 2015). In effect, an online survey of 35 statements was developed and administered to respondents (see: Table 1).

The main task of the sales agents was to indicate whether they agree or disagree with a statement displayed on the screen. Their declarative response was recorded in a form of 0 and 1 answers. Simultaneously the time (number of milliseconds) needed to provide each response was recorded to indicate the strength and accessibility of the attitude expressed. All surveyed employees were divided into two subgroups: above average-performing agents (n=18) and average-performing agents (n=83). Subgroups were defined based on the actual company's operational data (ie. agents' individual sales records).

Response time data were adjusted to handle the extremely short or extremely long reactions, as they could indicate a lack of attention in the processing of the questions or inability to answer in a spontaneous manner (Greenwald, Nosek, & Banaji, 2003). Values lower than 500ms and higher than 5000ms were thus eliminated. Moreover, if a given respondent exhibited too short or too long responses for over 40% of the answers provided, he/she was excluded from the analysis as a person who did not comply with the instructions and did not pay sufficient attention to the tasks.

During the analysis, the milliseconds were converted to natural logarithms (Winer, 1971) and the extreme values were truncated. Next, the values were standardized into a scale from 0 to 100 for each respondent, where the bottom value indicates the slowest reaction a given respondent achieved and the top value indicates the fastest response. Then the results for every respondent were transformed as a product of declarative evaluation multiplied by standardized response time scores into the Confidence Index with the range from -100 to +100 (the valance was provided by the declarative answer). The Confidence Index was created for the two reasons: to merge explicit with implicit measures and to enable more advanced statistical computations.

Results

Table 1 presents all 35 tested statements and the average scores both groups achieved on both applied measures. The results for declarative data did not show any significant differences between the tested groups. The results for Confidence Index, inspected with the nonparametric Mann-Whitney test, yielded a significant difference between average- and above average-performing groups in the two statements: *I have a well-thought plan for every meeting* – Z=-2.002, p<0,05 (two-tailed) (Figure 1) and *The company helps me achieve my sales goals* – Z=-2,123, p<0,05 (two-tailed) (Figure 2)

Machine Learning Analysis

After the Synthetic Minority Oversampling Technique (SMOTE) was applied the data were subject to Random Decision Forests (Table 2). The strongest model was built based on the Confidence Index – the metric that consists of both types of data (declarative and response time scores) the AUC (Area under the ROC Curve) rate for such model is 0.97 with the precision rate 0.99. Alternatively, the model build solely with the usage of declarative scores (excluding the response time data) is significantly weaker with AUC=0.82 and precision around 0.76.

Results Interpretation

The research hypotheses has been confirmed. Merging of explicit and implicit measures in the form of the Confidence Index has identified attitudinal differences between two tested groups, whereas applying explicit measurements only found no such differences at all.

The sole declarative scores failed to identify any significant differences between average- and above average-performing agents, which suggest that in this study the authors have replicated the results the company had achieved with previously administrated traditional explicit questionnaires. A vast majority of sales representatives declared that they agree with most of the values. Such a situation might occur due to many factors that include social biases, eagerness to provide only 'good answers' or self-presentation. In effect, the declarative scores are not entirely truthful and can be skewed. It does not mean the re-

Table 1. Comparison between average- and above average-performing agents for declarative answers and for Confidence Index

ATTRIBUTE	DECLARATIVE SCORES (%)					CONFIDENCE INDEX		
	YES		NO		diff.			
	average (n=83)	above (n=18)	average (n=83)	above (n=18)		average (n=83)	above (n=18)	diff.
I can turn failure into a success	82	94	18	6	n.s.	12	21	n.s.
I like to lead the team	62	78	38	22	n.s.	8	22	n.s.
I am a charismatic person	78	94	22	6	n.s.	28	47	n.s.
I know competitive products well	88	89	12	11	n.s.	22	26	n.s.
I like to perform in public	30	44	70	56	n.s.	-21	-19	n.s.
I easily recognize the client's needs	87	94	13	6	n.s.	40	46	n.s.
I adapt my approach to the client's profile	99	100	1	0	n.s.	62	64	n.s.
I can build long-term relationships with clients	98	100	2	0	n.s.	85	87	n.s.
I can convince clients to agree with my opinion	96	100	4	0	n.s.	64	71	n.s.
I answer most client questions easily	94	100	6	0	n.s.	66	67	n.s.
I help clients get what they need	100	100	0	0	n.s.	81	77	n.s.
I can successfully convince clients to make a decision	95	94	5	6	n.s.	50	44	n.s.
I feel comfortable when talking with clients	99	100	1	0	n.s.	78	86	n.s.
I recommend my company to others as a good place to work	96	100	4	0	n.s.	67	66	n.s.
The company provides me with proper product training	35	29	65	71	n.s.	0	-14	n.s.
The company helps me achieve my sales goals	86	78	14	22	n.s.	**39**	**12**	**0.03**
There's a bright future ahead of my company	82	88	18	13	n.s.	46	58	n.s.
I feel proud to work for my company	89	100	11	0	n.s.	39	53	n.s.
I respect others	99	100	1	0	n.s.	83	76	n.s.
I am open to taking the advice of others	94	100	6	0	n.s.	64	66	n.s.
I can support others	98	100	2	0	n.s.	57	62	n.s.
People can rely on me	99	100	1	0	n.s.	60	51	n.s.
I am a friendly person	98	100	2	0	n.s.	83	83	n.s.
I have a positive attitude	99	100	1	0	n.s.	79	90	n.s.
I skillfully control my emotions	87	94	13	6	n.s.	28	20	n.s.
I am a seller who always fights to the end	95	89	5	11	n.s.	65	78	n.s.
I continue to sell, even after the client's first refusal	96	94	4	6	n.s.	43	43	n.s.
I stubbornly strive to close the deal	94	94	6	6	n.s.	26	35	n.s.
Client refusals motivate me to work more intensively	86	89	14	11	n.s.	33	28	n.s.
I persistently work on closing the deal, even with a difficult client	98	94	2	6	n.s.	31	37	n.s.
I have a well-thought plan for every meeting	69	83	31	17	n.s.	**11**	**32**	**0.05**
I actively deepen my knowledge about the product I sell	89	100	11	-	n.s.	43	59	n.s.
I collect additional information about the clients I'm meeting	87	94	13	6	n.s.	46	41	n.s.
I keep deadlines	95	94	5	6	n.s.	47	45	n.s.
I fulfill my duties in the best possible way	98	94	2	6	n.s.	80	74	n.s.

Figure 1. Comparison between average agents and above average agents for Declarative scores (left chart) and Confidence Index scores (right chart)

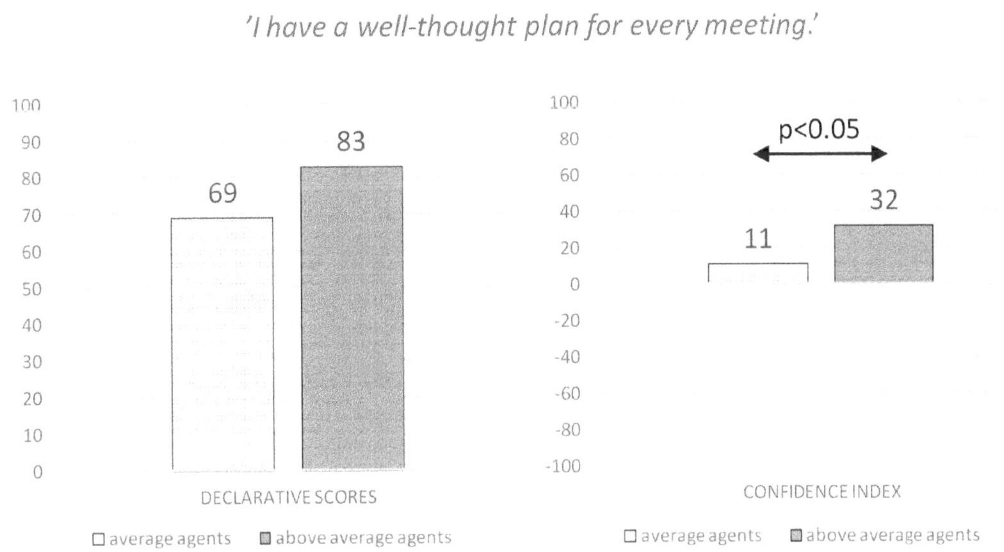

Figure 2. Comparison between average agents and above average agents for Declarative scores (left chart) and Confidence Index scores (right chart)

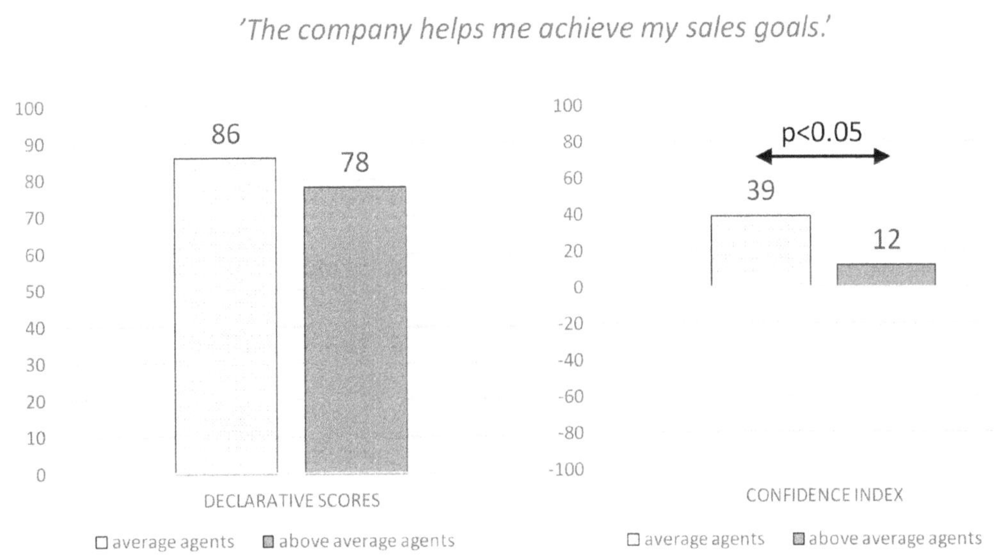

Table 2. Scores for Random Decision Forests models built with Declarative data (left column) and Confidence Index data (right column)

	DECLARATIVE SCORES	CONFIDENCE INDEX
AUC	0.82	0.97
Precision	0.76	0.99

spondents were not telling the truth, however, it indicates that on a conscious level some attitudes might be hard or even impossible to reach. Only the synergy of the declarative and response time data or the Confidence Index provides the differentiation one seeks.

Two key aspects of an effective sales agent were identified and eventually provided an answer to the "why" question i.e. what are the attitudes that differentiate the average and the above-average performing sales agents. The declarative answers alone would not identify these attitudes. Moreover, the machine learning analysis shows that the merge of explicit and implicit measures into the Confidence Index increases predictive power and makes more precise predictions.

DISCUSSION

The study described in this chapter confirmed that going beyond explicit declarations and enriching them with the implicit measures in the form of the Confidence Index did increase predictive validity and improve the attitude-behavior link. The results are in line with previous findings showing that response time measurement offers results which are less influenced by self-presentation bias or social desirability than traditional questionnaires (Greenwald & Krieger, 2006; Greenwald, Poehlman, Uhlmann, & Banaji, 2009). Moreover, in comparison to other implicit techniques the advantage of the Confidence Index is in departing from measuring associations in a form of the pairs of categories (Greenwald, McGhee, & Schwartz, 1998). The concern which is associated with the IAT usage that there is a possibility that negative beliefs may be obtained from people, who actually hold pejorative attitudes toward one issue from the pair, but also have positive or neutral attitudes toward the second studied issue from the set (Brendl, Markman, and Messner, 2001). Fortunately, in the Confidence Index tool this problem is eliminated as participants evaluate all study items separately. The Confidence Index tool also answers to another problem which is the possibility of studying one pair of beliefs at a time, which is not effective business-wise (Meissner et al., 2019). The new tool allows investigating multiple questions in one study, which shortens its duration and lowers financial resources spent on research.

From an exploratory perspective, thanks to machine learning, the results indicated that the response time score merged with the declarations score into the Confidence Index significantly improving the ability to predict the performance of the agents. Therefore, it can be a valuable expansion for traditional surveying techniques especially that the effort which is required to apply it is relatively low in comparison to other non-declarative techniques.

BUSINESS SOLUTIONS AND RECOMMENDATIONS

The study provided actionable insights for the company on how to improve sales team performance. Specific steps were advised to develop crucial characteristics of effective salespersons and then to facilitate and nourish them within the company. Moreover, the company gained knowledge of what aspects the future workshop sessions should be focused on and what other actions would be required to secure the success of the sales teams. The element that should be improved among average-performing agents was described by the statement *'I have a well-thought plan for every meeting.'* The response time score showed that for above average-performing agents this need is significantly accessible to them. It suggests they exercised this behavior more frequently than the average-performing agents. It seems that the ability to plan every meeting well is key to be an effective salesperson, at least in this case. It is worth to notice that during the implementation process, it is important that the agents should perceive this action as a success factor and not as a burden. Their motivation in this area needs to be strengthened but more importantly, it needs to be internalized. The agents should truly believe that planning the next meeting will bring them profits. It gives very actionable insights for the next steps. One can advise the company that they should organize workshops where the meeting-planning skill will be specifically practiced and the benefits of doing that will be presented in a simple, convincing and emotionally engaging way. Such workshops should also provide the tools to effectively structure or milestone a procedure of planning a meeting. To achieve higher internalization among the agents the procedure needs to fit each of the agent's daily routines and has to be seamlessly integrated with their other duties. Having those aspects fulfilled, successful implementation of this first insight should be achieved.

Thanks to the Confidence Index measures an even more surprising second insight was reached. The average-performing agents turned out to be more certain that the company helps them achieve their sales goals. The above average-performing agents had some doubts about this topic. It looks as if the above average-performing agents know their duties and see the best solutions to achieve their individual goals, better than might be done on a central level. One may speculate when the company tries to help them, the universal tools or solutions might not entirely fit agents' individual work-style. In a sense, their modus operandi may not be suitable for the style proposed by the company. It seems that the above average-performing agents follow folk wisdom: *'If you need a helping hand, you'll find one at the end of your arm.* They may have different expectations regarding '*helping them by the company.*' The organization should provide general guidelines and support for the agents' but then explore their needs, understand their processes and listen to their suggestions and learn from them for the future. The second insight may also suggest that above average-performing agents are more self-sustaining and independent than their less successful colleagues. These attitudes might be worth developing among other agents in the company.

With these two insights the company was in a position to design a precise action plan, including dedicated workshops to address and improve the confidence among the sales force team. They understood that the rational attitudes declared in the explicit questionnaire were not the only factor that had an impact on sales effectiveness. What was hidden was the confidence of the answers agents were providing. Without full commitment and engagement, the attitudes were just lip service, either when average-performing sales agents were claiming that they: '…have a well-thought plan for every meeting' or when the above average-performing agents declared that the company helps them achieve their sales goals. It seems that those answers were delivered just to 'satisfy' the company. Such declarations were probably given because the agents believed that they were the 'right answer' which the organization wanted to hear. However, because they were provided with hesitation or slow response time they had a weak impact on actual behavior.

The positive effects of the new strategy for agents' development (new training schedule, new bonus plan, nourishing the key attitudes), the company could observe in the year to year sales comparison as their revenues and profits exceeded expectations. The knowledge gathered in this study helped indeed to bridge the salesforce competency gaps and effectively improve their performance.

FUTURE RESEARCH DIRECTIONS

The Confidence Index measure allows to build a dedicated tool to identify key factors for effective performance in the form of a simple and fully automated application. Thanks to automation it will save time on survey preparation, data collection, data visualization, and reporting. Eventually, there will be advanced systems employed that enable the production of reports rich in recommendations and conclusions in a matter of seconds after fieldwork completion.

Such tool will be beneficial in various fields of science and business. It may be used managerially to monitor over time the level of key values among a sales force or to recruit candidates that have the highest entry potential. HR departments can use it to get more in-depth and accurate answers on topics such as employee satisfaction, adaptiveness to digital disruption or self-development. In marketing research, implicit measures enrich the whole field of the consumer experience - satisfaction, loyalty, brand perception or whenever performance of a given product, service or commercial want to be predicted. Brand strategy can benefit due to the finding of true purchase drivers and blockers on which the whole communication can be built. Communication can be perfected by understanding whether the goals are met and core values are persuaded on an emotional, implicit level – which will indicate higher effectiveness and thus higher ROI. In every aspect where filtering doubts out of declarative statements might bring benefits, the Confidence Index based tool should be a tremendous help and can elevate the understanding of human behavior to the next level bringing an actionable business insights.

CONCLUSION

In this chapter the authors has focused on the implicit tool that would reach beyond declarative reports and become most suitable and beneficial for business purposes. The Confidence Index tool that merges explicit with implicit response time based measures has been empirically proven to uncover findings invisible to explicit only measures. The tool seems a valuable option to business environment as it can be automated and carried out online thus the time, cost and effort needed to apply it is minimized. Moreover, the ability to run surveys online greatly increases their scalability (especially in comparison with the central location techniques such as fMRI, EEG or GSR) as they can be deployed in many countries at once and collect thousands of responses simultaneously, everything done in no time and from one's desk.

Toward the Intelligent Enterprise

Equipped with the Confidence Index based tools business researchers will be ready for a paradigm shift, soon to be expected under the name of the Intelligent Enterprise. Contemporary business understood well how it can benefit from its merge with science, especially now when artificial intelligence (AI) and digital technologies are booming and changing the way the world operates. Today, almost every aspect of a company can be measured. Operational data (O-data) provide information on what is going on within the organization. It answers the question 'What?' It provides details on aspects such as how many products have been sold. Where and when the sales are the best? Which sales team is the best? Which group of consumers are buying this product most often? Those and many more questions can be easily quantified in today's digital realm. However, even with all these information one still misses a very important piece of a puzzle, the 'Why' question. For this, the experience data (X-data) is needed - collected thanks to surveys in the form of consumers' or employees' feedback.

The Intelligent Enterprise emerges when those two sources of data – O and X – are integrated and this is already happening. While this article has been written, at least one company – SAP - is trying to merge those two worlds of data. So far all organizations worldwide have kept them in two separate silos. Soon, Intelligent Enterprises will charge their O+X data with AI advanced analytics to grow and prepare the most optimal and convenient solutions for their clients, customers, and employees. However, with the sole use of declarative scores for X data, they will contain the noise - external and internal biases triggered by social and cognitive determinants. Such noise should be filtered out. Just as Intelligent Enterprises merge operational with experiential data, within the latter the authors recommend merging declarative scores with implicit response time scores into the Confidence Index. Otherwise, the noisy declarative data might distort the models and could lead to false or incomplete conclusions and behavioral predictions. AI is as smart as the data provided to teach it, after all. This is where the experience in understanding the response time phenomenon gives a tremendous competitive advantage. Thanks to it – the experience data is more valuable, more truthful and easier to manage. Response time provides a double-check procedure allowing one to be one step ahead. The Confidence Index works in a similar way to a security ribbon in a banknote that tells if a currency is authentic and valuable or false and abused. Such a security ribbon indicates whether the feedback is clean and reliable or random and distorted. Knowing this one will or will not feed A.I. with X-data and therefore secure the most accurate understanding or prediction.

REFERENCES

Abdalla, M. M. I., Abdelal, M. S., & Soon, S. C. (2019). Attitude towards problem-based learning and its relationship with locus of control and academic self-concept among medical students. *Korean Journal of Medical Education*, *31*(1), 11–18. doi:10.3946/kjme.2019.114 PMID:30852857

Ajzen, I. (1991). The theory of planned behavior. *Organizational Behavior and Human Decision Processes*, *50*(2), 179–211. doi:10.1016/0749-5978(91)90020-T

Ajzen, I. (2008). Consumer attitudes and behavior. Handbook of Consumer Psychology, 1, 525-548.

Alhawari, Y., Verhoff, M. A., Ackermann, H., & Parzeller, M. (2019). Religious denomination influencing attitudes towards brain death, organ transplantation and autopsy—A survey among people of different religions. *International Journal of Legal Medicine*, 1–10. doi:10.100700414-019-02130-0 PMID:31418075

Alves, H. (2018). Sharing rare attitudes attracts. *Personality and Social Psychology Bulletin*, *44*(8), 1270–1283. doi:10.1177/0146167218766861 PMID:29637846

Ariely, D., & Berns, G. S. (2010). Neuromarketing: The hope and hype of neuroimaging in business. *Nature Reviews. Neuroscience*, *11*(4), 284–292. doi:10.1038/nrn2795 PMID:20197790

Bargh, J. A. (1994). The four horsemen of automaticity: Awareness, intention, efficiency, and control in social cognition. In R. S. Wyer Jr & T. K. Srull (Eds.), *Handbook of Social Cognition* (2nd ed., Vol. 1, pp. 1–40). Hillsdale, NY: Erlbaum.

Bargh, J. A. (1997). Automaticity of Everyday Life. *Advances in Social Cognition, 10*, 1–61.

Bornstein, R. F. (1989). Exposure and affect: Overview and meta-analysis of research, 1968-1987. *Psychological Bulletin, 2*(2), 265–289. doi:10.1037/0033-2909.106.2.265

Bornstein, R. F., & Pittman, T. S. (1992). *Perception Without Awareness*. New York: The Guilford Press.

Brendl, C. M., Markman, A. B., & Messner, C. (2001). How do indirect measures of evaluation work? Evaluating the inference of prejudice in the Implicit Association Test. *Journal of Personality and Social Psychology, 81*(5), 760–773. doi:10.1037/0022-3514.81.5.760 PMID:11708555

Brunel, F. F., Tietje, B. C., & Greenwald, A. G. (2004). Is the implicit association test a valid and valuable measure of implicit consumer social cognition? *Journal of Consumer Psychology, 14*(4), 385–404. doi:10.120715327663jcp1404_8

Chawla, N. V., Bowyer, K. W., Hall, L. O., & Kegelmeyer, W. P. (2002). SMOTE: Synthetic minority over-sampling technique. *Journal of Artificial Intelligence Research, 16*, 321–357. doi:10.1613/jair.953

Cooper, J., Blackman, S. F., & Keller, K. T. (2016). *The science of attitudes*. New York: Routledge.

Dieckmann, A., Unfried, M., Schreder, R., & Kissel, K. (2018). *How valid are response-time measures for capturing implicit brand attitudes?* GfK Working Paper Series, 7.

Dovidio, J. F., & Fazio, R. H. (1992). New technologies for the direct and indirect assessment of attitudes. In J. Tanur (Ed.), *Questions about survey questions: Meaning, memory, attitudes, and social interaction* (pp. 204–237). New York: Russell Sage Foundation.

Fabrigar, L. R., MacDonald, T. K., & Wegener, D. T. (2005). *The structure of attitudes. The handbook of attitudes, 80*. New York: Routledge.

Fazio, R. H., Powell, M. C., & Williams, C. J. (1989). The role of attitude accessibility in the attitude-to-behavior process. *The Journal of Consumer Research, 16*(3), 280–288. doi:10.1086/209214

Fazio, R. H., Sanbonmatsu, D. M., Powell, M. C., & Kardes, F. R. (1986). On the automatic activation of attitudes. *Journal of Personality and Social Psychology, 50*(2), 229–238. doi:10.1037/0022-3514.50.2.229 PMID:3701576

Fazio, R. H., & Williams, C. J. (1986). Attitude accessibility as a moderator of the attitude–perception and attitude–behavior relations: An investigation of the 1984 presidential election. *Journal of Personality and Social Psychology, 51*(3), 505–514. doi:10.1037/0022-3514.51.3.505 PMID:3761146

Fishbein, M., & Ajzen, I. (1975). *Belief, attitude, intention and behavior: An introduction to theory and research*. Reading, MA: Addison Wesley.

Gawronski, B., & Hahn, A. (2019). Implicit Measures: Procedures, Use, and Interpretation. In H. Blanton & G. D. Webster (Eds.), *Foundations of social psychological measurement*. New York: Taylor & Francis.

Glasman, L. R., & Albarracin, D. (2006). Forming attitudes that predict future behavior: A meta-analysis of the attitude-behavior relation. *Psychological Bulletin, 132*(5), 778–822. doi:10.1037/0033-2909.132.5.778 PMID:16910754

Greenwald, A. G. (1992). New Look 3: Unconscious cognition reclaimed. *The American Psychologist*, *47*(6), 766–779. doi:10.1037/0003-066X.47.6.766 PMID:1616174

Greenwald, A. G., & Banaji, M. R. (1995). Implicit Social Cognition Attitudes, Self-Esteem, and Stereotypes. *Psychological Review*, *102*(1), 4–27. doi:10.1037/0033-295X.102.1.4 PMID:7878162

Greenwald, A. G., Banaji, M. R., Rudman, L. A., Farnham, S. D., Nosek, B. A., & Mellott, D. S. (2002). A unified theory of implicit attitudes, stereotypes, self-esteem, and self-concept. *Psychological Review*, *109*(1), 3–25. doi:10.1037/0033-295X.109.1.3 PMID:11863040

Greenwald, A. G., & Krieger, L. H. (2006). Implicit bias: Scientific foundations. *California Law Review*, *94*(4), 945–967. doi:10.2307/20439056

Greenwald, A. G., McGhee, D. E., & Schwartz, J. L. (1998). Measuring individual differences in implicit cognition: The implicit association test. *Journal of Personality and Social Psychology*, *74*(6), 1464–1480. doi:10.1037/0022-3514.74.6.1464 PMID:9654756

Greenwald, A. G., Nosek, B. A., & Banaji, M. R. (2003). Understanding and using the implicit association test: I. An improved scoring algorithm. *Journal of Personality and Social Psychology*, *85*(2), 197–216. doi:10.1037/0022-3514.85.2.197 PMID:12916565

Greenwald, A. G., Poehlman, T. A., Uhlmann, E. L., & Banaji, M. R. (2009). Understanding and using the Implicit Association Test: III. Meta-analysis of predictive validity. *Journal of Personality and Social Psychology*, *97*(1), 17–41. doi:10.1037/a0015575 PMID:19586237

Holender, D. (1986). Semantic activation without conscious identification in dichotic listening, parafoveal vision, and visual masking: A survey and appraisal. *Behavioral and Brain Sciences*, *9*(1), 1–66. doi:10.1017/S0140525X00021269

Houben, K., & Wiers, R. W. (2008). Measuring implicit alcohol associations via the Internet: Validation of Web-based implicit association tests. *Behavior Research Methods*, *40*(4), 1134–1143. doi:10.3758/BRM.40.4.1134 PMID:19001405

Hussak, L. J., & Cimpian, A. (2018). Investigating the origins of political views: Biases in explanation predict conservative attitudes in children and adults. *Developmental Science*, *21*(3), e12567. doi:10.1111/desc.12567 PMID:28722292

Izuma, K., Shibata, K., Matsumoto, K., & Adolphs, R. (2016). Neural predictors of evaluative attitudes toward celebrities. *Social Cognitive and Affective Neuroscience*, *12*(3), 382–390. doi:10.1093can/nsw135 PMID:27651542

Jacoby, L. L., & Witherspoon, D. (1982). Remembering without awareness. *Canadian Journal of Psychology*, *36*(2), 300–324. doi:10.1037/h0080638

Kihlstrom, J. F. (2004). Implicit methods in social psychology. In C. Sansone, C. Morf, & A. Panter (Eds.), *The Sage handbook of methods in social psychology* (pp. 195–212). Thousand Oaks: Sage.

Kraus, S. J. (1995). Attitudes and the Prediction of Behavior: A Meta-Analysis of the Empirical Literature. *Personality and Social Psychology Bulletin*, *21*(1), 58–75. doi:10.1177/0146167295211007

Kruglanski, A., & Stroebe, W. (2012). *Handbook of the history of social psychology*. Philadelphia, PA: Psychology Press. doi:10.4324/9780203808498

Lakshminarayanan, B., Roy, D. M., & Teh, Y. W. (2014). Mondrian forests: Efficient online random forests. In Advances in neural information processing systems (pp. 3140-3148). Academic Press.

Li, T., Cheng, J., Xiong, T., Ye, J., & Zhang, Z. (2018). Research on Attitude Accessibility in Product Design Evaluation: Cognitive Features and Memory Network. In *Advances in Intelligent Systems and Computing*. Cham: Springer.

Likert, R. (1932). A technique for the measurement of attitudes. *Archives de Psychologie*, *140*, 5–55.

Luttrell, A., Stillman, P. E., Hasinski, A. E., & Cunningham, W. A. (2016). Neural dissociations in attitude strength: Distinct regions of cingulate cortex track ambivalence and certainty. *Journal of Experimental Psychology. General*, *145*(4), 419–433. doi:10.1037/xge0000141 PMID:26854498

Maison, D., & Oleksy, T. (2017). Validation of EEG as an Advertising Research Method: Relation Between EEG Reaction Toward Advertising and Attitude Toward Advertised Issue (Related to Political and Ideological Beliefs). In K. Nermend & M. Łatuszynska (Eds.), *Neuroeconomic and Behavioral Aspectsof Decision Making*. Springer Proceedings in Business and Economics. doi:10.1007/978-3-319-62938-4_18

Matukin, M. (2017). Physiological measures. In P. Dovas, L. Florentino, C. Grieve, H. Hofkirchner, C. Maclnnes, M. Matukin, B. Monteleone, S. Needel, R. Ohme, & P. Steidl (Eds.), Market Research revolution. CreateSpace.

Matukin, M., & Ohme, R. (2016). Implicit Measures of Attitudes in Market Research. In A. R. Thomas, N. A. Pop, A. M. Iorga, & C. Ducu (Eds.), *Ethics and neuromarketing: implications for market research and business practice* (pp. 113–123). Springer.

Matukin, M., & Ohme, R. K. (2017). How reaction time measurement empowers marketing and market research. In P. Dovas, L. Florentino, C. Grieve, H. Hofkirchner, C. Maclnnes, M. Matukin, B. Monteleone, S. Needel, R. Ohme, & P. Steidl (Eds.), Market Research revolution. CreateSpace.

Meissner, F., Grigutsch, L. A., Koranyi, N., Müller, F., & Rothermund, K. (2019). Predicting Behavior With Implicit Measures: Disillusioning Findings, Reasonable Explanations, and Sophisticated Solutions. *Frontiers in Psychology*, *10*, 10. doi:10.3389/fpsyg.2019.02483 PMID:31787912

Meyer, D. E., Osman, A. M., Irwin, D. E., & Yantis, S. (1988). Modern mental chronometry. *Biological Psychology*, *26*(1-3), 3–67. doi:10.1016/0301-0511(88)90013-0 PMID:3061480

Milliman, R. E., & Fugate, D. L. (1988). Using trust-transference as a persuasion technique: An empirical field investigation. *Journal of Personal Selling & Sales Management*, *8*(2), 1–7.

Murphy, S. T., Monahan, J. L., & Zajonc, R. B. (1995). Additivity of nonconscious affect: Combined effects of priming and exposure. *Journal of Personality and Social Psychology*, *69*(4), 589–602. doi:10.1037/0022-3514.69.4.589 PMID:7473021

Murphy, S. T., & Zajonc, R. B. (1993). Affect, cognition, and awareness: Affective priming with optimal and suboptimal stimulus exposures. *Journal of Personality and Social Psychology*, *64*(5), 723–739. doi:10.1037/0022-3514.64.5.723 PMID:8505704

Neely, J. H. (1991). Semantic priming effects in visual word recognition: A selective review of current findings and theories. In D. Besner & G. Humphreys (Eds.), Basic processes in reading: Visual word recognition (pp. 264-337). Hillsdale, NY: Erlbaum.

Nicolas, S., & Pins, D. (2014). Piéron's Law and the First Instruments for Measuring Reaction Time. *Bulletin de Psychologie*, (5): 385–407. doi:10.3917/bupsy.533.0385

Niedenthal, P. M., & Kitayama, S. (1994). *The heart's eye: emotional influences in perception and attention*. New York: Academic Press.

Nosek, B. A., & Banaji, M. R. (2001). The go/no-go association task. *Social Cognition*, *19*(6), 625–666. doi:10.1521oco.19.6.625.20886

Nosek, B. A., Greenwald, A. G., & Banaji, M. R. (2005). Understanding and using the Implicit Association Test: II. Method variables and construct validity. *Personality and Social Psychology Bulletin*, *31*(2), 166–180. doi:10.1177/0146167204271418 PMID:15619590

Nosek, B. A., Hawkins, C. B., & Frazier, R. S. (2011). Implicit social cognition: From measures to mechanisms. *Trends in Cognitive Sciences*, *15*(4), 152–159. doi:10.1016/j.tics.2011.01.005 PMID:21376657

Ohme, R. (1997). Social Comparison of Misfortune. *Polish Psychological Bulletin*, *28*(2), 189–201.

Ohme, R., Pochwatko, G., & Błaszczak, W. (1999). Paradygmat afektywnego poprzedzania: W poszukiwaniu nowej procedury badawczej. *Studia Psychologiczne*, *37*(1), 7–28.

Ohme, R. (2001). The implicit conditioning of consumer attitudes: Logo substitution effect. Polish Psychological Bulletin, 32(1).

Ohme, R. (2009). The unconscious as the third dimension in advertising. *American Academy of Advertising Newsletter*, *5*(4), 1–5.

Ohme, R., & Boshoff, C. (2019). The role of implicit learning in logo substitution. *Journal of Consumer Marketing*, *36*(5), 610–619. doi:10.1108/JCM-11-2017-2430

Ohme, R., Matukin, M., & Boshoff, C. (2016). Conscious and Subconscious Evaluation of Service Recovery Situation. In K. Plangger (Ed.), *Thriving in a New World Economy* (pp. 65–69). Cham: Springer. doi:10.1007/978-3-319-24148-7_20

Ohme, R., Matukin, M., & Pacula-Lesniak, B. (2011). Biometric measures for interactive advertising research. *Journal of Interactive Advertising*, *11*(2), 60–72. doi:10.1080/15252019.2011.10722185

Ohme, R., Reykowska, D., Wiener, D., & Choromanska, A. (2010). Application of frontal EEG asymmetry to advertising research. *Journal of Economic Psychology*, *31*(5), 785–793. doi:10.1016/j.joep.2010.03.008

Osgood, C. E. (1962). Studies on the generality of affective meaning systems. *The American Psychologist*, *17*(1), 10–28. doi:10.1037/h0045146

Plassmann, H., O'Doherty, J., & Rangel, A. (2007). A. Orbitofrontal cortex encodes willingness to pay in everyday economic transactions. *The Journal of Neuroscience: The Official Journal of the Society for Neuroscience*, *27*(37), 9984–9988. doi:10.1523/JNEUROSCI.2131-07.2007 PMID:17855612

Pornsakulvanich, V. (2017). Personality, attitudes, social influences, and social networking site usage predicting online social support. *Computers in Human Behavior, 76*, 255–262. doi:10.1016/j.chb.2017.07.021

Posner, M. I. (1978). Chronometric explorations of mind. Lawrence Erlbaum. Prislin, R., & Wood, W. (2005). Social influence in attitudes and attitude change. In D. Albarracin, B. T. Johnson, & M. P. Zanna (Eds.), *The handbook of attitudes* (pp. 671–706). Hillsdale, NJ: Erlbaum.

Project Implicit. (2019). *Take the IAT*. Retrieved from https://implicit.harvard.edu/implicit/

Project Implicit. (2019). *Project Implicit*. Retrieved from https://www.projectimplicit.net

Rieber, R. (Ed.). (2013). *Wilhelm Wundt and the making of a scientific psychology*. Springer Science & Business Media.

Roberge, M. (2015). *The Sales Acceleration Formula: Using Data, Technology, and Inbound Selling to go from $0 to $100 Million*. John Wiley & Sons.

Ross, A., & Tyler, M. (2011). *Predictable Revenue*. PebbleStorm.

Rüsch, N., Corrigan, P. W., Todd, A. R., & Bodenhausen, G. V. (2010). Implicit self-stigma in people with mental illness. *The Journal of Nervous and Mental Disease, 198*(2), 150–153. doi:10.1097/NMD.0b013e3181cc43b5 PMID:20145491

Schacter, D. L. (1987). Implicit memory: History and current status. *Journal of Experimental Psychology. Learning, Memory, and Cognition, 13*(3), 501–518. doi:10.1037/0278-7393.13.3.501

Shamim, S., Cang, S., & Yu, H. (2019). Impact of knowledge oriented leadership on knowledge management behaviour through employee work attitudes. *International Journal of Human Resource Management, 30*(16), 2387–2417. doi:10.1080/09585192.2017.1323772

Sternthal, B., Phillips, L. W., & Dholakia, R. (1978). The persuasive effect of scarce credibility: A situational analysis. *Public Opinion Quarterly, 42*(3), 285–314. doi:10.1086/268454 PMID:10297222

Strick, M., Van Baaren, R. B., Holland, R. W., & Van Knippenberg, A. (2009). Humor in advertisements enhances product liking by mere association. *Journal of Experimental Psychology. Applied, 15*(1), 35–45. doi:10.1037/a0014812 PMID:19309215

Thomas, S. R., Burton Smith, R., & Ball, P. J. (2007). Implicit attitudes in very young children: An adaptation of the IAT. *Current Research in Social Psychology, 13*(7), 75–85.

Thurstone, L. L. (1928). Attitudes can be measured. *American Journal of Sociology, 33*(4), 529–554. doi:10.1086/214483

Townslet, R. R., & Trimble, O. C. (1935). An electrically timed exposure apparatus with chronoscope connections. *The Journal of General Psychology, 13*(2), 466–471. doi:10.1080/00221309.1935.9917898

Triandis, H. C., & Fishbein, M. (1963). Cognitive interaction in person perception. *Journal of Abnormal and Social Psychology, 67*(5), 446–453. doi:10.1037/h0038494 PMID:14081887

Uleman J. S. & Bargh J. A. (1989). *Unintended thought.* New York: Guilford Press.

Winer, B. (1971). *Statistical Principles in Experimental Design* (2nd ed.). McGraw-Hill.

Yukl, G., Kim, H., & Falbe, C. M. (1996). Antecedents of influence outcomes. *The Journal of Applied Psychology*, *81*(3), 309–317. doi:10.1037/0021-9010.81.3.309

Zajonc, R. B. (1968). Attitudinal effects of mere exposure. *Journal of Personality and Social Psychology*, *9*(2, Pt.2), 1–27. doi:10.1037/h0025848

Zajonc, R. B. (1980). Feeling and thinking: Preferences need no inferences. *The American Psychologist*, *35*(2), 151–175. doi:10.1037/0003-066X.35.2.151

Zajonc, R. B. (1984). On the primacy of affect. *The American Psychologist*, *39*(2), 117–124. doi:10.1037/0003-066X.39.2.117

Zanna, M. P., Fazio, R. H., & Ross, M. (1994). The persistence of persuasion. *Beliefs, reasoning, and decision making: Psycho-logic in honor of Bob Abelson*, 347-362.

KEY TERMS AND DEFINITIONS

Attitude: A set of emotions, beliefs, and behaviors toward a particular object, idea, person, thing, or event and can have either a positive or negative valence. There are two kinds of attitudes: explicit attitudes that are conscious beliefs and implicit attitudes that are unavailable to self-report or introspection.

Attitude-Behavior Link: A theory that explains conditions when attitudes influence behavior. The strength (the confidence) with which an attitude is held is a good predictor of behavior and can be assessed thanks to the response time measurement.

Confidence: An attitude related feature that is connected with such phenomena as attitude strength or attitude accessibility. The higher the confidence the stronger and more accessible the attitude will be. Confidence can be measured with implicit tools that are utilizing response time measurement. It is directly linked with these aspects of attitudes that drive behaviour and can be used as an indicator of the strength of the attitude-behaviour relationship.

Confidence Index: A standardized index in which declarative responses are weighted by their response time. It reflects how confident an attitude is. This merge of explicit and implicit measures enabled more advanced statistical computations. Confidence Index works in a similar way to a security ribbon in a banknote and indicates whether the answer is authentic and valuable or false and abused.'

Explicit: (a) explicit or conscious processes - mental operations, opinions or judgments that can be retrospectively reported or intentionally recalled, e.g. viewpoint on a movie. (b) explicit or direct measures - approaches used to gather conscious answers, where respondents are aware what is examined (e.g. declarative opinion) and how it is examined (e.g. by a 7 point scale). Explicit measures might be prone to various biases (e.g. social norms).

Implicit: (a) Implicit or unconscious processes - traces of past experience that are unavailable to self-report or introspection, e.g. stereotypes; (b) Implicit or indirect measures – approaches used to enhance understanding of attitude formation, associations, strength and accessibility, especially when respondents are unable or unwilling to name the sources of influence on their behavior or opinion. During the testing procedure respondents are unaware of what is examined (e.g. stereotypes) and how it is examined (e.g. by measuring response time).

Intelligent Enterprise: An organization in which operational (hard) data (e.g., actual sales level) are continuously integrated with experiential (soft) data (e.g., consumer feedback) to understand "what" happens and "why" it happens.

Response Time: The time our mental system needs to process information, it can be used as a measure of the time course of mental operations in the human nervous system. As a theoretical background has been continuously used and developed since late 1800. It stormed the academic world and was popularized thanks to application in such approaches as Priming or Implicit Association Test.

Chapter 24
The Neuromarketing Revolution:
Bringing Science and Technology to Marketing Insight

Elissa Moses
BrainGroup Global, USA

Kimberly Rose Clark
https://orcid.org/0000-0003-4712-0475
Dartmouth College, USA

ABSTRACT

This chapter examines the advent of the neuromarketing revolution, which over the past 10 years changed the way market research is conducted worldwide to include nonconscious measures in everyday studies. It required a form of technology transformation as traditional researchers and marketers came to accept that nonconscious response and emotion are critical in driving brand perceptions and behaviors. Moreover, it demanded a steep learning curve for understanding and adopting new types of scientifically driven methodologies such as EEG and Biometrics. Now with experience and extensive research by academics and practitioners, neurometrics are considered of high value for understanding consumer response and of great potential value for improving prediction leveraging AI and machine learning.

INTRODUCTION

Every once in a great while, a significant sea change occurs in an industry that alters the way it operates universally, impacting ways of doing business and expectations for what can be delivered. Usually the change is driven by a combination of technology breakthroughs and pure science. We have seen this with telecommunications and the introduction of the cell phone, television with the breakthrough of on demand viewing and now marketing and market research with the seismic leap in applying understand-

DOI: 10.4018/978-1-7998-3115-0.ch024

Copyright © 2020, IGI Global. Copying or distributing in print or electronic forms without written permission of IGI Global is prohibited.

ing the Neuroscience of brain processing, how to measure emotions and the role they play in consumer decision making.

The game changing phenomenon for marketers and researchers was the discovery that emotion and the nonconsious response patterns are not only significant, but dominating influencers of decision making and behavior. Moreover, the research methods of neuroscientists and behavioral scientists were adaptable to business making the ability to measure emotions and nonconscious response a reality as never before. This budding revolution was enabled by scientific advancements not only in Neuroscience, but also in related fields of Cognitive Psychology, Behavioral Economics, Machine Learning and Predictive Analytics.

Hence, over the last 15 years, nonconscious methodologies have emerged to measure consumer response to marketing stimuli and rapidly developed to be vastly improved in terms of ease of use, affordability, speed and scalability. As a result, industry adoption has gone from use by only the most innovative and experimental researchers primarily at large corporations usually designated for experimental or special projects, to widespread usage *among the majority of industry market researchers, agencies and vendors.* According the industry's GRIT report, 56% of researchers use nonconscious methods and another 25% are interested in trying them (*GreenBook Market Leaders Report*, 2019).

Over a short period of time, the field of Neuromarketing, applied neuroscience for understanding and predicting consumer response, has gone from being a questionable interloper, to an academic and commercial discipline of great interest and high expectations. Business has joined forces with academics to bring a superior understanding of the drivers of consumer decision making and behavior and how to apply these insights for optimized marketing offers.

This chapter provides an overview of the field's rapidly evolving history, key methods adopted, examples of organizational integration models for traditional and nonconscious measures in brand research, seminal studies in academia and corporate research and a discussion of the field's continued bright trajectory.

Ultimately, this is a story of science and technology adoption that ultimately changed the course of marketing practices and is continuing to evolve. No longer a resisted or "special occasion" approach, neuroscientific and other nonconscious emotional and behavioral response measures have achieved success by becoming an everyday occurrence where most studies have some kind of nonconscious component baked in as standard for evaluation marketing elements of any kind including advertising, concepts, packaging, shopper behavior, etc. In this regard, neuromarketing is a revolution (Choi et al., 2016) Ironically, we all *feel* we understand emotion, but in truth, there is no scientific consensus on the definition of the term. What is agreed upon is that emotion is a physiological reaction that starts deep in the center of the brain as electrical responses (neurons firing), and chemical changes in the amygdala which is part of the limbic system located in the temporal lobe. Emotional response is complex, a type of multiphase or chain reaction that is also informed by other brain functions such as cognitive response, memory retrieval and attention. These physiological reactions are largely measurable and enable marketers to understand overall positive versus negative responses (known as valence) in fractions of a second as they correspond to moments in stimuli exposure such as the scene in an ad or the score of a football game. The pre-frontal cortex (toward the front of your skull and under the forehead) also plays an important role in registering and modulating emotional response. This is considered the location for establishing the well-known "fight or flight" response when people feel threatened. It is also adapted as a "lean in" vs. "lean back" reaction reflecting elements of interest or likeability. Activation patterns in the left prefrontal cortex are more associated with a strong motivation to engage with a stimulus and activity in the right prefrontal cortex has been found to correspond to a motivation to avoid a stimulus

(Choi et al., 2016; Marox et al., 2001). Hence when neuromarketers talk about emotional measurement, they are referring usually to measurement of nonconscious physiological reactions to stimuli that can be convergent with, or contrary, to stated reactions and lend layers of insight into understanding a consumers' total response.

It should also be noted that "emotions" are not the same thing as "feelings." Feelings are often experienced through compound emotions and defined by conscious definitions. These definitions take into consideration a cognitive evaluation, memory associations, and judgments. Emotions may take longer to form and can be are complex such as jealously, optimism, loyalty and disappointment. They are different in contrast to immediate responses of excitement, positive and negative valence, anger, etc.

Neuromarketing Methods

The Neuromarketing research sector is based upon the foundation of available new methods for nonconsious response. This section summarizes some of the key approaches that have become mainstream to the market research industry.

The Established Methods: For decades, market research was built upon asking people questions, primarily in surveys, focus groups and by observing their purchase and brand behavior. It is critically important for marketers to understand how consumers and customers think and feel about their brands, products and marketing efforts, especially advertising which is intended to motivate them to buy. And yet, there was widespread recognition that consumer feedback could not always be trusted to be predictive or reliable. People are biased in their response, often eager to please, sometimes embarrassed to be candid, uncertain regarding how they really feel and likely to change their minds. Hence marketing decisions based upon consumer question asking has been historically riddled with doubt and uncertainty. If an ad was killed or a new product was launched, was it really the right decision based upon research with so much imprecision? After all, the success rate of new product success is conventionally acknowledged to be astonishingly low. According to Harvard Business School professor Clayton Christensen, only 5% of new products succeed each year out of 30,000 introduced (*Clay Christensen's Milkshake Marketing*, 2011). Hence the angry creative director who likely feels that traditional copy testing might kill his ad for what he perceives to be "no good reason" may actually be right. This means that traditional research methods, while illuminating, are grossly inadequate when they do not accurately reflect emotional response which now can be measured with these new types of tools and methods.

Neuroscientific Methods: Several methods were adapted from the Neuroscience labs to provide reliable and meaningful insights for marketers that capture nonconsious emotional response. The following methods are lead tools in the neuromarketer's toolbox.

1. **EEG** (Electroencephalogram) measures the patterns of electrical responses in the brain. Depending upon the location of the electrodes, activation can be translated into attention, positive/negative valence, cognitive load (thinking) and memory encoding. EEG is considered the most sensitive of neuromarketing measures (short of using fMRI which is significantly more expensive and difficult to administer for standard market research.)

2. **Biometrics:** The term "Biometrics" historically refers to identifying physiological characteristics such as fingerprints or retina patterns. However, in Neuromarketing the definition is applied to non-direct brain physiological response patterns such as heart rate, galvanic skin response (GSR) which is sweat, eye tracking, etc. Neuromarketers use heart rate and GSR to determine second by second arousal (or excitement) generated by marketing stimuli. They use eye tracking to measure attention to very specific visual elements.
3. **Facial Coding:** Perhaps it is intuitive, but we all seem to be able to speak the emotional language of the face (from the smallest babies to our oldest family members), we can recognize basic human emotions the world over. Happiness, anger, fear, disgust, sadness, surprise and contempt are considered to be the seven universal emotions that can be easily deciphered by our facial expressions as classified by Professor Paul Ekman. Automated Facial Coding as a research tool uses machine learning to interpret the patterns on our face using a computerized overlay web of coordinates. In this way, the software can decipher the highest probability emotion that is being expressed at a given point in time - usually in response to marketing stimuli such as advertising or media content. Over time, huge data bases have been amassed by the two leading Facial Coding firms, Realeyes and Affectiva (and others) to establish insights into viewing patterns and normative ranges for meaningful interpretation. Two things should be noted, however.

One, is that facial expressions, unlike most other neurometric phenomenon that are measured, can be somewhat controlled by individuals. The role of facial expressions historically is considered to have evolved as a social communication mechanism and can be exaggerated or suppressed depending upon the objectives. Hence the often-big reaction to birthday gifts (whether we really like them on not) and the notion of the "poker face" when it is not in our interest to let others know what we think of our cards. In solo viewing situations, consumers often do not register big emotional reactions, although they do respond with consistency, discrimination and reliability. This means that if an adequate sample size is used that there is significant differentiation between stimuli or parts of stimuli and that the reactions are repeatable if tested again among a comparable sample.

Secondly, it should be noted that as of late, some academic controversy has arisen suggesting that cultural differences may make facial response patterns to be less universal than original thought to be. None the less, after many thousands of ad tests and huge data bases, the technique is considered by most neuromarketing professionals to be a reliable method for capturing specific emotions and is applied with worthwhile results. Moreover, facial coding, along with EEG and Biometrics have been found in R&D experimentation to be promising for prediction of ad effectiveness. This will be discussed in more detail later in this chapter.

4. **Implicit or Reaction Time Testing:** IAT (Implicit Association Test) or IRT (Implicit Reaction Time) methodologies have been designed to capture the strength of association between ideas, objects or attributes at the nonconscious level. The method consists of variations on a timed association test with multiple variations. However, the core concept is that the faster a participant is at linking two items, the more closely they are associated in the respondent's mind. Hence it may be a way of finding out favorability, key attributes or images on a deeply held level. In simple terms, the method is one of conviction or certainty. If asked to rate a product for its attributes such as Apple on "innovation", it is likely that most people will answer affirmatively. However, when asked on a timed basis, there may be evidence of hesitation which could suggest a budding crack

in perceptions for any number of reasons (J.Moli, 2016; *Neuromarketing News & Blog—NMSBA*, 2015; Ohme, R., 2016). In this respect, the tool is especially useful for differentiation and identification of conflict when people say yes but perhaps mean "no". The method was first developed as an aid to understanding racial prejudice in the NY Police Department by two leading academics Anthony Greenwald and Mahzarin Banaji. (Brunel et al., 2004; Mitchell et al., 2003; Nosek et al., 2007). The method and its many versions are now used all over the world for underlying perceptions regarding brands, ads, political candidates and almost every type of issue or marketing stimuli.

5. **Eye Tracking:** Eye tracking is actually one of the oldest neuromarketing tools having been established in the early 1980's as a useful tool for attention and noticeability, especially for print ads and store shelf design. However, the tool has evolved to offer many forms from stationary, online and mobile. Eye Tracking is a reliable method that can provide great accuracy for determining where people look and how long their eyes linger on specific elements and what the pattern is from element to element and sometimes back again. It is particularly useful for understanding how consumers navigate web sites. The results provide a number of key statistics, as well as heat maps which are color coded to reveal where the most people looked within a visual.

In addition to these six commonly used tools, there are other methods that are considered to provide nonconsious measurement but are either currently less developed/not yet validated (e.g. voice analytics, pupillometric asymmetry response, posture, thermal imaging) or narrowly used because of cost and level of complexity (e.g. fMRI, fEMG).

Most large market research firms (e.g. Ipsos, Nielsen, Kantar, etc.) now offer most of these primary tools in embedded into new types of service offers that include survey questions or qualitative research and are designed to provide comprehensive understanding of consumer response at the conscious and nonconsious levels combined.

Neuromarketing History - The Creation of a New Research Sub-Industry

In the beginning, there was a substantial doubt regarding the trustworthiness and practical value of nonconscious measures. In its infancy, neuromarketing practitioners could only promise that they would provide rich diagnostics for better understanding of consumer response and drives. Later, with further data, studies across varying neuro methodologies began to have convergent results indicating that better predictions of market performance could be made for advertising effectiveness, consumer preference and choice behavior with the use of or inclusion of neurometrics. Hence in less than 15 years, the field of Neuromarketing has gone from being the proverbial "new kid on the block", to an academic and commercial discipline of great value and reliability. Business has joined forces with academics to bring a superior understanding of the drivers of consumer decision making and behavior and how to apply these insights for optimized marketing offers.

From a more scientific perspective, Consumer Neuroscience harnesses both theoretical principles and applied measures from the decision and affective neurosciences, along with psychophysiology and vision research, in order to explain and predict consumption behaviors. This discipline organically links several subfields of neuroscientific inquiry, including neuroeconomics, social and affective neuroscience and Neuromarketing. While Neuroeconomics and Social and Affective Neuroscience focus on academic queries, Consumer Neuroscience and Neuromarketing concentrate on the application of theory for commercial purposes. Specifically, Neuromarketing focuses on research related to the success metrics of specific marketing techniques with the goal of brand and communication strategy optimization.

Taken together, this emerging field comprises both direct and peripheral measures of neural processing related to consumption behaviors. For example, direct measures of changes in cortical (scalp) electrical response or changes in cerebral blood flow allow for an understanding of neural processing dynamics that occur "upstream" from consumption behaviors. Peripheral measures serve as "downstream" proxies of neural processes, namely skin conductance, facial affect, pupillometric response, and cardiac signals. By measuring these in-moment responses to branded products or experiences, Consumer Neuroscience complements traditional commercial research measures such as self-report, which can often be inaccurate or biased regarding intentions or actual purchase patterns.

All told, Consumer Neuroscience represents a unique field drawing from niche neuroscience-oriented disciplines by focusing on the consumer and the innumerable factors that affect individual preferences and consumption behavior.

MAIN FOCUS OF THE CHAPTER

Advancing the Industry through Academic and Commercial R&D Research

As the marketing industry became more at ease with and reliant on the new types of data being provided to help optimize and select among marketing options for ads, packages, programing, products, etc., R&D studies were also being conducted by forward thinking clients, research companies and academics. These new studies, some of which are summarized here for illustration, expand our thinking about what is knowable based on neuro and nonconscious measurement and create the foundation for expectations that neuro data will enable us to improve our predictive capabilities with greater accuracy and reliability. Some of these studies elucidate various aspects of consumer behavior including academic and business studies on predicting consumer choice (Genevsky et al., 2017), prediction of in-market advertising efficacy Ehrenburg-Bass Institute, MediaScience (Bellman et al., 2017; Varan et al., 2015), Realeyes and others, Media Optimization (*CPC_Neuroscience_EN_150717.pdf*, 2015), Temple University (Venkatraman et al., 2015) and others, Creating Fandom (Merchant Mechanics, *The Neurological Effects of South Park | Viacom Fan Theory*, 2016.), and Harnessing Shopper Mood States (Moses et al., 2018).

A. Breakthroughs for Neuro-Prediction of Choice

Prediction of choice is the holy grail for marketers who aim to influence and maximize understanding of consumer behavior. Classically, the best measure has been reduced to the 5-point purchase intent scale ranging from "definitely will buy" to "definitely will not buy" or some such variation. None-the-less, this simple direct question has proven empirically to be relatively good for discrimination between options but not as good for predicting actual behavior. With studies like the one summarized below, academics such as Carolyn Yoon (University of Michigan) and Brian Knutson (Stanford university) have used fMRI, which details brain activity in a laboratory setting, to enhance behavioral prediction well beyond conscious questioning.

Synopsis:

"When Brain Beats Behavior: Neuroforecasting Crowdfunding Outcomes"

Authors: Alexander Genevsky of the Rotterdam School of Management, Erasmus University, Carolyn Yoon of the Stephen M. Ross School of Business, University of Michigan and Brian Knutson of the Psychology Department, Stanford University, Stanford

Study Overview: The findings from this study support the notion that signatures in brain activity related to basic choice scale more accurately to market-level behavioral outcomes than do traditional assessments that are based on individual choices. In this research, neural activity related to choice was used to determine the behavioral outcomes of market level crowdfunding weeks following the study. During the study, researchers presented participants with different crowdfunding opportunities while measuring neural activity in reward circuits found in the nucleus accumbens (NAcc) and for decision making centers in the medial prefrontal cortex (mPFC). Results showed that medial prefrontal cortex predicted individual choices to fund on a trial-to-trial basis in the neuroimaging sample, but the NAcc activity generalized to forecast market funding outcomes weeks later measured by donations levels to specific crowd-funded opportunities. The extent to which basic neural profiles can predict the aggregate crowd donation behaviors has implications for more accurate applications in the realms of commercial and policy-related research success metrics.

B. Using Neuro Data to Better Predict Ad Performance

This is an example of a pivotal study conducted with the Mars Corporation, an early adopter of neuroscience market research applications, on the potential for biometrics to predict ad performance in-market. Studies such as this one, along with others in conjunction with Mars and Realeyes, etc. established the foundation for Neuroprediction of in-market advertising performance.

Synopsis:

"What Makes a Television Commercial Sell? Using Biometrics to Identify Successful Ads

Demonstrating Neuromeasures' Potential On 100 Mars Brand Ads with Single-Source Data

Authors: Steven Bellman, Magda Nenycz-Thiel, Rachel Kennedy, Laurent Larguinat, Bruce McColl, Duane Varan

Study Overview: This study demonstrates the potential of certain neurological measures—in particular, biometrics—to identify television advertisements that successfully lead to sales. The researchers, who represent academia and industry, used direct measures of what they believe matters most to marketers: in-market sales response (from single-source data). To the authors' knowledge, the dataset is the largest ever studied: more than 100 consumer-packaged-goods advertisements for 20 Mars, Inc., brands, combined with laboratory testing from more than 1,000 respondents. The goal of the research, funded by Mars, was to identify evidence-based measures to inspire improved advertising practice and to explore the factors behind advertising effectiveness.

C. Optimizing Media Mix Plans Leveraging Neuro Insights

How do today's consumers consciously and nonconsciously engage with different forms of advertising media – direct mail, email, display and pre-roll video, specifically? Do integrated media campaigns that combine direct mail and digital advertising have the same consumer impact as digital-only campaigns? And what effects does the sequencing of direct mail and digital advertising in integrated campaigns bring to bear on engagement? The following study was commissioned by Canada Post, and conducted in collaboration with research companies Ipsos (Elissa Moses) and Neurons (Thomas Ramsøy) to explore the relative value of multiple media channels for creating attention and engagement in brand messaging and to guide optimization of multi-channel media plans (*CPC_Neuroscience_EN_150717.pdf*, 2016).

Synopsis:

"CONNECTING FOR ACTION A Neuromarketing Look at How Direct Mail Works with Digital Advertising In Integrated Campaigns to Optimize Consumer Attention, Emotional Engagement and Brand Recall"

Authors: Canada Post

Study Overview: The findings from this integrated media study advance our understanding of the role of direct mail, email, display and pre-roll in integrated campaigns and shed new light on how media sequencing can optimize campaign impact.

Direct mail offers a personal, sensory experience that effectively captures and sustains consumer attention, triggers the emotions that drive action, and optimizes recall. It can even earn brands a visible and lasting presence in their customers' homes. When combined with digital media in integrated campaigns, direct mail amplifies consumer attention, emotional engagement and brand recall. Its impact is strongest when used as a follow-up, suggesting direct mail can be a powerful agent for propelling customers forward through the purchase funnel. Email enforces key marketing messages and promotes recall, helping keep brands and offers top-of-mind. However, it elicits low levels of motivation, and over-communication can lead to consumer disengagement. Direct mail mitigates email fatigue by improving emotional engagement with the medium. It also maximizes brand recall when used as a follow-up. Display can stir excitement and motivation in consumers. However, it only captures brief sparks of their attention, at best, leading to low action and recall. Direct mail brings greater attention to display, improving recall. With its personal, portable format, direct mail connects consumers with media, content and offers across channels, amplifying their impact. It's the combination of physicality, data and connectivity that makes direct mail the power channel for customer activation.

D. Creating Fandom to Support Brands

Understanding the motivators of fandom allows for an unprecedented lens with which to assess different ways to determine how popular broadcast content is consumed. Though popular show content remains a constant, fans of that content resonate with the material and storylines in fundamentally different ways than non-fans or casual viewers of the same content. Content creators now have the ability to harness specific portions of a show, such as routine elements, music, and portions of a storyline to best resonate with its fan base. With the findings of this research, show creators also now have the ability to create novel content to carefully connect to fans by leveraging the more impactful elements of the initial show. Moreover, those on the fence about a specific show can be better spoken to by altering content to best resonate with this group. Moving into a world where dynamic digital content is a bourgeoning capability of broadcast providers, show creators will ever more have the ability to understand audience preference and tailor content at key moments to persuade continued viewership across fans and nonfans.

Synopsis:

"Inside the Brain of a Fan: Decoding the Neurological Effects of Fandom"

Authors: Kimberly Rose Clark of the Psychological and Brain Sciences, Dartmouth College and Matthew Tullman, Merchant Mechanics.

Study Overview: In this study, researchers utilized functional magnetic resonance imaging (fMRI) neuroimaging technology to study the brain activity of hardcore fans and non-fans of Comedy Central's *South Park* during a single episode. Significant differences in brain activity were found between the ways in which hardcore fans and non-fans experience show content. Specifically, when participants watched the title sequence of South Park, fans experienced significant increases in nucleus accumbens (NAcc) activity, related to reward processing (Knutson et al., 2003). This brain area has also been implicated in addiction and drug reinforcement. The NAcc activity that occurred during the title sequence suggests that fans have a learned response to associate the show's opening content with reward that did not occur in non-fans viewing the same opening content. Further, neurologic profiles in the temporoparietal junction (TPJ) associated with empathic response (Bruneau et al., 2012) and perspective taking (Morishima et al., 2012) were found to be differentially active in fans as compared to non-fans during portions of the show that were written to elicit empathy from viewers. This suggests that fans have a unique resonance with certain moments during the episode that were associated with increased identification and internalization more so than non-fans who experienced the same content.

E. Influencing Shopper Behavior Through Environmental Mood Factors

Marketers are in constant quest of enhancing the shopper experience at retail to optimize potential for sales. There is need for research that explores the potential for mood influence and other types of positive arousal with broader marketing and retail environments to establish predictive outcomes. This following study created a retail test/control experiment where the test sample was given a Verbena Daisy upon entering a large US Supermarket by a nicely dressed young man under the auspices of "Customer Appreciation Day." Using eye tracking, biometrics, voice analytics and behavioral metrics (# of items purchased, dollar value of shopper basket, etc.) it was determined that the phenomenon of getting a flower as a gift increased time spent in the aisles, items picked up, items purchased, etc. and significantly decreased price sensitivity.

"FLOWER POWER! THE INFLUENCE OF AN IN-STORE GIFT ON EMOTIONAL AROUSAL AND SHOPPER BEHAVIOR"

Authors: Elissa Moses, Ipsos, Laura Beavin, Ipsos PhD, Lisa Zaval, PhD, Ipsos and Kirk Hendrickson, Eye Faster

Study Overview: The current research employed a range of methods including biometrics, behavioral and attitudinal measures to explore whether presenting an unexpected flower to the shopper can influence response and behavior in the store with respect to emotional arousal, shopper satisfaction, and shopping behavior with respect to visual price fixation, basket size, and total spending.

Using a multi-method experimental protocol, the research evaluated a new approach for influencing shopper perceptions and behavior at the point of purchase. The study revealed that giving the gift of a flower early in the shopping experience significantly boosts the shopper's emotional arousal, reduces visual attention to price, improves shopping enjoyment, and increases touch-to-purchase conversion rates, compared to the no-gift control condition. These findings should encourage retailers and manufacturers to consider creative ways to improve emotion through possible "on the spot" emotional triggers

The Advancement of a New Field of Research

Since the early 2,000's a major sea change has been occurring in the market research industry. Essentially there has been a shift away from only asking rational questions with the expectation that consumers can answer accurately regarding how they feel and expect to behave, to capturing emotional response to all types of marketing stimuli with new types of nonconscious measures. This revolution was enabled by scientific advancements in Neuroscience, Cognitive Psychology, Behavioral Economics, Machine Learning and Predictive Analytics. The essential shift in perspective was based on the "eureka" insight that consumer influence and decision making is dominated by nonconscious emotional drivers. Now with academic breakthroughs for new nonconscious measures and method applications, including EEG, Biometrics, Facial Coding, Implicit Reaction Time Testing (IAT), etc., the market research industry and the marketing clients they serve now have the means to measure what is recognized to be critically important beyond rational questioning.

With the advent of new methods, there is also the advancement of practical issues that had to be addressed to make leveraging neuro measures a viable option in everyday market research. First there is the issue of "reliability" or "test/retest validity." This means that if a neuro study is repeated, the results and implications will be largely the same, similar to studies done with questions among quantitative samples. Without this, neuro measures would be useless because it means they could not be relied upon for consistent conclusions. With the right sample sizes and designs, all of the highly popular nonconsious methodologies described herein have proven to be reliable.

Many issues have to be addressed whenever there is a major change in practices. Hence, we review how the industry handled maintaining scientific validity and ground truth, addressing concerns over sample size, test re-test reliability and overall question of ethics. As with most successful technology disrupters, nonconscious measurement and the industry of Neuromarketing which it produced, is a story of scientific discovery, business innovation, initial resistance and ultimately transformation.

Along the same lines are the establishment of "ground truths" which illustrate independently and with face validity that neuro measures are indeed measuring what they purport to capture. This can be, for example, asking recall of items viewed when memory encoding via EEG is recorded for comparison or validating the emotion coding of a stimulus by asking what emotions the stimuli evoke. In essence, ground truth testing is a way of seeking independent validation.

Beyond scientific certainty, new types of measures for commercial application have to pass a number of practicality hurdles with respect to affordability, scalability and speed. Over the last 10+ years since Neuromarketing has arrived at the scene, methods have gotten much cheaper (typical of newest technology) applications have become more portable and simple enabling neuro research to be done largely anywhere throughout the world and the speed of processing has defied expectations to make many neuro study results available in real-time. All of the practical hurdles to adoption have been overcome enabling nonconscious measurement to become a fixture of mainstream research, embraced in one capacity or another by the majority of the major brand marketers the world over.

However, all of the above is rarely enough to pave the way for acceptance and success. Foremost is the need to establish the ultimate value proposition that drives change. When asking an industry to adopt new behavior, there needs to be an outstanding reason of measurable significance and on an emotional level, great desirability. Fortunately, this hurdle was achieved.

And yet, this is still not enough. To achieve enduring change, any obstacles have to be addressed and removed. With the case of neuroscience applications to market research and the use of nonconsious measurement, reasonable questions were raised regarding the ethics of neuro research practices.

The term neuroethics was first defined in 2002 to describe a field that connects the disciplines of the neurosciences, medical bioethics, cognitive science, public policy, law, and philosophy (Roskies, 2002; Trabulsi et al., 2017). The breadth of the field has provided for the consideration of complex ethical issues at an abstract and highly philosophical level, allowing for debate on the semantics of terminology as the field has crystallized (Baumeister & Bargh, 2014). As the neuromarketing industry continues to gain traction with a wider arena of clients, there is a growing need to consider a pragmatic focus on potential ethical issues that may arise from commercially applied neuroscience measures. The breadth of neuroethics must now comprise both academically oriented philosophical questions as well as application-centred considerations. Indeed, some academic institutions, practitioners, and client-side adopters have begun to understand this and put into place rules and language concerning the commercial use of applied measures of neuroscience (Al Pop et al., 2014; Thomas et al., 2016). In general, these rules speak to the need for the ethical treatment of human participants, focusing on informed consent and assurances of personal data protection to maintain participant privacy following participation in neuromarketing research.

In the realm of neuroscientific research for market research applications, several ethical and legal issues must be taken into consideration. The following is a list of key historical concerns by category:

Research Subjects:

- *Privacy* (with respect to identity, data and also possible findings regarding personal characteristics such as drug use or brain tumors)
- *Comfort* (does the equipment or protocol cause any discomfort, pain, or distress?)
- *Safety* (Is the experience 100% safe from causing any temporary or permanent harm to the subject?)
- *Influence* (Is the research experience likely to cause unusual influence over the subject with respect to attitudes and behavior?)

2. Marketers/Clients:

- *Responsible Conclusions and Recommendations* (Are the findings and insights presented without exaggeration, based on responsible designs with adequate sample size and expectation of repeatability?)

3. Company:

- *Liability* (Is any inappropriate risk being taken in any aspect of the research that could make the research company or end user vulnerable to liability? Does the research follow all established company policies, governmental laws and guidelines, as well as industry standards and codes both for neuro-based research and market research in general?)
- *Strategic Partnership Issues* (Is the IP of each firm properly protected? Are these safeguards in place to prevent client poaching?)

4. The Public

- *Influence* (Are insights from the research likely to cause inordinate influence - beyond the realm of conventional marketing - over consumers or other targets with respect to attitudes and behavior?)

SOLUTIONS AND RECOMMENDATIONS

After over a decade of examination and debate, the answers to all of the above questions were deemed to be ether favorable or manageable, provided that the same ethical standards of market research were applied to neuromarketing research as well. And the more familiar the industry became with neuromarketing methods and findings, the more open and accepting the professionals became until a tipping point occurred. Greenbook, the annual market research industry wide trends study, reported that nonconscious measurements, the foundation of the Neuromarketing research industry, were no longer a unique methodology, but a category of methods that are now embraced for conventional use, by leading brands the world over (*GreenBook Market Leaders Report*, 2019).

FUTURE RESEARCH DIRECTIONS

The Future: Advances Through Artificial Intelligence, Machine Learning, and Other New Technology Advances

Despite rapid change in a relatively short period, the advent of machine learning, artificial intelligence (AI), and predictive analytics promise to metamorphosize the research industry to become a superpower of understanding and prediction. And yet, it is possible that some current neuro methods will become obsolete or others are shown to be far superior in predictive power and practical considerations. In this regard, the race is on. Already some companies are claiming to be able to make market success predictions for new concepts using a relatively small amount of nonconscious data and artificial intelligence. For instance, the use of machine learning on large data sets is enabling the identification of new metrics such as body angle and head tilt with facial coding as contributory factors in being able to better predict ad performance. The key to the next frontier, predicting marketing effectiveness, will dwell with the ability to harness large data sets along with client and business organization's willingness to share data. Restriction to data access is currently the biggest obstacle to achieving breakthroughs in prediction and must be encouraged industry wide.

CONCLUSION

The game changing phenomenon for marketers and researchers was the discovery that emotion and the nonconsious response patterns are not only significant but dominating influencers of decision making and behavior. This chapter examined the rise and continued growth of the neuromarketing industry over the course of 2010-2020. The field has changed the way market research is conducted worldwide to include nonconscious measures in everyday studies. The integration of mixed methodologies that include in-moment responses to branded content, and credence to emotional influencers of behavior, are critical in this still relatively young field. Neuromarketing allows for a more precise understanding and prediction of brain and body responses that drive brand perceptions and behaviors. A summary of neuromarketing methods was presented that illustrates the more common-use tools in the industry, many of which are often used in conjunction with mixed methodological testing. A synopsis of several seminal studies was discussed to highlight contributions and collaborations in and across academic and industry use of neuroscientific tools. Several ethical issues were presented that have arisen in tandem with the field of neuromarketing, centered on neuromarketing vendors, study participants, and client end users of neuro-based data. Finally, a consideration of the future of the neuromarketing field is presented that highlights the increase in predictive power of brain and body data when integrated with artificial intelligence and a need for client-centered use of data to predict consumer behavior.

REFERENCES

Al Pop, N., Dabija, D.-C., & Iorga, A. M. (2014). Ethical responsibility of neuromarketing companies in harnessing the market research-A global exploratory approach. *Amfiteatru Economic*, *16*(35), 26.

Baumeister, R., & Bargh, J. (2014). Conscious and Unconscious. Toward an Integrative Understanding of Human Mental Life and Action. *Dual-Process Theories of the Social Mind,* 35–49.

Bellman, S., Nenycz-Thiel, M., Kennedy, R., Larguinat, L., McColl, B., & Varan, D. (2017). What Makes a Television Commercial Sell? Using Biometrics to Identify Successful Ads: Demonstrating Neuromeasures' Potential On 100 Mars Brand Ads with Single-Source Data. *Journal of Advertising Research*, *57*(1), 53–66. doi:10.2501/JAR-2016-051

Bruneau, E. G., Pluta, A., & Saxe, R. (2012). Distinct roles of the 'shared pain' and 'theory of mind' networks in processing others' emotional suffering. *Neuropsychologia*, *50*(2), 219–231. doi:10.1016/j.neuropsychologia.2011.11.008 PMID:22154962

Brunel, F. F., Tietje, B. C., & Greenwald, A. G. (2004). Is the implicit association test a valid and valuable measure of implicit consumer social cognition? *Journal of Consumer Psychology*, *14*(4), 385–404. doi:10.120715327663jcp1404_8

Choi, D., Sekiya, T., Minote, N., & Watanuki, S. (2016). Relative left frontal activity in reappraisal and suppression of negative emotion: Evidence from frontal alpha asymmetry (FAA). *International Journal of Psychophysiology*, *109*, 37–44. doi:10.1016/j.ijpsycho.2016.09.018 PMID:27693504

Clay Christensen's Milkshake Marketing. (2011, February 14). *HBS Working Knowledge*. https://hbswk.hbs.edu/item/clay-christensens-milkshake-marketing

CPC_Neuroscience_EN_150717.pdf. (n.d.). Retrieved March 10, 2020, from https://www.canadapost.ca/assets/pdf/blogs/CPC_Neuroscience_EN_150717.pdf

Genevsky, A., Yoon, C., & Knutson, B. (2017). When Brain Beats Behavior: Neuroforecasting Crowdfunding Outcomes. *The Journal of Neuroscience: The Official Journal of the Society for Neuroscience*, *37*(36), 8625–8634. doi:10.1523/JNEUROSCI.1633-16.2017 PMID:28821681

GreenBook Market Leaders Report. (n.d.). Retrieved March 10, 2020, from https://grit.greenbook.org/

Knutson, B., Fong, G. W., Bennett, S. M., Adams, C. M., & Hommer, D. (2003). A region of mesial prefrontal cortex tracks monetarily rewarding outcomes: Characterization with rapid event-related fMRI. *NeuroImage*, *18*(2), 263–272. doi:10.1016/S1053-8119(02)00057-5 PMID:12595181

Marox, E., Rodríguez, H., Yañez, G., Bernal, J., Rodríguez, M., Fernández, T., ... Guerrero, V. (2001). Broad band spectral measurements of EEG during emotional tasks. *The International Journal of Neuroscience*, *108*(3–4), 251–279. doi:10.3109/00207450108986517 PMID:11699193

Mitchell, J. P., Nosek, B. A., & Banaji, M. R. (2003). Contextual variations in implicit evaluation. *Journal of Experimental Psychology. General*, *132*(3), 455–469. doi:10.1037/0096-3445.132.3.455 PMID:13678378

Moli, J. P. (n.d.). *5 claves del Neuromarketing World Forum 2016*. Retrieved March 11, 2020, from http://brainandmarketing.blogspot.com/2016/01/5-claves-del-nmf-2016.html

Morishima, Y., Schunk, D., Bruhin, A., Ruff, C. C., & Fehr, E. (2012). Linking brain structure and activation in temporoparietal junction to explain the neurobiology of human altruism. *Neuron*, *75*(1), 73–79. doi:10.1016/j.neuron.2012.05.021 PMID:22794262

Moses, E., Beavin, L., Zaval, L., & Hendrickson, K. (2018). *The influence of an in-store gift on emotional arousal and shopper behavior*. Academic Press.

Neuromarketing News & Blog—NMSBA. (n.d.). Retrieved March 10, 2020, from https://nmsba.com/neuromarketing/news-blog?q=&p=2

Nosek, B. A., Smyth, F. L., Hansen, J. J., Devos, T., Lindner, N. M., Ranganath, K. A., ... Greenwald, A. G. (2007). Pervasiveness and correlates of implicit attitudes and stereotypes. *European Review of Social Psychology*, *18*(1), 36–88. doi:10.1080/10463280701489053

Ohme, R. (2016). *Neuromarketing World Forum, Speakers*. Neuromarketing World Forum. https://www.neuromarketingworldforum.com/info/videos/2016

Roskies, A. (2002). Neuroethics for the new millenium. *Neuron*, *35*(1), 21–23. doi:10.1016/S0896-6273(02)00763-8 PMID:12123605

The Neurological Effects of South Park | Viacom Fan Theory. (n.d.). Retrieved March 10, 2020, from http://fantheory.viacom.com/inside-the-brain/index.html

Thomas, A. R., Pop, N. A., Iorga, A. M., & Ducu, C. (2016). *Ethics and neuromarketing: Implications for market research and business practice*. Springer.

Trabulsi, J. F., Cordero-Merecuana, M., Somarriba, D., & Garcia-Garcia, M. (2017). Ethics in Consumer Neuroscience. *Consumer Neuroscience*, 303.

Varan, D., Lang, A., Barwise, P., Weber, R., & Bellman, S. (2015). How Reliable Are Neuromarketers' Measures of Advertising Effectiveness? Data from Ongoing Research Holds No Common Truth among Vendors. *Journal of Advertising Research*, *55*(2), 176–191. doi:10.2501/JAR-55-2-176-191

Venkatraman, V., Dimoka, A., Pavlou, P. A., Vo, K., Hampton, W., Bollinger, B., ... Winer, R. S. (2015). Predicting advertising success beyond traditional measures: New insights from neurophysiological methods and market response modeling. *JMR, Journal of Marketing Research*, *52*(4), 436–452. doi:10.1509/jmr.13.0593

KEY TERMS AND DEFINITIONS

Cognitive Neuroscience: The scientific field that is concerned with the study of the biological processes and aspects that underlie cognition, with a specific focus on the neural connections in the brain which are involved in mental processes.

Consumer Neuroscience: Is the combination of consumer research with modern neuroscience. The goal of the field is to find neural explanations for consumer behaviors. Unlike traditional market measures which rely on conscious recall of past experience or deliberative beliefs regarding future behaviors, consumer neuroscience relies on in-moment measures of central and peripheral nervous system processes that often occur outside of conscious awareness.

Crowd Sourced Data: Data simultaneously collected across a group of individuals.

Decision Making: The ability to make choices in certain and uncertain conditions.

Electroencephalography (EEG): EEG is a test used to evaluate the electrical activity in the brain. An EEG tracks and records brain wave patterns that are highly time locked to a stimulus.

Emotion: A natural instinctive state of mind deriving from one's circumstances, mood, or relationships with others.

Facial Action Unit Coding (FACs): FACs refers to a set of facial muscle movements that correspond to a displayed emotion.

Facial Electromyography (fEMG): Facial EMG refers to an electromyography (EMG) technique that measures muscle activity by detecting and amplifying the tiny electrical impulses that are generated by muscle fibers on the face when they contract and relax.

Functional Magnetic Resonance Imaging (fMRI): Functional magnetic resonance imaging or functional MRI (fMRI) measures brain activity by detecting changes associated with blood flow. This technique relies on the fact that cerebral blood flow and neuronal activation are coupled. When an area of the brain is in use, blood flow to that region also increases.

Functional Near Infrared Spectroscopy (fNIRS): Is a non-invasive imaging method involving the quantification of chromophore concentration resolved from the measurement of near infrared (NIR) light attenuation or temporal or phasic changes.

Haptics: The use of technology that stimulates the senses of touch and motion, especially to reproduce in remote operation or computer simulation the sensations that would be felt by a user interacting directly with physical objects.

Implicit Association Task (IAT): Is a measure within social psychology designed to detect the strength of a person's subconscious association between mental representations of objects (concepts) in memory on the basis of response time.

ISDN: Interdisciplinary symposia for decision neuroscience.

Judgements: The ability to generate estimates (guesses) regarding magnitudes and probabilities.

Neuromarketing Science and Business Association (NMSBA): Global organization aimed to increase awareness and utility of applied neuroscience across various commercial sectors.

Psychonomics: The science of the laws relating the mind to the organism's internal and external environment.

Sentiment Analysis: The process of computationally identifying and categorizing opinions expressed in a piece of text, especially in order to determine positive, negative, or neutral attitudes associated with test element.

Skin Conductance (Galvanic Skin Response): The psychophysiological phenomenon that the skin momentarily becomes a better conductor of electricity when either external or internal stimuli occur that are physiologically arousing.

Somatic Marker Hypothesis: Feelings in the body that are associated with emotions, such as the association of rapid heartbeat with anxiety or of nausea with disgust that strongly influence subsequent decision-making.

Stand-Off Measures: Measures captured from the consumer without having to physically touch the individual's person. Examples of stand-off measures include video and thermal cameras.

Thermal Imaging: The technique of using the heat given off by an object to produce an image of it, or to locate it, or to detect changes in health or emotion associated with a given stimulus.

Compilation of References

Aaker, J. (1997). Dimensions of brand personality. *JMR, Journal of Marketing Research, 34*(3), 347–356. doi:10.1177/002224379703400304

Abdalla, M. M. I., Abdelal, M. S., & Soon, S. C. (2019). Attitude towards problem-based learning and its relationship with locus of control and academic self-concept among medical students. *Korean Journal of Medical Education, 31*(1), 11–18. doi:10.3946/kjme.2019.114 PMID:30852857

Abeliotis, K., Koniari, C., & Sardianou, E. (2010). The profile of the green consumer in Greece. *International Journal of Consumer Studies, 34*(2), 153–160. doi:10.1111/j.1470-6431.2009.00833.x

ACCENTURE. (2014). *Circular advantage: innovative business models and technologies to create value in a world without limits to growth.* Available at: www.accenture.com/t20150523T053139__w__/ us en/_acnmedia/Accenture/ Conversion Assets/DotCom/Documents/Global/PDF/Strategy_6/ Accenture-Circular-Advantage-Innovative-Business-Models-Technologies-Value-Growth.pdf

Adams, D., Watkins, C., & White, M. (2008). *Planning, public policy and property markets* (Vol. 21). John Wiley & Sons.

Ahmad, N. (2017). *Indicators on global value chains: A guide for empirical work.* OECD Statistics Working Papers, 2017/08.

Ajzen, I. (2008). Consumer attitudes and behavior. Handbook of Consumer Psychology, 1, 525-548.

Ajzen, I. (1985). From intentions to actions: A theory of planned behavior. In *From intentions to actions: A theory of planned behavior* (pp. 11–39). Springer. doi:10.1007/978-3-642-69746-3_2

Ajzen, I. (1991). The theory of planned behavior. *Organizational Behavior and Human Decision Processes, 50*(2), 179–211. doi:10.1016/0749-5978(91)90020-T

Ajzen, I., Heilbroner, R. L., Fishbein, M., & Thurow, L. C. (1980). *Understanding Attitudes and Predicting Social Behaviour*. Prentice Hall PTR.

Al Pop, N., Dabija, D.-C., & Iorga, A. M. (2014). Ethical responsibility of neuromarketing companies in harnessing the market research-A global exploratory approach. *Amfiteatru Economic, 16*(35), 26.

Alcaro, A., Carta, S., & Panksepp, J. (2017). The affective core of the self: A neuro-archetypical perspective on the foundations of human (and animal) subjectivity. *Frontiers in Psychology, 8*, 1424. doi:10.3389/fpsyg.2017.01424 PMID:28919868

Alexander, M. (1996). *The Shock of Arrival: Reflections on Postcolonial Experience*. Boston: South End Press.

Alexandre, B., Navarro, J., Reynaud, E., & Osiurak, F. (2019). Which cognitive tools do we prefer to use, and is that preference rational? *Cognition, 186*(February), 108–114. doi:10.1016/j.cognition.2019.02.005 PMID:30771701

Alhawari, Y., Verhoff, M. A., Ackermann, H., & Parzeller, M. (2019). Religious denomination influencing attitudes towards brain death, organ transplantation and autopsy—A survey among people of different religions. *International Journal of Legal Medicine*, 1–10. doi:10.100700414-019-02130-0 PMID:31418075

Ali, I. (2019). Personality traits, individual innovativeness and satisfaction with life. *Journal of Innovation & Knowledge*, *4*(1), 38–46. doi:10.1016/j.jik.2017.11.002

Allaway, D. (2012). *Briefing Paper: Sustainable Consumption and Waste Prevention*. Retrieved January 10, 2020 from https://www.oregon.gov/deq/FilterDocs/2050-SustConsumpWastePrevention.pdf

Allen, B. P. (2006). Personality theories: development, growth, & diversity (5th ed.). London: Routledge.

Allen, M., Springer, T., & Waller, N. (1995). Implicit Pricing Across Residential Rental Submarkets. *The Journal of Real Estate Finance and Economics*, *11*(2), 137–151. doi:10.1007/BF01098658

Al-Mawrid, B. (2010). *A Modern Arabic-English Dictionary*. Beirut, Lebanon: Dar El-IlmLilmalayin.

Almeida, C., Karadzic, V., & Vaz, S. (2015). The seafood market in Portugal: Driving forces and consequences. *Marine Policy*, *61*, 87–94. doi:10.1016/j.marpol.2015.07.012

Almeida, J. F., Costa, A. F., & Machado, F. L. (1994). Recomposição socioprofissional e novos protagonismos. In A. Reis (Ed.), *Portugal: 20 Anos de Democracia* (pp. 307–330). Lisbon: Círculo de Leitores.

Almond, G. A., & Verba, S. (1963). *The Civic Culture: Political Attitudes and Democracy in Five Nations*. SAGE Publications. doi:10.1515/9781400874569

Alves, H. (2018). Sharing rare attitudes attracts. *Personality and Social Psychology Bulletin*, *44*(8), 1270–1283. doi:10.1177/0146167218766861 PMID:29637846

Amaldoss, W., & Jain, S. (2005). Conspicuous consumption and sophisticated thinking. *Management Science*, *51*(10), 1449–1466. doi:10.1287/mnsc.1050.0399

American Express Retail Monitor. (2018). *Annual Report 2018*. Retrieved from https://ir.americanexpress.com/

Andersen, L. F. (2015). The spatial and experiential dimensions of coastal zone tourism in Denmark. In A. Lorentzen, K. T. Larsen, & L. Schrøder (Eds.), *Spatial Dynamics in the Experience Economy* (pp. 174–190). Abingdon: Routledge.

Andersson Cederholm, E. (2004). The Use of Photo-elicitation in Tourism Research: Framing the Backpacker Experience. *Scandinavian Journal of Hospitality and Tourism*, *4*(3), 225–241. doi:10.1080/15022250410003870

Andreasen, A. R., Goldberg, M. E., & Sirgy, M. J. (2012). Foundational research on consumer welfare: Opportunities for a transformative consumer research agenda. In Transformative consumer research for personal and collective well-being, (pp. 25-65). Academic Press.

Andrews, C. J. (2007). Rationality in Policy Decision Making. In F. Fischer, G. Miller, & M. Sidney (Eds.), Handbook of Public Policy Analysis: Theory, Politics and Methods (pp. 161–172). Taylor & Francis.

ANEEL- Agência Nacional de Energia Elétrica. (2019). *Retrospectiva ANEEL*. Retrieved from https://www.aneel.gov.br/

Angelou, M. (2019). Staff spotlight. *Policy & Practice*, (19426828). Retrieved from http://search.ebscohost.com/login.aspx?direct=true&db=a9h&AN=135974225&site=eds-live

Ansaloni, F., Claros, A., Marquina, R., Pyszny, F., Quispe, J., & Zapata, J. (2006). Análisis del ingreso agricola proveniente de la producción de carne de camélidos sudamericanos en los paises latinoamericanos: resultados preliminares de una comparación de estudios de caso. In C. Renieri, E. Frank, & O. Toro (Eds.), *Camélidos Sudamericanos Domésticos: investigaciones recientes* (pp. 313–333). Lima, Peru: DESCO.

Anselin, L. (1988). *Spatial Econometrics: Methods and Models*. Boston: Kluwer. doi:10.1007/978-94-015-7799-1

Anselin, L. (2002). Under the Hood: Issues in the Specification and Interpretation of Spatial Regression Models. *Agricultural Economics*, *27*(3), 247–267. doi:10.1111/j.1574-0862.2002.tb00120.x

Anselin, L. (2010). Thirty years of spatial econometrics. *Papers in Regional Science*, *89*(1), 3–25. doi:10.1111/j.1435-5957.2010.00279.x

Antonini, M., Torres, D., Cristofanelli, S., Polidori, P., & Renieri, C. (2006). Calidad de la carne y carcasa de la llama (Lama glama) y la alpaca (Lama pacos) peruanas. In C. Renieri, E. Frank, & O. Toro (Eds.), *Camelidos sudamericanos domésticos. Investigaciones recientes* (pp. 113–123). Lima, Peru: DESCO.

Aplin, G. (2007). World Heritage Cultural Landscapes. *International Journal of Heritage Studies*, *13*(6), 427–446. doi:10.1080/13527250701570515

Appadurai, A. (1986). Introduction: Commodities and the Politics of Value. In The Social Life of Things: Commodities in Cultural Perspective. Melbourne: Cambridge University Press.

Applebaum, K. (1998). The sweetness of salvation: Consumer marketing and the liberal-bourgeois Theory of Needs. *Current Anthropology*, *39*(3), 323–349. doi:10.1086/204737

Arcadis (EURONEXT: ARCAD), Global Design & Consultancy. (2019). *People-centric mobility is key to the future success of cities*. https://www.arcadis.com/en/global/news/latest-news/2019/06/people-centric-mobility-is-key-for-the-future-success-of-cities/

Ariely, D., & Berns, G. S. (2010). Neuromarketing: The hope and hype of neuroimaging in business. *Nature Reviews. Neuroscience*, *11*(4), 284–292. doi:10.1038/nrn2795 PMID:20197790

Arli, D., Tkaczynski, A., & Anandya, D. (2019). Are religious consumers more ethical and less Machiavellian? A segmentation study of Millennials. *International Journal of Consumer Studies*, *43*(3), 263–276. doi:10.1111/ijcs.12507

Armstrong, C. M., Niinimäki, K., Kujala, S., Karell, E., & Lang, C. (2015). Sustainable product-service systems for clothing: Exploring consumer perceptions of consumption alternatives in Finland. *Journal of Cleaner Production*, *97*(June), 30–39. doi:10.1016/j.jclepro.2014.01.046

Arnold, M. J., & Reynolds, K. E. (2003). Hedonic shopping motivations. *Journal of Retailing*, *79*(2), 77–95. doi:10.1016/S0022-4359(03)00007-1

Arnott, R. (1987). Economic theory and housing. In G. Duranton, V. Henderson, & W. Strange (Eds.), Handbook of regional and urban economics (vol. 2). Elsevier Science Publishers.

Arnott, D., & Gao, S. (2019a). Behavioral economics for decision support systems researchers. *Decision Support Systems*, *122*(February), 113063. doi:10.1016/j.dss.2019.05.003

Arnott, D., & Pervan, G. (2005). A Critical Analysis of Decision Support Systems Research. *Journal of Information Technology*, *20*(2), 67–87. doi:10.1057/palgrave.jit.2000035

Arnould, E., & Thompson, C. (2005). Consumer Culture Theory (CCT): Twenty Years of Research. *The Journal of Consumer Research*, *31*(4), 868–882. doi:10.1086/426626

Arora, R., & Singer, J. (2006). Customer satisfaction and value as drivers of business success for fine dining restaurants. *Services Marketing Quarterly*, *28*(1), 89–102. doi:10.1300/J396v28n01_05

Arrondel, L., & Lefebvre, B. (2001). Consumption and investment motives in housing wealth accumulation: A French study. *Journal of Urban Economics*, *50*(1), 112–137. doi:10.1006/juec.2000.2209

Arts, J. W. C., Frambach, R. T., & Bijmolt, T. H. A. (2011). Generalizations on consumer innovation adoption: A meta-analysis on drivers of intention & behavior. *International Journal of Research in Marketing*, *28*(2), 134–144. doi:10.1016/j.ijresmar.2010.11.002

Ascencio, L. M., González-Ramírez, R. G., Bearzotti, L. A., Smith, N. R., & Camacho-Vallejo, J. F. (2014). A Collaborative supply chain management system for a maritime port logistics chain. *Journal of Applied Research and Technology*, *12*(3), 444–458. doi:10.1016/S1665-6423(14)71625-6

Ashworth, G. J. (2000). Heritage, Tourism and Places: A Review. *Tourism Recreation Research*, *25*(1), 19–28. doi:10.1080/02508281.2000.11014897

Ashworth, G. J. (2003). Heritage, identity and places: For tourists and host communities. In S. Singh, D. J. Timothy, & R. K. Dowling (Eds.), *Tourism in Destination Communities* (pp. 79–97). Wallingford: CABI. doi:10.1079/9780851996110.0079

Atalay, H. (1999). *Inglizce-Türkçe Sözlük*. Ankara: Türk Dili Kurumu.

Atkins, K. G., & Kim, Y.-K. (2012). Smart shopping: Conceptualization and measurement. *International Journal of Retail & Distribution Management*, *40*(5), 360–375. doi:10.1108/09590551211222349

Atkins, K. G., Kumar, A., & Kim, Y.-K. (2016). Smart grocery shopper segments. *Journal of International Consumer Marketing*, *28*(1), 42–53. doi:10.1080/08961530.2015.1082080

Attié, E., & Meyer-Waarden, L. (2018). The acceptance process of the Internet of Things: How to improve the acceptance of the IoT technology? In Smart Marketing With the Internet of Things. doi:10.4018/978-1-5225-5763-0

Atwal, G., & Williams, A. (2009). Luxury brand marketing – The experience is everything! *Journal of Brand Management*, *16*(5), 338–346. doi:10.1057/bm.2008.48

Aviles, M. (2016). *De donde venimos los cholos*. Lima, Peru: Seis Barral.

Awad, N. F., & Krishnan, M. S. (2006). The personalization privacy paradox: An empirical evaluation of information transparency and the willingeness to be profiled online for personalization. *Management Information Systems Quarterly*, *30*(1), 13–28. doi:10.2307/25148715

Ayadi, N., Paraschiv, C., & Vernette, E. (2017). Increasing consumer well-being: Risk as potential driver of happiness. *Applied Economics*, *49*(43), 4321–4335. doi:10.1080/00036846.2017.1282142

Ayeni, B. (2003). The design of spatial decision support systems in urban and regional planning (pp. 20–33). Academic Press.

Azevedo Filho, E. T., Palma, M. A. M., Perestrelo, M., da Hora, H. R. M., & Lira, R. A. (2019). The pre-salt layer and challenges to competitiveness in Brazil: Critical reflections on the local content policy in the oil and gas Sector. *The Extractive Industries and Society*, *6*(4), 1168–1173. doi:10.1016/j.exis.2019.09.009

Azevedo, G., & Gates, A. (2019). Wake Up! The World Is Out of Balance and If You Do Nothing You Are Part of the Problem: An Interview With Henry Mintzberg. *Journal of Management Inquiry*, *28*(2), 180–186. doi:10.1177/1056492618761811

Backx, J., Hilberath, C., Messenböck, R., & Morieux, Y. H. S. (2017). Mastering Complexity Through Simplification: Four Steps to Creating Competitive Advantage. *Boston Consulting Group*. Retrieved from https://www.bcg.com/publications/2017/people-organization-operations-mastering-complexity-through-simplification.aspx

Bagnall, G. (2003). Performance and Performativity at Heritage Sites. *Museum & Society*, *1*(2), 87–103. doi:10.29311/mas.v1i2.17

Bagwell, L. S., & Bernheim, B. D. (1996). Veblen effects in a theory of conspicuous consumption. *The American Economic Review*, *86*(3), 349–373.

Baiburin, A. (1983). *Jhilishche v obrjadakh i predstavleniax vostochnix slavjan* [Dwelling in rites and performances of Eastern Slavs]. Leningrad: Nauka.

Bailey, A., Mishra, A., & Tiamiyu, M. (2016). GREEN consumption values and Indian consumers' response to marketing communications. *Journal of Consumer Marketing*, *3*(7), 562–573. doi:10.1108/JCM-12-2015-1632

Balconi, M., Sebastiani, R., & Agioletti, L. (2019). Sensory marketing: Perspectives on benefits consumers'grapple in choosing greener products. *Global Journal of Commerce & Menagement Perspective*, *11*, 1–14.

Ballerstadt, R. (2010). *The postcolonial Citizen, the Intellectual Migrant*. New York: Peter Lang Publishing, Inc. doi:10.3726/978-1-4539-0057-4

Bandura, A. (1986). *Social foundations of thought and action: A social cognitive theory*. Prentice-Hall, Inc.

Bandyopadhyay, R. (2008). Nostalgia, identity and tourism: Bollywood in the Indian Diaspora. *Journal of Tourism and Cultural Change*, *6*(2), 79–100. doi:10.1080/14766820802140463

Barbosa, D., & Stanley, H. E. J. S. B. (1866). *A Description of the Coasts of East Africa and Malabar in the Beginning of the Sixteenth Century*. Hakluyt Society.

Baregheh, A., Rowley, J., & Sambrook, S. (2009). Towards a multidisciplinary definition of innovation. *Management Decision*, *47*(8), 1323–1339. doi:10.1108/00251740910984578

Bargh, J. A. (1994). The four horsemen of automaticity: Awareness, intention, efficiency, and control in social cognition. In R. S. Wyer Jr & T. K. Srull (Eds.), *Handbook of Social Cognition* (2nd ed., Vol. 1, pp. 1–40). Hillsdale, NY: Erlbaum.

Bargh, J. A. (1997). Automaticity of Everyday Life. *Advances in Social Cognition*, *10*, 1–61.

Barilliance. (2015). The most effective types of personalized product recommendations. *Barilliance*. Retrieved from https://www.barilliance.com/the-most-effective-types-of-personalized-product-recommendation

Barlow, J., & Duncan, S. (1992). Markets, states and housing provision: Four European growth regions compared. *Progress in Planning*, *38*, 93–177. doi:10.1016/0305-9006(92)90006-2

Barnett, T., Pearson, A. W., Pearson, R., & Kellermanns, F. W. (2015). Five-factor model personality traits as predictors of perceived & actual usage of technology. *European Journal of Information Systems*, *24*(4), 374–390. doi:10.1057/ejis.2014.10

Barska, A. (2018). Millennial consumers in the convenience food market. *Management*, *22*(1), 251–264. doi:10.2478/manment-2018-0018

Bartels, D. M., & Johnson, E. J. (2015). Connecting cognition and consumer choice. *Cognition*, *135*, 47–51. doi:10.1016/j.cognition.2014.11.024 PMID:25527275

Bartels, J., & Reinders, M. J. (2011). Consumer innovativeness & its correlates: A propositional inventory for future research. *Journal of Business Research, 64*(6), 601–609. doi:10.1016/j.jbusres.2010.05.002

Barthel, R., Hudson-Smith, A., & de Jode, M. (2015). Future retail environments and the internet of things (IoT). London Global University, UCL.

Barth, F. (1969). *Ethnic Groups and Boundaries*. Boston: Little Brown.

Bartnik, R., Wilhelm, M., & Fujimoto, T. (2018). Introduction to innovation in the East Asian automotive industry: Exploring the interplay between product architectures, firm strategies, and national innovation systems. *Technovation, 70–71*, 1–6.

Basu, S., & Thibodeau, T. G. (1998). Analysis of spatial autocorrelation in house prices. *The Journal of Real Estate Finance and Economics, 17*(1), 61–85. doi:10.1023/A:1007703229507

Bathmanathan, V., Rajadurai, J., & Sohail, M. S. (2018). Generational Consumer Patterns: A Document Analysis Method. *Global Business and Management Research, 10*(3), 958–970. Retrieved from http://search.ebscohost.com/login.aspx?direct=true&db=bth&AN=133618190&site=eds-live

Batista, P. (2019). *The interaction structure of e-territorial systems: territory, housing market and spatial econometrics / A estrutura de interação de um sistema e-territorial. Território, mercado de habitação e econometria espacial*. Universidade de Aveiro.

Bauer, M. M. (2013). *Estudo Sobre a Evidenciação Ambiental e Social Voluntárias das Empresas de Capital Aberto em Relatórios Anuais*. Tese de Doutorado. Universidade Feevale.

Bault, N., & Rusconi, E. (2020). The Art of Influencing Consumer Choices: A Reflection on Recent Advances in Decision Neuroscience. *Frontiers in Psychology, 10*, 3009. doi:10.3389/fpsyg.2019.03009 PMID:32038387

Baumeister, R., & Bargh, J. (2014). Conscious and Unconscious. Toward an Integrative Understanding of Human Mental Life and Action. *Dual-Process Theories of the Social Mind,* 35–49.

Baunach, M., Martins Gomes, R., Malenko, M., Mauroner, F., Batista Ribeiro, L., & Scheipel, T. (2018). Smart mobility of the future – a challenge for embedded automotive systems. *Elektrotech. Inftech., 135*(4-5), 304–308. doi:10.100700502-018-0623-6

BCG - Boston Consulting Group. (2018). *Complicatedness Survey: BCG's Complicatedness Survey pinpoints problem areas.* Retrieved from https://www.bcg.com/capabilities/smart-simplicity/complicatedness-survey.aspx

BCG - Boston Consulting Group. (2019). *Risk Management &Compliance in the Financial Industry.* Retrieved from https://www.bcg.com/industries/financial-institutions/risk-management.aspx

BCG - Boston Consulting Group. (2020a). *The New Globalization: A Collection.* Retrieved from https://www.bcg.com/featured-insights/thought-leadership-ideas.aspx

BCG - Boston Consulting Group. (2020b). *What will it take to win in the 2020s?* Retrieved from https://www.bcg.com/featured-insights/winning-the-20s/overview.aspx

Bechara, A., Tranel, D., & Damasio, H. (2000). Characterization of the decision-making deficit of patients with ventromedial prefrontal cortex lesions. *Brain, 123*(11), 2189-2202. doi:10.1093/brain/123.11.2189

Bedeian, A. G., & Wren, D. A. (2001). Most influential management books of the 20th Century. *Organizational Dynamics, 29*(3), 221–225. doi:10.1016/S0090-2616(01)00022-5

Belk, R. W. (1988). Possessions and the extended self. *The Journal of Consumer Research*, *15*(2), 139–168. doi:10.1086/209154

Bellman, S., Nenycz-Thiel, M., Kennedy, R., Larguinat, L., McColl, B., & Varan, D. (2017). What Makes a Television Commercial Sell? Using Biometrics to Identify Successful Ads: Demonstrating Neuromeasures' Potential On 100 Mars Brand Ads with Single-Source Data. *Journal of Advertising Research*, *57*(1), 53–66. doi:10.2501/JAR-2016-051

Beratšová, A., Krchová, K., Gažová, N., & Jirásek, M. (2018). Framing and Bias: A Literature Review of Recent Findings. *Central European Journal of Management*, *3*(2), 23–32. doi:10.5817/CEJM2016-2-2

Bercea, M. D. (2013). *Quantitative versus qualitative in neuromarketing research*. MPRA Paper No. 44134.

Berger, J., Humphreys, A., Ludwig, S., Moe, W. W., Netzer, O., & Schweidel, D. A. (2020). Uniting the Tribes: Using Text for Marketing Insight. *Journal of Marketing*, *84*(1), 1–25. doi:10.1177/0022242919873106

Berger, P., Berger, B., & Kellner, H. (1974). *The Homeless Mind*. New York: Vintage books.

Berghaus, S., & Back, A. (2016). Stages in digital business transformation: results of an empirical maturity study. *MCIS 2016 Proceedings*, 22. https://aisel.aisnet.org/mcis2016/22

Beriss, D. (2019). Food: Location, Location, Location. *Annual Review of Anthropology*, *48*. doi:10.1146/annurev-anthro-102317-050249

Berridge, K., & Robinson, T. (2016). Liking, wanting, and the incentive-sensitization theory of addiction. *The American Psychologist*, *71*(8), 670–679. doi:10.1037/amp0000059 PMID:27977239

Berry, C. J., Paganelli, M. P., & Smith, C. (2013). *The Oxford Handbook of Adam Smit*h. OUP Oxford. Retrieved from https://books.google.pt/books?id=D7Bef_1f_w0C

Betsch, T., & Haberstroh, S. (2005). *The routines of decision making* (T. Betsch & S. Haberstroh, Eds.). Lawrence Erlbaum Associates.

Beverland, M. (2004). Uncovering "theories-in-use": Building luxury wine brands. *European Journal of Marketing*, *38*(3/4), 446–466. doi:10.1108/03090560410518648

Beverland, M. (2005). Crafting brand authenticity: The case of luxury wines. *Journal of Management Studies*, *42*(5), 1003–1029. doi:10.1111/j.1467-6486.2005.00530.x

Beverland, M. (2006). The 'real thing': Branding authenticity in the luxury wine trade. *Journal of Business Research*, *59*(2), 251–258. doi:10.1016/j.jbusres.2005.04.007

Bhattacharjee, A., Castro, E., Maiti, T., & Marques, J. (2016). Endogenous Spatial Regression and Delineation of Submarkets: A New Framework with Application to Housing Markets. *Journal of Applied Econometrics*, *31*(1), 32–57. doi:10.1002/jae.2478

Bhattacharjee, A., Castro, E., & Marques, J. (2012). Spatial Interactions in Hedonic Pricing Models: The Urban Housing Market of Aveiro, Portugal. *Spatial Economic Analysis*, *7*(1), 133–167. doi:10.1080/17421772.2011.647058

Bhattacharjee, A., & Holly, S. (2013). Understanding interactions in social networks and committees. *Spatial Economic Analysis*, *8*(1), 23–53. doi:10.1080/17421772.2012.722669

Bhattacherjee, A. (2000). Acceptance of e-commerce services: The case of electronic brokerages. *IEEE Transactions on Systems, Man, and Cybernetics*, *30*(4), 411–420. doi:10.1109/3468.852435

Bilsky, W., & Schwartz, S. H. (1994). Values & personality. *European Journal of Personality*, *8*(3), 163–181. doi:10.1002/per.2410080303

Blair, A. J., Atanasova, C., Pitt, L., Chan, A., & Wallstrom, Å. (2017). Assessing brand equity in the luxury wine market by exploiting tastemaker scores. *Journal of Product and Brand Management*, *26*(5), 447–452. doi:10.1108/JPBM-06-2016-1214

Boano, C., Römer, K., Bloem, R., Witrisal, K., Baunach, M., & Horn, M. (2016). Dependability for the Internet of things: From dependable networking in harsh environments to a holistic view on dependability. *E&I Elektrotechnik und Informationstechnik*, *133*(7), 304–309. doi:10.100700502-016-0436-4

Bocken, N. M., Short, S. W., Rana, P., & Evans, S. (2014). A literature and practice review to develop sustainable business model archetypes. *Journal of Cleaner Production*, *65*, 42–56. doi:10.1016/j.jclepro.2013.11.039

Boglioti, E., Lyon, V., & Morieux, I. (2016). The Smart Solution to the Productivity Paradox. *The Boston Consulting Group*. Retrieved from https://www.bcg.com/publications/2016/technology-digital-people-organization-smart-solution-productivity-paradox.aspx

Boncinelli, F., Dominici, A., Gerini, F., & Marone, E. (2019). Consumers wine preferences according to purchase occasion: Personal consumption and gift-giving. *Food Quality and Preference*, *71*, 270–278. doi:10.1016/j.foodqual.2018.07.013

Bonn, M. A., Joseph-Mathews, S. M., Dai, M., Hayes, S., & Cave, J. (2007). Heritage/Cultural Attraction Atmospherics: Creating the Right Environment for the Heritage/Cultural Visitor. *Journal of Travel Research*, *45*(3), 345–354. doi:10.1177/0047287506295947

Bordarie, J., & Gaymard, S. (2015). Social Representations and Public Policy: Influence of the Distance from the Object on Representational Valence. *Open Journal of Social Sciences*, *03*(09), 300–305. doi:10.4236/jss.2015.39038

Borg, J., Costa, P., & Gotti, G. (1996). Tourism in European heritage cities. *Annals of Tourism Research*, *23*(2), 306–321. doi:10.1016/0160-7383(95)00065-8

Bornstein, R. F. (1989). Exposure and affect: Overview and meta-analysis of research, 1968-1987. *Psychological Bulletin*, *2*(2), 265–289. doi:10.1037/0033-2909.106.2.265

Bornstein, R. F., & Pittman, T. S. (1992). *Perception Without Awareness*. New York: The Guilford Press.

Bostancı, S. & Yıldırım, S. (2020). A Conceptual Study on Sustainable Communities and Ecological Citizenship. *IGDIR University Journal of Social Sciences*, (5), 203-218.

Bourdieu, P. (1979). *La Distinction. Critique Sociale du Jugement*. Paris: Éditions du Minuit.

Bourne, L. S. (1981). *The geography of housing*. London, UK: Edward Arnold.

Boyd, S. (2002). Cultural and Heritage Tourism in Canada: Opportunities, Principles and Challenges. *Tourism and Hospitality Research*, *3*(February), 211–233. doi:10.1177/146735840200300303

Bozkurt, E. (2009). *Conseptualising "Home". The Question of belonging among Turkish Families in Germany*. Frankfurt, New York: Campus Verlag.

Brendl, C. M., Markman, A. B., & Messner, C. (2001). How do indirect measures of evaluation work? Evaluating the inference of prejudice in the Implicit Association Test. *Journal of Personality and Social Psychology*, *81*(5), 760–773. doi:10.1037/0022-3514.81.5.760 PMID:11708555

Brennen, S., & Kreis, D. (2014). *Digitalization and digitalization*. http://culturedigitally.org/2014/09/digitalization-and-digitalization

Brewer, J., & Trentmann, F. (2006). *Consuming cultures, global perspectives: historical trajectories, transnational exchanges*. Retrieved from https://books.google.pt/books?id=XACSAAAAIAAJ

Brewer, M. B. (1979). In-group bias in the Minimal Intergroup Situation: A Cognitive-Motivational Analysis. *Psychological Bulletin*, *86*(2), 307–324. doi:10.1037/0033-2909.86.2.307

Brewer, M. B., & Hewstone, M. (2004). *Social cognition*. Blackwell Publishing Ltd.

Brodbeck, F. C., Kerchreiter, R., Mojzisch, A., & Schulz-Hardt, S. (2007). Group decision making under conditions of distributed knowledge: The information asymmetries model. *Academy of Management Review*, *32*(2), 459–479. doi:10.5465/amr.2007.24351441

Brown, H. D. (1994). *Principles of Language Learning and Teaching*. Englewood Cliffs, NJ: Prentice-Hall.

Brown, T. C. (1984). The Concept of Value in Resource Allocation. *Land Economics*, *60*(3), 231–246. doi:10.2307/3146184

Bruneau, E. G., Pluta, A., & Saxe, R. (2012). Distinct roles of the 'shared pain'and 'theory of mind'networks in processing others' emotional suffering. *Neuropsychologia*, *50*(2), 219–231. doi:10.1016/j.neuropsychologia.2011.11.008 PMID:22154962

Brunel, F. F., Tietje, B. C., & Greenwald, A. G. (2004). Is the implicit association test a valid and valuable measure of implicit consumer social cognition? *Journal of Consumer Psychology*, *14*(4), 385–404. doi:10.120715327663jcp1404_8

Bruner, G. C. II, & Kumar, A. (2005). Explaining consumer acceptance of handheld internet devices. *Journal of Business Research*, *58*(5), 553–558. doi:10.1016/j.jbusres.2003.08.002

Bruwer, J., Saliba, A., & Miller, B. (2011). Consumer behaviour and sensory preference differences: Implications for wine product marketing. *Journal of Consumer Marketing*, *28*(1), 5–18. doi:10.1108/07363761111101903

Buchraschwili, P. (2014). *Nicholas Marr – 150*. Tbilisi: Amirani.

Bukhrashvili, P. (2013)., House" in ancient Georgia. In *Proceedings of III international congress of Caucasiologists* (pp. 27-28). Tbilissi: Iv. Javakhishvili Tbilisi State University.

Bukhrashvili, P. (2001). *Kartli and Kakheti in the last quarter of the 18th and beginning of the 19th centuries*. Tbilisi: Amirani.

Bukhrashvili, P. (2003). *For a delimitation of the place of the phenomenon of dwellings in the daily life and culture of the Georgian people in the past (An attempt at Paleo Ethnological study)*. Tbilisi: Amirani.

Bukhrashvili, P. (2005). *Sacxovrisi qartveli eris yofasa da kulturashi zvelad* [Dweling in the life and culture of the ancient Geirgians]. Tbilisi: Amirani.

Bukhrashvili, P. (2014). *Saint George the great Knight*. Tbilisi: Amirani.

Bulz, A. C., Stapleton, A., Lewoc, B., & Bulz, N. (2015). On a Master-plan Towards a Cognitive Science Networking Religion, Conflict and Peacebuilding and Technology, Culture and International Stability. *IFAC*, *48*(24), 183–188. doi:10.1016/j.ifacol.2015.12.080

Bundy, A. (2017). Preparing for the future of Artificial Intelligence. *AI & Society*, *32*(2), 285–287. doi:10.100700146-016-0685-0

Burmann, C., Halaszovich, T., Schade, M., & Hemmann, F. (2017). *Identity-based brand management*. Wiesbaden: Springer Gabler. doi:10.1007/978-3-658-13561-4

Burnett, J., & Moriarty, S. E. (1998). *Introduction to marketing communication: an integrated approach*. Prentice Hall.

Butler, R.W. (2011). It's only make believe: the implications of fictional and authentic locations in films. *Worldwide Hospitality & Tourism Themes, 3*(2), 91 – 101.

Buxrashvili, P. (2005). *Dwelling in the Life and Culture of Ancient Georgia*. Tbilisi.

Caceres Cabana, Y. (1998). *Estudio de la comercialización de carne de alpaca. Mercados y Fuentes* (Unpublished master dissertation). Universidad nacional de San Agustin de Arequipa, Arequipa, Peru.

Caceres Cabana, Y. (2002). *Análisis del sistema de valor de carne del sub sector de carne de alpaca y llama* (Unpublished doctoral dissertation). Universidad Nacional Agraria La Molina, Lima, Perú.

Caceres Cabana, Y. (2012). El Uso de la Radio para Mejorar la Respuesta Local a la Variabilidad Climática: el Caso de los Criadores de Alpacas de la Región Andina del Perú. Manchester, Reino Unido: Nexus for ICTS, Climate Change and Development (NICCD).

Caceres Cabana, Y. (2019). Aspectos cualitativos que influyen en el consumo de carne de alpaca en el sector turismo. Papper presented at Seminario nacional: Carne de camélidos: potencialidades, politicas y consume, Arequipa, Perú.

Cacioppo, J. T., Petty, R. E., Kao, C. F., & Rodriguez, R. (1986). Central and peripheral routes to persuasion: An individual difference perspective. *Journal of Personality and Social Psychology, 51*(5), 1032. Doi:10.1037/0022-3514.51.5.1032

Cahill, S. E., Duveen, G., & Lloyd, B. (1990). *Social Representations and The Development of Knowledge* (Vol. 20). Academic Press.

Cairney, P., & Weible, C. M. (2017). The new policy sciences: Combining the cognitive science of choice, multiple theories of context, and basic and applied analysis. *Policy Sciences, 50*(4), 619–627. doi:10.100711077-017-9304-2

Can, A. (1990). The Measurement of Neighbourhood Dynamics in Urban House Prices. *Economic Geography, 66*(3), 254. doi:10.2307/143400

Caprara, G. V., Schwartz, S., Capanna, C., Vecchione, M., & Barbaranelli, C. (2006). Personality & Politics: Values, Traits, & Political Choice. *Political Psychology, 27*(1), 1–28. doi:10.1111/j.1467-9221.2006.00447.x

Carling, G., Cronhamn, S., Farren, R., Aliyev, E., & Frid, J. (2019). The causality of borrowing: Lexical loans in Eurasian languages. *PLoS One, 14*(10), 1–33. doi:10.1371/journal.pone.0223588 PMID:31665148

Carneiro, J., Conceição, L., Martinho, D., Marreiros, G., & Novais, P. (2016). Including cognitive aspects in multiple criteria decision analysis. *Annals of Operations Research.*

Carrier, J. (1995). *Gifts and Commodities: Exchange and Western Capitalism since 1770*. London: Routledge.

Carrus, G. A., & Caddeo, P. (2008). *Science Direct*. Retrieved 5 2, 2018, from The Role of Ethnic Identity and Perceived Ethnic Norms in Purchase of Ethnic Food Products: http://www.sciencedirect.com

Carter, C. (2017). The Oxytocin–Vasopressin Pathway in the Context of Love and Fear. *Frontiers in Endocrinology, 8*, 8. doi:10.3389/fendo.2017.00356 PMID:29312146

Carter, P. (1992). *Living in New Country, History, Travelling and Language*. London: Faber and Faber.

Carugati, F. F. (1990). From social cognition to social representations in the study of intelligence. In Social Representations and The Development of Knowledge (pp. 126–143). doi:10.1017/CBO9780511659874.008

Cassell, J. (2019). Artificial intelligence for a social world: The underlying mission is to better understand social interaction and to build machines that work more collaboratively and effectively with humans. *Issues in Science and Technology VO, 35*(4), 29.

Catry, B. (2003). The great pretenders: The magic of luxury goods. *Business Strategy Review*, *14*(3), 10. doi:10.1111/1467-8616.00267

Ceballos, L. M., & Bejarano, M. (2018). Value segmentation of adolescents: A performance of appearance. *International Journal of Fashion Design. Technology & Education*, *11*(2), 148–159. doi:10.1080/17543266.2017.1352039

Çelik, H. E., & Yilmaz, V. (2011). Extending the Technology Acceptance Model for Adoption of E-shopping by Consumers in Turkey. *Journal of Electronic Commerce Research*, *12*(2), 152–164.

CES Las Vegas. (2018). *Toyota Motor Corporation, President Akio Toyoda - Speech.* Press event presentation. https://global.toyota/en/album/videos/20566886

Chadha, S. (2018). *The CMO of 2020: navigating the journey towards digital marketing maturity in APAC.* https://bit.ly/2UGzakO

Chaib, M. (2015). Social representations, subjectivity and learning. *Cadernos de Pesquisa*, *45*(156), 359–371.

Chamber, L. (2001). *Culture After Humanism: History, Culture, Subjectivity.* New York: Routledge.

Chan Kim, W., & Mauborgne, R. (2005). *Blue Ocean Strategy: How to create uncontested market space and make the competition irrelevant.* Boston: Harvard Business Review Press.

Chan, K. (2000). Market Segmentation of Green Consumers in Hong Kong. *Journal of International Consumer Marketing*, *12*(2), 7–24. doi:10.1300/J046v12n02_02

Chao, C., Reid, M., & Mavondo, F. T. (2012). Consumer innovativeness influence on really new product adoption. *Australasian Marketing Journal*, *20*(3), 211–217. doi:10.1016/j.ausmj.2012.02.001

Chatzidakis, A., Kastanakis, M., & Stathopoulou, A. (2014). Socio-Cognitive Determinants of Consumers' Support for the Fair Trade Movement. *Journal of Business Ethics*, *133*(1), 95–109. doi:10.100710551-014-2347-9

Chawla, N. V., Bowyer, K. W., Hall, L. O., & Kegelmeyer, W. P. (2002). SMOTE: Synthetic minority over-sampling technique. *Journal of Artificial Intelligence Research*, *16*, 321–357. doi:10.1613/jair.953

Chen, I. S. (1998). Travel Motivation of Heritage Tourists. *Tourism Analysis*, *2*, 213–215.

Chesbrough, H. (2007). Business model innovation: It's not just about technology anymore. *Strategy and Leadership*, *35*(6), 12–17. doi:10.1108/10878570710833714

Chesbrough, H. (2010). Business model innovation: Opportunities and barriers. *Long Range Planning*, *43*(2-3), 354–363. doi:10.1016/j.lrp.2009.07.010

Chiu, C. M., Wang, E. T., Fang, Y. H., & Huang, H. Y. (2014). Understanding Customers' Repeat Purchase Intentions in B2C e-Commerce: The Roles of Utilitarian Value, Hedonic Value and Perceived Risk. *Information Systems Journal*, *24*(1), 85–114. doi:10.1111/j.1365-2575.2012.00407.x

Chkoniya, V., Madsen, A. O., & Coelho, T. (2019). The impact of information and communication technologies in fish consumption in Portugal: Building a support for the coming generations. *Economia Agro-Alimentare*, *21*(3), 855–872. doi:10.3280/ECAG2019-003016

Chkoniya, V., & Mateus, A. (2019). Digital Category Management: How Technology Can Enable the Supplier-Retailer Relationship. In D. Simões, B. Barbosa, & S. Filipe (Eds.), *Smart Marketing With the Internet of Things* (pp. 139–163). Hershey, PA: IGI Global. doi:10.4018/978-1-5225-5763-0.ch008

Choi, D., Sekiya, T., Minote, N., & Watanuki, S. (2016). Relative left frontal activity in reappraisal and suppression of negative emotion: Evidence from frontal alpha asymmetry (FAA). *International Journal of Psychophysiology*, *109*, 37–44. doi:10.1016/j.ijpsycho.2016.09.018 PMID:27693504

Chrisafis, A. (2002, May 6). Tourism on standby for Bollywood boom. *The Guardian*, p. 3.

Christodoulides, G., Michaelidou, N., & Li, C. H. (2009). Measuring perceived brand luxury: An evaluation of the BLI scale. *Journal of Brand Management*, *16*(5-6), 395–405. doi:10.1057/bm.2008.49

Chudik, A., Pesaran, M. H., & Tosetti, E. (2011). Weak and strong cross-section dependence and estimation of large panels. *The Econometrics Journal*, *14*(1), C45–C90. doi:10.1111/j.1368-423X.2010.00330.x

Chung, H., & Lee, E. (2017). Store Brand Quality and Retailer's Product Line Design. *Journal of Retailing*, *82*(4), 349–355. doi:10.1016/j.jretai.2006.08.008

Cirella, G. T., Bąk, M., Kozlak, A., Pawłowska, B., & Borkowski, P. (2019). Transport innovations for elderly people. *Research in Transportation Business & Management*, *30*. doi:10.1016/j.rtbm.2019.100381

Clark, R. A., & Goldsmith, R. E. (2006). Interpersonal influence & consumer innovativeness. *International Journal of Consumer Studies*, *30*(1), 34–43. doi:10.1111/j.1470-6431.2005.00435.x

Clark, W. A. V., & Onaka, J. L. (1983). Life Cycle and Housing Adjustment as Explanations of Residential Mobility. *Urban Studies (Edinburgh, Scotland)*, *20*(1), 47–57. doi:10.1080/713703176

Clay Christensen's Milkshake Marketing. (2011, February 14). *HBS Working Knowledge*. https://hbswk.hbs.edu/item/clay-christensens-milkshake-marketing

Cleveland, M., Laroche, M., Pons, F., & Kastoun, R. (2009). Acculturation and Consumption: Textures of Cultural Adaptation. *International Journal of Intercultural Relations*, *33*(3), 196–212. doi:10.1016/j.ijintrel.2008.12.008

Clinton, L., & Whisnant, R. (2019). Business Model Innovations for Sustainability. In *Managing Sustainable Business* (pp. 463–503). Dordrecht: Springer. doi:10.1007/978-94-024-1144-7_22

Coase, R. H. (1937). The Nature of the Firm. *Economica*, *4*(16), 386–405. doi:10.1111/j.1468-0335.1937.tb00002.x

Coelho, T., Chkoniya, V., & Queiroga, A. P. (2018, January). Quem são os Jovens Portugueses? Como consomem e como compram? *Distribuição Hoje*, 21–24. Retrieved from https://www.distribuicaohoje.com/insights/quem-sao-os-jovens-portugueses-como-consomem-e-como-compram/

Cognition, X. (2018). *CogX 2018 - Pre Primary Care.* Retriever from: https://www.youtube.com/watch?v=T_qslD7rAWs

Cohen, L., Manion, L., & Morrison, K. (2002). *Research methods in education.* Routledge.

Colaferro, C. A., & Crescitelli, E. (2014). A contribuição do Neuromarketing para o Estudo do Comportamento do Consumidor. *Brazilian Business Review*, *11*(3), 130–153. doi:10.15728/bbr.2014.11.3.6

Compeau, D. R., & Higgins, C. A. (1995). Computer self-efficacy: Development of a measure and initial test. *Management Information Systems Quarterly*, *19*(2), 189–211. doi:10.2307/249688

Constantine, C. (2015). *Landlords must adapt to demands of savvy customers.* Estate Gazette.

Cooper, J., Blackman, S. F., & Keller, K. T. (2016). *The science of attitudes.* New York: Routledge.

Corrado, L., & Fingleton, B. (2012). Where is the economics in spatial econometrics? *Journal of Regional Science*, *52*(2), 210–239. doi:10.1111/j.1467-9787.2011.00726.x

Costa, J., Dentinho, T., & Nijkamp, P. (2010). *Mercado Fundiário e Habitação. Compêndio de Economia Regional: Teoria, Temática e Políticas (1)*. Principia.

Costa, P. T., & McCrae, R. R. (1980). Influence of Extraversion and Neuroticism on Subjective Well-Being: Happy and Unhappy People. *Journal of Personality and Social Psychology*, *38*(4), 668–678. doi:10.1037/0022-3514.38.4.668 PMID:7381680

Cotte, J., Ratneshwar, S., & Mick, D. G. (2004). The times of their lives: Phenomenological & metaphorical characteristics of consumer timestyles. *The Journal of Consumer Research*, *31*(2), 333–345. doi:10.1086/422112

Coucke, N., Vermeir, I., Slabbinck, H., & Van Kerckhove, A. (2019). Show Me More! The Influence of Visibility on Sustainable Food Choices. *Foods*, *8*(6), 186. doi:10.3390/foods8060186 PMID:31151326

CPC_Neuroscience_EN_150717.pdf. (n.d.). Retrieved March 10, 2020, from https://www.canadapost.ca/assets/pdf/blogs/CPC_Neuroscience_EN_150717.pdf

Crappell, C. (2015). The ABCs of Gen X, Y(P), Z. *American Music Teacher*, *65*(3), 40–43. Retrieved from http://search.ebscohost.com/login.aspx?direct=true&db=a9h&AN=111188950&site=eds-live

CRISE. (2007). *Fluid Identities Exploring Ethnicity in Peru*. Oxford, UK: Maritza Paredes.

CRISE. (2010). *Ethnicity and the Persistence of Inequality*. Oxford, UK: Rosemary Thorp & Maritza Paredes.

Cristini, H., Kauppinen-Raisanen, H., Barthod-Prothade, M., & Woodside, A. (2017). Toward a general theory of luxury: Advancing from workbench definitions and theoretical transformations. *Journal of Business Research*, *70*, 101–107. doi:10.1016/j.jbusres.2016.07.001

Cristofanelli, S., Antonini, M., Torres, D., & Polid. (2004). Meat and Carcass quality from Peruvian llama (Lama glama) and alpaca (Lama pacos). *Meat Science*, 589-593. doi:10.1016/S0309-1740(03)00174-8

Csíkszentmihályi, M. (1975). *Beyond Boredom and Anxiety: Experiencing Flow in Work and Play*. San Francisco: Jossey-Bass.

Csutora, M. (2012). One more awareness gap? The behaviour-impact-gap problem. *Journal of Consumer Policy*, *35*(1), 145–163. doi:10.100710603-012-9187-8

Cubbin, J. (1970). *A hedonic approach to some aspects of the Coventry housing market*. Coventry, UK: University of Warwick, Department of Economics.

Cudahy, B. J. (2006). *The Containership Revolution: Malcom McLean's 1956 Innovation Goes Global*. Retrieved from http://onlinepubs.trb.org/onlinepubs/trnews/trnews246containerrevolution.pdf

Cuellar, I., Nyberg, B., Maldonado, M., & Roberts, R. E. (1997). Ethnic Identity and Acculturation in a Young Adult Mexican-Origin Population. *Journal of Community Psychology*, *25*(6), 535–549. doi:10.1002/(SICI)1520-6629(199711)25:6<535::AID-JCOP4>3.0.CO;2-O

Curran, J. M., & Meuter, M. L. (2007). Encouraging existing customers to switch to self-service technologies: Put a little fun in their lives. *Journal of Marketing Theory and Practice*, *15*(4), 283–298. doi:10.2753/MTP1069-6679150401

Cyert, R. M., & DeGroot, M. H. (1987). *Bayesian Analysis and Uncertainty in Economic Theory*. Rowman & Littlefield. doi:10.1007/978-94-009-3163-3

Czinkota, M., & Ronkainen, I. (1995). *International Marketing*. The Dryden Press.

D'Alessio, M., De Pascalis, V., Guarino, A., & Zimbardo, P. G. (2003). Testing Zimbardo's Stanford Time Perspective Inventory (STPI) - Short Form: An Italian Study. *Time & Society*, *12*(2-3), 333–347. doi:10.1177/0961463X030122010

d'Hauteville, F., Goldsmith, R. E., & Flynn, L. R. (1998). Theory & measurement of consumer innovativeness. *European Journal of Marketing*, *32*(3), 340.

Dabholkar, P. A. (1996). Consumer evaluations of new technology-based self-service options: An investigation of alternative models of service quality. *International Journal of Research in Marketing*, *13*(1), 29–51. doi:10.1016/0167-8116(95)00027-5

Dabholkar, P. A., & Bagozzi, R. P. (2002). An attitudinal model of technology-based self-service: Moderating effects of consumer traits and situational factors. *Journal of the Academy of Marketing Science*, *30*(3), 184–201. doi:10.1177/0092070302303001

Dael, N., Perseguers, M., Marchand, C., Antonietti, J., & Mohr, C. (2016). Put on that colour, it fits your emotion: Colour appropriateness as a function of expressed emotion. *Quarterly Journal of Experimental Psychology*, *69*(8), 1619–1630. doi:10.1080/17470218.2015.1090462 PMID:26339950

Dahlkild, N. (1991). *Fra sommervilla til feriehytte: Om århundredskiftets og mellemkrigstidens fritidsbebyggelser. Byplanhistoriske Noter (23).* København: Dansk Byplanlaboratorium.

Dai, W. (2010, May). *Consumer Oriented Supply Chain Management Based on Mobile Agent System.* Paper presented at the 4th International Conference on New Trends in Information Service and Service Science, Gyeongju, South Korea.

Damasio, A. (2000). *The feeling of what happens: Body and emotion in the making of consciousness.* Fort Worth, TX: Harcourt College Publishers.

Damasio, A. R., Everitt, B. J., Bishop, D., Roberts, A. C., Robbins, T. W., & Weiskrantz, L. (1996). The somatic marker hypothesis and the possible functions of the prefrontal cortex. *Philosophical Transactions of the Royal Society of London. Series B, Biological Sciences*, *351*(1346), 1413–1420. doi:10.1098/rstb.1996.0125 PMID:8941953

Damasio, A. R., Tranel, D., & Damasio, H. C. (1991). Somatic markers and the guidance of behavior: Theory and preliminary testing. In H. S. Levin, H. M. Eisenberg, & A. L. Benton (Eds.), *Frontal lobe function and dysfunction* (pp. 217–229). Oxford University Press.

Darmstadt, I. H. K. (2017). *Vor Ort erfolgreich bestehen. Ein Leitfaden für den stationären Einzelhandel* [Successful on site. A guideline for the stationary retail trade]. https://www.darmstadt.ihk.de/produktmarken/standortpolitik/branchen/Handel_Absatzwirtschaft/Brancheninformationen/Check-Liste-fuer-den-stationaeren-Einzelhandel/3639562

Daugstad, K. (2008). Negotiating Landscape in Rural Tourism. *Annals of Tourism Research*, *35*(2), 402–426. doi:10.1016/j.annals.2007.10.001

Davies, G. (1994). What Should Time Be? *European Journal of Marketing*, *28*(8), 100–113. doi:10.1108/03090569410067604

Davis, B., & Pechmann, C. (2013). Introduction to the special issue on transformative consumer research: Developing theory to mobilize efforts that improve consumer and societal well-being. *Journal of Business Research*, *66*(8), 1168–1170. doi:10.1016/j.jbusres.2012.08.008

Davis, F. D. (1989). Perceived usefulness, perceived ease of use, & user acceptance of information technology. *Management Information Systems Quarterly*, *13*(3), 319–340. doi:10.2307/249008

Davis, P. (2005). Places, "Cultural Touchstones" and the Ecomuseum. In G. Corsane (Ed.), *Heritage, Museums and Galleries*. Abingdon: Routledge. doi:10.4324/9780203326350_chapter_28

De Barnier, V., Falcy, S., & Valette-Florence, P. (2012). Do consumers perceive three levels of luxury? A comparison of accessible, intermediate and inaccessible luxury brands. *Journal of Brand Management, 19*(7), 623–636. doi:10.1057/bm.2012.11

De Langen, P. (2003). *The Performance of Seaport Clusters: a framework to analyse clusters performance and an application to the seaport clusters in Durban, Rotterdam and the lower Mississippi* (Unpublished doctoral dissertation). Erasmus Research Institute Management, Rotterdam School of Management, Erasmus University Rotterdam.

De Mooij, M. K. (2010). *Global marketing & advertising: underst&ing cultural paradoxes*. Los Angeles: Sage.

de Oliveira, A. (2004). *Análise do investimento em sistemas e tecnologias da informação e da comunicação*. Lisboa: Sílabo.

Deci, E. L., & Ryan, R. M. (2002). *Handbook of self-determination research*. Rochester, NY: University of Rochester Press.

Dekhne, A., Hastings, G., Murnane, J., & Neuhaus, F. (2019, April). Automation in Logistics: Big opportunity, bigger uncertainty. *The McKinsey Quarterly*.

Delloitte. (2014). *The Millennial Survey 2014*. Retrieved from http://www2.deloitte.com/al/en/pages/about-deloitte/articles/2014-mil-lennial-survey-positive-impact.html

Dennis, C., Brakus, J. J., Gupta, S., & Alamanos, E. (2014). The effect of digital signage on shoppers' behavior: The role of the evoked experience. *Journal of Business Research, 67*(11), 2250–2257. doi:10.1016/j.jbusres.2014.06.013

Denzin, N. K., & Lincoln, Y. S. (2011). *The SAGE Handbook of Qualitative Research*. SAGE Publications Inc.

Desai, J. (2004). *Beyond Bollywood: The cultural politics of South Asian diasporic film*. New York: Routledge.

Desai, J. (2004). *Beyond Bollywood: The cultural politics of South Asian diasporic film*. New York: Routledge. doi:10.4324/9780203643952

Descola, P. (2017). ¿Humano, demasiado humano? / Human, Too Human? *Desacatos*, (54), 16–27. doi:10.29340/54.1737

DESCOSUR. (2016). *Linea Base Proandino*. Arequipa, Peru: DESCOSUR.

Devaraj, S., Easley, R. F., & Crant, J. M. (2008). How Does Personality Matter? Relating the Five-Factor Model to Technology Acceptance & Use. *Information Systems Research, 19*(1), 93–105. doi:10.1287/isre.1070.0153

Devasagayam, P. R., Buff, C. L., Aurand, T. W., & Judson, K. M. (2010). Building brand community membership within organizations: A viable internal branding alternative? *Journal of Product and Brand Management, 19*(3), 210–217. doi:10.1108/10610421011046184

DeWaal, F. (2010). *The age of empathy*. New York: Harmony Books.

DeYoung, C. (2014). A cybernetic big five theory for personality psychology. *Personality and Individual Differences, 60*, S18. doi:10.1016/j.paid.2013.07.381

Diamantopoulos, A., Schlegelmilch, B. B., Sinkovics, R. R., & Bohlen, G. M. (2003). Can socio-demographics still play a role in profiling green consumers? A review of the evidence and an empirical investigation. *Journal of Business Research, 56*(6), 465–480. doi:10.1016/S0148-2963(01)00241-7

Dieckmann, A., Unfried, M., Schreder, R., & Kissel, K. (2018). *How valid are response-time measures for capturing implicit brand attitudes?* GfK Working Paper Series, 7.

Diener, E. (1984). Subjective Well-Being. *Psychological Bulletin, 95*(3), 542–575. doi:10.1037/0033-2909.95.3.542 PMID:6399758

Docapesca, (2020). *Mission and Strategy*. Retrieved from www.docapesca.pt/pt/docapesca/missao-e-estrategia.html

Doğan, A. (1995). *Osmanlıca Türkçe sözlük*. Ankara: Akcag Yayınları.

Dohmen, T., Falk, A., Huffman, D., & Sunde, U. (2018). On the relationship between cognitive ability and risk preference. *The Journal of Economic Perspectives*, *32*(2), 115–134. doi:10.1257/jep.32.2.115 PMID:30203932

Dolan, P., Peasgood, T., & White, M. (2008). Do We Really Know What Makes Us Happy? A Review of the Economic Literature on the Factors Associated with Subjective Well-Being. *Journal of Economic Psychology*, *29*(1), 94–122. doi:10.1016/j.joep.2007.09.001

Dollar. (2019). Invisible Links: Value chains transform manufacturing and distort the globalization debate. *Finance & Development, 56*(2), 50-53.

Dominik, T., Dostál, D., Zielina, M., Šmahaj, J., Sedláčková, Z., & Procházka, R. (2018). Libet's experiment: A complex replication. *Consciousness and Cognition*, *65*, 1–26. doi:10.1016/j.concog.2018.07.004 PMID:30007132

Donaldson, T., & Dunfee, T. W. (1994). Toward a Unified Conception of Business Ethics: Integrative Social Contracts Theory. *Academy of Management Review*, *19*(2), 252–284. doi:10.5465/amr.1994.9410210749

Dopson, A. (2007). Environmental Citizenship: Towards Sustainable Development. *Sustainable Development*, *15*(5), 276–285. doi:10.1002d.344

Douglas, M. (2002). *The World of Goods: Towards an Anthropology of Consumption*. Routledge. Retrieved from https://books.google.pt/books?id=goBCb-RGfU4C

Douglas, M. (2001). *Purity and Danger*. New York, NY: Routdledge. (Original work published 1966)

Douglas, M., & Isherwod, B. (1996). *The World of Goods towards an anthropology of consumption*. New York, NY: Routledge.

Dovidio, J. F., & Fazio, R. H. (1992). New technologies for the direct and indirect assessment of attitudes. In J. Tanur (Ed.), *Questions about survey questions: Meaning, memory, attitudes, and social interaction* (pp. 204–237). New York: Russell Sage Foundation.

Doyle, J., & Thomason, R. H. (1999). Background to Qualitative Decision Theory. *AI Magazine*, *20*(2), 55–68.

Drucker, P. F. (1964). *Managing for results. Economics task and risk-taking decision*. Retrieved from https://books.google.pt/books?id=ZMj2uQEACAAJ

Du Cros, H., & McKercher, B. (2015). *Cultural Tourism* (2nd ed.). Routledge.

Duarte, A. (2012). Emergência e Queda das Novas Classes Médias: a Improvável Consolidação das suas Práticas de Consumo. In C. M. Silva & J. V. Aguiar (Eds.), Classes, Políticas e Culturas de Classe (pp. 165-181). V. N. Famalicão: Edições Húmus/Universidade do Minho.

Duarte, A. (2009). *Experiências de Consumo. Estudos de caso no interior da Classe Média*. Porto: Universidade do Porto Editorial.

Duarte, A. (2011). *O Consumo para os Outros: Os Presentes como Linguagem de Sociabilidade*. Porto: Universidade do Porto Editorial.

Duarte, A. (2015). The Short Life of the New Middle Classes in Portugal. *Anthropologica*, *57*(2), 557–570.

Dubey, B. (2008, Oct. 18). Bollywood, pied piper for tourists. *Times of India*.

Dubois, A., & Gadde, L. E. (2002). Systematic combining: An abductive approach to case research. *Journal of Business Research*, *55*(7), 553–560. doi:10.1016/S0148-2963(00)00195-8

Dubois, B., Laurent, G., & Czellar, S. (2001). *Consumer rapport to luxury: Analyzing complex and ambivalent attitudes*. Academic Press.

Dubois, B., & Paternault, C. (1995). Observations - Understanding the world of international luxury brands - The dream formula. *Journal of Advertising Research*, *35*(4), 69–76.

Duralia, O. (2018). Integrated Marketing Communication and Its Impact on Consumer Behavior. *Studies in Business & Economics*, *13*(2), 92–102. doi:10.2478be-2018-0022

Dwyer & Patel. (2002). *Cinema India: The visual culture of Hindi film*. Rutgers University Press.

Eastman, J. K., & Goldsmith, R. E. (1999). Status Consumption in Consumer Behavior: Scale Development and Validation. *Journal of Marketing Theory and Practice*, *7*(3), 41.

Easymile. (n.d.). https://www.easymile.com

Eberhart, A. K., & Naderer, G. (2017). Quantitative and qualitative insights into consumers' sustainable purchasing behaviour: A segmentation approach based on motives and heuristic cues. *Journal of Marketing Management*, *33*(13/14), 1149–1169. doi:10.1080/0267257X.2017.1371204

Ebrahim, H. (2008). *From Ghetto to Mainstream: Bollywood in South Africa*. Taylor and Francis, Unisa Press.

Eccles, R. G., & Klimenko, S. (2019). The Investor Revolution. *Harvard Business Review*. Retrieved from http://search.ebscohost.com/login.aspx?direct=true&db=edb&AN=135981990&site=eds-live

Economics, O. (2019). *Country Economic Forecasts*. Retrieved from https://www.oxfordeconomics.com/my-oxford/publications/399091

Edson, G. (2004). Heritage: Pride or passion, product or service? *International Journal of Heritage Studies*, *10*(4), 333–348. doi:10.1080/1352725042000257366

Eglash, R., Robert, L., Bennett, A., Robinson, K. P., Lachney, M., & Babbitt, W. (2019). Automation for the Artisanal Economy: Enhancing the Economic and Environmental Sustainability of Crafting Professions with Human-Machine Collaboration. *AI & Society*. doi:10.100700146-019-00915-w

EIA- U.S. Energy Information Administration. 2020. *Analysis - Energy Sector Highlights*. Retrieved from https://www.eia.gov/international/overview/country/BRA

Eisenegger, C., Naef, M., Snozzi, R., Heinrichs, M., & Fehr, E. (2010). Prejudice and truth about the effect of testosterone on human bargaining behaviour. *Nature*, *463*(7279), 356–359. doi:10.1038/nature08711 PMID:19997098

EIU - The Economist Intelligence Unit. (2020). *Brazil Economy, Politics and GDP Growth Summary*. Retrieved from http://country.eiu.com/Brazil?utm_content=buffer3fe2c&utm_medium=social&utm_source=plus.google.com&utm_campaign=buffer#

El Hedhli, K., Chebat, J.-C., & Sirgy, J. (2013). Shopping well-being at the mall: Construct, antecedents, and consequences. *Journal of Business Research*, *66*(7), 856–863. doi:10.1016/j.jbusres.2011.06.011

Elhorst, J. P. (2014). *Spatial Econometrics: From Cross-Sectional Data to Spatial Panels*. Berlin, Germany: Springer. doi:10.1007/978-3-642-40340-8

Elsawah, S., Guillaume, J. H. A., Filatova, T., Rook, J., & Jakeman, A. J. (2015). A methodology for eliciting, representing, and analysing stakeholder knowledge for decision making on complex socio-ecological systems: From cognitive maps to agent-based models. *Journal of Environmental Management, 151*, 500–516. doi:10.1016/j.jenvman.2014.11.028 PMID:25622296

Eltis – The Urban Mobility Observatory. (n.d.). https://www.eltis.org/discover/case-studies/shared-mobility-enabling-maas-milans-sump European Commission (2012) Cars 21 High Level Group Final Report 2012 ec.europa.eu/growth/content/vision-2020-recommendations-help-car-industry-reach-new-heights-0_en

Eom, H. B., & Lee, S. M. (1990). A Survey of Decision Support System Applications (1971–April 1988). *Interfaces, 20*(3), 65–79. doi:10.1287/inte.20.3.65

EPE - Empresa de Pesquisa Energética. (2019). *Anuário Estatístico de Energia Elétrica.* Retrieved from http://www.epe.gov.br/

Epley, N., & Gilovich, T. (2006). The anchoring-and-adjustment heuristic : Why the adjustments are insufficient. *Psychological Science, 17*(4), 311–318. doi:10.1111/j.1467-9280.2006.01704.x PMID:16623688

Ericksen, P. J. (2008). Conceptualizing food systems for global environmental change research. *Global Environmental Change, 18*(1), 234–245. doi:10.1016/j.gloenvcha.2007.09.002

Ettenson, R., Conrado, E., & Knowles, J. (2013). Rethinking the 4 P's. *Harvard Business Review.*

Euromonitor International. (2018). *Digital disruption in retail.* https://blog.euromonitor.com/digital-disruption-in-retail/

European Commission. (2019). *Mobility and Transport.* https://ec.europa.eu/transport/themes/urban/urban_mobility_en

European Commission. (2020). *The EU Fish Market 2019 edition is out: everything you wanted to know about the EU market for fish and seafood.* Retrieved from https://ec.europa.eu/fisheries

Evergage. (2018). 2018 Trends in personalization. *Evergage.* Retrieved from https://www.evergage.com/wp-content/uploads/2018/04/Evergage-2018-Trends-in-Personalization-Survey.pdf

Everitt, B. S., Landau, S., Leese, M., & Stahl, D. (2011). *Cluster Analysis.* New York: John Wiley & Sons. Ltd. doi:10.1002/9780470977811

EWEA - The European Wind Energy Association. (2019). *Reports.* Retrieved from https://www.ewea.org/

Fabrigar, L. R., MacDonald, T. K., & Wegener, D. T. (2005). *The structure of attitudes. The handbook of attitudes, 80.* New York: Routledge.

Facchini, F., Digiesi, S., & Mossa, G. (2020). Optical dry port configuration for container terminals: A non-linear model for sustainable decision making. *International Journal of Production Economics, 219*, 164–178. doi:10.1016/j.ijpe.2019.06.004

Falk, P., & Campbell, C. (1997). *The Shooping Experience.* London, UK: Sage Publications.

Fayol, H. (1999). *Administration industrielle et générale. Dunod.* Retrieved from https://books.google.pt/books?id=HqsCHAAACAAJ

Fazio, R. H., Powell, M. C., & Williams, C. J. (1989). The role of attitude accessibility in the attitude-to-behavior process. *The Journal of Consumer Research, 16*(3), 280–288. doi:10.1086/209214

Fazio, R. H., Sanbonmatsu, D. M., Powell, M. C., & Kardes, F. R. (1986). On the automatic activation of attitudes. *Journal of Personality and Social Psychology, 50*(2), 229–238. doi:10.1037/0022-3514.50.2.229 PMID:3701576

Fazio, R. H., & Williams, C. J. (1986). Attitude accessibility as a moderator of the attitude–perception and attitude–behavior relations: An investigation of the 1984 presidential election. *Journal of Personality and Social Psychology*, *51*(3), 505–514. doi:10.1037/0022-3514.51.3.505 PMID:3761146

Fedigan, L. (2015). Dominance rank in primates. In P. Whelehan & A. Bolin (Eds.), *The International Encyclopedia of Human Sexuality* (pp. 305–306). Oxford: John Wiley & Sons, Ltd. doi:10.1002/9781118896877.wbiehs116

Ferrara, I. & Serret, Y. (2008). Introduction. *OECD Journal: General Papers, Special Issue: Household Behaviour and the Environment, 2008*(2), 5-18.

Fiala, J., Toufarová, I., Mokrý, S., & Souček, M. (2016). Perception of local food labelling by generation z:an eye-tracking experimente. *European Journal of Business Science and Technology*, *2*(2), 152–159. doi:10.11118/ejobsat.v2i2.65

Fiddes, N. (1991). *Meat: a natural symbol*. London, UK: Routledge.

Fiddes, N. (1994). Social Aspects of Meat Eating. *The Proceedings of the Nutrition Society*, *53*(2), 271–280. doi:10.1079/PNS19940032 PMID:7972141

Fieldhouse, P. (1986). *Food & Nutrition: Customs & Culture*. Croom Helm. Retrieved from https://books.google.pt/books?id=TicOAAAAQAAJ

Fiestas, M. M., Viedma, M. I., Fernández, J. S., & Rios, F. J. M. (2015). A Psychophysiological Approach For Measuring Response to Messaging How Consumers Emotionally Process Green Advertising. *Journal of Advertising Research*.

Fingleton, B. (2003). Externalities, Economic Geography, and Spatial Econometrics: Conceptual and Modeling Developments. *International Regional Science Review*, *26*(2), 197–207. doi:10.1177/0160017602250976

Finland Futures Research Centre. (2019). *A Scenario for the future of the peruvian agri - food sector 2030, focusing on andean native crops*. Turku, Finland: Author.

Fischler, C., Nemer, M., & France, N. (2011). *Manger mode d'emploi: entretiens avec Monique Nemer*. Fondation Nestlé France. Retrieved from https://books.google.pt/books?id=ePGyngEACAAJ

Fischler, C. (1988). Food, self and identity. *Information*, *27*(2), 275–292. doi:10.1177/053901888027002005

Fishbein, M., & Ajzen, I. (1975). *Belief, attitude, intention and behavior: An introduction to theory and research*. Reading, MA: Addison Wesley.

Fishbein, M., & Ajzen, I. (1975). *Belief, Attitude, Intention and Behavior: An Introduction to Theory and Rresearch*. Reading, MA: Addison-Wesley.

Fisher, C. E., & … . (2010). *Defining neuromarketing: practices and professional challenges*. Harvard Review Psychiatry Perspective.

Fisher, H., Island, H., Rich, J., Marchalik, D., & Brown, L. (2015). Four broad temperament dimensions: Description, convergent validation correlations, and comparison with the Big Five. *Frontiers in Psychology*, *6*, 6. doi:10.3389/fpsyg.2015.01098 PMID:26284018

Fjeldstad, Ø. D., & Snow, C. C. (2018). Business models and organization design. *Long Range Planning*, *51*(1), 32–39. doi:10.1016/j.lrp.2017.07.008

Fontana, A., & H. Frey, J. (1995). *Interviewing: The art of science*. Academic Press.

Foroudi, P., Gupta, S., Sivarajah, U., & Broderick, A. (2018). Investigating the effects of smart technology on customer dynamics and customer experience. *Computers in Human Behavior*, *80*, 271–282. doi:10.1016/j.chb.2017.11.014

Forsyth, D. R. (2010). *Group Dynamics*. Cengage Learning.

Foss, N. J., & Saebi, T. (2018). Business models and business model innovation: Between wicked and paradigmatic problems. *Long Range Planning*, *51*(1), 9–21. doi:10.1016/j.lrp.2017.07.006

Foulquier, E., & Maugeri, S. (2012). The Port as a Territory: An Excepctional Space or a Common Good? Discussing Deficiency in Port Governance. *Investigación y Desarrollo*, *20*(1), 32–53.

Fox, A. K., & Royne, M. B. (2018). Private information in a social world: Assessing consumers' fear and understanding of social media privacy. *Journal of Marketing Theory and Practice*, *26*(1-2), 72–89. doi:10.1080/10696679.2017.1389242

Foxall, G., Bhate, S., Pallister, J., Szmigin, I., Bagozzi, R. G., & Maddock, S. (1995). Consumer innovativeness & cognitive style. *European Journal of Marketing*, *29*(5), 6.

Frankish, K. (2010). Dual-Process and Dual-System Theories of Reasoning. *Philosophy Compass*, *5*(10), 914–926. doi:10.1111/j.1747-9991.2010.00330.x

Freeman, A. M. (1979). The hedonic price approach to measuring demand for neighbourhood characteristics. In D. Segal (Ed.), *The economics of neighbourhood*. Cambridge, MA: Elsevier. doi:10.1016/B978-0-12-636250-3.50015-5

Freimuth, V. S., & Mettger, W. M. (1990). Is there a Hard to Reach audience? *Public Health Reports*, *105*(3). PMID:2113680

Freud, S. (2018). The Uncanny. *Dialogues in Philosophy, Mental and Neuro Sciences*, *11*(2), 84–100. Retrieved from http://search.ebscohost.com/login.aspx?direct=true&db=a9h&AN=135254124&site=eds-live

Frow, P., & Payne, A. (2011). A stakeholder perspective of the value proposition concept. *European Journal of Marketing*, *45*(1/2), 223–240. doi:10.1108/03090561111095676

FuiYeng, W. & Yazdanifard, R. (2015). Green Marketing: A Study of Consumers' Buying Behavior in Relation to Green Products. *Global Journal of Management and Business Research: E Marketing*, *15*(5).

Fuller, J. B., Raman, M., Wallenstein, J. K., & de Chalendar, A. (2019). Your Workforce Is More Adaptable Than You Think. *Harvard Business Review*. Retrieved from http://search.ebscohost.com/login.aspx?direct=true&db=edb&AN=135981992&site=eds-live

Fu, R., Collier, M., Yin, L., & Christiansen, P. (2017). *Artificial Intelligence: Healthcare's New Nervous System*. Accenture.

Gachet, A., & Haettenschwiler, P. (2003). *Developing Intelligent Decision Support Systems: A Bipartite Approach*. Berlin: Springer.

Gade, D. W. (2013). Llamas and Alpacas as "Sheep" in the Colonial Andes: Zoogeography Meets Eurocentrism. *Journal of Latin American Geography*, *12*(2), 221–243. doi:10.1353/lag.2013.0009

Gainer, B. (1995). Ritual and Relationships: Interpersonal Influences on Shared Consumption. *Journal of Business Research*, *32*(3), 253–260. doi:10.1016/0148-2963(94)00050-O

Gallegos, R. (2013). Indice productivos de alpacas del Centro de Investigación y Producción La Raya. *Journal of High Andean Research*, *15*(02), 255–262. doi:10.18271/ria.2013.8

Galster, G. (1996). William Grigsby and the Analysis of Housing Sub-markets and Filtering. *Urban Studies (Edinburgh, Scotland)*, *33*(10), 1797–1805. doi:10.1080/0042098966376

Gao, L., & Bai, X. (2014). A unified perspective on the factors influencing consumer acceptance of internet of things technology. *Asia Pacific Journal of Marketing and Logistics*, *26*(2), 211–231. doi:10.1108/APJML-06-2013-0061

Garaus, M., Wolfsteiner, E., & Wagner, U. (2016). Shoppers' acceptance and perceptions of electronic shelf labels. *Journal of Business Research, 69*(9), 3687–3692. doi:10.1016/j.jbusres.2016.03.030

Garcia, R., & Calantone, R. (2002). A critical look at technological innovation typology & innovativeness terminology: A literature review. *Journal of Product Innovation Management, 19*(2), 110–132. doi:10.1111/1540-5885.1920110

Garia-Fodor, M., & Csiszárik-Kocsír, Á. (2018). The validity of value-based consumer behavioral models in the financial consciousness of the z generation. Online Journal Modelling the New Europe, (27), 107–131. doi:10.24193/OJMNE.2018.27.05

Gartner. (2018). 2018 State of personalization report. *Gartner*. Retrieved from https://www.gartner.com/en/documents/3892113/2018-state-of-personalization-report

Gaston, B. (1994). *The poetics of Space*. Boston: Beacon Press. (Original work published 1958)

Gatignon, H., & Robertson, T. S. (1985). A Propositional Inventory for New Diffusion Research. *The Journal of Consumer Research, 11*(4), 849–867. doi:10.1086/209021

Gawronski, B., & Hahn, A. (2019). Implicit Measures: Procedures, Use, and Interpretation. In H. Blanton & G. D. Webster (Eds.), *Foundations of social psychological measurement*. New York: Taylor & Francis.

Geissdoerfer, M., Bocken, N. M., & Hultink, E. J. (2016). Design thinking to enhance the sustainable business modelling process–A workshop based on a value mapping process. *Journal of Cleaner Production, 135*, 1218–1232. doi:10.1016/j.jclepro.2016.07.020

Geissdoerfer, M., Vladimirova, D., & Evans, S. (2018). Sustainable business model innovation: A review. *Journal of Cleaner Production, 198*, 401–416. doi:10.1016/j.jclepro.2018.06.240

Gelareth, S., Maculan, N., Mahey, P., & Monemi, R. (2013). Hub-and-spoke Network Design and Fleet Deployment for String Planning of Liner Shipping. *Applied Mathematical Modelling, 37*(5), 3307–3321. doi:10.1016/j.apm.2012.07.017

Gelderman, C. J., Paul, W. T., & Van Diemen, R. (2011). Choosing self-service technologies or interpersonal services—The impact of situational factors and technology related attitudes. *Journal of Retailing and Consumer Services, 18*(5), 414–421. doi:10.1016/j.jretconser.2011.06.003

Genevsky, A., Yoon, C., & Knutson, B. (2017). When Brain Beats Behavior: Neuroforecasting Crowdfunding Outcomes. *The Journal of Neuroscience: The Official Journal of the Society for Neuroscience, 37*(36), 8625–8634. doi:10.1523/JNEUROSCI.1633-16.2017 PMID:28821681

Gerstberger, C., & Yaneva, D. (2013). *Statistics in focus 2/2013 - Analysis of EU-27 household final consumption expenditure*. Eurostat.

Getis, A., & Ord, J. K. (1992). The Analysis of Spatial Association by Use of Distance Statistics. *Geographical Analysis, 24*(3), 189–206. doi:10.1111/j.1538-4632.1992.tb00261.x

Giampieri, A., Ling-Chin, J., Ma, Z., Smallbone, A., & Roskilly, A. P. (2020). A review of the current automotive manufacturing practice from an energy perspective. *Applied Energy, 261*, 114074. doi:10.1016/j.apenergy.2019.114074

Giddens, A. (1992). *As Consequências da Modernidade*. Oeiras: Celta Editora.

Gilmore, F. (1999). *Brand Warriors: Corporate Leaders Share Their Winning Strategies*. Profile Books.

Gilovich, T., Kumar, A., & Jampol, L. (2015). A Wonderful Life: Experiential Consumption and the Pursuit of Happiness. *Journal of Consumer Psychology, 25*(1), 152–165. doi:10.1016/j.jcps.2014.08.004

GirlFromBlupo. (2018, April 6). *Dear Amazon, I bought a toilet seat because I needed one. Necessity, not desire. I do not collect them. I am not a toilet seat addict. No matter how temptingly you email me, I'm not going to think, oh go on then, just one more toilet seat, I'll treat myself* [Twitter Post]. Retrieved from https://twitter.com/GirlFromBlupo/status/982156453396996096?s=20

Glasman, L. R., & Albarracin, D. (2006). Forming attitudes that predict future behavior: A meta-analysis of the attitude-behavior relation. *Psychological Bulletin*, *132*(5), 778–822. doi:10.1037/0033-2909.132.5.778 PMID:16910754

Global Economic Governance Africa. (2017). *E-commerce country case study South Africa*. http://www.gegafrica.org/publications/e-commerce-country-case-study-south-africa

Goel, L., Junglas, I., Ives, B., & Johnson, N. (2012). Decision-making in-socio and in-situ: Facilitation in virtual worlds. *Decision Support Systems*, *52*(2), 342–352. doi:10.1016/j.dss.2011.09.001

Goffman, E. (1983). The Interaction Order. *American Sociological Review*, *48*(1), 1–17. doi:10.2307/2095141

Goldsmith, R. E., & Foxall, G. R. (2003). The measurement of innovativeness. In *The measurement of innovativeness* (pp. 321–330). Elsevier. doi:10.1016/B978-008044198-6/50022-X

Gomes, R. M., Baunach, M., Malenko, M., Ribeiro, L. B., & Mauroner, F. (2017): A co-designed RTOS and MCU concept for dynamically composed embedded systems. OSPERT'17.

Gonçalves, V. C., Ribeiro Mendes, F., Sardinha, I. D., & Rodrigues, R. (2015). Twenty years after the Porter Report for Portugal. *Competitiveness Review*, *25*(5), 540–554.

Gonzalez, C. (2017). Decision-Making: A Cognitive Science Perspective. In S. E. F. Chipman (Ed.), *The Oxford Handbook of Cognitive Science* (pp. 264–270). Elsevier.

Goodwin, N., Nelson, J. A., Ackerman, F., & Weisskopf, T. (2008). *Consumption and the Consumer Society. Instructor's Notes And Exam Questions. GDAE Teaching Modules on Social and Environmental Issues in Economics*. Medford, MA: Global Development And Environment Institute Tufts University.

Gorbunov, R. D., Rauterberg, M., & Barakova, E. I. (2019). A cognitive model of social preferences in group interactions. *Integrated Computer-Aided Engineering*, *26*(2), 185–196. doi:10.3233/ICA-180590

Govindan, K. (2018). Sustainable consumption and production in the food supply chain: A conceptual framework. *International Journal of Production Economics*, *195*, 419–431. doi:10.1016/j.ijpe.2017.03.003

Gowda, R., & Fox, J. (2002). *Judgments, Decisions, and Public Policy* (R. Gowda & J. C. Fox, Eds.). https://ebooks.cambridge.org/ref/id/CBO9780511584206retrieved

Goyal, A. P., Bansal, S., & Srivastava, S. (2018). Sensory marketing: Perspectives on benefits consumers'grapple in choosing greener products. *Sustainability*, *7*, 61–73.

Graedel, T., & Allenby, B. (1998). *Industry ecology and Automobile*. Prentice Hall.

Grafton-Small, R. (1987). Marketing, or the anthropology of consumption. *European Journal of Marketing*, *21*(9), 66–71. doi:10.1108/EUM0000000004717

Graham, B., Ashworth, G. J., & Tunbridge, J. E. (2000). *A Geography of Heritage: Power, Culture and Economy*. London: Arnold.

GreenBook Market Leaders Report. (n.d.). Retrieved March 10, 2020, from https://grit.greenbook.org/

Green, P. E., & Srinivasan, V. (1990). Conjoint analysis in marketing: New developments with implications for research and practice. *Journal of Marketing*, *54*(4), 3–19. doi:10.1177/002224299005400402

Greenwald, A. G. (1992). New Look 3: Unconscious cognition reclaimed. *The American Psychologist*, *47*(6), 766–779. doi:10.1037/0003-066X.47.6.766 PMID:1616174

Greenwald, A. G., & Banaji, M. R. (1995). Implicit Social Cognition Attitudes, Self-Esteem, and Stereotypes. *Psychological Review*, *102*(1), 4–27. doi:10.1037/0033-295X.102.1.4 PMID:7878162

Greenwald, A. G., Banaji, M. R., Rudman, L. A., Farnham, S. D., Nosek, B. A., & Mellott, D. S. (2002). A unified theory of implicit attitudes, stereotypes, self-esteem, and self-concept. *Psychological Review*, *109*(1), 3–25. doi:10.1037/0033-295X.109.1.3 PMID:11863040

Greenwald, A. G., & Krieger, L. H. (2006). Implicit bias: Scientific foundations. *California Law Review*, *94*(4), 945–967. doi:10.2307/20439056

Greenwald, A. G., McGhee, D. E., & Schwartz, J. L. (1998). Measuring individual differences in implicit cognition: The implicit association test. *Journal of Personality and Social Psychology*, *74*(6), 1464–1480. doi:10.1037/0022-3514.74.6.1464 PMID:9654756

Greenwald, A. G., Nosek, B. A., & Banaji, M. R. (2003). Understanding and using the implicit association test: I. An improved scoring algorithm. *Journal of Personality and Social Psychology*, *85*(2), 197–216. doi:10.1037/0022-3514.85.2.197 PMID:12916565

Greenwald, A. G., Poehlman, T. A., Uhlmann, E. L., & Banaji, M. R. (2009). Understanding and using the Implicit Association Test: III. Meta-analysis of predictive validity. *Journal of Personality and Social Psychology*, *97*(1), 17–41. doi:10.1037/a0015575 PMID:19586237

Griggs, D., Stafford-Smith, M., Gaffney, O., Rockström, J., Öhman, M. C., Shyamsundar, P., ... Noble, I. (2013). Sustainable development goals for people and planet. *Nature*, *495*(7441), 305–307. doi:10.1038/495305a PMID:23518546

Grihault, N. (2003). Film tourism - The global picture. *Travel & Tourism Analyst*, *5*, 1–22.

Grimm, P. (2005). Ab components' impact on brand preference. *Journal of Business Research*, *58*(4), 508–517. doi:10.1016/S0148-2963(03)00141-3

Gronhaug, K., Gilly, M., & Penazola, L. (1993). Barriers and Incentives in Consumer Acculturation. *European Advances in Consumer Research*, *1*, 278–286.

Groupe Renault. (2019). *EZ-Flex and La Poste: Trial for Last Mile Deliveries*. Press Release. Retrieved from https://media.group.renault.com/global/en-gb/groupe-renault/media/pressreleases/21225825/renault-ez-flex-une-premiere-experimentation-avec-la-poste

Grunert, K. G., Brunsø, K., Bredahl, L., & Bech, A. C. (2001). Food-Related Lifestyle: A Segmentation Approach to European Food Consumers BT - Food, People and Society: A European Perspective of Consumers' Food Choices. Berlin: Springer Berlin Heidelberg. doi:10.1007/978-3-662-04601-2_14

Gummesson, E., Mele, C., Polese, F., Nenonen, S., & Storbacka, K. (2010). Business model design: Conceptualizing networked value co-creation. *International Journal of Quality and Service Sciences*.

Günther, M., Kacperski, C., & Krems, J. F. (2020). Can electric vehicle drivers be persuaded to eco-drive? A field study of feedback, gamification and financial rewards in Germany. *Energy Research & Social Science*, *63*, 101407. doi:10.1016/j.erss.2019.101407

Gupta, S. (2009). *Branding and Advertising*. Global India Publications.

Gursoy, D., Chi, O. H., Lu, L., & Nunkoo, R. (2019). Consumers acceptance of artificially intelligent (AI) device use in service delivery. *International Journal of Information Management, 49*, 157–169. doi:10.1016/j.ijinfomgt.2019.03.008

Guyader, H., Ottosson, M., & Witell, L. (2016). You can't buy what you can't see: Retailer practices to increase the green premium. *Journal of Retailing and Consumer Services, 34*, 319–325. doi:10.1016/j.jretconser.2016.07.008

GWEC - Global Wind Energy Council. (2019). *Global Wind Report 2018*. Retrieved from www.gwec.net

Habermas, J., & Fultner, B. (2002). *On the Pragmatics of Social Interaction: Preliminary Studies in the Theory of Communicative Action*. MIT Press. Retrieved from https://books.google.pt/books?id=CQtDResLBQ8C

Haeusel, H. G. (2011, March). *The scientific foundation of the Limbic approach*. Retrieved from https://www.nymphenburg.de/tl_files/pdf/LimbicScience110220.pdf

Haeusel, H. G. (2008). *Think Limbic*. Freiburg: Haufe Gruppe.

Halbwachs, M. (1992). *On Collective Memory*. Chicago: Academic Press.

HALKIER. (1999). B. Consequences of the politicization of consumption: The example of environmentally friendly consumption practices. *Journal of Environmental Policy and Planning*, (1): 25–41.

Hall. (2016). Exploring wine knowledge, aesthetics and ephemerality: clustering consumers. *International Journal of Wine Business Research, 28*(2), 134-153. doi:10.1108/IJWBR-09-2015-0044

Hall, M. C., & Page, S. J. (2006). Coastal and Marine Recreation and Tourism. In M. C. Hall & S. J. Page (Eds.), *The Geography of Tourism and Recreation: Environment, place and space* (3rd ed., pp. 291–314). Abingdon: Routledge. doi:10.4324/9780203420249

Handa, M., & Gupta, N. (2009). Gender Influence on the Innovativeness of Young Urban Indian Online Shoppers. *Vision: The Journal of Business Perspective, 13*(2), 25–32. doi:10.1177/097226290901300203

Han, H., & Lee, J. (2008). A Study on the KBS TV drama winter sonata and its impact on Korea's Hallyu tourism development. *Journal of Travel & Tourism Marketing, 24*(2-3), 115–126. doi:10.1080/10548400802092593

Hansen, L. A., & Jensen, M. B. (2014). To be demolished or protected – bunkers from concrete blocks to cultural heritage. In Bunkers – Atlantvoldens perspektiver i Danmark. Odense.

Hansen, L. A. (2014). *"All is data" – the ontological status of empirical material in tourism. In Tourism Methodologies - New Perspectives, Practices and Procedures*. CBS Press.

Harber, K. D., Zimbardo, P. G., & Boyd, J. N. (2003). Participant Self-Selection Biases as a Function of Individual Differences in Time Perspective. *Basic and Applied Social Psychology, 25*(3), 255–264. doi:10.1207/S15324834BASP2503_08

Harjani, P. (2011). India's tourists flock to Spain. *CNN.com*. Retrieved from http://www.cnngo.com/mumbai/life/indian-movie-boostsspanish-tourism-694426

Harris, L., & Westin, A. F. (1991). *Harris-Equifax Consumer Privacy Survey 1991*. Atlanta: Equifax Inc.

Harvey, D. (2006). Space as a Keyword. In N. Castree & D. Gregory (Eds.), *David Harvey: A Critical Reader*. Oxford, UK: Blackwell Publishing Ltd. doi:10.1002/9780470773581.ch14

Hastie, R., & Dawes, R. M. (2010). *Rational Choice in an Uncertain World: The Psychology of Judgment and Decision Making*. SAGE Publications.

Haws, K. L., Winterich, K. P., & Naylor, R. W. (2014). Seeing the world through GREEN-tintedglasses: Green consumption values and responses to environmentally friendly products. *Journal of Consumer Psychology*, *24*(3), 336–354. doi:10.1016/j.jcps.2013.11.002

HDE. (2018). *Online-Monitor*. https://www.einzelhandel.de/online-monitor

Heine, K., Atwal, G., Crener-Ricard, S., & Phan, M. (2018). Personality-driven luxury brand management. *Journal of Brand Management*, *25*(5), 474–487. doi:10.105741262-018-0090-8

Heinemann, G. (2017). *Die Neuerfindung des stationären Einzelhandels - Kundenzentralität und ultimative Usability für Stadt und Handel der Zukunft* [The reinvention of the stationary retail trade - customer centrality and ultimate usability for the city and trade of the future]. Wiesbaden: Springer-Verlag. doi:10.1007/978-3-658-15862-0

Heinonen, J. (2018). Conjoint fMRI method for shortening analysis time. *Cogent Psychology*, *5*(1), 1446254. doi:10.1080/23311908.2018.1446254

Hellström, T. (2004). Innovation as social action. *Organization*, *11*(5), 631–649. doi:10.1177/1350508404046454

Henderson, J. V., & Ioannides, Y. M. (1983). A model of housing tenure choice. *The American Economic Review*, *73*(1), 98–113.

Hengstler, M., Enkel, E., & Duelli, S. (2016). Applied artificial intelligence and trust, the case of autonomous vehicles and medical assistance devices. *Technological Forecasting and Social Change*, *105*, 105–120. doi:10.1016/j.techfore.2015.12.014

Hennigs, N., Wiedmann, K. P., Klarmann, C., Strehlau, S., Godey, B., Pederzoli, D., ... Oh, H. (2012). What is the Value of Luxury? A Cross-Cultural Consumer Perspective. *Psychology and Marketing*, *29*(12), 1018–1034. doi:10.1002/mar.20583

Hernandez, V., & Pedersen, T. (2017). Global value chain configuration: A review and research agenda. *BRQ Business Research Quarterly*, *20*(2), 137–150. doi:10.1016/j.brq.2016.11.001

Hertz, F. (1944). *Nationality in History and politics*. London: Kegan Paul Trench, Trubner and Co.

Hesse, A. (2019). Digitalisierung, Omnichanneling und Local-Commerce-Modelle aus Sicht des lokal-stationären Einzelhandels [Digitization, omnichanneling and local commerce models from the point of view of local-stationary retailing]. In Wissenschaftliche Schriften des Fachbereichs Wirtschaftswissenschaften, Hochschule Koblenz - University of Applied Sciences, Nr. 29.

He, X., Zhan, W., & Hu, Y. (2018). Consumer purchase intention of electric vehicles in China: The roles of perception & personality. *Journal of Cleaner Production*, *204*, 1060–1069. doi:10.1016/j.jclepro.2018.08.260

Hidalgo, C., & Hausmann, R. (2009). The building blocks of economic complexity. *Proceedings of the National Academy of Sciences of the United States of America*, *106*(26), 10570–10575. doi:10.1073/pnas.0900943106 PMID:19549871

Hidalgo-Mora, J. J., García-Vigara, A., Sánchez-Sánchez, M. L., García-Pérez, M.-Á., Tarín, J., & Cano, A. (2020). The Mediterranean diet: A historical perspective on food for health. *Maturitas*, *132*, 65–69. doi:10.1016/j.maturitas.2019.12.002 PMID:31883665

Higgins, E. T., & Bargh, J. A. (1987). Social Cognition and social perception. *Annual Review of Psychology*, *38*(1), 369–425. doi:10.1146/annurev.ps.38.020187.002101 PMID:3548576

Hill, R., & Keegan, J. (2002). *War at Sea in the Ironclad Age*. Cassell Military.

Hilton, J. (2018). Transforming the way we access and use transportation and mobility services. *Automotive Industries*. Retrieved from http://search.ebscohost.com/login.aspx?direct=true&db=bth&AN=138283403&site=eds-live

Hird, J., & Kvistgaard, P. (2010). *Oplevelsesrum: Turisme, kulturarv og oplevelser - et krydsfelt*. Århus, Denmark: Forfatterne og Academica.

Hirsch, M. (2012). The development of the retail environment in South Africa. *Retail Mark*, *8*(1), 82–85.

Hirschman, E. C. (1980). Innovativeness, Novelty Seeking, & Consumer Creativity. *The Journal of Consumer Research*, *7*(3), 283–295. doi:10.1086/208816

Hirschman, E., & Holbrook, M. (1982). Hedonic consumption: Emerging concepts, methods and propositions. *Journal of Marketing*, *46*(3), 92–101. doi:10.1177/002224298204600314

Hirsh, J., Kang, S., & Bodenhausen, G. (2012). Personalized Persuasion. *Psychological Science*, *23*(6), 578–581. doi:10.1177/0956797611436349 PMID:22547658

Hirunyawipada, T., & Paswan, A. K. (2006). Consumer innovativeness & perceived risk: Implications for high technology product adoption. *Journal of Consumer Marketing*, *23*(4), 182–198. doi:10.1108/07363760610674310

HLPF. (2018). *2018 HLPF Review of SDGs implementation: SDG 12 - Ensure sustainable consumption and production patterns*. Retrieved November 10, 2019 from https://sustainabledevelopment.un.org/content/documents/196532018backgroundnotesSDG12.pdf

Hobson, K. (2008). Sustainable Consumption in the United Kingdom: The "Responsible" Consumer and Government at "Arm's Length". *Journal of Environment & Development*, *13*(2), 121–139. doi:10.1177/1070496504265013

Hoch, S. J., Kunreuther, H. C., & Gunther, R. E. (Eds.). (2001). *Wharton on making decision*. John Wiley & Sons, Inc.

Hock, C. R. (1962). *The Four Temperaments*. Milwaukee: The Pallotine Fathers, Inc.

Hodder, I. (2018). Things and the Slow Neolithic: The Middle Eastern Transformation. *Journal of Archaeological Method and Theory*, *25*(1), 155–177. doi:10.100710816-017-9336-0

Hodgins, D. C., & Engel, A. (2002). Future time perspective in pathological gamblers. *The Journal of Nervous and Mental Disease*, *190*(11), 775–780. doi:10.1097/00005053-200211000-00008 PMID:12436018

Hoffman, D. L. (2012). Internet indispensability, online social capital, and consumer well-being. In Transformative consumer research for personal and collective well-being. New York, NY: Routledge.

Hoffman, D. L., Novak, T. P., & Peralta, M. (1999). Building consumer trust online. *Communications of the Advanced Conferences & Meetings, 42*(4), 80-85.

Hoffmann, S., & Soyez, K. (2010). A cognitive model to predict domain-specific consumer innovativeness. *Journal of Business Research*, *63*(7), 778–785. doi:10.1016/j.jbusres.2009.06.007

Hofstede, G., Hofstede, G., & Minkov, M. (2010). Cultures and organizations: Software of the mind (3rd ed,). Johanneshov: MTM.

Hogg, M. A., & Tindale, R. S. (2001). *Group Processes*. In Blackwell Handbook of Social Psychology. Blackwell Publishing Ltd.

Holak, S. L., & Lehmann, D. R. (1990). Purchase Intentions & the Dimensions of Innovation: An Exploratory Model. *Journal of Product Innovation Management*, *7*(1), 59–73. doi:10.1111/1540-5885.710059

Holbrook, M. B., & Schindler, R. M. (1994). Age, Sex, & Attitude Toward the Past as Predictors of Consumers' Aesthetic Tastes for Cultural Products. *JMR, Journal of Marketing Research*, *31*(3), 412–422.

Holender, D. (1986). Semantic activation without conscious identification in dichotic listening, parafoveal vision, and visual masking: A survey and appraisal. *Behavioral and Brain Sciences*, *9*(1), 1–66. doi:10.1017/S0140525X00021269

Holsapple, C. (2008). *DSS Architecture and Types. In Handbook on Decision Support Systems*. Berlin: Springer Berlin Heidelberg.

Holt, D., Quelch, J., & Taylor, E. (2004). How Global Brands Compete. *Harvard Business Review*, *82*, 68–75,136. PMID:15449856

Holtzman, J. (2006). Food and Memory. *Annual Review of Anthropology*, *35*(1), 361–378. doi:10.1146/annurev.anthro.35.081705.123220

Hong, W., & Thong, J. (2013). Internet privacy concerns: An integrated conceptualisation and four empirical studies. *MIS Quaterly*, *37*(1), 275–298. doi:10.25300/MISQ/2013/37.1.12

Hootsuite. (2019). *The global state of digital in 2019*. https://hootsuite.com/resources/digital-in-2019

Houben, K., & Wiers, R. W. (2008). Measuring implicit alcohol associations via the Internet: Validation of Web-based implicit association tests. *Behavior Research Methods*, *40*(4), 1134–1143. doi:10.3758/BRM.40.4.1134 PMID:19001405

Hourani, G. F., & Carswell, J. (1995). *Arab Seafaring in the Indian Ocean in Ancient and Early Medieval Times*. Princeton University Press.

Howland, P. J. (2013). Distinction by proxy: The democratization of fine wine. *Journal of Sociology (Melbourne, Vic.)*, *49*(2-3), 325–340. doi:10.1177/1440783313481746

Hsee, C. K., Yang, Y., Li, N., & Shen, L. (2009). Wealth, Warmth, and Well-Being: Whether Happiness Is Relative or Absolute Depends on whether It Is about Money, Acquisition, or Consumption. *JMR, Journal of Marketing Research*, *46*(3), 396–409. doi:10.1509/jmkr.46.3.396

Huang, M.-H., Rust, R., & Maksimovic, V. (2019). The Feeling Economy: Managing in the Next Generation of Artificial Intelligence (AI). *California Management Review*, *61*(4), 43–65. doi:10.1177/0008125619863436

Huang, R., Lee, S. H., Kim, H. J., & Evans, L. (2015). The impact of brand experiences on brand resonance in multichannel fashion retailing. *Journal of Research in Interactive Marketing*, *9*(2), 129–147. doi:10.1108/JRIM-06-2014-0042

Hu, D. (2013). Approaches to the Archaeology of Ethnogenesis: Past and Emergent Perspectives. *Journal of Archaeological Research*, *21*(4), 371–402. doi:10.100710814-013-9066-0

Hudson, S., & Ritchie, B. (2006a). Promoting destinations via film tourism: An empirical identification of supporting marketing initiatives. *Journal of Travel Research*, *44*(4), 387–396. doi:10.1177/0047287506286720

Hudson, S., & Ritchie, J. R. B. (2006). Film tourism and destination marketing: The case of Captain Corelli's Mandolin. *Journal of Vacation Marketing*, *12*(3), 256–268. doi:10.1177/1356766706064619

Hurt, H. T., Joseph, K., & Cook, C. D. (1977). Scales for the measurement of innovativeness. *Human Communication Research*, *4*(1), 58–65. doi:10.1111/j.1468-2958.1977.tb00597.x

Hussak, L. J., & Cimpian, A. (2018). Investigating the origins of political views: Biases in explanation predict conservative attitudes in children and adults. *Developmental Science*, *21*(3), e12567. doi:10.1111/desc.12567 PMID:28722292

Iacobucci, G. (2018). Babylon app increases CCG's costs. *BMJ (Clinical Research Ed.)*, *360*(8137), k221. doi:10.1136/bmj.k221 PMID:29339378

IBGE - Instituto Brasileiro de Geografia e Estatistica. (2020). *Estatísticas*. Retrieved from https://www.ibge.gov.br/

ICLEI- Local Governments for Sustainability. (2015). *From MDGs to SDGs: What are the Sustainable Development Goals.* ICLEI BRIEFING SHEET - Urban Issues, No. 01

Icomos. (1999). https://www.icomos.org/charters/tourism_e.pdf

Iglesias, O., Ind, N., & Alfaro, M. (2013). The organic view of the brand: A brand value co-creation model. *Journal of Brand Management, 20*(8), 670–688. doi:10.1057/bm.2013.8

Ignatenko, A., Raei, F., & Mircheva, B. (2019). *Global Value Chains: What are the Benefits and Why Do Countries Participate?* IMF Working Papers, WP/19/18.

IMF - International Monetary Fund. (2019). *World Economic Outlook Reports.* Retrieved from https://www.imf.org/

Immonen, M., & Sintonen, S. (2015). Evolution of technology perceptions over time. *Information Technology & People, 28*(3), 589–606. doi:10.1108/ITP-12-2013-0219

Im, S., Mason, C. H., & Houston, M. B. (2007). Does innate consumer innovativeness relate to new product/ service adoption behavior? The intervening role of social learning via vicarious innovativeness. *Journal of the Academy of Marketing Science, 35*(1), 63–75. doi:10.100711747-006-0007-z

INE - Instituto Nacional de Estatística. (2012). *Estatísticas da Pesca: 2011.* Lisboa: INE.

INE - Instituto Nacional de Estatística. (2018). *Estatísticas da Pesca: 2017.* Lisboa: INE.

INE - Instituto Nacional de Estatística. (2019). *Estatísticas da Pesca: 2018.* Lisboa: INE.

Ingold, T. (2019). Art and anthropology for a sustainable world. *Journal of the Royal Anthropological Institute, 25*(4), 659–675. doi:10.1111/1467-9655.13125

Ingram, J. (2011). A food systems approach to researching food security and its interactions with global environmental change. *Food Security, 3*(4), 417–431. doi:10.100712571-011-0149-9

Inman, J., & Nikolova, H. (2016). *Shopper-Facing Retail Technology: An Adoption Decision Calculus.* Academic Press.

Instituto Nacional de Defensa de la Competencia y de la protección de la Propiedad Intelectual. (2005). *Carne y productos cárnicos. Definiciones, requisitos y clasificación de las carcasas y carne de alpacas y llamas.* Lima, Peru: INDECOPI.

Instituto Nacional de Defensa de la Competencia y de la Protección de la Propiedad Intelectual. (2006). *Norma Técnica Peruana 201.059: 2006. Carne y productos cárnicos. Charqui. Requisitos.* Lima, Peru: INDECOPI.

Instituto Nacional de Estadística e Informática. (2012). *IV Censo Nacional Agropecuario.* Lima, Peru: INEI.

International Cocoa organization. (2020). *Quarterly Bulletin of Cocoa Statistics.* Retrieved from https://www.icco.org/

International Coffee Organization. (2020). *Trade Statistics - January 2020.* Retrieved from http://www.ico.org/

International Institute for Sustainable Development. (2012). *Sustainable Development Timeline.* Retrieved November 10, 2019 from https://www.iisd.org/pdf/2012/sd_timeline_2012.pdf

Israel, R. (2018). Mobility-as-a-service: The coming transportation revolution. *FS Private Wealth: Journal of Family Office Investment.* Retrieved from http://search.ebscohost.com/login.aspx?direct=true&db=bth&AN=135702114&site=eds-live

Izuma, K., Shibata, K., Matsumoto, K., & Adolphs, R. (2016). Neural predictors of evaluative attitudes toward celebrities. *Social Cognitive and Affective Neuroscience, 12*(3), 382–390. doi:10.1093can/nsw135 PMID:27651542

Jackson, T., & Michaelis, L. (2003). *Policies for Sustainable Consumption. Sustainable Development Commission.* Retrieved November 10, 2019 from https://pdfs.semanticscholar.org/b5f9/70330c8b0d02044a00b665a4e27f613a131d.pdf

Jacoby, L. L., & Witherspoon, D. (1982). Remembering without awareness. *Canadian Journal of Psychology*, *36*(2), 300–324. doi:10.1037/h0080638

Jagarnath, V. (2004). The politics of urban segregation and Indian cinema in Durban. In P. Kaarsholm (Ed.), *City flicks: Indian cinema and the urban experience*. Calcutta: Seagull Books.

Jamal, T., & Kim, H. (2005). Bridging the interdisciplinary divide: Towards an integrated framework for heritage tourism research. *Tourist Studies*, *5*(1), 55–83. doi:10.1177/1468797605062715

James, W. (1890). The Principles of. *Psychology*, *2*, 94.

James, W. (1988). Possessions and extended self. *The Journal of Consumer Research*, 139–165.

Jastrzebska, E. (2017). The Responsible Consumer As An Answer To New Sustainable Development Challenges. *Ekonomia I Środowisko*, *1*(60), 198-206.

Jedrychowski, W., Perera, F., Mrozek-Budzyn, D., Flak, E., Mroz, E., Sochacka-Tatara, E., & Spengler, J. D. (2010). Higher Fish Consumption in Pregnancy May Confer Protection against the Harmful Effect of Prenatal Exposure to Fine Particulate Matter. *Annals of Nutrition & Metabolism*, *56*(2), 119–126. doi:10.1159/000275918 PMID:20134157

Jenkins, O. H. (1999). Understanding and Measuring Tourist Destination Images. *International Journal of Tourism Research*, *1*(1), 1–15. doi:10.1002/(SICI)1522-1970(199901/02)1:1<1::AID-JTR143>3.0.CO;2-L

Jennings, G. (2010). *Tourism Research*. Milton, Queensland, Australia: John Wiley & Sons Australia Ltd.

Jephson, C., & Morgen, H. (2014). *Creating Global Opportunities: Maersk Line in Containerisation 1973-2013*. Cambridge University Press. doi:10.1017/CBO9781139795340

Jha, S. K. (2011). *Silsila, Lamhe are my Favourites: Yash Chopra*. Retrieved from: http://articles.timesofindia.indiatimes.com/2011-06- 27/news-interviews/29708368_1_yash-chopra-dhool-ka-phool-veer-zaara

Jiang, F., Jiang, Y., Zhi, H., Dong, Y., Dong, Q., & Li, H. (2017). Artificial intelligence in healthcare: Past, present & future. *Stroke and Vascular Neurology*, *2*(4), 230–243. doi:10.1136vn-2017-000101 PMID:29507784

Jodelet, D. (2008). Social representations: The beautiful invention. *Journal for the Theory of Social Behaviour*, *38*(4), 411–430. doi:10.1111/j.1468-5914.2008.00383.x

Johar, M. G. M., & Awalluddin, J. A. A. (2011). The Role of Technology Acceptance Model in Explaining Effect on e-Commerce Application System. *International Journal of Managing Information Technology*, *3*(3), 1–14. doi:10.5121/ijmit.2011.3301

Johnson, M. W., Christensen, C. M., & Kagermann, H. (2008). Reinventing your business model. *Harvard Business Review*, *86*(12), 57–68.

Kafentzis, K., Mentzas, G., Apostolou, D., & Georgolios, P. (2004). Knowledge marketplaces: Strategic issues and business models. *Journal of Knowledge Management*, *8*(1), 130–146. doi:10.1108/13673270410523961

Kahneman, D. (2011). *Thinking, fast and slow*. New York: Farrar, Straus and Giroux.

Kahneman, D., Slovic, P., & Tversky, A. (1982). *Judgment under uncertainty: heuristics and biases*. Cambridge University Press. doi:10.1017/CBO9780511809477

Kahneman, D., Tversky, A., Foundation, R. S., & Press, C. U. (2000). *Choices, Values, and Frames*. New York: Russell sage Foundation. Cambridge University Press. doi:10.1017/CBO9780511803475

Kain, J., & Quigley, J. M. (1975). A Theory of Urban Housing Markets and Spatial Structure. *Housing Markets and Racial Discrimination: A Microeconomic Analysis* (1), 9–55.

Kamenidou, I. C., Mamalis, S. A., Pavlidis, S., & Bara, E.-Z. G. (2019). Segmenting the Generation Z Cohort University Students Based on Sustainable Food Consumption Behavior: A Preliminary Study. *Sustainability, 11*(3), 837. doi:10.3390u11030837

Kanger, L., Geels, F. W., Sovacool, B., & Schot, J. (2019). Technological diffusion as a process of societal embedding: Lessons from historical automobile transitions for future electric mobility. *Transportation Research Part D, Transport and Environment, 71*, 47–66. doi:10.1016/j.trd.2018.11.012

Kant, I. (1999). *Critique of pure reason*. Cambridge University Press.

Kapferer, J. N. (1997). Managing luxury brands. *Journal of Brand Management, 4*(4), 251–259. doi:10.1057/bm.1997.4

Kapferer, J. N. (2004). *The new strategic brand management: creating and sustaining brand equity long term*. London: Kogan Page.

Kapferer, J. N. (2012). Abundant rarity: The key to luxury growth. *Business Horizons, 55*(5), 453–462. doi:10.1016/j.bushor.2012.04.002

Kapferer, J. N. (2014). The artification of luxury: From artisans to artists. *Business Horizons, 57*(3), 371–380. doi:10.1016/j.bushor.2013.12.007

Kapferer, J. N., & Valette-Florence, P. (2016). Beyond rarity: The paths of luxury desire. How luxury brands grow yet remain desirable. *Journal of Product and Brand Management, 25*(2), 120–133. doi:10.1108/jpbm-09-2015-0988

Kapferer, J. N., & Valette-Florence, P. (2018). The impact of brand penetration and awareness on luxury brand desirability: A cross country analysis of the relevance of the rarity principle. *Journal of Business Research, 83*, 38–50. doi:10.1016/j.jbusres.2017.09.025

Kapoor, K. K., Dwivedi, Y. K., & Williams, M. D. (2015). Empirical Examination of the Role of Three Sets of Innovation Attributes for Determining Adoption of IRCTC Mobile Ticketing Service. *Information Systems Management, 32*(2), 153–173. doi:10.1080/10580530.2015.1018776

Karahoca, A., Karahoca, D., & Aksoez, M. (2018). Examining intention to adopt to internet of things in healthcare technology products. *Kybernetes, 47*(4), 742–770. doi:10.1108/K-02-2017-0045

Karande, K., & Merchant, A. (2012). The Impact of Time & Planning Orientation on an Individual's Recreational Shopper Identity & Shopping Behavior. *Journal of Marketing Theory and Practice, 20*(1), 59–72. doi:10.2753/MTP1069-6679200104

Kardes, F. R., Herr, P. M., & Nantel, J. (2005). *Applying social cognition to consumer-focused strategy* (F. R. Kardes, P. M. Herr, & J. Nantel, Eds.). Lawrence Erlbaum Associates.

Karmarkar, U. S., & Pitbladdo, R. (1995). Service markets and competition. *Journal of Operations Management, 12*(3-4), 397–411. doi:10.1016/0272-6963(94)00014-6

Kastanakis, M. N., & Balabanis, G. (2012). Between the mass and the class: Antecedents of the "bandwagon" luxury consumption behavior. *Journal of Business Research, 65*(10), 1399–1407. doi:10.1016/j.jbusres.2011.10.005

Kaul, S. (2005). Impact of performance and expressiveness value of store service quality on the mediating role of satisfaction. *IIMA*, 3.

Kavaliers, M., Ossenkopp, K., & Choleris, E. (2018). Social neuroscience of disgust. *Genes Brain & Behavior, 18*(1), e12508. doi:10.1111/gbb.12508 PMID:30062689

Keller, K. L. (2009). Managing the growth tradeoff: Challenges and opportunities in luxury branding. *Journal of Brand Management, 16*(5-6), 290–301. doi:10.1057/bm.2008.47

Keller, K. L. (2016). Unlocking the Power of Integrated Marketing Communications: How Integrated Is Your IMC Program? *Journal of Advertising, 45*(3), 286–301. doi:10.1080/00913367.2016.1204967

Keller, L. K. (2013). *Strategic brand management: building, measuring, and managing brand equity* (4th ed.). London: Pearson.

Kenning, P., & Plassmann, H. (2005). NeuroEconomics: An overview from an economic perspective. *Brain Research Bulletin, 67*(5), 343–354. doi:10.1016/j.brainresbull.2005.07.006 PMID:16216680

Kerney, M., Smaers, J., Schoenemann, P., & Dunn, J. (2017). The coevolution of play and the cortico-cerebellar system in primates. *Primates, 58*(4), 485–491. doi:10.100710329-017-0615-x PMID:28620843

Khaw, M. W., Grab, D. A., Livermore, M. A., Vossler, C. A., & Glimcher, P. W. (2015). The measurement of subjective values and its relation to contigent valuation and environmental public goods. *PLoS One, 10*, 7.

Kidd, C., & Hayden, B. (2015). The Psychology and Neuroscience of Curiosity. *Neuron, 88*(3), 449–460. doi:10.1016/j.neuron.2015.09.010 PMID:26539887

Kiesler, C. A., & Kiesler, S. B. (1969). *Conformity*. Menlo Park: Addison-Wesley.

Kihlstrom, J. F. (2004). Implicit methods in social psychology. In C. Sansone, C. Morf, & A. Panter (Eds.), *The Sage handbook of methods in social psychology* (pp. 195–212). Thousand Oaks: Sage.

Kim, W. C., & Maubourge, R. (1997). Value innovation. *Harvard Business Review*, (1).

Kim, J., & Forsythe, S. (2008). Adoption of virtual try-on technology for online apparel shopping. *Journal of Interactive Marketing, 22*(2), 45–59. doi:10.1002/dir.20113

Kim, J., & Johnson, K. K. (2015). Brand luxury index: A reconsideration and revision. *Journal of Fashion Marketing and Management, 19*(4), 430–444. doi:10.1108/JFMM-05-2015-0043

Kim, S., & O'Connor, N. (2011). A cross-cultural study of screen-tourists' profiles. *Worldwide Hospitality and Tourism Themes, 3*(2), 141–158. doi:10.1108/17554211111123005

Kim, W. C., & Mauborgne, R. (1999). Strategy, value innovation, and the knowledge economy. *MIT Sloan Management Review, 40*(3), 41.

Kim, W., Anthony Di Benedetto, C., & Lancioni, R. A. (2011). The effects of country & gender differences on consumer innovativeness & decision processes in a highly globalized high-tech product market. *Asia Pacific Journal of Marketing and Logistics, 23*(5), 714–744. doi:10.1108/13555851111183101

Kim, W., Smolders, A., Brengman, M., Luyten, K., & Schöning, J. (2017). The path-to-purchase is paved with digital opportunities: An inventory of shopper-oriented retail technologies. *Technological Forecasting and Social Change, Elsevier, 124*(C), 228–242. doi:10.1016/j.techfore.2016.11.023

Kirshenblatt-GimbletT, B. (2004). Intangible heritage as metacultural production. *Museum International, 56*(1/2), 52–65. doi:10.1111/j.1350-0775.2004.00458.x

Kishwar, M. (Ed.). (2004). *Manushi. India Together- Revised Version of a Presentation at the Conference of India.* Retrieved from: http://www.indiatogether. org/manushi/issue139/idea.htm

Kiss, K., Ruszkai, C., & Takács-György, K. (2019). Examination of Short Supply Chains Based on Circular Economy and Sustainability Aspects. *Resources, 8*(4), 161. doi:10.3390/resources8040161

Klarin, T. (2018). The Concept of Sustainable Development: From its Beginning to the Contemporary Issues. *Zagreb International Review of Economics & Business, 21*(1), 67–94. doi:10.2478/zireb-2018-0005

Klink, R. R., & Athaide, G. A. (2010). Consumer Innovativeness & the Use of New versus Extended Br& Names for New Products. *Journal of Product Innovation Management, 27*(1), 23–32. doi:10.1111/j.1540-5885.2009.00697.x

Klotz, C., & Akinalp, C. (2013). Identifying Limbic Characteristics on Twitter. In *The 9th International Conference on Computing and Information Technology. Advances in Intelligent Systems and Computing*, (vol. 209, pp. 19-27). Springer. 10.1007/978-3-642-37371-8_6

Knudsen, D. C. (2012). Insiders and Outsiders in Thy. In A. K. Soper, C. E. Greer, & M. M. Metro-Roland (Eds.), Landscape, Tourism, and Meaning (p. 109-119). Ashgate.

Knudsen, D. C., & Greer, C. E. (2008). Heritage Tourism, Heritage Landscapes and Wilderness Preservation: The Case of National Park Thy. *Journal of Heritage Tourism, 3*(1), 18–35. doi:10.1080/1743873X.2008.9701248

Knutson, B., Fong, G. W., Bennett, S. M., Adams, C. M., & Hommer, D. (2003). A region of mesial prefrontal cortex tracks monetarily rewarding outcomes: Characterization with rapid event-related fMRI. *NeuroImage, 18*(2), 263–272. doi:10.1016/S1053-8119(02)00057-5 PMID:12595181

Koblenz Stadtmarketing. (2017). *Shopping & Genuss* [Shopping and enjoyment]. https://www.koblenz-stadtmarketing.de/shopping-genuss/

Kolb, M. (2018). *What Is Globalization?* Retrieved from https://www.piie.com/microsites/globalization/what-is-globalization

Kolb, M., & Trade and Investment Policy Watch (2018). *What Is Globalization?* Retrieved from https://www.piie.com/microsites/globalization/what-is-globalization

Kooij, D., Kanfer, R., Betts, M., & Rudolph, C. W. (2018). Future Time Perspective: A Systematic Review & Meta-Analysis. *The Journal of Applied Psychology, 103*(8), 867–893. doi:10.1037/apl0000306 PMID:29683685

Kotler, P., Kartajata, H., & Setiawan, I. (2017). Marketing 4.0 – Moving from traditional to digital. Academic Press.

Kotler, P. (2019). The market for transformation. *Journal of Marketing Management, 35*(5/6), 407–409. doi:10.1080/0267257X.2019.1585713

Koufaris, M. (2002). Applying the technology acceptance model and flow theory to online consumer behavior. *Information Systems Research, 13*(2), 205–223. doi:10.1287/isre.13.2.205.83

Koul, S., & Eydgahi, A. (2017). A systematic review of technology adoption frameworks & their applications. *Journal of Technology Management & Innovation, 12*(4), 106–112. doi:10.4067/S0718-27242017000400011

Kraus, S. J. (1995). Attitudes and the Prediction of Behavior: A Meta-Analysis of the Empirical Literature. *Personality and Social Psychology Bulletin, 21*(1), 58–75. doi:10.1177/0146167295211007

Kripalani. (2007). Trendsetting and product placement in Bollywood film: Consumerism through consumption Top of Form, New Cinemas: *Journal of Contemporary Film, 4*(3), 197-215.

Kruglanski, A., & Higgins, E. T. (2007). *Social Psychology: Handbook of Basic Principles. Political Psychology* (Vol. 29). The Guilford Press.

Kruglanski, A., & Ajzen, I. (1983). Bias and error in human judgment. *European Journal of Social Phsycologysycology, 13*(1), 1–44. doi:10.1002/ejsp.2420130102

Kruglanski, A., Shah, J. Y., Fishbach, A., Friedman, R., Chun, W. Y., & Sleeth-Keppler, D. (2002). A theory of goal systems. *Advances in Experimental Social Psychology, 34*, 331–372. doi:10.1016/S0065-2601(02)80008-9

Kruglanski, A., & Stroebe, W. (2012). *Handbook of the history of social psychology*. Philadelphia, PA: Psychology Press. doi:10.4324/9780203808498

Kruse, R. J. II. (2005). The Beatles as place makers: Narrated landscapes in Liverpool, England. *Journal of Cultural Geography, 22*(2), 87–114. doi:10.1080/08873630509478240

Kuehnhanss, C. R. (2019). The challenges of behavioural insights for effective policy design. *Policy and Society, 38*(1), 14–40. doi:10.1080/14494035.2018.1511188

Kuisma, T., Laukkanen, T., & Hiltunen, M. (2007). Mapping the reasons for resistance to Internet banking: A means-end approach. *International Journal of Information Management, 27*(2), 75–85. doi:10.1016/j.ijinfomgt.2006.08.006

Kulturstyrelsen; Udvikling Fyn; VisitAalborg; VisitDenmark; VisitAarhus; Wonderful Copenhagen. (2014). slks.dk/fileadmin/user_upload/Projektbeskrivelse_godkendt_17_december_2014.pdf

Kulviwat, S., Bruner, G. C. II, Kumar, A., Nasco, S. A., & Clark, T. (2007). Toward a unified theory of consumer acceptance of technology. *Psychology and Marketing, 24*(12), 1059–1084. doi:10.1002/mar.20196

Kumagai, K., & Nagasawa, S. (2017). The effect of selective store location strategy and self-congruity on consumers' apparel brand attitudes toward luxury vs. non-luxury. *Journal of Global Fashion Marketing*, 8(4), 266–282. doi:10.1080/20932685.2017.1348241

Kumar, A., Sah, B., Singh, A. R., Deng, Y., He, X., Kumar, P., & Bansal, R. C. (2017). A review of multi criteria decision making (MCDM) towards sustainable renewable energy development. *Renewable and Sustainable Energy Reviews, 69*, 596–609. . doi:10.1016/j.rser.2016.11.191retrieved

Kurtoğlu, A. (2005). Mekansal Bir Olgu Olarak Hemlşehrilik ve Bir Hemşehrilik Mekanı Olarak Dernekler. *European Journal of Turkish Studies*. https://journals.openedition.org/ejts/375

Kurzweil, R. (2010). *The Singularity Is Near: When Humans Transcend Biology*. Prelude Books.

Kvale, S. (2007). *Doing Interviews*. London, UK: SAGE Publications Ltd. doi:10.4135/9781849208963

Kvistgaard & Hird. (2016). *kvistgaardoghird.dk*. Accessed 5. 6. 2016 at http://kvistgaardoghird.dk/#home-section-forsking

Kwon, J., Seo, Y., & Ko, D. (2016). Effective Luxury-Brand Advertising: The ES-IF Matching (Entity-Symbolic Versus Incremental-Functional) Model. *Journal of Advertising, 45*(4), 459–471. doi:10.1080/00913367.2016.1226995

Lakshminarayanan, B., Roy, D. M., & Teh, Y. W. (2014). Mondrian forests: Efficient online random forests. In Advances in neural information processing systems (pp. 3140-3148). Academic Press.

Lal, P. (2004). *Bollywood ain't world cinema*. http://www.greencine.com/article?act ion=view&articleID=125

Lancaster, K. J. (1966). A new approach to consumer theory. *Journal of Political Economy*, *74*(2), 132–157. doi:10.1086/259131

Lane, B. W. (2019). Revisiting 'An unpopular essay on transportation:' The outcomes of old myths and the implications of new technologies for the sustainability of transport. *Journal of Transport Geography*, *81*, 102535. doi:10.1016/j.jtrangeo.2019.102535

Lang, N. S., & Mauerer, S. (2010). *Winning the BRIC Auto Markets: Achieving Deep Localization in Brazil, Russia, India, and China.* Retrieved from www.bcg.com

Langley, A. (1999). Strategies for theorizing from process data. *Academy of Management Review*, *24*(4), 691–710. doi:10.5465/amr.1999.2553248

Larkin, B. (2002). Indian flms and Nigerian lovers: media and the creation of parallel modernity. In *The anthropology of globalization: A reader*. Malden: Blackwell Publishing.

Laroche, M., & Sadokierski, R. W. (1994). Role of confidence in a multi-brand model of intentions for a high involvement service. *Journal of Business Research*, *29*(1), 1–12. doi:10.1016/0148-2963(94)90022-1

Larsen, G., & Lawson, R. (2013). Consumer Rights: An Assessment of Justice. *Journal of Business Ethics*, *112*(3), 515–528. doi:10.100710551-012-1275-9

Lassar, W. M., Manolis, C., & Lassar, S. S. (2005). The relationship between consumer innovativeness, personal characteristics, & online banking adoption. *International Journal of Bank Marketing*, *23*(2), 176–199. doi:10.1108/02652320510584403

Laukkanen, T. (2016). Consumer adoption versus rejection decisions in seemingly similar service innovations: The case of the Internet and mobile banking. *Journal of Business Research*, *69*(7), 2432–2439. doi:10.1016/j.jbusres.2016.01.013

Lazaris, C., & Vrechopolous, A. (2014). 'From Multichannel to Omnichannel' retailing: review of the literature and calls for research. *2nd International Conference on Contemporary Marketing Issues (ICCMI)*, 18-20.

Leaver, R. A. (2019). Die Lieder by Martin Luther [review]. *Notes*, *75*(4), 701–704. doi:10.1353/not.2019.0053

Lebel, R. (2017). Moving Beyond Fight and Flight: A Contingent Model of How the Emotional Regulation of Anger and Fear Sparks Proactivity. *Academy of Management Review*, *42*(2), 190–206. doi:10.5465/amr.2014.0368

LeDoux, J. E. (2000). Emotion circuits in the brain. *Annual Review of Neuroscience*, *23*(1), 155–184. doi:10.1146/annurev.neuro.23.1.155 PMID:10845062

Lee, E. J., Kwon, G., Shin, H. J., Yang, S., Lee, S., & Suh, M. (2014). The Spell of Green: Can Frontal EEG Activations Identify Green Consumers? *Journal of Business Ethics*, *122*(3), 511–521. doi:10.100710551-013-1775-2

Lee, I., & Lee, K. (2015). The Internet of Things (IoT): Applications, investments, and challenges for enterprises. *Business Horizons*, *58*(4), 431–440. doi:10.1016/j.bushor.2015.03.008

Lefebvre, H. (1991). *The production of space*. Oxford, UK: John Wiley & Sons Ltd.

Leicht, T., Chtourou, A., & Ben Youssef, K. (2018). Consumer innovativeness & intentioned autonomous car adoption. *The Journal of High Technology Management Research*, *29*(1), 1–11. doi:10.1016/j.hitech.2018.04.001

Leiva, F. M., & Carmona, D. G. (2019). Sparking interest in restaurant dishes? Cognitive and affective processes underlying dish design and ecological origin. An fMRI study. *Physiology & Behavior*. PMID:29908937

Lengwiler, Y. (2009). *The Origins of Expected Utility Theory. In Vinzenz Bronzin's Option Pricing Models*. Berlin: Springer Berlin Heidelberg.

Lennings, C. J., & Burns, A. M. (1998). Time perspective: Temporal extension, time estimation, & impulsivity. *The Journal of Psychology*, *132*(4), 367–380. doi:10.1080/00223989809599271 PMID:9637020

LeSage, J. P. (2014). What Regional Scientists Need to Know about Spatial Econometrics. *The Review of Regional Studies*, *44*(1), 13–32. doi:10.2139srn.2420725

LeSage, J. P., & Pace, R. K. (2014). The biggest myth in spatial econometrics. *Econometrics*, *2*(4), 217–249. doi:10.3390/econometrics2040217

LeSage, J., & Pace, R. (2009). *Introduction to Spatial Econometrics* (1st ed.). Boca Raton, FL: Chapman & Hall/CRC. doi:10.1201/9781420064254

Levinas, E. (1997). *Time and the other* (R. Cohen, Trans.). Pittsburgh: Duquesne University Press.

Lewin, K. (1951). Field Theory of Social Science: Selected Theoretical Chapters. *The Annals of the American Academy of Political and Social Science*, *276*(1), 146–147. doi:10.1177/000271625127600135

Lewis, G. (1992). Musseums and their precursors: A Brief Wold Survey. Manual of Curaorship, 2, 1-26.

Lezak, M. D., Howieson, D. B., Bigler, E. D., & Tranel, D. (2012). *Neuropsychological assessment* (5th ed.). USA: Oxford University Press.

Libet, B. (1996). Cerebral time factors in conscious and unconscious mental functions. *Journal of Clinical Neurophysiology*, *13*(4), 350. doi:10.1097/00004691-199607000-00027

Likert, R. (1932). A technique for the measurement of attitudes. *Archives de Psychologie*, *140*, 5–55.

Limayem, M., Khalifa, M., & Frini, A. (2000). What Makes Consumers Buy from Internet? A Longitudinal Study of Online Shopping, *IEEE Transactions on Systems. Man & Cybernetics: Part A*, *30*(4), 421–432. doi:10.1109/3468.852436

Lim, C. M., Brun, A., Runyan, R., & Kim, Y.-K. (2013). Segmenting luxe-bargain shoppers using a fuzzy clustering method. *International Journal of Retail & Distribution Management*, *41*(11/12), 848–868. doi:10.1108/ijrdm-01-2013-0012

Lin, C.-H. (2011). Personality, Value, Life Style and Postmodernism Consumer Behavior: A Comparison Among Three Generations. *International Journal of Organizational Innovation*, *3*(3), 203–230. Retrieved from http://search.ebscohost.com/login.aspx?direct=true&db=bth&AN=59220375&site=eds-live

Lindič, J., & Marques da Silva, C. (2011). Value proposition as a catalyst for a customer focused innovation. *Management Decision*, *49*(10), 1694–1708. doi:10.1108/00251741111183834

Lindner Radons, D., Flores Battistella, L., & Zampieri Grohmann, M. (2016). Geração e gênero como moderadores no comportamento de compra pró-ambiental. *Pensamiento & Gestión*, (41), 148–171. Retrieved from http://search.ebscohost.com/login.aspx?direct=true&db=bth&AN=122029597&site=eds-live~

Lindstrom, M. (2008). *Buyology: truth and lies abaut why we buy*. New York: Doubleday.

Lipton, B. (2015). *The biology of belief.* Hay House Publishing.

Li, T., Cheng, J., Xiong, T., Ye, J., & Zhang, Z. (2018). Research on Attitude Accessibility in Product Design Evaluation: Cognitive Features and Memory Network. In *Advances in Intelligent Systems and Computing*. Cham: Springer.

Li, W. S. (2018). Strategic Value Analysis: Value Search. In *Strategic Management Accounting* (pp. 159–170). Singapore: Springer. doi:10.1007/978-981-10-5729-8_9

Li, Y. J., Haws, K. L., & Griskevicius, V. (2019). Parenting Motivation and Consumer Decision-Making. *The Journal of Consumer Research*, *45*(5), 1117–1137. doi:10.1093/jcr/ucy038

Lockley, L. (1950). Notes on the history of marketing research. *Journal of Marketing*, *14*(5), 733–736. doi:10.1177/002224295001400511

Lorenzen, M., & Täube, F. A. (2008). Breakout from Bollywood? The roles of social networks and regulation in the evolution of Indian film industry. *Journal of International Management*, *14*(3), 286–299. doi:10.1016/j.intman.2008.01.004

Lorenzi-Cioldi, F., & Clémence, A. (2004). Group processes and the construction of social representations. In M. B. Brewer & M. Hewstone (Eds.), *Social cognition* (pp. 298–320). Academic Press.

Loroz, P. S., & Helgeson, J. G. (2013). Boomers and their Babies: An Exploratory Study Comparing Psychological Profiles and Advertising Appeal Effectiveness Across Two Generations. *Journal of Marketing Theory and Practice*, *21*(3), 289–306. doi:10.2753/MTP1069-6679210304

Lovgren, S. (2004, January 21). Bollywood: Indian films splice Bombay, Hollywood. *National Geographic News*. Retrieved online from http://news.nationalgeographic.com/news/2004/01/0121_040121_bollywo odfilms.html

Lowe, B., Dwivedi, Y. K., & d'Alessandro, S. (2019). Consumers and technology in a changing world. *European Journal of Marketing*, *53*(6).

Lowenthal, D. (1972). *Geography, Experience, and Imagination. In Tourism Business Frontiers: Consumers, Products and Industry* (pp. 211–219). Butterworth-Heinemann.

Lu, J., Zhang, G., Ruan, D., & Wu, F. (2007). *Multi-Objective Group Decision Making* (Vol. 6). https://www.worldscientific.com/worldscibooks/10.1142/p505retrieved

Luiz, M. (2017). *"A Simplificação como Protagonista do Sucesso Empresarial", as part of the "Presente para o Futuro" compilation, a Project that presents expectations and perceptions of The Boston Consulting Group Brazil partners for the coming 20 years*. The Boston Consulting Group.

Lu, J., Yao, J. E., & Yu, C. (2005). Personal innovativeness, social influences & adoption of wireless Internet services via mobile technology. *The Journal of Strategic Information Systems*, *14*(3), 245–268. doi:10.1016/j.jsis.2005.07.003

Lu, M. T., Preston, J. B., & Strick, P. L. (1994). Interconnections between the prefrontal cortex and the premotor areas in the frontal lobe. *Research Systems Neuroscience*, *V341*(3), 375–392. doi:10.1002/cne.903410308 PMID:7515081

Luna, D., & Gupta, S. F. (2001). An integrative framework for cross-cultural consumer behavior. *International Marketing Review*, *18*(1), 45–69. doi:10.1108/02651330110381998

Luttrell, A., Stillman, P. E., Hasinski, A. E., & Cunningham, W. A. (2016). Neural dissociations in attitude strength: Distinct regions of cingulate cortex track ambivalence and certainty. *Journal of Experimental Psychology. General*, *145*(4), 419–433. doi:10.1037/xge0000141 PMID:26854498

Lynn, M. (1991). Scarcity effects on value: A quantitative review of the commodity theory literature. *Psychology and Marketing*, *8*(1), 43–57. doi:10.1002/mar.4220080105

Macionis, N. (2004). Understanding the film-induced tourist. In *International Tourism and Media Conference Proceedings*. Melbourne, Australia: Tourism Research Unit, Monash University.

Macionis, N., & O'Connor, N. (2011). How can the film-induced tourism phenomenon be sustainably managed? *Worldwide Hospitality and Tourism Themes*, *3*(2), 173–178. doi:10.1108/17554211111123032

Macionis, N., & Sparks, B. (2009). Film-induced tourism: An incidental experience. *Tourism Review International*, *13*(2), 93–101. doi:10.3727/154427209789604598

MacKenzie, I., Meyer, C., & Noble, S. (2013). *How retailers can keep up with consumers*. Retrieved from https://www.mckinsey.com/industries/retail/our-insights/how-retailers-can-keep-up-with-consumers

MacLean, P. D. (1990). *The triune brain in evolution: Role in paleocerebral functions*. New York: Plenum Press.

Maclennan, D. (1977). Some Thoughts on the Nature and Purpose of House Price Studies. *Urban Studies (Edinburgh, Scotland)*, *14*(1), 59–71. doi:10.1080/00420987720080061

Maclennan, D., & Tu, Y. (1996). Economic Perspectives on the Structure of Local Housing Systems. *Housing Studies*, *11*(3), 387–406. doi:10.1080/02673039608720864

Madden, R. (2010). *Being Ethnographic*. London: Sage.

Madsen, A. O., & Chkoniya, V. (2019). Fish Consumption in the Age of the Information Society - The Evolution of the Fish Sector in Portugal. *European Journal of Social Sciences, 2*. Retrieved from http://journals.euser.org/index.php/ejss/article/view/4251

Madsen, A. O., & Chkoniya, V. (2019). Tendencies Regarding Fish Consumption – The Case of Portugal (Europe's Leader & 3rd in the World). *European Journal of Interdisciplinary Studies, 6*(1), 33–50.

Madsen, A. O., & Chkoniya, V. (2019a). Fish Consumption in the Age of the Information Society - The Evolution of the Fish Sector in Portugal. *European Journal of Social Sciences, 2*(2). Retrieved from http://journals.euser.org/index.php/ejss/article/view/4251

Madsen, A. O. (2014). *La influencia del sistema del mercado en comportamiento: el caso del pescado en Portugal y Dinamarca*. Universidad Rey Juan Carlos.

Madslien, J. (2017). Intelligent mobility. *Professional Engineering*. Retrieved from http://search.ebscohost.com/login.aspx?direct=true&db=bth&AN=123453640&site=eds-live

Maersk. (2019). *Maersk to Accelerate Growth in Logistics and Services*. Retrieved from https://www.maersk.com/news/articles/2019/05/16/maersk-to-accelerate-growth-in-logistics-and-services

Maison, D., & Oleksy, T. (2017). Validation of EEG as an Advertising Research Method: Relation Between EEG Reaction Toward Advertising and Attitude Toward Advertised Issue (Related to Political and Ideological Beliefs). In K. Nermend & M. Łatuszynska (Eds.), *Neuroeconomic and Behavioral Aspectsof Decision Making*. Springer Proceedings in Business and Economics. doi:10.1007/978-3-319-62938-4_18

Makri, K., & Schlegelmilch, B. B. (2017). Time orientation & engagement with social networking sites: A cross-cultural study in Austria, China & Uruguay. *Journal of Business Research*, *80*, 155–163. doi:10.1016/j.jbusres.2017.05.016

Malhotra, K., & Birks, D. F. (2007). *Marketing research: an applied approach*. Harlow, UK: Pearson Education Limited. doi:10.1108/S1548-6435(2007)3

Malhotra, N. K., Kim, S. S., & Agarwal, J. (2004). Internet Users' Information Privacy Concerns (Iuipc): The Construct, the Scale, and a Causal Model. *Information Systems Research*, *15*(4), 336–355. doi:10.1287/isre.1040.0032

Mamulia, G. (1979). *Klasobrivi sazogadoebisa da saxelmcopos chamokalibeba Qartlshi* [The Emergence of Ckass Society and State in ancient Kartli (Iberia)]. Tbilisi: Mecniereba.

Mancall, P. C., & Weiss, T. (1999). Was Economic Growth Likely in Colonial British North America? *The Journal of Economic History*, *59*(1), 17–40. doi:10.1017/S0022050700022270

Manning, P. (2008). Materiality and Cosmology: Old Georgian Churches as Sacred, Sublime, and Secular Objects. *Ethnos: Journal of Anthropology*, *73*(3), 327–360. doi:10.1080/00141840802324011

Mansor, A. A. A., & Isa, S. M. (2018). The Impact of Eye Tracking on Neuromarketing for Genuine Value-Added Applications. *Global Business and Management Research, 10*, 1–11.

Mansori, S., Sambasivan, M., & Md-Sidin, S. (2015). Acceptance of novel products: The role of religiosity, ethnicity and values. *Marketing Intelligence & Planning, 33*(1), 39–65. doi:10.1108/MIP-03-2013-0050

Manyika, J., Chui, M., Bughin, J., Dobbs, R., Bisson, P., & Marrs, A. (2013). *Disruptive technologies: Advances that will transform life, business, and the global economy*. McKinsey Global Institute.

Marketing Week. (2019). *Marketing effectiveness survey*. Retrieved from https://www.marketingweek.com/carlsberg-demographics-waterwipes-5-things-that-mattered-this-week-and-why/

Markman, A. B., & Brendl, C. M. (2005). Goals, Policies, Preferences, and Actions. In F. R. Kardes, P. M. Herr, & J. Nantel (Eds.), *Applying social cognition to consumer-focused strategy* (pp. 183–199). Lawrence Erlbaum Associates.

Marková, I. (2017). The making of the theory of social representations. *Cadernos de Pesquisa, 47*(163), 358–374.

Markowitz, L. (2012). Highland Haute Cuisine: The Transformation of Alpaca Meat. In E. Elizabeth Finnis (Ed.), *Reimagining Marginalized Foods*. Tucson, AZ: The University of Arizona Press. doi:10.2307/j.ctt1814g4b.5

Marox, E., Rodríguez, H., Yañez, G., Bernal, J., Rodríguez, M., Fernández, T., ... Guerrero, V. (2001). Broad band spectral measurements of EEG during emotional tasks. *The International Journal of Neuroscience, 108*(3–4), 251–279. doi:10.3109/00207450108986517 PMID:11699193

Marques, J. (2012). *The notion of space in urban housing markets* (PhD thesis). Universidade de Aveiro.

Marques, J., Castro, E., & Bhattacharjee, A. (2012). Methods and models for analysis of the urban housing market. In Emerging Challenges for Regional Development and Evolving Infrastructure Networks and Space. Edward Elgar.

Marques, J., Wolf, J., & Borges, M. (2018). Modelling the urban transformation at local scale. *Rivista Urbanistica Informazioni*, 80–83.

Marques, J., Wolf, J., & Borges, M. (2018). Modelling the urban transformation at local scale. Rivista Urbanistica Informazioni, dall'Istituto nazionale di Urbanistica, 80–83.

Marques, J., Borges, M., Batista, P., Gonçalves, C., & Wolf, J. (2019). Drivers and models to support policies of territorial transformation. *Conference Proceedings on the 4th International Conference on CHANGING CITIES: Spatial, Design, Landscape & Socio-economic Dimensions*.

Martin, D., & Schouten, J. (2012). *Sustainable marketing*. Upper Saddle River, NJ: Pearson Prentice Hall.

Mary Douglas and Baron Isherwood. (1979). *The World of Goods*. Routledge.

Maslow, A. H., Frager, R., Fadiman, J., McReynolds, C., & Cox, R. (1970). Motivation and personality (Vol. 2). Harper & Row.

Matta, R. (2013). Native Eating: The Modern Roosts of Peruvian Food Heritage. *Anthropology of Food, 8*(S8). doi:10.4000/aof.7361

Matthyssens, P., & Vandenbempt, K. (2008). Moving from basic offerings to value-added solutions: Strategies, barriers and alignment. *Industrial Marketing Management, 37*(3), 316–328. doi:10.1016/j.indmarman.2007.07.008

Mattos, K. M. C., & Mattos, A. (2004). Valoração econômica do meio ambiente: uma abordagem teórica e prática. São Carlos: Editora Rima.

Matukin, M. (2017). Physiological measures. In P. Dovas, L. Florentino, C. Grieve, H. Hofkirchner, C. Maclnnes, M. Matukin, B. Monteleone, S. Needel, R. Ohme, & P. Steidl (Eds.), Market Research revolution. CreateSpace.

Matukin, M., & Ohme, R. K. (2017). How reaction time measurement empowers marketing and market research. In P. Dovas, L. Florentino, C. Grieve, H. Hofkirchner, C. Maclnnes, M. Matukin, B. Monteleone, S. Needel, R. Ohme, & P. Steidl (Eds.), Market Research revolution. CreateSpace.

Matukin, M., & Ohme, R. (2016). Implicit Measures of Attitudes in Market Research. In A. R. Thomas, N. A. Pop, A. M. Iorga, & C. Ducu (Eds.), *Ethics and neuromarketing: implications for market research and business practice* (pp. 113–123). Springer.

Maury, C. (2007). *Social representations: A tool box Literature review.* Report for the Project n° 0288848-2 co funded by the European Commission within the Sixth Framework Progra.

Maymand, M., & Razmi, R. (2017). On the Effect of the Congruence between the Brand Image and Brand Personality on the Consumers' Brand Preference and Purchase Intent: A Case Study of Aquafina Bottled Water. *International Journal of Economic Perspectives*, *11*(1), 1369–1383.

Mayyas, A., Qattawi, A., Omar, M., & Shan, D. (2012). Design for sustainability in automotive industry: A comprehensive review. *Renewable & Sustainable Energy Reviews*, *16*(4), 1845–1862. doi:10.1016/j.rser.2012.01.012

McAdams, D., & Pals, J. (2006). A new Big Five: Fundamental principles for an integrative science of personality. *The American Psychologist*, *61*(3), 204–217. doi:10.1037/0003-066X.61.3.204 PMID:16594837

McCants, A. E. C. (2007). Exotic goods, popular consumption, and the standard of living: Thinking about globalization in the early modern world. *Journal of World History*, *18*(4), 433. doi:10.1353/jwh.2008.0008

McCosh, A. M., & Correa-Perez, B. A. (2006). *The optimization of what? Intelligent decision-making support systems.* London: Springer.

McCracken, G. (1986). Culture and Consumption: A theoretical account of the structure and movement of the cultural meaning of consumer goods. *The Journal of Consumer Research*, *13*(1), 71–84. doi:10.1086/209048

McCracken, G. (1988). *Culture and Consumption.* Bloomington: Indiana University Press.

McCrae, R. R., Costa, P. T. J., Ostendorf, F., Angleitner, A., Hrebícková, M., Avia, M. D., ... Smith, P. B. (2000). Nature over nurture: Temperament, personality, & life span development. *Journal of Personality and Social Psychology*, *78*(1), 173–186. doi:10.1037/0022-3514.78.1.173 PMID:10653513

McGhie, A. (2012). *Brand is a four letter word: positioning and the real art of marketing.* Charleston: Advantage Media Group.

McGrath, R. G. (2010). Business models: A discovery driven approach. *Long Range Planning*, *43*(2-3), 247–261. doi:10.1016/j.lrp.2009.07.005

McKinsey & Company. (2017). *How Shared Mobility will change the Automotive Industry April 2017 chapter.* https://www.mckinsey.com/industries/automotive-and-assembly/our-insights/how-shared-mobility-will-change-the-automotive-industry

McKinsey. (2013). *Disruptive technologies: advances that will transform life, business, and the global economy.* https://www.mckinsey.com/insights/business_technology/disruptive_technologies

MDGMONITOR. (n.d.). *Category: Sustainable Development Goals.* Retrieved November 10, 2019 from https://www.mdgmonitor.org/sustainable-development-goals/

Mecheril, P., & Teo, T. (Eds.). (1997). Rassismuserfahrungen von Anderen Deutschen-eine Einzelfallbetrachtung. Psychologie und Rassismus, 175-201.

Meining, D. W. (1979). *Symbolic landscapes. I D. W. Meinig, The Interpretation of Ordinary Landscapes* (pp. 164–192). Oxford: Oxford University Press.

Meissner, F., Grigutsch, L. A., Koranyi, N., Müller, F., & Rothermund, K. (2019). Predicting Behavior With Implicit Measures: Disillusioning Findings, Reasonable Explanations, and Sophisticated Solutions. *Frontiers in Psychology*, *10*, 10. doi:10.3389/fpsyg.2019.02483 PMID:31787912

Merchant, A., Rose, G., & Rose, M. (2014). The Impact of Time Orientation on Consumer Innovativeness in the United States and India. *Journal of Marketing Theory and Practice*, *22*(3), 325–338. doi:10.2753/MTP1069-6679220307

Meyer, G. (1890, Oct. 6). Die Deutschamerikaner. Festschrift zur Feier des Deutschamerikanischen Tages in Milwauke. Winsconsin.

Meyer, D. E., Osman, A. M., Irwin, D. E., & Yantis, S. (1988). Modern mental chronometry. *Biological Psychology*, *26*(1-3), 3–67. doi:10.1016/0301-0511(88)90013-0 PMID:3061480

Meyer-Rochow, V. B. (2009). Food taboos: Their origins and purposes. *Journal of Ethnobiology and Ethnomedicine*, *5*(18). PMID:19563636

Michelfelder, D. P. (2011). Dirty Hands, Speculative Minds, and Smart Machines. *Philosophy & Technology*, *24*(1), 55–68. doi:10.100713347-010-0009-0

Midgley, D. F., & Dowling, G. R. (1993). A Longitudinal Study of Product Form Innovation: The Interaction between Predispositions & Social Messages. *The Journal of Consumer Research*, *19*(4), 611–625. doi:10.1086/209326

Miles, R. E., & Snow, C. C. (1986). Organizations: New concepts for new forms. *California Management Review*, *28*(3), 62–73. doi:10.2307/41165202

Miles, R. E., Snow, C. C., Meyer, A. D., & Coleman, H. J. Jr. (1978). Organizational strategy, structure, and process. *Academy of Management Review*, *3*(3), 546–562. doi:10.5465/amr.1978.4305755 PMID:10238389

Mill, J. S. (1998). Utilitarianism (R. Crisp, Ed.). Oxford: Oxford University Press.

Mill, J. S. (2012). Utilitarianism. Spark Notes Editors.

Miller, A. (2019). The intrinsically linked future for human and Artificial Intelligence interaction. *Journal of Big Data*, *6*(1), 38. doi:10.118640537-019-0202-7

Miller, D. (1987). *Material Culture and Mass Consumption*. Oxford: Basil Blackwell.

Milliman, R. E., & Fugate, D. L. (1988). Using trust-transference as a persuasion technique: An empirical field investigation. *Journal of Personal Selling & Sales Management*, *8*(2), 1–7.

Milne, G., & Culnan, M. (2004). Strategies for Reducing Online Privacy Risks: Why Consumers Read (Or Don't Read) Online Privacy Notices. *Journal of Interactive Marketing*, *18*(3), 15–29. doi:10.1002/dir.20009

Ming, Z. (2018, Sept.). Alibaba and the Future of Business: Lessons from China's innovative digital giant. *Harvard Business Review*.

Ministerio de Agricultura y Riego. (n.d.). *Hoy se celebra el Dia Nacional de la Alpaca.* Lima, Peru: MINAGRI.

Ministerio de la Cultura. (2011). *Lima, Cocina e identidad La culinaria peruana como patrimonio cultural inmaterial.* Lima, Peru: Government Printing Office.

Minnema, A., Bijmolt, T. H. A., Gensler, S., & Wiesel, T. (2016). To Keep or Not to Keep: Effects of Online Customer Reviews on Product Returns. *Journal of Retailing*, *92*(3), 253–267. doi:10.1016/j.jretai.2016.03.001

Minocha, S., & Stonehouse, G. (2006). The "learning trap": A Bollywood frame from strategic learning. *Management Decision*, *44*(10), 1344–1362. doi:10.1108/00251740610715687

Minor-Cooley, D., & Brice, J. (2007). The Problems with Ethnic Identification and Its Potential in Cross-Cultural Marketing. *Academy of Marketing Science Review*, *11*(9), 1–9.

Mintzberg, H. (1973). *The Nature of Managerial Work. Harper & Row.* Retrieved from https://books.google.pt/books?id=9HmdkQEACAAJ

Mintzberg, H. (1990). The Manager's Job: Folklore and Fact. *Harvard Business Review Reprint Service.* Retrieved from https://books.google.pt/books?id=NAUXnQEACAAJ

Mintz, S. W. (2001). Comida e Antropologia – uma breve revisão. *Revista Brasileira de Ciências Sociais*, *16*(47), 31–41. doi:10.1590/S0102-69092001000300002

Mintz, S. W., & Du Bois, C. M. (2002). The Anthropology of Food and Eating. *Annual Review of Anthropology*, *31*(1), 99–119. doi:10.1146/annurev.anthro.32.032702.131011

Mitchell, D. W., & Bruckner Coles, C. (2004). Establishing a continuing business model innovation process. *The Journal of Business Strategy*, *25*(3), 39–49. doi:10.1108/02756660410536991

Mitchell, J. P., Nosek, B. A., & Banaji, M. R. (2003). Contextual variations in implicit evaluation. *Journal of Experimental Psychology. General*, *132*(3), 455–469. doi:10.1037/0096-3445.132.3.455 PMID:13678378

Mittal, V., & Kamakura, W. (2001). Satisfaction, repurchase intent, and repurchase behavior: Investigating the moderating effect of customer characteristics. *JMR, Journal of Marketing Research*, *38*(1), 131–142. doi:10.1509/jmkr.38.1.131.18832

Modi, S., Spulber, A., & Jin, J. (2018). Impact of automated, connected, electric, and shared (ACES) vehicles on design, materials, manufacturing and business models.

Moli, J. P. (n.d.). *5 claves del Neuromarketing World Forum 2016*. Retrieved March 11, 2020, from http://brainandmarketing.blogspot.com/2016/01/5-claves-del-nmf-2016.html

Monroe, R. W., & Barrett, P. T. (2019). The Evolving B2B E-Commerce and Supply Chain Management: A Chronological Mémoire. *Journal of Business and Management*, *25*(1), 49–67. doi:10.6347/JBM.201903_25(1).0003

Montag, C., & Panksepp, J. (2017). Primary emotional systems and personality: An evolutionary perspective. *Frontiers in Psychology*, *8*, 464. doi:10.3389/fpsyg.2017.00464 PMID:28443039

Montagrin, A., & Sander, D. (2016). Emotional memory: From affective relevance to arousal. *Behavioral and Brain Sciences*, *39*, 39. doi:10.1017/S0140525X15001879 PMID:28347365

Mont, O. (2004). Institutionalisation of sustainable consumption patterns based on shared use. *Ecological Economics*, *50*(1-2), 135–153. doi:10.1016/j.ecolecon.2004.03.030

Montreuil, B., Ballot, E., & Fontane, F. (2012). An Open Logistics Interconnection Model for the Physical Internet. *Information Control Problems in Manufacturing*, *14*(1), 327–332. doi:10.3182/20120523-3-RO-2023.00385

Moore, G. C., & Benbasat, I. (1991). Development of an instrument to measure the perceptions of adopting an information technology innovation. *Information Systems Research*, *2*(3), 173–191. doi:10.1287/isre.2.3.192

Moorhead, G., Ference, R., & Neck, C. P. (1991). Group Decision Fiascoes Continue: Space Shuttle Challenger and a Revised Groupthink Framework. *Human Relations*, *44*(6), 539–550. doi:10.1177/001872679104400601

Morhart, F., Malar, L., Guevremont, A., Girardin, F., & Grohmann, B. (2015). Brand authenticity: An integrative framework and measurement scale. *Journal of Consumer Psychology*, *25*(2), 200–218. doi:10.1016/j.jcps.2014.11.006

Morieux, Y. (2011). Smart rules: Six ways to get people to solve problems without you. *Harvard Business Review*, *89*, 78–84, 86,136. PMID:21939130

Morin, C. (2011). Neuromarketing: The new science of consumer behavior. *Society*, *48*(2), 131–135. doi:10.100712115-010-9408-1

Morishima, Y., Schunk, D., Bruhin, A., Ruff, C. C., & Fehr, E. (2012). Linking brain structure and activation in temporoparietal junction to explain the neurobiology of human altruism. *Neuron*, *75*(1), 73–79. doi:10.1016/j.neuron.2012.05.021 PMID:22794262

Morley, D. (2000). *Home, Territories, Media, Mobility and Identity*. London: Routledge.

Morley, D., & Robins, K. (1995). *Spaces of Identity: Global Media, Electronic Landscapes and Cultural Boundaries*. London: Routledge.

Morris, M., Schindehutte, M., & Allen, J. (2005). The entrepreneur's business model: Toward a unified perspective. *Journal of Business Research*, *58*(6), 726–735. doi:10.1016/j.jbusres.2003.11.001

Morse, J. M. (1991). Evaluating Qualitative Research. *Qualitative Health Research*, *1*(3), 283–286. doi:10.1177/104973239100100301

Mortelmans, D. (2005). Sign values in processes of distinction: The concept of luxury. *Semiotica*, *157*(1-4), 497–520.

Moscovici, S. (1988). *Notes towards a description of Social Representations*. Academic Press.

Moscovici, S. (2001). Why a Theory of Social Representation? In K. Deaux & G. Philogène (Eds.), *Representations of the social: Bridging theoretical traditions* (pp. 8–35). Oxford: Blackwell.

Moses, E., Beavin, L., Zaval, L., & Hendrickson, K. (2018). *The influence of an in-store gift on emotional arousal and shopper behavior*. Academic Press.

Mueller, S., & Lockshin, L. (2008). *How important is wine packaging for consumers? On the reliability of measuring attribute importance with direct vebal versus indirect visual methods*. Academic Press.

Muller, C. C., & Woods, R. H. (1994). An expanded restaurant typology. *The Cornell Hotel and Restaurant Administration Quarterly*, *35*(3), 27–37. doi:10.1177/001088049403500312

Mundel, J., Huddleston, P., & Vodermeier, M. (2017). An exploratory study of consumers' perceptions: What are affordable luxuries? *Journal of Retailing and Consumer Services*, *35*, 68–75. doi:10.1016/j.jretconser.2016.12.004

Munshi, N. (2012). *Spain's starring role in Bollywood movie a boon to tourism*. Retrieved February 11, 2013 from: http://adage.com/article/globalnews/ spain-s-starring-role-bollywood-movie-a-boon-tourism/232511/

Murphy, S. T., Monahan, J. L., & Zajonc, R. B. (1995). Additivity of nonconscious affect: Combined effects of priming and exposure. *Journal of Personality and Social Psychology*, *69*(4), 589–602. doi:10.1037/0022-3514.69.4.589 PMID:7473021

Murphy, S. T., & Zajonc, R. B. (1993). Affect, cognition, and awareness: Affective priming with optimal and suboptimal stimulus exposures. *Journal of Personality and Social Psychology*, *64*(5), 723–739. doi:10.1037/0022-3514.64.5.723 PMID:8505704

Murrell, A. & Mingrone, M. (1994). Correlates of temporal perspective. *Perceptual & Motor Skills,* 78 (3), 1331-1334.

Museer, S. (2014). *sydvestjyskemuseer.dk*. Accessed 10. 7. 2016 at https://www.sydvestjyskemuseer.dk/da/besoeg-museerne/museet-ribes-vikinger/

Museer, S. (2015). Projectdescription - pulje til udvikling af museumsområdet og museernes opgavevaretagelse. Kulturarvsformidling og kystturisme - et umage par? Esbjerg, Denmark.

Museet for Varde By og omegn. (2016). http://sargaanja.wix.com/vamhjemmeside

Musso, F. & Palmeira, M. (2017). *3Rs of Sustainability and the impact on consumer behaviour and people's values.* 24th Recent Advances in Retailing & Services Science Conference - EIRASS 2017.

Naci, H., & Ioannidis, J. P. A. (2015). Evaluation of Wellness Determinants and Interventions by Citizen Scientists. *Journal of the American Medical Association, 314*(2), 121. doi:10.1001/jama.2015.6160 PMID:26068643

Nadeem, W., Juntunen, M., & Juntunen, J. (2017). Consumer segments in social commerce: A latent class approach. *Journal of Consumer Behaviour, 16*(3), 279–292. doi:10.1002/cb.1632

Naganna, N., & Pankajakshi, R. (2019). Globalization & Marketing with Environmental Sustainability: A Holistic Resource-Centric Analysis with Reference to Corporatization. Bhavan's International. *The Journal of Business, 2*, 3–50.

Nair, R. (2016). Study on Economic Regulation of Collaborative Strategies among Container Shipping Companies Following Repeal of European Union Regulation 4056/86. *The Asian Journal of Shipping and Logistics, 32*(2), 89–97. doi:10.1016/j.ajsl.2016.05.002

Nascimento, A., & Gonçalves, R. (2017). *Porto de Sines: 3ª fase de ampliação do molhe leste: análise custo-benefício do investimento* (Unpublished technical report). CEGEA, Centro de Estudos em Gestão e Economia Aplicada – Universidade Católica Portuguesa.

Nascimento, A., Costa, A., Santos, F., & Cruz, C. (2016). *Terminais portuários e infra-estruturas logísticas em Portugal: análise da oportunidade para construção de um novo terminal de águas profundas.* Retrieved from: https://cciporto.com/downloads/acp_terminaisportuarios.pdf

Nascimento-Schulze, C. M., & Carmago, B. V. (2000). Psicologia social, representações sociais e métodos. *Temas em psicologia social, 8*(3), 287–299.

Navya. https://www.navya-corp.com/index.php/en/

Neely, J. H. (1991). Semantic priming effects in visual word recognition: A selective review of current findings and theories. In D. Besner & G. Humphreys (Eds.), Basic processes in reading: Visual word recognition (pp. 264-337). Hillsdale, NY: Erlbaum.

Neto, L. A., De, D., Diretor, C., Bueno, F., Schaefer, A.-R. M., Bernardini-Assessor Da, M., … Zanella, C. (2010). *ABIMAQ - Associação Brasileira da Indústria de Máquinas e Equipamentos.* Retrieved from www.abimaq.com

Neuromarketing News & Blog—NMSBA. (n.d.). Retrieved March 10, 2020, from https://nmsba.com/neuromarketing/news-blog?q=&p=2

Ngo, L. V., & O'Cass, A. (2013). Innovation and business success: The mediating role of customer participation. *Journal of Business Research, 66*(8), 1134–1142. doi:10.1016/j.jbusres.2012.03.009

Nguyen, H. V., Nguyen, C. H., & Hoang, T. T. B. (2018). Green consumption: Closing the intention-behavior gap. *Sustainable Development, 27*(1), 118–129. doi:10.1002d.1875

Nicolas, S., & Pins, D. (2014). Piéron's Law and the First Instruments for Measuring Reaction Time. *Bulletin de Psychologie*, (5): 385–407. doi:10.3917/bupsy.533.0385

Nida, E. (1998). Language, Culture and Translation. Foreign language Journal, 29-33.

Niedenthal, P. M., & Kitayama, S. (1994). *The heart's eye: emotional influences in perception and attention*. New York: Academic Press.

Niles-Hofmann, L., & Celentano, A. (2015). Learning Insights From Digital Body Language. *Chief Learning Officer*. Retrieved from http://search.ebscohost.com/login.aspx?direct=true&db=edb&AN=108887204&site=eds-live

Nobre, H., & Simões, C. (2019). NewLux Brand Relationship Scale: Capturing the scope of mass-consumed luxury brand relationships. *Journal of Business Research*. doi:10.1016/j.jbusres.2019.01.047

Noel, L., Zarazua de Rubens, G., Kester, J., & Sovacool, B. K. (2018). Beyond emissions and economics: Rethinking the co-benefits of electric vehicles (EVs) and vehicle-to-grid (V2G). *Transport Policy*, *71*, 130–137. doi:10.1016/j.tranpol.2018.08.004

Norbury, A., & Husain, M. (2015). Sensation-seeking: Dopaminergic modulation and risk for psychopathology. *Behavioural Brain Research*, *288*, 79–93. doi:10.1016/j.bbr.2015.04.015 PMID:25907745

Normann, R., & Ramirez, R. (1993). From Value Chain to Value Constellation: Designing Interactive Strategy. *Harvard Business Review*, *71*(4), 65–77. PMID:10127040

North, D. C. (1984). Transaction Costs, Institutions, and Economic History. *Journal of Institutional and Theoretical Economics*, 7–17.

Nosek, B. A., & Banaji, M. R. (2001). The go/no-go association task. *Social Cognition*, *19*(6), 625–666. doi:10.1521oco.19.6.625.20886

Nosek, B. A., Greenwald, A. G., & Banaji, M. R. (2005). Understanding and using the Implicit Association Test: II. Method variables and construct validity. *Personality and Social Psychology Bulletin*, *31*(2), 166–180. doi:10.1177/0146167204271418 PMID:15619590

Nosek, B. A., Hawkins, C. B., & Frazier, R. S. (2011). Implicit social cognition: From measures to mechanisms. *Trends in Cognitive Sciences*, *15*(4), 152–159. doi:10.1016/j.tics.2011.01.005 PMID:21376657

Nosek, B. A., Smyth, F. L., Hansen, J. J., Devos, T., Lindner, N. M., Ranganath, K. A., ... Greenwald, A. G. (2007). Pervasiveness and correlates of implicit attitudes and stereotypes. *European Review of Social Psychology*, *18*(1), 36–88. doi:10.1080/10463280701489053

Noteboom, T. (2008). *The Relationship Between Seaports and the Intermodal Hinterland in Light of Global Supply Chains: European Challenges*. OECD/International Transport Forum, Discussion Paper, 2008-10.

Noteboom, T. (2010). Concentration and the Formation of Multi-port Gateway Regions in the European Container Port System: An update. *Journal of Transport Geography*, *18*(4), 567–583. doi:10.1016/j.jtrangeo.2010.03.003

Novak, T. P., Hoffman, D. L., & Young, F. (2000). Measuring the Customer Experience in Online Environments: A Structural Modeling Approach. *Marketing Science*, *19*(1), 22–44. doi:10.1287/mksc.19.1.22.15184

Nowak, L., Thach, L., & Olsen, J. E. (2006). Wowing the millennials: Creating brand equity in the wine industry. *Journal of Product and Brand Management*, *15*(5), 316–323.

Nueno, J. L., & Quelch, J. A. (1998). The mass marketing of luxury. *Business Horizons*, *41*(6), 61.

Núñez, R., Allen, M., Gao, R., Miller Rigoli, C., Relaford-Doyle, J., & Semenuks, A. (2019). What happened to cognitive science? *Nature Human Behaviour*. PMID:31182794

Nunnally, J. C. (1975). Psychometric theory—25 years ago & now. *Educational Researcher*, *4*(10), 7–21.

Nuttin, J. (2014). *Future time perspective & motivation: Theory & research method*. Psychology Press. doi:10.4324/9781315802244

O'Reilly, K. (2009). *Key Concepts in Ethnography*. London: Sage.

Ocasio, W. (1997). Towards an attention-based view of the firm. *Strategic Management Journal*, *18*(S1), 187–206. doi:10.1002/(SICI)1097-0266(199707)18:1+<187::AID-SMJ936>3.3.CO;2-B

OCE - The Observatory of Economic Complexity. (2019). *Brazil*. Retrieved from https://oec.world/en/profile/country/bra

OECD. (2008). Promoting Sustainable Consumption. Good Practices In OECD Countries. OECD Publications.

Oh, H., Fiore, A. M., & Jeoung, M. (2007). Measuring experience economy concepts: Tourism applications. *Journal of Travel Research*, *46*(2), 119–132. doi:10.1177/0047287507304039

Ohme, R. (2001). The implicit conditioning of consumer attitudes: Logo substitution effect. Polish Psychological Bulletin, 32(1).

Ohme, R. (2016). *Neuromarketing World Forum, Speakers*. Neuromarketing World Forum. https://www.neuromarketingworldforum.com/info/videos/2016

Ohme, R. (1997). Social Comparison of Misfortune. *Polish Psychological Bulletin*, *28*(2), 189–201.

Ohme, R. (2009). The unconscious as the third dimension in advertising. *American Academy of Advertising Newsletter*, *5*(4), 1–5.

Ohme, R., Pochwatko, G., & Błaszczak, W. (1999). Paradygmat afektywnego poprzedzania: W poszukiwaniu nowej procedury badawczej. *Studia Psychologiczne*, *37*(1), 7–28.

Ohme, R., & Boshoff, C. (2019). The role of implicit learning in logo substitution. *Journal of Consumer Marketing*, *36*(5), 610–619. doi:10.1108/JCM-11-2017-2430

Ohme, R., Matukin, M., & Boshoff, C. (2016). Conscious and Subconscious Evaluation of Service Recovery Situation. In K. Plangger (Ed.), *Thriving in a New World Economy* (pp. 65–69). Cham: Springer. doi:10.1007/978-3-319-24148-7_20

Ohme, R., Matukin, M., & Pacula-Lesniak, B. (2011). Biometric measures for interactive advertising research. *Journal of Interactive Advertising*, *11*(2), 60–72. doi:10.1080/15252019.2011.10722185

Ohme, R., Reykowska, D., Wiener, D., & Choromanska, A. (2010). Application of frontal EEG asymmetry to advertising research. *Journal of Economic Psychology*, *31*(5), 785–793. doi:10.1016/j.joep.2010.03.008

Oliveira, A. (2007). A Discussion of Rational and Psychological Decision-Making Theories and Models: The Search for a Cultural-Ethical Decision-Making Model. *Electronic Journal of Business Ethics and Organization Studies Scenarios*, *12*(2), 12–17. http://ejbo.jyu.fi/pdf/ejbo_vol15_no1.pdfretrieved. Retrieved from http://ejbo.jyu.fi/pdf/ejbo_vol15_no1.pdf

Oliveira, J. H. C. (2014). Neuromarketing and sustainability: Challenges and opportunities for Latin America. *Latin American Journal Management for Sustainable Development*, *1*(1), 35–42. doi:10.1504/LAJMSD.2014.059779

Oliveira, T., Thomas, M., Baptista, G., & Campos, F. (2016). Full length article: Mobile payment: Underst&ing the determinants of customer adoption & intention to recommend the technology. *Computers in Human Behavior*, *61*, 404–414. doi:10.1016/j.chb.2016.03.030

Oliver, E. W. (1973). Markets and Hierarchies: Some Elementary Considerations. *The American Economic Review, 63*(2), 316–325.

Oliver, E. W. (2002). The Theory of the Firm as Governance Structure: From Choice to Contract. *The Journal of Economic Perspectives, 16*(3), 171–195. doi:10.1257/089533002760278776

Olwig, K. F. (2004). Ecotourism and authenticity [Comment]. *Current Anthropology, 45*(4), 491–492.

Oneplanetwork. (n.d.a). *Sustainable Consumption and Production: an operational approach to sustainability.* Retrieved November 10, 2019 from https://www.oneplanetnetwork.org/sites/default/files/briefings_on_scp.pdf

Oneplanetwork. (n.d.b). *What is SCP?* Retrieved November 10, 2019 from https://www.oneplanetnetwork.org/about/what-scp

ONU. (1988). *Relatório Brundtland "Nosso Futuro Comum".* Assembleia Geral da ONU.

OPEP - Organization of the Petroleum Exporting Countries. (2019). *Oil Market Report.* Retrieved from https://www.opec.org/opec_web/en/publications/338.htm

Organización de las Naciones Unidas para la Alimentación y la agricultura. (2005). *Desarrollo de productos con carne de alpaca.* Lima, Peru: FAO.

Orth, U. R., & Malkewitz, K. (2008). Holistic package design and consumer brand impressions. *Journal of Marketing, 72*(3), 64–81. doi:10.1509/jmkg.72.3.64

Osgood, C. E. (1962). Studies on the generality of affective meaning systems. *The American Psychologist, 17*(1), 10–28. doi:10.1037/h0045146

Ostrander, G. M. (1956). The Colonial Molasses Trade. *Agricultural History, 30*(2), 77–84.

Ostrom, E. (1998). Theory of Collective Action A Behavioral Approach to the Rational Choice Presidential Address, American Political Science Association. *The American Political Science Review, 92*(1), 1–22. doi:10.2307/2585925

Oswald, R. L. (1999). Culture Swapping: Consumption and the Ethnogenesis of Middle-Class Haitian Immigrants. *The Journal of Consumer Research, 25*(4), 303–318. doi:10.1086/209541

Otnes, C., Lowrey, T. M., & Shrum, L. J. (1997). Toward and Understanding of Consumer Ambivalence. *The Journal of Consumer Research, 24*(1), 80–93. doi:10.1086/209495

Oxford College of Marketing. (2016). *Digital disruption: what is it and how does it impact businesses?* https://blog.oxfordcollegeofmarketing.com/2016/02/22/what-is-digital-disruption/

Paavola, J. (2001). Economics, ethics and green consumerism. In Exploring sustainable consumption: Environmental policy ant the social sciences. Oxford: Elsevier Science.

Paço, A., Shiel, C., & Alves, H. (2018). A New Model for Testing Green Consumer Behaviour. *Journal of Cleaner Production.* doi:10.1016/j.jclepro.2018.10.105

Padmanabhan, G. (2010). Jive to the beat. *The Hindu.*

Paelinck, J., & Klaassen, L. (1979). *Spatial Econometrics.* Farnborough, UK: Saxon House.

Pahl, R. (1995). *After Success. Fin de Siècle Anxiety and Identity.* Cambridge: Polity Press.

Pallister, J. G., & Foxall, G. R. (1998). Psychometric properties of the Hurt-Joseph-Cook scales for the measurement of innovativeness. *Technovation, 18*(11), 663–675. doi:10.1016/S0166-4972(98)00070-4

Palmer, C. (2002). Christianity, Englishness and the southern English countryside: A study of the work of H.J.Massingham. *Social & Cultural Geography*, *3*(1), 25–38. doi:10.1080/14649360120114125

Panday, P. N., & Panday, S. (2018, March). *Leadership Strategies for supply chain Management*. Paper presented at the 3rd Global Leadership Research Conference 2018, Amity Business School, Noida, India.

Panksepp, J. (1998). *Affective neuroscience: The foundations of human and animal emotion*. New York, NY: Oxford University Press.

Panksepp, J. (2006). Emotional endophenotypes in evolutionary psychiatry. *Progress in Neuro-Psychopharmacology & Biological Psychiatry*, *30*(5), 774–784. doi:10.1016/j.pnpbp.2006.01.004 PMID:16554114

Panksepp, J. (2010). Affective neuroscience of the emotional BrainMind: Evolutionary perspectives and implications for understanding depression. *Dialogues in Clinical Neuroscience*, *12*(3), 533–545. PMID:21319497

Panksepp, J., & Biven, L. (2012). *The Norton series on interpersonal neurobiology. The archaeology of mind: Neuro-evolutionary origins of human emotion*. New York, NY: W. W. Norton & Company.

Panksepp, J., & Harro, J. (2004). The future of neuropeptides in biological psychiatry and emotional psychopharmacology: Goals and strategies. In J. Panksepp (Ed.), *Textbook of Biological Psychiatry* (pp. 627–660). Hoboken, NJ: Wiley.

Pantano, E., & Timmermans, H. (2014). What is smart for retailing? *Procedia Environmental Sciences*, *22*, 101–107. doi:10.1016/j.proenv.2014.11.010

Pardot. (2020). *B2B Marketing Trends | Insights from the Frontlines of B2B Marketing*. Retrieved from https://www.pardot.com/

Paris Motor Show. (2018). *Groupe Renault – Company's CEO Thierry Bolloré - Speech*. Press event presentation.

Park, G., Schwartz, H. A., Sap, M., Kern, M. L., Weingarten, E., Eichstaedt, J. C., & Seligman, M. E. P. (2017). Living in the Past, Present, and Future: Measuring Temporal Orientation With Language. *Journal of Personality*, *85*(2), 270–280. doi:10.1111/jopy.12239 PMID:26710321

Parment, A. (2013). Generation Y vs. Baby Boomers: Shopping behavior, buyer involvement and implications for retailing. *Journal of Retailing and Consumer Services*, *20*(2), 189–199. doi:10.1016/j.jretconser.2012.12.001

Parnell, G. S., Bresnick, T., Tani, S. N., & Johnson, E. R. (2013). *Handbook of Decision Analysis*. Wiley. doi:10.1002/9781118515853

Parry, J. H. (2010). *The Age of Reconnaissance: Discovery, Exporation and Settlement, 1450-1650*. Orion.

Pearce, D. G., & Kirk, D. (1986). Carrying capacities for coastal tourism. *Industry and Environment*, *9*(1), 3–6.

Perugini, M., & Bagozzi, R. (2001). The role of desires and anticipated emotions in goal directed behaviours: Broadening and deepening the theory of planned behaviour. *British Journal of Social Psychology*, *40*(1), 79–98. doi:10.1348/014466601164704 PMID:11329835

Peterson, R. A. (2005). In search of authenticity. *Journal of Management Studies*, *42*(5), 1083–1098. doi:10.1111/j.1467-6486.2005.00533.x

Pettersson, E., & Turkheimer, E. (2013). Approach temperament, anger, and evaluation: Resolving a paradox. *Journal of Personality and Social Psychology*, *105*(2), 285–300. doi:10.1037/a0033046 PMID:23773039

Pfeffer, J. (1981). *Power in organizations*. Marshfield: Pitman.

Phau, I., & Prendergast, G. (2000). Consuming luxury brands: The relevance of the 'Rarity Principle'. *Journal of Brand Management, 8*(2), 122–138. doi:10.1057/palgrave.bm.2540013

Phelps, J. E., D'Souza, G., & Nowak, G. J. (2001). Antecedents and consequences of consumer privacy concerns: An empirical investigation. *Journal of Interactive Marketing, 15*(4), 2–17. doi:10.1002/dir.1019

Phelps, J. E., Nowak, G. J., & Ferrell, E. (2000). Privacy concerns and consumer willingness to provide personal information. *Journal of Public Policy & Marketing, 19*(1), 27–41. doi:10.1509/jppm.19.1.27.16941

Philipp, S. F. (1992). Time orientation & participation in leisure activities. *Perceptual and Motor Skills, 75*(2), 659–664. doi:10.2466/pms.1992.75.2.659 PMID:1594428

Pighi, P. (2017, January 18). Por qué a muchos peruanos les cuesta reconocerse como cholos. *BBC News Mundo*. Retrieved from https://www.bbc.com/mundo/noticias-america-latina-37489332

Pinto, D.C., Nique, W.M. & da Silva Anana, E. (2011). Green consumer values: how do personal values influence environmentally responsible water consumption? *International Journal of Soncumer Studies, 35*(2), 122-131.

Pirtskalava, E. (2019). Being here and there: a case study of Muslim Meskhetians` identity and belonging, formation and reconstruction in the United States. Caucasus Survey, 7(7), 44-59.

Pitskhelauri, K. A. (1973). *Agmosavlet saqartvelos tomta istoriis ziritadi problemebi dzv. c XV-VII s.s* [Main issues of the history of tribes of Eastern Georgia (BC XV-VII cc)]. Tbilisi: Mecniereba.

Pitt, J. (2019). Transparent Ownership of Mobility-as-a-Service [Editorial]. *IEEE Technology and Society Magazine, 38*(2), 5–8. doi:10.1109/MTS.2019.2913064

Plassmann, H., O'Doherty, J., & Rangel, A. (2007). Orbitofrontal cortex encodes willingness to pay in everyday economic transactions. *The Journal of Neuroscience: The Official Journal of the Society for Neuroscience, 27*(37), 9984–9988. doi:10.1523/JNEUROSCI.2131-07.2007 PMID:17855612

Pligt, J. (1999). Decision making. In A. Manstead & M. Hewstone (Eds.), *The Blackwell encyclopedia of social psychology*. Oxford: Blackwell.

Policy Studies Institute. (2006). *Designing policy to influence consumers: Consumer behaviour relating to the purchasing of environmentally preferable goods.* Project under the Framework contract for economic analysis ENV.G.1/FRA/2006/0073 – 2nd.

Pollakowski, H. (1995). Data Sources for Measuring House Price Changes. *Journal of Housing Research, 6*(3), 377–387.

Pollard, J. (2019). *The use and reuse of stone circles: fieldwork at five Scottish monuments and its implications.* Archaeological Journal; doi:10.1080/00665983.2019.1596354

Poria, Y. (2010). *The Story behind the Picture: Preferences for the Visual Display at Heritage Sites. In Culture, Heritage and Representation.* Surrey, UK: Ashgate Publishing Limited.

Poria, Y., Butler, R., & Airey, D. (2003). The Core of Heritage Tourism. *Annals of Tourism Research, 30*(1), 238–254. doi:10.1016/S0160-7383(02)00064-6

Pornsakulvanich, V. (2017). Personality, attitudes, social influences, and social networking site usage predicting online social support. *Computers in Human Behavior, 76*, 255–262. doi:10.1016/j.chb.2017.07.021

Porter, M. E. (2001). Strategy and the Internet. *Harvard Business Review.* Retrieved from http://search.ebscohost.com/login.aspx?direct=true&db=bth&AN=4147416&site=eds-live

Porter, M. E., & Kramer, M. R. (2019). Creating shared value. In *Managing sustainable business* (pp. 323–346). Dordrecht: Springer. doi:10.1007/978-94-024-1144-7_16

Porter, M., & Siggelkow, N. (2008). Contextuality within activity systems and sustainability of competitive advantage. *The Academy of Management Perspectives*, *22*(2), 34–56. doi:10.5465/amp.2008.32739758

Portilho, F., (2005). Consumo sustentável: limites e possibilidades de ambientalização e politização das práticas de consumo. *Cadernos EBAPE.BR – Edição Temática – FGV*, *3*(3), 1 – 12.

Portuguesa, R. (2018). *Para uma nova geração de políticas de habitação*. Academic Press.

Posner, M. I. (1978). Chronometric explorations of mind. Lawrence Erlbaum. Prislin, R., & Wood, W. (2005). Social influence in attitudes and attitude change. In D. Albarracin, B. T. Johnson, & M. P. Zanna (Eds.), *The handbook of attitudes* (pp. 671–706). Hillsdale, NJ: Erlbaum.

Power, D. J. (2008). Decision support systems: a historical overview. In *Handbook on decision support systems 1* (pp. 121–140). Springer. doi:10.1007/978-3-540-48713-5_7

Power, D. J. (2008). *Decision Support Systems: A Historical Overview. In Handbook on Decision Support Systems 1*. Berlin: Springer Berlin Heidelberg.

Prahalad, C. K., & Ramaswamy, V. (2004). Co-creation experiences: The next practice in value creation. *Journal of Interactive Marketing*, *18*(3), 5–14. doi:10.1002/dir.20015

Prayoga, T., & Abraham, J. (2016). *Behavioral Intention to Use IoT Health Device: The Role of Perceived Usefulness*. Facilitated Appropriation, Big Five Personality Traits, & Cultural Value Orientations.

Price, J., Gardner, R. Jr, Wilson, D., Sloman, L., Rohde, P., & Erickson, M. (2007). Territory, rank and mental health: The history of an idea. *Evolutionary Psychology*, *5*(3), 531–554. doi:10.1177/147470490700500305

Project Implicit. (2019). *Project Implicit*. Retrieved from https://www.projectimplicit.net

Project Implicit. (2019). *Take the IAT*. Retrieved from https://implicit.harvard.edu/implicit/

Prusak, L. (1996). The knowledge advantage. *Planning Review*, *24*(2), 6–8. doi:10.1108/eb054546

Pryce, G. (2013). Housing Submarkets and the Lattice of Substitution. *Urban Studies (Edinburgh, Scotland)*, *50*(13), 2682–2699. doi:10.1177/0042098013482502

Puska, P., Kurki, S., Lähdesmäki, M., Siltaoja, M., & Luomala, H. (2018). Sweet taste of prosocial status signaling: When eating organic foods makes you happy and hopeful. *Apettite.*, *121*(1), 348–359. doi:10.1016/j.appet.2017.11.102 PMID:29180074

Püsküllüoğlu, A. (2007). *Türkçe Sözlük*. İstanbul: Can Yayınları.

PWC. (2018). *Five trends transforming the automotive industry*. Available from: https://www.pwc.at/de/publikationen/branchen-und-wirtschaftsstudien/eascy-five-trends-transforming-the-automotive-industry_2018.pdf

PWC. (2018). *Five Trends transforming the Automotive Industry*. https://eu-smartcities.eu/sites/default/files/2018-03/pwc-five-trends-transforming-the-automotive-industry.compressed.pdf

Pynnönen, M., Hallikas, J., & Ritala, P. (2012). Managing customer-driven business model innovation. *International Journal of Innovation Management*, *16*(04), 1250022. doi:10.1142/S1363919612003836

Quelch, J. A. (1987). Marketing the premium product. *Business Horizons*, *30*(3), 38–45.

Quester, P. G., & Wendt-Eccles, J. V. (2002). The Influence of Perceived Cultural Differences on Marketing Managers' strategic Decision making. An Explorary Study. *Journal of Asia-Pacific Marketing*, *1*(2), 47–62.

Quijano, A. (2003). Notas sobre raza y democracia en los países andinos. *Revista Venezolana de Economía y Ciencias Sociales*, *9*(1), 53–59.

Qu, Y., Li, M., Jia, H., & Gua, L. (2015). Developing More Insights on Sustainable Consumption in China Based on Q Methodology. *Sustainability*, *7*(10), 14211–14229. doi:10.3390u71014211

Rajadhyaksha, A. (2003). The "Bollywoodization" of the Indian cinema: Cultural nationalism in a global arena. *Inter-Asia Cultural Studies*, *4*(1), 25–39. doi:10.1080/1464937032000060195

Rajagopalan, S. (2005). *A taste for Indian films: negotiating cultural boundaries in post- Stalinist Soviet society* (PhD thesis). Indiana University.

Rakic, T., & Chambers, D. (2012). Introducing visual methods to tourism studies. In T. Rakic & D. Chambers (Eds.), *An introduction to visual research methods in tourism* (pp. 4–14). Abingdon, UK: Routledge.

Ram, A. (2018). *Babylon signs digital health deal with Samsung*. Retrieved from https://search.proquest.com/docview/2072565216

Rama, T. (2013). Phonotactic Diversity Predicts the Time Depth of the World's Language Families. *PLoS One*, *8*(5), 1–9. doi:10.1371/journal.pone.0063238 PMID:23691003

Randsborg, K. (2000). National History, Non-national Archaeology: The Case of Denmark. Oxford Journal of Archaeology, 19(2), 211–22.

Rangan, S., & Adner, R. (2001). Profits and the Internet: Seven Misconceptions. *MIT Sloan Management Review*. Retrieved from http://search.ebscohost.com/login.aspx?direct=true&db=bth&AN=4834377&site=eds-live

Ranyard, R., Crozier, R., & Svenson, O. (1997). *Decision making. Cognitive models and explanations*. Taylor & Francis.

Rappoport, L. (2010). *How We Eat: Appetite, Culture, and the Psychology of Food*. ECW Press. Retrieved from https://books.google.pt/books?id=srj_y0b8Mh8C

Rea, A. (2019). Reading Through the Ages: Compare all five generations of adult readers to ensure you're giving all your patrons what they want. *Library Journal*. Retrieved from http://search.ebscohost.com/login.aspx?direct=true&db=edsglr&AN=edsgcl.609310951&site=eds-live

Redler, J. (2018). *Die Store Brand: Einkaufsstätten als Marken verstehen, aufbauen und steuern* [The store brand: understanding, building and managing shopping stores as brands]. Wiesbaden: Springer. doi:10.1007/978-3-658-09709-7

Reed, K., & Ryan, P. (2019). Lessons from the past and the future of food. *World Archaeology*, *51*(1), 1–16. doi:10.1080/00438243.2019.1610492

Rempel, S. (2007, Mar. 8). Now it's the Indian dream; middle class drives economy expected by IMF to surpass the U.S. by 2050. *The Toronto Star*.

Rempel-Clower, N. L. (2007). Role of orbitofrontal cortex connections in emotion. *Annals of the New York Academy of Sciences*, *1121*(1), 72–86. doi:10.1196/annals.1401.026 PMID:17846152

Renko, S., & Druzijanic, M. (2014). Perceived usefulness of innovative technology in retailing: Consumers' and retailers' point of view. *Journal of Retailing and Consumer Services*, *21*(5), 836–843. doi:10.1016/j.jretconser.2014.02.015

Research and Markets. (2015). *Retail IoT Market Growth and Forecast 2015 to 2020*. Accessed from http://www.marketsandmarketsblog.com/retail-iot-market.html

Reyneke, M., Pitt, L., & Berthon, P. R. (2011). Luxury wine brand visibility in social media: An exploratory study. *International Journal of Wine Business Research*, *23*(1), 21–35. doi:10.1108/17511061111121380

Reynolds, T. J., & Olson, J. C. (2001). *Understanding consumer decision making: The means-end approach to marketing and advertising strategy*. Academic Press.

Reynolds, T. J., & Phillips, J. M. (2019). The Strata Model Predicting Advertising Effectiveness: A Neural-Network Approach Enhances Predictability of Consumer Decision Making. *Journal of Advertising Research*, *59*(3), 268–280. doi:10.2501/JAR-2018-037

Richards, G. (2000). Tourism and the World of Culture and Heritage. *Tourism Recreation Research*, *25*(1), 9–17. doi:10.1080/02508281.2000.11014896

Richards, G. (2001). *Cultural Attractions and European Tourism*. Wallingford: CAB International. doi:10.1079/9780851994406.0000

Rieber, R. (Ed.). (2013). *Wilhelm Wundt and the making of a scientific psychology*. Springer Science & Business Media.

Riedy, C. (2018). Cross-Generational Counseling Strategies: Understanding Unique Needs of Each Generation. *Journal of Counselor Practice*, *9*(1), 6–23.

Rigby, D. K., & Tager, S. (2014). *Leading a digital transformation*. http://www.bain.com/publications/articles/leading-a-digital-transformation.aspx

Ringberg, T., & Reihlen, M. (2008). Towards a socio-cognitive approach to knowledge transfer. *Journal of Management Studies*, *45*(5), 912–935. doi:10.1111/j.1467-6486.2007.00757.x

Ringkøbing-SKJERN Museum. (2016). *levendehistorie.dk*. Accessed 10. 7. 2016 at http://levendehistorie.dk/Forside-11

Ritchie, C. (2009). The culture of wine buying in the UK off-trade. *International Journal of Wine Business Research*, *21*(3), 194–211.

Rivera Medina, J., & Caceres Cabana, Y. (2016). *Línea de Base del Proyecto: Desarrollo sostenible de comunidades vulnerables en 3 provincias altoandinas de Arequipa y Puno*. Arequipa, Peru: DESCOSUR.

Rivera, T. (1979). Chicago literature: Fiesta of the Living, The Identification and Analysis of Chicago Literature. *Bilingual P/Editional Bilinguo*, 19-36.

Roberge, M. (2015). *The Sales Acceleration Formula: Using Data, Technology, and Inbound Selling to go from $0 to $100 Million*. John Wiley & Sons.

Roccas, S., Sagiv, L., Schwartz, S. H., & Knafo, A. (2002). The big five personality factors & personal values. *Personality and Social Psychology Bulletin*, *28*(6), 789–801. doi:10.1177/0146167202289008

Rodrigues, J. (2018). Smartphones: fundamentally reshaping today's teenagers: iGen: Why today's super-connected kids are growing up less rebellious, more tolerant, less happy: and completely unprepared for adulthood (Jean M. Twenge). *Church. Communication and Culture VO*, *3*(1), 75–79. doi:10.1080/23753234.2018.1429223

Roehrich, G. (2004). Consumer innovativeness: Concepts & measurements. *Journal of Business Research*, *57*(6), 671–677. doi:10.1016/S0148-2963(02)00311-9

Rogers, E. M. (1983). *Diffusion of Innovations*. New York: The Free Press.

Rogers, E. M. (2003). *Diffusion of innovations* (5th ed.). New York: Free Press.

Rolls, E. T., Hornak, J., Wade, D., & McGrath, J. (1994). Emotion-related learning in patients with social and emotional changes associated with frontal lobe damage. *Journal of Neurology, Neurosurgery & Psychiatry, 57*(12), 1518-1524. Doi:10.1136/jnnp.57.12.1518

Rosen, S. (1974). Hedonic Prices and Implicit Markets: Product Differentiation in Pure Competition. *Journal of Political Economy, 82*(1), 35–55. doi:10.1086/260169

Roskies, A. (2002). Neuroethics for the new millenium. *Neuron, 35*(1), 21–23. doi:10.1016/S0896-6273(02)00763-8 PMID:12123605

Ross, A., & Tyler, M. (2011). *Predictable Revenue*. PebbleStorm.

Rössel, J., & Pape, S. (2016). Who has a wine-identity? Consumption practices between distinction and democratization. *Journal of Consumer Culture, 16*(2), 614–632. doi:10.1177/1469540514536192

Rossiter, J. R., & Chan, A. M. (1998). Etnicity in Business and Consumer Behavior. *Journal of Business Research, 42*(2), 127–134. doi:10.1016/S0148-2963(97)00113-6

Rothenberg, J., Galster, G., Butler, R. V., & Pitkin, J. K. (1991). *The Maze of Urban Housing Markets: Theory, Evidence and Policy*. Chicago, IL: University of Chicago Press.

Roy, S. K., Balaji, M. S., Sadeque, S., Nguyen, B., & Melewar, T. C. (2016). Constituents and consequences of smart customer experience in retailing. *Technological Forecasting and Social Change*.

Roy, S., Guha, A., & Biswas, A. (2015). Celebrity endorsements and women consumers in India: How generation-cohort affiliation and celebrity-product congruency moderate the benefits of chronological age congruency. *Marketing Letters, 26*(3), 363–376. doi:10.100711002-015-9354-1

Rubio-Godoy, M., Aunger, R., & Curtis, V. (2007). Serotonin – A link between disgust and immunity? *Medical Hypotheses, 68*(1), 61–66. doi:10.1016/j.mehy.2006.06.036 PMID:16928421

Rubira-García, R., Puebla-Martínez, B., & Gelado-Marcos, R. (2018). Social representations in studying information, knowledge, and mediations: A critical review. *Social Sciences, 7*(12), 256. doi:10.3390ocsci7120256

Rumelt, R. P. (2012). Good strategy/bad strategy: The difference and why it matters. *Strategic Direction, 28*(8).

Rüsch, N., Corrigan, P. W., Todd, A. R., & Bodenhausen, G. V. (2010). Implicit self-stigma in people with mental illness. *The Journal of Nervous and Mental Disease, 198*(2), 150–153. doi:10.1097/NMD.0b013e3181cc43b5 PMID:20145491

Russo, J. E., & Schoemaker, P. J. H. (1990). *Decision traps : ten barriers to brilliant decision-making and how to overcome them*. Simon & Schuster.

Ryan, R. M., & Deci, E. L. (2001). On Happiness and Human Potentials: A Review of Research on Hedonic and Eudaimonic Well-Being. *Annual Review of Psychology, 52*(1), 141–166. doi:10.1146/annurev.psych.52.1.141 PMID:11148302

Ryden, D. (2001). Producing a Peculiar Commodity: Jamaican Sugar Production, Slave Life, and Planter Profits on the Eve of Abolition, 1750-1807. *The Journal of Economic History, 61*(2), 504–507. doi:10.1017/S0022050701268107

RYSTAD. (2019). *Energy Annual Review of World Oil Recoverable Resources*. Retrieved from https://www.rystadenergy.com/

Sabaei, D., Erkoyuncu, J., & Roy, R. (2015). A review of multi-criteria decision making methods for enhanced maintenance delivery. *Procedia CIRP, 37*, 30–35. doi:10.1016/j.procir.2015.08.086

Sachs, G. (2020). *Insights: Through the Trough*. Retrieved from https://www.goldmansachs.com/insights/pages/eurozone-outlook-2020.html

Saczina, M. (2019). Neuroscience in Linguistic Patterns of Communication Campaigns for Environmental Sustainability. Designing Sustainable Technologies. *Products and Policies*, *14*(1), 109–118.

Saidani, M., Yannou, B., Leroy, Y., & Cluzel, F. (2018). Heavy vehicles on the road towards the circular economy: Analysis and comparison with the automotive industry. *Resources, Conservation and Recycling*, *135*, 108–122. doi:10.1016/j.resconrec.2017.06.017

Salazar, R. D. (2001). Comida y Cultura: Identidad y significado en el mundo Contemporâneo. *Estudios de Asia y Africa*, *36*(1), 83–108.

Salesforce Inc. (2017). The Power of Personalized Shopping. *Salesforce.com Inc*. Retrieved from https://www.salesforce.com/products/commerce-cloud/resources/resources-assets-for-filter/the-power-of-personalized-shopping/

Sammells, C. (1998). Folkore, food, and national identity: Urban legends of llama meat in La Paz, Bolivia. *Contemporary Legend*, *1*, 21–54.

Sandy, C. J., Gosling, S. D., & Durant, J. (2013). Predicting Consumer Behavior and Media Preferences: The Comparative Validity of Personality Traits and Demographic Variables. *Psychology and Marketing*, *30*(11), 937–949. doi:10.1002/mar.20657

Sanjur, D. (1982). *Social and cultural perspectives in nutrition*. Englewood Cliffs, N.J.: Prentice-Hall. Retrieved from https://catalog.hathitrust.org/api/volumes/oclc/7572902.html

Santos, M. C. de O. (2007). A Representação Social da Moradia [The Social Representation of the Housing]. *Estudos e Pesquisas em Psicologia*, *7*(2), 336–341. pepsic.bvsalud.org/pdf/epp/v7n2/v7n2a18.pdf

Santos, R.O.J., Oliveira, J.H.C., Moura, J., Giraldi, E., & Bruno, A.R. (2015). *Public policies and selective visual attention: The effectiveness of awareness messages among young people about the consumption of alcoholic beverages in Brazil*. Academic Press.

Sapolsky, R. (2017). *Behave*. London: Vintage.

Saunders, M. N. K., Lewis, P., & Thornhill, A. (2012). *Research methods for business students* (6th ed.). Harlow, UK: Pearson.

Savage, M., Leroux, B., Rouanet, H., & Warde, A. (2008). Class and Cultural Division in the UK. *Sociology*, *42*(6), 1049–1072. doi:10.1177/0038038508096933

Saxon, W. (2001). M. P. McLean, 87, Container Shipping Pioneer. *The New York Times*.

Scarles, C. (2012). Eliciting embodied knowledge and response: Respondent-led photography and visual autoethnography. In T. Rakic & D. Chambers (Eds.), *An introduction to visual research methods in tourism* (pp. 70–91). Abingdon, UK: Routledge.

Schacter, D. L. (1987). Implicit memory: History and current status. *Journal of Experimental Psychology. Learning, Memory, and Cognition*, *13*(3), 501–518. doi:10.1037/0278-7393.13.3.501

Schiffauer, W. (1997). *Die Ehre in der Türkischen Kultur*. Berlin: Die Ausländerbeauftragte des Senats.

Schiffman, L. G., & Wisenblit, J. (2015). Consumer behavior (11th ed.). Harlow: Pearson.

Schmidt, H. J. (2015). *Markenführung* [Brand management]. Wiesbaden: Springer.

Schmidt, H. J., Mason, R., Steenkamp, P., & Mugobo, V. (2017). Does brand orientation contribute to retailers' success? An empirical study in the South African market. *Journal of Retailing and Consumer Services*, *38*, 210–222. doi:10.1016/j.jretconser.2017.06.012

Schouten, F. F. (1995). *Heritage as historical reality. In Heritage, Tourism and Society* (pp. 21–31). London: Mansell.

Schouten, F. F. (2007). Cultural Tourism: Between Authenticity and Globalization. In G. Richards (Ed.), *Cultural Tourism: Global and Local Perspectives*. Binghamton, NY: Haworth Hospitality Press.

Scott, R. (2001). *Institutions and organizations*. Thousand Oaks: Sage.

Selby, M. (2010). People-Place-Past: The Visitor Experience of Cultural Heritage. In E. Waterton & S. Watson (Eds.), *Culture, Heritage and Representation*. Surrey, UK: Ashgate Publishing Limited.

Seligman, M. E. P. (2011). *Flourish: A Visionary New Understanding of Happiness and Well-being*. New York: The Free Press.

Sell, R., Rassõlkin, A., Wang, R., & Otto, T. (2019). Integration of autonomous vehicles and Industry 4.0. *Proceedings of the Estonian Academy of Sciences*, *68*(4), 389–394. doi:10.3176/proc.2019.4.07

Seo, Y., & Buchanan-Oliver, M. (2015). Luxury branding: The industry, trends, and future conceptualisations. *Asia Pacific Journal of Marketing and Logistics*, *27*(1), 82–98. doi:10.1108/apjml-10-2014-0148

Serova, E., & Bagiev, G. (2012). Intelligent information technologies and systems in the systemic research of marketing space. In *ICMLG2016-4th International Conference on Management, Leadership and Governance: ICMLG2016* (p. 296-303). Academic Conferences and Publishing Limited.

Serova, E., & Krichevsky, M. (2015). Intelligent Models and Systems in Spatial Marketing Research. *Electronic Journal of Information Systems Evaluation*, *18*(2), 159–171.

Servicio Nacional de Sanidad Agraria. (2020). *Estado Situacional de los mataderos con respecto a la autorización sanitaria*. Lima, Peru: SENASA.

Servicio Nacional de Sanidad Agraria. (n.d.). *Estado Situacional de los mataderos con respecto a la autorización sanitaria*. Lima, Peru: SENASA.

Shah, G. R. (2012). The man who sparked Bollywood's love of foreign locales. *The New York Times Global Edition: India*. Retrieved online from: http://india.blogs.nytimes.com/2012/10/23/the-man-who-sparkedbollywoods- love-of-exotic-locales/

Shahiduzzaman, M., Kowalkiewicz, M., Barrett, R., & McNaughton, M. (2017). *Digital business: towards a value-centric maturity model*. Academic Press.

Shamim, S., Cang, S., & Yu, H. (2019). Impact of knowledge oriented leadership on knowledge management behaviour through employee work attitudes. *International Journal of Human Resource Management*, *30*(16), 2387–2417. doi:10.1080/09585192.2017.1323772

Sharma, S. (2017). Innovation in Marketing. *International Journal of Business and Management*, *3*, 1897–1912.

Sherman, E., Schiffman, L.G., & Mathur, A. (2001The Influence of Gender on the New Age Elderly's Consumption Orientations. *Psychology and Marketing*, *18*(10), 1073–1089. doi:10.1002/mar.1044

Sheth, J. N., Newman, B. I., & Gross, B. L. (1991). Why we buy what we buy: A theory of consumption values. *Journal of Business Research*, *22*(2), 159–170.

Sheth, J. N., Newman, B. I., & Gross, B. L. (1991a). *Consumption Values and Market Choices: Theory and Applications.* Cincinnati, OH: South-Western Publishing Co.

Sheth, J. N., Sethia, N. K., & Srinivas, S. (2011). Mindful consumption: A customer centric approach to sustainability. *Journal of the Academy of Marketing Science, 39*(1), 21–39. doi:10.100711747-010-0216-3

Shieh, L.-F., Chang, T.-H., Fu, H.-P., Lin, S.-W., & Chen, Y.-Y. (2013). Analyzing the factors that affect the adoption of mobile services in Taiwan. *Technological Forecasting and Social Change, 87*, 80–88. doi:10.1016/j.techfore.2013.11.004

Shimp, T., & Sharma, S. (1987). Consumer Ethnocentrism: Construction and Validation of the CETSCALE. *Journal of Marketing, 25*(8), 280–289. doi:10.1177/002224378702400304

Shin, D. (2010). The effects of trust, security & privacy in social networking: A security-based approach to understand the pattern of adoption. *Interacting with Computers, 22*(5), 428–438. doi:10.1016/j.intcom.2010.05.001

Shipp, A. J., Edwards, J. R., & Lambert, L. S. (2009). Conceptualization & measurement of temporal focus: The subjective experience of the past, present, & future. *Organizational Behavior and Human Decision Processes, 110*(1), 1–22. doi:10.1016/j.obhdp.2009.05.001

Silva, A. C. S. (2019). *Potencial da Neuroeconomia para criação de estratégias de Implementação de marketing e políticas ambientais* (Dissertação, MBA em Gestão Ambiental). Universidade Federal do Paraná, Brasil.

Silva, C. G., Brito, R. M. M., Monteiro, A., Leal, J. A. F., Furtado, A., Andrade, N., ... Alconchel, M. P. (2014). SOCIENTIZE participatory experiments, dissemination and networking activities in perspective. *Human Computation, 2*(2), 119–135. doi:10.15346/hc.v1i2.4

Silvera, D. H., & Laufer, D. (2005). Recent Developments in Attribution Research and Their Implications for Consumer Judgments and Behavior. In F. R. Kardes, P. M. Herr, & J. Nantel (Eds.), Applying social cognition to consumer-focused strategy (pp. 53–77). Lawrence Erlbaum Associates.

Silverstein, M. J., & Fiske, N. (2003). Luxury for the masses. *Harvard Business Review, 81*(4), 48.

Simon, H. A., & Newell, A. (1971). Human problem solving: The state of the theory in 1970. *The American Psychologist, 26*(2), 145–159. doi:10.1037/h0030806

Simon, Z. B. (2018). (The impossibility of) acting upon a story that we can believe. *Rethinking History, 22*(1), 105–125. doi:10.1080/13642529.2017.1419445

Simoons, F. (1994). *Eat Not this Flesh: Food Avoidances from Prehistory to the Present.* University of Wisconsin Press. Retrieved from https://books.google.pt/books?id=JwGZTQunH00C

Sims, C. A. (1986, Winter). Are forecasting models usable for policy analysis? *Quarterly Review of the Federal Reserve Bank of Minneapolis*, 2–16.

Singh, K., & Best, G. (2004). Film-induced tourism: motivations of visitors to the Hobbiton movies set as featured in the lord of the rings. In *International tourism and media conference proceedings*. Tourism Research Unit, Monash University.

Sivarajah, U., Irani, Z., & Weerakkody, V. (2015). Evaluating the use and impact of Web 2.0 technologies in local government. *Government Information Quarterly, 32*(4), 473–487. doi:10.1016/j.giq.2015.06.004

Sjostrom, T., Corsi, A. M., & Lockshin, L. (2016). What characterises luxury products? A study across three product categories. *International Journal of Wine Business Research, 28*(1), 76–95. doi:10.1108/ijwbr-05-2015-0017

Slots- og Kulturstyrelsen. (2016). *slks.dk*. Accessed 30. 5. 2016 at https://slks.dk/presse-nyt/pressemeddelelser/2016/kulturturister-vil-ogsaa-have-strand-shopping-og-storbyliv/

Smith, S. M. & Trivelli, C. (2001). *El Consumo Urbano de Alimentos Andinos Tradicionales*. Lima, Peru: Coleccion Minima 40.

Smith, A. (2019). *The Wealth of Nations*. BookRix.

Smith, E. R., & Semin, G. R. (2007). Situated Social Cognition. *Current Directions in Psychological Science*, *16*(3), 132–135. doi:10.1111/j.1467-8721.2007.00490.x

Smith, M. (2007). Space, Place, and Placelessness in the Culturally Regenerated City. In G. Richards (Ed.), *Cultural Tourism: Global and Local Perspectives*. Binghamton, NY: Haworth Hospitality Press.

Smith, M. K. (2003). *Issues in Cultural Tourism Studies*. London: Routledge. doi:10.4324/9780203402825

SMMT. (2017). *The digitalisation of the UK automotive industry*. Academic Press.

Snihur, Y., & Wiklund, J. (2019). Searching for innovation: Product, process, and business model innovations and search behavior in established firms. *Long Range Planning*, *52*(3), 305–325. doi:10.1016/j.lrp.2018.05.003

Soleas, G. J., Diamandis, E. P., & Goldberg, D. M. (1997). Wine as a biological fluid: History, production, and role in disease prevention. *Journal of Clinical Laboratory Analysis*, *11*(5), 287–313. doi:10.1002/(sici)1098-2825(1997)11:5<287:Aid-jcla6>3.0.Co;2-4 PMID:9292395

Solomon, M. R. (2018). Consumer behavior: buying, having, & being (12th ed.). Harlow, UK: Pearson.

Solomon, M. R. (1983). The role of products as social stimuli: A symbolic interactionism perspective. *The Journal of Consumer Research*, *10*(3), 319–329. doi:10.1086/208971

Sorescu, A., Frambach, R. T., Singh, J., Rangaswamy, A., & Bridges, C. (2011). Innovations in retail business models. *Journal of Retailing*, *87*, S3–S16. doi:10.1016/j.jretai.2011.04.005

Sovacool, B. K., Rogge, J.-C., Saleta, C., & Masterson-Cox, E. (2019). Transformative versus conservative automotive innovation styles: Contrasting the electric vehicle manufacturing strategies for the BMW i3 and Fiat 500e. *Environmental Innovation and Societal Transitions*, *33*, 45–60. doi:10.1016/j.eist.2019.02.004

Sovacool, B., & Brossmann, B. (2014). The rhetorical fantasy of energy transitions: Implications for energy policy and analysis. *Technology Analysis and Strategic Management*, *26*(7), 837–854. doi:10.1080/09537325.2014.905674

Sözlük, T. (2007). *Türk Dil Kurumu*. Retrieved 12 10, 2012, from www.tdk.gov.tr: www.tdk.gov.tr

Sproesser, G., Ruby, M. B., Arbit, N., Akotia, C. S., Alvarenga, M. dos S., Bhangaokar, R., & Renner, B. (2019). Understanding traditional and modern eating: The TEP10 framework. *BMC Public Health*, *19*(1). doi:10.118612889-019-7844-4

Stankevich, A. (2017). Explaining the Consumer Decision-Making Process: Critical Literature Review. *Journal of International Business Research and Marketing*, *2*(6), 7–14. doi:10.18775/jibrm.1849-8558.2015.26.3001

Stark, D., & Clippinger, J. (1999). Heterarchy: Distributing Intelligence and Organizing Diversity. In J. Clippinger (Ed.), *The Biology of Business: Decoding the Natural Laws of Enterprise*. San Francisco, CA: Jossey-Bass.

Statista. (2017). *Percentage of Global Research and Development Spending in 2017, by Industry*. Available at: https://www.statista.com/statistics/270233/percentage-of-global-rundd-spending-by-industry/

Stayman, D., & Deshpande, R. (1989). Siatuational Ethnicity and Consumer Behavior. *The Journal of Consumer Research*, *16*(3), 361–371. doi:10.1086/209222

Steenkamp, J. E. M., & Gielens, K. (2003). Consumer & Market Drivers of the Trial Probability of New Consumer Packaged Goods. *The Journal of Consumer Research*, *30*(3), 368–384. doi:10.1086/378615

Sterling, J. (2012). The Carbon Footprint of the Shipping Industry - More Than Shipping. *Politiken*. Retrieved from https://www.morethanshipping.com/green-shipping/

Sternthal, B., Phillips, L. W., & Dholakia, R. (1978). The persuasive effect of scarce credibility: A situational analysis. *Public Opinion Quarterly*, *42*(3), 285–314. doi:10.1086/268454 PMID:10297222

Stolarski, M., Fieulaine, N., & van Beek, W. (2015). *Time perspective theory; Review, research, & application*. Cham: Springer International. doi:10.1007/978-3-319-07368-2

Storm, E. (2003). Regionalism in History. *European History Quarterly*, *33*(2), 251–265. doi:10.1177/02656914030332005

Stoycheva, S., Marchese, D., Paul, C., Padoan, S., Juhmani, A., & Linkov, I. (2018). Multi-criteria decision analysis framework for sustainable manufacturing in automotive industry. *Journal of Cleaner Production*, *187*, 257–272. doi:10.1016/j.jclepro.2018.03.133

Strand, H. (2016). *hvidbjerg.dk*. Accessed 10. 7. 2016 at http://www.hvidbjerg.dk

Straszheim, M. (1974). Hedonic estimation of housing market prices: A further comment. *The Review of Economics and Statistics*, *56*(3), 404–406. doi:10.2307/1923985

Strathman, A., Gleicher, F., Boninger, D. S., & Edwards, C. S. (1994). The consideration of future consequences: Weighing immediate & distant outcomes of behavior. *Journal of Personality and Social Psychology*, *66*(4), 742–752. doi:10.1037/0022-3514.66.4.742

Streimikiene, D. (2015). Quality of life and housing. *International Journal of Information and Education Technology (IJIET)*, *5*(2), 140–145. doi:10.7763/IJIET.2015.V5.491

Strick, M., Van Baaren, R. B., Holland, R. W., & Van Knippenberg, A. (2009). Humor in advertisements enhances product liking by mere association. *Journal of Experimental Psychology. Applied*, *15*(1), 35–45. doi:10.1037/a0014812 PMID:19309215

Stroinska, M., & Cecchetto, V. (2003). *Exile, Language and Identity. The Role of Language in the Re-construction in Exile*. Frankfurt am Main: Peter Lang.

Stull, W. J. (1975). Community environment, zoning, and the market value of single-family homes. *The Journal of Law & Economics*, *18*(2), 535–557. doi:10.1086/466822

Sturges, D. (2016). Rethinking the City. *Automotive Design & Production*. Retrieved from http://search.ebscohost.com/login.aspx?direct=true&db=bth&AN=115873558&site=eds-live

Sui, D. Z. (2004). Tobler's first law of geography: A big idea for a small world? *Annals of the Association of American Geographers*, *94*(2), 269–277. doi:10.1111/j.1467-8306.2004.09402003.x

Suo, H., Wan, J., Zou, C., & Liu, J. (2012). Security in the Internet of Things: A Review. *Proceedings of the International Conference on Computer Science and Electronics Engineering*, 648-652. 10.1109/ICCSEE.2012.373

Su, R., Tay, L., & Diener, E. (2014). The Development and Validation of the Comprehensive Inventory of Thriving (CIT) and the Brief Inventory of Thriving (BIT). *Applied Psychology. Health and Well-Being*, *6*(3), 25171. doi:10.1111/aphw.12027 PMID:24919454

Surel, Y. (2000). The role of cognitive and normative frames in policy-making. *Journal of European Public Policy*, *7*(4), 495–512. doi:10.1080/13501760050165334

Sustainable Development Commission. (n.d.). *History of SD*. Retrieved November 10, 2019 from http://www.sd-commission.org.uk/pages/history_sd.html

Sustainable Development Goals Knowledge Platform. (n.d.). *United Nations Conference on Sustainable Development, Rio+20.* Retrieved November 10, 2019 from https://sustainabledevelopment.un.org/rio20

Svendsen, G. B., Johnsen, J. K., Almas-Sorensen, L., & Vitterso, J. (2013). Personality & technology acceptance: The influence of personality factors on the core constructs of the Technology Acceptance Model. *Behaviour & Information Technology*, *32*(4), 323–334. doi:10.1080/0144929X.2011.553740

Tafesse, W., & Korneliussen, T. (2013). Examining the effect of using multiple media tools on the marketing performance of organizations in a trade campaign environment. *Journal of Marketing Communications*, *19*(3), 215–227. doi:10.1080/13527266.2011.619556

Tagliabue, J. (2010). A beloved Bollywood extra draws Indians. *The New York Times.* Retrieved from: https://www.nytimes.com/2010/07/12/world/europe/12swiss.html?_r=0

Tajfel, H. (1981). *Human Groups and Social Categories: Studies in Social Psychology.* Cambridge: Cambridge University Press.

Talke, K., & Heidenreich, S. (2014). How to overcome pro-change bias: Incorporating passive and active innovation resistance in innovation decision models. *Journal of Product Innovation Management*, *31*(5), 894–907. doi:10.1111/jpim.12130

Taras, V., Kirkman, B., & Steel, P. (2010). Examining the impact of culture's consequences: A three-decade, multilevel, meta-analytic review of Hofstede's cultural value dimensions. *The Journal of Applied Psychology*, *95*(3), 405–439. doi:10.1037/a0018938 PMID:20476824

Tari, A. (2011). Z generáció. Budapest: Tercium Könyvkiadó.

Tauber, E. M. (1972). Why do people shop? *Journal of Marketing*, *36*, 46–49.

Taylor, F. W. (2010). The Principles of Scientific Management. *Cosimo, Incorporated.* Retrieved from https://books.google.pt/books?id=G_vTmZvRkhEC

Taylor, C., & Barber, N. A. (2016). How will my wine purchase decision be viewed by others? *Journal of Wine Research*, *27*(3), 202–225. doi:10.1080/09571264.2016.1173533

Teece, D. J. (2018). Business models and dynamic capabilities. *Long Range Planning*, *51*(1), 40–49. doi:10.1016/j.lrp.2017.06.007

Teece, D., Pisano, G., & Shuen, A. (1997). Dynamic Capabilities and Strategic Management. *Strategic Management Journal*, *18*(7), 509–533. doi:10.1002/(SICI)1097-0266(199708)18:7<509::AID-SMJ882>3.0.CO;2-Z

Teng, J. T. C., & Ramamurthy, K. (1993). Group Decision Support Systems: Clarifying The Concept And Establishing A Functional Taxonomy. *INFOR*, *31*(3), 166–185. doi:10.1080/03155986.1993.11732225

Teng, L., & Laroche, M. (2007). Building and testing models of consumer purchase intention in competitive and multicultural environments. *Journal of Business Research*, *60*(3), 260–268. doi:10.1016/j.jbusres.2006.09.028

Terlau, W., & Hirsch, D. (2015). Sustainable Consumption and the Attitude-Behaviour-Gap Phenomenon - Causes and Measurements towards a Sustainable Development. *International Journal on Food System Dynamics*, *6*(3), 159–174.

Tesseras, L. (2013). A Business Opportunity That's Only a Click Away. *Marketing Week.* Retrieved from http://search.ebscohost.com/login.aspx?direct=true&db=bth&AN=89984421&site=eds-live

Thach, L., Charters, S., & Cogan-Marie, L. (2018). Core tensions in luxury wine marketing: The case of Burgundian wineries. *International Journal of Wine Business Research*, *30*(3), 343–365. doi:10.1108/IJWBR-04-2017-0025

The Economist. (2009). Brazil takes off. *Economist*, (8657). Retrieved from https://www.economist.com/leaders/2009/11/12/brazil-takes-off

The Economist. (2019, June 13). The World is not flat, Special Report: Global Supply Chains. *The Economist*.

The Federal Government. (2018). National Programme on sustainable Consumption, From Sustainable Lifestyles towards Social Change. Federal Ministry for the Environment, Nature Conservation, Building and Nuclear Safety, Bonn, Germany.

The Neurological Effects of South Park | Viacom Fan Theory. (n.d.). Retrieved March 10, 2020, from http://fantheory.viacom.com/inside-the-brain/index.html

Thévenot, L. (2001). Organized Complexity. *European Journal of Social Theory*, *4*(4), 405–425. doi:10.1177/13684310122225235

Thidell, A. (n.d.). *Sustainable Consumption And Green Lifestyles Definitions And Concepts*. https://mst.dk/media/mst/68633/Background%20paper%20A%20-%20Session%201.pdf

Thogersen, J., & Schrader, U. (2012). From Knowledge to Action—New Paths Towards Sustainable Consumption. *Journal of Consumer Policy*, *35*(1), 1–5. doi:10.100710603-012-9188-7

Thomas, A. R., Pop, N. A., Iorga, A. M., & Ducu, C. (2016). *Ethics and neuromarketing: Implications for market research and business practice*. Springer.

Thomas, S. R., Burton Smith, R., & Ball, P. J. (2007). Implicit attitudes in very young children: An adaptation of the IAT. *Current Research in Social Psychology*, *13*(7), 75–85.

Thornton, P. H., & Ocasio, W. (2008). Institutional Logics. In R. Greenwood, C. Oliver, R. Suddaby, & K. Sahlin-Andersson (Eds.), *The sage handbook of organizational institutionalism* (pp. 99–129). SAGE Publications. doi:10.4135/9781849200387.n4

Thurstone, L. L. (1928). Attitudes can be measured. *American Journal of Sociology*, *33*(4), 529–554. doi:10.1086/214483

Tiago, M. T. P. M. B., & Veríssimo, J. M. C. (2014). Digital marketing and social media: Why bother? *Business Horizons*, *57*(6), 703–708. doi:10.1016/j.bushor.2014.07.002

Timmermans, H., Molin, E., & Noortwijk, L. (1994). Housing choice processes: Stated versus revealed modelling approaches. *Netherlands Journal of Housing and the Built Environment*, *9*(3), 215–227. doi:10.1007/BF02496997

Timmins, C., & Schlenker, W. (2011). Reduced-Form Versus Structural Modeling in Environmental and Resource Economics. *Annual Review of Resource Economics*, *1*(1), 351–380. doi:10.1146/annurev.resource.050708.144119

Timothy, D. J., & Boyd, S. W. (2006). Heritage Tourism in the 21st Century: Valued Traditions and New Perspectives. *Journal of Heritage Tourism*, *1*(1), 1–14. doi:10.1080/17438730608668462

Tobler, W. (2004). On the First Law of Geography: A Reply. *Annals of the Association of American Geographers*, *94*(2), 304–310. doi:10.1111/j.1467-8306.2004.09402009.x

Toch, E., Wang, Y., & Cranor, L.F. (2012). Personalization and privacy: a survey of privacy risks and remedies in personalization-based systems. *Science & Business Media*, 203-220.

Todor, R. D. (2014). The importance of branding and rebranding for strategic marketing. *Bulletin of the Transilvania University of Braşov*, *7*(56), 60–64.

Toffler, A. (1973). Future Shock. *Saturday Evening Post*. Retrieved from http://search.ebscohost.com/login.aspx?direct=true&db=a9h&AN=17947865&site=eds-live

Tooke, N., & Baker, M. (1996). Seeing is believing: The effect of film on visitor numbers to screened locations. *Tourism Management*, *17*(2), 87–94. doi:10.1016/0261-5177(95)00111-5

Törőcsik, M., Szűcs, K., & Kehl, D. (2015). Lifestyle Segments in Generation Z – A New Approach to Identify Groups among Youth. *International Journal of Business Insights & Transformation*, *9*(1), 64–68. Retrieved from http://search.ebscohost.com/login.aspx?direct=true&db=bth&AN=131717881&site=eds-live

Toronchuk, J., & Ellis, G. (2007a). Disgust: Sensory affect or primary emotional system? *Cognition and Emotion*, *21*(8), 1799–1818. doi:10.1080/02699930701298515

Toronchuk, J., & Ellis, G. (2007b). Criteria for basic emotions: Seeking DISGUST? *Cognition and Emotion*, *21*(8), 1829–1832. doi:10.1080/02699930701334419

Toronchuk, J., & Ellis, G. (2013). Affective neuronal selection: The nature of the primordial emotion systems. *Frontiers in Psychology*, *3*, 589. doi:10.3389/fpsyg.2012.00589 PMID:23316177

Townslet, R. R., & Trimble, O. C. (1935). An electrically timed exposure apparatus with chronoscope connections. *The Journal of General Psychology*, *13*(2), 466–471. doi:10.1080/00221309.1935.9917898

Trabulsi, J. F., Cordero-Merecuana, M., Somarriba, D., & Garcia-Garcia, M. (2017). Ethics in Consumer Neuroscience. *Consumer Neuroscience*, 303.

Tracy, S. J. (2013). *Qualitative research methods: collecting evidence, crafting analysis, communicating impact*. Chichester, UK: Wiley-Blackwell.

Transport & Environment Brief Report. (2017). *Does Sharing cars really reduce car use?* https://www.transportenvironment.org/sites/te/files/publications/Does-sharing-cars-really-reduce-car-use-June%202017.pdf

Transport & Environment Press Report. (2017). *35 million dirty diesels are driving on Europe's roads today, new research finds*. https://www.transportenvironment.org/press/35-million-dirty-diesels-are-driving-europe%E2%80%99s-roads-today-new-research-finds

Transport & Environment Press Report. (2017). *Fixing Dieselgate in Europe (Briefing report May 2015)*. https://www.transportenvironment.org/sites/te/files/publications /2017_05_Fixing_Dieselgate_in_Europe.pdf

Transport & Environment. (2016). *Dieselgate: Who? What? How? (Study report September 2016)*. Author. https://www.transportenvironment.org/publications/dieselgate-who-what-how

Transport & Environment. (2017). *Does Sharing cars really reduce car use? - June 2017 - Transport & Environment Brief Report (ITF OECD, 2016; BEUC, 2016)*. https://www.transportenvironment.org/sites/te/files/publications/Does-sharing-cars-really-reduce-car-use-June%202017.pdf

Tress, G. (2002). Development of Second-Home Tourism in Denmark. *Scandinavian Journal of Hospitality and Tourism*, *2*(2), 109–122. doi:10.1080/15022250216289

Triandis, H. C., & Fishbein, M. (1963). Cognitive interaction in person perception. *Journal of Abnormal and Social Psychology*, *67*(5), 446–453. doi:10.1037/h0038494 PMID:14081887

Trimi, S., & Berbegal-Mirabent, J. (2012). Business model innovation in entrepreneurship. *The International Entrepreneurship and Management Journal*, *8*(4), 449–465. doi:10.100711365-012-0234-3

Troncoso-Pantoja, C. (2019). Comidas tradicionales: Un espacio para la alimentación saludable. *Perspectivas en Nutricion Humana*, *21*(1), 105–114. doi:10.17533/udea.penh.v21n1a08

Truong, Y., McColl, R., & Kitchen, P. J. (2009). New luxury brand positioning and the emergence of Masstige brands. *Journal of Brand Management*, *16*(5/6), 375–382. doi:10.1057/bm.2009.1

Tsanava, A. (1992). *Qartuli Mitologia* [Georgian Mythology]. Tbilisi: Merani.

Tuan, Y. F. (1972). *Topophilia: Personal Encounters with the Landscape. In Man, Space, and Environment*. Oxford: Oxford University Press.

Tuan, Y. F. (1974a). Space and Place: Humanistic Perspective. *Progress in Geography*, *6*, 233–246.

Tuan, Y. F. (1974b). *Topophilia: A Study of Environmental Perception, Attitudes, and Values*. Englewood Cliffs, NJ: Prentice-Hall, Inc.

Tuesta, A. V. (2013). *La riqueza exportadora de nuestra Sierra*. Lima, Peru: Sierra Exportadora.

Tuite, K. (1999). On the etymology and earliest social significance of ts'ats'loba", Amirani. *Journal of the International Caucasologigal Research Institute*, *I*, 13–19.

Tuite, K. (2007). Dialect Change: Convergence and Divergence in European Languages/How New Languages Emerge. *Journal of Linguistic Anthropology*, *17*(2), 314–316. doi:10.1525/jlin.2007.17.2.314

Tuite, K. (2017). Love stories: Language, private love, and public romance in Georgia. *Journal of the Royal Anthropological Institute*, *23*(1), 216–217. doi:10.1111/1467-9655.12576

Tukker, A., & van den Berg, C. (2017). Product-services and competitiveness. In *New Business for Old Europe* (pp. 35–71). Routledge. doi:10.4324/9781351280600-3

Türkçe Sözlük. (1998). Ankara: Türk Dili Kurumu.

Turnbull, O. H., Bowman, C., Shanker, S., & Davies, J. (2014). Emotion-based learning: Insights from the Iowa Gambling Task. *Frontiers in Psychology*, *162*(5). doi:10.3389/fpsyg.2014.00162 PMID:24711796

Turow, J., Hennessy, M., & Bleakley, A. (2008). Consumers' Understanding of Privacy Rules in the Marketplace. *The Journal of Consumer Affairs*, *42*(3), 411–424. doi:10.1111/j.1745-6606.2008.00116.x

Tversky, A., & Kahneman, D. (1974). Judgment under Uncertainty: Heuristics and Biases. *Science*, *185*(4157), 1124–1131. doi:10.1126cience.185.4157.1124 PMID:17835457

Tversky, A., & Kahneman, D. (1981). The Psychology of Preferences tend to follow regular patterns that can be described mathematically. *Scientific American*, *246*, 160–173.

Tversky, A., & Kahneman, D. (1986). Rational Choice and the Framing of Decisions. *The Behavioral Foundations of Economic Theory*, *59*(4), 251–278. doi:10.1086/296365

Tylor, E. (1876, Jan. 6). Dammann`s Race-photographs. *Nature*.

Tyng, C., Amin, H., Saad, M., & Malik, A. (2017). The Influences of Emotion on Learnıng and Memory. *Frontiers in Psychology*, *8*, 8. doi:10.3389/fpsyg.2017.01454 PMID:28883804

UC Davis / ITDP. (2017). *Three Revolutions in Urban Transportation May 2017 – report*. https://steps.ucdavis.edu/wp-content/uploads/2017/05/STEPS_ITDP-3R-Report-5-10-2017-2.pdf

Ukon, M., Bezerra, J., Cheng, S., Aguiar, M., Xavier, A., & Le Corre, J. (2013). Brazil: Confronting the Productivity Challenge. *Boston Consulting Group*. Retrieved from https://www.bcg.com/publications/2013/globalization-leadership-talent-brazil-confronting-productivity-challenge.aspx

Uleman J. S. & Bargh J. A. (1989). *Unintended thought.* New York: Guilford Press.

Ulver, S. (2019). From Mundane to Socially Significant Consumption: An Analysis of How Foodie Identity Work Spurs Market Formation. *Journal of Macromarketing, 39*(1), 53–70. doi:10.1177/0276146718817354

UN (United Nations). (2015). *Transforming Our World: The 2030 Agenda For Sustainable Development.* A/RES/70/1. Retrieved November 10, 2019 from https://sustainabledevelopment.un.org/content/documents/21252030%20Agenda%20for%20Sustainable%20Development%20web.pdf

UN (United Nations). (2019). *The contribution of consumer protection to sustainable consumption.* TD/B/C.I/CPLP/17. Trade and Development Board, Trade and Development Commission, Intergovernmental Group of Experts on Consumer Protection Law and Policy, Fourth session, Geneva, 8 and 9 July 2019, Item 3 (a) of the provisional agend.a

UNCTAD. (2017). *Achieving the Sustainable Development Goals through Consumer Protection.* UNCTAD/DITC/CPLP/2017/2.

UNCTAD. (2019). *Handbook of Statistics*. United Nations.

UNDP. (2018). *2018 Statistical update: United Nations Development Programme Human Development Reports.* http://hdr.undp.org/en/2018-update

UNEP (United Nations Environment Programme). (2015). *Sustainable Consumption and Production.* Global edition. Author.

UNEP. (2009). *Mainstreaming Sustainable Consumption and Production and Resource Efficiency into Development Planning.* DTI/1235/PA.

UNESCO. (1972). *Convention Concerning the Protection of the World Cultural and Natural Heritage*. Paris: UNESCO.

Unidad de coordinación de emergencias y rehabilitaciòn. (2008). *¿Cuál ha sido el Impacto en 2008 de las Bajas Temperaturas en la Agricultura y Ganadería Altoandina?* Lima, Peru: Organización de las Naciones Unidas para la agricultura y la alimentación FAO en el Perú.

United Nations Human Settlements Programme (UN-Habitat). (2017). *Human Rights in Cities Human Rights in Cities.* Author.

UNPD. (n.d.). *Millennium Development Goals*. Retrieved November 10, 2019 from https://www.undp.org/content/undp/en/home/sdgoverview/mdg_goals.html

Urry, J. (1990). *The tourist gaze*. London: Sage.

Urry, J. (2002). *The Tourist Gaze: The New Edition*. London: Sage Publications.

Vala, J. (2012). Dynamics and dilemmas in social psychology: Social relations, identities and cognition. *Portuguese Journal of Social Science, 11*(1), 3–14. doi:10.1386/pjss.11.1.3_1

Vala, J., & Castro, P. (2013). Pensamento social e representações sociais e psciologia social do conhecimento quotidiano. In J. Vala & M. B. Monteiro (Eds.), *Psicologia Social*. Fundação Calouste Gulbenkian.

Van Boven, L., & Gilovich, T. (2003). To Do or to Have? that Is the Question. *Journal of Personality and Social Psychology, 85*(6), 1193–1202. doi:10.1037/0022-3514.85.6.1193 PMID:14674824

Van der Heijden, H. (2004). User acceptance of hedonic information systems. *Management Information Systems Quarterly, 28*(4), 695–704. doi:10.2307/25148660

Van der Hoven, E. (2013). *Fact sheet- Ethics Subgroup IoT-Version 4.01*. Delft University of Technology Chair Ethics Subgroup IoT Expert Group.

Van Everdingen, Y. M., & Waarts, E. (2003). The Effect of National Culture on the Adoption of Innovations. *Marketing Letters*, *14*(3), 217–232. doi:10.1023/A:1027452919403

Van Liere, K. D., & Dunlap, R. E. (1981). Environmental concern: Does it make a difference? How it's measured? *Environment and Behavior*, *13*(6), 651–676. doi:10.1177/0013916581136001

Varan, D., Lang, A., Barwise, P., Weber, R., & Bellman, S. (2015). How Reliable Are Neuromarketers' Measures of Advertising Effectiveness? Data from Ongoing Research Holds No Common Truth among Vendors. *Journal of Advertising Research*, *55*(2), 176–191. doi:10.2501/JAR-55-2-176-191

Vargo, S. L., & Lusch, F. R. (2017). Service-dominant logic 2025. *International Journal of Research in Marketing*, *34*(1), 46–67. doi:10.1016/j.ijresmar.2016.11.001

Venkatesh, V., & Bala, H. (2008). Technology acceptance model 3 and a research agenda on interventions. *Decision Sciences*, *39*(2), 273–315. doi:10.1111/j.1540-5915.2008.00192.x

Venkatesh, V., & Davis, F. D. (2000). A theoretical extension of the technology acceptance model: Four longitudinal field studies. *Management Science*, *46*(2), 186–204. doi:10.1287/mnsc.46.2.186.11926

Venkatesh, V., Morris, M. G., Davis, G. B., & Davis, F. D. (2003). User Acceptance of Information Technology: Toward a Unified View. *Management Information Systems Quarterly*, *27*(3), 425–478. doi:10.2307/30036540

Venkatraman, M. P., & Price, L. L. (1990a). Differentiating Between Cognitive & Sensory Innovativeness: Concepts, Measurement, & Implications. *Journal of Business Research*, *20*(4), 293–315. doi:10.1016/0148-2963(90)90008-2

Venkatraman, V., Dimoka, A., Pavlou, P. A., Vo, K., Hampton, W., Bollinger, B., ... Winer, R. S. (2015). Predicting advertising success beyond traditional measures: New insights from neurophysiological methods and market response modeling. *JMR, Journal of Marketing Research*, *52*(4), 436–452. doi:10.1509/jmr.13.0593

Verhallen, T. M. M., & Robben, H. S. J. (1994). Scarcity and preference - An experiment on unavailability and product evaluation. *Journal of Economic Psychology*, *15*(2), 315–331. doi:10.1016/0167-4870(94)90007-8

Verhoef, P. C., Lemon, K. N., Parasuraman, A., Roggeveen, A., Tsiros, M., & Schlesinger, L. A. (2009). Customer Experience Creation: Determinants, Dynamics and Management Strategies. *Journal of Retailing*, *85*(1), 31–41. doi:10.1016/j.jretai.2008.11.001

Verhoef, P. C., Stephen, A. T., Kannan, P. K., Luo, X., Abhishek, V., Andrews, M., ... Zhang, Y. (2017). Consumer connectivity in a complex, technology-enabled, and mobile-oriented world with smart products. *Journal of Interactive Marketing*, *40*, 1–8. doi:10.1016/j.intmar.2017.06.001

Vermeir, I., & Verbeke, W. J. (2006). Sustainable Food Consumption: Exploring the Consumer "Attitude – Behavioral Intention" Gap. *Journal of Agricultural & Environmental Ethics*, *19*(2), 169–194. doi:10.100710806 005 5485 3

Verneau, F., & Griffith, C. J. (2016). *Consumer behaviour in a changing world: food, culture & society*. Bradford, UK: Emerald.

Victoria's Palace. (2016). *victoriaspalace.dk*. Accessed 10. 7. 2016 at http://www.victoriaspalace.dk/shop/frontpage.html

Vieira, G., Kliemann Neto, F., & Ribeiro, D. (2015). The Rationalization of Port Logistics Activities: A Study at Port of Santos (Brazil). *International Journal of e-Navigation and Maritime Economy*, *2*, 73-86.

Vigneron, F., & Johnson, L. (2004). Measuring perceptions of brand luxury. *Journal of Brand Management*, *11*(6), 484-506.

Vigneron, F., & Johnson, L. W. (1999). A review and a conceptual framework of prestige-seeking consumer behavior. *Academy of Marketing Science Review*, *1*(1), 1–15.

VisitDenmark, Videncenter for Kystturisme, & Region Syddanmark. (2014). *Ferie i Kystdanmark - warum nicht?* TNS Gallup.

VisitDenmark. (2016a). *Kulturturisme i Danmark: Kyst- og naturturister & Storbyturister*. København: VisitDenmark.

VisitDenmark. (2016b). *International markedsføring af Danmark som rejsemål - Notat med fokus på kulturoplevelser. VisitDenmark*. København: VisitDenmark.

VisitDenmark. (2016c). https://www.visitdenmark.dk/sites/default/files/vdk_images/PDF-and-other-files/Analyser/2016/status_paa_turisternes_overnatninger_i_danmark-2015.pdf

Voelklein, C., & Howarth, C. (2005). A review of controversies about social representations theory: A British debate. *Culture and Psychology*, *11*(4), 431–454. doi:10.1177/1354067X05058586

Wakefield, K. L., & Baker, J. (1998). Excitement at the mall: Determinants and effects on shopping response. *Journal of Retailing*, *74*(4), 515–540. doi:10.1016/S0022-4359(99)80106-7

Walk, K. (1998). *How to write a comparative analysis*. https://writingcenter.fas.harvard.edu/pages/how-write-comparative-analysis

Wallendorf, M., & Reilly, M. D. (1983). Ethnic Migration, Assimilation and Consumption. *The Journal of Consumer Research*, *10*(3), 292–302. doi:10.1086/208968

Wall, H., Campbell, C., Kaye, L., Levy, A., & Bhullar, N. (2019). Personality profiles and persuasion: An exploratory study investigating the role of the Big-5, Type D personality and the Dark Triad on susceptibility to persuasion. *Personality and Individual Differences*, *139*, 69–76. doi:10.1016/j.paid.2018.11.003

Wang, Y., & Ruhe, G. (2007). The Cognitive Process of Decision Making. *Journal of Cognitive Informatics and Natural Intelligence, 1*(2), 73–85.

Wang, C. (2017). Consumer acceptance of self-service technologies. *International Journal of Market Research*, *59*(6), 787–802. doi:10.2501/IJMR-2017-048

Wang, G., Dou, W., & Zhou, N. (2008). Consumption attitudes & adoption of new consumer products: A contingency approach. *European Journal of Marketing*, *42*(1), 238–254. doi:10.1108/03090560810840998

Wang, J., & Fung, R. Y. (2015). Dynamic appointment scheduling with patient preferences and choices. *Industrial Management & Data Systems*, *115*(4), 700–717. doi:10.1108/IMDS-12-2014-0372

Wang, J.-J., Jing, Y.-Y., Zhang, C.-F., & Zhao, J.-H. (2009). Review on multi-criteria decision analysis aid in sustainable energy decision-making. *Renewable & Sustainable Energy Reviews*, *13*(9), 2263–2278. doi:10.1016/j.rser.2009.06.021

Wansink, B., & Sobal, J. (2007). Mindless eating. *Environment and Behavior*, *39*(1), 106–123. doi:10.1177/0013916506295573

Waterman, A. M. C. (2003). Mathematical Modeling as an Exegetical Tool: Rational Reconstruction. In *A Companion to the History of Economic Thought*. Malden, MA: Blackwell Publishing Ltd. doi:10.1002/9780470999059.ch37

Watkins, C. (2001). The Definition and Identification of Housing Submarket. *Environment & Planning*, *33*(12), 2235–2253. doi:10.1068/a34162

WBCSD (World Business Council for Sustainable Development). (2011). *A vision for sustainable consumption, Innovation, collaboration, and the management of choice*. Retrieved November 10, 2019 from http://docs.wbcsd.org/2011/10/AVisionForSustainableConsumption.pdf

Webster, C. (1991). Attitudes Towards Marketing Practices: The Effects of ethnic Identification. *Journal of Applied Business Research*, *7*(2), 107–116. doi:10.19030/jabr.v7i2.6251

Webster, C. (1994). Effects of Ethnic Identification on Marital Rols in the Purchase Decision Process. *The Journal of Consumer Research*, *21*(2), 319–331. doi:10.1086/209400

Weijters, B., Rangarajan, D., Falk, T., & Schillewaert, N. (2007). Determinants and outcomes of customers' use of self-service technology in a retail setting. *Journal of Service Research*, *10*(1), 3–21. doi:10.1177/1094670507302990

Weismantel, M. J. (1988). *Food, Gender, and Poverty in the Ecuadorian Andes*. Philadelphia, PA: University of Pennsylvania Press.

Welch, C., Piekkari, R., Plakoyiannaki, E., & Paavilainen-Mäntymäki, E. (2011). Theorising from case studies: Towards a pluralist future for international business research. *Journal of International Business Studies*, *42*(5), 740–762. doi:10.1057/jibs.2010.55

Wellman, M. P., & Doyle, J. (1991). Preferential Semantics for Goals. *Proceedings of the 9th National Conference in Artificial Intelligence*, 698–703.

Western Cape Government. (2015). *Socio-economic profile Stellenbosch municipality*. www.westerncape.gov.za

Westin, A. (1967). *Privacy and Freedom*. New York: Atheneum.

Wetherall, K., Robb, K., & O'Connor, R. (2019). Social rank theory of depression: A systematic review of self-perceptions of social rank and their relationship with depressive symptoms and suicide risk. *Journal of Affective Disorders*, *246*, 300–319. doi:10.1016/j.jad.2018.12.045 PMID:30594043

White, K., Hardisty, D. J., & Habib, R. (2019). The Elusive Green Consumer. *Harvard Business Review*. Retrieved from http://search.ebscohost.com/login.aspx?direct=true&db=edb&AN=137120584&site=eds-live

White, A. (2007). A "Consuming" Oppression: Sugar, Cannibalism and John Woolman's 1770 Slave Dream. *Quaker History*, *96*(2), 1–27. doi:10.1353/qkh.2007.0003

Whitfield, K. (2015). *Quick Guide to Sustainable Development: History and Concepts*. Retrieved November 10, 2019 from http://www.assembly.wales/research%20documents/qg15-003%20-%20sustainable%20development%20history%20and%20concepts/qg15-003.pdf

Whiting, L. S. (2008). Semi-structured interviews: Guidance for novice researchers. *Nursing Standard*, *22*(23), 35–40. doi:10.7748/ns2008.02.22.23.35.c6420 PMID:18323051

Whittle, C., Whitmarsh, L., Haggar, P., Morgan, P., & Parkhurst, G. (2019). User decision-making in transitions to electrified, autonomous, shared or reduced mobility. *Transportation Research Part D, Transport and Environment*, *71*, 302–319. doi:10.1016/j.trd.2018.12.014

Widyaningsiha, N., Tjiptoherijantob, P., Widanarkob, S., & Seda, F. (2015). Linkage model between sustainable consumption and household waste management. *Procedia Environmental Sciences*, *28*, 195–203. doi:10.1016/j.proenv.2015.07.026

Wiedmann, K. P., Hennigs, N., & Siebels, A. (2009). Value-Based Segmentation of Luxury Consumption Behavior. *Psychology and Marketing*, *26*(7), 625–651. doi:10.1002/mar.20292

Wilson, F. (2010). Indians and Mestizos: Identity and Urban Popular Culture in Andean Peru. *Journal of Southern African Studies*, *26*(2), 239–253. doi:10.1080/03057070050010093

Winer, B. (1971). *Statistical Principles in Experimental Design* (2nd ed.). McGraw-Hill.

Wolf, H. L., Morrish, S. C., & Fountain, J. (2016). A conceptualization of the perceptions and motivators that drive luxury wine consumption. *International Journal of Wine Business Research*, *28*(2), 120–133. doi:10.1108/ijwbr-09-2015-0038

Wolf, J., Borges, M., Marques, J. L., & Castro, E. (2019). Smarter Decisions for Smarter Cities: Lessons Learned from Strategic Plans. In C. Rego & M. I. Sánchez-hernández (Eds.), *New Paths of Entrepreneurship Development: The Role of Education, Smart Cities and Social Factors* (pp. 7–30). Springer. doi:10.1007/978-3-319-96032-6_2

Wood, S. L. & Swait, J. (2002). Psychological Indicators of Innovation Adoption: Cross-Classification Based on Need for Cognition & Need for Change. *Journal of Consumer Psychology, 12*(1), 1-13.

Woodward, L. (2007). *Understanding Material Culture*. London: Sage. doi:10.4135/9781446278987

Wooldridge, J. (2008). *Introductory econometrics: A modern approach* (4th ed.). Mason, OH: Cengage Learning.

World Bank. (2020). *Brazil*. Retrieved from https://www.worldbank.org/en/country/brazil

World Economic Forum. (2015). *Is this the future of the internet of things?* https://www.weforum.org/agenda/2015/11/is-this-future-of-the-internet-of-things/

World Economic Forum. (2018). *Electric vehicles for smarter cities: the future of energy and mobility*. http://www3.weforum.org/docs/WEF_2018_%20Electric_For_Smarter_Cities.pdf

Wrona, T., Ladwig, T., & Gunnesch, M. (2013). Socio-cognitive processes in strategy formation - A conceptual framework. *European Management Journal*, *31*(6), 697–705. doi:10.1016/j.emj.2013.07.005

WTO. (2019). *Global Value Chain Development Report: technological innovation, supply chain trade, and workers in a globalized world*. Geneva, Switzerland: The World Trade Organization.

Wüenderlich, N. V., Heinonen, K., Ostrom, A. L., Patricio, L., Sousa, R., Voss, C., & Lemmink, J. G. A. M. (2015). Futurizing smart service: Implications for service researchers and managers. *Journal of Services Marketing*, *29*(6/7), 442–447. doi:10.1108/JSM-01-2015-0040

Xue, H., & Lin, Y. (2017). The omni-channel consumer segmentation method based on consumption data stream mining. 2017 IEEE 2nd International Conference on Big Data Analysis (ICBDA)(, Big Data Analysis (ICBDA), 2017 IEEE 2nd International Conference On. 10.1109/ICBDA.2017.8078814

Xu, H., Luo, X., Carroll, J. M., & Rosson, M. B. (2011). The Personalization Privacy Paradox: An Exploratory Study of Decision Making Process for Location-Aware Marketing. *Decision Support Systems*, *51*(1), 42–52. doi:10.1016/j.dss.2010.11.017

Yale, P. (1991). *From Tourist Attractions to Heritage Tourism*. Huntingdon: Elm.

Yan, G. R., & Yusniza, K. (2016). Moving Towards Sustainable Consumption: A Study of Reduce, Reuse and Recycle (3Rs) Adoption among Malaysians. *"Marketing to the Bottom of the Pyramid in Emerging Markets" - Vol. 3 IBAICM-2016: Third International Conference on Marketing.*

Yang, Q.Z., Zhou, J. & Xu, K. (2014). A 3R Implementation Framework to Enable Circular Consumption in Community, *International Journal of Environmental Science and Development*, *5*(2).

Yıldırım, S. (2018). Roles And Responsibilities In Sustainable Development Goals. *International Congress of Management, Economy and Policy, 201*, 425-433

Yıldırım, S., & Candan, B. (2015). Segmentation of Green Product Buyers Based on Their Personal Values and Consumption Values. *Environmental Values, 24*(5), 641–661. doi:10.3197/096327115X14384223590212

Yıldırım, S., & Yıldırım, D. Ç. (2020). *Achieving Sustainable Development Through a Green Economy Approach. In Advanced Integrated Approaches to Environmental Economics and Policy: Emerging Research and Opportunities* (pp. 1–22). IGI Global Pub.

Yıldırım, S., Yıldırım, D. Ç., & Gedikli, A. (2016). Sustainable Consumption Trends in the World in the Context of Green Economy and Sustainability. In M. M. Erdoğdu, T. Arun, & I. H. Ahmad (Eds.), *Handbook of Research on Green Economic Development Initiatives and Strategies* (pp. 66–84). IGI Global. doi:10.4018/978-1-5225-0440-5.ch004

Yi, M. Y., Jackson, J. D., Park, J. S., & Probst, J. C. (2006). Understanding information technology acceptance by individual professionals: Toward an integrative view. *Information & Management, 43*(3), 350–363. doi:10.1016/j.im.2005.08.006

Yin, R. K. (2011). *Applications of case study research*. Thousand Oaks, CA: Sage Publications.

Young, A., & Young, R. (2008). Measuring the effects of film and television on tourism to screen locations: A theoretical and empirical perspective. *Journal of Travel & Tourism Marketing, 24*(2-3), 195–212. doi:10.1080/10548400802092742

Young, W., Hwang, K., McDonald, S., & Oates, C. J. (2010). Sustainable Consumption: Green Consumer Behaviour When Purchasing Products. *Sustainable Development, 18*, 20–31.

Yukl, G., Kim, H., & Falbe, C. M. (1996). Antecedents of influence outcomes. *The Journal of Applied Psychology, 81*(3), 309–317. doi:10.1037/0021-9010.81.3.309

Zajonc, R. B. (1968). Attitudinal effects of mere exposure. *Journal of Personality and Social Psychology, 9*(2, Pt.2), 1–27. doi:10.1037/h0025848

Zajonc, R. B. (1980). Feeling and thinking: Preferences need no inferences. *The American Psychologist, 35*(2), 151–175. doi:10.1037/0003-066X.35.2.151

Zajonc, R. B. (1984). On the primacy of affect. *The American Psychologist, 39*(2), 117–124. doi:10.1037/0003-066X.39.2.117

Zakhariuk, O. (1977). O ponjatii, fact" v arxeologicheskoi hauke [On the concept of "fact" in archaeological science]. *Sovetskaja Arkheologia., 4*, 21–27.

Zaman, A. U. (2015, March). A comprehensive review of the development of zero waste management: Lessons learned and guidelines. *Journal of Cleaner Production, 91*, 12–25. doi:10.1016/j.jclepro.2014.12.013

Zanna, M. P., Fazio, R. H., & Ross, M. (1994). The persistence of persuasion. *Beliefs, reasoning, and decision making: Psycho-logic in honor of Bob Abelson*, 347-362.

Zemke, R. R., & Raines, C. (2012). Generations at Work: Managing the Clash of Veterans. Baby Boomers, Xers, and Nexters in You Workplace. Academic Press.

Zhang, J., & Mao, E. (2016). From Online Motivations to Ad Clicks and to Behavioral Intentions: An Empirical Study of Consumer Response to Social Media Advertising. *Psychology and Marketing, 33*(3), 155–164. doi:10.1002/mar.20862

Zhang, L., & Wu, Y. (2012, December). Market segmentation and willingness to pay for green electricity among urban residents in China: The case of Jiangsu Province. *Energy Policy, 51*, 514–523. doi:10.1016/j.enpol.2012.08.053

Zhao, H. H., Gao, Q., Wu, Y. P., Wang, Y., & Zu, X. D. (2014, January 15). What affects green consumer behavior in China? A case study from Qingdao. *Journal of Cleaner Production*, *63*, 143–151. doi:10.1016/j.jclepro.2013.05.021

Zhao, R., & Zhong, S. (2015). Carbon labelling influences on consumers' behaviour: A system dynamics approach. *Ecological Indicators*, *50*, 98–106. doi:10.1016/j.ecolind.2014.08.030

Zhao, Y., Ni, Q., & Zhou, R. (2018a). Review: What factors influence the mobile health service adoption? A meta-analysis & the moderating role of age. *International Journal of Information Management*, *43*, 342–350. doi:10.1016/j.ijinfomgt.2017.08.006

Zimbardo, P. G., & Boyd, J. N. (1999). Putting Time in Perspective: A Valid, Reliable Individual-Differences Metric. *Journal of Personality and Social Psychology*, *77*(6), 1271–1288. doi:10.1037/0022-3514.77.6.1271

Zinkhan, G. M., & Braunsberger, K. (2004). The complexity of consumers' cognitive structures and its relevance to consumer behavior. *Journal of Business Research*, *57*(6), 575–582. doi:10.1016/S0148-2963(02)00396-X

Zmud, J., & Arce, C. (1992). The Ethnical and Consumption Relationship. *Advances in Consumer Research. Association for Consumer Research (U. S.)*, *19*, 443–449.

Zralek, J., & Burgiel, A. (2020). Prospects for a Sustainable Future: Mapping Sustainable Behaviors According to Consumer Perceptions. *Review of Business*, *40*(1), 35–50. Retrieved from http://search.ebscohost.com/login.aspx?direct=true&db=bth&AN=141137614&site=eds-live

About the Contributors

Paata Bukhrashvili has defended doctoral dissertation in 1989 in Pre- and Protohistory at the Georgian National Academy of Sciences on the topic of "The Dwelling in the Ethnic Mode of Life". Was a Doctoral Candidate at the State University of Tbilisi between 1985-1989. Graduated from Tbilisi State University School of History (Diploma Excellent) in 1976-1983. Has worked at Ilia State University as a Professor and Dean of School of Humanities and Cultural Studies between 2006-2010. Was Director of the International Caucasological Scientific Research Institute in 1997. Was Professor of Ethnology at Ivane Javakhishvili Tbilisi State University of between 1990-2006. Professor of Caucasian History at State Pedagogical University of Tbilisi in 1994-2006. Was a Professor of Georgian History at Technical University of Tbilisi 1988-1994. Senior Researcher of Kakhetian Archeological Expedition at Archeological Research Center, Georgian Academy of Sciences during 1983-2006.

Valentina Chkoniya received her PhD in Technical Sciences by Murmansk State Technical University, Russia, in 2003. Actually, she is a professor at the University of Aveiro, member of GOVCOPP, Portugal, and managing partner of VT Mar (company in the marketing intelligence market). Valentina Chkoniya is a highly professional and experienced professor with a deep understanding and knowledge regarding the business, based on a deep strategic perspective and building on more than 20 years of experience. Her current research interests include data analysis, decision support systems, marketing research, consumer behaviour and information technologies for retail.

Ana Oliveira Madsen was born in Portugal and, while attending the Administration and Management degree at the Universidade Católica do Porto, she has done one semester at the Aarhus Business School - Denmark. She ended up living for 7 years in Denmark, where she taught Consumer Behaviour at Syddansk University, where she was enrolled as a non-tenured associate professor at the Department of Environment and Business Economics. She holds a Ph.D. degree in "Market Systems and Consumption" from the Universidade Rey Juan Carlos, Madrid, Spain. Since 2012 she has been enrolled as a teacher at Universidade Católica Portuguesa and in 2016 she became part of the Católica Porto Business School. Since 2019 she is part of CEGE (a research center whose members are the most productive researchers at Católica Porto Business School). Currently, Ana is doing research in the fields of fish consumption, market institutions, Portuguese Economy, Business and Consumer Behaviour. She is married and has 2 daughters.

* * *

Marlene Almeida holds a degree in International Relations field of Economics and Politics (Universidade do Minho, Braga, Portugal) and got a D.E.S. in Management (ICHEC Brussels Management School, Belgium). Based in Brussels and working for a major automotive company for over 14 years. Current research interests include trends scouting activities, future city landscape studies, technologies driving quality of life.

Giorgi Antadze has an MBA and MSc International Marketing Graduate and is a prospect PhD student. Currently working as the Global Investment Analyst at Wavemaker in London, UK.

Elodie Attié is a PhD graduate at the Toulouse School of Management. Her main research interest is technology acceptance and use of the Internet of Things and smart technologies, and the influence of technologies on consumer well-being. She is one author of a book chapter about the acceptance of smart homes.

Eric Bachié is an engineer in theorical chemistry and scientific computing. He has started his career in computer sciences in the bank field. Then he continued in the industrial field. Since 14 years, he worked in PLM (Product Lifecycle Management) and since 4 years, he specialized in the IoT (Internet of Things) and innovation for Percall. His work experience is totally oriented around customers needs, finding the best solution to digitalize the companies he works for. In 2018, He has developed the concept of connected stores after a long scoping phase to detect the customers uses and needs in partnership with the CETI (European Center of textiles innovative). He is a passionate creator of new activities, new deliveries model and people development.

Paulo Batista has a PhD on E-Planning, a joint phd degree from University of Aveiro, University of Lisbon and Lisbon New University. Moreover, he has a degree in Regional and Urban Planning and a degree in Regional and Urban Planning (specialization in public policies), both from the University of Aveiro. He is a researcher at University of Aveiro, as a member of Governance, Competitiveness and Public Policy Research Unit since 2012 (GOVCOPP). He develops its research work in the Research Group in Territory and Innovation (GETIN_UA), from which he is a member since 2008. His research activity has involved the participation in housing planning and housing market analysis projects at urban scales, for which he is involved on the development of decision support tools.

Arnab Bhattacharjee is Professor of Economics and Director, Spatial Economics and Econometrics Centre (SEEC) in Heriot-Watt University - United Kingdom. Has two Ph.Ds: i) in Statistics from the Indian Statistical Institute, Kolkata, India; and, ii) in Economics, University of Mumbai, Mumbai, India. He worked for 5 years at the Reserve Bank of India and in recent years was professor at Cambridge University, St Andrews University, Dundee University. Currently is professor at Heriot-Watt Edinburgh. His work focuses on microeconomics, panel data analysis and spatial econometrics. In this context it has been addressing issues related to housing, demography and other economic processes with particular emphasizes on spatial dimension of this phenomena.

Monique Borges has a master degree in Regional and Urban Planning and a degree in Public Administration (specialization in public policies), both from the University of Aveiro. Presently she is a PhD student in the Doctoral Program of Public Policy in the same University. She is a Research fellow in the GETIN_UA - Research Group in Territory and Innovation - since 2009 and member of the decision support systems group of the GOVCOPP - Research Unit for Governance, Competitiveness and Public Policy of the University of Aveiro - since 2013. Her research activity has involved the participation in strategic planning projects at regional and local levels, as well as the development of decision support methodologies and tools.

Elisabed Bzhalava is Doctor of Philology and associate professor at Ivane Javakhishvili Tbilisi State University. Her research fields are Language, Sociolinguistic and Linguo Culturology. Dr. Elisabed Bzhalava takes part in international conferences, workshops and seminars, is the co-author of Turkish Language Textbook, "Georgian-Turkish-Russian Phrase-Book" for Meskhetian repatriates and "Short Course of Georgian Language for Turkish people (Video Lessons) and author of many articles. Dr. Elisabed Bzhalava was a scholarship holder of Erasmus Mundus credit mobility program -2019- guest Teacher at Cadiz University; 2018-guest Teacher at Afyon Kocatepe University; 2016 -The postgraduate scholarship at Ca' Foscari University and 2016- Moldova State University -"Possibilities and limits, Challenges and Obstacles of Transferring CEE EU pre-accession Best Practices and Experience to Moldova's and Georgia's pre-accession Process, 2014 - Vilnius university. At different times gave lectures at the following universities -2019-Cadiz University; 2018- Afyon Kocatepe University; 2002- School of foreign language (Ankara/Turkey); 2001- School of foreign language (Istanbul/Turkey)). She Knows Georgian, Russian, Turkish and English languages.

Yezelia Danira Caceres is an Economist, Master in Agribusiness and currently works as an ordinary professor at the Faculty of Economics of the National University of San Agustín de Arequipa, Peru. Likewise, in their professional performance they highlight the contributions in: Analysis of the instrument for measuring institutional capacity. Case study: Pampacolca 2018 Prepared as a product of the CIES 2017 Economic and Social Research Consortium research contest Theoretical contributions for the analysis of competitiveness and the value chain in micro and small companies. Ilustro 2018, vol 9 ISSN: 2311-4126 The use of information and communication technologies for the improvement of agricultural production in the Arequipa region 2014 - Research Contest Consortium for Economic and Social Research CIES "The use of ICT for key industries in the southern economic corridor: alpaca and coffee. Enhancing the Competitiveness of SMEs in the Southern Economic Corridor in Peru (2012) KDS Korean Development Strategy Using the radio to improve the local responses to climate variability, Center for Development and Informatics (CDI) of the University of Manchester, UK (2012)

José Luís Cacho is CEO of APS – Ports of Sines and the Algarve Authority, S.A. and President of APLOP - Association of Portuguese Speaking Ports. The Port of Sines is an open deep-water sea port with excellent maritime access, without restrictions, leading the Portuguese port sector in the volume of cargo handled, and offering unique natural characteristics to receive any type of vessels. He also was member of the Monitoring Committee of the Logistics Platforms National Network Plan, a member of the Monitoring Group for the rail link to the Port of Aveiro and of the Committee on Accreditation of Civil Engineering Graduation at the University of Trás-os -Montes e Alto Douro (UTAD), by the Engineers Order between. He was also member of the Biology Department Council, of the University of Aveiro, while being a member of the Council General of the University of Coimbra. He was CEO of APA - Port of Aveiro Authority, S.A., where he had already been Member of the Board of Directors and CEO of APFF - Port of Figueira da Foz Authority, S.A. and President of APP – Portugal Ports Association.

Eduardo Anselmo de Castro has a PhD in Regional Economics from the University of Aveiro, a MSc in Local Geography, Local and Regional Planning from the University of Lisbon and a degree in Civil Engineering from the University of Coimbra. Currently he is Vice-Rector at the University of Aveiro, where is an Associate Professor, at the Department of Social, Political and Territorial Sciences. He lectures under-graduated and graduated courses of Regional Economics and Planning, Social and Economic Analysis, Environmental Economics and Policy and Project Evaluation. Presently, he is member of the research unit on Governance, Competitiveness and Public Policy (GOVCOPP). Moreover, he was member, and most of the times coordinator, of research teams of the University of Aveiro participating in several European and National sponsored projects in the fields of Analysis of Social and Economic impacts of ICT, Regional Development and Innovation Policies, Decision Support Tools development (combining the demographic, economic, environmental and spatial dimensions).

Kimberly Clark is a Behavioral Neuroscientist, Researcher, and Lecturer in The Department of Psychological and Brain Sciences and Affiliated Faculty in the Cognitive Science Progam at Dartmouth College; Co-Founder & CRO, Merchant Mechanics; serves government, commerce, advertising, and social media industry blue-chip clients. Dr. Clark also serves as Co-Founder and CEO of Bellwether Citizens Response, a research consultancy to advance political and sustainability-focused communications. Dr. Clark is widely published in academic and industry journals.

Teresa Coelho is Chairman of the Board of Directors of Docapesca – Portos e Lotas, S.A. since 2016. She holds a law degree from University of Coimbra and a master's degree in Human Resources Management from Paris School of Management. Teresa Coelho has developed work in the field of fisheries since 1996 in public and governmental institutions, namely at the Ministry of Justice ant the Secretaries of State for Fisheries, Forests and Home Affairs.

Alice Duarte has a PhD in Anthropology of Complex Societies at ISCTE - University Institute of Lisbon, Master in Anthropology, Specialization in Ethno-Museology, University of Minho and Degree in Social and Cultural Anthropology at Universidade Nova de Lisboa. She is a full professor and member of the respective scientific committees of the Doctorate Program in Heritage Studies and Master in Museology by FLUP/ UPorto (Portugal). Full Professor of Master in African Studies and Master in History and Heritage by FLUP / UP. Integrated Researcher at ISUP - Institute of Sociology, University of Porto. Areas of interest and publication: consumption as cultural practice, museums and museology, heritage and integrated development, in which he guides several theses of the 3rd and 2nd cycles. On these topics has two books published and several articles distributed by various national and international magazines.

Elizaveta Fainshtein is a postgraduate student, Department of Management, National Research University Higher School of Economics (HSE). The supervisor of studies is Professor Valery Gordin. National Research University Higher School of Economics, 16, Soyuza Pechatnikov Street, St. Petersburg, 190121, Russian Federation. Research interests: strategic marketing, business modeling and business management in the organization. Taught the discipline "Fundamentals of International Business" in English at the National Research University Higher School of Economics; was the attaché of the Nobel laureate in economics, Sir Christopher Pissarides (Scopus Author ID: 6603439301), (professor of economics at the London School of Economics UCL) while working at SPIEF'16.

Elissa Fernandes is a pharmacist from Universidade Federal do Rio Grande do Sul. Graduate Student at the Neuroscience Program – RS – Brazil.

Carlos Figueiredo is a member of the Executive Board of Directors of Docapesca - Portos e Lotas, S.A. since 2017. He is an economist with a degree in Economics from the Instituto Superior de Economia of the Technical University of Lisbon. Carlos Figueiredo has developed management work in several public and private institutions, namely at the Institute for Nature Conservation and Biodiversity, Institute of Financing for Agriculture and Fisheries, I.P., and at the International Fund for Agricultural Development.

Paola Figueiró has a PhD in Business Administration from Universidade Federal do Rio Grande do Sul – RS – Brazil, Adjunct Professor at the Post Graduate Program in Business Administration at Feevale University - RS-Brazil.

Sara Gonzalez, anthropologist, graduated at FCSH-Universidade Nova de Lisboa and a Master´s Degree in Sociology, specialization in Communities and Social Dynamics at the same University. Is currently in the project CRiCity - Children and their right to the city.

Barbora Gulisova holds the Erasmus Mundus master's degree European Master in Tourism Management (2016). She is currently a Ph.D. Fellow at University of Southern Denmark and has previously worked as a self-employed consultant, associated with the INSETUR (Higher institute of tourism research), and Campus Turisme, both at the University of Girona.

Lulu Anne Hansen holds a Ph.D. in History. She has previously taught at the centre for Tourism Innovation and Culture at University of Southern Denmark and now holds a position as Head of History and Interpretation at Museum of Southwest Jutland. She has previously published on topics relating to history and heritage management.

Andreas Hesse is Professor of Marketing at Koblenz University of Applied Science. Andreas has an outstanding managerial experience in various management positions. In his teaching and research, he is interested in digital commerce and green marketing.

Katharina Sophie Kuehn received her Master's Degree in Sociology and Neuromarketing from the Université de Genève, Switzerland and Otto-Friedrich-University of Bamberg, Germany in 2010. During and following her studies, Katharina trained and worked in the team of one of Germany's pioneering neuroscientists in business and bestselling author, Dr. Hans-Georg Häusel. She published her thesis on the social construction of brands (Die soziale Konstruktion von Marken) at VdM Verlag Dr. Müller, in German language. Katharina has consulted to leading retailers and manufacturers across Europe and Asia Pacific and most recently joined the Winning Group as Chief Strategy Officer, where her work combines science, technology and strategy to drive the growth and development of the Group's e-commerce, technology, logistics and retail brands. She writes and presents globally on the neuroscience of personality and the non-conscious nature of human decision-making, including at TedX in 2018. Katharina was ranked number #5 in Internet Retailing Australia's Top 50 People in E-Commerce in 2019.

Manuel Luiz is Managing Director and Partner at the Boston Consulting Group (BCG), Rio de Janeiro office (Brazil). He joined BCG in September 2001, as an Associate, in Lisbon (Portugal). He transferred to Brazil by mid-2011 and before that, Manuel spent almost two years in the BCG South Cone system, based in Santiago (Chile). He is a Core Member of the Energy Practice and he is the People and Organization Practice node in Brazil. Manuel has worked extensively in the change management, organizational design and human resources topics. Mr. Luiz obtained his MBA from MIT – Sloan School of Management (Cambridge, MA) in 2007. Also, he has a degree in Business Management from Universidade Católica Portuguesa, Centro Regional do Porto (2001), where he graduated first of his Class. Other professional experience includes consulting for Tatweer Dubai, a Governmental company within Dubai, UAE. Manuel is married and has 2 young children (António, 7 years old and Francisco, 5) enjoys exercising (triathlon), following sports (soccer, baseball, rugby) and travelling.

Liraz Margalit, PhD, is a Social Psychologist who specializes in Behavioral Design and Decision Making. She integrates Neuropsychology and Behavioral Economics perspectives to analyze User behavior and deliver actionable insights for business stakeholders. Liraz is a lecturer at the IDC and a worldwide keynote speaker. Her consumer behavior research was awarded with the OBE, Online Business Excellence for 2016 as well as the Best of Neuromarketing and was chosen as CMSWire contributor of the year 2017. Her research papers and studies can be found in top business magazines such as Entrepreneur, TechCrunch and Forbes. She also writes an ongoing blog for Psychology Today named "Behind Online Behavior".

Joao Marques is assistant professor at the Department of Social, Political and Territorial Sciences of the University of Aveiro, lecturing courses in the areas of Urban and Regional Planning (in the field of quantitative methods and techniques to support decision making). PhD in Social Sciences by the University of Aveiro, he did a MsC in Innovation and Regional Development Policies, and his graduation studies in Urban and Regional Planning by the same university. In 1999, he joined the research group CEIDET- Centre for Studies in Innovation and Territorial and Industrial Dynamics. Currently he is member of the research group on Planning and Innovation (GETIN_UA); and of the Research Unit in Governance, Competitiveness and Public Policies (GOVCOPP). He has been developing research in the fields of strategic spatial planning, spatial competitiveness analysis, studies related to higher education and economic models for regional development. His current area of interest is the development of tools and methodologies to support the decision in public policy. The application of these methodologies covers various issues (housing, demographics, mobility, planning, equipment and infrastructure, employment etc.) and various territorial levels (local to national scale).

Luís Marques is Invited Auxiliar Professor at Católica Porto Business School (since 2011) and Board Member at Rangel Invest, S.A. (since 2014). PhD (2013) and MSc (2002) in Business Sciences at Faculty of Economics, University of Porto. Degree in Accounting and Audit (1997) at University of Aveiro. Former Board Member at Aveiro Port Authority (2005 to 2014) and also Director of Finance (2000 to 2005). Former PwC (1995 to 1999) and CFA, SROC (1994 to 1995) collaborator. Former Invited Assistant of Corporate Finance at University of Aveiro (2008 to 2011) and Invited Professor of Strategy at IPAM (2004 to 2010).

Michał Matukin is a social psychologist working with neuroscientific research methods since 2007. Expert in continuous measurement of emotion and attention. Experienced psychologist and researcher involved in the application of new technologies such as response latency measures, electroencephalography, electromyography, galvanic skin response, and eye-tracking to the marketing field. His research focuses on applied affective neuroscience, including the usage of high technologies in the daily routine of marketers. He cooperates with Universities and Academic professionals in order to enhance our understanding of human behavior and decision making. He established neuroscientific laboratories in Beijing, China (Renmin University) and in Capetown, South Africa (University of Stellenbosh).

Juan Medina is an Agricultural Engineer, graduated from the National University of San Cristóbal de Huamanga, master's degree in Agribusiness granted by the National Agrarian University La Molina (Lima, Peru), master's degree in Local Development granted by the University of Andalusia (Seville, Spain), Evaluation Specialist Social Projects awarded by Los Andes University (Bogotá, Colombia) and post-graduate degrees in local development, project management, public management in Israel (Asia), Portugal (Europe) and Egypt (Africa). In relation to his professional experience, he has more than 20 years, has developed professional work as an external agent for inspection of social projects with the FONCODES (PCM), Institutional strengthening specialist in the National Council of Decentralization CND (PCM / Agorah), Regional Export Committee Manager (MINCETUR); PRONAA Zonal Chief (MIDIS), Chief of General Services in Civil Defense-INDECI (PCM), Public Manager of the National Civil Service Authority SERVIR (PCM), Lead Evaluator of the National Agricultural Research Program PNIA (MINAGRI); mainly. Experience in higher education in undergraduate Universidad Tecnológica del Perú and Universidad Continental. Experience in postgraduate higher education National University San Cristóbal de Huamanga and National University San Agustín de Arequipa.

Raquel Filipa do Amaral Chambre de Meneses holds a Ph.D. in Business Science from the University of Porto, where she teaches in the area of strategy and international marketing. She researches in the same area, attending international conferences and having several book chapters and papers published in scientific peer review journals. Currently, she is the director of Master in Marketing at University of Porto.

Nuno Metello de Nápoles has a BA in Marketing Management by Instituto Português de Administração de Marketing and a Master's degree in Sales Management from Faculdade de Economia do Porto. He is in charge of Sales & Marketing of Clube Reserva 1500 since 2017, a wine club for Sogrape Vinhos customers, the largest wine producer in Portugal and already considered the best wine producer in the world.

Lars Meyer-Waarden is Professor at the Toulouse School of Management. His main research interests are Customer Relationship Management, loyalty programs as well as Consumer Empowerment and Well-Being through digital products and services. He is the author of a book about the efficiency of loyalty programs, and has published lots of articles about these issues in international journals as in New York Wall Street Journal, Journal of Retailing, Journal of the Academy of Marketing Science, Journal of Marketing Management, European Journal of Marketing, Journal of Service Marketing, Journal of Business Research, Journal of Retailing and Consumer Services, Technological Forecasting and Social Change, International Journal of Electronic Commerce.

Elissa Moses is a Neuromarketing Pioneer, Behavioral Strategist, Founder & CEO, BrainGroup Global, former CEO Ipsos Neuro & Behavioral Science, renown brand and advertising strategist with expertise in youth, innovation and emotion. Published book and academic journal author; frequent global speaker. Partner in Bellwether Citizen Response and Hark Connect. MS Technology Management, Columbia University and AB Human Behavior, University of Chicago.

Virimai Victor Mugobo is holder of doctoral degree in Marketing with a special focus on the strategic brand management for nations. He is a researcher with a keen interest investigating on how African nations can become sustainable and competitive through the adoption and application of strategic branding strategies. Virimai has more than 15 years' experience in the higher education and training field and he is currently the Acting Head of Department and Senior Lecturer in the Retail Business Management Department at the Cape Peninsula University of Technology.

Alvaro Nascimento is Professor of Economics and Finance at Católica Porto Business School – having been dean from 2008 to 2013 – and member of the board of Católica Luanda Business School. Non-executive director on several boards: president of the Board of the Auditing and Finance Committee of Sonae MC, non-executive director at NORS, member of the Auditing Committee at Unicer, president of the Advisory Board of the Portuguese Regulatory Authority for Water and Waste (ERSAR), and board member of FAE (Portuguese Association of Corporate Managers). In the past he served as Chairman of Caixa Geral de Depósitos, president of the Auditing Committee at Banco Carregosa, independent director of Euronext Lisbon, and the Portuguese Institute for Corporate Governance (IPCG). He holds a PhD in Banking and Finance – Cass Business School (London) – and a MSc in Internal Trade and Finance – University of Lancaster (UK). He was a research fellow at London Business School on regulation and competition. He has research and publications in finance, telecommunications and competition and regulation. Professional consultant on competition to private organisations and government agencies, such as the Portuguese Competition Authority, Health and Telecom Regulators. He is regularly invited to deliver presentations, seminars and conferences to professional audiences in subjects linked to asset valuation, risk management, corporate governance, and regulation of the financial and telecommunications sectors.

Helena Nobre is Ph.D. in Business Sciences from the University of Porto in association with Boston University. She is an Assistant Professor of Management at the University of Aveiro (Portugal) and Senior Research Fellow at GOVCOPP (University of Aveiro). Her main research interests are branding and consumer behavior. She has several papers published in indexed Journals and conferences proceedings, a book and some book chapters. She is Associate Editor of the Review of Business Management (Web of Science). She taught several topics in Management in Portugal and abroad, namely in Boston University, as Adjunct Assistant Professor. She has experience in international companies.

Rafal Ohme (PhD) is a psychologist, expert in emotions, communication and consumer neuroscience. He is a professor at Business School at Stellenbosch University in South Africa. He held a Fulbright scholarship at Kellogg School of Management, at Stanford University he conducted research on unconscious emotions. Awarded by the President and the Prime Minister of Poland, a finalist of EY Entrepreneur of the Year 2015 program. Founder of NEUROHM, a smart tech company which licenses new research tools for HR, sales, marketing & PR. Author of articles, chapters and books including Mind

Spa (2019), Emo Sapiens (2017), Unconscious Affect (2007), Subliminal Facial Information (2003), and trilogy Automaticity (2001, 2003, 2003). Writes for Forbes.

Nino Okrostsvaridze is Doctor of Philosophy in History at Tbilisi Ilia State University. Her research fields are History, Ethnology and Eastern studies. Works on the issues of migration, identity and memory of Turkish Georgians living in Germany and Turkey. Dr. Nino Okrostsvaridze takes part in international conferences, workshops and seminars, is the author of monograph-"Family and Family life of Turkish Georgians: The Case of Hayriye Village population, Inegol Region, Turkey", and co-author of work "Georgian Cultural heritage monuments of Artaani (sample of fortification, cultural communication and household architecture)". Conducted scientific researches and expeditions in Turkey and Germany. Dr. Nino Okrostsvaridze is a scholarship holder of "Shota-Rustaveli scientific Foundation and German federation "DAAD" scholarship at Jena, Friedrich—Schiller University, (2019-guest researcher-an expert of Georgian Muslims in Turkey and Germany) 2019 - Erasmus grant in Portugal, Aveiro University, 2017-George Mason University - Mason-Georgia Policy Research and Methods. 2016- Shota Rustavely national foundation, 2012-scholarship of "Universities Coimbra Group at Friedrich-Schiller University, Jena Germany". Since 2009 is a member of "International Caucasological Research Institute". Delivers lectures at ilia State University and the University of Georgia, Knows Georgian, English, Turkish and Russian languages.

Alexandre Quevedo is Assistant Professor in the Department of Surgery and Orthopedic at the Universidade Federal do Rio Grande do Sul (UFRGS), Brazil. He is faculty in the Neuroscience Graduate Program, and in the Postgraduate Program in Dentistry (UFRGS). His dental degree is from Universidade Federal de Pernambuco (UFPE), Brazil. He was a Fellow in the Orofacial Pain Clinic at the University of Kentucky (U.S.A.). He received a Ph.D. degree in Neurobiology and Anatomy from the Wake Forest University (W.F.U.)(U.S.A.). He did postdoctoral training in Neuroscience at the W.F.U. and in Pharmacology at the UFRGS. His research interests focus on the central pain processing and top-down factors related to pain modulation.

Daniela Quevedo has a PhD in Water Resources and Environmental Sanitation from Universidade Federal do Rio Grande do Sul – RS – Brazil, Adjunct Professor at the Post-Graduate Program in Business Administration and in the Post Graduate in Environmental Quality at Feevale University - RS- Brazil.

Holger J. Schmidt is Professor of Marketing at Koblenz University of Applied Science. He also is a Visiting Professor at EM Strasbourg Business School and lectures regularly at CPUT in Cape Town. In his teaching and research, he is passionate about brands.

Nandini Sen is an academic researcher at Heriot Watt University, School of Social Sciences. Her book 'Urban Marginalisation in South Asia: Waste Pickers in Calcutta' was published by Routledge, 2018. Her Article ' Women and Gender in Short Stories by Rabindranath Tagore' was published by Anthropological Journal of European Culture, 2016. She has reviewed both project proposals, book chapters and articles for esteemed publishers and journals.

Elena Serova is Candidate of Sciences (PhD), Associate Professor, Department of Management, National Research University Higher School of Economics (HSE). National Research University Higher School of Economics, 16, Soyuza Pechatnikov Street, St. Petersburg, 190121, Russian Federation. Research interests: Business Analysis and Decision Making, Strategic Management, Innovation Management, Business Modeling and Business Models, Spatial Economy. Teaching courses in bachelor, master, PhD, MBA and further education programs. Academic advisor of Bachelor Thesis, Master Degree Thesis, and PhD Thesis.

Santosh Singh is commercial lead, APM Terminals, AP Moller Maersk Group. Based in APM Terminals' headquarters in Den Haag, Netherlands. Working on uncovering the unseen role of container shipping on globalization, on consumer behaviour and on changing patterns of consumer behaviour in the world. Head of Commercial – India, Middle East and Africa Region & Global Key Client Director - APM Terminals

Pieter Steenkamp is a Lecturer in the marketing department of the Cape Peninsula University of Technology in Cape Town. His research focuses on brand management.

Paula Wicher is a researcher with an academic background in psychology and social neuroscience and a co-author of scientific papers related to social mimicry and emotional intelligence. Has hands-on experience with different types of quantitative and qualitative research, data analysis, interpretation and dissemination of results. She is interested in the application of different research methods in business.

Seda Yıldırım was born in 1983. She graduated from Kocaeli University, Department of Business Administration in 2006. She completed her postgraduate and doctoral education at the Department of Business Administration, Kocaeli University, Production Management and Marketing. She worked as a research assistant in Kocaeli University between 2010-2013 and as an assistant professor in Recep Tayyip Erdoğan University between 2013-2016. Since 2017, she has been working as an Associate Professor at Namık Kemal University. Her current research interests include sustainable development, green marketing, sustainable consumption, Islamic economics, marketing culture, and values. She works as an editorial board member and arbitrator in various journals. She also studies as a member of the organizing committee of various international congresses (İCOMEP, ENSCON, İSEFE).

Index

J

K

L

M

N

O

P

R

S

T

V

W

Y

Purchase Print, E-Book, or Print + E-Book

IGI Global's reference books are available in three unique pricing formats:
Print Only, E-Book Only, or Print + E-Book.
Shipping fees may apply.

www.igi-global.com

Recommended Reference Books

ISBN: 978-1-5225-6201-6
© 2019; 341 pp.
List Price: $345

ISBN: 978-1-5225-7262-6
© 2019; 360 pp.
List Price: $215

ISBN: 978-1-5225-8003-4
© 2019; 216 pp.
List Price: $205

ISBN: 978-1-5225-5763-0
© 2019; 304 pp.
List Price: $205

ISBN: 978-1-5225-6980-0
© 2019; 325 pp.
List Price: $235

ISBN: 978-1-5225-7808-6
© 2019; 397 pp.
List Price: $215

Do you want to stay current on the latest research trends, product announcements, news and special offers?
Join IGI Global's mailing list today and start enjoying exclusive perks sent only to IGI Global members.
Add your name to the list at **www.igi-global.com/newsletters.**

Publisher of Peer-Reviewed, Timely, and Innovative Academic Research

IGI Global
DISSEMINATOR OF KNOWLEDGE

www.igi-global.com Sign up at www.igi-global.com/newsletters facebook.com/igiglobal twitter.com/igiglobal linkedin.com/igiglobal

Ensure Quality Research is Introduced to the Academic Community

Become an IGI Global Reviewer for Authored Book Projects

The overall success of an authored book project is dependent on quality and timely reviews.

In this competitive age of scholarly publishing, constructive and timely feedback significantly expedites the turnaround time of manuscripts from submission to acceptance, allowing the publication and discovery of forward-thinking research at a much more expeditious rate. Several IGI Global authored book projects are currently seeking highly-qualified experts in the field to fill vacancies on their respective editorial review boards:

Applications and Inquiries may be sent to:
development@igi-global.com

Applicants must have a doctorate (or an equivalent degree) as well as publishing and reviewing experience. Reviewers are asked to complete the open-ended evaluation questions with as much detail as possible in a timely, collegial, and constructive manner. All reviewers' tenures run for one-year terms on the editorial review boards and are expected to complete at least three reviews per term. Upon successful completion of this term, reviewers can be considered for an additional term.

If you have a colleague that may be interested in this opportunity, we encourage you to share this information with them.

IGI Global Proudly Partners With eContent Pro International

Receive a 25% Discount on all Editorial Services

Editorial Services

IGI Global expects all final manuscripts submitted for publication to be in their final form. This means they must be reviewed, revised, and professionally copy edited prior to their final submission. Not only does this support with accelerating the publication process, but it also ensures that the highest quality scholarly work can be disseminated.

English Language Copy Editing

Let eContent Pro International's expert copy editors perform edits on your manuscript to resolve spelling, punctuaion, grammar, syntax, flow, formatting issues and more.

Scientific and Scholarly Editing

Allow colleagues in your research area to examine the content of your manuscript and provide you with valuable feedback and suggestions before submission.

Figure, Table, Chart & Equation Conversions

Do you have poor quality figures? Do you need visual elements in your manuscript created or converted? A design expert can help!

Translation

Need your documjent translated into English? eContent Pro International's expert translators are fluent in English and more than 40 different languages.

Hear What Your Colleagues are Saying About Editorial Services Supported by IGI Global

"The service was very fast, very thorough, and very helpful in ensuring our chapter meets the criteria and requirements of the book's editors. I was quite impressed and happy with your service."

– Prof. Tom Brinthaupt, Middle Tennessee State University, USA

"I found the work actually spectacular. The editing, formatting, and other checks were very thorough. The turnaround time was great as well. I will definitely use eContent Pro in the future."

– Nickanor Amwata, Lecturer, University of Kurdistan Hawler, Iraq

"I was impressed that it was done timely, and wherever the content was not clear for the reader, the paper was improved with better readability for the audience."

– Prof. James Chilembwe, Mzuzu University, Malawi

Email: customerservice@econtentpro.com

www.igi-global.com/editorial-service-partners

IGI Global
DISSEMINATOR OF KNOWLEDGE
www.igi-global.com

Celebrating Over 30 Years of Scholarly Knowledge Creation & Dissemination

CELEBRATING 30 years EST. 1988 Academic Publishing Excellence

InfoSci®-Books

A Database of Over 5,300+ Reference Books Containing Over 100,000+ Chapters Focusing on Emerging Research

InfoSci®-Books Database

The **InfoSci®-Books** database is a collection of over 5,300+ IGI Global single and multi-volume reference books, handbooks of research, and encyclopedias, encompassing groundbreaking research from prominent experts worldwide that span over 350+ topics in 11 core subject areas including business, computer science, education, science and engineering, social sciences and more.

Open Access Fee Waiver (Offset Model) Initiative

For any library that invests in IGI Global's InfoSci-Journals and/ or InfoSci-Books databases, IGI Global will match the library's investment with a fund of equal value to go toward **subsidizing the OA article processing charges (APCs) for their students, faculty, and staff** at that institution when their work is submitted and accepted under OA into an IGI Global journal.*

INFOSCI® PLATFORM FEATURES

- No DRM
- No Set-Up or Maintenance Fees
- A Guarantee of No More Than a 5% Annual Increase
- Full-Text HTML and PDF Viewing Options
- Downloadable MARC Records
- Unlimited Simultaneous Access
- COUNTER 5 Compliant Reports
- Formatted Citations With Ability to Export to RefWorks and EasyBib
- No Embargo of Content (Research is Available Months in Advance of the Print Release)

**The fund will be offered on an annual basis and expire at the end of the subscription period. The fund would renew as the subscription is renewed for each year thereafter. The open access fees will be waived after the student, faculty, or staff's paper has been vetted and accepted into an IGI Global journal and the fund can only be used toward publishing OA in an IGI Global journal. Libraries in developing countries will have the match on their investment doubled.*

Budget Friendly · InfoSci-Books · InfoSci-Videos · InfoSci-Journals

To Learn More or To Purchase This Database:
www.igi-global.com/infosci-books
eresources@igi-global.com • Toll Free: 1-866-342-6657 ext. 100 • Phone: 717-533-8845 x100

IGI Global
DISSEMINATOR OF KNOWLEDGE
www.igi-global.com

IGI Global
DISSEMINATOR OF KNOWLEDGE
www.igi-global.com

Publisher of Peer-Reviewed, Timely, and Innovative Academic Research Since 1988

IGI Global's Transformative Open Access (OA) Model: How to Turn Your University Library's Database Acquisitions Into a Source of OA Funding

In response to the OA movement and well in advance of Plan S, IGI Global, early last year, unveiled their OA Fee Waiver (Offset Model) Initiative.

Under this initiative, librarians who invest in IGI Global's InfoSci-Books (5,300+ reference books) and/or InfoSci-Journals (185+ scholarly journals) databases will be able to subsidize their patron's OA article processing charges (APC) when their work is submitted and accepted (after the peer review process) into an IGI Global journal.*

How Does it Work?

1. When a library subscribes or perpetually purchases IGI Global's InfoSci-Databases including InfoSci-Books (5,300+ e-books), InfoSci-Journals (185+ e-journals), and/or their discipline/subject-focused subsets, IGI Global will match the library's investment with a fund of equal value to go toward subsidizing the OA article processing charges (APCs) for their patrons.

   Researchers: Be sure to recommend the InfoSci-Books and InfoSci-Journals to take advantage of this initiative.
2. When a student, faculty, or staff member submits a paper and it is accepted (following the peer review) into one of IGI Global's 185+ scholarly journals, the author will have the option to have their paper published under a traditional publishing model or as OA.
3. When the author chooses to have their paper published under OA, IGI Global will notify them of the OA Fee Waiver (Offset Model) Initiative. If the author decides they would like to take advantage of this initiative, IGI Global will deduct the US$ 1,500 APC from the created fund.
4. This fund will be offered on an annual basis and will renew as the subscription is renewed for each year thereafter. IGI Global will manage the fund and award the APC waivers unless the librarian has a preference as to how the funds should be managed.

Hear From the Experts on This Initiative:

"I'm very happy to have been able to make one of my recent research contributions, 'Visualizing the Social Media Conversations of a National Information Technology Professional Association' featured in the *International Journal of Human Capital and Information Technology Professionals*, freely available along with having access to the valuable resources found within IGI Global's InfoSci-Journals database."

– **Prof. Stuart Palmer**,
Deakin University, Australia

For More Information, Visit: www.igi-global.com/publish/contributor-resources/open-access or contact IGI Global's Database Team at eresources@igi-global.com.

Are You Ready to **Publish Your Research?**

IGI Global
DISSEMINATOR OF KNOWLEDGE

IGI Global offers book authorship and editorship opportunities across 11 subject areas, including business, computer science, education, science and engineering, social sciences, and more!

Benefits of Publishing with IGI Global:

- Free one-on-one editorial and promotional support.
- Expedited publishing timelines that can take your book from start to finish in less than one (1) year.
- Choose from a variety of formats including: Edited and Authored References, Handbooks of Research, Encyclopedias, and Research Insights.
- Utilize IGI Global's eEditorial Discovery® submission system in support of conducting the submission and blind review process.
- IGI Global maintains a strict adherence to ethical practices due in part to our full membership with the Committee on Publication Ethics (COPE).
- Indexing potential in prestigious indices such as Scopus®, Web of Science™, PsycINFO®, and ERIC – Education Resources Information Center.
- Ability to connect your ORCID iD to your IGI Global publications.
- Earn royalties on your publication as well as receive complimentary copies and exclusive discounts.

Get Started Today by Contacting the Acquisitions Department at:

acquisition@igi-global.com

www.igi-global.com/infosci-ondemand

InfoSci®-OnDemand

Continuously updated with new material on a weekly basis, InfoSci®-OnDemand offers the ability to search through thousands of quality full-text research papers. Users can narrow each search by identifying key topic areas of interest, then display a complete listing of relevant papers, and purchase materials specific to their research needs.

Comprehensive Service

- Over 125,000+ journal articles, book chapters, and case studies.
- All content is downloadable in PDF and HTML format and can be stored locally for future use.

No Subscription Fees

- One time fee of $37.50 per PDF download.

Instant Access

- Receive a download link immediately after order completion!

"It really provides an excellent entry into the research literature of the field. It presents a manageable number of highly relevant sources on topics of interest to a wide range of researchers. The sources are scholarly, but also accessible to 'practitioners'."

- Lisa Stimatz, MLS, University of North Carolina at Chapel Hill, USA

"It is an excellent and well designed database which will facilitate research, publication, and teaching. It is a very useful tool to have."

- George Ditsa, PhD, University of Wollongong, Australia

"I have accessed the database and find it to be a valuable tool to the IT/IS community. I found valuable articles meeting my search criteria 95% of the time."

- Prof. Lynda Louis, Xavier University of Louisiana, USA

Recommended for use by researchers who wish to immediately download PDFs of individual chapters or articles.

www.igi-global.com/e-resources/infosci-ondemand

IGI Global DISSEMINATOR OF KNOWLEDGE

www.igi-global.com

www.ingramcontent.com/pod-product-compliance
Lightning Source LLC
LaVergne TN
LVHW080405011026
849161LV00009B/2351
* 9 7 8 1 7 9 9 8 3 1 1 5 0 *